AN INTRODUCTION TO MICROECONOMICS

MICHAEL WATTS
Purdue University

HAYDEN-McNEIL PUBLISHING, INC.

Printed in the United States of America

10 9 8 7 6 5 4 3 2 1

ISBN 1–881592–10–3

HAYDEN-MCNEIL PUBLISHING, INC.
340 N. Main, Suite 204
Plymouth, MI 48170

Acknowledgments

Although this is a draft version of a slightly longer and considerable more polished book yet to come, the material that is here has been in preparation for several years, and has been improved both in form and content by the efforts of many people.

In formatting, revising, and especially in meeting the schedule to get this version printed, major thanks go to Jo Ellen Hayworth, who temporarily gave up her part-time status to work for Hayden-McNeil Publishing. Nancy Vollmer pitched in too, as she often does.

Mike Elia and Ed Millman provided extensive editorial help, improving nearly every page at least a little, and the overall manuscript substantially (but as I always have to remind them, only on net). Patrick Olson at Hayden-McNeil was remarkably enthusiastic, patient, and flexible -- very rare and desirable qualities in the publishing industry, or any other.

A "Maymester" class I taught at Purdue University in 1989, and a dozen instructors and hundreds of students in 1991-92 used even earlier versions of the book, and helped to improve it in matters large and small. My own teachers also played an important role in shaping what is here and how it is presented -- though they wouldn't always agree with the choices I have made. Bob Smith at the University of Nevada - Las Vegas, and formerly of Louisiana State University, deserves special mention among those many past instructors.

Finally, a lot of time out of my life has been given over to writing this tome. That was a cost I paid by choice, but which often spilled over to my family as well. The plan is to substitute future time with them to make up for what was taken away; but of course that's never the same thing. I greatly appreciate their patience, understanding, and encouragement.

TABLE OF CONTENTS

A Note to Students on Chapter Features

The constraint of one-color printing severely limits the number and kinds of layout features that can be used to help you make your way through this book. However, there are several devices included here that will be more useful if you know what they are, and how to look for them, before you start reading the chapters.

After a one-page introduction, you come to the 17 regular chapters and one Appendix (a review of graphical analysis following Chapter 1). Each of the chapters begins with a short, boxed feature that starts with the phrase "In This Chapter ...." These are brief introductions of the major concepts and themes introduced in the chapters, which also link each chapter with the material that has come before and, in some cases, with topics to be covered in later chapters.

Each chapter is divided into two to four (usually three) major sections, which are identified by large, boldface, and centered section titles:

Major Section Titles

After each of these headings, a paragraph or two in *italics* briefly describes the concepts introduced in the section, and why that material is important. Use these paragraphs as "advance organizers" for what you are about to read.

The major sections are in turn broken down into several (usually three, but sometimes more or fewer) subsections. The subsection headings are left justified and set off by spaces:

Subsection Headings

Occasionally, but not often, a subsection will have sub-subsections, identified by underlined topic headings at the start of a paragraph directly in the text, or by numbered entries.

New concepts are identified using all capital letters in italics: *NEW CONCEPTS*. Each of these terms is defined in the text at or very near that point, and again in the Glossary at the end of the book.

At least one Case Study is provided after the standard textual material in each chapter. These are usually applications or extensions of material presented in the chapter, sometimes theoretical, sometimes empirical, sometimes biographical, and in some cases simply descriptions and basic analysis of current economic events or issues. The examples and applications in the Case Studies are usually developed more fully than they could be in the main body of the chapters, and at least in later chapters deal with somewhat more topical and controversial issues.

At the end of each chapter (and the Appendix to Chapter 1), a brief Chapter Summary is provided which again indicates the major concepts introduced in the chapter with all capital letters in italics. Items in the chapter summaries are also numbered, and paired with items that have the same number in the Review and Discussion Questions that immediately follow. In other words, if there are 10 items in a chapter summary, there will be 10 review and discussion questions. The first question deals with the same material covered in the first entry in the Chapter Summary, the second question with the second entry in the summary, and so on.

1

Economics -- What's in It for You?

The Economic World Around You

No one comes to their first college courses in economics as a blank slate, with little or no personal experience in economic matters to draw on *or* to color their opinions on various economic issues. Instead, you have actively participated in an economic system from a very young age -- certainly as a consumer, and probably as an employee and a voter, too.

Taking economics courses may not change the decisions you make in each of these roles, at least in many situations and markets. In fact, the economic models and analysis you will study in this book are assumed to work whether or not the decision makers involved have studied economics; and an extensive literature of empirical (statistical) studies supports that assumption. Nor is there hard evidence to show that understanding economics will significantly improve your chances of making your own fortune, which is even more depressing (at least to economists). So the question of what's in it for you is by no means an idle one -- just what can you hope to get out of your first economics courses?

Perhaps the two most important things basic courses and textbooks on economics have to offer are: 1) an understanding of how the different parts of the economic system fit and ultimately work together -- e.g., how prices for different goods and services are related, and different kinds of markets are linked together; and 2) an appreciation for the way economists think about the world, in terms of analyzing economic decisions and problems. Economic forces are pervasive, and the work that economists do is now regularly discussed by business and political leaders, and in the media. Unemployment, poverty, inflation, rent controls, trade and budget deficits, discrimination in hiring practices, the OPEC cartel, technological change, free-trade agreements, support programs for agricultural products, foreign investment, stock market booms and busts, the productivity "crisis" -- the list of economic issues facing individuals and nations in the modern world seems to grow longer each year, and each decade. That means understanding economics has become a required part of being an informed and articulate citizen in the modern world. As the Nobel laureate economist George Stigler once wrote,

> ...(T)hat the public does concern itself most frequently with economic questions...is a true and persuasive reason for its possessing economic literacy. In the best of all worlds it might be most desirable to have musical or theological literacy, but in ours the public wants to talk about money. Although the public cannot have universal literacy, this is no reason for possessing no special knowledge at all. The public has chosen to speak and vote on economic problems, so the only question is how intelligently it speaks and votes.[1]

By and large over the last century, economists have felt that the public doesn't speak and vote very intelligently about economics. The best evidence of such shortcomings can be found as you go through your economics courses, and this textbook, by looking for situations where something you thought was true turns out to be false. In those cases, you will find that widespread belief in economic arguments that just aren't so usually results from a failure to trace through the long-run consequences of some action, and to consider the secondary effects of a change in one market in terms of "feedbacks" to others. That's part one of our rationale for studying basic economic concepts, and real-word applications of those ideas.

The second part has to do with the economic way of thinking, and the body of work that economists have done over the past two centuries. Some of that work has come to serve as the foundation of scientific management practices in the area of corporate finance and strategic planning. Other work by economists informs public policy debates, both by evaluating current government programs and predicting how consumers, workers, and firms will react to new policies.

Taken together, that's more than enough material to cover in an introductory course on economics.

---

[1]"The Case, if Any, for Economic Education," *Journal of Economic Education*, Spring 1970, p. 7.

Chapter 1
Facing Up To Scarcity

In This Chapter...

we introduce scarcity, the fundamental economic problem; several ways of dealing with that problem; and the basic supply-and-demand framework economists use to analyze problems that individuals and governments must face because of scarcity.

Scarcity: The Fundamental Economic Problem

Scarcity, the fundamental economic problem, exists because human wants are unlimited relative to the economic resources available to satisfy them. Because of scarcity, people must make choices about how those resources will be used, and those choices always entail an opportunity cost.

Wants

The average life expectancy for people born in the United States today is about 75 years. During that lifetime, an average American will consume approximately 82,000 meals; live in a dozen or more houses or apartments; buy hundreds of shirts and pairs of pants and shoes; travel hundreds of thousands of miles in cars, planes, trains, and boats; enjoy any number of the good things in life, such as movies, plays, concerts, stereo systems, and amusement parks; and use up literally years of leisure time. The first, and most basic point in economics is that none of these activities will be free. Every time you buy something, or use something you bought earlier, or even goof off for a day and just lay around vegetating, there is an economic cost to be paid.

Does that imply that economists are opposed to consumption and leisure activities, or in particular to luxuries such as big houses, meals at fine restaurants, or expensive cars and stylish clothes? Hardly. Economists usually measure economic progress, both for individuals and nations, by the degree to which people's material *WANTS* are satisfied -- and satisfied by expensive luxury items as well as plain, basic things that all people buy and use. The most famous economist of the first half of this century, John Maynard Keynes, was asked shortly before his death whether he would do anything differently if he could relive his life. Keynes, whom you will meet again in later chapters, replied that he would drink more champagne.

As social scientists, economists make no value judgments about people's wants. In philosophy or political science courses you may learn about schemes that claim to improve human welfare by favoring the use of certain kinds of goods and services, or by discouraging others. But in courses on economics, and in economic studies of human behavior, wants are treated as bits of information, and not a call for moral approval or disapproval. Of course, economists recognize that some goods and services are declared illegal through the political process. But it would be naive to ignore the fact that billions of dollars are spent each year on such illegal goods and activities, and that whole industries exist because a large number of people want and pay for these illegal products.

The last two centuries have seen an unprecedented increase in the production and consumption of goods and services, at least in economically developed and industrialized nations such as the United States. Middle class American families today are far better off in material terms than families were just three or four generations ago. Nevertheless, today's families aspire to still more comfort, variety, and leisure. Similarly, most poor families in the United States now have greater and far more regular access to food, clothing, shelter, and leisure activities than the vast majority of all of the people who have ever lived on this planet; but they clearly want more goods and services. And even the wealthy have wish lists they would fill if they earned an extra million or so.

Human wants, whether satisfied by legal or illegal products, or unsatisfied by either, are a powerful force in economic affairs. They constitute the starting point of the study of economics.

Productive Resources

All *GOODS* and *SERVICES* are economic resources in the general sense that they satisfy human wants. But economists limit their definition of *PRODUCTIVE RESOURCES* to include only the resources that can be used to produce goods and services. Therefore, productive resources are also known as the *FACTORS OF PRODUCTION*.

There are four different kinds of productive resources, as you will soon see, but they all share one common problem -- there aren't enough of them to make enough goods and services to satisfy all human wants. Using the most modern technology and all of the resources available in the world, neither the most profitable business managers nor the wisest government leaders could produce enough products to make the peoples of the world say "Stop, we have enough!"

Economists identify four categories of productive resources: land, labor, capital, and entrepreneurship.

LAND refers to all natural resources -- those produced with no human effort -- including virgin forests, the oceans, and petroleum and mineral deposits, as well as the mountains and fields of earth that most people think of when the term land is used.

LABOR includes all routine kinds of human effort to produce goods and services, including many tasks done in jobs that non-economists often classify as management rather than labor. In fact, the only kind of human effort that economists don't consider labor is the special category of human endeavor known as entrepreneurship, which is defined below.

CAPITAL refers to products that are produced in order to make other goods and services faster or more efficiently. It includes tools, industrial machinery, and factory buildings, but is not limited to those physical inputs. In particular, a special form of capital is known as *HUMAN CAPITAL*, which refers to education, training, on-the-job experience, and health and fitness programs, which all increase a worker's ability to produce goods and services. On the other hand, while *MONEY* is often referred to as capital in the financial press, economists do not count it as capital, or any factor or production, because it does not directly produce goods and services. To be sure, money has value to an economy in making it easier for people to buy the things they want, now and in the future. But you can't produce goods or services with money until you transform it into real resources -- i.e., into land, labor, capital, and entrepreneurship. So economists will sometimes refer to money as *FINANCIAL CAPITAL*; but they refuse to classify it as a productive resource.

ENTREPRENEURSHIP is the the human activity that entails accepting the personal or financial RISKS involved in producing goods and services. For example, when products don't sell producers incur monetary losses. Under this definition of entrepreneurship, the owner of a small taco stand who risks his or her life savings qualifies as an entrepreneur (although the time spent making tacos and cleaning up is traditional labor, not associated with risk-taking). On the other hand, a senior executive at a large firm who is paid to make routine decisions following well defined policies is not being entrepreneurial, even if the executive earns several hundred thousand dollars a year.

Everyone controls *some* productive resources that can be used to make goods or services, and to earn money to buy products that will satisfy *some* of their wants. The money they earn from theses productive resources has special names in economics: the payment for land is called *RENT*, the payment for labor is known as *WAGES* or *SALARIES,* the payment for capital resources is *INTEREST,* and the payment for entrepreneurship is *PROFIT.* Clearly, both the wants and resources sides of economists' picture of *SCARCITY* are important. And *ECONOMICS* is concerned, most basically, with the ways people and nations deal with the fundamental economic problem of scarcity.

Choice and Opportunity Cost

If you can't have all of the goods and services you want, how do you get the most satisfaction from the things you can have? Economists have developed several important ideas to help answer that pervasive and persistent question. One key principle is that resources used to make one product can't be used to make something else at the same time. For example, if you decide to use your land to grow trees, you can't use the same land to grow wheat, or to build a barn on. If you use wood to make paper, you can't use that wood to make furniture or houses. Using paper to print an economics textbook requires giving up the opportunity to use that paper to print a new novel. People must choose among their economic alternatives, by evaluating which alternatives are the most satisfying or profitable.

In real rather than monetary terms, the cost of using a resource in one way is giving up the next most valuable way it could have been used. Economists call this the *OPPORTUNITY COST* of an economic choice. For example, suppose you have the time and cash required to: buy a used car; or take a skiing vacation in Colorado; or visit your future spouse in Medicine Lodge, Kansas, on your spring break. You have decided to do one of these three things, but you only have enough time and money to do one of the three. Rank the alternatives, in terms of which you would do first, which you would do next if you could, and which you would do last. You will use your resources to carry out your highest-ranked choice, and only the choice you ranked second will be your opportunity cost.

Every economic choice involves alternative uses of scarce resources, and has an opportunity cost. In fact, economists define an *ECONOMIC GOOD* or *SERVICE* as one that is available only if something must be given up to get it. Free goods -- such as sand to someone in the Sahara Desert or the air you breathe as you read this book -- aren't economic goods if they are truly free, which means that *no one* had to give up anything to get them. Of course, if you receive a new car as a gift that doesn't mean that the car isn't an economic good, because whoever gave the car to you had to give up something to get it.

Costs for economic goods can be shifted, but they can't be ignored or made to disappear. Economists are fond of saying "There's no such thing as a free lunch," because the resources used to provide the lunch could have been used to make other goods or services, and because somebody must ultimately pay for the meal.

Careful economic decisions entail a thorough consideration of the costs and benefits involved. The costs ultimately are measured by what is given up in using resources to satisfy a particular want; the benefits ultimately derive from the satisfaction of that want. This probably strikes you as simple common sense. But you will see throughout this book that the costs and benefits of a choice are often hidden, indirect, or different in future years rather than in the immediate present.

Suppose, for example, that you want to earn $15,000 to buy a car, and that suggests getting a job. But the fastest way to earn the money may be to invest in a training program that will qualify you for a higher paying job. Ironically, you first buy -- or more precisely invest in -- the job training, even though what you really want is a car. And note too that a major part of the cost of the training program will be what you could have earned now in a lower-paying job, which you have to give up while you complete the training. Even in a simple example like this one, some of the costs and decisions involve subtle and often unseen factors.

Hidden costs also face our national policymakers. For example, taxes on foreign autos help U.S. auto producers by increasing the prices U.S. consumers must pay for the foreign cars. That makes the imported cars less attractive, compared to cars produced in the United States. But these taxes on imported cars hurt the consumers who face higher prices, *and* other businesses which experience declining sales when consumers pay more for cars. Those lost sales in other businesses are part of the real cost of the tax on imported cars.

Sometimes consumers, business leaders, and public officials must make decisions when it is impossible to get precise information on what the costs and benefits of their alternative choices will be. Consider, for example, business executives trying to predict all of the things that might happen in response to an increase in the price of their product. Or in some cases, choices made by individuals affect others who may or may not know that they are being helped or hurt by these actions. For example, the value of your property may increase because your neighbors improved the external appearance of their property, even though you don't help to pay for those improvements.

Economics offers a framework for decisionmaking in all of these situations, based on the careful consideration of all relevant costs and benefits of alternative choices. While some observers have described economics as the dismal science because it attempts to cost out private actions and public policies that sometimes involve such controversial issues as compensation for physical injuries and the loss of human life, even in those cases it is almost always true that some choices are better than others. So, in the face of the enduring and perhaps even eternal problem of scarcity, the ultimate message of economics is not to despair because we can't have everything we want, but to do the best we can with what we do have.

Lessening the Burden of Scarcity

The burdens of scarcity can be reduced, but not eliminated. Four of the most important ways that have evolved to deal with scarcity are: 1) specialization and the division of labor, which makes both labor and capital resources more productive; 2) voluntary exchanges, which allow both buyers and sellers to gain, and direct resources to their most valued economic uses; 3) investing in physical and human capital, which requires a decrease in current consumption levels but increases the future stock of productive resources and productivity levels; and 4) technological innovation, or discovering new ways to produce products, including entirely new products.

Specialization and Comparative Advantage

If your last name is Smith, there is a good chance that one of your ancestors worked as a blacksmith. Similar links to occupations are indicated by such surnames as Farmer, Wheeler, Cooper, Merchant, and Carpenter, and when many surnames from other languages are translated into English. Most of these names originated centuries ago, to be sure; but even today when people meet for the first time they often ask each other "Where do you work?", "What do you do?", or "What are you majoring in?".

From an economic point of view, what is important about this is that people limit the kind of work they do. *SPECIALIZATION* and, in particular, dividing the work of producing and selling a product into a large number of discrete steps, allows workers to become more skilled at a particular task. That also lets employers match workers with tasks they do well, which in turn encourages the development of specialized tools and assembly-line techniques. All of this results in greater production from a given resource base and improves material living standards -- particularly for middle-class families, since mass production both permits and requires mass consumption.

In an economy with high levels of specialization, workers and nations must decide exactly how they should specialize. That depends, in large part, on the resources and talents they have been provided by nature, or acquired through education, training, and experience. Many of us might like to specialize in playing center field for the New York Yankees, trombone for the London Philharmonic Orchestra, or the lead role in the lavish sequel to *Gone With The Wind*. But it's foolish to pursue these jobs if you can't hit a curveball, keep a stiff upper lip, or cry convincingly on command.

When someone can do one of these things very well -- and only one thing -- it's fairly easy for them to decide how they should specialize. But what about people who are capable of doing many different jobs well, or nations with resource bases that allow them to produce large quantities of many different products? What, specifically, should they produce? We will present a formal answer to this question in later chapters, but for now let's look at two examples to see, in general terms, what such an economic choice entails.

We will begin with a favorite example of economists -- a person who happens to be the best lawyer *and* the best typist in a community. If this person's goal is to earn the highest income, will it pay to work as a lawyer *and* type his or her own legal papers, or to work for others strictly as a typist? Probably not, because to do so would require giving up time that could be used to work as an attorney. Of course, if the wage rate for typists is high enough, compared to the wage rate for lawyers, it will be financially advantageous for our worker to work as a typist. But that isn't likely, and even if that did happen the worker would then specialize in typing, and do no work as a lawyer. Only if the return for an hour of work as a typist is exactly equal to the return for an hour of work as a lawyer *might* it be in this person's financial interest to do both typing and an attorney's work. In the most likely scenario, he or she will specialize as a lawyer and hire someone else to do the typing, even though the secretary who is hired will not type as fast and accurately as our hypothetical attorney-typist.

The same general pattern holds true for nations. What a country produces, and what it imports and exports, will reflect choices to specialize and maximizing its material well being. A technologically advanced nation rich in natural, human, and capital resources like the United States might well be able to produce more of all agricultural and manufactured products than a smaller, less developed nation like, say, Colombia. For example, let's suppose that in the United States 100 times more automobiles can be produced than in Colombia. Furthermore, using greenhouses, hydroponics, and other techniques, suppose that twice as much coffee could be grown in the United States than in Colombia, but only by using the same set of resources that could be used to make the automobiles. Although it is possible for U.S. producers to make more of either good under normal circumstances they will, like the attorney-typist, specialize to maximize their economic standard of living.

You can quickly get a sense of this kind of decision by looking at Table 1-1, which presents a situation in which the production of automobiles is cheaper in the United States than in Columbia. It is cheaper because the opportunity cost is smaller, in terms of the amount of coffee that must be given up to produce a car. Conversely, the opportunity cost of producing coffee is lower in Columbia, because fewer automobiles must be given up to grow a ton of coffee. In this situation, both countries benefit if the United States produces cars for itself *and* Columbia, and Columbia produces coffee for itself *and* for the United States. That way the opportunity costs of producing both goods are minimized, and the lower costs keep the prices consumers pay lower than they would be if each country tried to produce all of its own coffee and all of its own automobiles.

Table 1-1
Specialization and Opportunity Cost

U.S. Production Alternatives		Colombia Production Alternatives	
Cars (In Thousands)	Coffee (In Thousands)	Cars (In Thousands)	Coffee (In Thousands)
0	1000	0	500
200	800	2	400
400	600	4	300
600	400	6	200
800	200	8	100
1000	0	10	0

U.S. Opportunity Costs	Columbian Opportunity Costs
1000 cars cost 1 ton of coffee	1000 cars cost 50 tons of coffee
1 ton of coffee costs 1000 cars	1 ton of coffee costs 20 cars

Using hypothetical data, this table shows how many cars and tons of coffee the United States and Colombia can produce in various combinations, using the same quantity of productive resources. For each 200,000 additional cars produced, the United States must use up resources that could have been used to grow 200 tons of coffee. Therefore, the opportunity cost of 1,000 cars in the United States is one ton of coffee, and the opportunity cost of one ton of coffee is 1,000 cars. In Colombia, to produce 2,000 more cars the production of coffee must be cut by 100 tons, so the opportunity cost of 1,000 cars is 50 tons of coffee, and the opportunity cost of one ton of coffee is 20 cars. Clearly, it costs less coffee to make cars in the United States, and it costs less cars to grow coffee in Colombia.

Economists say that the attorney-typist enjoys an *ABSOLUTE ADVANTAGE* in the production of both kinds of work, which simply refers to the ability to produce more units of output than another producer, using the same quantity of resources. So if Table 1-1 is based on production levels that are obtained using an equal quantity of productive resources, the United States also has an absolute advantage in the production of both cars and coffee. But despite these absolute advantages, producers should specialize in the one product for which they have a *COMPARATIVE ADVANTAGE* -- which means the product they can produce at a lower opportunity cost.

To review: the lawyer has a comparative advantage in legal work, the secretary in typing, the United States in automobiles, and Colombia in coffee.

Through specialization the material standard of living can be improved for the attorney *and* the secretary, and for *both* nations, because total production can be increased. In fact, as much or more of *each* product can be produced. For example, if the United States imports 200 tons of coffee from Colombia instead of producing it, then the United States can produce 200,000 more cars. To produce the 200 tons of coffee that the United States would import instead of producing, Columbia gives up the production of only 4,000 cars. Hence, the total production of coffee stays the same, but automobile production increases by 196,000. As long as Colombia gets more than the 4,000 cars it gives up to grow the additional coffee it will be better off; and as long as the United States pays less than the 200,000 cars it would have to give up to grow this amount of coffee it will be better off. Picking a trading ratio between these two points -- e.g., say the United States agrees to pay Columbia 100,000 cars for 200 tons of coffee -- the United States will pay 100,000 cars less for its coffee, and Columbia gets 96,000 more cars than it would by giving up this much coffee to produce its own cars. The key point is that both countries gain by specializing and trading.

However, there are also costs associated with specialization which have long been recognized, even by economists who argue strongly that specialization and trade is one of the most effective ways to increase the wealth of all nations. Adam Smith, widely regarded as the first great economist, wrote in 1776 that

> In the process of the division of labor, the employment of the far greater part of those who live by labor...comes to be confined to a few very simple operations.... But the understandings of the greater part of men are necessarily formed by their ordinary employments. The man whose whole life is spent in performing a few simple operations...has no occasion to exert his understanding, or to exercise his invention.... He naturally loses, therefore, the habit of such exertion, and generally becomes as stupid and ignorant as it is possible for a human creature to become.[1]

Recognizing this, many workers who can afford to do so choose occupations in which they are not forced to specialize in a rigid manner. And similarly, some U.S. businesses have recently found that their workers' jobs were too narrowly specialized to maintain efficient production over a long period of time. Following the widely publicized examples of certain Japanese firms, the U.S. businesses achieved productivity gains by allowing workers to change jobs periodically, or to perform several tasks instead of one repetitive operation. Many countries have also adopted policies that limit specialization, for such reasons as maintaining cultural diversity, or promoting national defense and political stability, even if it is known that this will reduce their material standard of living.

Nevertheless, it should be clear that modern, industrialized nations with high levels of income and wealth differ considerably from less developed nations in their degree of specialization. In very poor nations, for example, most shops are likely to be small general stores rather than the specialty shops and huge department stores that are common in wealthy nations and cities.

Growth in world population and income, improvements in global communications and transportation technologies, the explosion of technical knowledge, and the development of worldwide financial markets have all increased the importance of, and the opportunities for, economic specialization by workers, businesses, and nations. Despite its inherent drawbacks, specialization is one of the oldest and most effective means of dealing with scarcity.

---

[1]*The Wealth of Nations*, E. Cannan, ed., (Chicago: University of Chicago Press, 1976), Volume I, pp. 302-03.

Exchange and Transaction Costs

Specialization and *EXCHANGE* are complementary, and indeed inseparable activities. The reason for that is simple: If you specialize you don't produce everything you consume, so you have to get the rest from someone else. The butcher depends on the baker to produce bread, and in turn the baker depends on the butcher for meat. That means they have to be able to exchange their products, as well as those made by carpenters, tailors, physicians, etc., to make any extensive degree of specialization possible.

There are several different ways to transfer resources from one person to another, including stealing, charitable programs, or income redistribution schemes adopted through the political process. But in many nations, including the United States, the most common and important type of economic exchanges are voluntary transactions made in markets, where one thing of value is traded for another.

In such dealings, say when you buy a soft drink for 50 cents, you indicate that you would rather have the soft drink than the 50 cents, or anything else you could buy with this money. Whoever sells the soft drink to you would rather have the 50 cents. A basic principle of economics is that voluntary exchange takes place only when both parties involved in the exchange expect to gain from the transaction.

You may not appreciate the importance of this mutual gain through voluntary exchange unless you recognize how different it is from many day-to-day activities. For example, mutual gain does not occur in scorekeeping for games of chance or sport. Whether the game is poker or football, when one player or team's position improves the others playing the game are, at least relatively speaking, worse off.

Perhaps because of these common experiences in which one person's gain is another person's loss, there is a common misperception that the result of most exchanges between consumers and businesses is a net loss for the consumer and a net gain for the business, especially if the business is a foreign firm. However, most purchases are made from a wide range of potential buyers. In other words, in most transactions between consumers and producers both parties know exactly what they are getting and giving up. Most importantly, again, neither buyers nor sellers make deals unless they expect to gain.

From this discussion, you should see that anything that makes voluntary exchanges easier and less expensive to conduct will contribute to a nation's economic well being. Conversely, conditions that discourage voluntary exchange will reduce or limit that well-being. Economists label many such impediments to voluntary exchange *TRANSACTIONS COSTS*.

Transactions costs include any cost to buyers or sellers that is not included in the *PRICE* of a traded good or service. For example, the lack of a widely accepted currency limits the ability of buyers and sellers to meet and agree on the terms of an exchange. Without a standard currency, both parties face higher costs in determining that whatever goods are being used as payment are genuine and have a certain value. There are also, frequently, higher freight and security costs for carrying these items around in public. And, of course, not everyone is in the market for a particular good or service, but everyone accepts currency because it can be used to purchase all other goods and services. So the lack of currency makes it harder for sellers to find buyers, and reduces the amount of trading that is done.

Another kind of transactions costs are consumers' transportation costs in making their purchases -- e.g., in driving to a shopping center or to a particular seller's place of business. Producers' transportation costs are not considered transaction costs, however, because they are incorporated directly into a product's selling price. Clearly, sellers who don't cover these costs in the prices for their goods will soon be out of business. But note that better roads, bridges, airports and modes of transportation will lower these costs, both for producers and consumers.

The most important transactions costs for many exchanges are acquiring information about product availability, quality, and price, and about sellers' location, reputation, and customer policies. These costs reduce the level of well being that could be achieved if such information were freely available to everyone, and could be costlessly stored and used. In fact, though, information is a scarce good, and many resources are used to provide information to consumers more efficiently. Both private firms and government agencies are in the business of making information more widely available, and serving consumers and businesses by lowering these and other transaction costs. For example, the U.S. Treasury provides currency, and many private companies provide "money substitutes" such as travellers' checks and credit cards. Other companies transport people and products all over the world, and several government agencies assist those activities, too. There are also many laws prohibiting fraud and requiring full disclosure of key facts in several kinds of exchanges, such as interest rates charged on loans.

All of this is done, in large part, because lowering transactions costs makes it possible for a specialized worker or company to serve a larger number of customers. That expands opportunities for voluntary exchange and specialization, which alleviates the problem of scarcity.

Investing for the Future

Material standards of living have risen dramatically in the United States and other industrialized nations over the past 200 years. Economic historians estimate that in 1970 the average income of U.S. citizens was about 12 times higher than it was in 1770, and rose somewhat faster from 1870 to 1970 than it did from 1770 to 1870.[2] Over these same two centuries, many studies suggest that all income groups -- rich and poor -- experienced broadly similar levels of gain. Or as President John F. Kennedy said, economic growth served as "a rising tide that lifts all boats." However, the economic growth and prosperity achieved in economically developed nations has not uniformaly transferred to the rest of the world. Most people in the world today still live at income levels below the official U.S. poverty line.

Industrialized nations have demonstrated that investment in human and capital resources and improvements in technology play a major role in achieving a higher material standard of living. Nevertheless, technological advances and improving capital and human resources are not free activities. They are paid for in two key ways: 1) directly, by reducing current consumption of goods and services -- since we can't consume now what we put aside to produce more goods and services in the future, and 2) indirectly, through new kinds of pollution and the disruption of established patterns of employment, schooling, government, and social custom.

Over long periods of time, nations which have devoted substantial resources to capital investment and technological advancement have achieved higher rates of economic growth than nations which have not paid these costs. That isn't meant to suggest that the process of economic development is this simple, or that many other economic, demographic, and political issues are not involved. However, it is clear that investment and technology can be important weapons in the struggle to deal with the basic economic problem of scarcity.

The next topic to consider is how economists measure the scarcity of various goods and services, and the factors that make some products relatively more scarce than others. Then, in later chapters, these measures will be used to predict how consumers, workers, firms, and governments will respond to the challanges and opportunities they face in trying to satisfy some, but not all, of their wants.

Measuring Scarcity

Although scarcity exists because human wants exceed the ability to satisfy them using all available resources, it is very hard to observe and measure precisely either human wants or, when defined so broadly, productive resources. By replacing wants with the concept of demand, and then replacing resources with the concept of supply, economists can predict the effects of a wide range of possible events on the market value of a given product, which is the economic measure of the product's relative scarcity.

Demand

DEMAND is a schedule representing the quantities of a product that consumers are willing and able to purchase at all possible prices, over some particular period of time. The *LAW OF DEMAND* was intuitively known and

---

[2]Simon Kuznets, "Two Centuries of Economic Growth: Reflections on U.S. Experience," *American Economic Review*, February 1977, p. 5.

accepted by many ordinary consumers and producers, and by popular authors, long before there were professional economists to state it as an economic law. It is, simply, that people are willing and able to buy more of a product as its price decreases, and less as its price increases. For example, if the price of hamburgers drops from $1.50 to $1.00, customers will usually increase the number of hamburgers they buy each month.

QUANTITY DEMANDED is a more formal name for the amount of a product consumers buy at any particular price. Economists often state the law of demand by saying that price and quantity demanded are inversely related. In making that statement, they assume that price is the only major factor affecting consumers' purchasing decisions for that product that is changing. We will relax that assumption and consider other variables that influence these purchases in Chapters 2 and 3. Here, the law of demand is illustrated in Figure 1-1. (Look at that graph before reading on. If you don't feel comfortable interpreting the figure, you should now read the appendix on graphical techniques at the end of this chapter.)

Figure 1-1
The Law of Demand

Demand Schedule

Price	Quantity Demanded
10	1
9	2
8	3
7	4
6	5
5	6
4	7
3	8
2	9
1	10

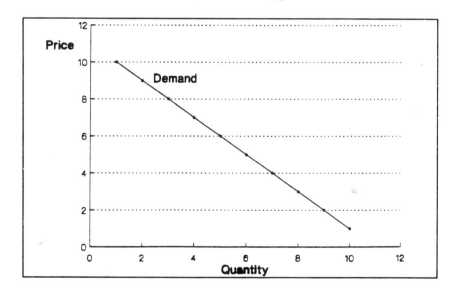

The most basic law of economics is that people are willing to buy more of a product at a lower price and less at a higher price in a given period of time, other things being equal.

While you may well accept the law of demand as simple common sense, it is important for you to understand the three reasons why it holds: the substitution effect, the income effect, and diminishing marginal utility.

The *SUBSTITUTION EFFECT* refers to the fact that as the price for a product increases it becomes more expensive, relative to the prices of other products which consumers can use to satisfy their same general wants. When that happens, consumers buy more of these other, lower-priced substitute products, and less of the product they originally wanted, which is now selling at a higher price.

For example, let's say you are in the mood for some fresh fruit and a thick steak. You go to the store planning to buy some apples and T-bone steaks, but when you arrive you find that the clerk has just finished raising the prices on these two goods. What do you do? Perhaps you decide to buy exactly the same quantities you had originally planned to buy. But many consumers will either buy fewer T-bones steaks and apples, or switch entirely to other kinds of meat and fruit. In fact, the effect would be much the same if the clerk had posted an "unadvertised special" lowering the prices of oranges and lobster tails, instead of raising the prices of T-bones and apples. Either way, the *relative* prices of T-bones and apples have increased.

The substitution effect is stronger in cases where there are many close substitutes for the good in question. Nevertheless, economists are regularly amazed at how creative people can be in finding substitutes for virtually any product when they want to. For example, swimming pools became an important substitute for gasoline for some families in the mid-1970s. At that time, gasoline prices were rising steeply in response to production cutbacks in the market for crude oil, initiated by the Organization of Petroleum Exporting Countries (OPEC). These higher prices led many families to cancel vacations that required extensive driving. A few families used their vacation funds to build home swimming pools instead. Even more consumers switched to smaller, more fuel-efficient cars, and bought houses or rented apartments nearer their place of employment. Despite widespread claims that gasoline was a necessity which people would have to buy at any price, gasoline sales declined by as much as seven per cent a year in many regions of the country after the price increases.

A comparative handful of products, such as insulin for a diabetic, have few close substitutes (although medical researchers have recently developed new types of synthetic insulin). But products with only one or two close substitutes are rare indeed, given consumers' creativity in satisfying their wants in different ways, and producers' creativity in building better mousetraps and competing products. Therefore, the substitution effect always leads people to consider buying less of a product when its price increases, and more when its price falls.

The *INCOME EFFECT* is another reason for the inverse relationship between price and quantity demanded, at least for most goods. If the price of a good you buy increases while your income, measured in money terms, does not, then in real terms your purchasing power has declined. How will this affect the amount of the product you buy? That depends on whether the product is what economists define as a normal good or an inferior good.

As real income rises, people buy more of a *NORMAL GOOD* and less of an *INFERIOR GOOD*. T-bone steaks and Ferraris are, for most consumers, normal goods. Generic beer and hamburger supplements are, for many consumers, inferior goods. As the names suggest, most products are normal goods.

The income effect reinforces the substitution effect for all normal goods, by leading consumers to buy more of those products when their prices decrease and less when their prices increase. For example, if automobile and housing prices decrease, this makes many people wealthier in real terms, and increases the number of these products they buy. But for inferior goods the income effect works against the substitution effect, leading consumers to buy more of an inferior product when its price rises, and less when its price falls. If the price of boxed macaroni dinners goes up, for example, a graduate student spending 50% of her income on this product will be poorer in real terms. In that case, the income effect can lead her to buy more macaroni dinners, while the substitution effect will lead her to buy less due to the higher relative price of the product, which makes pot pies and other substitute products more attractive. The substitution effect is almost always, if not literally always, larger than the income effect; so demand curves for inferior goods are still downward sloping[3].

The *LAW OF DIMINISHING MARGINAL UTILITY* is the third reason economists give to explain the law of demand. *MARGINAL UTILITY* refers to the additional satisfaction associated with the consumption of one more, or one less, unit of a product. In fact, you will see the idea of marginal changes in consumption, production, costs,

---

[3]The possible exception to this rule, known as a Giffen good, is discussed in Chapter 6.

and several other variables as you read through this textbook, and in all of those cases *MARGINAL* refers to the change in the total value of those variables when one unit is added to or subtracted from the total.

Here, the law of diminishing marginal utility suggests that as people consume more and more units of a product in a given time period, the satisfaction derived from each additional unit will eventually begin to decline. In other words, the fourth hamburger you eat in an hour is likely to give you less additional satisfaction than the third hamburger did, and the tenth will be less satisfying than the ninth. It is not claimed that, over some range, the additional satisfaction from consuming more units of a product can not initially rise. You may well derive more pleasure from your second golf lesson in a week than from your first lesson. However, if you continue to increase the number of lessons you take each week, the law of diminishing marginal utility suggests that you will eventually reach a point where the next lesson you take will be less pleasing to you than the previous lesson was.

For goods that are subject to this economic law, it is reasonable to expect an inverse relationship between price and quantity demanded. In effect, consumers will not be willing to pay as much for the 20th gallon of water they use each day as they would be for the first gallon, because they use it to do things that are much less important and satisfying to them. The first gallon purchased will be used for activities that provide a great deal of satisfaction, such as drinking and cooking. So even if water was very expensive, most consumers would probably still buy at least a little of it. At lower prices, however, consumers are willing to buy more water, for uses that do not provide as much satisfaction -- such as washing clothes and cars, watering their lawns, running fountains, or keeping pet fish.

You might ask, "Are there any goods which are not subject to the law of diminishing marginal utility?" Maybe, at least for some people. Think of a miser's satisfaction from money, even when he saves his millionth or billionth dollar. Or consider the antique car collector who is about to corner the market on Stanley Steamers (the cars, not the carpet cleaners). Such collectors may value the next units they acquire more than they do the previous units they have "consumed."

So if there are exceptions to the law of diminishing marginal utility, does that mean the quantity demanded of these goods will not decrease as their price decreases? Not at all, since the substitution and (for normal goods) income effects will still support the law of demand. And, of course, most consumers aren't miserly collectors of money or other goods.

The law of demand is, therefore, a stronger and more general law than the law of diminishing marginal utility. The demand relationship is, in fact, one of the most important in all of economics. Together with the law of supply it provides the most basic way to measure the scarcity of different products, in terms of what consumers must give up to get them.

Supply

The *LAW OF SUPPLY* is deceptively simple. Most people intuitively accept its basic proposition: that producers are willing to sell more units of a product at higher prices than at lower prices. From this statement we derive upward-sloping supply curves, such as the example shown in Figure 1-2, and the idea that, like demand, *SUPPLY* refers to a schedule of quantities associated with all possible prices for a product.

QUANTITY SUPPLIED refers to the amount producers supply at a given price. Once again, we assume for now that all other major factors that affect supply decisions remain constant, and relax that assumption in later chapters.

Despite its apparent simplicity, the law of supply is based on two rather sophisticated ideas: diminishing marginal returns and comparative advantage. For starters, you must understand that diminishing marginal returns and, therefore, the law of supply, apply only to short-run situations.

Economists define the *SHORT RUN* as a time period when the amount of at least one resource used to produce a product is fixed, and can not be changed. The *LONG RUN* is a period long enough to vary all productive resources, including factory space, any large machines used in production, and the amount and location of a firm's land inputs. Short-run production and supply decisions therefore refer to those made and implemented while at least one input (typically capital or land) is fixed.

Figure 1-2
The Law of Supply

<u>Supply Schedule</u>

Price	Quantity Supplied
10	10
9	9
8	8
7	7
6	6
5	5
4	4
3	3
2	2
1	1

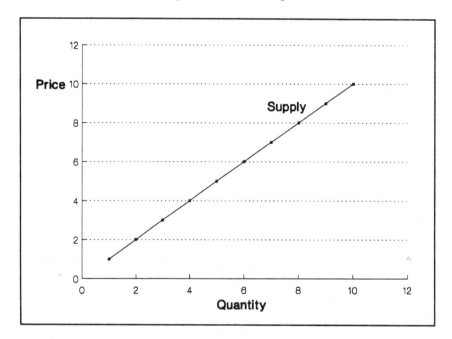

This graph and table indicate a direct relationship between price and the quantity of a product supplied in a given period of time. Other things being equal, producers will make and offer to sell more units of a product when the price of the product increases, and fewer units when the price decreases.

Note that under these definitions, the long run will be a longer period of time for producing some products, such as electricity, than for other goods, such as tacos. To build a new plant to produce electricity may take as long as 10 or 20 years, depending on whether the plant is to be conventionally or nuclear powered. Building a new taco stand may only take a few days or a few hours. Therefore, when economists talk about the short run in the context of producing a product, they may mean a day, week, month, year, or even decades; it all depends on the product.

But given that qualification, consider a short-run production process for virtually any kind of good or service. *THE LAW OF DIMINISHING MARGINAL RETURNS* states that as more and more units of a *VARIABLE INPUT* are added to at least one *FIXED INPUT*, eventually the additional units of *output* that can be produced by using one more unit of the variable *input* will decline. Suppose, for example, that we want to increase the production of tacos in the short run, and we do so by adding more workers to our same old taco stand. The addition of each new worker may well increase total output. However, after some point, each new worker will produce less *additional* output than the previous new worker.

This situation is shown in Table 1-2. Notice that the total output of tacos continues to increase as more units of labor are hired. However, it initially increases rapidly, and then the rate of increase tapers off -- the first labor unit increases output by 20 units, whereas the seventh increases output by only one unit. The change in total output resulting from the addition of one unit of labor -- i.e., the *MARGINAL PRODUCT* of labor -- becomes smaller and smaller. The law of diminishing marginal returns is at work.

Table 1-2
A Production Schedule for Tacos with Diminishing Marginal Returns

Units of Labor	Units of Capital	Number of Tacos	Change in Output -- Marginal Product Of Labor
0	10	0	--
1	10	20	20
2	10	35	15
3	10	45	10
4	10	52	7
5	10	57	5
6	10	60	3
7	10	61	1

Using hypothetical data, this table shows the quantities of tacos that can be produced in a given time period by adding more units of labor to a fixed quantity of capital resources. Note that each additional unit of labor produces fewer additional units of output.

Why does the marginal product of labor diminish? And what does this have to do with the supply schedule? It happens because the fixed input is being spread out more and more thinly across a growing number of variable inputs. More workers are trying to use one stove and a fixed amount of floor space at the taco stand. And the same thing happens as more employees are hired to work a fixed number of acres on a farm, or to work with a fixed number of machines in a factory. On average, as more workers are hired they each have less machinery or land or factory space to use, and with less of the fixed input to work with their productivity declines. The amount each new worker adds to total output gets smaller and smaller, and this is true even if the last worker hired is just as qualified and hard working as all the workers hired before.

For a time, the advantages of letting workers specialize may offset the diminishing returns -- we will work through examples of those cases in later chapters. Eventually, though, the effects of spreading the fixed input so thinly become too powerful to escape. But remember, diminishing returns is only a short-run concept, built on the assumption of at least one fixed input. It doesn't apply in the long run, when all inputs are variable.

The link between the law of diminishing marginal returns and the short-run supply schedule is the increased cost of producing additional units of output. This is easy to show with the taco example. Assume all workers are equally skilled and motivated in these jobs, and that we pay each unit of labor in Table 1-2 at a rate of $4 per hour. To keep things simple, also assume that the stove, hot sauce, and all other resources used to make the tacos are given to us by the American Society for the Preservation of Independent Taco Stands (ASPITS). Then labor is our only cost, and we have the simple cost schedules shown in Table 1-3. Strictly because of the law of diminishing marginal returns, the per unit cost of producing tacos increases as the quantity supplied increases.

Table 1-3
A Short-Run Production Schedule and Rising Per Unit Costs

Units of Labor	Number of Tacos	Total Cost	Average (Per Unit) Cost
0	0	$ 0	.00
1	20	4	.20
2	35	8	.23
3	45	12	.27
4	52	16	.31
5	57	20	.35
6	60	24	.40
7	61	28	.46

The law of diminishing marginal returns implies that per-unit production costs will rise as producers increase the level of output. That is shown using average costs here -- a more precise link between per unit costs and supply is reviewed in Chapter 9.

The same thing happens if producers have to begin hiring inputs that are less well suited to the production of their product -- such as farmland that is less fertile in producing a certain crop, or workers that are not as skillful or well trained in producing a firm's product. In those cases, producing more output requires using and paying for more of the less productive resources, which increases production costs. Putting this in terms of the example you saw earlier, in our discussion of Table 1-1, it is equivalent using all of Columbia's resources to produce coffee and then, if demand is sufficiently high, using some of the United States' resources to grow coffee, too. As you saw, coffee grown in the United States will be more expensive than coffee grown in Columbia, due to the higher opportunity cost of decreased automobile production. That is another way of saying that resources in the United States are not as well suited to producing coffee, and that using them for that purpose will raise unit production costs. Such cases are another application of the idea of comparative advantage, this time in terms of its impact on supply decisions related to product price.

From a bottom-line standpoint, both diminishing marginal returns and comparative advantage mean that producers will only be willing and able to sell more units of output when the prices of their products increase enough to cover the higher per unit production costs. This link between higher output and higher unit costs is *the* reason that the short-run supply schedule slopes upward and to the right, as shown earlier in Figure 1-2.

You will see many short-run supply schedules in your economics courses, so take the time now to understand what lies behind them. Long-run supply curves are not as widely used and are introduced much later, in Chapter 10.

Market Prices

With your new understanding of short-run supply and demand schedules, we can now discuss how market measures of relative scarcity are determined.

MARKETS are places where buyers and sellers exchange money, products, and related information on product price, quality, and availability, among other product characteristics. In some cases, markets are simply a set of technological arrangements (usually telephone, computer, or video networks) on which information and some financial products -- such as stocks and bonds -- are traded.

Individual buyers and individual sellers rarely have the information reflected by overall *MARKET SUPPLY* or *MARKET DEMAND* schedules, which show how much all producers and all consumers in a market will sell or buy, respectively, at all possible prices. But they do each know how much they are personally willing and able to buy or sell. They begin to make those transactions and then, impersonally and automatically, the market "adds

17

up" the production signals from what may be thousands of individual sellers, and the spending signals from what may be millions of individual buyers, to establish what the total quantity supplied and the total quantity demanded of a product will be at different prices. Economists describe this process as the horizontal summation of individual supply and demand schedules to find, respectively, market supply and demand curves. It is illustrated in Figure 1-3.

Figure 1-3
Deriving Market Demand From Individuals' Demand Schedules

Price	Units Purchased by Consumer #1	+	Units Purchased by Consumer #2	+	Units Purchased by Consumer #3	=	Market Quantity Demanded
$10	0		0		1		1
9	0		1		1		2
8	1		1		1		3
7	1		1		2		4
6	1		2		2		5
5	2		2		2		6
4	2		2		3		7
3	2		3		3		8
2	3		3		3		9
1	3		3		4		10

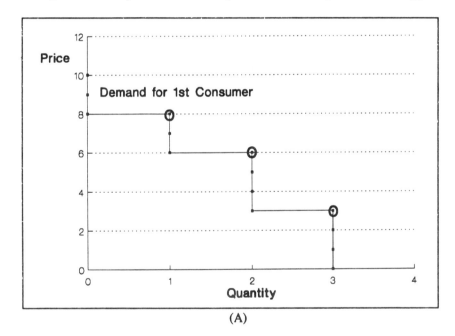

(A)

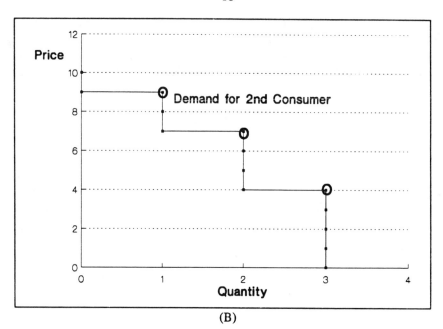

(B)

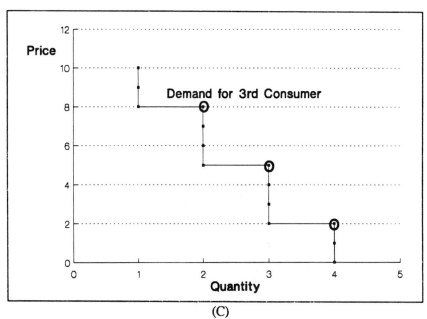

(C)

19

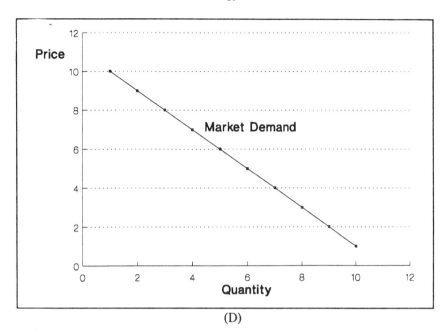

(D)

Market demand schedules for most goods and services are derived by adding up the quantity demanded at each price from the individual demand schedules for all consumers in the market. For simplicity, we assume here that there are only three consumers of this product in the market, whose individual demand curves are shown in the three panels labeled A-C. The market demand curve shown in panel D is found by horizontally summing up those three schedules, to find the total quantity demanded at each possible price. Individual demand curves are often "lumpy" and discontinuous, as shown, even when the market demand curve is much smoother.

Once we have these market schedules, something interesting happens when we plot both the market supply and market demand curves for a product on the same graph. Specifically, there is a single intersection point for the two schedules, which means that there is a unique price at which the quantity supplied exactly equals the quantity demanded. This is shown in Figure 1-4. Since it is the first example of an intersection point in this book, it is only fair to warn you that in introductory economics courses whenever two lines cross something important is almost always going on.

The price at which a market supply curve and a market demand curve intersect is called the *MARKET CLEARING PRICE*, because at that one price the market is literally cleared of buyers or sellers. Everyone who is willing and able to buy at this price finds someone willing and able to sell, and everyone who is willing and able to sell at this price finds a buyer. That isn't true at any other price. Specifically, at any price above the market clearing price, the quantity supplied will exceed the quantity demanded. At any price below the market clearing price, the quantity demanded will exceed the quantity supplied.

There are strong market pressures for a price to increase whenever quantity demanded exceeds quantity supplied, and for prices to fall when quantity supplied exceeds quantity demanded. Because of that, as long as market supply and demand curves are unchanged, the market clearing price exhibits a considerable degree of built-in stability. A price above the market clearing price is driven down by these market forces, and a price below the market clearing price is driven up. That automatic tendency to balance quantity supplied and quantity demanded, and for markets to stabilize at the one price at which that occurs, is reflected in another common name for the market clearing price, the *EQUILIBRIUM* price.

Note well that the equilibrium or market clearing price is found and maintained without establishing committees or passing laws to set and adjust prices. In fact, you will see how such laws often destabilize markets in Chapter 4. But here be sure you understand how, when individual buyers and sellers are allowed to act in their own best economic interests, market prices for thousands of products are automatically set at the levels that clear markets of both buyers and sellers.

Market clearing prices are the most basic measures of the relative scarcity of different goods and services. They tell consumers what they must give up to buy each product, and they tell producers what they will get when they sell a unit of a product. The demand side of the market is based on consumers' wants and their actions to satisfy those wants by purchasing goods and services. The supply side of the market is based on producers' decisions to use resources to produce certain goods and services instead of others, in their own search for higher income and the satisfaction they derive from doing a certain job.

Figure 1-4
Marketing Clearing -- or Equilibrium -- Price and Quantity

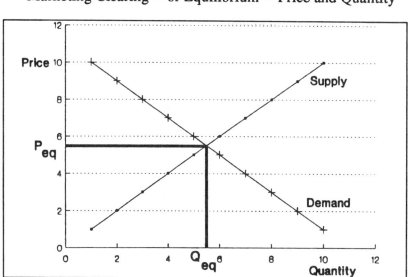

At the equilibrium or market clearing price, P_{eq}, quantity supplied equals quantity demanded. All buyers who are willing and able to buy at this price can do so, and all sellers who are willing and able to sell at this price are able to find buyers. There are no excess units demanded or supplied at this price -- i.e., no "leftover" buyers or sellers.

Products that are very scarce will have high market clearing prices, and those that are not very scarce will have low market clearing prices. That holds true whether the products in question are legal or illegal, or good or bad according to the value judgments of different observers. For example, some people find it upsetting that a gallon of milk has a lower market price than a gallon of aged Kentucky bourbon, or that professional football players are paid more than most lawyers, teachers, and engineers. They argue that teachers should be worth more than ill-mannered tennis players, or at least that philosophy professors should be paid the same as accounting and finance professors. Such arguments are *NORMATIVE* in nature and, as such, are not weighed in the operations of the market unless people spend their dollars in ways that support these feelings. We will address these issues in more detail in Chapter 2. Here, it is important for you to understand that economic scarcity depends only on how much of a product can be made available at different prices, relative to how much of the product people are willing to buy at those prices. Milk and teachers are certainly important, even in countries where market prices for these products are relatively low. But they are simply more abundant than products like bourbon and professional athletes, in comparison to the amounts people want and are spending to get them. In other words, they are less scarce.

One last re-statement, for emphasis: Relative scarcity determines the market prices of goods and services. But that does not mean that economists see scarcity and price as the only characteristics of a product, or the full measure of a product's impact on the human experience. To illustrate that, consider one final example and question. Nothing is more important in maintaining life than air to breathe, but is that air scarce? Will it command a high market price? (Note that we are only talking about air to breathe -- not machine-cooled air in the summer, or heated air in the winter, or clean, unpolluted air in heavily populated and industrialized areas, such as Los Angeles.)

An economist can easily answer that question by drawing the supply and demand curves for breathing air, and at this point you should be able to do the same thing, or at least understand the graph. Here's a hint: a scarce good is one that is *not* available to everyone freely, which is to say that the quantity demanded exceeds the quantity supplied at a price of zero. Look at Figure 1-5, now, to see the relative position of supply and demand curves for breathing air. If you don't find what you expected to see there, review this section before going on.

Figure 1-5
Breathing Air Is Not a Scarce Good

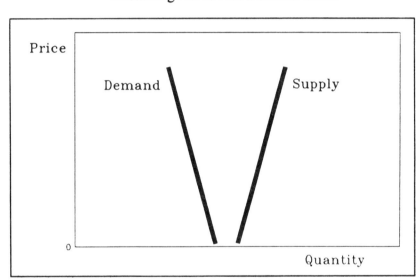

Under normal circumstances, the supply of breathing air exceeds the demand at all possible prices. Even at a price of zero the quantity supplied is greater than the quantity demanded, reflecting the fact that if you want more air all you have to do is breathe faster and more deeply.

Case Study #1
A Graphical Picture of Scarcity: The Production-Possibilities Frontier

A simple way to illustrate the concepts of scarcity, choice, and opportunity cost is with the two graphs shown in Figure 1-6, which represent *PRODUCTION-POSSIBILITIES FRONTIERS* that all individuals, nations, and producing units must face.

We will discuss the differences in these two graphs shortly. First, though, you must understand the ways in which they are alike. The straight line in the top graph and the curve in the bottom graph are both boundaries or frontiers which separate production areas that are attainable from those that are unattainable. The areas representing what is attainable include all combinations of the two kinds of products shown on the axes which an individual (or region or nation) can produce with available resources and technology. The region representing what is unattainable is beyond (up and to the right, graphically) current production limits. Points directly on the production-possibilities frontier (PPF) represent complete production efficiency using all available resources. Points below the frontier indicate inefficient production, or a failure to fully use some resources.

In both graphs we have assumed that a nation could produce either 100 units of consumer goods (such as food and clothing) or 100 units of capital goods (such as factories and machines) if it decided to use *all* of its available resources to produce only one of these products. In other words, the nation can make either 100 units of consumer goods or 100 units of capital goods, but not both. It can also choose to produce different combinations of the two products, as shown by the various points on the PPF schedules. But note that whenever we move along either PPF we produce more units of one product and fewer units of the other. That is precisely the idea of an opportunity cost.

Points inside the production-possibilities frontiers are places we would rather not be. They represent output levels at which some resources are unemployed, or at least underemployed and not used at peak efficiency. It would be possible to produce more of both kinds of outputs if all resources were used fully and efficiently. To economists such waste in the production process is a kind of economic sin, because it makes the problem of scarcity worse than it has to be.

Now consider the significance of the straight line and the curved line in the two graphs -- the things that make them different. The slope of the straight line in the top graph is constant, meaning that at every point on the frontier the same amount of one good must be given up to produce an additional unit of the other good. In other words, no matter what the level of production, the opportunity cost of producing more units of either good does not vary.

The bowed out production-possibilities frontier in the bottom graph suggests something very different. There, the amount of capital goods that must be given up to produce an extra unit of consumer goods increases as we move down along the schedule and devote more and more resources to the production of consumer goods. This happens when some resources are better suited to the production of one kind of product than the other. The producers of consumer goods represented in the bottom graph will, at first, hire the resources best suited to making consumer goods; but as the pressure to make more and more consumer goods increases they will also start to hire resources that are really better suited to produce capital goods. Therefore, the cost of producing additional units of consumer goods will rise as we move down along the frontier toward the point where the nation is producing only consumer goods. The same thing happens, in reverse, if we devote more and more resources to the production of capital goods -- they become increasingly expensive in terms of the consumer goods sacrificed to produce each additional unit of capital goods.

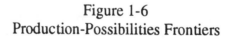

Figure 1-6
Production-Possibilities Frontiers

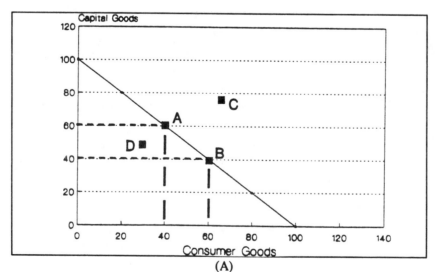

(A)

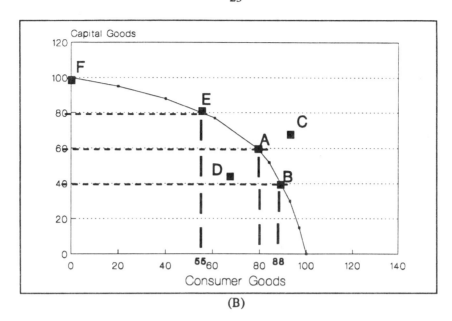

(B)

Each point on the lines in the graphs shows a different combination of consumer goods and capital goods that a nation can produce using all of its available resources. In both graphs, therefore, points A and B represent full-employment alternatives. The benefits and costs of moving between two points on the production-possibility frontier is measured in terms of gains in one product and sacrifices of the other. Point C, like all points above and to the right of the production-possibilities frontiers, is currently unattainable though desirable, which illustrates the concept of scarcity. At point D, and all other points inside the production-possibilities frontiers, at least some resources are unemployed or inefficiently used.

The top graph (panel A) assumes that resources are equally productive and suitable for use in making either kind of output. The bottom graph (panel B) results if some resources are better suited to the production of one kind of product than the other. Note that in moving from B to A on this graph, the cost of producing 20 additional units of capital goods is 8 units of consumer goods. But between points E and F, where most of the nation's resources are already being used to produce capital goods, the cost of producing 20 more units of capital goods has risen to 55 units of consumer goods. In panel A, the cost of one more unit of consumer goods is *always* one unit of capital goods.

It would be nice to move from point A to point C in either graph. After all, at point C the country gets more of both goods than at point A. Sadly, that is not possible given the available resources and the current state of technology. The production-possibilities frontiers show the *maximum* level of outputs that can be produced assuming that all resources are used fully and at peak production efficiency. Over time, however, a country can shift its production-possibilities frontier outward (upward and to the right) by producing more capital goods. And countries that produce more capital goods today will be able to shift their production- possibilities frontier outward faster than countries that produce more consumer goods. By cutting back on current consumption, a country can develop more productive resources and enjoy a higher standard of living in the future. Again, that's all part of the notion of opportunity cost -- but extended to show that sometimes current benefits have future costs, and future benefits have current costs. This is shown in Figure 1-7.

Figure 1-7
The Cost of Investing, and the Cost of Not Investing

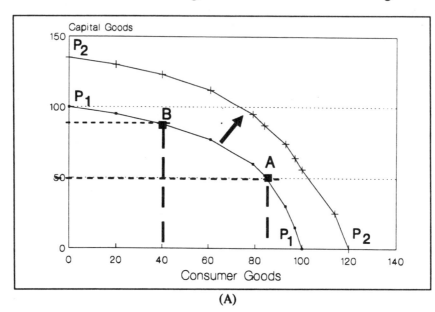

(A)

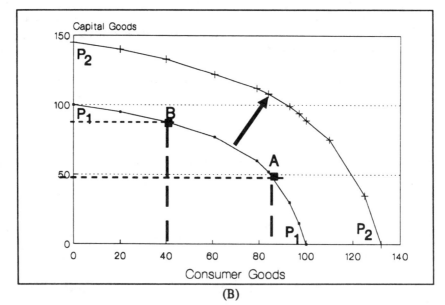

(B)

Suppose two countries currently face the same production-possibilities frontier, labeled P_1 in both panel (A) and panel (B). One country, shown in panel (A), chooses to produce at point A, and consumes more goods and services than the other country, shown in panel (B), which chooses to produce at point B and invest in more capital goods by consuming less today. Over time, the second nation is likely to see a larger outward shift in its production-possibilities frontier, to P_2, and a larger increase in its future standard of living. That is, in fact, an important part of the story some economists see when they compare the experience of the United States and Japanese economies in the post-World War II period. There are costs and benefits associated with both policies.

Case Study #2
Scarcity and Economic Systems: Market, Traditional, and Command

An economic system is a set of social arrangements used to answer the three basic economic questions that arise from the fundamental economic problem of scarcity:

1) What products will be produced?
2) How will those products be produced?
3) Who will consume the products that are produced?

A *MARKET ECONOMY* is a decentralized economic system in which individuals own and exchange goods, services, and productive resources. Producers make available those goods and services which they believe they can sell at prices high enough to cover their costs, including a return (profit) for accepting the entrepreneurial risks they face. How products are produced depends both on available production technologies and the prices of productive resources, which are established in separate markets for land, labor, capital, and entrepreneurship. The question of who will consume products is also answered in large part by two sets of market-determined prices -- the prices for the goods and services people want to consume and the prices for the resources people sell to earn incomes. Incomes are, of course, used to purchase the products people consume.

A market economy may seem familiar and even old-fashioned to students who have grown up surrounded by such institutions, but our understanding of how markets provide a *system* of economic coordination and organization is a relatively recent development -- no more than a few hundred years old. Other types of economic systems for coordination and social planning were understood much earlier. In fact, throughout history, traditional and command systems have probably influenced more nations and generations than market systems. But there is far more diversity among traditional and command economies than there is among market economies. For example, unregulated markets work essentially the same way in New York, Hong Kong, Nuevo Laredo, or Istambul today as they did in ancient Athens. However, the traditional economy of medieval Europe exhibits many key differences from the traditional economic systems of certain groups of Eskimos or Australian aborigines. Similarly, the command system economy used in the Soviet Union from 1960-1990 was considerably different in detail from the command economies used in China or Cuba in those same years, or in ancient Sparta.

Nevertheless, what distinguishes a *TRADITIONAL ECONOMY* is its reliance on custom and long-established forms of production, employment, and other social arrangements, such as legal and religious systems. In a traditional economy, farmers' children usually grow up to be farmers, and prices this year are usually what they were last year. The strongest arguments supporting legal claims involving economic resources or other issues is to show that your position is consistent with the way things have been done for "time out of mind." Wages and prices may well be set in laws or regulations, which typically reinforce a broader social (often religious) code that endorses and attempts to ensure stability in nearly all facets of life.

In traditional economies, what will be produced is basically what has always been produced, and production methods and distribution questions are dealt with in a similar way. Scarcity is still a central feature of economic life, but it is perhaps more accepted in these economies in the sense that there is little or no emphasis on improving production methods from generation to generation, and even less on raising material living standards for the masses. Whether that is because the people in such societies are "by nature" less materialistic than the average person in a market economy, or because they tend to live in poorer societies where saving, education, and capital investments are simply less feasible, less remunerative, or both, is the subject of a long-standing debate between economists and anthropologists. Traditional economies are not represented today among the highly developed and industrialized nations (as you might expect), but they are sometimes found among third world nations, and they were much more numerous in earlier centuries.

The key feature of a *COMMAND ECONOMY* is some form of *centralized* economic planning, usually by a committee of economic and industrial experts or political leaders, or some combination of both. To be sure, there is also planning in market and traditional economies, but in market systems economic planning is highly decentralized, and usually occurs at the individual household or firm level.

In some command economies, but not all, large enterprises such as factories, department stores, hospitals, and schools are owned by the government. But what really puts the element of command in a command economy is highly centralized economic planning.

The central planning group in a command economy makes the major decisions on what is to be produced, and how, by establishing production quotas for various firms and products. Who will consume the products that are produced is also generally determined by the central planners, primarily by setting wages and product prices.

Based only on a casual, sightseeing trip to two different nations with different economic systems, it might be difficult to tell the difference between a command economy and a market economy with comparable levels of per capita income and economic development. You might well see factories, retail stores, schools, hospitals, and a wide range of goods and services for sale in both nations. However, the process used to answer the three basic economic questions is quite different in the two systems, and even the prices you see in the two economies do very different things. To see that, let's compare the price of a loaf of bread in a market economy and in a command economy.

In the market economy, the price measures the relative scarcity of the bread and is determined by the willingness of farmers, bakers, and retailers to supply their products and resources, and the purchasing decisions made by millions of consumers. In the command economy, the price is set by central planners.

In the market economy, if at some initial price the quantity demanded exceeds the quantity supplied, then the price of bread will rise, producers will see this higher price and respond by bringing more bread to the market, while consumers see the higher price as a signal to reduce their consumption of bread. If the higher prices persist because people have decided to begin eating more bread, eventually more people and firms will become bread producers. Then, over time, more resources will be used to make bread instead of other products.

In the command economy, when the quantity demanded exceeds the quantity supplied, the initial result will be that bread disappears from the grocery shelves, and long lines will form whenever new shipments do arrive from the bakery. The same thing might happen, briefly, in a market economy, until sellers independently take their cue from the lines and raise the price, which decreases the quantity demanded *and* makes bakers willing to produce more bread. However, in a command economy the lines do not automatically result in an increase in the price of bread -- that requires some action by the central planning group, which may or may not choose to raise the price.

In some command economies, the prices of basic food staples like bread become a serious political issue as well as an economic concern. Central planners may find it socially and personally advantageous to keep these prices low, even though the shelves remain empty most of the time and lines remain long when some bread is available. And even if the price is raised to eliminate the lines, that may or may not lead to a higher level of output of bread because the production decision is largely divorced from the pricing decision in a command economy. In the Soviet Union, for example, a *TURNOVER TAX* was sometimes imposed on products to limit the quantity demanded, but the revenues from that tax did not necessarily flow to the producers of those products. To produce more in a command system requires either a decision by the planning group to increase production quotas, together with an increase in the allocation of productive resources to these uses, or new incentive programs to encourage or threaten workers and managers to meet existing quotas.

Supporters of the market system stress the freedom and efficiency achieved by letting people buy whatever they can afford that makes them happiest, and letting firms produce whatever they can sell profitably to consumers in competition with other firms. Along these lines, Adam Smith noted that most producers will be led to provide the kinds of products people want, at reasonable prices and with reasonably courteous service, simply because if they don't someone else will. For the same reason, workers will work diligently and employers will pay the market rate of wages to their workers. All of this doesn't happen because consumers, workers, producers, and employers are all generous and altruistic in their business and financial dealings, but *because* they are rational and self-interested. And that in itself leads to important social benefits. In a famous passage in *The Wealth of Nations*, Smith wrote that

> ...(I)t is only for the sake of profit that any man employs a capital in the support of industry; and he will always, therefore, endeavour to employ it in the support of that industry of which the produce is likely to be of the greatest value, or to exchange for the greatest quantity either of money or of other goods.

27

But the annual revenue of every society is always precisely equal to the exchangeable value of the whole annual produce of its industry.... As every individual, therefore, endeavours...so to direct that industry that its produce may be of the greatest value, every individual necessarily labours to render the annual revenue of society as great as he can. He generally, indeed, neither intends to promote the public interest, nor knows how much he is promoting it. ...(H)e intends only his own security; and by directing that industry in such a manner as its produce may be of the greatest value, he intends only his own gain, and he is, as in many other cases, led by an invisible hand to promote an end which was no part of his intention. Nor is it always the worse for the society that it was no part of it. By pursuing his own interest he frequently promotes that of the society more effectually than when he really intends to promote it. I have never known much good done by those who affected to trade for the public good.[4]

Those who favor command economies believe such systems eliminate wasteful practices associated with firms competing for business, such as advertising and bankruptcies. Further, they say command economies lead to a more equal and equitable distribution of income, and reduce expenditures on bad or useless goods and services produced in market economies, such as high fashion clothing and decadent forms of entertainment and publications. Many of these issues will be considered in more detail in later chapters. What is important for you to see now is that different kinds of economic systems have evolved to deal with the problem of scarcity, and they deal with that problem in substantially different ways.

You should also recognize that, in practice, all modern economic systems include some features of market, traditional, and command systems, and so may be described as *MIXED ECONOMIES*. Still, it is often more useful and informative to note the differences in the systems -- for example, by describing the United States' greater reliance on markets to answer the three basic economic questions, and China's greater reliance on command and central planning -- than it is to describe these and all other systems as mixed economies.

Chapter Summary

1) *SCARCITY* is the fundamental economic problem; it results because human *WANTS* are relatively unlimited, while only a limited quantity of *RESOURCES* is available to satisfy those wants.

2) An economic *GOOD* or *SERVICE* is one that satisfies wants but is not available at a zero price -- i.e., someone must give up something to use the product.

3) Because of scarcity, using an economic good or service to satisfy any particular set of wants implies that it can not be used to satisfy other wants. The *OPPORTUNITY COST* of using a product or resource in a given way is its highest-valued alternative use.

4) The four basic categories of productive resources are *LAND*, *LABOR*, *CAPITAL*, and *ENTREPRENEURSHIP*. Land includes all natural resources. Labor includes all routine human effort involved in the production of goods and services. Capital goods are those used to produce other goods and services; *HUMAN CAPITAL* is produced by investments in education, training, and health care which make workers more productive. Entrepreneurship involves risk taking, and producing goods and services with the hope that they can be sold at prices high enough to cover all opportunity costs of the resources used in production.

5) *SPECIALIZATION* and the division of labor increase the productivity of available resources and diminish the burden of scarcity.

---

[4]Smith, Volume I, pp. 477-78.

28

6) *COMPARATIVE ADVANTAGE* refers to the idea of producing goods and services at the lowest possible cost, including opportunity costs. When individuals, regions, and nations specialize along the lines of their respective comparative advantages, worldwide production levels are maximized. There are, however, important disadvantages to this level of specialization that must also be considered.

7) Lowering the *TRANSACTIONS COSTS* of making exchanges increases the potential size of the *MARKETS* that can be served by producers, which expands opportunities for specialization and the division of labor.

8) Voluntary *EXCHANGE* takes place because buyers and sellers can mutually benefit by trading with each other.

9) Investment in capital goods, human capital, and technology are additional means of promoting increased production and economic growth. However, this investment is not free; it requires a reduction in current consumption levels and entails risk.

10) *DEMAND* is a schedule relating each possible price for a product with the quantity consumers are willing and able to buy at that price. As the price increases, other things being equal, the *QUANTITY DEMANDED* will decrease.

11) Demand curves and schedules show an inverse relationship between price and quantity demanded because of *INCOME* and *SUBSTITUTION EFFECTS*, and the *LAW OF DIMINISHING MARGINAL UTILITY*.

12) *SUPPLY* is a schedule relating the possible prices for a product with the quantity producers are willing and able to sell at each of those prices. As the price increases, other things being equal, the *QUANTITY SUPPLIED* will increase.

13) The *SHORT-RUN* supply curve shows a direct relationship between price and quantity supplied because of the *LAW OF DIMINISHING MARGINAL RETURNS* and comparative advantages in the use of various factors of production. The short run is defined as a time period in which at least one factor of production is fixed, implying that the short run will be a longer period of time in some production processes than in others.

14) The one price at which quantity demanded will equal quantity supplied is known as the *MARKET CLEARING or EQUILIBRIUM PRICE*. This price is the market measure of the relative scarcity of a product.

15) (Case Study #1) *PRODUCTION-POSSIBILITIES FRONTIERS* show how many units of two goods, or two classes of goods, an individual, nation, or other production unit can produce using all available resources. These schedules and graphs can be used to illustrate the basic concepts of scarcity, choice, and opportunity cost.

16) (Case Study #2) There are three basic types of *ECONOMIC SYSTEMS*: *MARKET*, *TRADITIONAL*, and *COMMAND*. Each of these systems provides a mechanism to deal with the fundamental economic problem of scarcity by generating answers to three basic questions: What goods and services will be produced? How will they be produced? and Who will consume them?

Review and Discussion Questions

1) Do you agree that human wants for material goods and services are unlimited, relative to the resources available to satisfy those wants? Can you offer examples of individuals or nations of people whose wants were apparently not unlimited? Are some kinds of goods and services better described as needs rather than wants?

2) Is clean air an economic or free good?

3) What is your opportunity cost of reading this book, taking this course, and enrolling in college? Are the costs the same for your classmates? Why or why not?

4) To what category of productive resources would each of the following people and items be assigned by an economist?

a)	A physician	b)	An accountant	c)	A ditchdigger
d)	A farmer	e)	A stock broker	f)	A restaurant owner
g)	A hammer	h)	A bank building	i)	A car
j)	A milk cow	k)	A virgin forest	l)	A bag of garbage

5) What are the major benefits and costs associated with the departmental specialization and division of labor used at the college or university you are attending?

6) Comparing the U.S. economy to those of Japan and Saudi Arabia, where do you suspect the comparative advantages for these nations lie in terms of the production of goods and services? Specifically, what goods are they most likely to import and export?

7) How would the adoption of a global language and currency affect the extent of worldwide trade? Would you endorse such innovations?

8) When the United States trades wheat with Saudi Arabia in exchange for oil, who benefits? If the United States restricts the number of Japanese cars that may be sold in the United States, who benefits? Does anyone lose in either of these two situations?

9) What countries do you believe have invested most in new technology and capital goods over the past 10-20 years? Why might they have invested more than other countries? How could you measure or approximate the amount of this investment?

10) If tuition at your college or university tripled next year, would you still come to the same school? Would all of your classmates? Would the reaction of next year's juniors and seniors be likely to differ from those of freshmen and sophomores? Would the average number of courses taken by those who do attend be likely to change?

11) How would the substitution and income effects, and the law of diminishing marginal utility, be at work in question #10?

12) Would the short-run supply of crude oil in the world energy market be upward sloping, like the curve presented in Figure 1-2? Why or why not?

13) Can labor ever be a fixed factor of production, and if so does this make the law of diminishing marginal returns apply, as in cases where land or capital is the fixed input?

14) What causes a product to become more or less scarce? How is this reflected in the market clearing price of the product?

15) (Case Study #1) Explain how production-possibilities frontiers can, or cannot, be used to illustrate the following concepts:

a) Scarcity   b) Choice   c) Opportunity Cost
d) Investment   e) Price   f) Comparative Advantage

16) (Case Study #2) How would the following events be resolved in market, traditional, and command economies?

a) A three-year drought leads to a 20% decrease in food supplies.
b) For some reason, 10,000 more men's shirts are produced than people are willing to buy at current prices.
c) A leading inventor wants to get a new machine produced.
d) People begin saving 20% more this year than they did last year.
e) The percentage of the population over 50 years of age begins to grow rapidly.

Appendix to Chapter 1: Graphical Analysis

In this Appendix...

we provide a basic primer on two-dimensional, Cartesian graphs for students who have not worked with these tools in other courses. This also serves as a basic review of those techniques for students who have used them before, and shows some of the particular applications of graphical analysis that economists most often employ, including measurements of slope along both straight and curved lines, and calculating areas from sections of graphs representing different economic variables.

If you flip through the pages of this book, you will quickly get the idea that economists are fond of using graphs. In fact, a few years ago T-shirts proclaiming "Economists do it graphically" were big sellers at their conventions, which just goes to show that nobody ever went broke underestimating the taste of American economists. It also means you won't do well in this course until you become comfortable and competent with two-dimensional graphs (also called Cartesian graphs, after the French mathematician and philosopher Rene Descartes). Most students have worked with such graphs at least since their first high school course in algebra; but even if you haven't, don't panic. They aren't difficult to understand and use.

Graphs are used to show a *relationship* between variables. When you look at a graph, therefore, the first thing to do is identify what variables are involved in the relationship that is shown. To do that, just read the labels on the graph's axes.

For example, consider the labels on the axes of the three panels in Figure 1-8. The labels in the first panel promise a graph that will depict the relationship between price and quantity supplied, the second a graph of the relationship between total costs (measured in dollars) and the number of units of a product produced (total product), and the third graph will show what happens to the quantity of a product produced as a firm hires more units of labor. You can tell all of that just by reading the labels on the axes, even without looking at the curves that will be drawn in these graph spaces later. That illustrates why, if an axis is not labeled, we have absolutely no idea about what that axis represents, or what any line drawn in that graph space would show. So any time you draw a graph on an exam or quiz, or just to study the material in this course, remember that the first step is to *label your axes!*

The next step is to mark in the scale you are using on the axes, usually starting with a zero value at the point where the two axes intersect, known as the origin. Economists are most often interested in very general relationships between variables, from ranges where very small amounts of two variables are involved all the way up to levels where very large amounts are considered. Therefore, if no specific scales are shown on an axis, we will assume a graph is drawn depicting unit values of zero at the origin, with steadily increasing values as we move up the vertical axis, or rightward on the horizontal axis.

Figure 1-8
Preparing to Graph Three Economic Relationships

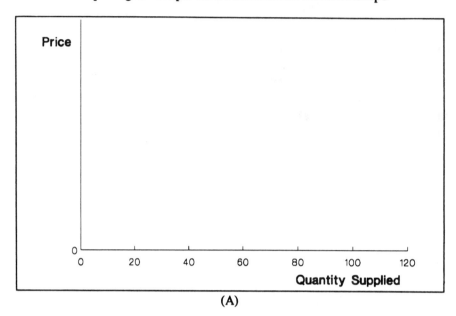

(A)

(B)

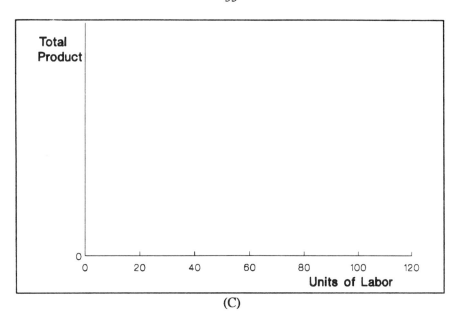

(C)

The graphs that would be drawn on the three sets of axes shown here are called, respectively, a demand curve, a total cost curve, and a total product curve. They show the relationship between the variables indicated on the two axes for each of the graphs.

Once you have read or labeled the axes on a graph, and determined the scale of values on the axes, your most important job is to understand the relationship that is shown between these variables in the graph. The key thing to remember here is that a graph is simply another way to show pairs of values that could be shown in a table, instead of a graph. For example, consider the demand schedule and curve shown in Figure 1-9.

Note that both the numerical schedule and graph show the same paired combinations of price and quantity demanded, which could each be read as "at a price of 10, 1 unit is demanded each week; at a price of 9, 2 units are demanded," etc. More formally, each point on the graph corresponds to one of the numbered pairs in the form (P,Q_d), designating price and quantity demanded in this example, but more generally as (Y,X), since mathematicians call the vertical axis the Y axis and the horizontal axis the X axis. Each pair of points in the table is plotted on the graph by moving up the vertical axis for whatever distance that represents the positive value for Y in the table, and then right (on or parallel to the horizontal axis) the appropriate distance for a positive value of X.

All of the numbered pairs from the table in Figure 1-9 are shown in the graph, and the line drawn through these points in the graph also shows all of the possible pairs *between* the ten that are listed in the table. For example, at a price of 9 1/2 the quantity demanded is 1 1/2. This demonstrates one important advantage graphs enjoy over tables: a graph can represent continuous ranges of data out to infinity, and show the infinite number of points in a finite range, such as all the points on the demand curve between data points (10,1) and (9,2), as shown in Figure 1-9. Tables, obviously, can only show a finite number of data entries. That is one major reason why economists are so fond of using graphs to describe very general relationships. Another reason is that graphs are a visual picture of the relationship between variables, and so are easier to remember, and often much easier to work with, than a long series of numbers in a table.

Figure 1-9
The Simple Law of Demand

Price	Quantity Demanded Per Week
10	1
9	2
8	3
7	4
6	5
5	6
4	7
3	8
2	9
1	10

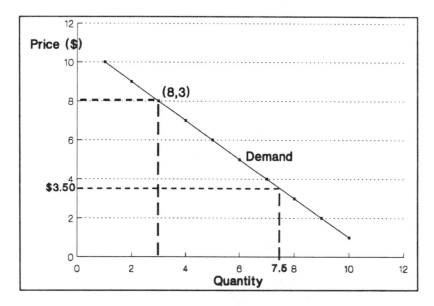

This is the same table and graph presented in Figure 1-1. The pairs of data points shown in the table have been plotted on the graph. For example, the pair (8,3) is 8 units up on the price axis and 3 units to the right on the quantity axis. All of the resulting points are connected to suggest that it would also be possible to buy fractional quantities of the product and pay prices between the integers shown in the table. In particular, note that at a price of $3.50 the quantity demanded is 7 1/2.

In the graphs in Figure 1-10, for example, we start with the axes shown in Figure 1-8, but add all the right curves in all the right places. The graph in panel (A) of this figure shows the quantity of a product supplied increasing as price increases; the graph in panel (B) shows the total costs of production rising as more units of output are produced, but not always at the same rate; and the graph in panel (C) shows that hiring more units of labor will usually increase the amount of a product that is produced -- but not always, and not always at the same rate. This discussion of the rate at which a curve rises or falls as we move out along the axes of a graph leads us to the next key topic in reading and understanding a graph: the concept of slope.

35

Figure 1-10
Graphs of Three Economic Relationships

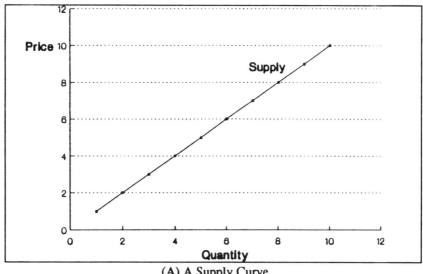

(A) A Supply Curve

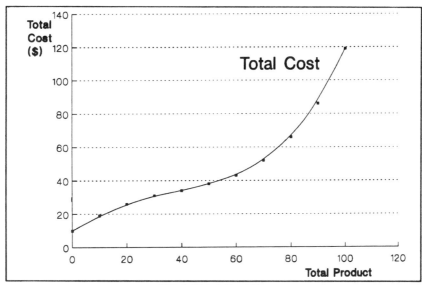

(B) A Total Cost Curve

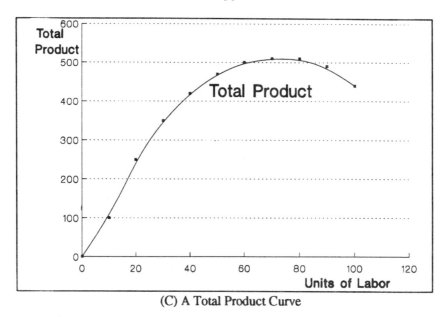

(C) A Total Product Curve

Don't worry about understanding why the graphs shown here look the way they do -- the economic relationships involved are explained in other sections of this book. But be sure you do understand what these graphs are indicating about the changes in the values for one variable that are associated with changes in the value of the variable shown on the other axis. For example, in the first graph quantity supplied increases as price increases; in the second graph, production costs increase as a firm's output level increases; and in the last graph, using more labor usually increases the amount of a product that a firm can produce -- but only up to a point.

Slope

The slope of a line is simply its "rise" divided by its "run" over some range of values on the two axes. This is shown in Figure 1-11, where the rise is labelled ΔY and the run ΔX. A Δ is the symbol (the Greek letter delta) that mathematicians use to represent "the change in." Note that the slope of a line that rises as we move from left to right on the horizontal axis -- such as a supply curve, or the graph shown in panel (A) of Figure 1-11 -- is positive. That simply means that an increase in the value of the variable shown on the vertical axis (such as price on a supply curve) is associated with an increase in the value of the variable measured on the horizontal axis (such as quantity supplied, for the supply curve). So in general terms, we say the two variables on such graphs are directly related, meaning that a positive change on the Y axis is associated with a positive change on the X axis.

Notice that the total cost and total product schedules shown in Figure 1-10 are also positively sloped over most of their ranges, reflecting a direct relationship between values of the two variables shown on the axes for each of those graphs. Everywhere except just to the right of the highest level of output for the total product schedule, the value of one variable always increases as the value of the other variable increases.

However, schedules such as demand curves and the line shown in panel (B) of Figure 1-11 have negative slopes. That is, a positive change in the run of the schedule is associated with a negative change in the rise of the line, or *vice versa*. Using the specific example of a demand curve, as a good's price increases (on the vertical axis), quantity demanded decreases (on the horizontal axis). In more general terms this is known as an inverse relationship, to indicate that the two variables move in opposite directions as their values change.

At several points in your economics coursework you will be asked to develop numerical estimates of slope as well as simple, qualitative, indications of whether slope is positive or negative. In the two graphs shown in Figure 1-11, you should find it easy to calculate the slopes for each of the curves shown. Taking the rise over the run over any range on these straight lines, we find the slope of the first line is +1, and the slope of the second line is -1/2.

Figure 1-11
Determining the Slope of a Straight Line

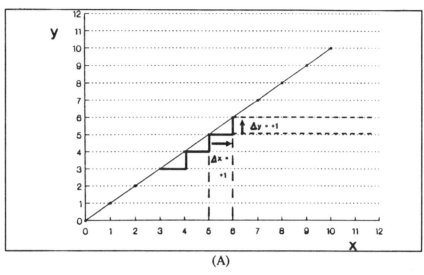

(A)

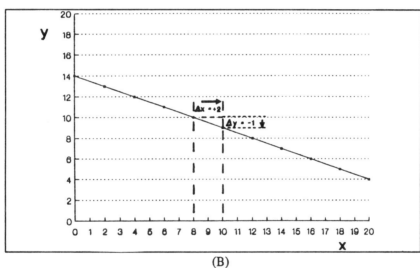

(B)

For the linear schedule shown in panel (A), a one-unit change in value on the x axis is always associated with a one-unit change in value on the y axis. That is,

$$\frac{\text{rise}}{\text{run}} = \frac{+\Delta y}{+\Delta x} = \frac{+1}{+1}$$

so the slope of this line is +1.

In panel (B), a two-unit increase on the x axis is always associated with a one unit decrease on the y axis, or

$$\frac{\text{rise}}{\text{run}} = \frac{-\Delta y}{+\Delta x} = \frac{-1}{+2}$$

so the slope of this line is -1/2.

The two graphs in Figure 1-12 take more thought and explanation. The slope of the first graph is 0, which simply indicates that this function is all run and no (i.e., zero) rise. The second graph is said to have an infinite slope, based on the fact that it is all rise and no run. (Technically, the rise-over-the-run rule would lead you to try to divide by zero, which you probably know is undefined -- a mathematical "no-no." But we are only cheating a bit in this case because, as the line approaches a perfectly vertical position and the run gets closer and closer to zero, the slope of the line approaches infinity.)

Figure 1-12
Two Extreme Cases: Zero and Infinite Slopes

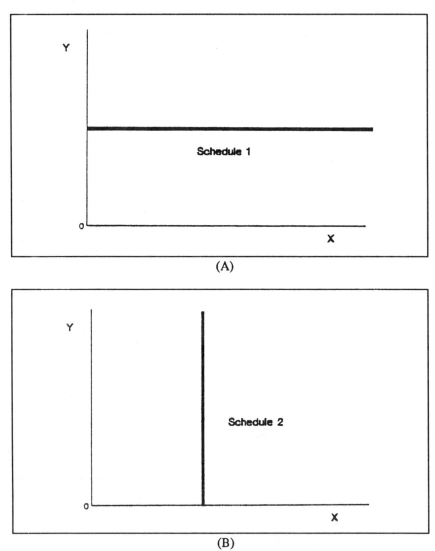

(A)

(B)

In the first graph (Schedule 1), regardless of how much X increases there is no change in the Y variable. Therefore, the slope of any such horizontal line is zero. On the other hand, a vertical line (Schedule 2) represents an infinite slope since it is all rise and no run. Technically, the slope approaches infinity as the line becomes more and more vertical, but is undefined if it becomes perfectly vertical.

Along nonlinear (i.e., curved) lines, slope is not constant, and in fact may be different at every point on the line. We can still approximate the slope over any range of such lines using the rise-over-the-run rule; but that estimate will be more accurate for small changes in the values of X and Y than for large changes. This is demonstrated in Figure 1-13. Note that in the extreme case of measuring slope at a particular *point* on a curved line, the slope will be equal to the slope of the straight line that is tangent to the non-linear function at that point. (A tangent to a point on a curved line is the straight line that touches the curved line only at that particular point, as shown at point d in Figure 1-13.)

Figure 1-13
Approximating the Slope of a Curved (Non-Linear) Line

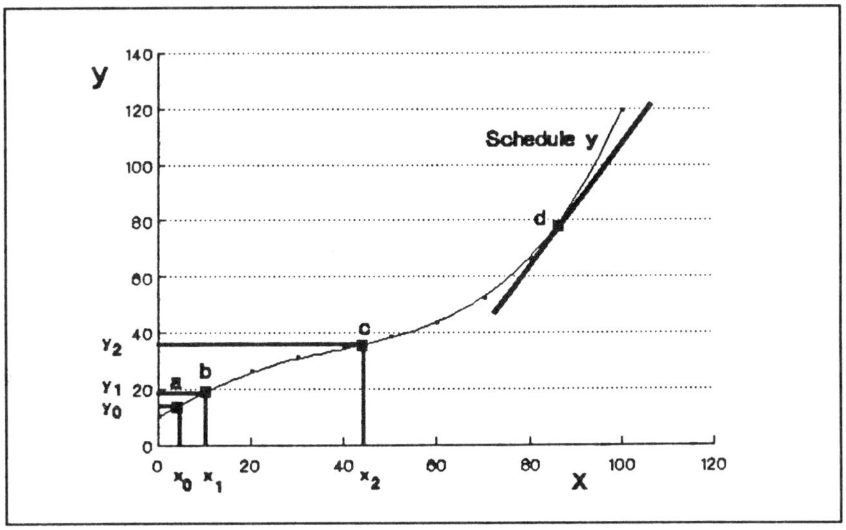

We can estimate the slope of this nonlinear function using the rise-over-the-run rule. From point a to point c, the approximate slope is $\frac{Y_2 - Y_0}{X_2 - X_0}$, which is actually the slope of the straight line found by connecting points a and c. We get a more accurate estimate using this method for smaller changes in X and Y, e.g., between points a and b. In fact, at a single point on the curve, the slope is exactly equal to the slope of the straight-line tangent to the curve at that point, as shown at point d.

Notice too that as we move up the curve shown in panel (A) of Figure 1-14, the slope of the tangents to that line become steeper and steeper. That illustrates the idea of a schedule which is increasing at an increasing rate, which is exactly what certain kinds of economic cost functions do, at least over part of their ranges. In panel (B) of the same Figure, we have drawn a schedule which increases at a decreasing rate, to illustrate that the series of tangents will have flatter and flatter slopes as we move up and to the right on the curve. You will see several economic functions which behave this way in your economics courses, too -- including the largest and most important segments of most total product schedules.

Figure 1-14
Schedules That Increase at Increasing or Decreasing Rates

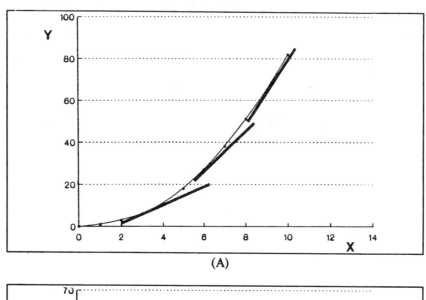

(A)

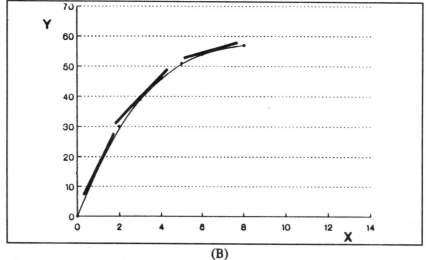

(B)

Moving along a curved line, the slope of the line will not be constant -- it may be increasing or decreasing. In panel (A), tangents to the curve become steeper and steeper at higher values on the x and y axes, indicating that the slope of the curve is constantly increasing, and that values on the y axis increase at an increasing rate as we move outward on the x axis.

In panel (B), the values on the y axis also increase constantly as we move outward on the x axis, but at a decreasing rather than increasing rate. This indicates that the slope of the curve is decreasing as we move to higher values on the curve, and that is shown clearly by the decreasing slope of tangents to the curve as we move along it going away from the origin.

Maximum and Minimum Values

Now consider the two graphs shown in Figure 1-15. Note that Schedule 1 starts from the origin with positive slope, rises for a time (to X_0), and then takes on a negative slope and ultimately falls back to zero. Schedule 2 is an inverted version of Schedule 1. At first it falls with negative slope, then levels off (at X_1), and finally rises with a positive slope. Any smooth, unbroken curve that takes on first a positive and then a negative slope must, in fact, have a leveling-off point. The slope of the curve at that point is always zero, and that point always represents the maximum value of the Y variable over the range of such an inverted U-shape like the curve shown as Schedule 1. Or, the leveling-off point will show the minimum value of the Y variable for a U-shaped curve like Schedule 2. You can see that by drawing the tangents to these curves at their maximum and minimum points. In both cases the tangents are horizontal, which means they have a slope of zero. Remember this little mathematical tidbit, because in economics you will often be concerned with maximizing some things (such as profits and personal satisfaction) and minimizing others (such as costs).

Calculating Values for Geometric Areas

It is also important for you to see how certain values of costs, profits and other variables can be represented and measured by areas in a graph. This is usually a simple matter of finding an area identified by one or more straight lines or curves -- the trick is to determine which lines and which curves, and then to apply some simple mathematical formulas to determine the value of that area.

For example, look at the example shown in Figure 1-16. Given the standard demand curve like the ones used in this chapter, suppose we wanted to know what total revenue a firm facing this demand curve would take in *if* it charged a price of $5. The demand curve shows us that at this price 6 units of output will be sold in the time period represented by the schedule, and that means total revenues will be $30 ($6 times 5 units sold). Graphically, we can show this by drawing in a horizontal line from the point representing $5 on the price axis to the corresponding point on the demand schedule, line BC. Dropping a line from that point on the demand curve perpendicularly to the quantity axis completes the rectangle labeled ABCD in the graph, where the line segments AB and CD are each $5 high, and the segments BC and AD are each 6 quantity units wide. Recalling that the area of a rectangle is equal to height times width, we confirm that the area of ABCD is $30.

It is an easy step from this point to subtract from area ABCD some other area that represents the firm's costs of producing six units of output. Assuming an average cost of $3 per unit, as shown in Figure 1-17, we get a new rectangle representing costs, labeled AEFD, with a height of $3 and a width of 6 units. Total costs -- the area of rectangle AEFD -- are therefore $18. And even more interesting from an economic standpoint is that the firm's profits are represented by rectangle EBCF, which has a height of $2 ($5 - $3, or line segment AB minus line segment AE), and a width of 6 units (for the line segments labelled EF and BC). The firm's profits are, therefore, $12 ($2 per unit times 6 units). Graphically we have, in effect, subtracted rectangle AEFD from rectangle ABCD, following the formula: Profits = Total Revenues - Total Costs. You will see this problem again later in this book, using more realistic (which is to say somewhat more complex) graphs. However, the basic economic and mathematical principles involved do not change.

Figure 1-15
Determining Maximum and Minimum Values of U-Shaped Functions

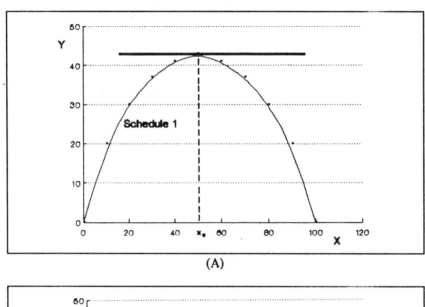

(A)

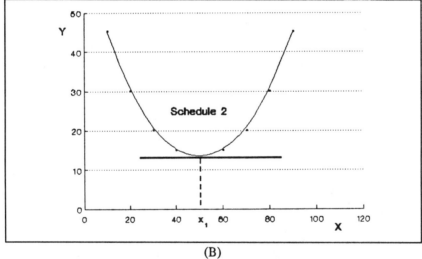

(B)

A horizontal line is tangent to the two graphs above at their respective maximum (Schedule 1) and minimum (Schedule 2) points, in terms of values measured on the Y axis. The slopes of the horizontal lines *and* of the two Schedules at these points of tangency are always zero.

43

Figure 1-16
Using Graphs to Calculate Areas of Dollar Values

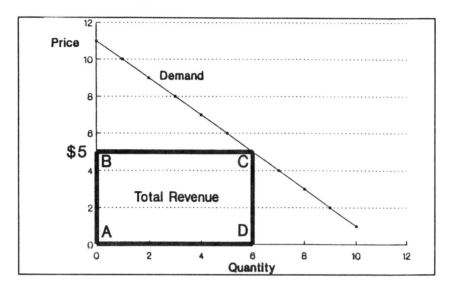

A firm facing the demand curve shown above can earn total revenues of $30 by selling 6 units of output for $5 each.

Figure 1-17
Calculating Costs and Profits Using Graphs

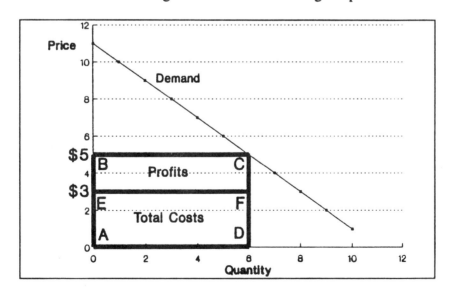

From the $30 of total revenue represented by area ABCD, the firm pays costs of $3 per unit, represented by area AEFD, and earn profits of $12, as shown by area EBCF.

Lying With Graphs

While graphs can be powerful analytical tools and aids to understanding, when used improperly they can mislead and confuse. For example, the apparent steepness of a schedule can be manipulated simply by changing the scale or starting points of the axes, as shown in Figure 1-18. Someone trying to argue that producers are responding to rising prices by producing much more output might choose to use the graph shown in panel (A), while someone arguing that producers are producing only a little more would prefer to use the graph in panel (B). But in fact, the two graphs show *exactly* the same data points. The only difference is that panel (A) uses a scale of hundreds on the horizontal axis, while panel (B) uses a scale of thousands. The obvious moral of this example is: Let the careful reader beware, and draw his or her own conclusions -- don't just passively accept other people's ideas, statements, or graphs.

The story graphs tell can also be made to look very different by omitting values from one or both axes, as shown in Figure 1-19. Starting the vertical axis at a value of 4% in panel (B), rather than at 0% as in panel (A), makes the fluctuations in unemployment rates plotted on the graphs *look* much more extreme. But once again, exactly the same data points are plotted in these two graphs. And although the numbers are the same, deleting some values on the vertical axis makes the story *look* very different. Watch for this trick whenever you are reading reports that have a certain point of view to sell -- reputable writers will put slash marks or some other device on any axis where some values have been dropped, to alert their readers rather than mislead them.

An even more deliberate attempt to lead readers down the primrose path -- or at least a more careless use of data -- occurs when someone selects an unrepresentative sample of observations and claims that they are representative of the general pattern that holds for the variables involved. For example, the two graphs in Figure 1-20 show the interest rates paid on 10-year U.S. Treasury Bonds over two different time periods, from 1977-1981 in the first graph, and from 1953-1988 in the second graph. The claim that interest rates on these bonds always rise from year to year could be supported by the first graph, but clearly refuted by the second. In other words, the uniformly increasing rates observed in the shorter time period were not representative of the more variable pattern observed over the longer period of years, even though an unscrupulous broker selling stocks and bonds might tell customers they were. There are many cases in economics where we don't expect data from a particular time period to be representative of more general trends. For example, patterns observed in periods of great upheaval or war, such as the 1930s and 1941-45, are often not representative of trends and relationships observed in more normal periods.

Figure 1-18
Confusing Steepness and Scale

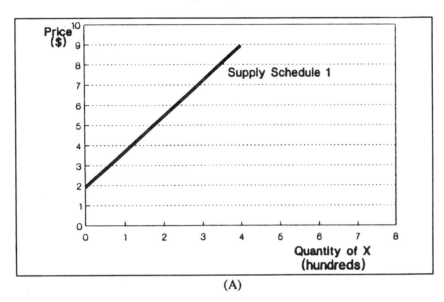

(A)

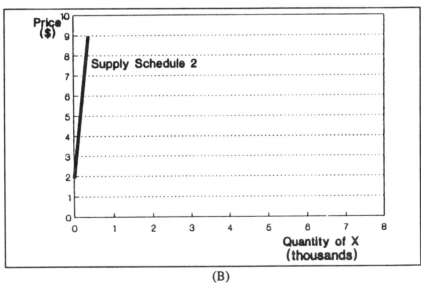

(B)

Despite the fact that Supply Curve 2 looks much steeper than Supply Schedule 1, in fact they are plotted from exactly the same data points. The apparent difference in the values and steepness of the schedules results from the different quantity scales used on the horizontal axes in the two graphs.

Figure 1-19
Omitting Values on an Axis

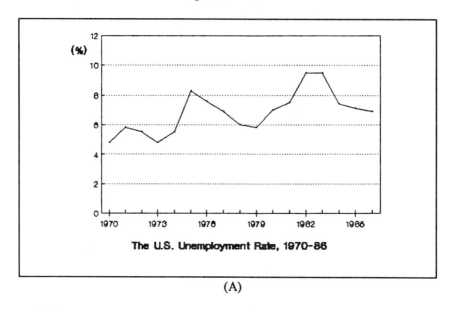

(A)

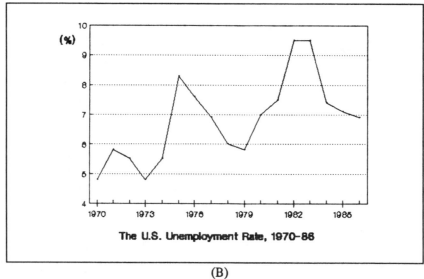

(B)

Here the schedule shown in panel (B) appears to vary much more dramatically than the schedule shown in panel (A). Again, however, both graphs plot the same data points. The difference this time is that the vertical axis on panel (B) starts at 4%, not 0%.

Figure 1-20
Unrepresentative Samples

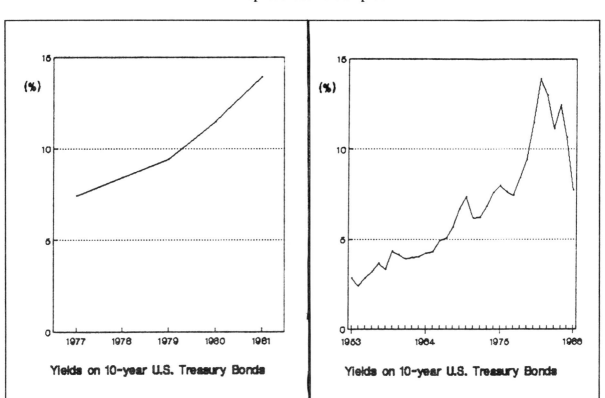

(A)   **(B)**

By limiting the number of observations reported and carefully selecting the base period used for comparisons or as a starting point, writers may convince gullible readers that a variable usually or uniformly follows a particular trend, when in fact the long-run pattern is very different or much less predictable. For example, interest rates rose steadily from 1977-1981, as shown in panel (A), but behaved much more erratically over longer periods of time, as shown in panel (B).

Winston Churchill once identified three kinds of lies: "lies, damn lies, and statistics." If Churchill had studied more economics, he might well have added "graphical analysis" as a fourth kind of lie. But statistics (discussed at a very basic level in the next chapter) and graphical analysis are too important and, when used properly, too helpful to our understanding of the economic world around us to dismiss so lightly. So we prefer the homespun wisdom which states that "figures don't lie, but liars figure." In other words, you have to learn about graphs and statistics, if only to know when someone is playing fast and loose with facts and figures.

Finally, be warned that just being able to read a graph doesn't mean you understand all of the key features of the economic relationship between the variables that are shown this way. We will spend many pages in several later sections of this book developing the economic assumptions and understandings that lie behind each of the functions that were used in this appendix. But using the basic graphical techniques presented here will allow you to understand and use these concepts faster, and often with more precision than you could with only verbal or tabular information.

48

Appendix Summary

1) Graphs are regularly used in economics to depict functional relationships between two variables, and to analyze where a function will be maximized, minimized, or equal to some specified value, given various economic conditions and constraints. A graph is constructed by plotting out all of the paired combinations of points for the two variables shown on a graph's axes, and the positions of those paired points are determined by the functional statement of the economic relationship between those variables. For example, the law of demand indicates that the quantity of a product demanded will decrease when the price of the product increases. That relationship establishes the general shape of a demand curve -- it falls from left to right when price is plotted on the Y axis and quantity values are shown on the X axis.

2) Over any range of a straight line, the slope of the line is its rise (measured on the Y axis) divided by its run (measured on the X axis). For a curved line, the slope is different at different points of the line; but it can still be estimated using the rise-over-the-run rule. These estimates will be more accurate over small ranges on the curve than over large ranges. In fact, at a particular point on the curve the slope of the line is precisely equal to the slope of the tangent to the curve at that point.

3) Horizontal lines have a slope of 0; vertical lines have an infinite slope. Curved lines which rise and then fall will reach their maximum value on the Y axis at the point where their slope (and the slope of the tangent to the curve) is 0. Similarly, curved lines which fall and then rise reach their minimum value on the Y axis when the slope of the line (and the tangent) is 0.

4) The Y-axis values on a curved line which rises and always becomes steeper as we move rightward on the X axis increase at an increasing rate. On a curve which always rises but becomes less steep at higher values on the X axis, the Y-axis values increase at a decreasing rate.

5) Areas in a graph are often used to identify and measure the value of various economic variables, such as revenues, costs, profits and losses. These areas may even be added together or subtracted from each other to obtain additional information that is important to the economic analysis of situations involving individual consumers or businesses, or the economic performance of the national economy.

6) While graphs are important and useful tools in conducting economic analysis and conveying information about economic trends and conditions, they can be intentionally or inadvertently misused to confuse unsuspecting readers. Major problems that can lead to such misinformation and misinterpretation include: a) confusing steepness and scale on graphs using different values on one or both axes; b) omitting values on one or both axes to change the appearance of a line that is plotted on a graph; and c) using an unrepresentative sample of data to estimate a relationship, and then claiming that those results are typical for most other periods.

Review and Discussion Questions

1) Draw out the graphs associated with each of the columns of Y data shown below, using the same column of data points for the X axis in each of those graphs:

X	Y_1	Y_2	Y_3	Y_4	Y_5
0	0	18	0	0	0
1	3	15	1	6	4
2	6	12	3	11	6
3	9	9	6	15	7
4	12	6	10	18	6
5	15	3	15	20	4
6	18	0	21	21	0

2) a) Calculate the slopes for schedules Y_1 and Y_2 shown in the table for question #1.

    b) Estimate the slopes for schedules Y_3 and Y_4, first over the range from X = 1 to X = 6, and then over the range from X = 2 to X = 3. Over these respective ranges, which of those estimates is a more accurate estimate of the slopes of these curves at the points directly on these schedules?

3) What is the slope of the tangent to schedule Y_5, shown in the table in question #1, at the point X = 3, Y_5 = 7?

4) Draw a series of tangents to the graphs for schedules Y_3 and Y_4, shown in the table for question #1. What happens to the slopes of those tangents along the schedules moving away from the origin, and what does that indicate about the values on those two schedules?

5) Assume that the points shown in the X and Y_2 columns in the table for question #1 represent the demand curve for some product. Calculate, and show graphically, the amount of money that consumers would spend for the product if the price were set at $9. If the costs of producing the products to satisfy that demand were $7 per unit, what profits would the producers of this product earn? Show that area on your graph as well.

6) Using the Y_1 and Y_2 schedules shown in question #1, show how changing the scale of the X and/or Y axis can make graphs of those schedules look steeper or flatter. With schedule Y_5, omit Y values from 0 to 3 to present a one-sided view of the relationship between X and Y values for this schedule.

Chapter 2
Building and Using Economic Models

In This Chapter...

we explain the basic steps economists follow in building and testing models of the behavior of individuals and organizations. While the use of these models sometimes contributes to the public image of economists as people who are "ivory tower" theorists and uncommonly argumentative, it has also led to substantial improvements in our understanding of economic activities and problems.

The Rules Economists Play By: An Introduction

Economic methodology is the set of methods and rules economists follow in selecting what issues to study, and in evaluating the theoretical and empircal (statistical) evidence about the factors that influence those issues. This methodology plays an important role in distinguishing economics from other fields of study, and in making it possible for economists to understand and appraise work done by other economists -- even those who study very different kinds of topics and problems. For example, the two major branches of economics are microeconomics and macroeconomics. Microeconomists study the behavior of individual consumers, producers, or markets, while macroeconomists study the overall workings of the national, or even world, economy. But that classification is based on the different kinds of problems and variables studied in the two sub-fields, not different procedures or rules in building and evaluating the economic models used in the two areas.

Consensus and Dissention Among Economists

Economists don't always agree with each other. At least not according to playwrite George Bernard Shaw, who claimed that "If all the economists in the world were laid end to end, they wouldn't reach a conclusion." Or according to former President Reagan, who said that an economist's version of *Trivial Pursuit* would feature 3000 answers to 100 questions.

Nevertheless, many prominent economists have written books, articles, and countless after-dinner speeches arguing that there is a high degree of consensus among economists on such controversial issues as the free trade versus buy American debate; price controls on housing, energy, and basic food items to assist low-income families; legal limits on wage and price increases to control inflation; the most promising kind of welfare reform and poverty-assistance programs; and new approaches to pollution control and related environmental issues. There are, in fact, occasional surveys of economists from the United States and other countries, which repeatedly identify many such areas where economist do agree, and some where they do not.

The areas of agreement usually, but not always, have been achieved by economists who study microeconomic problems and issues; the highly publicized disagreements are most common in the area of macroeconomics. Let's look at those two areas to see why that is true.

Microeconomics

MICROECONOMICS deals with the actions of individual consumers and families, or of individual businesses, or of an industry of firms which produce similar or identical products. Those actions are influenced by the economic *INCENTIVES* facing these units, and by the information available to them about the likely effects of the alternative choices they might make. So microeconomists study such problems as how a consumer makes spending and saving choices, how firms producing similar products compete, how labor markets and labor unions function, or how best to reduce a family's poverty and a firm's pollution.

The methods, models, and data that economists have developed in studying such problems have been consistent and powerful enough to achieve a high degree of consensus in terms of the way these problems are perceived, even to the point of economists agreeing on a wide range of public policy recommendations to deal with the problems. Public policies are laws, regulations, or government assistance programs enacted by a legislative body. These policies are adopted based in part on testimony of those who would be affected by the programs, and by government and private experts on such programs -- including economists. On microeconomic issues, even when economists' recommendations are rejected in Washington or in other seats of government as being politically naive or ivory-tower impractical, at least the economists send out a clear and largely consistent message.

There are, of course, some important microeconomic issues over which economists strongly disagree, as you will see in later chapters. But these disagreements are the exceptions, rather than the rule.

Macroeconomics

MACROECONOMICS deals with aggregated variables that measure the activity of the national or global economy as a whole, rather than an individual household or business unit's economic activity. For example, macroeconomists study the average level of all prices instead of the price for one good or service, and the national production level of all goods and services rather than the equilibrium quantity in a single market for a particular product. Macroeconomists also study such problems as inflation, unemployment, and improving living standards for all people in a nation through the process of economic growth.

Money, interest rates, and the banking system play key roles in macroeconomic studies. Money is important in macroeconomics because it is the commodity which represents generalized purchasing power, or the ability to buy all other goods and services. Interest rates are important because they represent the price of money and a financial cost of investments in factories, machinery, and other capital goods. The banking system is crucial in macroeconomics because that is where money is created and destroyed as loans are made and paid off, and influenced by policy actions of the central bank (in the United States, the Federal Reserve System).

Macroeconomic concepts and issues were not extensively and systematically studied by economists before this century. In fact, it was John Maynard Keynes, the champagne drinker you met in Chapter 1, who launched macroeconomics as a distinct sub-discipline of economics in the 1930s, with a major assist from the public outcry to "do something" to deal with the Great Depression.

Partly because macroeconomics is newer than microeconomics, and partly because its problems involve a larger number of variables, institutions, and simultaneously determined factors than the problems usually studied in microeconomics, consensus is not yet a characteristic of work in macroeconomics. Nevertheless, macroeconomists today have developed much better data on the performance of national economies than was available just 30 or so years ago. Because of this, and the development of several different kinds of macroeconomic models, there is now considerable professional agreement on policies that can greatly reduce the chances of anything as drastic as the Great Depression, or the triple-digit inflations of other places and times, ever afflicting the U.S. economy again. Yet macroeconomists are still divided among several major *competing* schools of thought. And the predictions and recommendations offered by economists to deal with routine or even moderately severe macroeconomic problems are often widely disparate and contradictory, reflecting the different analytical ideas of advocates from the different schools.

When you study macroeconomics, you will see how very intelligent people with similar educational training, interests, and experience can look at the same data and reports, see the same national and world conditions, and come to very different conclusions. At times this may reflect differences in personal values, related to ideas on what problems facing the nation are most serious. But quite often there are direct disagreements on what policies are most effective in dealing with a particular problem or problems. If you like nice, clean, simple answers to nice, clean, simple problems, you probably won't want to be a macroeconomist. But if you like to deal with the big picture, get in the middle of important but often controversial issues with lots of rough edges and some factors beyond your control, macroeconomics may well be the field for you.

The Economic Method

Despite these differences between microeconomics and macroeconomics they are, all things considered, more alike than different. They both accept scarcity, choice, and opportunity costs as the basic economic facts of life. And they both use the same basic methods and procedures to try to prove that one explanation of some phenomenon is better than another, or that one model predicts future developments better than others. In other words, there is fundamental agreement among most economists about the basic kinds of problems involving material resources, and what the rules of evidence should be in analyzing these problems and developing answers for them. Those rules are the subject of the remainder of this chapter.

Economic Models and the Positive vs. Normative Distinction

Theoretical models of economic activity are built up from claims about the cause-and-effect relationships between two or more variables. Once constructed, those models are used to predict what will happen in the part of the economic system they describe as the values of the variables included in the models change. A model is tested and evaluated on several criteria, including the logical and mathematical consistency of its individual and combined assertions about cause-and-effect relationships, and ultimately by whether its predictions conform to behavior that is observed in the economy. Deciding which activities and problems to study with such models reflects normative judgments by economists about what things are most interesting and important to understand.

Stating a Problem and Hypotheses

It could happen to you: You walk into your first economics class and your instructor says your term project is to build a simple economic model and test it. Your model must somehow relate to a real world problem, and it will count as 30% of your grade in the course. This isn't how you planned to spend your weekends, but how do you start your project?

An economic model is either built to address a particular problem that people want to solve (e.g., persistent unemployment), or to better understand how some economic process works (e.g., the factors that influence supply and demand in a certain market). Therefore, your model must first pass the "So what?" test: Does anyone care enough about the topic you are addressing to be interested in your model and its ability to explain or predict? This ultimately involves a normative decision about what ought to be, because your choice of a problem will implicitly be based on a claim that something is wrong enough to justify the use of resources to try to help fix it, or your choice of the process you model on the implicit claim that it is important enough to try to understand in more detail.

Assuming your model passes the so what test, your next task is to identify the specific questions you will attempt to answer with it. For example, you may decide to work on the general problem of predicting future price levels for a commodity, such as pork bellies. Your specific question might be how changes in suppliers' inventories are related to changes in product prices. By stating this specific question, you are beginning to form an economic theory, or hypothesis, about how two or more variables are related. You will have formed your theory when you suggest or assert the nature of that relationship -- e.g., that increases in inventories will lead to future decreases in price.

An economic model is made up of a logically consistent and reasonably complete set of these theoretical statements, dealing with the specific topic you have chosen to study. Of course any model written out in a few pages can't include everything that goes on in the real world situations you are studying, but as one noted economic theorist said, the art of developing a good model is "knowing how to simplify one's description of reality without neglecting anything essential...."[1]

---

[1]James S. Duesenberry, *Business Cycles and Economic Growth*, (McGraw-Hill Book Co., 1958), pp. 14-15

54

In our pork belly example, if you can show that, say, changes in inventory levels usually lead to changes in product prices, or that changes in product prices are likely to lead to changes in the level of inventories firms will want to hold, or both, you will have developed a model. What you will have shown, in effect, or at least argued, is that some variables are *INDEPENDENT VARIABLES*, and others *DEPENDENT VARIABLES*. Dependent variables are those which change as a result of changes in other variables. Variables which cause the dependent variables to change are known as independent variables. So, for example, in the laws of supply and demand you saw in Chapter 1, quantity supplied and quantity demanded are the dependent variables, while price is the independent variable. That is, changes in the price of a product lead to changes in the quantity of the product supplied and demanded.

In specifying these theoretical statements or hypotheses, you are exclusively concerned with what are known as *POSITIVE STATEMENTS* -- statements that deal with "the way things are," not *NORMATIVE* questions or beliefs on "the way things ought to be." No matter how extreme or shocking an idea may seem, in this stage of model building your only concern is whether or not it helps you explain the questions you are trying to answer. If you have to explain the demand for silver bullets by treating the phases of the moon as an independent variable, so be it.

Normative or moral concerns in the model-building stage don't help, and in fact may hinder. One famous example of this occurred when Galileo was forced to recant a new theory in astronomy -- that the earth rotated around the sun -- after testing it with observations made using early models of the telescope. Galileo's claims violated religious leaders' endorsement of the Ptolemeic system of astronomy, in which the earth was believed to be the physical center of the universe. As a normative system of religious values the Ptolemeic system may or may not have been superior to Galileo's world view. As positive, scientific theory, it was doomed to fail as more evidence like Galileo's became available, and as a physically correct understanding of the solar system became more important to such practical endeavors as navigation, transportation, and communication.

Predictions and Falsification

A strong theory provides testable predictions that can be used to develop empirical evidence which supports or refutes the theory. However, some theories include predictions or assertions that cannot be tested, at least not at the time they are originally developed. That's true of theories developed by eminent scientists -- such as Albert Einstein, whose theory of relativity could only be tested in some aspects after experiments in low-gravity environments were possible -- as well as bright and lovable eccentrics like Charles Fourier, who claimed in the 19th century that his plans for new economic systems based on voluntary cooperation would work because they were already successful on the planet Herschel. Theories which cannot be tested or refuted by observation must be accepted or rejected on the grounds of pure deductive logic -- i.e., on the basis of the internal consistency of the arguments and how they relate to other models and facts which are accepted as true -- or as a simple matter of faith.

Theories which yield predictions that don't come true, or that do not conform to relevant observations from historical and contemporary experience, are usually not long for the world as mainstream science. However, in the social sciences such theories have the disconcerting knack of showing up in slightly different language from one generation to the next, and then enduring with few or no changes if the ideas attract wealthy or powerful sponsors. As Keynes wrote

> ...the ideas of economists and political philosophers, both when they are right and when they are wrong, are more powerful than is commonly understood. Indeed, the world is ruled by little else. Practical men, who believe themselves to be quite exempt from any intellectual influences, are usually the slaves of some defunct economist. Madmen in authority, who hear voices in the air, are distilling their frenzy from some academic scribbler of a few years back.[2]

General Theory of Employment, Interest and Money, (Harcourt, Brace & World: New York, 1964), p. 383. ...lished in 1936.

When this happens, the often slow and tedious process of refuting these theories begins again for the scientific community.

Incomplete and inaccurate theories can be exposed and rejected based on their own poor performance, but they are rarely abandoned until better theories appear. Kenneth Arrow, a Nobel laureate in economics, tells a wonderful story about working as an Army meteorologist during World War II, and being asked to provide a long-range weather forecast for an island in the Pacific which U.S. forces were scheduled to invade in several months. Arrow and his group of forecasters candidly told their general that the evidence consistently showed that such forecasts were unreliable. The general replied that he already knew that, but went on to say that he still needed the forecast "for planning purposes."

Some leading writers who study problems in scientific methodology and the philosophy of knowledge claim that no theories are ever finally proved. Instead, they claim, we move closer to the truth by constantly testing all new and currently accepted models, and rejecting those that are not consistent with empirical data. Therefore, when you present your model to your instructor at the end of the semester, you will want to be able to say that the hypotheses you are offering seem logical, reasonably complete, and are not refuted by your observations of the economic world around you. In other words, you won't claim that you have established new truths once and forever, but you will want to be able to say that your model is not refuted by a careful look at the empirical evidence you had at your disposal.

There are other tests which you may be able to apply to your model, and which are expected to be applied regularly to the models developed by professional economists. We will discuss several of these tests later in this chapter. But first, we will complete our discussion of how normative concerns are involved in determining whether a model passes the "so what" test, and in determining precisely what evidence should be used to evaluate a model's effectiveness.

Economic Goals and Trade-offs

It's not controversial to say that the goal of economics, and all other fields of study, is to make the world a better place. The problem is, what do we mean by "better"? With well deserved modesty, economists admit that their discipline is not, can not, and will never be, the source of any ultimate answer to this question.

What economists do say is that there appear to be several goals involving the production, consumption, and distribution of material resources which most people seem to accept as contributing to the ultimate goals of a better world -- however the ultimate goals are defined. The economic goals are not considered to be of equal importance by all people, certainly; but virtually everyone seems to accept them as valid and important to some degree. Broadly defined, the economic goals can be stated as economic freedom, efficiency, growth, security, and justice. Each of these goals is briefly defined in Table 2-1; and each is considered in a wide range of examples throughout the text. Understanding these economic goals, and the idea of trade-offs among them, is a key part of determining what passes the "so what" test, and what doesn't.

The goals listed in the table are sometimes mutually attainable, but often in conflict with one another. For example, policies designed to promote economic growth may reduce economic security. In one such case, building a new interstate highway may reduce travel time and transportation costs to previously remote areas of a state or city, bringing new products, businesses, and opportunities to residents in these areas. That promotes economic growth. But the new traffic routes may well kill off some businesses located on the old routes into these areas, causing workers at those firms to lose their jobs, and some property values to fall sharply through no real fault of the owners. That reduces economic security for those who are displaced by the new highway system.

At times, *TRADE-OFFS* also arise in trying to achieve any one of these economic goals. The most often-discussed example of this involves the possible trade-off facing nations and, in particular, policy makers such as the President, Congress, and central banking officials, between higher inflation and lower unemployment. Both of these problems affect the goal of economic security. You will study the debate and evidence related to this possible tradeoff in courses on macroeconomics.

Table 2-1
Basic Economic Goals

Economic Efficiency -- Producing goods and services at the lowest possible cost, and at the optimal level of output.

Economic Freedom -- The right to acquire, hold, and dispose of economic resources through the process of voluntary exchange, according to one's own interests and abilities.

Economic Growth -- A sustained increase over time in the real value of goods and services produced in a nation, often stated on a per capita basis.

Economic Justice -- Equity or fairness in the distribution and exchange of economic resources.

Economic Security -- Protection from economic hazards such as poverty, unemployment, and inflation.

Methodological Individualism

Moving further into the uneasy world of normative issues, it is clear that in considering trade-offs that affect more than one person we must deal with fundamental problem of measuring the costs and benefits associated with the changes in some set of circumstances. Typically, economists working in market-oriented, democratic nations like the United States measure these costs and benefits assuming three things:

1) That changes in the material circumstances of all individuals should be counted.
2) That those changes can often be measured most effectively using the market values of the goods and services produced and consumed in the economic system. And
3) That in economic affairs people will regularly do what they perceive to be in their own best interests.

Models based on these assumptions represent an approach known as *METHODOLOGICAL INDIVIDUALISM*. Such models are often used simply because it is difficult to get reliable economic data consistent with other approaches. In other words, a key advantage to this approach is that the market prices of goods and services are comparatively easy to observe and use in economic analysis. Also, as you saw in Chapter 1, market prices reflect the purchasing decisions of individual consumers and producers, which is consistent with the first assumption of methodological individualism.

Another apparent advantage of this approach is that these assumptions seem to strike many people in modern market societies as somehow inoffensive and exclusively positive in nature. Yet several facets of the assumptions are normative, and at least potentially controversial on those grounds. For example, observers from aristocratic nations or eras might say it is foolish to count dollar units of things produced to satisfy unrefined and uneducated individuals in the same way and with the same weight as products made for, or at the direction of, those in more elevated social stations. That wording no doubt offends many people who believe in democratic principles. But if you consider the specific examples of treating dollars spent for the production of "adult" films and magazines or the more tasteless gossip magazines sold at supermarket checkout lines as equal to dollars directed at the production of classic music, dance, or theatre, the aristocratic sentiments may seem a bit more reasonable, at least in some respects.

In fact, the statement that all individuals' preferences should be counted equally is no less normative than the statement that some individuals' preferences should count more than others. Furthermore, economic models *can* be constructed or adapted to yield predictions and policy recommendations for societies in which aristocratic, spiritual, or even dictatorial tastes are the ultimate standard of value, rather than market-determined prices which reflect the aggregated decisions of individual consumers and producers. And these non-individualist models are perfectly reasonable in a purely scientific sense: their predictions can be generated with standard propositions about cause-and-effect relationships that are strictly positive in nature. But in using the predictions from these and other models to develop or evaluate public policy proposals, normative standards are always involved, if only in determining whose spending and welfare counts, and how it will be measured.

Without developing additional positive concepts, models, and data, discussions on these normative aspects of evaluating models or setting public policy tend to be unending and unfruitful, generating more heat than light. Even with the additional tools many normative debates have never, and probably will never, be resolved. Fortunately, however, most economic issues are amenable to extensive amounts of positive analysis as well as normative debate.

It turns out, for example, that many policies designed to achieve some normative goal are ineffective (totally or relative to alternative policy measures), or even perverse in terms of producing exactly the opposite effects from those intended. For instance, increases in the minimum wage designed to increase the income of young and unskilled workers can, under some conditions, make both of these groups worse off because firms hire fewer workers when their wages are increased. In such cases, two economists who disagree on many other issues and policies may well agree in opposing a piece of legislation, based strictly on the positive analysis of its consequences. In fact, that is not an uncommon occurrence.

Keep this discussion of normative goals and issues clear, along with the basic distinction between positive and normative propositions and arguments, as you study economic problems, models, and public policy proposals. At the very least, recognize when some statement or claim is positive, and when it is normative.

Choosing the Most Appropriate Model

Economic models are judged by the accuracy of their predictions, not the degree of detail and realism in their assumptions. In fact, economists tend to favor models with a few, broad assumptions -- which often seem very unrealistic -- because they apply to a wider range of cases and are easier and less costly to use or explain than more complex and realistic models. However, the issue of what model to use to analyze an economic problem is ultimately determined by deciding what kinds of questions the model will be expected to answer.

Simplification and Abstraction

What makes an airplane an airplane, or a bank a bank, or a business a business? There are many different sizes and types of airplanes and banks and businesses, but there are also certain key features that indicate to us that a thing is a member of a certain categories of things -- like airplanes or banks -- and not a member of other categories. Do those key features alone provide a realistic picture of an airplane or bank or business? If not, can they help us answer questions we might want an economic model to answer about the behavior of a business, consumer, or government agency? That depends on the kinds of questions you want to ask, and the degree of detail and realism you want in the answers from your model. Deciding that helps you choose the right kind of model in the first place, in economics and in any other science.

Suppose, for example, your assignment had been to make a class presentation based on a model airplane, rather than an economic model. At least in this case you know you can buy such a model in a toy or hobby shop. But being the thoughtful student you are, when you get to the store you don't just buy the big, plastic model of the B-2 bomber -- complete with 116 movable parts, four sheets of decals, and a flexible toy pilot -- that you see in the store window. Instead, you walk around the store and come to the shelf where cheap, balsa-wood airplanes are displayed. If only to save a few dollars, you begin to think about the two different models.

The B-2 plastic model is much more detailed and, based on external appearances, looks more like the real airplanes that carry people, bombs, and other cargo. It is, in fact, a fine *DESCRIPTIVE MODEL* of the B-2 bomber. But it doesn't look like other kinds of planes, and it can't fly in any sense that comes close to the way that real airplanes do. On the other hand, the balsa models don't look much like any real airplanes, but they do capture more of the *functional* characteristics of real airplanes: the shape and slope of the wings are designed to provide lift, the rubber band and plastic propeller provide thrust, and the shape and weight of the plane result in drag and resistance as it moves through the air. If you accept the idea that the most important and general characteristic of real airplanes is that they fly, then the balsa kit is a better *ANALYTICAL MODEL* of airplanes than the more detailed (and expensive) plastic models.

Most economic models focus more on analysis than on description, but some are much more descriptive and realistic than others. And just as with the model airplanes, the more descriptive and detailed an economic model is, the less general it will be. Even model builders face trade-offs.

All model builders *must* use assumptions to simplify the many things observed in the real world, and clear away everything but the most important variables that influence the problem they have chosen to study. That makes their models abstract and unreal, but without this abstraction and simplification models end up being just as complicated as the real-world situations they are designed to explain -- and no more useful in terms of analyzing those situations to understand and predict outcomes in similar situations. In building your model, then, you wouldn't even try to incorporate all the details of the process you are studying. Instead, you would simplify down to the underlying, fundamental relationships, and try to explain what causes the related variables to interact as they do.

Fitting Models to Particular Questions: General vs. Detailed Predictions

Now we turn to the decision of exactly what questions you want your model to answer, because that will determine the kind of model you will build. If you want your model to provide predictions about the linkages between product inventories and product prices in many different industries and time periods, you will need a very general model that focuses on such basic questions as what all kinds of businesses try to accomplish, and how inventories and prices influence what they are trying to do. If these questions can be answered in clear, meaningful ways, your model will probably be both very general and very useful, despite the fact that it will also be very abstract and simplified *because* you have designed it to address such a wide range of firms.

But suppose you choose to study the inventory-price question in a narrower setting, say in the U.S. auto industry since 1970. You might begin with the kind of general model we just discussed, but you will almost certainly refine that model to incorporate many of the specific features of this particular industry during this particular period of time. For example, interest rates might be more important in your model of auto inventories than they were in the general model for all kinds of products. And gasoline prices might be important to include here even if they weren't treated at all as a separate variable in the more general model. Or you may decide that while profit maximization is a major goal of most firms in most historical periods, it seems that since 1970 most U.S. auto firms have attempted to maintain their "market share," which is to say the percentage of all new cars sold each year.

By incorporating such assumptions into your model you move to a more focused and, of course, narrower model of the price-inventory relationship in a particular setting. If your refined model is a good one, it will give you more extensive and accurate information and predictions about the auto industry than the more general model described earlier. Those results, however, will not be applicable to nearly as many other firms and situations.

BEHAVIORAL MODELS are even more specific, often dealing with how the individual decision makers in a particular firm, household, or government agency go about their business. It might be, for example, that to fully explain the level of car inventories held by the Chrysler Corporation in the late 1980s, you would have to analyze how confident and aggressive Lee Iacocca, Chrysler's Chief Executive Officer (CEO) at that time, felt about Chrysler's future. That could have been influenced by a number of things, such as Chrysler *and* industry sales levels, as well as Iaccoca's plans to have Chrysler acquire smaller firms in and out of the auto business, sales of Iaccoca's best-seller autobiography, and perhaps even developments related to his marriage and personal life. Here, if your model is successful, you would develop better information about the Chrysler Corporation than you would using more general models. Again, however, what you gain in precision would cost you in terms of how useful the model will be in explaining the actions of other firms and industries, or even of the Chrysler Company with a different CEO.

Evaluating Alternative Models

An economic model is more accurate if it predicts future actions more accurately than other models, or explains past and present facts more precisely or fully. For example, macroeconomic models that forecast unemployment and inflation rates better than others are superior to those that yield less accurate predictions, and a model of the effect of railroads on the growth of the American West is more accurate than other models if it explains more precisely the changes that occurred in prices for land, shipping fees and tonnage on railroads and canals, and so forth. In this most basic sense, economic models are judged by their conclusions and predictions, *not* by the degree of realism in the assumptions that underlie them. That is a key thing to remember as you set out to evaluate any economic model. But there are other factors to consider, too.

The first pertains to *INDUCTIVE* theories and models -- those developed from the observation of facts, or on previous studies that were based on or tested against empirical data. Inductive models must be tested against data that is not the same data used in developing the theory. For example, it is not legitimate to look at the data on prices and inventories in the automobile industry for the period from 1930-1940, use those observations to estimate the relationship between those two variables, and then test the theory by seeing how well it explains the relationship in this same time period. It *would* be appropriate, however, to build the theory based on data from 1930-40, or from 1950-1970, and then test it by seeing how well it predicts this relationship in, say, the period from 1970 to the present. Intuitively, it seems more likely that the estimates based on 1950-1970 data would be more accurate in predicting what happened, both because 1930-1940 was an atypical decade for the auto industry (given the Great Depression), and because the data from 1950-1970 probably reflect other structural changes in the industry that occurred after 1940. But intuition is only a weak substitute for an empirical test to see which model works best.

DEDUCTIVE MODELS are developed through introspection, logic, mathematics, or all of the above. For example, an economist might build up a theory of consumption expenditures based on the factors that are most important in shaping his or her own spending, and express those relationships in terms of mathematical equations that include variables to represent prices of goods and services and consumers' incomes. Those equations might then be manipulated to suggest what will happen when prices, incomes, or other variables in the model experience changes in values, perhaps due to some outside influence such as a drought that raises the price of agricultural products. Like inductive models, deductive models are tested by the accuracy of their predictions of future events, or the extent to which they explain current or past events.

Both inductive and deductive models, and combinations of the two, can be useful. And there are abundant examples in fact and fiction of both inductive and deductive types of scientists and scientific work. David Ricardo was the first prominent deductive economist. His friend Thomas Malthus was a prominent inductive economist. Their even more famous predecessor, Adam Smith, brilliantly combined both approaches. In fiction, for the Trekkies among you, Mr. Spock relies primarily on deductive methods, while Dr. McCoy and Mr. Scott more often use the inductive approach to solving a problem. (Captain Kirk relies mostly on his skills as an inter-galactic womanizer.)

A more philosophical problem in evaluating both inductive and deductive models is choosing between different models which seem to predict with equal accuracy. In such cases, economists typically use the model with the least restrictive set of assumptions (which are not necessarily the most realistic, in terms of reflecting all details of the economic activity that is modeled), because that model is more likely to apply to a wider range of cases. That is simply a case of adopting a plain balsa-wood model of airplanes, rather than a model with more decals and features designed to duplicate the features of a particular kind of airplane.

Put differently, economists tend to follow the rule of *"OCCAM'S RAZOR"* (named for the medieval English philosopher William of Occam), by choosing the model that is simplest and least expensive to use and explain. That reflects a natural (for economists) concern with economizing the use of scarce resources. But it also reflects a normative interest in keeping things "elegantly simple," a goal in many scientific and artistic fields. Einstein, for example, once told a group of students that good physics should be simple. When one of the students asked "But what if it isn't?" Einstein answered, "Then I wouldn't be interested in it."

Mathematics and Statistics in Economic Models

Building and evaluating economic models frequently requires advanced mathematical and statistical tools, just as in other natural, physical, and social sciences. But because the conditions economists face in testing their theories and models are different from those facing researchers in the 'pure,' experimental sciences, their procedures often differ, too. In particular, it is often impossible, or at least prohibitively expensive, for economists to run controlled experiments featuring random samples of individuals or businesses operating under laboratory conditions. Questions involving the basic rationality of individual behavior, and decision making at the margin, are also endemic to economic research. These issues further distinguish economic research from research in the natural and physical sciences.

Limited Uses of The Experimental Method

Periodically we hear of medical research on new drugs or surgical procedures which proves that these innovations are effective against some disease or chronic condition. If you read the fine print on such reports, you may be surprised to find that the proof is often based on trials involving a small number of patients (literally, at times, fewer than 100). Economic studies, on the other hand, often involve thousands of people and observations without proving any new breakthroughs. Do medical researchers know something that economists don't? Not really. The difference is that health researchers can more often conduct their tests under strictly-controlled, laboratory conditions, which eliminate influences from variables other than those they want to test. Economists must usually test their theories using observations that *are* influenced by forces other than the one or two variables at the heart of their theories. Their laboratory is usually the real world, where it is normally impossible to conduct controlled experiments under the sanitary conditions that physical and biological scientists often enjoy.

For example, a medical researcher who believes a certain drug may be effective will, after meeting appropriate safeguards, test it by giving the drug to randomly chosen members of a group of patients, while giving a placebo -- an inactive but identically appearing "drug" -- to another group of patients, who form what is called a control group. This allows direct comparisons between the two groups, which are alike in all biochemical respects except for which group receives the test drug, and which group doesn't. There are also studies in which neither the staff who provide the treatment to patients nor the patients themselves are told who is receiving the drug and who is isn't. These "double-blind" studies are designed to insure that all other aspects of the treatment provided to the two groups are identical, including the advice and attention provided by physicians and nurses. Under these strict conditions, if a significantly larger number of the treatment group than the control group improve or are cured, the drug is considered proven to be medically effective.

In economics it is difficult, and in some cases illegal, to expose human subjects to laboratory experiments involving economic variables such as prices, incomes, and employment status at levels that approach the real impact these variables can have on people's lives. Some experimental work has been done in economics despite these limitations, occasionally even using white rats as subjects (which turned out to obey the law of demand, at least in most situations). But it is highly debatable, of course, to say to what extent those findings apply to human economic behavior; so most work in the comparatively new field of experimental economics does employ human subjects. For example, one of the earliest experimental studies in economics involved the derivation of consumer preferences for different combinations of doughnuts and ball-point pens.[3] After a few false starts in the experimental design, it turned out that these preference schedules looked very much the way economic theorists had thought they would -- like the schedules you will see in Chapter 6.

Some prominent economists have called for the expanded use of experimental methods in assessing the effects of key public policy efforts, such as job-training programs for economically disadvantaged groups of women.[4] In

[3]K. R. MacCrimmon and M. Toda, "The Experimental Determination of Indifference Curves," *Review of Economic Studies*, October 1960, pp. 433-51.
[4]Orley Ashenfelter, "The Case for Evaluating Training Programs with Randomized Trials," *Economics of Education Review*, (Vol. 6, #4, 1987), pp. 333-38.

these studies, some applicants would be randomly choosen to participate in the training programs, and others go without training to serve as a control group. But that is still somewhat controversial, and certainly difficult and expensive to arrange. Practical considerations also make such studies impossible in many cases. For example, political approval and funding for such tests is not easy to secure when politicians are unwilling to subject their pet projects to such rigorous scrutiny.

If experimental studies are not feasible, economists usually evaluate public policy efforts such as job training programs, or an economic theory based on a particular variable, in the following way: First they try to specify all of the factors that might influence the variable they are studying. Then they collect real-world data that is varied and detailed enough to allow them to statistically sort out the effects of changes in each variable, including the one (or more) that is at the heart of the theory being tested, or which represents the effect of a public policy program. Finally, they test for the statistical significance of those key variables. The next section explains that process in greater detail.

Functional Relationships and Significant Variables

Physicists talk about actions that lead to predictable reactions. Computer scientists include "if/then" statements in their programs. And chemists, logicians and psychologists look for causes, effects, and catalysts. In all of these cases of scientific endeavor, the intent is to specify the nature of the linkage between two or more variables. In mathematical terms, this is known as stating a functional relationship.

We will write general functional relationships as mathematical statements using the notation

$$A = f(B,C,...)$$

to indicate that the variable A is a function of variables B, C, and any other variables specified within the parentheses. In this particular statement A is the dependent variable, while B, C, and any other variables specified are independent variables. In simpler language, the value of A depends, in some way, on the values of B, C, and any other independent variables.

As an example, let's look at the general statement

$$Q_d = f(P)$$

where Q_d represents the quantity of a good consumers are willing and able to buy. That depends on P, which represents the price of the good. So this is a general statement of the law of demand. To specify the demand relationship between Q_d and P for a particular product, we have to write a specific equation, such as

$$Q_d = 11 - P$$

This equation indicates that price and quantity demanded are inversely related along a linear schedule, meaning that the relationship between Q_d and P will be shown as a straight line that slopes downward to the right. In fact, this is the mathematical function represented graphically as the demand curve in Figure 1-1.

How could we discover such a specific relationship as $Q_d = 11 - P$? In most cases by going to the market for a product and observing changes in prices and purchasing behavior, or by surveying buyers to find out how many units of a product would be purchased at various price levels. The data points are plotted graphically, and the equation for the line that best fits the observations can then be estimated statistically.

For example, the technique of linear regression analysis, described briefly in Figure 2-1, finds the equation for a straight line which is closest to a given set of data points. In this case, we want a line that predicts quantity demanded at all possible prices with the least amount of error. To do that, we find the line that minimizes the sum of the squared vertical distance from each data point to the nearest point on the estimated line. (By using squared distances, all of the distance values are positive -- whether the line is above or below an observed data point -- and the computer or unfortunate researcher who has to calculate a regression line by hand simply looks for the line that yields the lowest positive value of the sum of those distances.) The procedure is linear because it only tries to fit a straight line to the data points. It is called regression analysis largely due to an historical quirk: One of the first and most famous statistical studies found that the average adult height of children born to parents of any given height tends to "regress" toward the average height of the population. In other words, it regresses toward the mean; and we've had that terminology ever since.

Figure 2-1
Regression Analysis

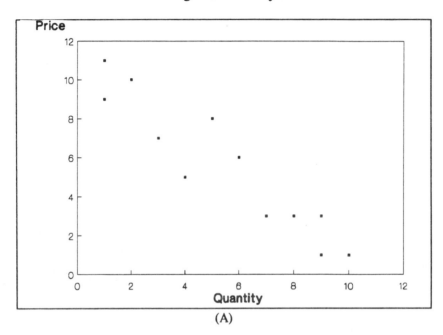

(A)

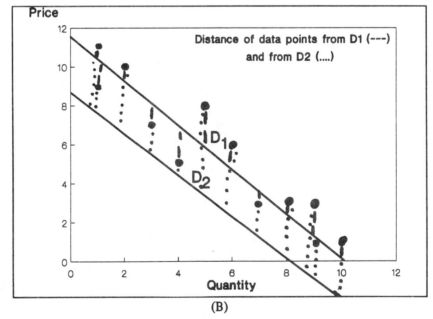

(B)

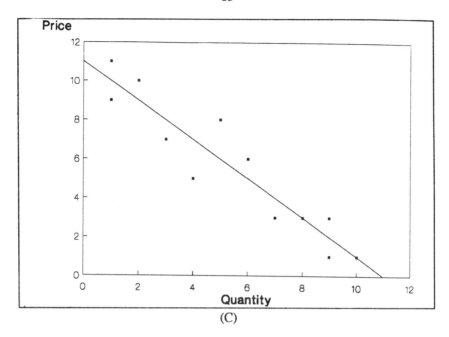

(C)

In panel (A), a series of points are plotted indicating price and quantity demanded combinations observed in a certain market, or collected in surveys and interviews of consumers, or both. Using these data points, a regression procedure fits different straight-line demand curves until it minimizes the sum of the squared vertical distances from each observed data point to the estimated demand line (as shown in panel B). For example, the line labeled D_1 in panel (B) is clearly a better fit than the line labeled D_2. When the best possible fit has been made (panel C), the estimated values of the intercept and slope terms for this line identify the mathematical function for the demand schedule in this particular market -- in this case, $Q_d = 11 - P$. The slope of this line is negative, confirming the inverse relationship between price and quantity demanded we expected, because of the law of demand.

Regression analysis also provides information which can be used to test whether or not the functional relationship between two variables, such as price and quantity demanded, is statistically significant. If the variables are not systematically related the slope of the fitted line will be zero, or very close to zero. If they are related, directly or inversely, the slope will be positive or negative, respectively, but significantly different from zero.

The convention in economics, as in most natural and social sciences, is to test at the five percent significance level. That means that, based on some assumption about the kind of distribution the observations used to estimate these slope values are drawn from (e.g., the bell-shaped "normal" distribution that is often used as a grading curve), in only five percent of cases would we claim to find a significant relationship where none really existed, due to chance variations in the data points that were collected. In many empirical studies hypotheses are also tested at the more stringent one percent level -- meaning that researchers must be even more certain that a suggested relationship between variables is not due to chance before they label it as statistically significant.

The signs and statistical significance of values estimated for individual variables in a regression analysis can support or reject theoretical propositions developed by economists and other researchers. That evidence, in turn, indicates whether certain variables should or should not continue to be included in future models of some economic problem or relationship. Other statistical tests are used to determine what part of the observed variation in the dependent variable is explained by including a particular independent variable, or group of variables, entered in a given format such as linear or non-linear equations. Very few economic relationships involve only a single independent variable, and many relationships are found not to follow simple linear forms. Those complexities require more sophisticated theoretical models and empirical tests. In Chapter 3, for example, we will allow variables other than price to enter into the basic supply and demand relationships.

But each level of reality and sophistication we add -- including each independent variable introduced in the model -- comes at the cost of greater complexity and potential new problems, such as those discussed in the following section.

Correlation, Causation, and Simultaneity

A few years ago, several researchers tried to figure out what helps students learn more economics, and also what makes them like the subject. For example, the researchers speculated that student IQ scores might well influence learning. And whether students chose to major in economics or some field of business might be a variable related to how much they liked economics. But it also seemed quite possible that how much students liked economics might affect how much they learned, while *at the same time* how much they learned could be affecting how much they liked the subject. What do you think? Does learning cause liking, or does liking cause learning? Or, is the answer to both these questions "Yes"? It turned out that students who learned more also reported on surveys that they liked the subject. But that *CORRELATION* -- the fact that students with high learning scores also had high "like economics" scores, and those with low scores in one area tended to have low scores in the other area, too -- was not sufficient to prove any particular pattern of *CAUSATION*. In other words, it didn't show which score rose first, causing the other score to rise, *if* in fact that kind of pattern was present in the data. How could you resolve this kind of question?

The theoretical and statistical problem here hinges on an even older one in economics, that was dealt with about 100 years ago by an economist named Alfred Marshall. Marshall is the economist who first used graphical analysis in a systematic way as a researcher and teacher. He's also the fellow who put price -- the independent variable -- on the vertical axis, and quantity -- the dependent variable -- on the horizontal axis. That's exactly opposite to the way mathematicians and most other scientists plot independent and dependent variables. But economists have followed Marshall's practice ever since, much to the chagrin of math and engineering students taking economics courses, among others.

Marshall did settle, once and for all, the major debate of his time concerning whether market price and output levels were ultimately determined by supply or demand. Obviously, Marshall said, theory tells us that this is a *SIMULTANEOUS RELATIONSHIP*, and he dismissed the whole debate by writing, "We might as reasonably discuss whether it is the upper or the under blade of a pair of scissors that cuts a piece of paper."[5]

Marshall recognized that the equilibrium price and equilibrium quantity for a product could be found when we have equations for both the supply schedule and demand schedule, for example

$$Q_d = 11 - P$$

and (following the supply schedule shown in Figure 1-2)

$$Q_s = P$$

At equilibrium, we know

$$Q_s = Q_d$$

so the right-hand sides of these two equations will also be equal. That gives us

$$2P = 11$$
$$\text{or } P = 5.5 \text{ and } Q = 5.5$$

[5]*Principles of Economics*, 8th ed., (Macmillan Publishers, London, 1977), p. 290.

Marshall thus gave economists a basic framework to model simultaneous relationships. But establishing whether or not one variable in these systems of equations *caused* values of another variable to change was often a more difficult problem. While statistical tests for causality across two or more data series have been developed in recent decades, in most cases the tests require observations taken over some period of time. That way it is possible to look at the pattern of *changes* in the variables that may be simultaneously related.

That has now been done in many studies, looking at many different variables. In particular, several researchers have found that student scores for liking economics are significantly increased when they learn more during their coursework, but changes in their learning scores are not significantly affected by changes in their attitudes.[6] So if you and your instructor want you to like economics more, the thing to do is make sure that you learn more economics.

Rationality and Homo Economicus

Mathematical and statistical tools are built up from a series of rationally defined relationships, such as $2 + 2 = 4$. Therefore, when economists began to apply advanced mathematical and statistical procedures to human actions, assuming that people behave as if they were following such functions, it was not surprising that the issue of how rational people really are arose. In fact, economists are often accused of assuming that the typical consumer, businessperson, and government official is a completely rational, self-interested agent -- *Homo Economicus*.

Economists usually defend the assumption of rational behavior as either accurate, efficient, or necessary. Specifically, most economic models incorporate the notion of rational behavior in the form of three basic assumptions:

1) Decision makers make economic choices from a set of given alternatives which are known to them.
2) The outcomes of these alternative choices are also known, at least in terms of which outcomes are most or least likely. And
3) Decision makers try to maximize or minimize some known function -- such as their own satisfaction in the case of consumer decisions, or production costs for any given level of output in the case of most businesses.

These assumptions can and have been tested statistically, by comparing the predictions of models that are built using them to the actions of consumers, businesses, and government officials. For example, as we noted earlier, researchers have found that under laboratory conditions rats generally exhibit downward sloping demand curves for food, and respond as economic models predict to the substitution and income effects discussed in Chapter 1. If rats are this rational, can't we expect humans to be even more so? In broad, general terms, the answer appears to be yes. Enough people seem to behave rationally in dealing with the kinds of problems economists are interested in to make the predictions based on rationality assumptions generally accurate, important, and useful. Even though no one may be completely rational all of the time, and some people may even be irrational all of the time, in dealing with the economic problems that make up the ordinary business of everyday life, it appears that most people and businesses do behave the way the rationality assumptions predict they will.

Researchers have, however, recently identified some interesting cases where the rationality assumptions do not perform so well. For example, when two psychologists[7] asked large samples of students to choose between two public policies designed to deal with a hypothetical outbreak of a contagious disease in a community of 600 people, they observed a response pattern that questions standard notions of rational behavior. One group of students was told that policy A would save 200 lives, while policy B had a one-third probability of saving 600 lives and a two-thirds probability of saving no lives. The second group of students was told that policy A would

---

[6]See Chapter 7 of W. E. Becker, Jr., and W. B. Walstad, eds., *Econometric Modeling in Economic Education Research*, Boston: Kluwer-Nijhoff Publishing, 1987.

[7]A. Tversky and D. Kahneman, "The Framing of Decisions and the Psychology of Choice," *Science*, (January 30, 1981), pp. 453-58.

result in 400 deaths, while policy B offered a one-third probability that no one would die and a two-thirds probability that 600 people would die. No other remedies were available.

If you are familiar with basic probability calculations you will recognize that the problem the students faced was numerically rigged. Despite the differences in wording, the two groups of students were dealing with exactly the same problem -- the expected number of deaths under both policies is identical. But because of the differences in the way the policy options were described, a large majority (72%) of the first group of students choose policy A, while an even larger majority (78%) of the second group chose policy B.

Economic theories (and those in many other social sciences) would have been in deep trouble if research had concluded that most humans are irrational in most of their actions. But identifying cases which suggest that the extent of this rationality is limited, or that the ability to make perfectly rational decisions is limited in practice if not in theory, only helps to identify some of the current frontiers of that body of knowledge. Optimization of well specified objectives in the face of well known constraints is an economic and mathematical ideal state, in some respects. But it is also a process that individual consumers, firms, and governments try to practice in many situations, with varying degrees of success.

Bounded Rationality

Findings that people do not always make choices in completely rational ways have led some economists, most notably Nobel laureate Herbert Simon, to develop models of *BOUNDED RATIONALITY*. While recognizing the usefulness of the traditional rationality assumptions in most settings, bounded-rationality models proceed by relaxing one or more of the three assumptions. In some cases they explore how consumers, business executives, or public officials use resources to *generate* or look for alternative courses of action, rather than assuming that all options are known. For other problems they examine the limits of current knowledge or people's ability to forecast the future. And in still other studies, they consider the computational difficulties associated with making certain types of choices, and how that affects our ability to know, or at least to achieve precisely, the specific functions we are trying to maximize.

Simon describes this approach as a "central theme in the behavioral approach to economics," which tries to "capture the actual process of decision as well as the substance of the final decision itself."[8] He suggests that for certain classes of problems bounded rationality models may be more accurate and fruitful than traditional models. If that is so, their results may justify the additional costs associated with using these models. Only time will tell how widely they will be used by other economists.

Optimization and Marginal Analysis

One final topic remains in our discussion of economic models -- a simple but subtle set of ideas which eluded economists until they were published independently in works by William Stanley Jevons, Leon Walras, Carl Menger, and Alfred Marshall in the late 19th century. They now form a central part of economic analysis, and are the basic reason that most economic theory can be expressed in mathematical models.

Known collectively as marginalism or *MARGINAL ANALYSIS*, in their most basic sense the ideas express the simple notion that few economic decisions are all-or-nothing propositions. Consumers increase their satisfaction by buying a few more units of some goods and services and a few less units of something else, not by tearing up their past shopping lists and purchasing a completely different bundle of products. Similarly, businesses typically adjust their revenue, cost, and profit positions by changing prices a little or by producing more units of some products and fewer units of others, not by producing all new products or by going out of business. There are, of course, occasionally such dramatic, all-or-nothing decisions that must be faced by consumers, businesses, or even

---

[8]"Bounded Rationality," in *The New Palgrave: A Dictionary of Economics*, J. Eatwell, M. Milgate, and P. Newman, eds., (Macmillian Press, Vol. 1, 1987), pp. 266-67.

governments. But most decisions can be stated in incremental terms: Will the company earn more profit by hiring 10, 11, or 12 workers? Will I be happier if I buy two, three, or four steaks this week? Will the country be better off, or will I have a better chance of getting re-elected, if we fund $5 billion, $6 billion, or $7 billion of water projects in the next federal budget?

The appropriate economic approach to answer these kinds of questions is to weigh the additional benefit -- that is the marginal benefit -- associated with the higher level of consumption, production, or federal spending against the additional cost -- the marginal cost -- of that increased activity. For example, say a firm increases its production and boosts sales by $10,000, but doing that increases its costs by $15,000. It is clear that this increase in production is not a profitable action for the firm. Or, suppose a consumer gets 10 units of satisfaction (however we choose to measure that) by spending an additional $10 on Brand X of a product, but only 5 units of additional satisfaction by spending the same amount on Brand Y. It's clear which of these two products he or she should would buy.

We will examine how consumers, businesses, and governments make these decisions at some length in later chapters. Our primary point here is simply to introduce the concept of choice at the margin. But we also want to make the related point that economic models are often used to link changes in the value of one variable with changes in the value of another. That is, we will be concerned with marginal changes in dependent and independent variables, not just the total values of the variables at one point in time.

Case Study #3
Evaluating the "Sunspot Theory"

In 1801, the British astronomer Sir William Herschel began to build a model linking the price of corn and a 10-year cycle in the level of sunspot activity that he and other astronomers had recently documented. Herschel and other astronomers eventually abandoned these attempts, so the job was left for economist William Stanley Jevons to do. He marshalled statistical evidence linking sunspot activity to grain prices, then linking the grain prices to production and international trade figures for the overall British economy, and from that linking sunspot activity to the recurring commercial crises that had afflicted England during the first 100 years of its industrial revolution.

Jevons had strong personal reasons to be interested in such questions. His father and grandfather were each bankrupted in different periods of downturn in the economy, and his own schooling was interrupted due to related financial problems. In fact, he never overcame anxieties related to financial ruin, and compulsively hoarded books and other commodities he expected to increase in value. Fifty years after his death (he drowned in 1882, at the age of 46), his children were still using supplies of wrapping paper he had purchased in the belief that growth in population and living standards would sharply increase the prices of basic products like paper and coal.

In Jevons' own lifetime, commercial crises had struck the British economy in 1825, 1836, 1847, 1857, and 1866 -- regularly and in approximately 10-year intervals. Jevons obtained historical data on prices for wheat and other commodities in these decades, and raised the possibility of a sunspot cycle in a public talk in 1875. But then he decided that the data did not support this linkage, and withdrew that paper on the sunspot theory from publication.

Three years later, based on more extensive data on the trade cycle in England, revised data from the astronomers on the average length of the sunspot cycles, and a new focus on grain prices *in India*, Jevons took the plunge. He conceded that such ideas seemed far-fetched at first glance; but he now begged readers of his article in *Nature* to believe that "I am perfectly convinced that these [ten-year] crises do depend upon meteorological variations of like period." His theoretical justification for this claim rested on statements that are not at all unreasonable for economies that are as extensively agrarian as India, and even England, were in the 19th century. Jevons claimed that

...the success of the harvest in any year certainly depends upon the weather, especially that of the summer and autumn months. Now, if this weather depends in any degree upon the solar period, it follows that the harvest and the price of grain will depend more or less upon the solar period, and will go through periodic fluctuations in periods of time equal to those of the sunspots.[9]

More specifically, Jevons recognized the work of a government statistician pointing to a ten-year cycle of famines in India, and linked those Indian crop failures to a drop in British *EXPORTS* to India, and thus to the British trade cycle. (The famines in India reduced income there, which decreased Indian purchases of British goods.) Jevons was surprised that the effects of the Indian failures did not impact the English economy *after* a *LAG* of one or two years, instead of developing simultaneously or even a bit after the initial declines in England were observed, since "the effect can not precede its cause." But his theory was clear as to which event must represent cause and which effect, and he found the statistical correspondence too compelling to ignore.

Shortly after Jevons' death, the statistical evidence on the sunspot cycles turned sharply less favorable to his theory of trade cycles. And as the relative importance of agriculture in industrial nations decreased, the theory seemed inherently more comical. Most importantly, other theories of the *BUSINESS CYCLE* emerged that explained these movements more accurately, and suggested public policy remedies for smoothing out the cycles far easier than models based on sunspots. So forever since, in spite of his many contributions in the study of economic theory, statistics, and other major economic problems of his time, Jevons has been remembered as the crackpot economist who thought sunspots controlled the macroeconomy.

Later theorists, however, have recognized both the strengths and weaknesses of Jevons' ideas. For example, Keynes noted that the sunspot theory was

...prejudiced by being stated in too precise and categorical a form. Nevertheless, Jevons's notion that meteorological phenomena play a part in harvest fluctuations, and that harvest fluctuations play a part (though more important formerly than today) in the trade cycle, is not to be lightly dismissed.[10]

Jevons' theory was also the basis for some recent work and tongue-in-cheek fun by economists. Using statistical tests to investigate causality linkages between sunspot activity and the U.S. business cycle, Richard Sheehan and Robin Grieves found that

We are forced to conclude that the U.S. economy has a significant impact on the sun but that sunspots have no influence on the economy. We were, of course, more than a little surprised to find that the U.S. economy has any influence on the sun. However, as [other economists] said so well, one "would have to be rather more pigheaded in order not to have the evidence change his views."[11]

Jevons would have appreciated the authors' deference in accepting empirical evidence before economic or meteorological theories (but perhaps not their sense of humor). More generally, remember that economic models are ultimately tested by their usefulness in predicting and explaining observable and measurable relationships. That approach to building and testing models is, in large part, the legacy of Jevons and other early economists.

Chapter Summary

1) *MICROECONOMICS* deals with the actions of individual consumers, firms, and industries. *MACROECONOMICS* studies the national economy and the aggregated actions of all households, businesses, and government units.

---

[9] "The Solar Period and the Price of Corn," 1875, published in Jevons' *Investigations in Currency and Finance*, H. Foxwell, ed., (Macmillan, 1884), pp. 194-5.
[10]*Essays in Biography*, Norton, 1963, pp. 279-80.
[11]"Sunspots and Cycles: A Test of Causation," *Southern Economic Journal*, Jan. 1982, pp. 776-77.

2) Economists disagree more on macroeconomic issues than on microeconomic issues. In both areas, disagreements may develop because of differences in normative goals associated with some policy, or due to inadequate and conflicting theories and evidence used to analyze economic problems.

3) Mainstream economists agree on the procedures used in building and testing economic models and theories. Specifically, theories and models are tested by how well they explain or predict, not by the degree of realism or detail in the assumptions on which they are based.

4) Economic theories are built by identifying a cause and effect relationship between two or more variables. Economic models usually combine two or more theories, to explain or test a broader set of relationships.

5) The usefulness of an economic model depends on how well it addresses individual and social problems, and helps people achieve their economic goals. Most models are concerned with goals that can be broadly classified as *ECONOMIC FREEDOM*, *EFFICIENCY*, *GROWTH*, *SECURITY*, and *JUSTICE*.

6) The kind of economic model used to analyze some topic or problem depends on the question(s) the model is expected to address. In general, there is a trade-off between the degree of detail in the predictions a model can provide and the range of cases to which it can be applied.

7) Most economic models: 1) assume that individuals and businesses try to maximize some measure of their own wellbeing; 2) treat units of spending and production as equal no matter what kind of person or firm provides it; and 3) use market prices of goods and services to evaluate the costs and benefits of a given change in economic circumstances. As a group, these assumptions represent the approach known as *METHODOLOGICAL INDIVIDUALISM*.

8) Empirical studies featuring controlled experiments and random samples are sometimes used to evaluate economic theories or policy measures. More often, economists must work with real-world data and try to separate out the effects of different influences on some measure of economic activity.

9) General functional statements and specific mathematical equations are used to specify the economic relationships between *INDEPENDENT* and *DEPENDENT VARIABLES*, or *SIMULTANEOUSLY-RELATED VARIABLES*.

10) Statistical tests are used to test the significance of individual variables in an economic model, and the ability of the overall model to explain the results of changes in the dependent variable(s) included in the model.

11) Economists' widespread use of the assumptions associated with methodological individualism, and their use of mathematical and statistical techniques in building and testing their models, have raised serious questions related to the issue of how rational people are in their economic dealings. While empirical studies support the idea that a broad range of decisions are made carefully and rationally, there also appear to be limits and exceptions to such behavior.

12) Most economic decisions are based on *MARGINAL ANALYSIS* -- comparing the costs and benefits of buying a few more or a few less units of particular goods and services, or doing a little more or little less of some other activity.

13) (Case Study #3) In the late 19th century, William Stanley Jevons argued that cyclical changes in price levels and national spending were caused by the pattern of sunspot activity. While this theory seems ludicrous to many, the proper test of it is its ability to explain and predict, not its basic assumptions (which were more plausible than most people think, at least in Jevons' day).

Review and Discussion Questions

1) Are consumption, saving, and investment microeconomic or macroeconomic activities?

2) Give an example of a possible normative disagreement for both a microeconomic and a macroeconomic topic or problem.

3) How do the procedures used by economists to build and test models differ from those employed by researchers who work in the natural sciences?

4) State what you consider to be a reasonable hypothesis linking each of the following pairs of variables:

   a) income and consumer spending   b) income and saving
   c) income and employment   d) imports and employment
   e) product price and profits   f) education and unemployment

5) Describe a public policy that might involve a trade-off between the goals of: a) economic freedom and security; b) economic efficiency and freedom; and c) economic growth and equity. Are there other economic goals you think are as important as the five discussed in this chapter? Explain.

6) Write two economic questions that would be answered most appropriately by a general theoretical model, and two more for a behavioral model.

7) Does the economic behavior of family units seem to fit the general assumptions of methodological individualism? Can you suggest decisions made by individual consumers, workers, and voters that seem to contradict these assumptions?

8) Describe how an experimental study might be used to test the law of demand. Discuss whether or not your study could work outside of a controlled, laboratory setting.

9) Express each of the hypotheses you developed in question #4 in functional notation, and then identify the dependent and independent variable in each of those statements. Would you expect each of those relationships to be: a) direct or inverse, and b) linear or non-linear? Explain why.

10) If a model includes what turns out to be a statistically significant variable, will the model itself be significant? Explain.

11) Have you ever made a decision that you thought was irrational at the time you made it? Have you made any that, looking back in time, seem now to be irrational? If you answered yes to either question, suggest why you made such decisions. Would you want your friends, teachers, or family to learn about these decisions?

12) How could decisions made at the margin help a consumer maximize his or her total satisfaction, or help a firm maximize its total profits?

13) (Case Study #3) Suppose you were developing a theory about tides and the position of the moon *before* Sir Issac Newton discovered gravity. Describe a likely process that might lead you to formulate such a theory, and how you might test your theory using no modern scientific instruments. Would the process you described be considered an example of inductive or deductive reasoning? Does this exercise make Jevons' sunspot theory seem more or less reasonable to you? Explain.

Chapter 3
Markets and "The Perennial Gale of Creative Destruction"

In This Chapter...

we examine factors which lead to shifts in supply and demand schedules, reflecting a change in the relative scarcity of a good or service. These changes in supply and demand lead to shortage and surplus conditions, and markets that are temporarily not in equilibrium. Equilibrium is restored through actions taken by both consumers and producers. One important market which has undergone dramatic shifts in supply over the past 20 years is the global oil market, which is reviewed in the Case Study for this chapter.

Change and the Marketplace

Many factors other than price must be considered to complete our understanding of supply and demand for a particular product. Changes in these non-price factors lead to shifts in supply and demand curves, which in turn lead to changes in equilibrium price and quantity. Successful producers and consumers learn how to adapt to these changes. Or, they can be even more successful if they anticipate the changes.

Sources of Accelerating Change

Students graduating from colleges and high schools are often told that, on average, they will change jobs six or more times in their lifetime. That's not a comforting thought to someone about to begin their first career. And all too often, the message about changing jobs in the future is delivered by speakers who have never changed jobs or careers, and who have little understanding of why such changes occur. While economists aren't known for frequent career jumps themselves, they have identified the following factors contributing to rapid change in labor markets and other sectors of modern economies:

* There are more people in the world today than ever before, with more combined productive and purchasing power, more extensive information about their economic opportunities, and greater ability to change how and where they currently work and live. In industrialized nations, consumers and workers have more resources at their disposal than in earlier centuries, when economic life was simpler and much poorer. Many people now have the wherewithal to start their own business, or a franchise business associated with a large national company. For most of those who do not, the range of occupational choices has broadened far beyond the basic agricultural and manufacturing jobs that accounted for the great majority of all employment through the first half of this century. And even in less developed nations the range of jobs available to some workers has dramatically diversified, and most people are more aware than ever before of different kinds of jobs and lifestyles in their own county, and in other nations.

* There is more capital today, created by and using ever more sophisticated technologies. More resources are specifically devoted to the discovery of new knowledge and technologies, and to the transfer of those techniques to industries and countries which have never used them before. As a result, old technologies, production processes, and skills become obsolete more rapidly than in the past. For example, newspapers and books are now composed and designed on computers, as are new clothing styles, automobiles, and chemicals. Genes and viruses are mapped, spliced, or otherwise transformed, and the commercial opportunities from doing this are searched out relentlessly. This has led to dramatically different kinds of products, such as new medicines and hybrid or bioengineered strains of grains and other agricultural crops. Electronic components and equipment

are made smaller, more powerful, and less expensive every year, and sometimes produced in rooms that are cleaner than hospital operating rooms. The electronics and computer revolutions have in turn allowed purchasing and earnings data for a country's population, and for customers of particular firms, to be collected and analyzed. That helps producers identify what new products are most likely to succeed, and how old products can be redesigned or repackaged to meet changing interests and competition from new products. In all of these cases, things that were technologically impossible or prohibitively expensive just a decade ago are now routine parts of doing business in a wide range of markets.

The higher average level of wealth in industrialized nations makes it possible for individuals and both public and private organizations to undertake more risk-taking investments and enterprises. Many new products and production methods, such as the high-tech, capital-intensive operations discussed above, are financed by private companies and the investors in these companies who purchase stocks and bonds directly, or indirectly through participation in retirement programs which make such investments. Other large-scale, "basic" research projects -- those not directed at any specific application but which may have very broad economic consequences in the future -- are publicly financed. For example, superconductivity research and basic physics experiments that explore fusion energy are today extensively subsidized by public funds, and while it is very difficult to predict what practical applications may evolve from this work in the future, the possible range of innovations is amazing. Past experience with such projects over the last century is illuminating in that respect. Think, for example, of the many spin-off products and technologies that have resulted from the U.S. and Soviet space programs of the 1950s - 1980s, including mundane items such as non-stick cookware as well as products more obviously related to space exploration, such as electronic communications and surveillance equipment.

Global markets have developed to the point that economic circumstances in any one nation are increasingly affected by conditions in other parts of the world. Better communications and transportation networks make it easier to move factories, capital, and jobs from one nation to another. The level of trade in consumer goods and services has also grown to unprecedented heights. Because of that, political events and changes in economic policies and conditions in one nation now affect other countries far more often and rapidly than ever before.

The market system itself encourages innovation by rewarding those who produce new products which are well received by consumers, and those who "build a better mousetrap" by finding better and less expensive ways to make existing products. New products regularly replace old ones in what economist Joseph A. Schumpeter aptly described as "the perennial gale of creative destruction." The creative side of the gale is the development and distribution of new products and production methods. The destruction side of the process is the wide-ranging and fast-paced change that makes many traditional products and occupations obsolete. In an economic sense, the same kind of gale buffets both markets for basic consumer products (including food, clothing, and shelter) and markets for more aesthetic endeavors (such as music, literature, film, or any of the art forms).

In Chapter 1, you studied the laws of supply and demand to see how the equilibrium price that measures the relative scarcity of a product is determined when supply and demand schedules are fixed and unchanging. Now you can see that it is unrealistic to assume that supply and demand do not change frequently. The material presented in Chapter 1 is an important starting point, but it must be expanded greatly before you can really use those theories to analyze most real-world markets.

The General Law of Demand

Using functional notation, the law of demand presented in Chapter 1 is

$$Q_d = f(P), c.p.$$

where the letters c.p. are an abbreviation for the Latin phrase *CETERIS PARIBUS*, which means other things being equal or everything else remaining unchanged. We read this equation as "quantity demanded is a function of price, other things being equal." We also know from the law of demand that price and quantity demanded are inversely related -- as price increases quantity demanded decreases, and as price decreases quantity demanded increases.

But there are many other factors that determine the level of demand for a good or service. Recognizing this, we can write the *GENERAL LAW OF DEMAND* as

$$Q_d = f(\, P, \overline{P_r}, \overline{Y}, \overline{T}, \overline{X_b}, \overline{N_b}\,), \text{ c.p.}$$

where

P_r represents the price of related goods and services (i.e., substitutes and complements),
Y represents consumers' income,
T stands for consumer tastes and preferences,
X_b indicates buyers' expectations of future prices for the product in question, and
N_b represents the number of buyers in the market.

The bars over the symbols representing the new variables that have been added to this equation are used to indicate that a specific value for these variables is associated with a specific level of demand for a product. For example, if the level of consumers' income changes the value of Y changes, and that will shift the level of demand. Or putting that another way, the bars over the symbols indicate that we assume the values of these variables don't change when we write down the values for a particular demand schedule, or draw a particular demand curve. But by stating the general law of demand we are recognizing explicitly that those values can change over time, and acknowledging that when they do we will have to re-write or re-draw the demand schedule.

Note also that even in our statement of the general law of demand we again include the *ceteris paribus* assumption. This recognizes that there are other variables besides the five listed here that may have at least a minor effect on the demand curves for a wide range of products, and that for some specific products other variables can be very important. For example, the demand for disposable diapers may be strongly affected by the number of people in a market area aged 17-35, and by the number of women in this group who hold full-time jobs. But we were not trying to specify the demand schedule for disposable diapers here, only a general form that can serve as a starting point for specifying the demand function for most goods and services -- including disposable diapers. So the specification of the general laws of supply and demand include only those variables which have a major impact on a wide range of products; the *ceteris paribus* assumption takes care of the rest.

The General Law of Supply

The *GENERAL LAW OF SUPPLY* is built around the same set of assumptions as the general law of demand but, as you might suspect, the factors that determine the position of a supply schedule are different from those that determine the position of a demand curve. The functional notation for the general law of supply is:

$$Q_s = f(\, P, \overline{C_\$}, \overline{S}, \overline{P_o}, \overline{X_s}, \overline{N_s}\,), \text{ c.p.}$$

where

$C_\$$ represents the cost of the resources (*inputs*) used to produce a good or service,
S represents the state of productive technologies for the product that is being made and offered for sale,
P_o stands for the price of other goods that producers could make and sell,
X_s indicates sellers' expectations concerning the future price of the product in question, and
N_s represents the number of sellers in the market.

Now that you have seen the statements of both the general law of supply and the general law of demand, we will consider each of the variables listed in those statements, which can shift supply or demand curves.

General Determinants of the Level of Demand

Demand for most products changes if there is a change in: 1) consumers' income, 2) prices of related goods, 3) consumers' tastes and preferences, 4) consumers' price expectations, or 5) the number of buyers in a market. The relative importance of these five factors will vary for different products, and there may be other factors important enough to include in considering the demand for particular goods or services. But these five factors influence market demand for virtually all products.

Income

The income effect associated with a change in the price of a product, discussed in Chapter 1, helps to explain why the demand curves for normal goods have a downward, negative slope. It is important to distinguish that kind of income effect from the result of a change in *INCOME* when the prices of the products a person consumes do not change. A consumer whose income increases is willing and able to buy more units of a normal good *at all possible prices*. That means for any normal good an increase in income leads to an increase in demand, which is shown as a rightward shift in the demand curve (see Figure 3-1). The slope of the demand curve may or may not change as it shifts, depending on how much people buy at each different price level with their higher level of income. But that is a level of detail which we cover in a later chapter. Here, the key point to see is that at all prices people bought more of the normal good as their income increased. Or put more briefly, the rise in income increased demand.

Of course for an inferior good just the opposite occurs. An increase in demand would result from a decrease in income, and a decrease in demand would result from an increase in income. Similarly, a decrease in demand is observed for normal goods when income decreases -- that is, quantity demanded falls *at all possible prices*. Graphically, this results in a leftward shift in the demand curve, as shown in Figure 3-2.

Prices of Related Goods and Services

As consumers, people deal with two distinct types of related goods: *COMPLEMENTS* and *SUBSTITUTES*. Complements are goods or services which are consumed together, such as cars and tires, tennis balls and tennis rackets, or cold drinks and any salty food. Substitutes are products which satisfy the same general set of wants and are therefore in competition for the same consumer dollars. Examples include Ford and Chevrolet automobiles, wine and beer, pork and beef, and household plastic wrap and aluminum foil.

A shift in the demand for a particular product occurs when the prices of its complements or substitutes change. This is pure common sense. Those who view apples and oranges as substitutes will buy fewer apples *at all possible prices* if the price of oranges decreases. And, since cameras and film are complementary goods, if the price of 35mm cameras decreases substantially, not only will more cameras be sold, more 35mm film will be sold *at all possible* prices for film.

An increase in the price of a product will increase the demand for its substitutes, and decrease the demand for its complements. A decrease in the price of a product will decrease the demand for substitutes and increase the demand for complementary goods.

Figure 3-1
An Increase in Demand

Price	D_1 (Quantity Demanded When Income = $20,000)	D_2 (Quantity Demanded When Income = $25,000)
$10	1	1.5
9	2	3.0
8	3	4.5
7	4	6.0
6	5	7.5
5	6	9.0
4	7	10.5
3	8	12.0
2	9	13.5
1	10	15.0

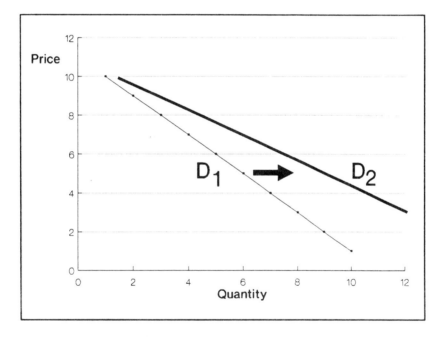

If consumers in a particular market enjoy a 25% increase in income while the prices of the products they consume remain constant, they will buy more units of all normal goods in a given period of time. At a price of $5, for example, the quantity demanded increases from 6 to 9 units. Demand has shifted from D_1 to D_2.

Figure 3-2
A Decrease in Demand

Price	D₁ (Quantity Demanded When Income = $20,000)	D₂ (Quantity Demanded When Income = $15,000)
$10	1	.5
9	2	1.0
8	3	1.5
7	4	2.0
6	5	2.5
5	6	3.0
4	7	3.5
3	8	4.0
2	9	4.5
1	10	5.0

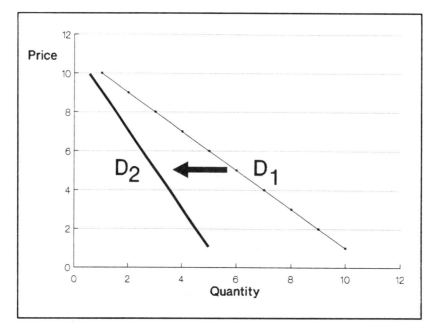

Here, consumers are shown responding to a decrease in income that occurs while the prices of the products they consume remain constant. *Ceteris paribus*, they would buy fewer units of all normal goods in a given period of time, so demand shifts from D_1 to D_2. At a price of $5, for example, quantity demanded would decrease from 6 to 3 units.

Consumer Tastes and Preferences

The winds of fashion are fickle, blowing sometimes "cool," sometimes "hot," sometimes rainbow pastels, sometimes earth tones, and always from changing directions. Today's high fashion may be tomorrow's rags, and *vice versa*. For some things, changes in *PREFERENCES* take centuries to evolve -- for example in language, where linguists and literary scholars have documented changes in the ways vowels are pronounced over a period of centuries. In other areas fashions change with the seasons, or even with the phases of the moon. In the last 30 years, Nehru jackets, pet rocks, paper dresses, hula hoops, disco music, Cabbage Patch dolls and video arcades are examples of "fad" items. But people in earlier ages were just as susceptible to the stylish appeal of such items as variegated tulips, new colors of dyes for togas, and Marco Polo's culinary discovery from China, spaghetti.

Psychologists may have better tools than economists to explain how and why these changes in *TASTES* occur. But economist must be concerned with the effects of shifts in the demand for products that are sensitive to changes in fashion. By definition, a fashionable item is one that experiences a short-term increase in demand due to changes in consumers' preferences. A good or service that goes "out of fashion" experiences a decrease in demand -- i.e., *at all possible prices* the quantity demanded falls.

Price Expectations of Buyers

Suppose you are going to take a trip to Europe next year, and you know that you will have to exchange some U.S. dollars for some British pounds before you go, or after you arrive in England. A financial advisor you trust tells you that she believes the price you will pay for pounds next year will be much lower than the price you would pay for pounds today. How does this affect your demand for pounds? Chances are, you will not buy pounds today, but wait until next year. If other consumers who have currently been buying pounds have similar *PRICE EXPECTATIONS*, the present demand for pounds will decrease.

On the other hand, if you expect the price of some good or service you intend to buy to go up in the future, you will probably try to buy it now at the current price, before the price increase takes effect. The quantity demanded will increase even though the price has not decreased -- a sure sign that demand has increased.

To summarize: Expectations of future price increases increase current demand for a product. Expectations of future price decreases decrease current demand.

Number of Buyers in the Market

All of the variables that determine the level of demand which we have reviewed to this point directly influence individual consumers' demand for products, and thereby affect the level of market demand -- the sum of the quantities all individual consumers demand at different prices. Another way market demand increases or decreases is when the size of the market changes as consumers move into or out of a market area.

As more consumers enter the market for a product the quantity demanded *at all possible prices* will increase. A decrease in demand results when significant numbers of consumers move out of a market area. In the last two decades, markets in many western and southern states have grown as a result of people moving to these states from other parts of the country, and even from other parts of the world. Demand for many products increased in these areas, but decreased in the areas that were losing population.

Table 3-1 summarizes our discussion of the general determinants of demand.

General Determinants of the Level of Supply

The supply of most products changes when there is a change in: 1) prices for productive resources, 2) production technologies, 3) prices of other goods and services, 4) price expectations of sellers, and 5) the number of sellers in a market. While other variables can have a major impact on the supply of particular products, these five affect the supply of virtually all goods and services.

Prices for Productive Resources

Suppliers will offer to sell more units of a product at all possible prices when the prices they must pay for land, labor, capital, and entrepreneurship decrease; they will offer to sell fewer units when the prices for these

Table 3-1
Determinants of Market Demand

Increases in Demand Are Caused By:

* Increased Income (for Normal Goods)   * Decreased Income (for Inferior Goods)

* Increases in the Prices of Substitute Products

* Decreases in the Prices of Complementary Products

* Favorable Changes in Consumers' Tastes and Preferences

* Expectations of Future Price Increases

* Increases in the Number of Consumers in the Market

Decreases in Demand Are Caused By:

* Decreased Income (for Normal Goods)   * Increased Income (for Inferior Goods)

* Decreases in the Prices of Substitute Products

* Increases in the Prices of Complementary Products

* Unfavorable Changes in Consumers' Tastes and Preferences

* Expectations of Future Price Decreases

* Decreases in the Number of Consumers in the Market

Each of the factors listed above leads to a shift in demand, which means that the amount of a product people are willing and able to buy changes *at all possible prices*.

---

productive resources increase. An important exception to this generalization are goods which can not be currently produced (e.g., authentic antiques or works by a deceased artist). Since these goods can't be produced, changes in the prices for productive resources will not directly affect their current supply.

But for more typical products that can be produced now, using available resources, an increase in supply resulting from lower prices for productive inputs is indicated by a new schedule relating price and quantity supplied. Specifically, it is represented by a rightward shift in the supply curve, as shown in Figure 3-3.

Similarly, a decrease in supply will result from an increase in the prices of the resources used to produce a good or service. This is indicated by a leftward shift of the supply curve, as shown in Figure 3-4. Just as we saw with shifts in demand, the slope of a supply curve may or may not change as it shifts in or out. That depends on such factors as production technologies and possible changes in the optimal mix of inputs (such as capital and labor) as output levels are changed, which we will review in later chapters. Here, the basic point for you to see is that an increase in supply refers to an increase in the quantity supplied *at all possible prices*. A decrease in supply occurs when the quantity supplied is reduced *at all price levels*.

Figure 3-3
An Increase in Supply

Price	S₁ (Quantity Supplied With High Resource Prices)	S₂ (Quantity Supplied With Low Resource Prices)
$10	10	15.0
9	9	13.5
8	8	12.0
7	7	10.5
6	6	9.0
5	5	7.5
4	4	6.0
3	3	4.5
2	2	3.0
1	1	1.5

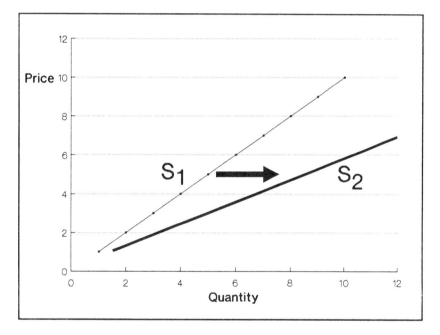

The hypothetical data presented in this table and graph depict an increase in the supply of a product resulting from a decrease in the price of the resources used to produce the product. An increase in supply means that the quantity supplied increases *at all possible prices* (from S_1 to S_2). For example, at a price of $5 the quantity supplied increases from 5 to 7.5 units.

Figure 3-4
A Decrease in Supply

Price	S_1 (Quantity Supplied With Low Resource Prices)	S_2 (Quantity Supplied With High Resource Prices)
$10	10	5.0
9	9	4.5
8	8	4.0
7	7	3.5
6	6	3.0
5	5	2.5
4	4	2.0
3	3	1.5
2	2	1.0
1	1	.5

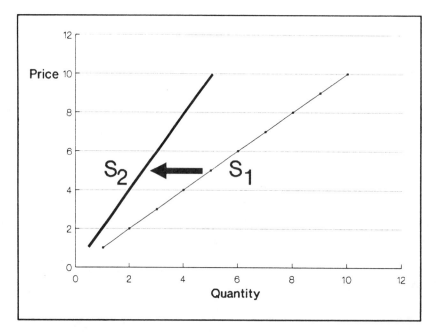

Here, over the range of *all possible prices* for a product, quantity supplied decreases as a result of an increase in the prices of the resources used to produce the product (from S_1 to S_2). At a price of $6, for example, quantity supplied decreases from 6 to 3 units.

Technology

There are two ways that technology increases supply: 1) by developing entirely new productive resources, or 2) by making existing resources more productive. When new products are invented or discovered, that technological change creates a supply where none previously existed at any price. While it may be possible to think of lost technologies that have resulted in us not being able to make things that people were once able to make -- perhaps Egyptian mummies, for example -- these cases are clearly limited in number and importance. Therefore, we will assume that technological change works only in the direction of increasing supply.

When existing resources are made more productive, a given quantity of inputs will produce more products after the technological change is applied to the production process. This has the same practical effect as a decrease in the price of the productive resources, which also leads to an increase in supply. But the prices of the inputs don't really change as an immediate result of technological progress. Instead, producers spend less for the resources because it now takes fewer inputs to make their final products. As a result, there is an increase in the quantity of the product producers are willing and able to offer for sale *at all possible prices*.

Prices of Other Goods and Services

In a market economy, producers are generally free to use their resources as they choose, to supply whatever legal products they care to produce. They are also free to move their resources out of the production of one good or service, and into the production of another. Many of them do just that when they feel they can earn a greater profit by supplying a different product.

For example, one barber we know left barbering in the 1970s when long hair styles for men became popular, and used the proceeds from the sale of his shop to buy a road-cleaning machine which he used to vacuum the runways of the local airport. At that time, air travel was becoming more popular and affordable, and after comparing his expected financial returns from barbering or from cleaning the runways, the basic pleasure he derived from the two businesses, and the relative financial and physical risks involved in the two pursuits, the barber decided to increase the supply of runway cleaning services and decrease the supply of haircuts.

In more general terms, when the prices of other products rise relative to the price of a certain product -- call it product X -- resources will be shifted away from the production of product X and its supply will decrease. Conversely, a decrease in the prices of other goods and services while the price of X remains constant will shift resources to the production of X, and increase the supply of this product.

Price Expectations of Sellers

Each year at harvest time, grain farmers around the country must decide whether to sell all or part of their crop. Many speculate each year that the price for wheat, corn, oats, etc., will go up in the future. These farmers choose to store some grain, withholding it from the market for a time. Their expectations that prices will rise in the future effectively decreases the amount of grain offered for sale at all possible prices today -- i.e., decreases the current supply of grain.

Of course, when suppliers believe the prices for their products are going to decrease in the future they try to sell more now, before the prices fall. In other words, there is an increase in the amount producers are willing and able to offer for sale *at all possible prices*.

To summarize: Expectations of future price increases decrease supply in the current time period. Expectations of future price decreases increase the current supply.

Number of Sellers in the Market

Just as market demand is found by adding up the quantities that all individual consumers' demand at different prices, market supply is the sum of all individual producers' supply schedules. Therefore, market supply will change when the number of suppliers changes significantly, *ceteris paribus*. As more producers enter a market the quantity supplied *at all possible prices* will increase. But when producers stop producing a good or service and exit from a market, the market supply curve will decrease, shifting to the left.

This is the only general determinant of supply we have discussed that does not affect supply schedules for individual producers, but only the number of individual curves that are added up to find the market level of supply. Of course, that is exactly the same situation that was seen earlier, in our discussion of the role of the number of consumers and the position of the market demand curve.

Table 3-2 summarizes our discussion of the general determinants of supply. Be sure you understand the material represented there and in Table 3-1 before you continue on in this chapter.

Table 3-2
Determinants of Market Supply

Increases in Supply Are Caused By:

* Decreases in the Prices of Productive Resources

* Technological Advancements

* Decreases in the Prices of Other Goods and Services

* Expectations of Future Price Decreases

* Growth in the Number of Producers in the Market

Decreases in Supply Are Caused By:

* Increases in the Prices of Productive Resources

* Increases in the Prices of Other Goods and Services

* Expectations of Future Price Increases

* Decline in the Number of Producers in the Market

Each of the factors listed above leads to a shift in supply, which means that the amount of a product producers are willing and able to offer for sale changes *at all possible prices*.

Using Supply and Demand Analysis: Some Basic Exercises

There are several things for you to understand about the effects of shifts in supply and demand curves. In particular, you must be able to distinguish the causes and consequences of a shift in a supply or demand curve from the causes and consequences of moving along a curve that does not shift. You must also see how shifts in supply and demand lead to new levels for equilibrium price and quantity. And you must be able to describe how a market adjusts from an old equilibrium position to a new one when supply or demand changes.

Changes in Supply and Demand vs. Changes in Quantity Supplied and Quantity Demanded

Now you have come to the distinction that drives some first-time economics students to despair, and others into careers as accountants. Beware! Many instructors put questions on this distinction on two or three exams in their courses, yet some students persist in getting them wrong. But forewarned is forearmed, so take the time to get this down pat now.

A change in demand is not the same thing as a change in the quantity demanded, and a change in supply is not the same thing as a change in quantity supplied. It's really a simple point -- the difficult thing is to understand why economists insist it is so important. Here's why: One refers to a *shift* of a curve, and the other to a *movement along* a curve. That's obviously a big difference graphically and conceptually, so we have signal that difference, too.

The distinction is easiest to see in a practical example, so let's say the quantity purchased from one time period to the next. That increase could be the result of a decrease in the price which case it would represent a downward movement along the demand curve, for example i b in panel (A) of Figure 3-5. But the increase in the quantity might also be the result of a shift of the demand curve, so that equilibrium output shifts from point a to point d in the same graph.   that case we know consumers are now willing to buy more of the product *at all prices* and that, *ceteris paribus*, the price of cars will soon increase. (To see that, simply sketch in a supply curve in this panel of Figure 3-5.) The movement from a to b is only a change in the *quantity demanded* of the product; the movement from a to d is a change in the *demand* for it.

Changes in any of the general determinants of supply or demand, which we reviewed in the earlier sections of this chapter, shift the entire supply or demand schedule. A change in the price of a product leads to a change in the quantity supplied and the quantity demanded of the product, as indicated by the laws of supply and demand, but not to a change in the entire supply or demand schedule.

Thomas Carlyle once compared economists to parrots which had been trained to answer "supply and demand" to any question, and in fact there is some justification in that unflattering comparison. It's correct at least in the sense that supply and demand analysis is such a basic and widely used tool in economics that it is crucial to establish language that clearly makes the distinction between a shift in the supply or demand curve and a movement along the curves. Learn the distinction between changes in demand and quantity demanded and supply and quantity supplied now -- before it costs you points on an exam.

Figure 3-5
Changes in Supply and Demand vs. Changes
in Quantity Supplied and Demanded

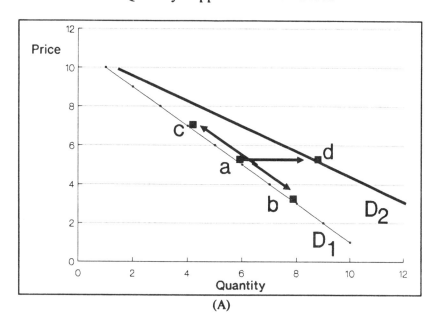

(A)

84

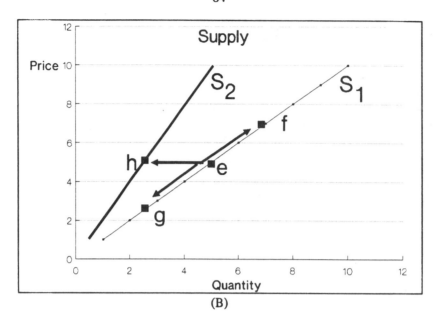

(B)

Movement from point a to point b in panel A depicts an increase in quantity demanded that would result from a decrease in the price of the hypothetical product. Movement from point a to point c represents a decrease in quantity demanded, resulting from an increase in the price of the product. Since demand curves and schedules show how much consumers will buy at all possible prices, any change in price simply results in a movement *along* the schedule or demand curve, not a shift in the schedule or curve. However, when quantity demanded changes even though there has been no change in price -- e.g., from point a to point d -- it is clear that we can no longer be on the original demand curve or schedule. The shift in the demand curve from D_1 to D_2 means that *at all possible prices* consumers are willing and able to buy more units of this product, and is caused by a change in some variable other than the price of this product.

The graph is panel B shows the corresponding distinction between a change in supply and quantity supplied. Moving from point e to points f or g represents an increase or decrease in quantity supplied, resulting from a change in the price of the product. Moving from point e to point h implies a decrease in supply, from S_1 to S_2.

The Possible Outcomes of Changes in Supply and Demand

Equilibrium price and quantity are changed by shifts in supply or demand, or both. Fortunately, there are only three things a supply or demand curve can do: increase, decrease or remain the same. So there are only nine possible combinations of the possible actions of the two curves, and nine possible outcomes for equilibrium price and quantity. These are shown in Table 3-3 and in Figure 3-6. You should work through each of these situations, and convince yourself that each case shown in the table is consistent with its corresponding graph in the figure.

Assuming you are like most students who take this course, the four cases where one schedule changes and the other doesn't (graphs B through E) will not be difficult for you to understand or remember. In fact, those four cases are summarized in a reasonably complete sense by the brief statement that, *ceteris paribus*, an increase in supply makes a product less scarce while an increase in demand makes a product more scarce, and *vice versa*.

The cases where both schedules shift (graphs F through I) are a little more complicated, and you may well have been surprised to see question marks denoting ambiguous changes in equilibrium price or quantity on these lines in the table. The reason for this ambiguity is simply that in these cases supply and demand shifts work in opposite and offsetting directions. Whether the equilibrium price or quantity will increase, decrease, or remain unchanged

Table 3-3
Possible Outcomes of Shifts in Supply and Demand

	Supply	Demand	Equilibrium Price	Equilibrium Quantity
a)	Unchanged	Unchanged	Unchanged	Unchanged
b)	Increases	Unchanged	Decreases	Increases
c)	Decreases	Unchanged	Increases	Decreases
d)	Unchanged	Increases	Increases	Increases
e)	Unchanged	Decreases	Decreases	Decreases
f)	Increases	Increases	?	Increases
g)	Increases	Decreases	Decreases	?
h)	Decreases	Increases	Increases	?
i)	Decreases	Decreases	?	Decreases

This table summarizes all possible combinations of shifts in supply and demand schedules, and the resulting effects on equilibrium price and quantity.

---

depends on whether the change in demand has a larger, smaller, or the same effect as the opposite change in supply.

Make sure you understand how shifts in supply and demand are related to the question of how scarce a good or service is. Then, if you see how separate shifts in supply or demand are related to changes in equilibrium price and quantity, it will not be difficult to reason your way through questions that involve simultaneous shifts to identify where these shifts are reinforcing and where they are offsetting.

Shortages and Surpluses

To this point, we have blithely used supply and demand models to move from one equilibrium position to another, assuming that when supply and demand change we move instantaneously and costlessly to the new equilibrium. That's not the way the world really works, so let's take some time to see what is involved in these adjustments.

Shortages

Consider an increase in demand, which you already know will result in a higher equilibrium price and quantity, *ceteris paribus*. But now we want to see *how* those new price and quantity level are achieved in the marketplace. Figure 3-7 shows the key steps in that process. After demand increases from D_1 to D_2, the first thing sellers will notice is that sales of the product have increased, even though the price for the product has not changed. Specifically, at the original equilibrium price, P_1, quantity demanded is now Q_2, and greater than the quantity supplied, Q_1.

86

Figure 3-6
Shifts in Supply and Demand:
Considering the Possibilities, Graphically

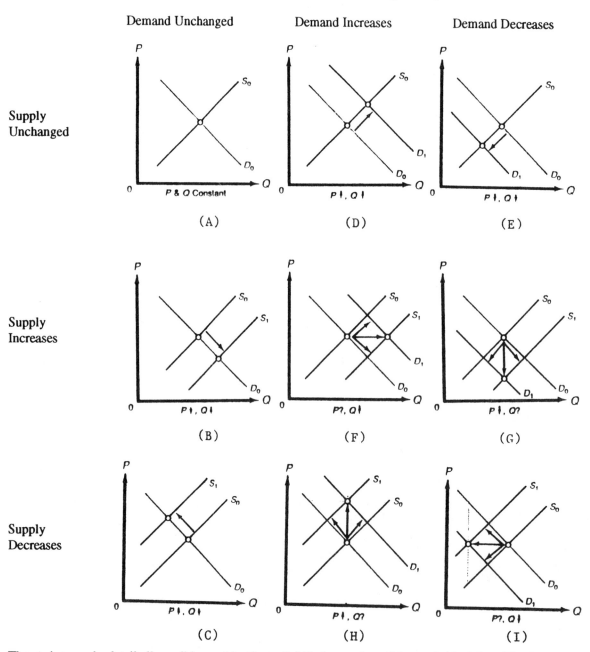

These nine graphs detail all possible combinations of shifts in supply and demand schedules. The four graphs that have the triple arrows denote the cases where the change in either equilibrium price or quantity will depend on the relative magnitudes of the shifts in supply and demand.

87

Figure 3-7
Shortages

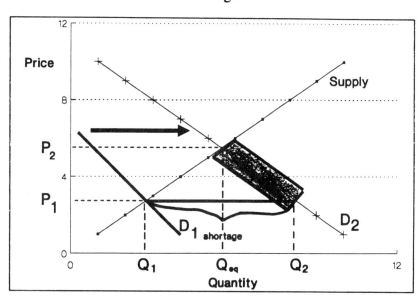

When demand increases from D_1 to D_2, equilibrium price increases from P_1 to P_2, *ceteris paribus*. However, it may take buyers and sellers some time to recognize that market demand has increased, and for price, production, and purchasing decisions to respond to these new conditions. If these responses are not instantaneous, at P_1 quantity demanded initially increases from Q_1 to Q_2, while quantity supplied remains at Q_1. A shortage equal to $Q_2 - Q_1$ units will exist, and a shortage of some amount will persist until the price rises to at least P_2. The shaded area of the demand curve indicates that even some buyers want to see prices increase when shortages occur, to insure that they can buy the product before it is sold out. Sellers are, of course, usually quite willing to oblige these buyers by raising the price.

Sellers still clear their shelves of the product -- in fact, they can't keep enough of it on hand. What isn't cleared in this market after the increase in demand is consumers who are willing and able to buy at the original price. In fact, as represented by the shaded area of the demand shown in Figure 3-7, some disappointed buyers are willing to pay more for the product than the buyers who show up early enough to get it, and willing to pay more than sellers require to provide additional units of the product. These buyers may even tell sellers that so, as you can imagine, it won't take sellers long to increase their price. But of course that is exactly what must happen to reach the new equilibrium. As the price rises quantity demanded falls and quantity supplied rises, until they are once again equal at the new equilibrium price. When the new equilibrium is achieved the market once again is cleared of both buyers and sellers -- everyone who wants to buy or sell the product *at that price* can do so.

The technical name for any situation in which quantity demanded exceeds quantity supplied at some price is a *SHORTAGE*. In other words, shortages occur *at any price* below the equilibrium price, since quantity demanded is greater than quantity supplied at all such prices. That also means that anything that raises equilibrium price will result in a shortage if the old equilibrium price continues to be charged in the market, even for a short time. So you should see that a shortage can develop, at least temporarily, when supply decreases as well as when demand increases. Both kinds of changes in market forces put upward pressure on equilibrium prices, and prices may not immediately rise to the new market-clearing level. Large, active, and efficient markets tend to adjust rapidly, but products that are traded less widely sometimes require more time to come back into balance, as will prices that are restricted in moving upward by contracts, laws, regulations, or even social traditions.

88

Note carefully that a shortage doesn't imply *anything* about how high or low the price for a product is. Diamonds are expensive -- which is to say they have a high equilibrium price -- because they are very scarce, not because a shortage condition exists in the market for diamonds. Similarly, a loaf of bread has a relatively low price because bread is not very scarce; but that doesn't mean that at times there can not be shortages of bread. As you have seen, shortages are indicated by rising prices, and by consumers who are willing and able to buy a product at its current price but can't find any to buy. The relative scarcity of a good or service is measured by its equilibrium price, compared to prices for other products. Something that has a high equilibrium price is more scarce than a good with a low equilibrium price, even when neither is in a shortage situation. A shortage of something exists when its price is below the equilibrium price, whether that equilibrium price is very high or very low. The basic point to see here is simply that scarcity and shortages are very distinct concepts.

Surpluses

The opposite of a shortage is a *SURPLUS*, and that occurs when quantity supplied exceeds quantity demanded at some price. In fact, a surplus occurs at any price above the equilibrium price for a product, and can develop (at least temporarily) as a result of a decrease in demand or, as shown graphically in Figure 3-8, an increase in supply.

Figure 3-8
Surpluses

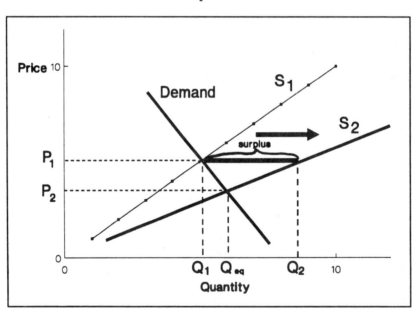

When supply increases from S_1 to S_2, equilibrium price will decrease from P_1 to P_2, *ceteris paribus*. Initially, at P_1, quantity supplied increases from Q_1 to Q_2, while quantity demanded remains at Q_1. A surplus equal to $Q_2 - Q_1$ units will exist, and persist until the price falls to at least P_2.

A surplus clears the market of buyers but not of the product. Everyone who is willing and able to buy at the original price -- the equilibrium price prior to the increase in supply -- can do so. But there are no longer enough buyers to purchase all that suppliers are producing at that price. Over time the product piles up on store shelves and in warehouses, or simply rots if it can't be stored. This naturally leads to downward pressure on prices in the form of clearance sales and occasionally even going-out-of-business sales. That pressure will continue until sellers realize it is better to sell their inventories for a lower price than to not sell them at all, and in doing so move toward the new, lower equilibrium price.

How fast prices adjust to new equilibrium conditions depends on many factors, which are featured in many discussions in later chapters of this book, and also in courses on macroeconomics.

Case Study #4
OPEC and the U.S. Economy

Almost any market could be used to show how the seemingly abstract concepts of supply and demand schedules are at work every day in the real world, but the world market for crude oil from the 1950s to the 1990s is a textbook author's dream. It offers a story involving vast sums of money, political intrigue and ineptitude, criminal behavior (including murder), wars, and even religion. While the events in this market were often painful and tragic for those who lived through them, they make for more memorable reading than most examples of changes in supply and demand. And surprisingly, the extraordinary events in this market developed from conditions that were initially quiet and peaceful, at least in this country.

In the early 1950s the United States was the world's largest producer of oil, and a net exporter of oil to other countries. The world demand for oil was growing steadily as a result of population growth and industrialization in both developed and underdeveloped nations. At the same time, however, there were discoveries of massive new crude oil reserves around the world and oil prices were falling, at least as compared to prices for all other goods and services. (In actual dollar terms, the prices for oil and most other goods rose slightly in this period, due to inflation. But the relative price of oil fell.) This situation, which forms the background for the rest of our story, is illustrated graphically in Figure 3-9. Although there were simultaneous increases in supply and demand, oil prices fell because the supply increases were proportionately larger than increases in demand.

During this period the United States adopted a series of *QUOTAS* and other restrictions on oil *IMPORTS*, which were supposed to encourage exploration and oil production in the U.S. But in practice, more oil was extracted from U.S. wells than was discovered, so U.S. oil reserves were depleted much faster than they otherwise would have been. In more cynical words, these public policies served to "drain America first."

The foolishness of those programs hit home in the 1970s, when the rate of increase in world demand for oil caught up to and surpassed the rate of increase in supply, and prices began to rise. Several factors contributed to this reversal. First, the 1960s and early 1970s saw faster and more consistent economic growth in many parts of the world. Second, there was a slowdown in the rate of new discoveries of oil reserves, reflecting the fact that the reserves which were easiest to find and bring into production had already been found and exhausted in many areas, while new discoveries were being made in more remote settings that were more expensive and environmentally difficult to develop. Some decrease in supply resulted from lost production in nations such as Libya, where oil reserves were seized from private oil companies by national governments. The companies which had contracted for the drilling rights in these nations often anticipated this "nationalization" of their contracts, and pumped more oil than they normally would have from these wells until the nationalization occurred. At that time production fell off to earlier levels, or even lower because some production skills and materials were temporarily lost when the oil companies were expelled and because the rapid pumping reduced the total amount of oil that could eventually be recovered from the wells.

Figure 3-9
The World Market for Oil in the 1950s and 1960s

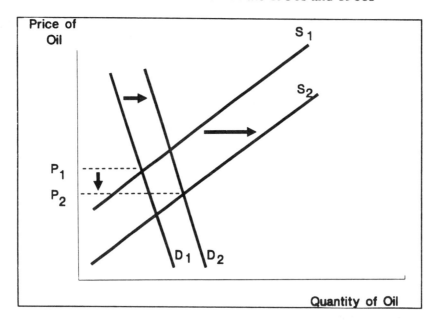

Because new discoveries outpaced the growth in demand for oil in this period, the price of oil fell relative to prices for other goods and services. This is shown by increases in supply that are greater than the increases in demand for oil products.

These factors set the stage for a dramatic jump in oil prices in 1973, ostensibly instituted by the Organization of Petroleum Exporting Countries (OPEC) to raise funds for Arabic nations fighting the Arab-Israeli war. (Most of the countries that belong to OPEC are Arabic nations.) Because of their continued support of Israel, the Netherlands and the United States were singled out for an *EMBARGO* of OPEC oil, which meant that direct shipments of oil from the OPEC nations to these two countries were temporarily suspended. However, the embargo had much less economic effect than the general price increases, because the embargoed nations could still buy oil (including oil originally produced in OPEC countries) from non-OPEC sources. But the OPEC nations did control over half of the worldwide output of crude oil, and their ability to influence oil prices was further strengthened by the United States' shift from an oil exporter to an oil importer. As if admitting that new fact of economic life, the United States belatedly dropped its oil import quotas in 1973, after its domestic production levels began to drop while its consumption had steadily increased.

By sharply cutting back on the amount of oil produced and sold by its member nations, OPEC was able to drive the price of oil up about 400% in a very short period of time. At the end of 1973, its members set a target price of $10 per barrel, and agreed not to *EXPORT* oil at lower prices. Frequent OPEC meetings were held to enforce the agreement, but virtually all production cutbacks were made by the OPEC nations with the largest oil reserves and comparatively small populations: Saudi Arabia, Kuwait, and the United Arab Emirates. Through the end of the 1970s, OPEC held the inflation-adjusted price for oil reasonably constant. Increased production from non-OPEC nations (responding to the higher price for oil) was offset by further cutbacks in OPEC production, again falling mainly on the Saudis. A simplified supply and demand picture of these developments is presented in Figure 3-10.

The rise in the price of oil had many substantial consequences. Oil-producing areas enjoyed large jumps in income and employment levels, while oil-consuming industries and households experienced dramatic cost increases. Energy substitutes (including insulation, double and triple-paned windows, and fuel-efficient machinery) faced large increases in demand that were reinforced by public subsidies for those who produced or consumed these products. Gas-guzzling cars and other offending symbols of "fuelishness" were penalized by falling prices in the marketplace, and further chastized, taxed, and regulated in the Congress. President Carter spoke to the nation from the White House on national television, symbolically wearing a sweater to encourage lower thermostat settings during winter and energy conservation. He later declared the quest for energy independence from foreign suppliers to be "the moral equivalent of war."

Figure 3-10
The World Oil Market in the 1970s

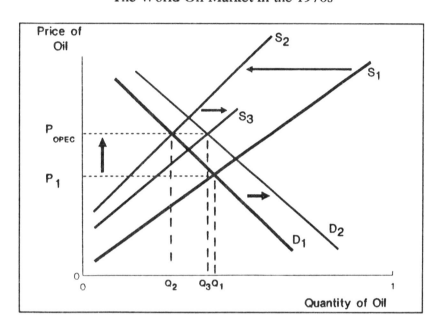

Due to restrictions in oil production in OPEC nations, the world supply of oil decreased from S_1 to S_2 in 1973, increasing the equilibrium price from P_1 to P_{OPEC} and decreasing the quantity of oil demanded from Q_1 to Q_2. In the rest of this decade, the world demand for oil continued to increase while the higher relative price of oil (compared to other products suppliers could produce and sell) attracted new oil producers -- especially non-OPEC producers. These changes are shown by the shift in demand from D_1 to D_2 and a second shift in supply, from S_2 to S_3. The equilibrium quantity stabilized around Q_3 with the equilibrium price (adjusted for inflation) relatively stable at P_{OPEC}.

Most oil-consuming nations allowed the price of oil products to rise, including Japan and other countries that import a far greater portion of their oil than the United States. And many nations continued to tax gasoline and other petroleum products at far higher rates than were charged in the United States. But for a time, the United States legally limited the price of gas and oil products below their new equilibrium levels. The most noticeable results of these policies were persistent shortages and long lines at gasoline stations. Waiting in lines is not something most people do well, and this case proved to be no exception. Fights broke out between people arguing about their places in line, and between customers and gas station attendants who tried to enforce the lines. In at least one case on the East coast, a person was shot and killed in one of these arguments.

The U.S. price controls were eventually abandoned (in stages), and by 1979 U.S. oil prices had risen to equal oil prices in other nations (except for international differences in taxes on petroleum products). There were also signs that those prices were beginning to fall, and likely to continue falling. In part that was due to increased supplies of non-OPEC oil: North Sea oil began reaching the market in 1975; in 1977 the Alaskan pipeline was completed and reversed the decline in U.S. oil production; and the Soviet Union, Norway, Mexico, and other countries were rapidly expanding their oil and natural gas production, exploration, and export activities. OPEC still controlled about half of the world's proven oil reserves, but that proportion was falling. Some observers, including several prominent economists, predicted imminent declines in oil prices. Instead, prices soon took their second major jump of the decade.

What the forecasters had failed to predict was the fall of the Shah of Iran and the rise (from exile in Paris) of the Ayatollah Khomeini and his Islamic Republic. They also didn't predict the rapid increase in world (and particularly U.S.) money supplies, which drove up prices for oil and other commodities that people viewed as insurance against inflation, such as real estate and precious metals.

By 1979, Iran was the second largest producer of oil in OPEC, with a daily output of more than five million barrels of oil. The Ayatollah's new regime initially denounced the former Shah's modernization programs and reliance on oil revenues, and Iranian production fell by over 66% to about 1.7 million barrels a day in 1980, and lower still in 1981. OPEC nations, especially those with oil production levels that greatly exceeded their own consumption levels, such as Saudi Arabia, decided *not* to produce more to offset the drop in Iranian oil supplies. A major factor in that decision appears to have been the fear of offending the Ayotollah, whose charismatic appeal to Islamic fundamentalists and revolutionaries had many people and political leaders worried about Iran "exporting terrorism" and coups.

The price increases that resulted from the Shah's overthrow and OPEC's decisions to maintain their current production levels were, at that point, easy to foretell. Through the early 1980s, the price for crude oil remained higher than it had before 1979, but again began dropping slightly over time in terms of inflation-adjusted dollars. In the long run, the 1979 price increases served to speed up production increases in non-OPEC nations, moves to conserve energy (i.e., decreases in the quantity of oil demanded), and the development of other types of energy. By 1985 OPEC's share of world oil production had fallen from 56% to 30%, and more than 20% of its production was being consumed by the OPEC nations themselves. In short, the group was losing power to oil consumers and other oil producers. Moreover, it was proving increasingly difficult to keep the nations which belonged to the OPEC *CARTEL* from producing and selling more oil as oil prices and revenues decreased, given the massive spending programs these countries had launced in times of higher oil prices, and which their leaders and populations quickly became accustomed to. Then, to the further detriment of OPEC's position, the long, bloody and expensive war between Iran and Iraq broke out, leading both of these nations to increase their oil production levels to get the cash required to continue the war. Our final graph depicting the world oil market, and illustrating these developments of the 1980s, is provided in Figure 3-11.

In 1986, the price of oil dropped briefly below $10 a barrel -- lower than the price OPEC had set at the peak of its power in the mid-1970s, even ignoring the substantial inflation that had occurred over the previous decade. (In other words, the $10 paid for a barrel in 1986 was worth a lot less than the $10 consumers were paying in 1973, because $10 bought fewer goods and services in 1986 than in 1973.) However, that low price overstated OPEC's weakness in some ways, because it resulted in part from an increase in production by Saudi Arabia that was designed to discipline the other OPEC members. The Saudis were, in effect, pointing out how low they could drive prices if the other members continued to ignore OPEC quotas and calls to restrict production.

By 1990, OPEC seemed in some ways to be in an even weaker position than it had enjoyed just a few years before, with slim prospects of ever recapturing its old dominance. However, another round of threats of increased production and lower prices from the Saudis, coupled with the gradual depletion of reserves in Alaskan and North Sea oil fields, and a renewed dependence on imported oil in the United States, briefly pushed oil above the $20 a barrel level in the first half of the year. That price had begun to slip again when Iraq (having recently agreed to a ceasefire in its war with Iran) invaded Kuwait in August of 1990. Kuwaiti and Iraqi production were almost immediately eliminated from the oil market due both to sharply decreased production in Kuwait and economic sanctions adopted by the United Nations (proposed by the United States and its allies), which included prohibitions against buying Iraqi oil and selling most kinds of products to Iraq. Oil prices temporarily shot up above $40 a barrel, even after other OPEC nations (especially Saudi Arabia) increased their output to fully offset the Iraqi and Kuwaiti production losses. Those short-run price increases primarily reflected concerns that such massive oil reserves were now controlled by the unpredictable regime in Iraq, led by President Saddam Hussein.

Figure 3-11
The World Oil Market in the 1980s

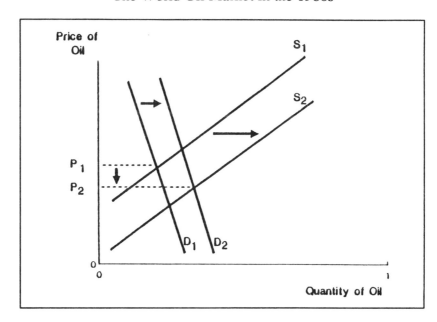

This graph represents OPEC's decline during the 1980s. Increases in world oil supplies, from S_1 to S_2, once again outstripped increases in demand, while OPEC's share of world crude oil production fell sharply. As a result, the equilibrium price of oil decreased even before adjusting for inflation.

Fears that oil fields and facilities might be destroyed if war broke out even led to some predictions that oil prices might rise as high as $100 a barrel. But when U.S. and United Nations forces began to bomb Iraq and Iraqui-occupied Kuwait in January of 1991, the initial effect was a drop in the price of oil, to about $20 a barrel. That indicated a sense of confidence in the military efforts to drive Iraq out of Kuwait and quickly restore the lost oil supplies to the market. The war was, in fact, ended quickly. But Iraqi forces set hundreds of Kuwaiti oil wells on fire as they retreated, so that this production (as well as Iraq's) was not quickly restored. It was, however, largely offset by increased production from other OPEC nations and non-OPEC producers. As the Kuwati production returned to the market the downward pressure on oil prices resumed -- market prices for OPEC oil in May of 1992 were about $18 a barrel.

Today, OPEC certainly remains as a key player in the world oil market, but not with as dominant a role as it enjoyed in the 1970s. In fact, while the oil market will probably never again look the way it did before 1970, it will likely never look the way it did in the 1970s, either.

There are far too many economic, political, and military variables involved to predict the future course of this market with any great confidence at this time, or in any great detail. But looking back at past events, even wars and coalitions such as OPEC have affected the market for oil in ways that are thoroughly consistent with the analysis provided by basic supply and demand models.

Chapter Summary

1) Many factors other than the price of a product cause short-run and long-run changes in the supply of or demand for it.

2) A market system establishes financial incentives to reward those who develop new products that consumers are willing and able to buy, or who develop better ways to make existing products. Those who continue to provide "old" products and services may experience declining income if the demand for these products decreases.

3) The demand for a product is a function of its price, holding constant such general determinants of demand as *INCOME*, the price of related goods (*COMPLEMENTS* and *SUBSTITUTES*), consumer *TASTES* and *PREFERENCES, PRICE EXPECTATIONS* of buyers, and the number of buyers in the market.

4) The supply of a product is a function of its price, holding constant such general determinants of supply as *INPUT* prices, technology, the price of other goods and services, the price expectations of sellers, and the number of sellers in the market.

5) Changes in one of the *GENERAL DETERMINANTS OF SUPPLY OR DEMAND* will lead to a shift in the entire supply or demand schedule. A change in the price of a product normally leads to a change in the quantity supplied and the quantity demanded of the product, but not to a change in the entire supply or demand schedule.

6) Changes in supply and demand result in new equilibrium price and quantity levels. However, sometimes simultaneous shifts in supply and demand are offsetting, and leave either the equilibrium price or quantity unchanged.

7) A *SHORTAGE* exists when, at a given price, quantity demanded exceeds quantity supplied. Shortages develop at all prices below the equilibrium price level, and lead to upward pressure on prices.

8) A *SURPLUS* exists when, at a given price, quantity supplied exceeds quantity demanded. Surpluses develop at all prices above the equilibrium price level, and lead to downward pressure on prices.

9) (Case Study #4) During the 1970s, OPEC was able to restrict the supply of oil to world markets. This initially resulted in higher prices for oil and significant decreases in the amount of oil consumed. Over time, the higher oil prices also resulted in the development of new supplies of oil and the increased use of oil substitutes. These increases in supply, coupled with decreases in oil consumption, led to declining oil prices and reduced OPEC's control over the world market for petroleum. However, political and military events have at times increased oil prices.

Review and Discussion Questions

1) What would you predict to happen to the price of automobiles if:

   a) the price of gasoline drops sharply?
   b) the cost of mass transit drops sharply?
   c) average incomes, adjusted for inflation, increase 25%?
   d) the media report that car prices will increase sharply next year?
   e) the number of consumers aged 16-70 declines?
   f) the United Auto Workers Union negotiates a contract raising its members' wages by 10%?
   g) engineers discover how to produce the same number of cars at U.S. auto plants using less electricity but current levels of all other resources?
   h) the number of world automobile producers is halved?
   i) military contracts to produce tanks suddenly become more lucrative?
   j) the supply and demand for cars both increase?

k) the supply and demand for cars both decrease?
l) the supply of cars increases while the demand decreases?
m) the demand for cars increases while the supply decreases?

2) In your opinion, what new product or service developed in your lifetime has made your life more different from your parents' lives than any other? What product developed in their lifetime made their lives most different from your grandparents' lives? How have new jobs been created by these products, and old jobs destroyed?

3) In one year, enrollments at a Big-10 university were about 32,000. The next year, tuition increased 6% while the inflation rate was only 4%, and enrollments increased to over 33,000. Does this refute the law of demand? Why or why not?

4) When Henry Ford built his factory in Detroit, he produced more cars by using new, assembly-line methods. This lowered the cost of producing a car by over 50%, and Ford sold more cars by lowering car prices. Does this refute the law of supply? Why or why not?

5) What's wrong with the following statement: "The price of oil fell 7% in 1977 and as a result the demand for oil increased by 12%."

6) What's wrong with this statement: "The price of Product X is the same today as it was two years ago. Therefore, we know that the supply and demand schedules for Product X haven't changed."

7) If there is a shortage for some good, is it scarce? If a good is scarce, is there a shortage of it?

8) If there is a surplus of a good, can it still be scarce? How are surpluses eliminated in markets where prices are not set by government laws or regulations?

9) (Case Study #4) How did OPEC's success in increasing the price of oil in 1973 set into motion forces which made it more difficult to maintain those higher prices in the 1980s?

Chapter 4
Elasticity, Price Controls, and Consumer and Producer Surplus

In This Chapter...

we extend the basic analysis of supply and demand to introduce three ideas that are important in a wide range of decisions made by private producers and consumers, and in numerous public policy issues:

Elasticity -- measures of responsiveness in the quantity of a product demanded or supplied when product prices or consumers' incomes change.

Price controls -- legal price ceilings or floors which make it impossible for prices to rise or fall automatically to market-clearing levels. And

Consumer and Producer Surplus -- measures of individuals' economic welfare used in evaluating public policies, or in assessing economic efficiency given any set of market-determined prices and incomes.

Elasticity

Supply or demand for a product is said to be elastic over a price range when a change in price, measured in percentage terms, leads to a greater change in quantity supplied or demanded, also measured in percentage terms. When the price change is greater than the quantity change, supply and demand are said to be inelastic. Similar measures are used to classify the responsiveness of the amount of a product consumers buy when their incomes change; but in that case there is also a question about the direction of the response: the quantity of normal goods demanded increases when incomes rise; the quantity of inferior goods demanded decreases. Similarly, in comparing the response in the quantity of one product demanded to a change in the price of a related good, these cross price elasticity measures are positive for substitute products, but negative for complements.

Price Elasticity of Supply and Demand

You already know that the quantity of a product demanded and supplied change when the price of the product changes, but by how much? And why is the quantity response to a certain price increase larger for some products than others? These questions are important in considering many practical issues, not just theoretical and academic concerns. For example, businesses care a great deal about how much sales of their products will fall when they raise prices, or how much sales will increase if they lower prices. And as you will see later in this chapter, these "how much" issues are crucial in determining who ultimately pays a tax levied on a product by the government. Businesses naturally try to pass those taxes on to consumers; but sometimes they can, and sometimes they can't. It all depends, like the answers to the other "how much" questions raised above, on the concept of *ELASTICITY*. This concept was formally developed by Alfred Marshall -- the same man who saw that supply and demand work together to set market prices like the two blades of a pair of scissors.

Marshall established the basic formulas to calculate *PRICE ELASTICITY COEFFICIENTS* -- measures of the responsiveness of quantity supplied or quantity demanded (that is, the changes in these variables) to changes in price. The greater the change in quantity supplied or demanded, compared to a given change in price, the greater the price elasticity coefficient. Or in other words, price elasticity coefficients (e_p) are calculated as:

$$e_p = \frac{\%\text{ change in quantity supplied or demanded}}{\%\text{ change in price}}$$

It is easy to see from this formula that the absolute value of the price elasticity coefficient will be greater than 1 if the percentage change in quantity is greater than the percentage change in price. It will be equal to 1 if the percentage changes in quantity and price are exactly equal. And, of course, it will be less than 1 if the percentage change in quantity is less than the percentage change in price.

This basic price elasticity formula also suggests that, because of the law of demand, direct calculations of price elasticity of demand coefficients will always be negative (since an increase in price leads to a decrease in quantity, and *vice versa*). Conversely, the law of supply implies that price elasticity of supply coefficients will always be positive (since price and quantity supplied move in the same direction). But because the price elasticity concept focuses on questions of how much quantity changes in response to price changes, what economists really care about is the relative size of the price and quantity changes. After all, they already know what direction quantity demanded and supply will move when price rises or falls. Therefore, economists typically express *all* price elasticity measures as a positive value (in effect, multiplying price elasticity of demand measures by -1). That allows them to use a simple classification system for all price elasticity coefficients, with only three basic categories:

$$\text{if } e_p > 1, \text{ supply or demand is } \textit{PRICE ELASTIC};$$
$$\text{if } e_p = 1, \text{ supply or demand is } \textit{UNITARY price ELASTIC};$$
$$\text{and if } e_p < 1, \text{ supply or demand is } \textit{PRICE INELASTIC}.$$

So, for example, if a 10% increase in the price of a product leads to a 5% decrease in quantity demanded and a 20% increase in quantity supplied,

$$e_p \text{ (Demand)} = \frac{5\%}{10\%} = .5 \text{ and } e_p \text{ (Supply)} = \frac{20\%}{10\%} = 2$$

In this price range -- where we move from the original price p to a price that is 10% higher -- we would say that demand is price inelastic, but supply is price elastic. A price elasticity coefficient of exactly 1 would indicate unitary price elasticity. By now, you should see that all of those elasticity categories are simply shorthand ways of describing whether the quantity response is greater than, less than, or equal to the price change that leads consumers and producers to change the amount of a product they are willing and able to buy and sell.

The qualifying phrase "in this price range" turns out to be an important consideration, because price elasticity for most products is different in different parts of the supply or demand schedule -- even when the supply or demand curve is a straight line. For example, consumers may be very sensitive to a change in the price of sirloin steaks from $3 to $4 a pound (in terms of how much they buy), but not as sensitive to an increase in price from $1 to $2 a pound. This leads to an important distinction: price elasticity coefficients are *not* equal to measures of slope on either supply or demand curves, and slope and elasticity are very different concepts. We will work through a numerical example shortly to show this. But first we must develop a more precise way to measure elasticity, and explain how and why it is used.

The Mid-point Formula for Arc Elasticity

A fundamental problem arises in using the general formula for price elasticity coefficients you just saw. The problem is we get different values over the same price and quantity ranges on a supply or demand curve, depending on whether we are looking at a price increase or a price decrease over that range. Suppose, for example, you wanted to calculate the price elasticity of supply for a certain product, working from the following observations: when price is $2, quantity supplied is 2 units; and when price is $4, quantity supplied is 5 units. Since a price increase from $2 to $4 is a 100% increase ((4-2)/2), and the resulting increase in quantity supplied from 2 to 5 units is a 150% increase ((5-2)/2), you would conclude that supply is price elastic in this price range, with a coefficient of 1.5 (150%/100%). But the same data points might represent a price and quantity decrease.

In that case, you would calculate the price decrease from $4 to $2 as a 50% decrease ((4-2)/4), and the related decrease in quantity supplied from 5 to 2 units as a 60% change ((5-2)/5). From these values, you would now conclude that price elasticity of supply is 60%/50% or 1.2. That gives us two different elasticities over the *identical* range of the supply schedule!

That kind of discrepancy obviously can't help in trying to conduct a careful economic analysis of what is going on in some market, even though the different estimates arose only because we used $2 and 2 units as the base values for the percentages in the first calculation, and $4 and 5 units as the base values in the second calculation. The problem is simply that the different bases yield different percentages for the elasticity formula, and therefore different elasticity coefficients.

To avoid this problem economists developed the *ARC ELASTICITY COEFFICIENT*, which provides a single measure of elasticity at the midpoint of a range on a supply or demand curve (or more technically, as the name suggests, for an arc of that curve) where the range is identified by some specific price change along these curves. To calculate arc elasticity measures, just take the mid-point of the price values and use it as the base for your calculations of the percentage change in price. Then do the same thing for the quantity values. That results in the following mid-point formula:

$$e_{p\text{(arc)}} = \frac{\dfrac{\text{change in quantity}}{\text{mid-point of the quantities}}}{\dfrac{\text{change in price}}{\text{mid-point of the prices}}}$$

Obviously the mid-point (or simple numerical average) of two values, X_1 and X_2, is $(X_1+X_2)/2$, and the change or difference in those two values can be written as ΔX (found by subtracting the smaller of the two numbers from the larger number). Therefore, we can write the mid-point formula for arc elasticity as:

$$e_p = \frac{\dfrac{\Delta Q}{\dfrac{(Q_1+Q_2)}{2}} \Bigg\} \text{Midpoint}}{\dfrac{\Delta P}{\dfrac{(P_1+P_2)}{2}} \Bigg\} \text{midpoint}}$$

where Q_1 is the quantity supplied or demanded at P_1, and Q_2 is the quantity associated with P_2.

We can now use this formula to find a unique arc elasticity coefficient in the example we worked through to start this section. It is clear that, whether we begin from $2 and 2 units or from $4 and 5 units: the change in price (ΔP) is $2; the change in quantity supplied (ΔQ) is 3 units; the mid-point of the two prices is $3; and the mid-point of the two quantity levels is 3.5. So $e_{p\text{(arc)}}$ is 3/3.5 divided by 2/3, or 1.29. Note that this value for arc elasticity lies between the two values, 1.2 and 1.5, which we calculated earlier. It isn't the precise value for price elasticity starting at either end point in this price and quantity range, but it is a reasonable estimate of the average value for e_p over this entire range of prices and quantities.

In Figure 4-1, it is shown that the arc elasticity coefficients change as we move along a linear demand curve. In particular, they are higher at high price ranges on the curve, and lower at low price ranges. The reasons for that pattern are explained a bit later, in the general discussion of what makes supply and demand for some products more elastic than supply and demand for other products. But just as a matter of simple logic, you should recognize here that the slope of a linear demand curve such as the one shown in Figure 4-1 *is* the same at every point or segment of the line, even though the elasticity coefficients change as we move along the demand curve. That demonstrates quite conclusively that slope and price elasticity aren't the same thing, and rarely have the same numerical values. Slope is simply the measure of rise over run, in direct numerical values; price elasticity is the measure of the *relative* responsiveness of quantity demanded or supplied to a change in price.

Figure 4-1
Slope vs. Elasticity

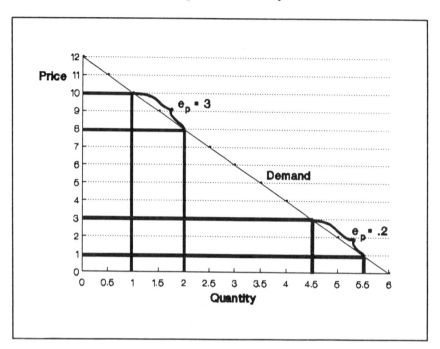

The slope of the demand curve shown above is -2. However, the mid-point formula for price elasticity of demand shows that in the price range from $1 to $3, the elasticity coefficient is .2. In the price range from $8 to $10, price elasticity = 3. Price elasticity changes at every point along a linear demand curve, and along most supply and non-linear demand curves. It is clearly *not* the same as the slope of a demand or supply curve.

The Point Elasticity Formula

Whenever possible -- which means, in practice, whenever enough information is available to estimate the formula for the demand or supply curve for a product -- economists also calculate *POINT ELASTICITY COEFFICIENTS*. These are the most precise estimates of elasticity, and naturally, the price and quantity point that is often of greatest interest to economists and policy makers is the current equilibrium point on both the supply and demand curve for a product.

Once you understand the arc elasticity formula, it's fairly easy to see how the point elasticity formula is derived, and what it represents. Just recognize that, in calculating an elasticity coefficient, taking smaller and smaller price changes also results in smaller changes in quantity demanded or supplied. Eventually, ΔP and ΔQ get so small (in mathematical terms, infinitesimal -- meaning almost but not quite zero) that P_1 and P_2 are essentially equal, and Q_1 and Q_2 are essentially equal. In effect, our price and quantity ranges have shrunk to a single point, at price P and quantity Q. When that happens, the arc elasticity formula becomes the point elasticity formula:

$$e_{P(point)} = \frac{\frac{\Delta Q}{Q}}{\frac{\Delta P}{P}} = \frac{\Delta Q}{\Delta P} \, X \, \frac{P}{Q}$$

This is called the *POINT ELASTICITY* formula, because we have essentially shrunk the price and quantity range down to a single point on the supply or demand curve. And because $\frac{\Delta Q}{\Delta P}$ is the reciprocal of the slope of a

linear demand or supply curve (that is, 1 over the slope), the formula for point elasticity is also given by

$$e_{P(point)} = \frac{1}{slope} \, X \, \frac{P}{Q}$$

To find the point elasticity on non-linear supply and demand curves, simply draw the straight line tangent to the curve at the point for the values of P and Q where you want to estimate price elasticity, and use the slope of that tangent line in the formula. (This is shown in Figure 4-2.) On both linear and non-linear curves, the point formula gives the most precise elasticity estimates, because it measures at a particular point rather than approximating elasticity over a range of different prices and quantities. But to calculate point elasticity, we have to know or be able to calculate the formula for the supply and demand curve, at least around the point on the curve for which we are trying to estimate price elasticity.

Figure 4-2
Point vs. Arc Elasticity

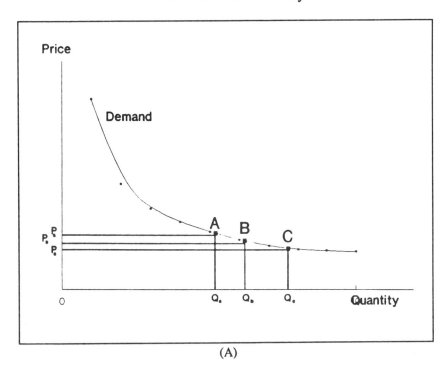

(A)

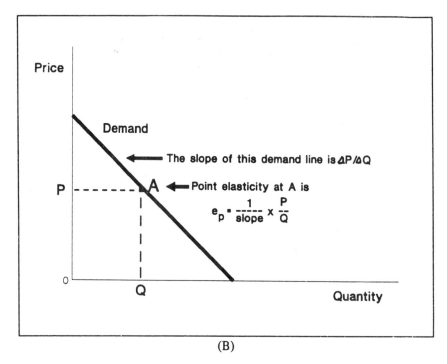

(B)

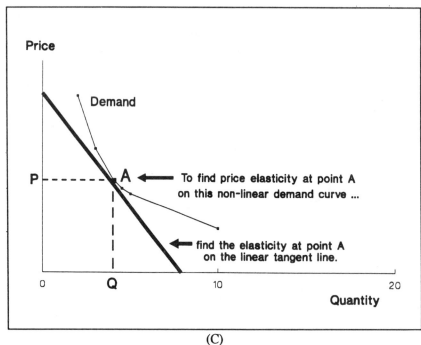

(C)

In panel (A), price elasticity of demand between points A and C can be approximated using the mid-point formula for arc elasticity, but that estimate is more accurate for points near the mid-point of this price range than for points near either extreme. When estimates can be made for smaller changes in price and quantity, as at points A and B, the arc elasticity estimates become more accurate -- closer to the point elasticity estimates in this price range -- and in particular the error for points away from the mid-point becomes less severe.

For infinitesimal changes in price and quantity, the point elasticity formula may be used to determine price elasticity at a specific point on a linear or non-linear supply or demand schedule. Point elasticity is equal to the reciprocal of the slope of a linear curve times $\frac{P}{Q}$, as shown in the middle graph (panel B). For non-linear curves, simply use the reciprocal of the slope of the straight line tangent to the curve at the price and quantity coordinate for the point to be estimated, as shown in the bottom graph (panel C).

Perfectly Elastic and Inelastic Supply and Demand Curves

Before considering the determinants of price elasticity, let's look at the most extreme cases of the concept, the perfectly elastic and perfectly inelastic supply and demand curves shown in Figure 4-3.

A vertical supply or demand curve is perfectly price inelastic, because there is no change in quantity regardless of how much price changes. The supply of original paintings by a deceased artist is perfectly inelastic, and the supply of land surface on the globe is nearly so. There probably aren't real world examples of market demand curves that are perfectly price inelastic (which would, after all, violate the law of demand). But as shown in Table 4-1, the demand for some products is strongly inelastic, especially in the short run when consumers don't have time to adjust their purchases of some products to changes in the products' prices. And individuals' demand curves for certain products are sometimes perfectly price inelastic over some ranges, even though the market demand curve is not. For example, an individual buyer might buy only one BMW convertible at a price of $40,000 *or* $30,000; but at the market level, more of these cars are sold at the lower price. In short, the individual buyer's demand curve was perfectly inelastic in this price range; the market demand curve was not.

A horizontal supply or demand curve is perfectly price elastic. For example, small firms in a large city can hire as many workers from most professions as they want at the market-determined wage rate in their labor market, which means the firms face a horizontal supply curve of labor. (The exceptions occur when these firms hire very specialized kinds of workers, such as professional athletes or physicians who are among a handful of doctors who know how to do a certain kind of operation.) In normal cases, a small firm that tries to pay anything lower than the market wage will find that no one is willing to work there; the workers simply go down the street to another firm that does pay the market wage rate. So even an infinitesimal decrease in the wage rate can lead to an infinite change in the quantity of labor supplied to the firm. Similarly, a small firm (such as a family farm) which sells its product in a large market may face a perfectly elastic demand curve. It can sell as much as it wants to at the market-determined price, but sales will fall to zero if it tries to charge even a penny more. In both of these examples, tiny changes in price lead to extremely large (in some sense total) changes in quantity.

Determinants of Price Elasticity of Demand

Economists have developed estimates of price elasticity for many different products over typical price ranges. As shown in Table 4-1, some goods and services exhibit greater price elasticity than others.

104

Figure 4-3
Perfectly Elastic and Inelastic Supply and Demand Curves

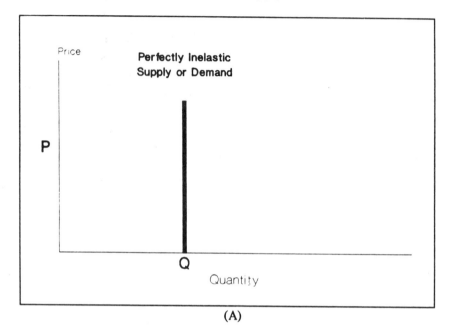

(A)

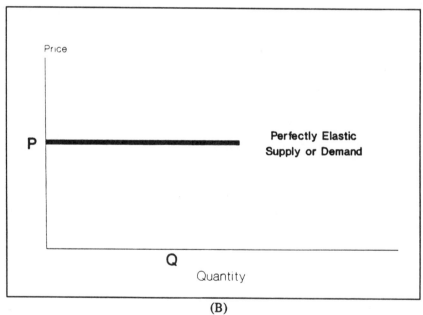

(B)

Vertical supply or demand curves are perfectly price inelastic because quantity supplied and demanded are completely unresponsive to changes in price. Horizontal supply and demand curves are perfectly price elastic, because a small change in price can cause quantity demanded or supplied to fall to zero. Some kinds of firms face perfectly elastic supply and/or demand curves.

Table 4-1
Price Elasticities of Supply and Demand for Various Products
(LR = Long Run; SR = Short Run)

Demand			Supply	
Fresh Tomatoes	4.6		Spinach (LR)	4.7
Radio & TV Repair (LR)	3.8		Green Peas (LR)	4.4
Movies (LR)	3.7		Cucumbers (LR)	2.2
Fresh Peas	2.8		Lima Beans (LR)	1.7
Canned Tomatoes	2.5		Cabbage (LR)	1.2
Electricity -- Residential (LR)	1.8	Elastic	Cauliflower (LR)	1.1
Foreign Travel by U.S. Citizens (LR)	1.8			
Canned Peas	1.6			
Auto Repairs	1.4			
Automobiles	1.35			
Auto Tires (LR)	1.2			
Electricity	1.2			
Beer	1.13			
		Unitary	Onions (LR)	1.0
Housing	1.0	Elastic	Carrots (LR)	1.0
			Beets (LR)	1.0
Shoes	.9		Cabbage (SR)	.36
Movies (SR)	.87		Onions (SR)	.34
Auto Tires (SR)	.8		Green Peas (SR)	.31
Taxi Rides	.6		Cucumbers (SR)	.29
Local Bus & Subway	.6		Spinach (SR)	.2
Jewelry & Watches (LR)	.6		Cauliflower (SR)	.14
Radio & TV Repair (SR)	.5		Carrots (SR)	.14
Jewelry & Watches (SR)	.4	Inelastic	Lima Beans (SR)	.1
Potatoes	.3			
Telephone	.25			
Theatre & Opera Tickets	.2			
Regular Coffee	.16			
Foreign Travel by U.S. Citizens (SR)	.1			
Electricity -- Residential (SR)	.1			
Hospitals & Physicians	.1			

Over longer periods of time, consumers and producers are able to adjust quantity demanded and supplied, respectively, more than they can in the short run. So time is one, but only one, determinant of price elasticity.

Sources: I. Demand: Coffee -- C. J. Huang, et. al., Summer 1980, *Quarterly Review of Economics and Business*; Vegetables -- D. M. Shuffert, U.S. Dept. of Agriculture Technical Bulletin #1105, 1954; Beer -- T. F. Hogarty and K. G. Elzinga, May 1972, *Review of Economics and Statistics*; Electricity -- L. Taylor, Spring 1975, *Bell Journal of Economics*, (now the *Rand Journal*); Housing -- R. F. Muth in *The Demand for Durable Goods*, H. Houthakker, ed., Univ. of Chicago Press, 1960; Automobiles -- G. C. Chow, *Demand for Automobiles in the U.S.*, North-Holland Publishing, 1957; Hospitals and Physicians -- J. P. Newhouse and C. E. Phelps in *The Role of Health Insurance in the Health Services Sector*, R. N. Rosett, ed., National Bureau of Economic Research, 1976; All

Other Products -- H. Houthakker and L. D. Taylor, *Consumer Demand in the United States*, Harvard University Press, 1970.

II. Supply: M. Nerlove and W. Addison, November 1958, *Journal of Farm Economics*.

There are four major determinants of the price elasticity of demand for a product (or, sometimes, for a broad group of products such as food or medical services):

1) the number of close substitutes for the product;
2) the average portion of the budget this product represents to buyers;
3) the time buyers have to adjust their purchases when the price of the product changes; and,
4) to a lesser and less certain degree, the extent that buyers view the product as either a luxury or necessity.

Most of these determinants are easy to understand on the basis of common sense. For example, products with few substitutes, such as heart transplants, are naturally going to be less sensitive to changes in price than products with many substitutes, such as a particular brand of running shoes or canned green beans. Similarly, the demand for a broad category of products, such as food, will be less elastic than the demand for a particular product in that category, such as bologna. There are few substitutes for all the products in this broad category of products (i.e., all foods), but within the category there are many substitutes for individual food products (such as hamburgers).

Salt is the classic example of a good that represents such a small part of most household budgets that retail demand for the product is largely insensitive to changes in its price. Conversely, because housing and automobiles are "big-ticket" items for most families, you should not be surprised to find that these products exhibit elastic or at least unitary elastic demand. You should also understand that some individual consumers of a product like salt may have a more elastic demand for it than most retail consumers. For example, salt is an important budget item for for some businesses, such as those doing certain chemical processes or making certain products. On the other hand, the business or wholesale demand for some other products can be less elastic than the retail demand. For example, maids have fewer substitutes, and may represent a smaller part of the total budget, for large hotel chains than for private households.

The time determinant of price elasticity of demand is illustrated by the short-run (SR) and long-run (LR) estimates for many of the items in Table 4-1. Most products show greater price elasticity in the long run than in the short run. That is because it takes time for consumers and businesses to adjust their consumption and production of most products, including electricity and gasoline. In the 1970s, dramatic price increases for crude oil drove the prices of these products up as well, with only minor immediate effects on their production and consumption. But over the next few years, as oil prices remained high, consumers made many adjustments, including: switching to smaller cars that used less gasoline; the re-gentrification of downtown residential areas located near peoples' workplaces; and buying energy-saving devices such as bicycles, better insulated windows and doors, and active and passive solar heating devices. The government even chipped in by letting taxpayers deduct some of the expenses of many energy-saving improvements for their homes and businesses. All these adjustments tended to make demand for these products more price elastic over time, as shown in Figure 4-4.

As noted earlier, the luxury/necessity determinant of price elasticity of demand is not as certain or precise in its effects as the other determinants. As a general rule, consumers have more discretion over purchases of luxury items than necessities, so we can expect greater responsiveness to price (i.e., higher price elasticity) for luxury goods. However, luxury items are consumed primarily by families with higher incomes, and are frequently found to be inelastic, as is the case for theatre and opera tickets (shown in Table 4-1). A major part of the difficulty here are the labels "luxury" and "necessity." One person's "need" may be another's luxury, and what a middle-income family claims to be a necessity may be a pure luxury item for a low-income family. Remember this determinant, but use it as economists do -- sparingly and cautiously.

Figure 4-4
Time and Price Elasticity of Demand

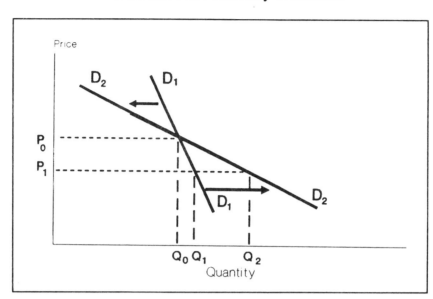

Demand curve D_1 is less elastic than demand curve D_2, because for any given price change there is a greater change in quantity demanded along D_2. For example, if price falls from P_0 to P_1, along D_1 quantity demanded increases from Q_0 to Q_1, but on D_2 the increase is from Q_0 to Q_2. When consumers have more time to adjust to price changes for a product, demand becomes more price elastic by shifting from, say, D_1 toward D_2.

Determinants of Price Elasticity of Supply

There are three basic determinants of price elasticity of supply:

1) the time producers have to adjust to price changes for a product;
2) the degree to which different factors of production are substitutable in producing a good or service, or in shifting from the production of some products to others; and,
3) how sensitive production costs are to changes in the level of output produced.

Long-run and short-run price elasticity of supply coefficients are shown for all items under the supply column in Table 4-1. With agricultural products, it is easy to see that once the planting season has passed, production is relatively inelastic. Farmers can increase production to some extent by using more fertilizer, herbicides, irrigation, etc.; but what they've planted limits what they will have to sell. To sell a lot more they have to plant and grow more, and that takes more time.

In manufacturing and service industries, the scenario is not as different from agriculture as you might expect. Given more time to adjust to a higher or lower price, *ceteris paribus*, producers will shift resources into markets where prices are rising, and out of markets where they are falling. The easier it is to shift resources into or out of the production process for a particular product, or to convert a production site from making one product to making another, the faster we will observe quantity supplied responding to price changes, and the larger those responses can be in a given period of time. Therefore, in those cases, price elasticity of supply will be high. Similarly, if the output of a product can be increased greatly without sharply increasing production costs, price elasticity of supply will be correspondingly greater, and *vice versa*.

Price Elasticity of Demand and Total Revenue

If you ask a business executive what the price elasticity of demand for his or her product is, you will most likely get a blank stare in return. Still, it's easy to show executives that they probably do know something about this concept, or at least that they certainly should care about it, because price elasticity for their product directly affects a firm's *TOTAL REVENUE*.

The easiest way to show the linkage between price elasticity of demand and total revenue is with the formula for total revenue, TR = P X Q, where P is price and Q is the quantity sold. The law of demand indicates that quantity demanded decreases when price increases, and *vice versa*. Showing that with simple arrow symbols, we have:

$$P(\uparrow) \text{ X } Q(\downarrow) = TR$$
$$\text{and}$$
$$P(\downarrow) \text{ X } Q(\uparrow) = TR$$

Next, remember that when demand is price elastic, the change in quantity demanded due to a price change is relatively larger than the price change, so total revenue changes in the same direction as quantity demanded. That is:

$$\text{For } e_p > 1: \quad P(\uparrow) \text{ X } Q(\downarrow) = TR(\downarrow)$$
$$\text{and}$$
$$P(\downarrow) \text{ X } Q(\uparrow) = TR(\uparrow)$$

When demand is price inelastic, the price change is relatively larger than the resulting change in quantity demanded, so total revenue changes in the same direction as price:

$$\text{For } e_p < 1: \quad P(\uparrow) \text{ X } Q(\downarrow) = TR(\uparrow)$$
$$\text{and}$$
$$P(\downarrow) \text{ X } Q(\uparrow) = TR(\downarrow)$$

At unitary elasticity ($e_p = 1$), price and quantity changes are exactly offsetting, so total revenue remains constant.

This establishes the useful, though somewhat imprecise, *TOTAL REVENUE TEST* for price elasticity. If you know the direction of a price change and the price elasticity of demand for a product, you can determine the direction of the related change in total revenue. Or, if you know how total revenue changes in response to a price change, you know whether demand for the product is price elastic, inelastic, or unitary elastic. The total revenue test doesn't tell you what the precise elasticity coefficient is, of course -- in an elastic range of demand, for example, total revenue will change in the same direction as quantity demanded whether e_p is 1.5 or 15. But at least you can use the test to establish whether e_p is greater than, less than, or equal to 1.

Price Elasticity and the Relationship Between
Total Revenue and Marginal Revenue

Total revenue schedules can be linear or nonlinear, as shown in Figure 4-5. A linear total revenue schedule indicates that the price for a product remains the same no matter how many units of output are sold. This is the total revenue schedule for a small firm selling its product in a large marketplace, in competition with many other firms selling identical products. In other words, this firm would be facing a perfectly elastic (horizontal) demand curve and would take the market price as a given.

Figure 4-5
Linear and Non-linear Total Revenue Schedules

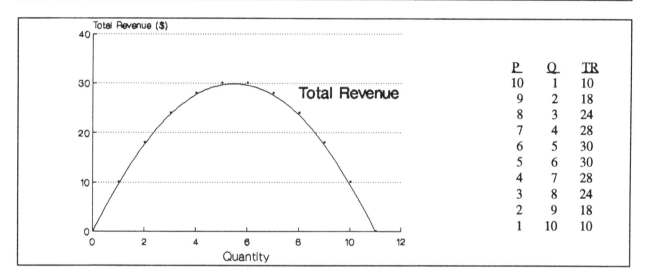

The total revenue schedule in the upper graph is for a firm that can sell as many units of its product as it chooses at a market-determined price (assumed to be $5 in this example). That price does not vary as a result of this one firm's sales, so the firm faces a perfectly price elastic demand curve, and its total revenue schedule will be a straight line. The lower graph shows a firm that faces a downward sloping demand curve for its output. In fact, the demand schedule in Figure 1-1 was used to generate this total revenue schedule.

A nonlinear total revenue schedule indicates firms that sell products different from those sold by other firms, or firms that are large relative to the total market for the kinds of products it sells. These firms will sell different quantities of their output at different prices, and must lower price to sell more. That is, these firms face downward-sloping demand curves.

The change in total revenue that results from selling an additional unit of output is called *MARGINAL REVENUE*, and a marginal revenue schedule can be derived for any total revenue schedule.

In the case where price is constant no matter how many units are sold, as represented by the linear total revenue schedule in Figure 4-5, marginal revenue is equal to the price for each unit of the product sold, which is always the same price. In other words, every time the firm sells one more unit of output, its total revenue goes up by the amount of that price. This is shown by the upper schedule in Figure 4-6, where marginal revenue is constant no matter how many units are sold.

Figure 4-6
Marginal Revenue Schedules

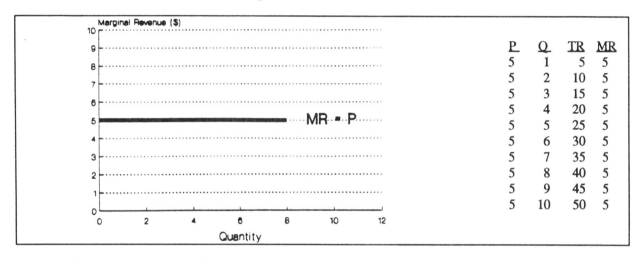

P	Q	TR	MR
5	1	5	5
5	2	10	5
5	3	15	5
5	4	20	5
5	5	25	5
5	6	30	5
5	7	35	5
5	8	40	5
5	9	45	5
5	10	50	5

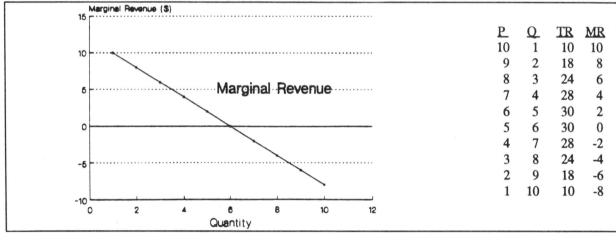

P	Q	TR	MR
10	1	10	10
9	2	18	8
8	3	24	6
7	4	28	4
6	5	30	2
5	6	30	0
4	7	28	-2
3	8	24	-4
2	9	18	-6
1	10	10	-8

Marginal revenue is the change in a firm's total revenue associated with a one-unit change in the quantity of output sold. The marginal revenue schedules shown above correspond to the total revenue schedules shown in Figure 4-5, which in turn were based on a horizontal demand curve (for the upper graph) and a downward-sloping demand curve (for the lower graph). Firms that can sell a little or a lot of their product without changing the product's market price will face a constant marginal revenue schedule equal to the market price for their product -- the amount they take in each time they sell an additional unit of output. Firms that produce and sell all or a large part of the total market output of some product will face downward-sloping demand and marginal revenue curves, because they can sell higher levels of output only by lowering their price.

The lower schedule in Figure 4-6 corresponds to the nonlinear total revenue schedule in Figure 4-5. Note that once the first unit of output is sold, this marginal revenue curve falls as the quantity sold increases. That happens because, whenever a firm faces a downward sloping demand curve, more units are only sold by decreasing the price for a product.

The total revenue at any level of sales can be found simply by adding up the marginal revenue for each unit sold up to and including the last unit. So as long as marginal revenue is positive, a firm's total revenue will increase as it sells more units of output. However, total revenue for many firms reaches a maximum and then falls, so it is clear in these cases that, at some point, marginal revenue must change from positive values to zero, and then become negative. Beyond that point, selling more units decreases total revenue. This pattern is a direct result of the kind of downward sloping demand curve represented by the price and quantity columns in the lower panels of Figures 4-5 and 4-6.

As shown earlier, the total revenue test for price elasticity indicates that, in the elastic range of a demand schedule, a price decrease leads to an increase in total revenue. Another way to say that total revenue is increasing is to say that marginal revenue is positive. Therefore, when marginal revenue is positive demand is price elastic -- consumers respond to the price decrease by buying relatively more of the product.

Conversely, when price decreases lead to decreases in total revenue -- in other words when marginal revenue is negative -- then demand is price inelastic. In these ranges of the demand curve there is a less than proportional change in quantity demanded in response to the change in price.

When total revenue does not change as price changes -- meaning marginal revenue is zero -- the price elasticity of demand is unitary. In these cases, the change in quantity demanded exactly offsets the change in price.

The general relationship between marginal revenue and price elasticity, in all three of these cases, is summarized in Table 4-2.

Table 4-2
Marginal Revenue and Price Elasticity of Demand

When Marginal Revenue is	e_p is
Greater Than 0	Greater Than 1
0	1
Less Than 0	Less Than 1

Income Elasticity and Cross Elasticity of Demand

The equilibrium level of quantity demanded is influenced by things other than changes in the price of a product, as you saw in Chapter 3. Two of the general determinants of the level of demand for some product are consumers' incomes and the prices of related goods -- when they change, that causes the entire demand curve to shift. Therefore, it may not surprise you to learn that economists have developed elasticity measures that quantify how much the quantity demanded of a good changes when there are changes in consumers' income, called the *INCOME ELASTICITY OF DEMAND*, or that quantify how much quantity demanded changes when there are changes in the prices of related goods and services, called the *CROSS-PRICE ELASTICITY OF DEMAND*.

The formula for income elasticity of demand (e_y) is similar to the price elasticity formula, except that now we are concerned with the responsiveness of the change in quantity demanded to a change in consumers' income, both measured in percentage terms:

$$e_y = \frac{\% \text{ change in quantity demanded}}{\% \text{ change in income}}$$

Unlike price elasticity estimates, however, income elasticity estimates can be either positive or negative numbers, because we have to allow for both normal and inferior goods. Normal goods are, by definition, those which people buy more of as their income increases, other things being equal. Inferior goods are those which people buy more of as their income falls, *ceteris paribus*. Therefore, income elasticity coefficients will be positive for normal goods, and negative for inferior goods.

Table 4-3 lists estimated income elasticity coefficients for a number of goods, but note that all but one of the products are normal goods, with positive income elasticity measures. That reflects the fact that, while many products are inferior goods for some individuals and families, at the market level there are usually even more consumers who view these products as normal goods. In countries where average incomes are steadily rising over time, products that are inferior goods at the market level will face steadily falling market demand, and eventually go out of production entirely.

Table 4-3
Income Elasticities of Demand for Various Products

Private Education	2.46	Normal Goods -- Income Elastic
New Cars	2.45	
Recreation & Amusement	1.57	
Alcoholic Beverages	1.54	
Furniture	1.48	
Books	1.44	
Dental Services	1.41	
Housing	1.04	
Clothing	1.02	
Beer	.93	Normal Goods -- Income Inelastic
Charitable Donations	.70	
Tobacco	.63	
Pharmaceuticals	.61	
Food	.53	
Electricity & Natural Gas	.50	
Fuels	.38	
Hospital & Physicians' Services	.09	
Margine	-.20	Inferior Good

Sources: Beer -- T. F. Hogarty and K. G. Elzinga, *Review of Economics and Statistics*, May 1972; Charitable Donations -- M. Feldstein and A. Taylor, *Econometrica*, November 1976; Hospital and physicians' services -- J. P. Newhouse and C. E. Phelps, *The Role of Health Insurance in the Health Services Sector*, R. N. Rossett, ed., National Bureau of Economic Research, 1976; All other products -- H. S. Houthakker and L. D. Taylor, *Consumer Demand in the United States*, Harvard University Press, 1970.

Cross-price elasticity of demand measures (e_{ab}) show the change in the quantity of one product demanded that occurs because of a change in the price of some other good or service. Once again, both the quantity and price changes are measured in percentage terms. Therefore, the formula for cross-price elasticity is:

$$e_{ab} = \frac{\% \text{ change in the quantity of good a demanded}}{\% \text{ change in the price of good b}}$$

Cross-price elasticity coefficients may also be either positive or negative, because two products may be complements or substitutes. A positive cross-price elasticity measure for two goods indicates that they are substitutes, because an increase in the price of one product (say coffee) results in an increase in the quantity demanded (and demand) for the other product (say tea), even though the price of the other product has not changed.

A negative cross-price elasticity measure suggests that two goods are complements (like cameras and film), because a drop in the price of one leads to an increase in the quantity demanded of the other product, even though its price has not changed. In other words, as you saw in Chapter 3, the demand for the second, complementary product increases as a result of the fall in the price of the first product.

Elasticity and Tax Incidence

Not only consumers and businesses have something at stake in elasticity measures; these concepts can also be crucial to political leaders. For example, most national governments levy excise taxes on certain products to help pay for government programs. A certain level of excise tax (say 10% of a product's price, or perhaps $1 tax per unit sold) will clearly produce more tax revenue when levied on products that are price inelastic than it will when levied on products that are highly price elastic, other things being equal. On the other hand, a legislator who wants to discourage the consumption of some product (say cigarettes or foreign cars) will get better results in terms of reduced consumption if demand for the product in question is highly elastic -- that is, quite responsive to price changes.

Legislators also worry about raising government revenues in ways that are perceived as fair -- or at least won't get them voted out of office. Elasticity concepts are important here, too, in determining who ultimately pays a tax, and in showing the difference between the *LEGAL* and *ECONOMIC INCIDENCE* of a tax. Legal incidence refers to those who, by law, are required to send the tax payments to the government. Economic incidence refers to those who ultimately pay the tax, by facing lower profits, higher prices, or lower wages and salaries. The legal and economic incidence are often different, because firms or landowners legally required to submit the tax revenues to the government can sometimes -- but not always -- "pass on" some or all of the tax payment to their customers in the form of higher prices, or to their employees in the form of lower wages.

To illustrate this, Figure 4-7 shows, using hypothetical data, what might happen if a $1 per gallon tax was passed on all gasoline sold in the United States. (Gasoline taxes are, in fact, collected by the federal and state governments in the United States. They do not yet total $1 a gallon here, but they do in many European nations.) Producers would face the same other production and distribution costs for this product as they did before this tax was levied. Therefore, they would have to collect $1 more for each gallon they sold to be as well off as they were before (ignoring any costs associated with collecting and paying the taxes). Graphically, this is shown by the leftward shift to the supply + tax curve, which is exactly $1 higher than the untaxed supply curve at all quantities. Does this mean that the market price of gasoline will increase by $1? Only if the demand for gasoline is perfectly price inelastic, like D_1.

In fact, although the short-run price elasticity of demand for gasoline is usually found to be strongly inelastic (most estimates of these coefficients range from .1 to .4), it is not perfectly inelastic. And over periods of a year or longer, the demand becomes much more responsive to price changes -- some estimates suggest five times more elastic. Over time, therefore, the demand for gasoline shifts from a relatively inelastic schedule, although not nearly as inelastic as D_1, to one that is much more elastic, like D_2. As shown in the graph, the shift from D_1 to D_2 makes it clear that the final market price will not be $1 higher than before the tax. That means producers eventually pay part of the tax, but shift a substantial part of it to consumers in the form of a higher price. *Ceteris paribus*, the more elastic the demand for gasoline, the smaller the increase in price would be, the less of the tax that would be passed on to consumers, and the more of the tax producers would have to pay out of their earnings. With the hypothetical schedules shown in Figure 4-7, assuming market demand is shown by D_2, the $1 tax increases the market price from $2 to $2.50. That shows that consumers end up paying half of the $1 tax, and producers pay the other half out of their earnings.

Figure 4-7
Tax Incidence and Price Elasticity of Demand

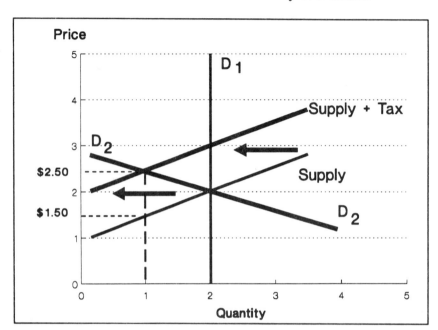

The shift from the original supply curve to the supply + tax schedule shows the effect of imposing a $1 per gallon tax on gasoline. Note that the vertical distance between the supply and supply + tax schedule at any quantity is $1.

If the demand for gasoline were perfectly inelastic (in reality, it isn't), as shown on D_1, the market price for gasoline would increase by $1 after the imposition of this tax, and consumers would bear the full economic incidence of the tax. If demand were more elastic, as shown by D_2, the market price for gasoline would increase by less than $1 after the tax. Here, hypothetically, consumers and producers are shown sharing the burden of the tax equally, paying 50 cents each. Before the tax, the market price paid by consumers and received by producers was $2. After the tax is imposed, consumers pay $2.50 at the new equilibrium point, with producers keeping $1.50 of this amount after remitting the $1 per gallon excise tax to the government.

But this is looking at only half of the story or, in Alfred Marshall's words, at only one blade of the scissors. Figure 4-8 shows that the more elastic supply is (now assuming a fixed demand curve to keep the analysis simple), the more of the excise tax producers are able to pass on to consumers in the form of higher prices, and the less of the tax producers will have to pay. In the extreme case, if supply was perfectly inelastic, producers would pay all of the tax; and if supply was perfectly elastic, they would pay none of it. But in nearly all markets neither supply nor demand is perfectly elastic or inelastic, and the degree to which a tax is passed on to consumers depends on the *relative* price elasticity of supply and price elasticity of demand. As shown in Figure 4-8, taxes on products with inelastic supply schedules, such as antiques, original art by deceased master painters, and land, are paid mainly by the sellers of these products. And as just shown in Figure 4-7, taxes on products with inelastic demand -- such as insulin, cigarettes, and salt -- are paid largely by consumers.

Figure 4-8
Tax Incidence and Price Elasticity of Supply

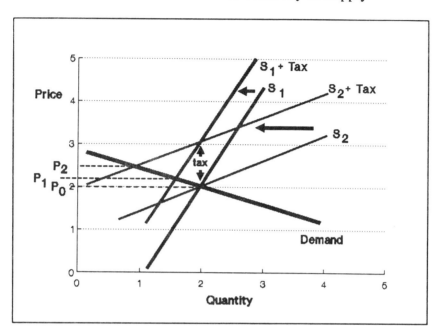

In the graph above, the supply curve labeled S_1 is less price elastic than the supply curve labeled S_2. Adding a $1 per unit excise tax to both supply curves shifts them both to the left, leaving them each vertically higher than the original supply curves by the amount of the tax.

Note that the pre-tax equilibrium price for either S_1 and S_2 was P_0. After the tax is imposed, price rises to P_1 if supply is less elastic (S_1), but to P_2 if supply is more elastic (S_2). *Ceteris paribus*, the more sensitive production decisions are to price changes -- in effect, the easier it is for producers to move their resources to some other endeavor -- the larger the share of the excise tax consumers will ultimately pay in the form of higher prices.

Price Controls

Through the political process, some groups of consumers are able to establish legal price ceilings for the products they buy, set below the equilibrium price that would prevail in a free market. Similarly, some groups of producers are able to establish legal price floors for the products they sell, at levels above the free-market equilibrium price. Some price ceilings are well intentioned efforts designed to help low-income groups, but they often have unexpected consequences in that regard. Some price floors are also well intentioned attempts to help farmers or other groups of producers subject to unpredictable changes in production conditions, or unfavorable long-term trends in the product prices that largely determine their incomes. But these price controls also lead to serious resource misallocations, which can be avoided by using other kinds of assistance programs.

Price Ceilings

Not everyone is as fond of the way markets work as economists. Most people just want the prices of the things they buy to be lower, and the prices of the things they sell to be higher. Several public opinion polls suggest people think high incomes *and* low prices are good, while low incomes *and* high prices are bad. The problem is, the wages that represent high incomes for workers are the *same* prices that firms must pay to the workers they hire, so paying high wages and incomes to workers increases prices for the goods and services workers and their families buy in their roles as consumers.

What market prices do so well, automatically, is reflect both sides of this tension in providing a measure of the relative scarcity of different kinds of workers, and of the many different goods and services they buy. But sometimes political bodies are convinced by especially needy or powerful groups, or even by charismatic individuals in prominent positions, to legally set a maximum price -- lower than the market price -- for some product or group of products. Examples of such *PRICE CEILINGS* include rent controls, usury laws on interest rates, and price controls on gasoline or other fuels. Let's examine the consequences of such policies, using the analytical tools we have developed thus far.

The most basic effect of a price ceiling is shown in Figure 4-9. In the absence of any price control, supply S and demand D would result in the equilibrium price and quantity P_{eq} and Q_{eq}, which would clear the market. But when price P_c, lower than P_{eq}, is imposed as the maximum legal price, quantity demanded increases to Q_d, while quantity supplied falls to Q_c. A shortage develops equal to $(Q_d - Q_c)$ units. (If P_c wasn't less than P_{eq}, the legally determined maximum price would have no practical consequences, and the market clearing price would prevail.) Some consumers will benefit by paying less for the product than the old, market-clearing price, since Q_c units will be sold at the lower price. But there will be other consumers who want to buy the product at this lower price, including some who were formerly buying the product at the higher, equilibrium price, who will have to go without it.

How great the shortage $(Q_d - Q_c)$ will be depends on: a) the difference between the price ceiling and what the equilibrium price would have been, and b) the price elasticities of supply and demand for the product. Suppose, for example, that both price elasticities are 2, and that the original equilibrium quantity is 100 units. A legal price ceiling that is set 10% below the market clearing price would lead to a 20% increase in quantity demanded -- roughly speaking from 100 to 120 -- and a 20% decrease in quantity supplied -- approximately from 100 to 80 units. That means there will be a shortage of about 40 units over the time period represented by these supply and demand schedules. In other words, about 80 units of the product will now available, compared to the 100 units that were sold before the price ceiling was imposed, and to the roughly 120 units that are demanded at the new, ceiling price.

Will those who called for the ceiling price be satisfied with the new conditions in this market? Only partly. While the lucky consumers of 80 units are happier, having paid a lower price, there are unhappy consumers willing and able to buy 40 additional units, but unable to find and buy the units at the lower price. There is also the problem of determining which people will get the 80 units, and which people won't.

That points out that an important consequence of price ceilings is to take away the market's ability to distribute products automatically, based simply on who is willing and able to buy and sell at different prices. Markets allow enormously complicated questions of resource allocation to be settled in a very decentralized and cost-efficient process. For example, by letting millions of individuals in New York City decide what they want to eat for lunch each day, and letting thousands of others decide what kind of restaurant services to offer to these consumers, we avoid the problems that would develop if there was a Central Planning Committee for Lunches in New York. But that doesn't mean that some other allocation system couldn't be used along with price ceilings.

Figure 4-9
Price Ceilings and Shortages

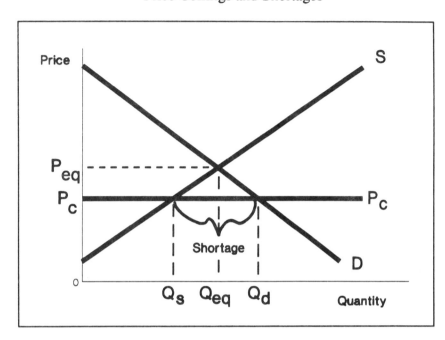

A legal price ceiling at P_c will result in a shortage equal to (Q_d - Q_c). Without the price restriction, price would rise to P_{eq} in this market, and the shortage would be eliminated.

One such allocation procedure is the time-honored custom of "first-come, first-served," otherwise known as standing in line. Under this scheme, those who happen to be at the right store at the right time -- when new shipments arrive -- will get the product, though they will often have to stand in line for hours to do so. Those who arrive too late will do without -- unless they can convince someone who did buy the product to sell some units to them, often illegally at a price greater than the legal ceiling price. These so-called "black markets" often develop when price ceilings are imposed, for the simple reason that some consumers are willing and able to pay a higher price for the product, as shown in Figure 4-10.

Even when illegal re-selling does not take place, first-come first-served schemes favor those who have more time to stand in line and search for the product, or those who can afford to hire someone to do so for them. That tends to be upper-income families, rather than the low-income groups many price ceilings are supposedly designed to help.

Coupon rationing is an alternative to first-come, first-served. In such a system, consumers must present a coupon or some other kind of token when they buy products that are price controlled, in addition to paying the ceiling price that has been set for the product. During World War II, U.S. consumers could not buy sugar, meat, gasoline, and tires or other rubber products without special ration coupons for these items that they received from the government. And in the 1970s, the United States government once again printed rationing coupons for gasoline (but this time never distributed them). The problem with these coupons is that they are expensive and cumbersome to print, distribute, collect, and verify. Counterfeit coupons may also appear unless appropriate counter-measures are taken. And, of course, some agency has to decide how many coupons everybody gets -- they may be distributed on a simple, per capita basis; but usually people in some areas or occupations get more coupons than others. For example, in World War II the government decided to give special allotments of gasoline and tire coupons to farmers and traveling salesmen.

Figure 4-10
Price Ceilings and Black Markets

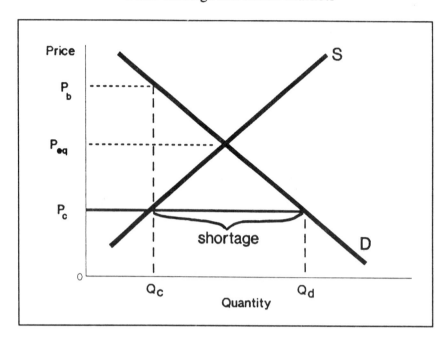

One consequence of the shortage (Q_d - Q_c) is that consumers are actually willing and able to pay a price of P_b for Q_c units, as shown on the market demand curve. Unless legal sanctions and enforcement provisions are sufficiently severe to prevent re-selling of the product, many of those who purchase some of the Q_c units at price P_c will try to gain by selling their units illegally for prices higher than P_c on black markets. If the black market becomes established and works very efficiently, all of the Q_c units will eventually be consumed by those who are willing to pay at least P_b for them, and the true price in this market will be higher than both the legal price ceiling *and* the equilibrium price that would prevail in the absence of any price controls.

Even more troublesome is the tendency for markets *in ration coupons* to develop, legally or illegally. If the coupons can be bought and sold, we end up in a position that is very different from what was intended by the price ceiling, as shown in Figure 4-11. The result there is very similar to what we just saw in Figure 4-10, describing black markets. Even with a coupon system, the maximum price that consumers are willing and able to pay for the lower quantity of the product supplied once the price ceiling is imposed is shown as P_s; and that is, in fact, the *total* price consumers will ultimately pay in this situation -- P_c to the suppliers of the product *plus* (P_s - P_c) for the ration coupons required to buy the product. In other words, we end up with a higher price for the product with price ceilings than we would without them (and a lower quantity produced), although a large part of the higher price now goes to pay for ration coupons. Moreover, the government (i.e., the taxpayer) is left with the bill for the printing, distribution, and enforcement costs of the coupons.

All of these problems have been observed whenever price ceilings are imposed -- they aren't hypothetical. For example, U.S. price ceilings on gasoline in the 1970s led to gross misallocations among consumers and producers, and a measurable stunting of economic growth in many areas of the nation. Similarly, rent controls make housing less available and lead to sharp declines in the quality of the housing that is rent-controlled. In fact, some economists who have studied rent controls have concluded that, short of nuclear weapons, they are the fastest and surest way to destroy a city's stock of rental properties. And price ceilings on interest rates which are supposedly designed to protect the poor from high interest rates tend to have precisely the opposite effect. They lead legal lenders to cut off *all* credit for those who don't have good credit ratings, steady jobs, and solid collateral -- i.e., the poor.

Figure 4-11
Price Ceilings With a Market For Ration Coupons

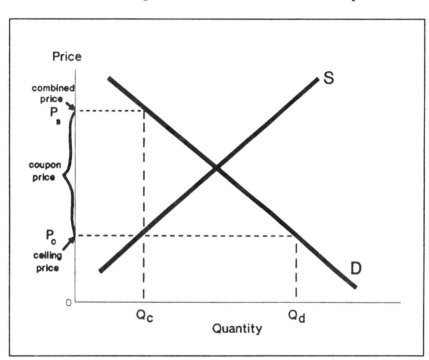

Perversely, price ceilings combined with an open market for ration coupons result in a higher total price -- the price of the product plus the price of the coupons required to buy the product. With product price limited to P_c, producers will supply quantity Q_c. But that quantity can and eventually will be sold at price P_s, because consumers will pay up to $(P_s - P_c)$ for the ration coupons they need to buy the available output. (Note that they are willing and able to pay a price of P_s for output Q_c; and since the ceiling price is set at P_c, they are willing to pay the difference, $P_s - P_c$, for the coupons.) The income from the coupons that are sold goes to those who sell coupons rather than to producers of the product. That means there are significant income redistribution effects of this policy.

Price Floors

Agricultural price supports and minimum wage laws are examples of *PRICE FLOORS* -- minimum prices, above the market equilibrium prices for some goods or services -- that are part of U.S. economic policy today. The effect of a price floor is illustrated in Figure 4-12, where a free market would lead to equilibrium price P_{eq} and clear the market. But a minimum price P_f, set higher than P_{eq}, reduces quantity demanded to Q_d and increases quantity supplied to Q_s. The price floor represents a subsidy to producers of this product, and as a result a surplus (Q_s - Q_d) develops. The size of the surplus depends, as with shortages under price ceilings, on the difference between P_f and P_{eq}, and on the price elasticities of supply and demand.

The workers or producer groups who lobby for a price floor may be helped by this kind of legal price support in one of two ways. If demand is price inelastic over the range from P_{eq} to P_f, the total revenue test tells us that raising the price to the price floor will result in higher total revenues for the producers of this product as a group, even though some producers who want to sell at the higher price will be unable to find buyers. In other words, some suppliers will gain and some will lose; but the overall gains to sellers will exceed the losses. On the other hand if, as in many past agricultural price support programs, the government not only enforces the price floor but also purchases the resulting surplus, then all of the suppliers gain. Given that outcome, why do most economists oppose price floors? The answer is, of course, based on the effects these programs have on consumers and taxpayers, and the production and consumption distortions that result when a price floor changes the relative prices of products.

Figure 4-12
Price Floors

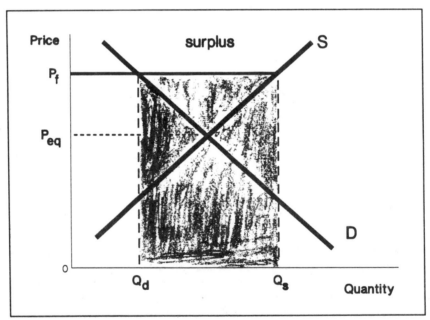

If a legal price floor is enforced at P_f, quantity supplied exceeds quantity demanded by (Q_s - Q_d). The price floor will increase producers' revenues if demand is price inelastic between P_{eq} and P_f, or if the government agrees to purchase the surplus output.

Consumers are hurt in several ways: they have to pay the higher price for the units of the product that they continue to buy; they have to cut back on the amount of the product they consume (from Q_{eq} to Q_d in Figure 4-12); they must switch some of their consumption to products they originally viewed as less desirable substitutes; and, if demand is price inelastic, they have to reduce their total expenditures for all other goods and services. Taxpayers have to pay to purchase the surplus, and to then store, destroy, or distribute the surplus in some other way.

Destroying products or letting them rot away is highly visible and politically dangerous -- particularly if the products are food items and there are hungry or starving people in the world. Storing products -- especially food products -- is costly; but distributing food surpluses can also be difficult and expensive. For example, in countries facing epidemic levels of starvation, the political climate is frequently so unsettled that aid programs to distribute surplus food products there are difficult, if not impossible. And domestic distribution programs in nations that adopt price floors must be done in such a way that the market sales that do take place at the price floor are not decreased -- otherwise, the government distributions will undercut the intended economic benefits of the price support program to producers. That was the reason why, when U.S. government stocks of surplus cheese were given away in the early 1980s, the cheese was distributed to the elderly and the poor in relatively small amounts (usually 5-pound blocks). The system was designed to get the products to people who otherwise wouldn't or couldn't buy them, in small enough quantities that they wouldn't re-sell them. Only in that (expensive) way could the surplus food be distributed without cutting into regular sales of the product at the existing price floors.

In the long run, production distortions can come to be the largest single cost of a price-support program, because resources are systematically shifted away from their most efficient uses. Producers are led by the higher prices to produce more of the subsidized products, and less of the products they would otherwise make or grow. At the same time, consumers facing the artificially high prices use less of these products than they otherwise would, use more of substitute products and, if demand is inelastic, buy fewer units of everything else. All these actions distort the results that would be achieved in free markets, and affect the prices of things we buy and use every day. Dairy products like milk and cheese, for example, aren't really as scarce as their current prices suggest; price supports just make them look that way.

A Brief Example: Price Supports and Production Distortions. The United States government sets price floors and other support programs for corn and other grains grown by U.S. farmers. While some U.S. production is thereby channeled to government purchases of surplus grain stocks (which probably won't go on forever), producers in other countries are establishing themselves in stronger positions in these and other agricultural markets as a result of the higher prices for U.S. grains.

By the late 1980s many agricultural researchers were concerned that U.S. farmers were losing their share of world soybean production to other nations, as they had already lost market share in world wheat, corn, and other grain markets, because of U.S. price supports for these products. The price supports result in higher prices for U.S. grain, and in particular higher prices relative to grain grown in many other countries. That makes foreign buyers less interested in purchasing U.S. grain; gives foreign producers a bigger market for their own crops; and even sets up incentives for U.S. companies that use grain in making their products to move their factories overseas, where they can purchase the cheaper foreign grain. The price supports for grain also threaten to weaken the U.S. position in the world market for soybeans, which was originally built up on rapid increases in U.S. soybean production and extensive research on different uses for this versatile crop. Why do price supports for wheat, corn, and other grains threaten the United States position as a leading soybean producer? Because American farmers can earn more by growing price-supported grains than by growing free-market soybeans, and that leaves the world market for soybeans more open to farmers from other countries.

The moral is: Short-run expedients often have long-run costs, and good politics is often bad economics. These are themes you will see often as you work through this book.

Price Controls and Income Distribution Policies

Are there better ways to help the groups that price controls are supposed to help -- such as farmers and the poor?

In later chapters, we will work through specific proposals for reform of the nation's welfare assistance programs which are endorsed by large numbers of economists, who range in their political views from the very conservative to the very liberal. In general, a key feature of these proposals is providing assistance in the form of direct income transfers or, equivalently, with reduced income taxes so that "take-home" income is increased. That minimizes the distortion of market prices for specific products, restoring the usefulness of those prices as measures of different products' relative scarcity, and as signals and incentives to producers and consumers. It also avoids the need for extensive government rationing and allocation systems on the one hand, and storage and

122

distribution systems for product surpluses on the other. Most fundamentally, direct income transfer programs make clear exactly what the assistance is costing taxpayers *and* how much the recipients are being helped.

Even direct income transfers introduce some distortions, inefficiencies, and special costs, as we will see in later chapters. But despite that, some kinds of assistance policies seem to be clearly better than others. Price controls on individual products have a long history of creating more problems than they solve, and creating more severe problems the longer they are enforced.

Supply, Demand, and Measures of Economic Welfare

Areas below the demand curve can be used to measure consumers' economic welfare -- that is, how much they value the satisfaction they derive from the consumption of different quantities of some good or service. Consumer surplus is a measure of how much greater the value of that satisfaction is than what consumers had to pay to acquire the products that are consumed. Similarly, producer surplus measures the difference between what producers are paid for selling some quantity of a product and the minimum prices that would have been required to make them willing to sell those units of output. Both of these concepts are important in evaluating a wide variety of public policies, as well as outcomes in markets for different goods and services.

Consumer Surplus

Oscar Wilde once defined a cynic as someone who knows the price of everything and the value of nothing. Given the importance economists attach to equilibrium price as the market measure of relative scarcity, they may seem to qualify as cynics under Wilde's definition. But that's a bum rap, because they also understand that market prices are measures of economic *VALUE IN EXCHANGE*, as opposed to measures of economic *VALUE IN USE*. Value in use is measured using equilibrium or market clearing price and an additional concept -- *CONSUMER SURPLUS*.

Consider the supply and demand curves in Figure 4-13. The equilibrium price for this particular product is $5, and at that price consumers are willing and able to buy 6 units (in whatever time period these schedules represent), but no more. In other words, they get just enough satisfaction from the 6th unit to make them willing to buy it at this price, but not enough satisfaction from the 7th unit to buy it. Furthermore, if the price increases just slightly while the demand curve remains unchanged, consumers will stop buying the 6th unit. That demonstrates that the satisfaction they get from the 6th unit is worth exactly $5 to them, *ceteris paribus*. But what about the satisfaction they get from the 1st through 5th units?

The demand curve suggests that consumers get *more* than $5 worth of satisfaction from every one of these units, even though they pay only $5 for each of them. Specifically, the demand curve shows that some consumer would be willing and able to pay $10 if he or she could get only one unit of this product in this time period, or $9 each if consumers could get only two units. So, given the market price of $5, the consumer who is willing to pay $10 for the 1st unit is said to enjoy $5 of consumer surplus on that unit; and the consumer who is willing to pay $9 for the 2nd unit of the product enjoys $4 of consumer surplus on that unit. Similarly, consumers derive $3, $2 and $1 of consumer surplus from the 3rd, 4th and 5th units.

If we assume that consumers can buy any fractional unit of the product shown in Figure 4-13, not just whole units, consumer surplus is graphically equal to the area of triangle ABC (because we add the consumer surplus associated with 1/4, 1/2, and 1 1/2 units, etc.). That triangle, as you can see, has a height of $6 along segment AB, and a width of 6 units along segment BC. That means the total area of the triangle is equal to $18, which is our estimate of consumer surplus in this particular market situation. It should be obvious to you that if changes in supply caused the market price for this product to rise, consumer surplus would diminish. Conversely, but again holding demand constant, a decrease in market price would lead to an increase in consumer surplus.

Figure 4-13
Consumer Surplus

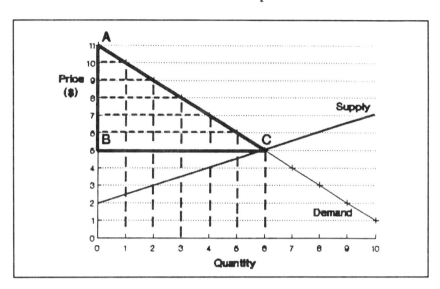

Consumer surplus for the first unit of this product sold at the market price of $5 is $5; for the second unit, $4; and $0 for the 6th unit. If fractional units of this product can be sold, as well as whole units, the total consumer surplus in this market is equal to the area ABC.

This shows that consumer surplus is the sum of the monetary values of the difference between what consumers actually pay for the units of the products they consume and the maximum amount they would have been willing to pay for these units. In other words, it is the sum of the difference between the value in use and the value in exchange for each unit of a product that is consumed.

For some products, such as water, this can be a very large sum -- consider how much you would be willing and able to pay for just enough water to keep yourself and your family alive if water suddenly became very scarce, and compare that to what you actually pay for water, even if you buy Perrier. Even though the first few units of water people consume are extremely important to them, because water is so abundant in most areas and its price is so low, people buy and use it to satisfy wants that are much less important to them, such as washing cars and sidewalks, or running flamingo lawn fountains. They don't get much consumer surplus from the last few units of water they buy; but they do get a lot from the first few units that are used for drinking, cooking, and bathing.

For other products, such as diamonds, consumer surplus is normally very small. That simply means that most consumers have to pay almost as much as they are willing and able to pay *for each unit* of diamonds they buy -- even the first units. This is, in fact, the example that made it clear to economists about 100 years ago that relative scarcity only determines value in exchange (or market value), not value in use. Diamonds have high prices because they are very scarce; but those prices capture almost all of the value in use associated with their consumption. Water has a low price because it isn't very scarce; but its value in use is very high, because people would be willing to pay a great deal more for the first units of water they use if they had to. To summarize: Market prices reflect scarcity and value in exchange; but if we want to know how much people really value the products they consume, we have to add their consumer surplus to estimate their value in use.

Understanding this helps to explain the diamond-and-water paradox that still upsets so many moralistic thinkers -- namely that the price of water (which is so good for people and even vital for life) should be so low, while diamonds (which are largely used to satisfy peoples' vanity) command such high prices. But really, would anyone be happier if the opposite were true -- with diamonds cheap and water expensive -- except those who owned large stocks of water?

A more technical point to understand, and a subtle one, is why the measure of consumer surplus shown in Figure 4-13 is only an approximation. That is true because, as we compare different price and quantity points along the demand curve, those points represent purchasing decisions that are influenced in part by the income effects associated with price changes (and especially large changes in prices). To get a precise measure of consumer surplus we would have to adjust for those effects, because income is one of the determinants of demand we want to hold constant in establishing the position of a demand curve *and* in determining a consumer's equilibrium level of satisfaction, which is based on the consumption of some combination of goods and services.

Fortunately, recent studies[1] have shown that in a wide range of cases the estimates of consumer surplus derived with the simple procedure of Figure 4-13 are useful and reasonably accurate, or easily adapted to be so. And the basic idea of consumer surplus -- that whenever consumers can purchase products at a given market price, the total value to them of the products they buy is often much greater than the amount they spend -- is in no way changed by these technical concerns.

Producer Surplus

In Chapter 1, you saw that when some inputs are fixed (that is, in the short run), producers will only sell more units of the goods and services they make when price increases enough to cover their rising per-unit costs of production. The positive, upward slope of the supply curve shown in Figure 4-14 reflects that fact. For example, producers are willing to make and sell two units rather than one unit only if the price per unit increases from $2.50 to $3. And at the market price of $5, producers are willing to sell six units, but no more. If the price falls even a little, they will no longer be willing to sell six units. From this we can say that the $5 price exactly covers their cost of producing the 6th unit, including some minimally acceptable level of profit. But what about the producers' returns on units 1 to 5, which they are willing to sell at lower prices?

The supply curve indicates that some producer is willing and able to sell the first unit of output at a price of only $2.50. So at a market price of $5, a *PRODUCER SURPLUS* of $2.50 will go to that supplier. The seller who was willing and able to offer the 2nd unit of output at a price of $3 will receive a producer surplus of $2, and so on up to the 6th unit which, we have seen, offers no such surplus to producers at this price. Note that the source of producer surplus on the first five units is simply the ability to provide those units at a lower cost. Higher levels of output are provided through more costly production, whether they are provided by a single producer or through the process of attracting new suppliers into this market with the lure of higher prices.

Producer surplus is the sum of the differences between the market price for a product and the minimum prices at which producers would be willing to sell each unit that is actually sold. This concept is, as you have undoubtedly noticed, the flip side of the notion of consumer surplus. And again, analagously, if any fractional quantities of this product can be produced and sold, as well as whole units, the total producer surplus is represented by area BCD in Figure 4-14. An increase in equilibrium price holding supply constant will obviously lead to an increase in producer surplus, while a decrease in price would have the opposite effect.

At the market price of $5, it is clear that the buyer and seller of the last unit sold are only just willing to undertake the exchange, since neither consumer nor producer surplus is gained from the transaction. However, those who buy and sell the other five units traded in this market do acquire consumer and producer surplus as a result of their trading. This demonstrates in a more formal sense a basic point we discussed in Chapter 1: Voluntary trade can benefit *both* buyers and sellers, and is not a zero-sum game. For example, for the fifth unit of output in Figure 4-14, at a market price of $5 the consumer gains $1 of consumer surplus, while the producer gains 50 cents of producer surplus on the same unit.

[1]Most notably Robert Willig's "Consumer's Surplus without Apology," *American Economic Review*, September 1976, pp. 589-97; and Jerry A. Hausman's "Exact Consumer's Surplus and Deadweight Loss," *American Economic Review*, September 1981, pp. 662-76.

Figure 4-14
Producer Surplus

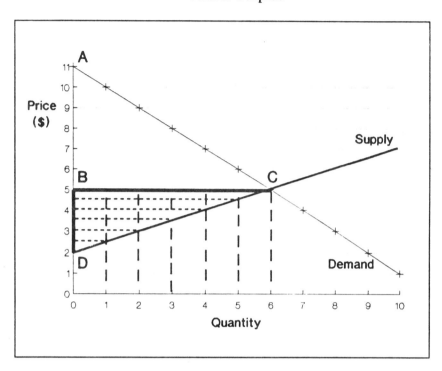

Producer surplus for the first unit of this product sold at the market price of $5 is approximately $2.50; for the second unit, $2; and $0 for the 6th unit. The total producer surplus in this market is equal to the area BCD, or $9.

Public Policy Programs and Measures of Economic Welfare

Consumer and producer surplus are important measures in many public policy discussions. For example, because producer surplus is the *excess payment* above the minimum price required to draw forth production from suppliers, it is possible to tax away some or all of the producer surplus without changing the quantities producers are willing to sell. That offers an attractive source of tax revenues to legislators and economists looking for ways to raise those revenues with minimal consequences on the economic incentives to produce and consume particular products. We will examine some of the taxes targeted at producer surpluses in later chapters.

Taxes which result in price increases for specific products, such as the excise tax discussed earlier in this chapter, as well as the tariffs discussed in Case Study #6 at the end of this chapter, must be evaluated using some measure of consumer and producer surplus. For one thing, the higher prices resulting from these product-specific taxes will, like any other increase in price while demand is constant, reduce consumer surplus. That means it is patently inadequate to measure the cost of these taxes to consumers and producers as simply the amount of tax revenue generated by the government.

In another setting, Figure 4-15 uses consumer surplus to show the most efficient toll on a publicly built bridge -- efficient in the sense of finding the toll that will maximize the combined economic welfare of producers and consumers. For simplicity, we assume that the cost of letting additional cars use the bridge once it is built is equal to zero, and that routine maintenance costs for the bridge will be incurred regardless of how little or how much it is used. In this special case, the supply of bridge crossings is perfectly inelastic; and if the bridge is just large enough to handle all existing traffic, then the supply and demand for crossings will intersect at quantity C, with an equilibrium price of zero. (If the bridge were smaller, some cars would be able to cross and others wouldn't when

126

the price is set at zero, which means that there would be a positive cost of letting cars use the bridge -- namely traffic jams.)

Under these assumptions, the total benefits associated with the use of the bridge are shown by the area of consumer surplus associated with this level of use, or area ABC in Figure 4-15. *Any* positive toll would reduce consumer surplus (for example, a toll of P_t reduces consumer surplus to area ADE), thereby reducing the benefits of using the bridge without affecting the costs associated with its use. That would be bad economics and, since toll bridges are also unpopular with voters, bad politics too.

Figure 4-15
Consumer Surplus and Toll Bridges

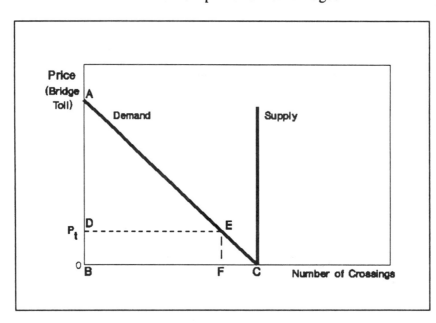

When cars can cross a bridge without causing repair costs or traffic jams, the fixed supply curve for the bridge intersects the demand curve at a price of zero, or lies entirely to the right of the demand curve. In these cases no toll should be charged for cars using the bridge, because a toll reduces the benefits derived from the bridge without affecting the costs of providing this service. For example, the toll P_t reduces consumer surplus from area ABC to area ADE, because it results in a decrease in the quantity of crossings. Even if the toll revenues (area DEFB) are used to provide other goods and services to consumers to offset the loss in consumer surplus, there is still a net loss (area ECF) associated with the toll.

This analysis suggests that in urban areas the only times that tolls may be efficient are during rush hours, and that in rural areas there should never be tolls. In fact, in 1938 economist Harold Hotelling concluded (optimistically), "This is [all] such plain common sense that toll bridges have now largely disappeared from civilized communities."[2] What Hotelling didn't anticipate was how difficult it would be, largely for political reasons, to re-introduce tolls when traffic congestion made the assumption of zero-cost crossings invalid. He also failed to predict the difficulty of assessing steep tolls on trucks and other heavy equipment, which have become dramatically heavier over the years and cause a disproportionate share of the damage to bridges and highways.

[2]"The General Welfare in Relation to Problems of Taxation and of Railway and Utility Rates," *Econometrica*, July 1938, p. 261.

While it is true that truckers pay special road taxes, some studies have suggested that they pay far less than they should in terms of the road and bridge damage they cause.

Another example of consumer and producer surplus measures in public policy debates involves the price controls discussed earlier in this chapter. Figure 4-16 is similar to Figure 4-9, which introduced the notion of a price ceiling. The difference here is that some additional costs of the price ceiling are shown in the form of lost producer surplus *and* lost consumer surplus. Note that there is some redistribution of benefits involved with these programs, as the decrease from the market price to the ceiling price causes an area that was producer surplus to become consumer surplus (area CGEF). However, there is also an area of *DEADWEIGHT LOSS*, where former benefits that existed partly as consumer surplus (area HBG) and partly as producer surplus (area GBE) disappear, in the sense that neither consumers nor producers continue to derive welfare from these product units. That happens simply because, at the price ceiling, fewer units of the product will be produced -- output falls from Q_{eq} to Q_c. Even though the demand curve suggests that some consumers would be willing and able to cover producers' costs in providing the units of output from Q_c to Q_{eq} *if* the producers were allowed to charge higher prices, they can't do that given the price ceiling. And neither producers nor consumers can benefit from goods or services that aren't produced.

Figure 4-16
Price Ceilings and "Deadweight Loss"

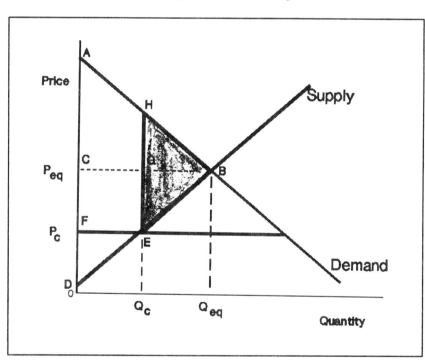

At the equilibrium price in this market, consumer surplus is shown by area ABC and producer surplus by area CBD. A legal price ceiling, P_c, changes consumer surplus to area AHEF, and reduces producer surplus to area FED. Area CGEF was part of producer surplus before the price ceiling, but becomes part of consumer surplus unless black markets and side payments for this product develop. The shaded area HBE represents a deadweight loss associated with the price ceiling, since production and consumption was reduced from Q_{eq} to Q_c units. Part of the deadweight loss (area HBG) was originally an area of consumer surplus, and part (area GBE) an area of producer surplus.

128

Case Study #5
Agricultural Price Supports

In many ways, technological change has made farming an easier job than it was just a few decades ago. While it is still true that farmwork is never finished -- livestock must be fed (and some of it milked) every day, which makes it hard to take a real day off, let alone a vacation -- at least plowing, planting, and harvesting can be done from air conditioned machinery. Fields are worked much faster by fewer hands, and improvements in breeding both plants and livestock have dramatically increased yields, as have new herbicides, pesticides, fertilizers, veterinary serivces, and other improvements in farming methods. Innovations as different as hail insurance and irrigation have even given farmers more protection from bad weather than they ever enjoyed before. That's the good news on the farm; but there's a lot of bad news, too.

The demand for food products largely depends on the number of people around to buy food, and to a lesser degree on the amount of income people can spend on food. Those things don't change very much from year to year, and even if the price of food changes significantly the amount of food bought stays pretty much the same. In other words, the demand for food is highly price inelastic.

That suggests a lot of stability in agricultural markets on the demand side; but the same thing can't be said about the other side of the market. The supply of food is also very price inelastic in the short run (e.g., see the estimates in Table 4-1), but cycles of good and bad weather can cause the supply curve for food products to shift up or down dramatically from year to year. And putting inelastic supply and demand curves together explains why market prices for farm products experience much larger variations than prices for products with more elastic supply and demand schedules, as shown in Figure 4-17. A given change in supply or demand schedules that are inelastic (as shown in panel A), leads to a greater change in product price than the same change with more elastic supply and demand curves (as shown in panel B), other things being equal.

Figure 4-17
Price Elasticity and Price Stability

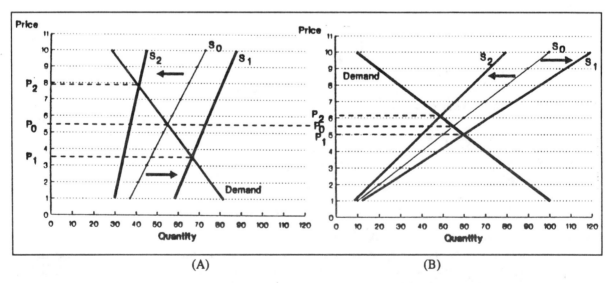

(A)   (B)

The supply and demand curves shown in panel (A) are much more price inelastic than the schedules shown in panel (B). The shifts to S_1 and S_2 in both graphs represent a 20% increase and decrease from S_0, respectively; but these shifts lead to much larger price fluctuations when supply and demand are price inelastic, as is the case with most agricultural products, than when they are elastic.

Large price swings for agricultural products mean large swings in farmers' incomes. That's one reason farmers have long lobbied for price stabilization programs for agricultural products. Another reason is linked to the productivity gains in agriculture noted earlier, which translated into large rightward shifts in supply over time, while demand increased relatively slowly. The relatively constant demand and increasing supply resulted in sharp decreases in market prices and, therefore, in total farm income. (Remember the total revenue test -- when demand is price inelastic, as for food, a decrease in price leads to a decrease in total revenue.)

Some farmers today support agricultural price *PARITY PROGRAMS*, in which the price supports for farm products are held equal to the current price of a basket of consumer goods and services that could be purchased at the same price as a basket of farm products in the period from 1910-14. For example, if the basket of consumer goods cost $100 in that time period, but now costs 10 times that amount, or $1,000, these farmers would request price-support programs that keep prices for agricultural products ten times higher than they were from 1910-14. Not surprisingly, however, farmers pick the period from 1910-14 because agricultural prices were relatively high in these years, compared to other goods and services.

As you have already seen, economists generally disapprove of using price supports to protect the income level of any occupational group, whether they be farmers, physicists, airline pilots, or blacksmiths. But the idea of providing some protection against short-term price swings (as opposed to long-term trends) that occur through no fault of the farmers is another matter. Some economists are more receptive to this kind of support, as long as it is provided in ways that do not severely disrupt the ability of market prices to serve as signals of the relative scarcity of these products, and as appropriate incentives to producers and consumers. With this background, let's take a quick look at the kinds of agricultural price support programs that have been used in the United States over the past 30-40 years.

Until 1973, price support programs consisted primarily of price floors combined with federal government purchases of the resulting surpluses. These are exactly the kind of programs described earlier in this chapter, in our discussion of Figure 4-12. The one major modification to this simple price floor model was a system of *PRODUCTION CONTROLS*, which were designed to limit the size of the surplus that the government had to buy. The effect of this modification is shown in Figure 4-18. To have any impact at all on surpluses, the level of production must be set and enforced at some point between Q_d and Q_s. Typically, agricultural production was controlled by directly limiting the acreage a farmer planted. This was enforced by requiring farmers to sign up before planting season, agreeing to the acreage limits in order to obtain the government's guaranteed price for crops that would be harvested in later months.

In 1973 and 1974, poor harvests in other countries and favorable movements in the price of the dollar on international currency markets led to sharp increases in U.S. farm exports (particularly to nations in the Soviet bloc, which we had not been trading with on a large scale prior to these years), and to sharp increases in the prices of most farm prices in general. For example, the price of a bushel of wheat rose from about $2 to over $5. Of course the best thing that can happen to any farmer is to have a bumper crop in a year when all other farmers have crop failures, and that's what happened to U.S. producers who grew wheat, corn, sugar cane, and many other farm products in these years. Some federal stocks of crop surpluses were sold in these years, to ease the upward pressures on prices; but as you can imagine this wasn't popular with farm groups. They liked the high prices, which meant higher incomes *and* higher values for farmland, the major asset of most working farms.

Figure 4-18
Using Production Limits With Price Floors

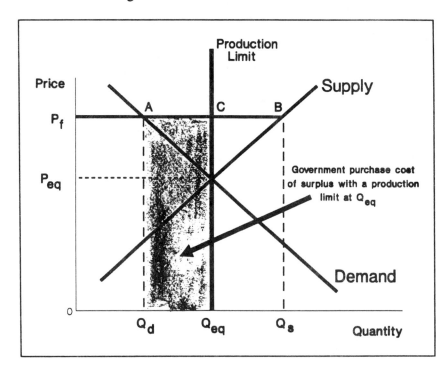

The government can reduce the amount of the surplus created, and thus the amount of product it must buy and somehow dispose of at the price floor P_f, by setting a production limit to the left of Q_s. We have assumed here that, by chance or by foresight, the controls were set at the equilibrium quantity. Note that this reduces, but does not eliminate, the costs of the price floor program -- from area ABQ_sQ_d to area $ACQ_{eq}Q_d$. Nor does it eliminate the production and consumption distortions that result from setting a price higher than the market price -- since P_f is higher than P_{eq}, this signals both producers and consumers that the product is more scarce than it really is.

The higher crop prices did lead to the adoption of a different kind of farm price support program in 1973 which, along with acreage restrictions and federal loan guarantees for farmers, is still offered today. The key feature of this program, as shown Figure 4-19, is that the government allows the equilibrium price and quantity to be set freely in the market, and then pays farmers the difference between a *TARGET PRICE* set by the government and the market price P_{eq} for each unit of output a farmer sells.

By limiting production -- *if* farmers can be convinced or coerced to plant Q_{eq}, rather than Q_t -- this type of program is designed to avoid, or at least to reduce, problems associated with government purchases of surplus products. Ironically, however, the program can lead to higher government payments to farmers than a system of price floors, surplus purchases, and production controls (shown in Figure 4-18). To see that, assume the market supply and demand schedules in Figures 4-18 and 4-19 are identical, that $P_f = P_t$, and that Q_d and Q_{eq} represent the same two levels of output in both figures. Then the target price program will be more expensive if demand is price inelastic. Why? Note that in Figure 4-18 the government's expenditures are equal to $P_f \times (Q_{eq} - Q_d)$. In Figure 4-19, the government payments will be equal to $(P_t - P_{eq}) \times Q_{eq}$. Substituting P_t for P_f in the first expression, we can eliminate the common area of $P_t \times Q_{eq}$ in both values to find that the relative size of the

131

payments depends on whether the area $P_t \times Q_d$ is greater than, less than, or equal to $P_{eq} \times Q_{eq}$. It is clear in Figure 4-18 that this question simply depends on the price elasticity of demand in this range.

Figure 4-19
"Target" Prices for Agricultural Products

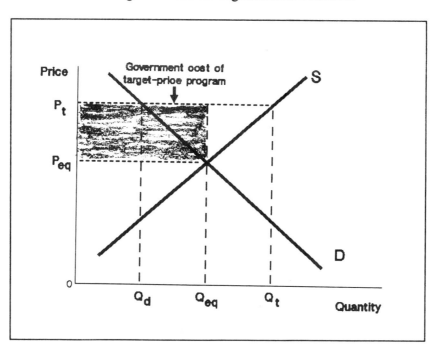

Under this system of price supports, the government allows the market price and quantity to be set at P_{eq} and Q_{eq}, as shown, and then pays producers the difference between the target price P_t and the market price for each unit of output they grow and sell. The program must be designed to hold production at Q_{eq} rather than Q_t, which farmers will grow if they correctly anticipate the target price and are not subject to production restrictions.

To see whether this kind of target-price program will require higher or lower support payments by the government than the price-floor program with production limits shown in Figure 4-18, assume $P_f = P_t$, and that Q_d and Q_{eq} are the same output levels in both graphs. Then:

<u>In Figure 4-18</u>
Government payments to farmers =
$P_f \times (Q_{eq} - Q_d) =$
$(P_t \times Q_{eq}) - (P_t \times Q_d)$

<u>In Figure 4-19</u>
Government payments to farmers =
$(P_t - P_{eq}) \times Q_{eq} =$
$(P_t \times Q_{eq}) - (P_{eq} \times Q_{eq})$

If $(P_t \times Q_d)$ is larger than $(P_{eq} \times Q_{eq})$, government payments will be smaller under the price floor and production limit program shown in Figure 4-18 than under the target price program shown here. That will be true if demand is price inelastic, as the demand for agricultural products typically is. You can see that in Figure 4-18 -- using the total revenue test, increasing price from P_{eq} to P_f (which we assume to be equal to P_t) will increase total revenues if demand is inelastic in this price range, which means that area $(P_f \times Q_d) = (Pt \times Q_d) > (Peq \times Q_{eq})$.

If demand is price inelastic, P_t X Q_d is the larger area, and since this is the value that is *subtracted* from the larger area P_t X Q_{eq} under the price ceiling support scheme, those payments will be less than the payments under the target price program. You have already seen that the demand for agricultural products tends to be price inelastic, which suggests that the payments to farmers will often be greater under the target price system. Remember, however, that this may be partly or wholly offset by reduced costs for storage and distribution of the surpluses generated under the price floor programs. And some observers suggest that target prices are administratively easier to change, and will eventually prove to be politically easier to phase out, than a system of price floors. In fact, the price supports were cut sharply in the 1980s, largely because of the federal government's attempts to limit the size of its own budget deficits. Still, the target-price subsidies appear to have become strongly entrenched over the past two decades, despite their inefficiency and unpopularity in some quarters.

Much of the current debate over the farm problem is emotionally based and largely misdirected, in the sense of hoping to preserve a way of life for the family farmer. Today, less than 3% of the U. S. population lives on farms, and most full-time farms are million-dollar operations whether they are owned by families, corporations, or families that have formed corporations. The only small farms left -- those of a few hundred acres or less -- are usually operated as part-time businesses or, in many cases, as hobbies of those who have full-time jobs doing something else.

If economists were asked to design an assistance program to help the few small family farms that are still operating, it would probably feature direct payments based on family income rather than crop production levels, be strictly capped in terms of the maximum income that leaves a family eligible for assistance, and also set a maximum amount that could be paid out to a single family or farm. Even that assumes a political decision will be made to continue to assist farmers, despite the fact that such assistance is not provided to independent plumbers, moviemakers, or workers in many other fields that are also risky.

Most economists have concluded that the American agricultural problem is compounded by a combination of bad public policies, political strength in the farming communities (which may decide as many as a third of all the elections to the U. S. Senate), and misunderstanding or ignorance among non-farm voters and representatives about the causes, financial costs, and long-term consequences of our current farm problems and policies.

Case Study #6
Tariffs and Quotas

TARIFFS are excise taxes levied on imported goods and services. They are among the oldest forms of taxation because they are easy to collect at major shipping ports, and offer the political attraction of apparently raising tax dollars from residents of other nations. *QUOTAS* are legal restrictions on the maximum quantity of certain goods that can be imported from other countries. Like tariffs, quotas restrict international trade, and at extreme levels can even eliminate it.

While the United States currently has, or did have in recent years, tariffs on such products as sugar, steel, chemicals, furniture, motorcycles, automobiles, electronic appliances, shoes, and other clothing, it has relied much more extensively on quotas, including "voluntary" quotas such as those agreed to by Japanese auto makers. (In practice, there is little difference in results between "voluntary" and involuntary quotas.)

Both tariffs and quotas ultimately affect price and quantity levels in a market, as shown in Figure 4-20. By making imported products more expensive, the tariffs and quotas help domestic producers facing foreign competition, including the workers in these U.S. industries. That is great news for these producers and workers, but it turns out to be bad news for some producers and workers in other U.S. industries, and especially for U.S. consumers. Consumers have to pay higher prices when supply and competition are restricted by tariffs and quotas; and if demand for those products is price inelastic, the producers of many other goods and services will see their sales fall as consumers spend more on the protected products and reduce their spending on other things. In the long run, tariffs and quotas also direct more resources into the production of products for which a nation does not have a comparative advantage, and away from those for which it does, simply because the price signals that producers and consumers see are distorted by the tariffs and quotas.

Figure 4-20
Comparing Tariffs and Quotas

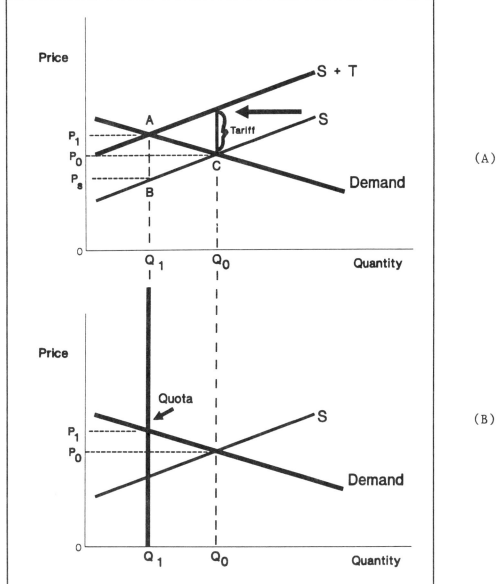

(A)

(B)

Both graphs show the foreign supply and domestic demand for a product in a nation which imports it. A tariff has the effect of shifting the supply curve leftward (top graph), as you saw in Figure 4-7. The post-tariff equilibrium price P_1 is greater than the original price P_0, though not by the full amount of the tax. The quantity of this product demanded decreases from Q_0 to Q_1 while the demand (and price) for similar products produced in the United States rise, due to this increase in the price of a close substitute. Area P_1ABP_s is the tax revenue generated by the tariff; it was formerly part foreign producer surplus and part domestic consumer surplus; area ABC is a "world" deadweight loss associated with the tariff. Domestic producers of this product (and their workers) gain from the losses of the foreign producers (and their workers), and from the losses of domestic consumers.

Quotas have similar, but not identical, results, as illustrated in the lower graph. Theoretically, a quota could be set that would increase price and decrease quantity demanded to the same levels that resulted from the tariff, as shown. The deadweight loss of both policies would thus be identical, but now the area that was tax revenue becomes entirely producer surplus (assuming no other actions are taken by governments in the exporting and importing nations, or by the foreign producers and their domestic competitors). This suggests why foreign producers of these products will sometimes agree to "voluntary" quotas, or at least prefer them to tariffs.

The empirical evidence on the costs of trade barriers is consistent with this theory, and at times astounding.[3] For example, the Council on Wage and Price Stability (now defunct) estimated in the late 1970s that a proposed tripling of the tariff on sugar would reduce consumer surplus by more than $260 million dollars a year. In the 1980s, sugar tariffs were so high that some companies imported sugar-coated breakfast cereals which were not subject to the sugar tariff, then refined the sugar out of those products and used it to make their own products.

Other studies have estimated the annual cost of saving each job in U.S. industries that are protected from foreign competition by the tariffs and quotas. Some of these estimates are: $45,000 per job in the textile industry; $60,000 per job in the sugar industry; $100,000 per job in both book manufacturing and the shoe industry; $105,000-$160,000 per job in the automotive industry; $220,000 per job in the dairy products industry; and $750,000 per job in the steel industry. The specific values in this listing are sensitive to changes in foreign exchange rates and other factors, but they indicate clearly that such job protection is very expensive -- few legislators would support direct cash payments to poor families at this level. But these aren't anti-poverty programs in any case; in fact, the workers and owners in these protected industries usually have above-average incomes.

Another way of costing out these programs focuses on how much more consumers must pay for protected products. A 1985 study[4] found that, in 1985, U.S. consumers paid 10% more for leather purses, 20% more for rubber boots and vinyl purses, 24% more for blue jeans, 33% more for an automobile, and 150% more for a box of candy than they would have if there were no tariffs and quotas in those industries.

Robert Crandall estimated that the "voluntary" quotas on Japanese cars increased their price by about $2,500 a car, which in turn led to an increase of about $1000 a car for U.S. models.[5] Alan Blinder pointed out that the additional revenues to U.S. producers from these price increases amounted to about $8 billion a year -- or roughly all of Detroit's profits in 1984 and 1985. Detroit's gain was other U.S. producers' loss, due to lower spending for non-auto products. But those losses didn't apply to Japanese car producers. They, and their American dealers, are estimated to have gained about $5 billion. So in effect, U.S. consumers paid about $13 billion to improve profits for American car companies by $8 billion. A direct cash subsidy would have been much cheaper -- if that was something we really wanted to do with $8 billion -- and would have left car prices closer to a true measure of the relative scarcity of automobiles.

The study by Hufbauer et al. estimated that the total cost of trade protection to 31 U.S. industries in 1984 exceeded $53 billion dollars, while the benefits to the American producers in these industries were about $40 billion. From the standpoint of the American taxpayer that's both a negative-sum game and an implicit tax -- paid by consumers in the form of higher product prices.

---

[3]For a very readable discussion of this issue, written from an "honest-liberal" point of view that nevertheless strongly opposes these trade restrictions, see Chapter 4 of Alan S. Blinder's, *Hard Heads, Soft Hearts: Tough-Minded Economics for a Just Society* (Reading, Massachusetts: Addison Wesley, 1987).

[4]Gary Hufbauer, Diane Berliner and Kimberly Elliot, *Trade Protection in the United States: 31 Case Studies*, Washington, D.C.: Institute for International Economics, 1986.

[5]"Import Quotas and the Automobile Industry: The Costs of Protectionism," *Brookings Review*, Summer 1984, pp. 8-16.

For over 200 years now virtually all professional economists, regardless of their political affiliation, have opposed nearly all tariffs and quotas. You should now understand why, although we hold a more complete discussion of these topics for a later chapter.

Chapter Summary

1) *ELASTICITY* measures compare the change in one variable to the change in some other variable, expressing all changes in percentage terms. *PRICE ELASTICITY OF DEMAND*, for example, is the percentage change in the quantity demanded for some product resulting from some percentage change in that product's price. *PRICE ELASTICITY OF SUPPLY* compares changes in quantity supplied and price for a given product. *INCOME ELASTICITY OF DEMAND* compares changes in the quantity of a product demanded to changes in consumers' incomes. And *CROSS-PRICE ELASTICITY OF DEMAND* compares changes in the quantity of one product demanded to changes in the price of some other good or service. Quantity responses to price changes are said to be *ELASTIC* if they are larger than the change in price. If the quantity response is relatively smaller, it is said to be *INELASTIC*. When both changes are equal, the response is said to be *UNITARY ELASTIC* in that price range.

2) Slope and elasticity are not identical. For example, on a linear demand curve where slope has the same value at every point, price elasticity has a different value at every point

3) When you know two discrete points on a supply or demand curve, you can estimate the average elasticity over the range of those two points, called *ARC ELASTICITY*, using the the *MID-POINT FORMULA*. Where it is possible to measure infinitesimal changes along a curve, you can determine the precise elasticity, called *POINT ELASTICITY*, at a particular point on a supply or demand curve.

4) The major determinants of *PRICE ELASTICITY OF DEMAND* for a product are: the number of close substitutes available for it, the portion of consumers' budgets that its purchases represent, the amount of time buyers have to adjust their purchases to price changes, and the extent to which buyers view it either as a luxury or necessity.

5) The major determinants of *PRICE ELASTICITY OF SUPPLY* for a product are: the amount of time producers have to adjust production in response to changes in its price; the degree to which different resources are substitutable in its production, and in the production of different goods and services; and how much changes in the quantity produced affect per unit production costs.

6) Perfectly price elastic supply and demand curves are horizontal; perfectly inelastic supply and demand curves are vertical.

7) When demand is price elastic, an increase in price results in a decrease in *TOTAL REVENUE*. When demand is price inelastic, price and total revenue change in the same direction. *MARGINAL REVENUE* -- the change in total revenue when one more unit of output is sold -- is positive when demand is price elastic, negative when demand is price inelastic, and zero when price elasticity of demand is unitary.

8) *INCOME ELASTICITY OF DEMAND* is positive for normal goods and negative for inferior goods. *CROSS-PRICE ELASTICITY OF DEMAND* is positive for substitutes and negative for complements.

9) The *ECONOMIC INCIDENCE* of a tax levied on a specific good or service is determined by the relative price elasticity of supply and demand for the product. If demand is relatively more elastic than supply, most of the tax will be paid by producers; if supply is relatively more elastic than demand, most of the tax will be paid by consumers.

10) A *PRICE CEILING* for a product will result in a shortage and distortions in its production, distribution, and consumption.

11) A *PRICE FLOOR* for a product will result in a surplus and distortions in the product's production, distribution, and consumption.

12) The political support for some price controls is motivated by an interest in redistributing income to help groups which are economically disadvantaged or especially vulnerable to changes in the economy. Most economists favor alternative social policies to accomplish these same ends, which entail fewer distortions in market prices and economic incentives.

13) *CONSUMER SURPLUS* is the difference between what was actually paid for a unit of a product and the maximum amount consumers would have been willing and able to pay for that unit.

14) *PRODUCER SURPLUS* is the difference between what a seller received for a unit of a product and the minimum amount that would have been required to make a producer willing to sell that unit.

15) Consumer and producer surplus both represent measures of *ECONOMIC WELFARE*, and can be used to demonstrate the mutual gains to buyers and sellers who engage in voluntary exchanges.

16) Price ceilings result in *DEADWEIGHT LOSS*, which is a loss in areas of consumer and producer surplus associated with curtailed production levels and a corresponding decrease in the volume of voluntary exchange.

17) (Case Study #5) Public assistance programs for farmers in the United States have, historically, been built around price floors, production quotas, and target prices, which have in turn spawned long-term problems in the allocation of resources.

18) (Case Study #6) *TARIFFS* and *QUOTAS* restrict voluntary exchange, and so result in deadweight losses by reducing the worldwide level of output of goods and services. The economic costs of these programs, measured in terms of costs per job saved or product price increases, are often extremely high.

Review and Discussion Questions

1) *Ceteris paribus*, would you prefer to be a producer of a product facing a price elastic or inelastic supply curve? Similarly, as a producer, would you prefer to face a price elastic or inelastic demand curve? What about your preferences as a consumer, in terms of facing either situation?

2) Suppose you know that the demand schedules for two products are linear, and that at current prices the demand for the first product is price elastic, while the demand for the second product is price inelastic. Which curve has the steepest slope?

3) If you knew the quantities of a product demanded at each of two prices, what formula would you use to calculate price elasticity of demand? If you knew the formula for the entire demand curve, which elasticity formula could you use to estimate price elasticity of demand at each of these two pairs of price and quantity coordinates? Would those elasticity coefficients be the same as the first estimate? Which elasticity coefficients would be most accurate? Why?

4) Explain why you think price elasticity of demand is elastic or inelastic, at current price levels, for each of the following products:

a) Home mortgages   b) Car loans
c) Private airplanes   d) Large commercial jetliners
e) Pizzas   f) Light beers
g) Heroin   h) Penicillin

5) Explain why you think price elasticity of supply would be elastic or inelastic, at current price levels, for each of the following products:

a) Concessions at the Super Bowl   b) Snowballs
c) Movies   d) Crude oil
e) Diamonds   f) Mink coats
g) Stradivarius violins   h) Turkeys

6) Can perfectly elastic and inelastic supply and demand curves shift and still be perfectly elastic or inelastic?

7) If you know the equilibrium price and quantity demanded before and after a shift in demand, can you use the total revenue test to determine whether demand is elastic, inelastic, or unitary elastic in this price range? Explain.

8) Is the income elasticity of demand likely to be positive or negative for the following products: apples, caviar, wine coolers, Napoleon brandies, used cars, and Hamburger Helper? Is the cross-price elasticity of demand likely to be positive or negative for each of the following pairs of goods and services: apples and oranges; VCRs and movie tickets; golf clubs and golf shoes; steaks and lobsters?

9) Based on the elasticity estimates provided in Table 4-1, will consumers or producers of green peas bear more of the economic incidence of an excise tax levied on this product? Illustrate that situation with a supply and demand diagram.

10) Do you think price ceilings on local telephone service and third and fourth-class postage are desirable policies? Why or why not? Why do you think such policies are in place today in the United States and some other countries? How would things change if these policies were abandoned? Illustrate that situation with a supply and demand diagram.

11) Are there any products which you would favor supporting with a price floor? Why or why not? Are you or your family involved in the production of any of the products you might have listed?

12) List your own criteria for determining who should receive income assistance from the federal government. Using that list, determine whether any of the price control programs described in this chapter, or any you may know about from other sources, seem to be effective ways of assisting those who meet your criteria.

13) Estimate how many pizzas, hamburgers, colas, and gallons of water you consume in one week. Then estimate your consumer surplus from these products. Will your consumer surplus for different units of the same product -- say the 2nd and 3rd pizza you consume -- always be the same? Why or why not?

14) Discuss, and show graphically, how a 50% drop in the price of a barrel of crude oil would affect the producer surplus derived from oil pumped on an offshore or Arctic rig, and oil pumped by the most efficient OPEC producer. (Hint: where are production costs for crude oil highest?)

15) Using the concept of consumer surplus, discuss the costs and benefits of charging all customers a flat monthly fee for telephone directory assistance services, compared to charging only those who use these services. For simplicity, assume a telephone company with only 10 customers, and specify a demand schedule and a per-call fee that falls somewhere in the middle of the price range you use in your hypothetical demand schedule.

16) Show graphically how the deadweight loss associated with an excise tax or price ceiling is affected by the price elasticity of demand (or supply) for the product in question.

17) (Case Study #5) Do you think farmers should benefit from government support programs not available to other kinds of producers? Why or why not?

18) (Case Study #6) Should voluntary trade by U.S. citizens who live in different states be restricted through any kind of tariffs or quotas? Can you think of any examples of how it is? How is this kind of trade different from trade between producers and consumers who live in different nations?

Chapter 5
Market Failure and Government Policy

In This Chapter...

we present an overview of the economic functions of government in a market economy. We first analyze several kinds of market failures that lead to government intervention, then discuss several reasons why government itself will often fail to allocate a nation's scarce resources efficiently.

Government and the Economy

Economists identify six broad areas where government has important economic roles to play even in market economies, though they often disagree on which specific policies should be used to fulfill those roles. In general terms, government intervention is warranted when private markets fail to provide the optimal allocation of resources to certain products or uses, or when overriding concerns with equity and the distribution of income among families establish a clear consensus favoring political modifications of market outcomes (e.g., through programs to transfer income and social services to the poor, the elderly, or the disabled). But the economic functions of government in a market economy are distinctly limited, and an economic justification for public intervention into particular markets is the exception, not the rule. In particular, for any policy of intervention to be justified on the grounds of economic efficiency, its benefits must be greater than or equal to its costs.

The Economic Functions of Government

Oliver Wendell Holmes, Jr. once described taxes as what we must pay for a civilized society. Economists agree, but only reluctantly. Their reluctance stems from their great respect for the ability of private markets to lead to the efficient production of most of the goods and services people want, and from their understanding of forces that lead to systematic inefficiencies in the decisions made by government officials and agencies.

That reluctance notwithstanding, economists have identified certain kinds of goods and services which private markets cannot produce at all, or will produce only at inefficient levels. One economic function of government is to determine the optimal price and quantity of these products, given their production costs and the overall value people place on them, and then take steps to bring about that level of production.

In other situations economic considerations are determined to be secondary to political, ethical, or religious concerns, so something that could plausibly be done on a market basis is set largely, if not wholly, outside the marketplace. For example, it is illegal to directly buy and sell votes in U.S. political elections, even though some candidates would undoubtedly be willing to make such purchases, and clearly many voters would be grateful for the opportunity to earn a few dollars quickly and legally by selling their votes. Or note that producers in market economies have the freedom to produce and sell whatever they want, *except* for certain kinds of products which the government has declared illegal -- such as slaves and narcotics. And recognize that during the past 75 years the government has played a much larger role in transferring income and providing basic levels of housing, food, education, and medical care to low-income families, largely because the extended family structure of earlier centuries (tied largely to agrarian-based economic systems) gave way to so-called nuclear and even single-parent families.

Today, most economists agree that the government must perform six broad functions to make a market economy work more efficiently, while also providing for those who are not able to care for themselves. How those functions can best be performed is often a matter of considerable controversy among economists, and everyone else. But knowing what these functions are, we can at least say that if a government action doesn't fit reasonably well within one of them, there is little *economic* justification for that action.

With that introduction, let's look quickly at the list of the basic economic roles of government in a market economy:

1) <u>Maintaining a Stable Legal and Social Environment.</u> Market transactions require that people be free to buy, sell, and own private property. Legal services (including police and, at the international level, the military) protect and extend the property rights that underlie a market economy. However, provisions which limit private property rights, such as *EMINENT DOMAIN* (laws that allow government to buy property even from those who don't want to sell it if the property is necessary to complete some public works project), are also often used by the government to undertake projects that expand markets and improve efficiency, such as interstate highways or railroad right-of-ways. Similarly, governments provide currencies, and establish standard systems of weights and measures which are recognized and accepted across a nation. That enhances the workings of a market economy by reducing the transactions costs of acquiring such information, thereby encouraging a greater volume of market exchanges and a higher degree of specialization.

2) <u>Maintaining Competition.</u> How efficiently a market economy functions and responds to consumers' wants is closely linked with the level of competition in product (output) and resource (input) markets. Legislation and government regulations can be used to promote and maintain competition. However, it is sometimes important to provide exemptions to these policies, in order to encourage special activities by producers. For example, the development of new products and production processes is promoted by awarding patents and copyrights to inventors and creative artists, which give them the exclusive legal right to produce their new products for a limited period of time. Without those legalized monopoly rights, there would be few economic incentives for people to develop and search for these new products in the first place, and the rate of technological progress would be slowed.

3) <u>Redistributing Income.</u> Some people do not have the assets or skills required to maintain a decent standard of living in a market economy. While private charities have provided for many of these individuals, U.S. public-assistance programs expanded rapidly from 1935-1970. Today, the notion that public assistance programs serve as the "safety net" for those in need has been accepted even by very conservative political administrations in the United States, and in other industrialized nations. But such programs inescapably involve transferring resources from some people to others, and alter the incentives to work and save both for those who receive the benefits and those who pay for them. Thus, this function stands clearly as an economic as well as a moral and ethical function of government.

4) <u>Providing Public Goods.</u> Products such as national defense and regional insect-control programs cannot be provided in private markets. Individual consumers following their own self-interests won't buy them voluntarily, which means private producers can't sell them in the marketplace. These public goods comprise an important class of market failures; and decisions about what quantity of these products to produce must be made through some governmental process. Once the output level has been set, however, public goods and other kinds of government services are often provided wholly or in part by private firms entering into contracts with the government. For example, contractors routinely build schools, prisons, weapons systems, and even space vehicles for the government.

5) <u>Adjusting for Externalities.</u> This class of market failures affects both "bad" things like pollution *and* "good" things like medical vaccines and education. Externalities occur whenever producers or consumers send incorrect signals to the marketplace about the costs of producing or the benefits of consuming a product. When that leads to a serious misallocation of resources, the government's role is to adjust the

market level of production and consumption -- not to entirely take over the decision process about how much should be produced, as it does in the case of public goods.

6) <u>Conducting Macroeconomic Stabilization Policies.</u> Today, governments in most industrialized nations account for over a third of all annual spending in those countries. Therefore, government spending and tax policies have a significant effect on national levels of unemployment, inflation, and economic growth, at least in the short run. Similarly, government policies affecting the supply of money and the availability of credit have major impacts nationally, and in some cases internationally. In fact, conducting stabilization policies has become one of government's most visible and controversial economic roles since the Great Depression. And from every corner of this controversy, enormous public pressures are brought to bear on political leaders to "do something" to improve the business climate during a recession or in times of high inflation.

Each of these economic roles of government is discussed in detail, and in a wide range of applications, later in this textbook. For now, this introductory overview is completed by describing how economists determine, from an economic point of view, whether a policy involving any of these six functions should be undertaken. That is done using *COST-BENEFIT ANALYSIS*, which means, as the name suggests, comparing a policy's costs with its benefits to judge its economic efficacy.

Cost-Benefit Analysis

Suppose a government agency decides to study whether it should clean up a lake that was polluted by a now-defunct mining company. Table 5-1 shows the agency's estimated costs and benefits of restoring the lake to different degrees of purity. Note that the total benefits of making the lake 100% clean exceed the total costs. Assuming these estimates are accurate in every respect, would it be good economic policy for the government to clean up the lake completely?

Table 5-1
Total Costs and Benefits of a Pollution Control Project[1]

Degree of Cleanup (%)	Total Costs ($)	Total Benefits ($)
0	0	0
20	1,000,000	50,000,000
40	3,000,000	90,000,000
60	8,000,000	115,000,000
80	23,000,000	130,000,000
100	55,000,000	140,000,000

The hypothetical data shown here indicate the estimated total costs and benefits associated with cleaning up a polluted lake. The benefits of the cleanup might include greater recreational use of the lake, improved land values around the lake, and health benefits to those who use the lake's waters for drinking, swimming, cleaning, etc.

The answer is, perhaps surprisingly, no. To see why, look at Table 5-2, which shows the *incremental* costs and benefits of cleaning up the lake in the same 20% steps that are shown in Table 5-1. Notice that initially

[1] This example is adapted from Otto Eckstein, *Public Finance*, Englewood Cliffs, N. J.: Prentice-Hall, 1964.

the incremental costs of making the lake a little cleaner are relatively low, while the incremental benefits from the first steps of the clean-up are quite high. But, by the time we get to improving the lake from 80% to 100% purity -- the last 20% of incremental cleanup -- the costs are quite high, while the benefits achieved by removing these last traces of pollution are relatively low. Cleanup beyond the 80% level of purity costs more than leaving the last 20% of the pollutants in the lake, which is to say more than the value of the benefits of that degree of additional cleanup.

Table 5-2
Incremental Costs and Benefits of a Pollution Control Project

Increments of Cleanup (%)	Costs per 20% Increment ($)	Benefits per 20% Increment ($)
0% - 20%	1,000,000	50,000,000
20% - 40%	2,000,000	40,000,000
40% - 60%	5,000,000	25,000,000
60% - 80%	15,000,000	15,000,000
80% - 100%	32,000,000	10,000,000

These data show the incremental costs and benefits of moving from one level of water purity to the next higher level. These are the relevant costs and benefits to compare in determining, in economic terms, how much the lake should be cleaned up -- not the total benefits vs. total costs for an "all-or-nothing" cleanup of 100% vs. 0%. As long as the incremental benefits are greater than the incremental costs, additional cleanup is economically efficient.

Cost-benefit analysis can be used to evaluate a wide range of public policy programs, including real-world pollution control. And very often, as in the example we used here, to eliminate the last incremental unit of pollution, illiteracy, discrimination, unemployment, inflation, murder, or drug traffic is far more expensive than getting rid of the first unit, or even the median unit. At the same time, although it may seem harsh logic, an occasional crime or oil spill or rise in prices doesn't disrupt a community nearly as much as regular occurrences of these problems. In other words, the first unit of any of these problems often does less harm (and so eliminating it provides less benefit) than additional units of the same problem. Human beings and the environment seem to be able to tolerate small amounts of pollution and other kinds of problems with few adverse effects, even though higher levels can have extremely serious consequences.

The general message from cost-benefit analysis of these kinds of problems is clear. From an economic perspective, there is an optimal amount of most "bads" that we should tolerate, and that level is reached when the costs of eliminating additional amounts of the bads exceed the benefits of purging them. In Table 5-2, for example, it clearly pays the government to undertake the 20, 40, and 60% clean-up programs; and, just as clearly, it does not pay to remove pollution beyond the 80% level. If the 80% to 100% clean-up work is done, in effect the government will be spending more to eliminate the remaining pollution than the pollution was costing in the first place.

Technically, the government should be indifferent about cleaning up the lake from 60% to 80% if it can only do so in these fixed, 20% increments, since the incremental costs and benefits of moving from 60% to 80% are identical. If, however, as shown in Figure 5-1, it is possible to clean up the water in much smaller increments of purity (e.g., 76, 77, 78, or 79%), then it will pay to clean the water *up to* the 80% level, where the incremental costs are exactly equal to the incremental benefits.

Figure 5-1
The Optimal Level of Pollution Cleanup

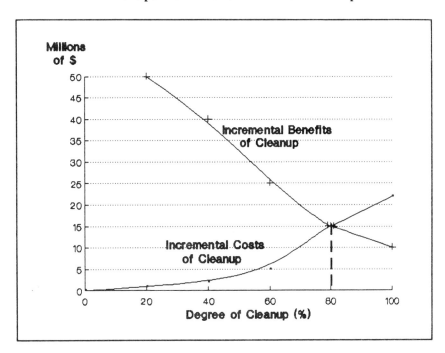

Based on the data in Table 5-2, this graph shows that economically efficient pollution control programs will end at a point that leaves some pollution in the environment. Clean-up efforts beyond this point (in this hypothetical example, 80% water purity) cost more than the costs of the pollution itself.

The conclusions derived from our comparison of incremental costs and benefits will also be reached by policy makers who determine the highest *net* benefits of the cleanup options shown in Table 5-1, by subtracting the total costs of such options from the total benefits. Since that sounds simple enough for even politicians to do, you may wonder how widely cost-benefit analysis is used by legislators. The answer is often but not always, and to an increasing degree. Many public works projects are now required by law to include such analysis when they are proposed (e.g., the water projects conducted by the Army Corps of Engineers that are controversial parts of most annual budgets for the federal government). But why is it not always used? And why do legislators sometimes vote against recommendations derived from such studies? There are several reasons.

First, cost-benefit analysis is itself controversial in several respects. A major concern to many people is that the analysis often requires estimates of the monetary value of human life, injury, or suffering, which they find offensive or immoral. On this point, economists counter that those who evaluate public policies *must* weigh these effects in any case, either implicitly or explicitly; and better decisions seem likely when costs and benefits are made explicit.

To see that, consider the following example: We know with certainty that if people travel in automobiles, lives will be lost on roads and highways. Moreover, the faster people drive their cars, *ceteris paribus*, the more lives will be lost. So no matter what speed limit we set, we are factoring human lives into the balance. That means a rational decision on the issue of setting speed limits will involve estimates of the number of lives that will be saved, as well as what it costs to save a life by imposing a lower speed limit. The careful researcher or policy maker will also compare the estimates of the costs of saving lives by lowering the speed limit to the estimated costs of other ways of saving as many, or even more, lives -- perhaps by requiring roll bars and inflatable air bags in all cars. Under any program some lives will be lost, so the question is never really at what speed limit can we

144

eliminate all deaths, but rather what level of deaths is, in a pragmatic sense, judged to be "best." It just isn't sensible to do all of the things that could be done to save lives, such as banning automobiles, because the cost is simply too high. Similarly, we could eliminate all train accidents involving cars, trucks, and school buses by building an underpass or overpass at every train crossing. But we don't, because that would use up too many resources (perhaps the equivalent of the nation's total output of goods and services for several years) that we want to use in other ways.

Some economic choices are inevitably dismal and depressing, but they all eventually have to be made -- sometimes by default, when politicians and voters decide to sidestep issues that make them uncomfortable. Unfortunately, ducking issues rarely leads to good economic policy, which is based on efficient ways to save both lives and scarce resources that can be used for other purposes.

Another problem with cost-benefit analysis is that it requires the availability of good data for estimating of the costs and benefits of a proposed program. On that count, human life isn't the only difficult variable to measure. For example, as you saw in Chapter 4, the concept of consumer surplus suggests that it is often improper to use market prices of products as estimates of their total value. So when resources are redistributed from some groups to others, as they often are in government spending and taxation programs, it is extremely difficult to quantitatively measure those effects. And as you will see in later chapters, when a future stream of costs and benefits must be included in a cost-benefit analysis, adjustments must be made to compare uncertain, future dollars that *may* be spent or received with current dollars that are certain to be received, spent, or taxed away.

Techniques have been developed to deal with many of these problems in preparing cost-benefit estimates; and cost-benefit studies have been completed for a wide range of public programs and policies. Some of these are summarized in Table 5-3. While these studies are by no means perfect, the real issue is whether those estimates are valuable enough to justify the costs of producing them -- and most economists believe they are.

Table 5-3
The Cost of Various Risk-Reducing Regulations Per Life Saved

Regulation	Year	Agency	Status*	Initial Annual Risk**	Annual Lives Saved	Cost Per Life Saved (Thousand of 1984$)
Steering Column Protection	1967	NHTSA	F	7.7 in 10^5	1,300.000	$ 100
Unvented Space Heaters	1980	CPSC	F	2.7 in 10^5	63.000	100
Oil & Gas Well Service	1983	OSHA-S	P	1.1 in 10^3	50.000	100
Cabin Fire Protection	1985	FAA	F	6.5 in 10^8	15.000	200
Passive Restraints/Belts	1984	NHTSH	F	9.1 in 10^5	1,850.000	300
Fuel System Integrity	1975	NHTSA	F	4.9 in 10^6	400.000	300
Trihalomethanes	1979	EPA	F	6.0 in 10^6	322.000	300
Underground Construction	1983	OSHA-S	P	1.6 in 10^3	8.100	300
Alcohol & Drug Control	1985	FRA	F	1.8 in 10^6	4.200	500
Servicing Wheel Rims	1984	OSHA-S	F	1.4 in 10^5	2.300	500
Seat Cushion Flammability	1984	FAA	F	1.6 in 10^7	37.000	600
Floor Emergency Lighting	1984	FAA	F	2.2 in 10^8	5.000	700
Crane Suspended Personnel Platform	1984	OSHA-S	P	1.8 in 10^3	5.000	900
Children's Sleepware Flammability	1973	CPSC	F	2.4 in 10^6	106.000	1,300
Side Doors	1970	NHTSA	F	3.6 in 10^5	480.000	1,300

Regulation	Year	Agency	Status*	Initial Annual Risk**	Annual Lives Saved	Cost Per Life Saved (Thousand of 1984$)
Concrete & Masonry Construction	1985	OSHA-S	P	1.4 in 10^5	6.500	1,400
Hazard Communication	1983	OSHA-S	F	4.0 in 10^5	200.000	1,800
Grain Dust	1984	OSHA-S	P	2.1 in 10^4	4.000	2,800
Benzene/Fugitive Emissions	1984	EPA	F	2.1 in 10^5	0.310	2,800
Radionuclides/Uranium Mines	1984	EPA	F	1.4 in 10^4	1.100	6,900
Asbestos	1972	OSHA-H	F	3.9 in 10^4	396.000	7,400
Benzene	1985	OSHA-H	P	8.8 in 10^4	3.800	17,100
Arsenic/Glass Plant	1986	EPA	F	8.0 in 10^4	0.110	19,200
Ethylene Oxide	1984	OSHA-H	F	4.4 in 10^5	2.800	25,600
Arsenic/Copper Smelter	1986	EPA	F	9.0 in 10^4	0.060	26,500
Uranium Mill Tailings/Inactive	1983	EPA	F	4.3 in 10^4	2.100	27,600
Acrylonitrile	1978	OSHA-H	F	9.4 in 10^4	6.900	37,600
Uranium Mill Tailings/Active	1983	EPA	F	4.3 in 10^4	2.100	53,000
Coke Ovens	1976	OSHA-H	F	1.6 in 10^4	31.000	61,800
Asbestos	1986	OSHA-H	F	6.7 in 10^5	74.700	89,300
Arsenic	1978	OSHA-H	F	1.8 in 10^3	11.700	92,500
Asbestos	1986	EPA	P	2.9 in 10^5	10.000	104,200
DES (Cattlefeed)	1979	FDA	F	3.1 in 10^7	68.000	132,000
Arsenic/Glass Manufacturing	1986	EPA	R	3.8 in 10^5	0.250	142,000
Benzene/Storage	1984	EPA	R	6.0 in 10^7	0.043	202,000
Radionuclides/DOE Facilities	1984	EPA	R	4.3 in 10^6	0.001	210,000
Radionuclides/Elemental Phosphorus	1984	EPA	R	1.4 in 10^5	0.046	270,000
Acrylonitrile	1978	OSHA-H	R	9.4 in 10^4	0.600	308,000
Benzene/Ethylbenzenol Styrene	1984	EPA	R	2.0 in 10^6	0.006	483,000
Arsenic/Low-Arsenic Copper	1986	EPA	R	2.6 in 10^4	0.090	764,000
Benezene/Maleic Anhydride	1984	EPA	R	1.1 in 10^8	0.029	820,000
Land Disposal	1986	EPA	P	2.3 in 10^8	2.520	3,500,000
EDB	1983	OSHA-H	P	2.5 in 10^4	0.002	15,600,000
Formaldehyde	1985	OSHA-H	P	6.8 in 10^7	0.010	72,000,000

* Proposed, rejected or final rule

** Annual deaths per exposed population. An exposed population of 10^3 is 1,000, 10^4 is 10,000 etc

Source: David L. Weimer and Aidam R. Vining, *Policy Analysis: Concepts and Practices*, 2nd ed., Englewood Cliffs, New Jersey: Prentice-Hall, 1992, pp. 302-03. Weimer and Vining derived the table from John F. Morrall, III, "A Review of the Record," *Regulation*, November/December 1986, pp. 25-34.

The final criticism of cost-benefit analysis we will discuss is the charge that it can lead to public planning in the form of one grand optimizing scheme or, conversely, as a haphazard ensemble of unrelated projects. The first charge condemns the mechanistic summing up and ranking of public policies to maximize the net value of governmental activity. The second charge suggests that adopting individual programs based on their net value can result in an overall government budget with no central goal or focus.

In response, many practitioners of cost-benefit analysis have adopted a planning-in-stages protocol that calls for the government to first establish a total budget which sets overall tax and spending levels that contribute to a coherent macroeconomic stabilization policy. By doing that, there is at least some guiding principle for the overall size of the budget. After that, cost-benefit analyses of specific programs are used to insure that relevant data are collected and studied before each program in the budget is adopted, to avoid wasting resources at the microeconomic level.

In its most basic sense, cost-benefit analysis is simply the careful and explicit study, and the direct comparison, of alternative public policies. The desirability of that approach strikes most economists as self-evident. With this general procedure understood, we are ready to examine some of the economic functions of government in more detail.

Public Goods

Most goods and services are what economists call private goods, products which can only be consumed by one person, or at least by only one person at a time. Whoever buys these goods and services in private markets makes the final decisions about how they will be used, and by whom. Public goods, however, are products which can be used by more than one person without reducing the amount of the product available to others (the classic example is national defense). Another important characteristic of public goods is that, once they are produced, it is impossible to keep anyone from using them -- even people who haven't help pay for them. That makes it impossible for firms to profitably produce and sell this kind of product in private markets, so the government must decide how much of them to produce, raising the funds to pay for them through taxes or public borrowing.

Rival and Non-rival Consumption

A basic characteristic of the *PRIVATE GOODS* you buy in the marketplace is that when you consume them, someone else can't. That applies to food, clothing, shelter, cars, and most of the other things you use. But not to everything. As you saw in Chapter 4, until traffic congestion becomes a problem you can use bridges and highways without reducing the amount of these goods available for others to use. The same is true for sidewalks, and even more for services like national defense, for which congestion isn't a problem. You can also take radio and TV signals from the air waves without reducing anyone else's opportunities to use these same products. And you can read a library book, watch a fireworks display, or look at a painting in a museum and the animals in zoos without "using up" these products, at least under normal circumstances. Such products, which we might say can be consumed jointly, are said to exhibit *NON-RIVAL CONSUMPTION*. This property is one technical characteristic of a public good. Private goods, on the other hand, usually exhibit the property of *RIVAL CONSUMPTION*, meaning consumption by one person precludes consumption by others.

For public goods subject to non-rival consumption, the same quantity of a product is available to all consumers in a given market area, even though each consumer may place a different value on the product. That means that the market demand for the product is not found by horizontally summing up the quantities that everyone in the market is willing and able to buy at various possible prices, as we did in Chapter 1 for private goods. Instead, we must vertically sum up the values that all consumers place on various quantities of the public good, as shown in Figure 5-2. We do that because once some quantity of the public good is produced, that same quantity can be used by everyone, and the true value of that quantity is therefore the value that all of the users taken together place on it.

Figure 5-2
Deriving The Market Demand for Public Goods

Quantity	Value of Output to Consumer #1	+	Value of Output to Consumer #2	+	Value of Output to Consumer #3	=	Total Value of Output
1	$5		$4		$3		$12
2	4		3		2		9
3	3		2		1		6
4	2		1		0		3
5	1		0		0		1
6	0		0		0		0

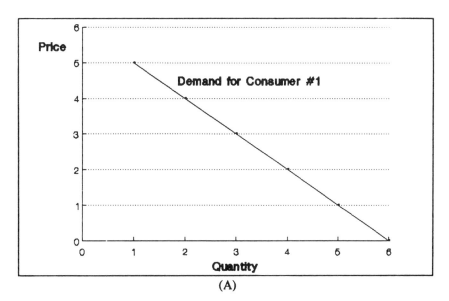

(A)

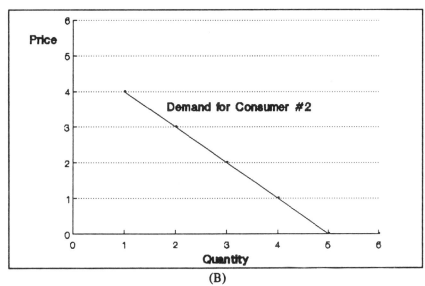

(B)

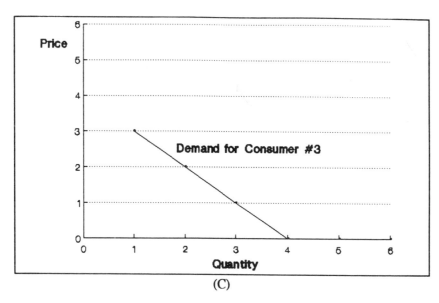

(C)

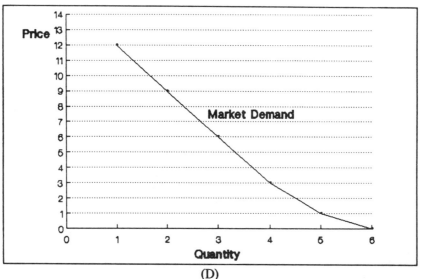

(D)

Assume there are only three consumers in a market, each with the demand schedules and curves for a non-rival public good as shown. If one unit of the product is produced it can be used by all three consumers, so the total market value of this unit is found by adding up the prices that all three consumers are willing and able to pay for this unit of output. The same procedure is repeated for the 2nd, 3rd, ... etc., units to derive the market demand curve. In effect, we *vertically* sum up the individual demand schedules, rather than *horizontally* summing them as we did for rival private goods in Figure 1-3.

A second consequence of non-rival consumption is that shrewd consumers will try to understate how much they personally value a public good, knowing that once it is produced it can be used by everyone, including those who have not helped to pay for it. They hope others will say they want the product and be charged the taxes or other fees required to provide it -- then they can use it, too, at little or no charge. This is the *FREE-RIDER* problem, which leads to the underproduction of goods and services that are non-rival in consumption. The underproduction occurs because, when free riders say they don't value new highways or schools or defense systems, legislators are less likely to vote for them.

This is the same problem producers face when they stage a public performance or fireworks display and then try to get the audience to pay for it by passing the hat: many who enjoyed the show don't chip in -- the free riders. Public television stations encounter the same problem, which is why they often ask for funds from their viewers by appealing both to their altruism ("help others see our fine programs") and guilt ("don't be a free rider -- pay for what you get").

But notice those who sell rival, private goods usually don't engage in such appeals. Why not?

The Non-Exclusion Principle

When it is possible to keep those who don't pay for a particular product from consuming it, its sales are based on the self-interest of buyers and sellers, and conducted through voluntary exchange. The free-rider problem disappears because consumers pay their money and take their choice of products -- but first they pay their money. Walt Disney bet that people would pay to see a fireworks display, *if* he bought enough land around his theme park so that customers had to pay to get in to be close enough to see the show. That worked better for him than passing the hat, and it works better for consumers, too, in the sense that they can be sure that a fireworks display is always available for them to see *if* they are willing to pay the price.

In short, private goods are subject to the *EXCLUSION PRINCIPLE*, meaning only those who pay for them get to use them; but public goods are subject to the *NON-EXCLUSION PRINCIPLE*, meaning once the good is produced, it can be used both by those who have helped to pay for it (through taxes, say), and by those who have not.

If public goods were not subject to the non-exclusion principle, then producers of those goods might be able to sell these products profitably to consumers in private markets. The problem is, it's impossible to avoid the free-rider problem for some goods and services -- and those products become public goods. For example, suppose you owned a firm that was able to destroy incoming ICBMs and cruise missiles, and you tried to sell these services door to door. Suppose you could even document that your missile defense services were effective and that the government's weren't, so there was a real incentive for people to buy your product. But as soon as you sold one policy to a survivalist family in a prosperous neighborhood, you would face a real problem: no one else in the neighborhood would buy from you. Once you contracted to protect one house in the neighborhood, your service, by its nature, will have to protect other houses in the area, even if their owners don't buy your product.

If you don't like to think about nuclear weapons, note that exactly the same problem faces a firm that might like to sell mosquito-extermination services in states like Minnesota and Louisiana, where abundant breeding grounds make regional control programs necessary. In effect, the mosquitos are just an insect version of the incoming missiles in the previous example. And once again, as soon as you sign one contract in an area, everyone else can free ride. The typical solution to this problem is to sell such products to a community or the nation as a whole, not to individuals -- in other words, to treat it as a public rather than a private good.

Privately operated fire protection companies that are used in many small communities face a related, but in this case solvable, problem with the non-exclusion principle. Suppose the company is called out to a client's home when a neighbor's house bursts into flames, and the neighbor is not a client. Once the equipment arrives, the neighbor rushes out and asks the firefighters to put out the fire, even agreeing to buy a policy on the spot. Would you do it if you ran the fire protection company? Not if you wanted to stay in business. If people know they can wait until they have a fire to buy your service, your membership list will shrink precipitously. The economics of the situation is clear -- you don't let the fire spread to your client's property, but you don't put it out. This isn't a hypothetical example; it has happened just this way, many times. When it does, the press typically gets a good story; some people are outraged and write to their local newspaper about greed and profits; and the fire service sells more policies. But for some reason the neighbor who didn't buy a policy in the first place is rarely described as being greedy for trying to save money by not buying insurance until the fire struck, even if he or she clearly had the resources to afford the service.

Of course fire protection can be, and usually is, provided publicly. This often results in fewer serious fires and lower insurance premiums, so the benefits of public fire service outweigh the costs of making fire protection services, which *can* be offered privately or voluntarily, a public entitlement program. But one cost of the public fire service is introducing the free-rider problem -- many people will favor better fire-protection services in the abstract, but be reluctant to approve the taxes required to pay for them unless the taxes fall largely on someone else.

The key point to remember about the non-exclusion principle is that when it applies to a product the product cannot be offered profitably by a private firm, unless it operates under a contract with a government agency.

Public, Quasi-public, and Quasi-private Goods

A pure public good is both non-rival in consumption and characterized by the non-exclusion principle. It *must* be provided by the government in a market economy, because (1) no private producer can supply it profitably, and (2) the government is better able to develop information about how much consumers value the product and collect the fees that pay for it. (Among the government's special tools for those purposes are public elections, taxes, laws and regulations, and the power to put people in jail.) However, not all of the products provided by governments are pure public goods. And some products provided by private firms have one, but not both, of the characteristics of a public good. Still other goods that have only one of these characteristics are provided by both public and private institutions. These are *QUASI-PUBLIC* and *QUASI-PRIVATE* goods, and the best way to understand these hybrid products that are neither fish nor fowl is by considering several examples.

Radio and television broadcasts over the airwaves are typically produced as quasi-private goods. These are certainly non-rival in consumption, and non-exclusionary to consumers (unless the signals are scrambled to those who don't rent a decoder). However, local broadcast stations and the national broadcasting networks can sell air time for commercials as a private, *EXCLUSIONARY GOOD* to firms that want to advertise their products. Firms that don't pay for the air time don't have their commercials broadcast, which allows broadcasting to be treated as a quasi-private good (subject to some special regulations and public licensing fees), despite exhibiting many of the characteristics of public goods.

Movies and books are also non-rival in consumption in many respects (as long as we consider only movies that don't sell out theatres, so that letting one person in doesn't prevent someone else from viewing the film). For movies, however, it has proven relatively easy to avoid the non-exclusion principle by building enclosed theatres with a turnstile at the entrance. (Customer turnstiles were first used in England by the father of one of Shakespeare's colleagues.) For many years, operators of drive-in theatres found that they could even let anyone see their pictures (for most kinds of movies) and still stay in business by making the movie sound track the exclusionary product they sold. Because the exclusion principle holds in these cases, these products can also be sold as quasi-private goods, despite having some characteristics of public goods. But note too that the public-good characteristics that these products exhibit largely explains why public libraries lend out books, movies, and records.

Roads, bridges, and waterways are products which also offer non-rival consumption, at least until traffic congestion becomes a problem. That is why these products are usually provided by government as quasi-public goods, even though they can be made exclusionary by collecting tolls and not allowing access to those who don't pay.[2] In fact, the government has adopted *USER FEES*, such as fuel taxes dedicated to highway construction and maintenance, to establish some degree of exclusionary consumption for these goods. These fees mean that those who benefit most from highways and bridges pay more for them, since people and firms who use the roads more pay more for fuel and fuel taxes, too. Concerns about national defense also had a role in the decision to develop a national highway system. For example, the construction of interstate highways in the United States was initiated under the Eisenhower administration, in large part because this former general had been impressed with the military advantages of the German *autobahn* in World War II.

Some goods are rival but non-exclusionary, typically when the property rights to those goods are non-existent or poorly defined. That is why buffalos, whales, eagles, and the rights to minerals and sunken treasures

---

[2]The public provision of transportation facilities is also supported because, as you saw in Chapter 1, transactions costs are substantially lowered by reducing or eliminating the time people spend waiting to pay these tolls, and private monopolies over strategically located sections of a road or river are eliminated by moving these services into the public sector.

in international waters have all been, at one time or another, subject to the unbridled rule of first come, first served. International treaties and other laws have been passed, sometimes too late, to make these goods exclusionary or to entirely prohibit their use and abuse. If such steps are not taken these resources are overused, even to the point of extinction in some cases. (See Case Study #7 following this chapter.)

Table 5-4

Rival and Exclusion Properties of Different Kinds of Goods

	Rival	Non-rival
Exclusionary	**Pure Private Goods:** e.g., food; clothing; housing; soldout entertainment events and travel on private carriers	**Quasi-Private Goods** (Excess Capacity): e.g., most movies and concerts; private roads and bridges; many trips on commercial planes, ships and buses; commercial radio and TV broadcasts
Non-exclusionary	**Quasi-Public Goods** (Poorly Defined Property Rights): e.g., public parks, wildlife, rivers and oceans, the air	**Pure Public Goods:** e.g., national defense, flood- and insect-control projects, fireworks displays in urban areas

Pure private goods are characterized by rival consumption and subject to the exclusion principle. Conversely, pure public goods are non-rival in consumption and subject to the non-exclusion principle. Most goods and services are pure private goods, traded in private markets with buyers and sellers facing well defined property rights. Some products, however, known as quasi-public or quasi-private goods, mix characteristics of both private goods and public goods.

To summarize: All goods and services can be classified as rival or non-rival in consumption, and exclusionary or non-exclusionary in their availability to those who do not pay for them. Most products are pure private goods which, in market economies, are supplied to consumers by privately owned firms. Only a few goods, such as national defense, are pure public goods. But various levels of government also provide a wide range of goods and services which have some, but not all, of the characteristics of pure public goods, such as roads and bridges. And even private firms provide some products that have some of the characteristics of public goods, such as television programs and movies.

There is also an economic justification for government intervention in private markets when there are positive or negative externalities associated with the production and/or consumption of a private good. In fact, this explains many of the largest and most important government programs in the United States and many other nations, involving such products as education, pollution control, and public health services. These externalities and related government policies are the subject of the following section.

Externalities

Externalities or third-party effects distort market prices and output levels, and result in the overallocation or underallocation of resources to certain uses. For example, if there is extensive pollution associated with the production and consumption of automobiles, too many cars will be produced unless the government acts to make producers and consumers take the costs of that pollution into account. And without public subsidies of the production or consumption of vaccines which prevent contagious diseases, too little of the vaccines will be produced. In cases like these there will be some private production the goods and services involved even if the government does not intervene -- but the market level of output will be inefficient unless the government uses taxes, fines, regulations, or subsidies to correct the signals that are sent to these markets by producers and consumers.

External Costs

An *EXTERNAL COST*, also known as a spillover cost, is associated with the production or consumption of a good or service but paid by someone other than the producers and consumers of that good or service. The classic example of this kind of third-party cost is pollution. Suppose, for example, that the city of Cincinnati dumps its wastes into the Ohio River. All the cities downstream that use river water as their water supply will bear higher costs, whether they purify the river water for drinking and recreational purposes; use the water without purifying it and pay the costs in the form of poorer health; or entirely avoid using the river water, by switching to a less convenient and more expensive source, such as well water. In effect, the people downriver will pay some of the costs of the people who live in Cincinnati, or any other city upstream which pollutes the river.

The same thing happens if a firm, such as a chemical factory, is the polluter. In either case the polluting organization behaves as if its operating costs do not include the pollution costs, which it transfers to others. (If the pollution affected *only* the employees and customers of the firm, with everyone recognizing its effects and agreeing on its consequences and costs, then there would be no external costs. Only the producers and consumers of the product would be affected by the pollution and its costs -- i.e., the pollution costs would be completely *internalized*.)

When external costs affect the market for some product, producers will supply too much of these products, because they do not bear some of the costs of production. Put differently, if producers did have to bear the external costs they would have to charge a higher price, resulting in lower sales and, therefore, lower production. In technical terms, that shows how external costs lead to an *OVERALLOCATION OF RESOURCES* to the organizations that are able to shift these costs to others. In the example of cities that dump wastes into rivers, the upstream cities grow larger than they should, and the communities downriver remain smaller than they should, because the wrong signals about the true costs of living in those towns and cities are be sent to the marketplace, and reflected in the prices (the costs of living) paid by those who work and live in them.

External costs affect the supply curve for a firm which shifts these costs to others, as shown in Figure 5-3. The firm's supply curve reflects only the *PRIVATE COSTS* that it pays to produce its products, not the external costs. But the total *SOCIAL COSTS* of their production include both the direct, private costs that the firm does pay (for raw materials, labor, capital, etc.) *and* the external costs shifted to third parties. Thus, the true supply curve for the producer lies to the left of its private-cost supply schedule, and calls for a higher equilibrium price and lower output level (given a typical demand curve for the firm's products).

Unless the government makes the firm and its customers take these external costs into account, the price will remain too low and the output level too high, because of the costs that are shifted over to third parties -- people who neither produce nor consume the product. There are several ways the government can correct this misallocation of resources, as you will see after we consider the opposite kind of market failure.

External Benefits

When the production or consumption of a good or service provides benefits to parties other than the producers and consumers of these products, that is called an *EXTERNAL BENEFIT*, or a spillover benefit.

Figure 5-3
External Costs

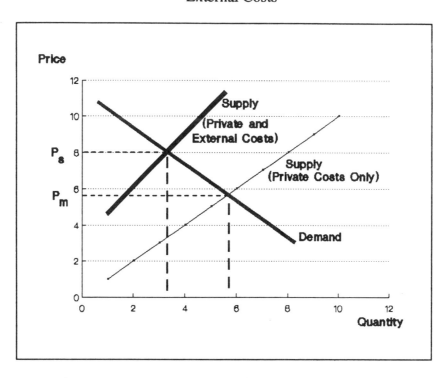

The market supply curve for a product only reflects the firm's private costs of producing its good or service, not the external costs associated with the production or consumption of that product. A higher price (P_s, rather than P_m) and lower level of output would prevail if the full social costs of production were reflected in the price of the product.

To illustrate what are perhaps the oldest examples of external benefits (and costs), once simply described as "neighborhood effects," consider two very different neighbors. One is every property owner's dream of a good neighbor, who spends heavily on improvements like landscaping and regular painting inside and (especially) outside his house, and has two well behaved children and no pets. The other neighbor is your worst nightmare, who keeps four junked cars in his front yard among unmowed "crops" of crabgrass and other weeds, has a menagerie of promiscuous pets and children who spend more time at your house (understandably) than their own, and a family that is apparently allergic to paint, soap, or household chores of any kind. The first neighbor will raise the property values of all houses in the neighborhood, not just his own -- generating external benefits -- while the other neighbor will decrease surrounding property values -- representing an external cost.

Other examples of products that provide external benefits include health vaccinations and screening tests for contagious diseases, bee hives located next to fruit orchards that rely on natural pollination, and education. Vaccines and screening tests not only benefit those who consume and produce them, they also reduce other peoples' chances of contracting the diseases they protect against. Similarly, a honey producer gains by selling the honey produced in this hobby or business, but the fruit farmer who lives next door benefits too, because the bees pollinate the fruit blossoms and increase the output of fruit.

Education is a somewhat controversial example of a service that provides external benefits, because a large part -- some say all, or nearly all -- of the benefits from education go directly to its producers (in the form of present income) and consumers (in the form of expected future income). However, most economists, educators, and political leaders claim that there are also *SOCIAL BENEFITS* gained from education, such as lower crime and unemployment rates, a more informed and politically sophisticated electorate, and a population that is more diverse and flexible in adapting to changing economic conditions.

As shown in Figure 5-4, the market demand curve for a product that generates external benefits is too far to the left, which is to say too low. That happens because the market only sees what people are willing and able to spend for this product, and that is determined by the private benefits they receive when they consume a product, not the external benefits that the production and consumption of the product provide to others. Given a typical supply schedule for the product, this results in price and output levels for the product that are lower than they would be if the external benefits were also taken into account. Thus, the economic effect of external benefits is an *UNDERALLOCATION OF RESOURCES* to the affected products.

Figure 5-4
External Benefits

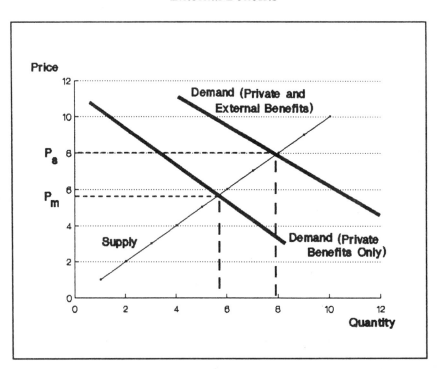

When external benefits occur in the production or consumption of a product, the observed demand curve for the product reflects only the private benefits of consuming the good or service. That leads to a lower market price (P_m) and level of output than would prevail if the full social benefits were reflected in the price (P_s) of the product.

It is theoretically possible for people who are going to paint their house or undertake a landscaping project to pass the hat among their neighbors, asking them to contribute as much as they will benefit from these improvements. But sadly, as you saw in our discussion of public goods, passing the hat is often not an efficient way of allocating resources. And clearly the transactions costs of contacting everyone who gains when you get a flu shot, figuring out how much they each have gained, and collecting that amount from each of them, makes it prohibitively expensive for you to privately correct this form of market failure. Fortunately, as with external costs, there are steps government agencies can take to correct these market failures.

155

Public Policies and Externalities

Many external costs and benefits are too trivial to justify government actions to correct the related misallocation of resources. But when externalities are pronounced and the misallocation of resources is significant the government can, and often does, act. To correct for the underallocation of resources associated with external benefits the government can subsidize either the production or the consumption of the products, or both. To correct for the overallocation of resources associated with external costs, the government can tax the producers or the consumers of the product, or both, or enforce regulations limiting or prohibiting spillover costs (e.g., by making public intoxication and driving under the influence of alcohol or other controlled substances a crime, or by requiring non-smoking zones in public areas). Exactly how the government decides to correct these problems does make a difference, however.

Adjusting for external benefits. When the government increases the allocation of resources to some product by subsidizing consumers, the subsidy shifts the demand curve for the product to the right. Providing vouchers that can only be used to buy a certain product (e.g., food stamps), or tax deductions or credits tied to the purchase of certain goods and services (e.g., deductions on mortgage payments for private homes, and credits for child-care expenses), lowers the final cost of these products to consumers, and so increases demand as shown in Figure 5-5.

When the government subsidizes producers of certain products (e.g., by giving tax credits for investments in new capital equipment), or directly engages in the production of certain goods or services (such as public education and health care programs), it shifts the supply curve to the right (also shown in Figure 5-5). Both approaches will increase the output of the affected products; but, as shown in Figure 5-5, the two approaches move the market price for a product in different directions. Consumer subsidies increase the price; producer subsidies lower it. Moreover, vouchers and other subsidies that increase demand tend to maintain consumer choice and greater variety in the kinds of output produced, while production subsidies and, in particular, direct government production of goods and services, have historically led to more standardization and concentration of production activities in those markets. (Again, think of public education.) What this shows is that, even if the underallocation of resources is remedied by government policies, the debate about the best way to provide these subsidies is likely to be long and contentious, involving political as well as economic considerations.

Adjusting for external costs. The overallocation problem associated with external costs can also be addressed with public policies aimed at producers or consumers, again with the effect of shifting (this time decreasing) either the supply or demand curve. Examples of this include excise taxes on alcohol and tobacco products, which burden both producers and consumers of these goods, as you saw in Chapter 4, and therefore reduce the production and consumption of the product that is taxed. Regulations that limit where these products may be sold and the quantity consumers can buy also have the effect of countering any overallocation of resources to these products.

In practice, most government policies concerned with external costs and overallocation problems are aimed at producers who are polluting, or thought to be polluting. That raises two interesting questions: 1) Why does pollution occur in the ways and places we find it occurring? and 2) Are *EFFLUENT TAXES*, taxes which rise as the amount of pollution a producer releases into the environment increases, more effective and economically efficient than regulations that directly limit or prohibit pollution?

The answer to the first question shows that pollution has something in common with the near-extinction of the buffalo, whale, and eagle. Specifically, pollution is usually observed where property rights are poorly defined and difficult to enforce -- in the air, rivers, and oceans. This suggests that public lakes are more likely to be littered and fished out than private ponds, because the pond owners have stronger and clearer economic incentives to keep their own property clean, manage their livestock resources carefully, and prosecute anyone who seriously abuses those assets. Conversely, while we may all be said to own a share of any public property, we aren't as likely to prosecute anyone we see littering in public parks and national forests, or to make them clean up their mess, as we would be if they dumped the same trash on our front yard.[3]

---

[3]The exceptions to this rule are generally small parks that are repeatedly used by the same, relatively small, group of people. So this exception really isn't an exception after all -- the people who use such parks develop a well-founded sense of *de facto* ownership over these resources.

Figure 5-5
Government Subsidies and External Benefits

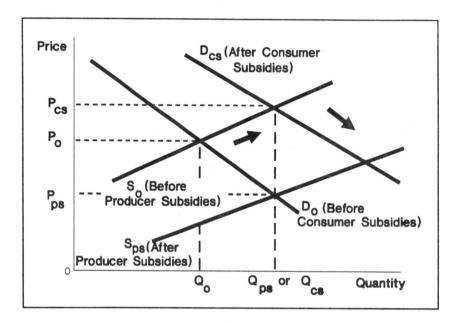

Subsidies to consumers shift the demand curve rightward; subsidies to producers shift the supply curve rightward. Both policies can correct the underallocation of resources that occurs when external benefits are present in the production or consumption of a product. But the different policies have different impacts on the prices of affected products, and in the number of producers and product features consumers can choose from in these markets. In this graph, consumer subsidies raise price from P_0 to P_{cs}; producer subsidies lower price from P_0 to P_{ps}. Either type of subsidy increases production above Q_0.

Though not shown here, taxes and fines on producers or consumers can be used to shift supply or demand curves leftward, to correct for the overallocation of resources due to external costs. Shifting either curve leftward reduces equilibrium production and consumption levels, but reducing supply increases price while reducing demand lowers price.

The second question, about using effluent taxes or regulations that directly limit the amount of pollution a firm can release, has a more complicated and qualified answer: When it is possible to accurately and inexpensively measure the effluents released into the air or water at a production site, and to estimate the costs associated with that pollution, effluent taxes are more efficient than direct regulation. When accurate monitoring at a particular production site is difficult and expensive, the regulation may be a better choice. Here's why.

The costs of a given amount of pollution are the same, whether the pollution is released into the environment by an old plant, a new plant, a large plant, a small plant, or a middle-aged, middle-sized plant. In other words, a ton of sulpher dioxide that goes up the smokestack and into a city's air will have the same effect no matter where it comes from. But the cost of reducing pollution by an identical amount may vary among these different kinds of facilities. And remember (as shown in our discussion of cost-benefit analysis), we don't want to spend more to reduce pollution by some amount than that pollution costs us in the first place, in the form of poorer health and property damage. That is the reason why, if it is easy to measure the pollution released at each plant site, the most efficient way to reduce pollution to its economically optimal level is to set the effluent fees at the level that

157

will reduce pollution to that amount, giving firms the option of reducing their pollution to avoid (or reduce) these tax payments, or to continue to pollute and pay higher taxes.

Plants that can reduce pollution at costs lower than the effluent tax will choose to do so, while those that can't will pollute and pay the tax. In other words, pollution will be reduced at the sites where it is least expensive to do so, and in that way the benefits of the cleaner environment are achieved at the lowest possible cost. The effluent tax simply has to be set at the level that makes polluters cut back up to the point where the costs of pollution reduction are equal to, but do not exceed, the benefits of the last degree of cleanup -- just as you saw earlier, in Figure 5-1. Note that even firms that decide not to install pollution-reduction equipment will pollute less after this policy is imposed because the taxes raise their costs of production, which decreases their supply (production levels) and, in turn, the amount of pollution they generate.

An across-the-board regulation that yields the same reduction in pollution (say one that requires all plants to lower pollution by 50%) would cost much more. Under that policy, some of the reductions have to be made in plants where it is more expensive to reduce pollution (often older plants). And at the same time, plants that would cut back more than 50% under the effluent tax system have no incentive to do so under this policy -- all they care about is meeting the new emission standards.

Effluent taxes provide the government revenues which, in theory, could be used to compensate those who are harmed by the pollution that is permitted. Another way of getting these revenues is for the government to determine what the optimal level of pollution is, and then auction off the rights to release that amount of pollution to the highest bidders (who, presumably, expect to get the greatest benefits from being allowed to pollute, by producing and selling their products.)

Although government auctions of pollution rights strike many economists as a neat idea, the thought of trying to explain a public auction for pollution rights to voters (particularly to members of the Sierra Club and the Audubon Society) brings fear to the hearts of most politicians and civil servants. As yet, this is not a widely used policy -- but then neither were free trade, flexible exchange rates, and an all-volunteer army when some economists first began supporting those policies. And in the early 1990s, policies were adopted that set up open markets for pollution permits in many U.S. cities. Under those programs there may or may not be initial auctions run by the government; but pollution permits are issued or sold, and firms can then buy or sell them in open markets. Firms that don't have enough permits to cover the amount of pollution they are releasing are fined, so they want to buy more permits. Firms releasing less than their permitted amount of pollution will, conversely, sell some of their "extra" permits to other firms. Permit prices will rise or fall depending on the number of permits the government issues (which is based on their estimate of the optimal amount of pollution) and current business conditions in an area (because when business is good, the polluting firms want to produce more). The higher the price of the permits rises, the more incentive there is for firms to reduce their pollution.

When the transactions costs of monitoring effluents and estimating the costs of different increments of pollution are very high, direct regulations may be more efficient than effluent taxes or auctions of pollution rights. The same is true for pollutants that are extremely toxic, because *any* traces of those substances can lead to substantial environmental and health costs.

In some cases, a combination of regulations, effluent taxes, and pollution permits may be the most effective way to reduce pollution to its optimal level. But that assumes, like everything else up to this point in the chapter, that the government will always search for the most efficient way to correct for market failures. And sadly, that's not always the case.

Public Choice Theory and Government Failure

Market failures such as public goods and externalities can lead to inefficient production and consumption levels unless the government intervenes in the affected markets. But government failure also distorts resource allocations. These failures occur because voters, public employees, and elected officials often pursue their own private interests, rather than promoting the public interest or economists' notion of optimal resource allocation. These sources of government failure are studied in the field of economics known as public choice theory.

Public Interest vs. Self-Interest

We have discussed how the government intervenes in the economy either to provide goods and services that private producers and markets can't, or because private markets fail to provide the optimum amount of some goods and services. But government intervention itself can fail to rectify market failures, and introduce entirely new kinds of distortions in the overall pattern of resource allocation in the economy. As two conservative economists, one of them a Nobel laureate, describe this problem:

> ...the very factors that produce the market failure also make it difficult for government to achieve a satisfactory solution. Generally, it is no easier for government to identify the specific persons who are hurt and benefited than for market participants, no easier for government to assess the amount of harm or benefit to each. Attempts to use government to correct market failure have often simply substituted government failure for market failure.... The imperfect market may do as well or better than the imperfect government.[4]

The idea of government failure is an old one -- perhaps nearly as old as government itself -- and one that is recognized not only by economists.[5] But in recent decades many economists, Nobel laureate James Buchanan being the most prominent, have developed what is known as *PUBLIC CHOICE THEORY* to analyze the sources of market failure, and to evaluate policies that might avoid or reduce that failure, including limits to the government's involvement in private markets. This approach analyzes the economic incentives facing politicians, government employees, and voters, to determine how much of their behavior is explained or predicted by these incentives. That is a sharp break from more traditional theories of government policy and political science, which assumed that "statesmen," civil servants, and citizens are motivated by a self-effacing concern for the public welfare, and in particular for the plight of the poor.

Several controversial conclusions have developed from the public choice analysis. For example, instead of describing people who don't vote in elections as apathetic or even bad citizens, public choice theorists point out that these people are probably making a rational economic choice. After all, voting is not a free activity -- it uses up time and transportation, scarce resources that have an opportunity cost. Furthermore, very few elections are decided by one vote, or even a few votes. In fact, national elections in the United States are rarely decided by fewer than several million votes. So unless a person views voting as a pleasurable activity, which is to say as an economic good in its own right, not voting is a rational choice *regardless* of the outcome of the election, because one person's vote will rarely change the outcome. This is especially true when eligible voters are comfortable with all of the leading candidates and propositions in an election; most voters can then free ride and let others bear the costs of the election process.

Most people who do vote do not carefully study all the issues involved in an election, nor the candidates' positions on these issues. Public choice theory predicts exactly that kind of behavior, because the payoff to voters of studying this material is so low. In effect, since voters have so little impact on the final outcome in large elections (whether or not they are well informed), they choose to be "rationally ignorant" about the issues and candidates. If they could sway the outcome, it would pay them to incur the costs of becoming better informed.

Think about the kinds of commercials and paid political announcements you see and hear during statewide or national elections. Most deal with images and broad themes, and only superficially with issues and facts, precisely because most voters have very little reason to learn more about the issues and facts, or any interest in doing so.

Elected officials and government employees also face personal incentives that frequently lead to actions and policies that work against the public interest. Their own wealth, power, and personal comfort are largely

---

[4] Milton and Rose Friedman, *Free to Choose*, New York: Harcourt Brace Jovanovich, Inc., 1979, pp. 214-18.
[5] See, for example, Henry Adams' nineteenth century novel, *Democracy*, and Joseph Heller's more recent *Good As Gold*.

associated with such things as large support staffs, plush offices, higher salaries, and appointments on high-visibility, low-work committees.[6] Politicians who are ambitious and hard working also have incentives to seek appointments on powerful and highly visible committees -- preferably those which determine the future of public projects that will bring new jobs and federal programs to their own districts (for example, a large military base or federal water projects). Once in place, the typical politician favors increases, not cuts, in these plums, and may well be willing to trade support for other politicians' pet projects to make that happen. It's called horse trading, logrolling, or "you scratch my back and I'll scratch yours"; but what makes it all more likely to happen is that the traders are spending tax dollars, not their own money.

In the Unites States, even after adjusting for inflation, government spending increased some 40 times from 1900 to 1970. There is no doubt that this rapid growth is tied, in some degree, to these public choice issues. Or as the writer H. L. Mencken put it, "Democracy is the theory that people deserve to get what they want, and get it good and hard." But just as surely, the increase reflects growing popular demands for government services, in part to deal with market failures which have expanded and become more complex as the economy has grown and become more internationalized.

As you will see in later chapters, the problems associated with bureaucratic growth are not limited to the public sector; both economists and sociologists have documented similar problems in large organizations as diverse as corporations, labor unions, foundations, and charities. But economists have identified other sources of government failure, more subtle and potentially even more serious, that are far less common in private organizations.

Special Interest Groups

Suppose after careful cost-benefit analyses are completed, two projects are each predicted to improve overall economic welfare in the United States by $2.5 billion dollars a year.

In one project, an excise tax will be levied on a few large firms whose products cause a mild new form of air pollution, which has the one negative property of making it harder to clean the soap and dirt rings off porcelain plumbing fixtures. Because those costs are widespread and small, it has been decided to use the revenues from the tax to lower each taxpayer's federal income tax by about $10 a year.

In the other project, everyone's federal taxes will be raised $10 a year to finance the construction and operation of a new dam and flood control project for several states in the Pacific Northwest.

Strictly from a cost-benefit standpoint, the two projects are judged to be equally deserving of public support. But politically, which is most likely to pass?

Clearly it pays the firms which will be subject to the new excise tax to organize and lobby heavily to defeat the first proposal; but few taxpayers (or elected officials) will be excited enough about the prospects of saving $10 on their taxes to make this their cause in life. In the second proposal, the tax costs are spread out so broadly that there is little incentive for any group to organize and oppose it, while the benefits are concentrated enough to guarantee a loud and loyal group of sponsors for the project.

How costs and benefits affect different people and firms helps explain why some laws pass (the new dam) and others don't (the taxes on polluting firms), regardless of whether cost-benefit analysis suggests that a program should be adopted or defeated.

This hypothetical example illustrates a classic case of *SPECIAL-INTEREST* groups. You can get the names and affiliations of key players in today's real world game of special interests by driving around Washington, D.C. or any state capital, reading the names on the doors of the non-government buildings. Or you can look up the industry, labor, educational, retail, financial, and farming trade associations (i.e., lobbies) listed in the yellow pages of the telephone directories in any capital city. Special interest groups undoubtedly provide valuable services to their members, and even to the process of democratic government, by keeping tabs on proposed legislation and changing conditions in their respective fields. But they can also distort the political decisions of a government and the allocation of economic resources by securing unwarranted subsidies, tax breaks, or regulatory

---

[6]The philosopher Bertrand Russell once described a bureaucrat as someone who likes to exercise authority and avoid work, and accomplishes both by regularly saying "No."

protection from competition for their constituents. The special interest groups do this either through direct lobbying or by providing campaign contributions and staffing assistance to sympathetic and malleable candidates running for public office.

Additional Sources of Government Failures

Several other features of the government sector make it possible for these distortions to endure:

First, the government doesn't face the same constraints on spending that individuals and businesses do. Governments can increase revenues by legislation (i.e., by raising taxes) or, at the federal level, by spending more money than it takes in for an indefinite number of years.

Second, the government doesn't face direct competition from producers who offer most of the same kinds of products it does. And even where there is some competition (e.g., from private schools), people who choose the private services must still pay taxes to support the public services.

Third, there is a built-in shortsightedness in government policies, resulting from elected and appointed officials wanting to sponsor programs that offer visible benefits now (before the next election), and postpone costs until the future (after election day, or better yet retirement).

Finally in this abbreviated list, the signals that policy makers get about what people want and how well public programs are working are often not as clear as the signals households and businesses have available to them.

This last point bears further discussion: You know better than anyone else what a hamburger is worth to you. And a company that sells hamburgers knows with every profit and loss statement just how well it is doing. The government doesn't usually have such data on individuals' satisfaction *or* clearcut profit and loss statements for its programs. In fact, to make things worse, it is often charged with the responsibility of providing services which are, by definition, unprofitable. Unlike businesses, the government can't always stop doing something just because a project is losing money. Instead, when a government program seems to be failing, its supporters often claim that it would be successful if it were only better funded; and more money and resources are often directed to government programs that haven't worked for just this reason. In the mid-1980s, for example, the Reagan administration wanted to sell off the government-owned Conrail system of freight railways to private companies, eliminating public subsidies of this service. But supporters of Conrail claimed there were many external benefits associated with the operation of the system, and that the subsidy costs weren't really substantial. Regardless of who was right, the debate itself was a classic example of the difficulties regularly faced when the government tries to eliminate a service it has provided for many years.

In a democratic political system, the electoral process is relied on to prevent these problems. But unfortunately, even the voting signals available to policy makers can be mixed and contradictory. For example, public opinion polls often report that people favor less government and lower public spending in general, yet want more spending on a wide array of the most expensive kinds of public services that are specifically listed in the polls. Election results on political candidates (which are viewed as signals about what voters want from government) and public policy issues are just as blurred. (See Table 5-5.)

Despite these mixed signals, political leaders must cast their votes and choose between the options that are available to them. And then, as they do this, another kind of distortion in the allocation of economic resources can occur.

Unintended Effects of Public Policies

The poet John Donne wrote that "No man is an island." Similarly, in economics no price is an island. Anything that affects one product's price is likely to set off a chain of reactions affecting many other products, including some that are seemingly unrelated. An important strength of the market allocation system is that these changes happen quickly, impersonally, and automatically, all the while providing signals to producers and consumers indicating how they can change their behavior to maximize their gains or minimize their losses. But in the public sector that's one of the problems facing policy makers, who would often like to be able to change only one particular price (to get more or less of some product produced and consumed), without affecting anything else. Because markets don't work that way, policy makers face the difficult task of trying to anticipate the full

Table 5-5
A Voting Paradox

Voters

Policies or Candidates on the Ballot	Lucy's Rankings	Desi's Rankings	Ethyl's Rankings
A	1st	2nd	3rd
B	2nd	3rd	1st
C	3rd	1st	2nd

Possible Election Pairings	Election Outcomes
A vs. B	A
B vs. C	B
A vs. C	C

If these three voters are a representative sample of the electorate, majority-rule elections will lead to an inconsistent set of public policies. If an election or referrendum is held between options A and B Lucy and Desi will vote for A, so we say A is preferred to B. If the election is held between options B and C Lucy and Ethyl vote for B, so we say B is preferred to C. If these social preferences were mathematically well behaved, or transitive, we would be able to say that since A is preferred to B, and B is preferred to C, A must be preferred to C. But that's not the way social preferences work. In this example, an election between options A and C shows that Desi and Ethyl vote for C, so C is preferred to A.

These voter intransitivities help to explain how the government finds itself simultaneously supporting programs that raise food prices and others that transfer income to the poor; programs that provide income transfers to unemployed workers and others that raise the minimum wage (which makes it more difficult for some unemployed workers to find jobs); programs that subsidize middle-income families (such as mortgage deductions and support for college tuition) and others that transfer income from middle to low-income families (such as food and rent-subsidy programs); or programs that subsidize tobacco farmers and others that provide public warnings about links between smoking, lung cancer, and heart attacks.

range of consequences associated with changes in the price and output levels of products they choose to subsidize or tax.

For political reasons, when a particular subsidy or tax is strongly supported by a large majority of voters, those consequences are sometimes ignored, at least for a time. In other cases, they simply aren't anticipated. For both of these reasons, policies intended to solve one problem will often create new ones in some other area, sometimes more serious than the original problem. Moreover, we sometimes see policies that work in the short run fail in the long run, or even lead to exactly the opposite effect from what was intended, because of reactions in other parts of the economy.

These unintended consequences of public policies can be comical, frustrating, or tragic. For example, the Occupational Safety and Health Administration (OSHA) is responsible for the bells and other noises you hear on trucks and other large vehichles when they are backing up. That regulation entails certain costs and benefits, and by itself is not particularly interesting. But at some work sites where workers were required by other OSHA guidelines to wear earplugs to protect against hearing loss, it turned out that workers could not hear the warning bells on the trucks. One regulation literally offset the other.

Other cases are more subtle, and serious. A few years ago, tough bumper regulations for new cars were imposed, aimed at reducing repair costs for low-impact accidents. Combined with other regulations requiring steel door panels, padded dashboards, shoulder belts, etc. -- all of which raised production costs and car prices -- drivers and passengers in automobiles were better protected in collisions than ever before. But because of this greater protection from low-speed crashes, researchers observed an increase in the number of this particular kind of crash, and more serious injuries among pedestrians who were hit by cars with these strengthened bumper systems.[7]

In another case, economists studied federal policies allowing air traffic controllers to take early retirement if their work history indicated high levels of stress and fatigue. Revisions to the policies in 1974 allowed controllers to establish a history of stress by reporting their own violations of the required air-space cushions between planes they were directing. Because the controllers weren't risking their careers in reporting their violations, and instead documented their own stress, the reported cases of "near misses" went up sharply. But most surprisingly -- except to economists -- the reported near misses went up more among controllers in the age group which had the most to gain financially from early retirement, not among the least experienced *or* the oldest controllers, as we might have expected if stress was the true cause of the near misses.[8]

What can we conclude, then, about the economic role of government in a market economy, given all of the problems of market failures and government failures reviewed in this chapter? Simply that neither markets nor governments are panaceas for all of the economic troubles of the world, which is why economists have to fall back on procedures like cost-benefit analysis to determine whether or not government should adopt a particular policy. And in recent years, public choice theory has added some additional insights to this general conclusion, by confirming that in both the public and private sectors people usually follow their own self-interests, altering their behavior in the face of different legal and economic constraints.

Case Study #7
Property Rights, Externalities, and the "Tragedy of the Commons"

In 1968 biologist Garrett Hardin published his influential essay, "The Tragedy of the Commons," in *Science* magazine. The content of this essay was drawn as much from economics and ethics as from the natural sciences, and dealt with issues such as world population growth for which, Hardin claimed, "no technical solutions are possible." Parts of the essay are consistent with the analysis of external costs, built around the example of publicly held resources like the village "*COMMONS*" of medieval Europe and colonial North America. These commons were much like public parks today, except that villagers had the right to graze their livestock there.

Hardin explained clearly why the commons were overgrazed: Each citizen derived all the benefits of allowing more of their animals to graze on the commons, but bore only a fraction of the cost of decreasing the amount of grass on the publically owned land (roughly equal to $1/n$, where n is the total number of animals on the commons). Thus, in the rational pursuit of self-interest (from an individual perspective), each villager grazes more and more animals on the commons, until it is ruined. That's the tragedy of a system that treats a finite economic resource as if it were unlimited, free, and publically owned.

Pollution, Hardin pointed out, is an example of the tragedy of the commons in reverse. Instead of taking away some resource (like grass) from the collectively-owned pool, people add a "bad" of some kind, since they bear only a small fraction of the cost of doing so. In Hardin's view, the failure to understand this logic of the commons is responsible for such contemporary problems as: demands by ranchers' associations to expand the sale of leases for grazing rights on public lands in western states; not limiting the number of visitors at some public parks; and "freedom of the seas" laws that led to overfishing and the near-extinction of many species of fish and whales.

Hardin also claimed that public policies and international aid programs that are intended to prevent famine and disease, assist the poor, and make education and other basic services available to all children, have greatly

---

[7]The seminal article in this area is Sam Peltzman's "The Effects of Auto Safety Regulation," *Journal of Political Economy*, August 1975, pp. 677-723.

[8]Michael E. Staten and John Umbeck, "Information Costs and Incentives to Shirk: Disability Compensation of Air Traffic Controllers," *American Economic Review*, December 1982, pp. 1023-37.

weakened the linkage between the ability of families (and nations) to support children and their decisions to increase world population. This has been done, Hardin said, to let people exercise their "freedom to breed." As a result, he feels the world's finite resource base has become a kind of commons for the global population, and advocates the revocation of such popular tenets as the United Nations' "Universal Declaration of Human Rights." That declaration, signed by dozens of nations, accepts the family as the "natural and fundamental" social unit, and the position that any decision about family size must rest with the family itself.

Hardin suggests that legal rights to increase family size, like the rights to use any commons, should be limited. Certificates to have children, like claims to land or areas of the seas and sea floors, could be bought and sold on private markets, giving producers and consumers incentives to treat these resources as scarce, not free. Policies and programs to distribute these rights among individuals and nations would be imperfect, Hardin admits, but in his view preferable to the consequences of unrestrained population growth or rushing to use up marine life and mineral deposits on the seabeds before somebody else gets them. The options to implement such policies include auctioning off the rights to have children or harvest from a certain area of the ocean, or allocating these rights on some other basis (such as merit, lotteries, first-come/first-served, or popular elections). The result would be to make something that was once a commonly held right, or entitlement, an exclusive and rival good.

The costs and benefits of such a program are, of course, difficult to evaluate. Some people view government intrusions into family concerns as particularly offensive, while others see the costs of continuing global population growth as an even more serious problem.

Unlike Hardin, most economists are guardedly optimistic about the net effects of population increases, given the current levels of world population relative to physical resources and labor productivity. (Labor productivity draws attention to the world population's role as a productive economic resource, not just its effect on consumption levels.)

There are, however, some prominent economists on the same side of this issue as Hardin. For example, Kenneth Boulding of the University of Colorado, who has written extensively in the area of ethics as well as economics (sometimes even in verse), uses the image of "spaceship earth" to stress finite resources and of a "lifeboat" to show the social setting for our economic and ethical choices. Boulding has also proposed a "greenstamp" distribution and resale program to allocate rights to childbearing.

For non-human resources, almost all economists agree with Hardin about the desirability of clarifying property rights to deal with the resource misallocations that occur when externalities are present. In fact, economist R. H. Coase from the University of Chicago showed that private bargaining can resolve externality problems if transactions costs, including the cost of clearly establishing property rights for one party or another, are negligible. Let's look at one of his examples in some detail.[9]

Consider a cattle rancher and a grain farmer with adjoining properties. Suppose it would cost $9 a year to build and maintain a fence between the rancher's pasture and the farmer's field, to prevent the rancher's cattle from trampling down any of the farmer's crop. Without a fence, say that 1 steer would ruin 1 ton of grain each year, 2 steers would ruin 3 tons a year, 3 steers would ruin 6 tons, and 4 steers would ruin 10 tons. (The assumption of increasing marginal costs with larger herds isn't crucial to this example, only that they remain positive.)

Assuming that each ton of the farmer's crops can be sold for $1, and that the rancher is liable for any damage that his cattle cause, then if the rancher keeps 3 or fewer steers he should not build a fence to contain his herd. Instead, he should pay the farmer for the crop damage the cattle cause, which is less than the $9 annual cost of the fence (6 tons x $1 per ton). If the rancher runs 4 or more steers, the $9 per year fence becomes cheaper than paying the crop damages (at least 10 tons x $1 per ton). However, it may be cheaper for the rancher to pay the farmer to stop planting crops in this field altogether, or just in areas where the cattle roam, rather than building the fence. That's because the farmer's profits are less than the $1 per ton price he receives for the grain, due to the costs of planting, growing, harvesting, and transporting the crop.

---

[9]Many other interesting and relatively non-technical applications are included in Coase's article, "The Problem of Social Cost," in *The Journal of Law and Economics*, October 1960, pp. 1-44.

Coase's example demonstrates three important points:

1)   The value of the lost crop production *can* be taken into account in determining the optimal size of the cattle herd -- in other words the externality can be effectively internalized.

2)   When the rancher bargains with the farmer to stop or restrict planting, and pays for only the net loss of the crop production, the farmer will be at least as well off as when he produces the crop and receives full compensation for whatever the cattle destroy. The rancher will be better off, because he pays lower damages.

3)   When the value of the additional beef production is greater than the value of the lost crops (even in cases where it does not pay to build the fence), it would be a misallocation of resources to give up the additional cattle to preserve the additional crops.

Once again, this example shows that we don't want to spend more than the cost of the external cost to eliminate it. Both the cattle and the crops have economic value, and the social or external cost occurs both because the ranch is where it is *and* the farm is where it is. While the legal problem may be to determine who bears the final liability in this case, that is entirely distinct from the economic problem of getting the highest net value of production from these scarce resources. Fortunately, the principals in this example have clear economic incentives to recognize that, and the resources available to achieve that result.

But now suppose that, for some reason, no legal liability for damages can be enforced. (Perhaps there is no effective legal system on the frontier territory where this example takes place. Or, in a modern setting, say there is a court system, but one so expensive that it won't pay the farmer to sue to get a ruling.) That means the farmer can't use the legal system to make the rancher pay for crop damage caused by the cattle. But if all other transactions costs between the farmer and rancher are still very low, the same economic incentives to bargain and produce the highest valued combination of outputs (grain *and* beef) from these resources are still present, and the final production level of both products will be exactly the same as in the case where the rancher can be held liable for damages!

What is different in this case is that the farmer has the incentive to pay the rancher up to $1 not to increase his herd from no steers to 1 steer; up to $2 not to increase his herd from 1 steer to 2 steers; and up to $3 not to go from 2 steers to 3. These payments will make the rancher factor in those costs of adding to his herd, just as the farmer had to recognize the value of the offer from the rancher to limit or stop planting when we assumed there was a legal liability for the herd's damage. If, after accounting for these costs, it still pays the rancher to run a herd of 4 or more steers, it would pay to build the fence to keep the cattle out of the farmer's fields, or to stop planting in these areas if that is cheaper, just as in the earlier scenario. The difference is that now the farmer pays to build the fence or gives up the profits from the lost grain production, not the rancher. (This is true so long as the net value of the farm's output is greater than $9. If it isn't, the farmer will stop farming altogether. Similarly, in the first scenario we implicitly assumed that the net value of the ranch at some positive level of output covered the liability costs the rancher had to pay to the farmer; if not, the rancher would stop ranching.)

This example demonstrates that, when transactions costs are low so that it is easy for all parties affected by an externality to negotiate with each other, private markets can function to attain the highest valued output of products even when externalities occur, and in the absence of court-enforced settlements. This insight is called the *COASE THEOREM*, although Coase himself was content to present examples demonstrating the range of applications of this idea, and the common failure of economists and courts to recognize it. He did not characterize his findings as a theorem or an economic law.

From a production and efficiency standpoint, Coase showed that externalities may not always call for governmental action. But from an distribution and equity perspective (e.g., judging whether it is fairer for the rancher or the farmer to pay for the herd's damages in the above example), or when transactions costs are high (e.g., when externalities affect a large number of producers and/or consumers, so that it would be very difficult and costly for them to negotiate with each other), government intervention to correct for externalities may well be warranted.

Chapter Summary

1) The economic functions of government in a market economy are to:
   a) Establish a legal and social environment which supports, within proscribed limits, the functioning of private markets.
   b) Enforce laws and regulations which maintain competition among producers.
   c) Redistribute income to assist low-income families;
   d) Determine the level of output of *PUBLIC GOODS* to be produced, and shift the resources required to produce them from the private to the public sector.
   e) Correct for the resource misallocations that occur when significant *EXTERNAL COSTS OR BENEFITS* are associated with the production or consumption of a product.
   f) Establish policies to smooth out cyclical variations in the performance of the national economy, and to promote full employment, a stable price level, and reasonable rates of economic growth.

2) The economic effectiveness of a public policy is determined by weighing its expected benefits against its expected costs. Using that criterion, the government should increase its support for a program as long as the additional benefits of doing so are greater than the additional costs.

3) A product exhibits *RIVAL CONSUMPTION* if one person's consumption of it prevents anyone else from using it. An *EXCLUSIONARY GOOD* is one that can be withheld from those who do not pay to use it. For example, food and clothing are both rival and exclusionary goods.

4) A *NON-EXCLUSIONARY GOOD* which is *NON-RIVAL* in consumption is a pure public good (e.g., national defense). A pure *PRIVATE GOOD* is both exclusionary and rival in consumption (e.g., a hamburger). Private producers can not profitably make and sell public goods in private markets because of the *FREE-RIDER* problem.

5) The market demand curve for a public good (or service) is calculated by vertically summing up the value placed on various quantities of it by all consumers who have access to it. This reflects the non-rival consumption properties of public goods.

6) Most products are private goods; only a few are pure public goods; and some products have one of the characteristics of both public and private goods. All products can be classified as rival or non-rival, and as exclusionary or nonexclusionary.

7) *EXTERNALITIES* exist whenever some of the costs or benefits associated with the production or consumption of a product fall to parties other than its producers and consumers. Externalities typically occur where property rights to some resource are not well defined, or are difficult and expensive to enforce.

8) *EXTERNAL COSTS* can result in an *OVERALLOCATION OF RESOURCES* to the production of some good or service. The overallocation may be corrected by government excise taxes on the producers or consumers of the product, such as *EFFLUENT TAXES* on pollution, or by regulations which directly limit the amount of these costs that can be passed on to others.

9) *EXTERNAL BENEFITS* can result in an *UNDERALLOCATION OF RESOURCES* to the production of some good or service. The underallocation may be corrected by government subsidies to the producers or consumers of the product.

10) There is an economically optimal level of many spillover costs, such as pollution, which is greater than zero because preventing it is also a costly activity. It is economically inefficient to spend more to prevent pollution or other types of external costs than the value of the costs themselves.

11) When monitoring costs and other transactions costs are low, effluent taxes are more efficient ways of reducing pollution than direct regulations, because they permit pollution to be reduced at the lowest possible cost.

12) While government has clear and important economic roles to play in dealing with market failures such as public goods and externalities, it too suffers from systematic failures that lead to resource misallocations. This makes it difficult to determine and establish the optimal output levels for public goods, or for products that lead to external costs or benefits.

13) The major sources of government failure are:

   a) Self-interested behavior by government employees and public officials.
   b) Citizens' ignorance of, or apathy for, public issues and candidates, extending to non-participation in elections.
   c) Incomplete or contradictory signals sent to public officials through the electoral process.
   d) Special interest groups able to influence legislation and candidates.
   e) The lack of competition in the government's production of goods and services.
   f) Poor measures of the success, failure, and true costs of government programs.
   g) The difficulty of designing public programs and policies that do not have unanticipated negative effects.

14) (Case Study #7) External costs can be reduced or eliminated, in many cases by extending property rights. R. H. Coase demonstrated that when property rights are clear and transactions costs are low, private exchanges can internalize externalities -- even if the legal liability of who is responsible for the damages of an external cost is not established or enforced.

Review and Discussion Questions

1) Give examples of government programs or laws at the federal, state, or local level which you believe are designed to fulfill each of the six economic roles of government. Can you give an example of a program or law that does not seem to be aimed at any of these six basic roles? If so, what?

2) Do you personally favor or oppose using cost-benefit analysis to evaluate the effectiveness of public policies dealing with issues which have important economic consequences? Why? Have you ever used this kind of procedure, at least on an intuitive basis, in making a personal decision?

3) List the five goods or services that represent the largest costs in your annual budget. Classify each of them as rival or non-rival and exclusionary or non-exclusionary. What goods and services, if any, are you currently able to use as a free rider?

4) a) Classify each of the products listed in your answer to question #3 as pure public, pure private, quasi-public, or quasi-private.
   b) Is information a public good? Why or why not?

5) Suppose the good shown in Figure 1-3 was a public rather than private good. Draw the market demand curve for that product, based on the individual schedules for the three consumers in this market.

6) List three major products provided by each level of government (federal, state, and local) in the United States today. Categorize each of these nine products as pure public, pure private, quasi-public, or quasi-private.

7) Can you give an example of an external cost and benefit occurring where all applicable property rights are well defined? Is this example different from those presented in the chapter, or more difficult to identify? Explain why or why not.

8) Give an example of a government subsidy which you believe represents an attempt to correct for an underallocation of resources associated with an external benefit. Give an example of another subsidy program which you believe is not linked to an externality.

9) Give an example of an external cost other than pollution, and discuss what public policies are, or might be, used to address this problem.

10) Is there an optimal level of academic cheating greater than zero? Explain.

11) Describe how an effluent tax on smoking in restaurants and offices might work. Compare this tax to direct regulations banning smoking in these areas, and speculate about their relative effectiveness.

12) Are the economic motivations of those who work in the public sector different enough from the motivation of those who work in the private sector to help explain government failure?

13) Which source of government failure discussed in this chapter do you think is most serious and widespread? Explain.

14) (Case Study #7) Describe a scenario in which an external benefit might be internalized through a process of voluntary exchange. How is your example similar to the example of the Coase Theorem provided in this case study?

Chapter 6
Behind the Demand Curve: Models of Consumer Choice

In This Chapter...

we introduce basic models of the process of consumer choice, and use those models to enhance and extend your understanding of the general concept of demand, discussed in previous chapters. Finally, in a case study, we show how consumer-choice models can be used to evaluate alternative public policies designed to assist low-income families.

Utility Theory

The utilitarian philosophers of the early nineteenth century claimed that numerical measures of pleasure and pain could be used to design laws and economic policies that would allow the government to guarantee 'the greatest good for the greatest number.' Early economists showed that, with the assumptions of cardinally measurable utility and diminishing marginal utility, they could establish models of rational consumer choice that generated downward sloping demand curves, provided distinct measures of value in use and value in exchange, and clarified the relationship between marginal utility and price elasticity of demand. Despite these achievements, many later economists were troubled by the very nature of the assumption that individuals could measure utility in cardinal terms, and that policy makers could then add such measures together to justify government interventions in the economy. This eventually led to the development of the models of consumer choice that are presented in later sections of this chapter; but the ideas developed under the utilitarian assumptions are still a simple and useful introduction to economists' attempts to understand and predict consumer behavior.

Total and Marginal Utility

UTILITY is the term economists use to represent the satisfaction an individual or household derives from the consumption of goods or services. Their use of this term dates back to the work of Jeremy Bentham and his colleagues, who established the utilitarian school of philosophy and social reform in the early nineteenth century.

We introduced the law of diminishing marginal utility in Chapter 1, and from that discussion you know that *TOTAL UTILITY* is the measure of the overall satisfaction derived from the consumption of a good or service in a specified time period, while *MARGINAL UTILITY* measures the change in total utility derived from consuming one more, or one less, unit of a product. For the great majority of products which are subject to diminishing marginal utility, the relationship between total and marginal utility follows the general pattern shown in Figure 6-1. Total utility increases as long as marginal utility is positive, and even at an increasing rate for the first units consumed if marginal utility is initially increasing. But once marginal utility begins to diminish, total utility increases at a decreasing rate. And if an individual should continue to consume units of some product until its marginal utility becomes negative, total utility will begin to fall. Of course, rational behavior suggests that people won't pay to consume a product that decreases their satisfaction, so we don't expect to observe that under normal circumstances.

The value for total utility can always be found by adding up the values for the marginal utility of each unit of the product that is being consumed, and this quantitative relationship between marginal and total values holds for any variable, not just utility. This is even easier to see when applied to something that is regularly measured, such as the production or cost levels you will study in later chapters, than to these abstract notions of utility. After all, you probably don't go around saying to yourself "That slice of pizza gave me 10 *UTILS* (as Bentham called them) of satisfaction, but the next piece will have a marginal utility of 7, bringing my total utility from this pizza to 17."

If it was possible to measure utility in cardinal numbers that we could reasonably add or subtract in this way (it isn't), it would also be easy to demonstrate that diminishing marginal utility leads to downward sloping demand curves, like those we used in earlier chapters. We will, in fact, show exactly that in the next section, before discussing more general and powerful models of consumer behavior that don't assume cardinally measurable utility. Fortunately, these newer and more defensible models can also be used to derive demand schedules, and to study other facets of consumer choice and public policies affecting household consumption decisions.

Figure 6-1
Total and Marginal Utility

Units Consumed	Total Utility	Marginal Utility
0	--	--
1	3	3
2	8	5
3	12	4
4	14	2
5	15	1
6	15	0
7	13	-2

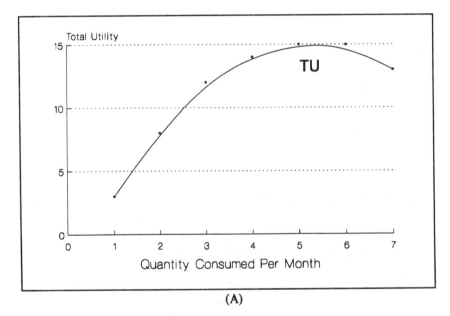

(A)

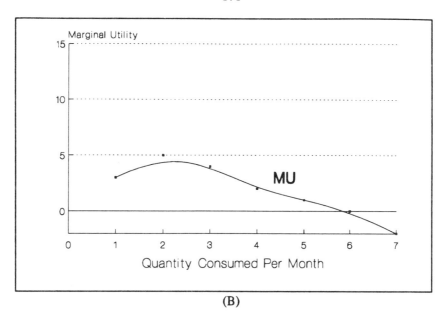

(B)

The graphs above are derived from the values shown in the table above them, which indicate how a consumer's total and marginal utility change as additional units of a product are consumed over a given period of time. Note that total utility increases as long as marginal utility is positive (units 1-5), even though marginal utility is decreasing over most of this range. Total utility is maximized when marginal utility is zero, which occurs when six units of this product are consumed. Total utility will decline if marginal utility becomes negative, which occurs if more than six units of this product are consumed in one month.

Diminishing Marginal Utility and Demand

Table 6-1 shows a consumer's total and marginal utility schedules for three products, A, B, and C, which we will assume are the only three products this individual consumes. We can use these schedules and the product prices shown there to determine how a consumer would maximize utility subject to a budget constraint. Doing this is useful because it shows the general logic involved such a decision process, and establishes the equilibrium conditions that must hold at the best possible consumption levels.

So, given the utility schedules in Table 6-1; prices for products A, B, and C of $30, $20, and $10, respectively; and a budget of $60 a week; how many units of each product should you consume in a week to maximize your total satisfaction?

If you divide your spending into $10 increments and look at the best set of purchases you can make, you find that with only $10 a week to spend you will buy one unit of Product C (obviously, since both A or B cost more than $10), and achieve a satisfaction level of 5 utils. But if you can spend $20 a week, you can afford to buy either one unit of B or two units of C. In this case, you get more satisfaction (10 utils) from the single unit of B than from two units of C. With $30 to spend, you are equally well off (at 15 utils) buying one unit of A *or* one unit of B and one unit of C, but either of those "consumption bundles" of products is superior to three units of C (which yield only 13.5 utils). At $40, however, you clearly should buy one unit of A and one unit of C to maximize your utility. For $50, the best you can do is buy one unit of A and one unit of B. Finally, spending your entire budget of $60 a week, your best possible choice given these prices and utility schedules is to buy one unit of all three products. No other possible spending pattern will equal or exceed this satisfaction level (30 utils).

Table 6-1
A Utility Maximization Problem

Product A ($30 each)			Product B ($20 each)			Product C ($10 each)		
Units	TU	MU	Units	TU	MU	Units	TU	MU
0	--	--	0	--	--	0	--	--
1	15	15	1	10	10	1	5	5
2	25	10	2	18	8	2	9.5	4.5
			3	24	6	3	13.5	4
						4	17	3.5
						5	20	3
						6	22.5	2.5

The utility schedules above are for a consumer who spends all of his or her income on three products -- A, B, and C -- which are each sold at the prices indicated. A particular combination of products will provide the highest level of satisfaction that the consumer can afford to reach. For example, spending a total budget of $60 in $10 blocks so that marginal utility per dollar is always as high as possible, this consumer will maximize total utility by consuming one unit of each of these three products.

While many consumers follow this kind of trial and error process to find the best way to use their scarce resources, if for no other reason than to find out how their satisfaction changes as they vary the level of their consumption of various products, there is a more general idea and procedure behind all of this. That is, simply, the idea that consumers try to get the highest possible level of satisfaction per dollar spent from all the goods they consume. In other words, that means they have to look at how much additional (marginal) utility they get by spending more dollars on one product, compared to the marginal utility they would get by spending those dollars on another product. Clearly, the product consumers should buy next is always one that gives them the highest marginal utility per dollar.

Algebraically, that means that to maximize total utility subject to some budget constraint consumers must set

$$\frac{MU_A}{P_A} = \frac{MU_B}{P_B} = ... \frac{MU_n}{P_n}$$

where MU_A is the marginal utility of product A, P_A is the price of product A, etc. If that is not done -- for example, if the marginal utility per dollar from the consumption of good A is higher than the marginal utility per dollar received from the consumption of good B, a consumer would gain satisfaction by shifting dollars from the purchase of B to the purchase of A. Doing this will reduce and eventually eliminate the inequality *if* both products are subject to the law of diminishing marginal utility and the prices of the two products remain fixed. As the consumer buys more units of A and fewer units of B, the marginal utility of A will fall, the marginal utility of B will rise, and the consumer will eventually reach an equilibrium point at a higher level of total satisfaction.

If a consumer is in equilibrium, as shown by the equation above, and the price of one of the products he or she is consuming changes, that will also lead to adjustments in purchases of these products. Specifically, assume that the price of B increases and that the consumer experiences diminishing marginal utility for these products over the relevant range of consumption choices, *ceteris paribus*. The higher price for B will lead the consumer to buy fewer units of B to restore the consumption equilibrium, and to use the funds no longer spent on B to buy more units of A.

All of this is, as you should recognize, an example of rational individual behavior which underpins the law of demand. But while it comforted some economists to know that these utilitarian maximization models yielded results that further supported the theory of market demand offered by Adam Smith and other early economists, who had never heard of marginal utility, major questions and problems with the utilitarian framework quickly arose. Many economists complained that people didn't (and couldn't) really calculate numerical measures of utility this way; that the utility from the consumption of one product was often affected by the level of consumption of other products (not perfectly independent, as the schedules we have used in these examples have assumed); and that interpersonal comparisons of utility could never be made just by comparing satisfaction indexes people claimed to derive from the consumption of different products. In broadest terms, many economists objected then and now to the kinds of social planning and policies that might be adopted if it was accepted that different people's utility could be measured and added together on some fixed scale, as discussed in the following boxed insert on Jeremy Bentham.

The Haunted House of Jeremy Bentham[1]

Jeremy Bentham's standing as a pioneer in systematically designing and analyzing laws and other social institutions using a democratic standard of providing "the greatest good for the greatest number" is secure even today, more than 200 years after his birth and the publication of his early works. But many of Bentham's ideas and actions have always generated controversy, inspiring enthusiastic devotees and equally energetic critics.

For example, Bentham engaged in several notorious personal eccentricities, such as letting a pet pig wander around his mansion; asking the London City Council to let him line his driveway with mummified human corpses that he found more "aesthetic" than flowers; and requiring the University of London to bring his own embalmed body (with a wax head) to its trustees' meetings -- if it wanted to receive the proceeds from his considerable estate. Then, like today, universities were often willing to accommodate wealthy donors, so the body did "attend" these meetings for many years with the Secretary's minutes noting that Bentham was "present but not voting." You can still see his body sitting in a glass case at the University, or you can read about this in a "Believe It Or Not" comic book entitled "The Demon in the Glass Cage." The other trustees finally objected to Bentham's constant abstentions and, after they were sure his estate was irrevocably theirs, ordered his body removed from their meetings. Some say Bentham's spirit protested, but that's another story and course.

In terms of recommendations on economic policies, many of Bentham's ideas concerning the importance of freely-determined market prices, including even interest rates on loans, were in line with those made by the usually less flamboyant economists of his day. But other aspects of utilitarianism, and particularly the idea that appropriate judgments about policies could be made simply by adding up the changes in utility of those who were affected by such initiatives, were (and remain) more disturbing to other economists, because they suggested a mechanistically and technologically driven system of central planning which allowed little consideration of personal rights and liberties. A famous example of Bentham's ideas for such centralized social arrangements was his "panopticon" -- a model for new prisons in which a guard stationed at the center of a network of mirrors could monitor the behavior of all of the prisoners in a cell block without being seen by them. Critics claim that many of Bentham's other ideas for social reforms would have set up similar "webs" to observe ordinary citizens, and to control or at least partially direct their behavior.

These complaints were, to a large extent, resolved by developing the indifference curve models you will soon study in this chapter. First, however, we want to digress just a bit to review the link between the utility measures we have just discussed and two other important concepts covered in Chapter 4: consumer surplus and price elasticity of demand.

---

[1]This title is borrowed from an essay on Bentham by the noted historian Gertrude Himmelfarb, which provides an excellent introduction and summary of Bentham's ideas. The essay is reprinted in Himmelfarb's *Victorian Minds*, New York: Alfred A. Knopf, 1968.

Utility, Consumer Surplus, and Price Elasticity of Demand

In Chapter 4 you saw that market prices are measures of economic value in exchange. Multiplied by the quantity of a product purchased in a given time period, they show the total *market* value of the products exchanged. But, due to the notion of consumer surplus -- which is based on the amount of satisfaction consumers receive from using each unit of a product, and measured by the maximum amount they would be willing and able to pay for each of these units -- that value may be very different from the value in use of these same products. Adding consumer surplus to the market or exchange value for a product, as shown in Figure 6-2, provides a dollar measure of the total value of all goods traded in a market that is based on this notion of total utility derived from consumption. The market or exchange price is *not* directly related to the total utility of that level of output, as you just saw in the previous section of this chapter, but rather to the marginal utility of the last unit of output produced. Understanding this can help you resolve several apparent paradoxes in economics, such as those depicted in Figures 6-3 and 6-4.

Figure 6-2
Market Values and Total Utility

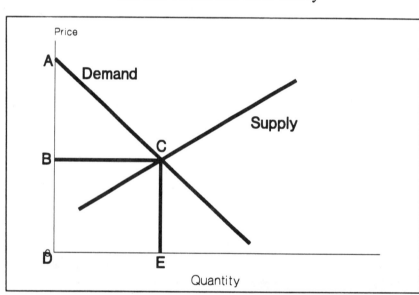

The economic value associated with the total utility derived from the consumption of a given level of output for some product includes both the areas of value in exchange (i.e., the market value), and consumer surplus. Consumer surplus is area ABC, as we saw in Chapter 4. Value in exchange is simply the area given by multiplying market price times equilibrium quantity, shown here as the rectangle BCED. Adding the two areas together provides a measure of economic value in use.

Great natural calamities (such as tornadoes, plagues, and earthquakes) or man-made tragedies (such as war and mass-scale arson) almost always drive up prices for housing and other products that survive the disasters. This plus the resulting expenditures for rebuilding sometimes leads to claims that disasters and war are generally "good business" for an economy, human suffering notwithstanding. And in some more technical respects those claims are plausible. For example, if the demand for housing is price inelastic over the range of prices that prevail before and after a major fire reduces the supply of housing in some city by 50%, as shown in Figure 6-3, the market value of the surviving houses would literally exceed that of all houses before the fire. Is that a sensible way to let markets operate, and to determine the economic value of a resource as important as housing?

Figure 6-3
Gaining By Losing, or Nero and the Market Value of Housing in Rome

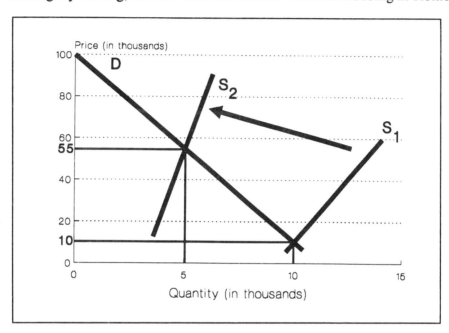

The graph above shows a sharp decrease in the supply of housing due to a major fire, from S_1 to S_2. If demand is price inelastic the total market value of housing after the fire (P X Q = $55,000 X 5,000 = $275 million) will be higher than it was before the fire ($10,000 X 10,000 = $100 million). Given that possible result, is it clear that Nero was crazy and/or a bad emperor? Probably -- remember to look at the measures of value in use as well as value in exchange.

In fact, this situation demonstrates two very different economic ideas, neither of which is particularly pernicious or strange. First, it shows once again that value in use is different from value in exchange. The decrease in the level of output and consumer surplus indicate clearly in Figure 6-3 that value in use does fall, while value in exchange may rise or fall, depending on the price elasticity of demand over this range of prices and outputs. Looking at the demand curve as the schedule of people's *marginal* willingness to pay for different output levels of housing, the total value of housing is simply the sum of the values under the demand curve for all of the units that are actually produced. That area does drop -- sharply -- as a result of the fire.

The second idea demonstrated by this example is that, after the leftward shift in supply caused by the fire, more consumers must pay a price closer to the maximum price they are willing and able to pay for housing. That's just another way of saying that consumer surplus has decreased, and that is to be expected since housing has become more scarce. But remember that the higher price also encourages faster rebuilding in the long run, leading many producers who do not usually build homes or offer housing services to do so, at least for a time. Temporary rent-controls could be used to limit "*WINDFALL PROFITS*" from housing that survived the fire, but such controls entail both costs and benefits, as we discussed in Chapter 4.

Our final example in this section deals with the relationship between price elasticity of demand and marginal and total utility. Many students are surprised to learn that the total utility associated with the consumption of a product is not directly involved in determining the product's coefficient of price elasticity.[2] To see this, think of a

---

[2]Though perhaps not those who remember the diamond and water paradox discussed in Chapter 4.

176

case in which the price of one product you consume, say CDs, increases while other prices do not. That means that, to reestablish your equilibrium position, you must adjust your consumption of CDs to the point where its marginal utility per dollar is the same as for all other products you consume. That may take a large or small adjustment in the quantity of the CDs you will buy at the new price, depending on whether your marginal utility schedule is relatively flat or steep over this range (i.e., on how fast marginal utility changes as you change your consumption).

If marginal utility changes rapidly as your consumption level changes, you will only have to make a small change in the quantity of the CDs you buy. Your demand will therefore be relatively price inelastic in this range, while the total utility you derive from CDs may change a little or a lot. That's the point -- we don't need to know what happens to total utility from the consumption of the product to know that you have acted rationally to reestablish an equilibrium position, only what happens to marginal utility.

If your marginal utility schedule is fairly constant for CDs, it will take a relatively greater change in quantity demanded to get you back to an equilibrium position, meaning that demand will be relatively more price elastic. Again, this doesn't tell us how much or how little your total utility from the consumption of CDs has changed, and no matter -- marginal utility is what's relevant. This is summarized in Figure 6-4.

Figure 6-4
Marginal Utility and Price Elasticity of Demand

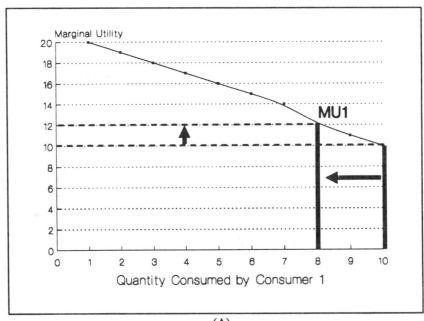

(A)

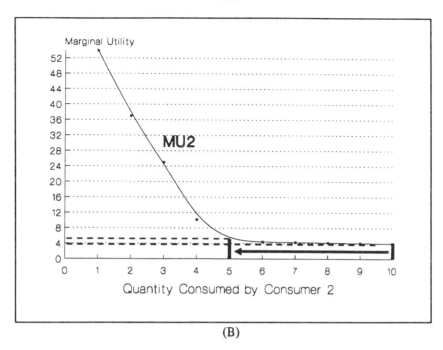

(B)

The graphs above show the marginal utility schedules for some identical product for two different consumers. In both graphs, it was assumed that the price of the product increased by 25%, and that both consumers then decided to reduce their consumption of the product so that marginal utility will increase 20% in order to reestablish an equilibrium level of consumption. (Marginal utility increases from 10 to 12 utils in panel A, and from 4 to 4.8 utils in panel B.)

To bring about the 20% increase in marginal utility, the first consumer (panel A) reduces quantity demanded by 20%, or from 10 units to 8 units over whatever period of time this consumption is measured. In panel B, the second consumer reduces consumption by 5 units, or 50% of his original level of quantity demanded.

The marginal utility schedules for these two consumers have also been constructed so that total utilities are equal when we compare them for two individuals, both before *and* after the adjustments for the price increase are made. (See review and discussion question #4, at the end of this chapter.) This shows again that price elasticity of demand is related to marginal utility, not to total utility.

Budget Constraint Schedules

What people can spend for goods and services is determined largely by their own incomes and by the market prices of the goods and services they consume. Taken together, those factors represent a constraint on consumers' purchasing behavior -- separating attainable and unattainable combinations or bundles of products. In that sense, budget constraint lines illustrate the basic idea of scarcity, as it affects an individual consumer or household, and the notion of relative prices for the two goods that are shown on the axes of these graphs.

Income and Prices

While most people don't think explicitly in terms of marginal utility when buying goods and services, they usually do consider product prices and how much money or income they have to spend. Prices and budget constraints are therefore the first things we will incorporate into our more general models of consumer choice, in which we do not assume that we can measure utility in cardinal terms such as utils, or any other units of satisfaction.

Graphically, a *BUDGET CONSTRAINT LINE* for a consumer is constructed using information on prices and income levels. Both the position and slope of this schedule is determined by the amount of income the consumer has to spend in the time period represented in the graph, and by the prices of the two goods shown on the axes, as shown in Figure 6-5.

For example, if a consumer (call her Sam) has $100 a week to spend on two products that sell for $10 and $5 per unit, respectively, she could buy, at most, 10 units a week of the first product (shown as good A in Figure 6-5) and 20 units a week of the second product (shown as good B). Every time Sam buys a unit of the first good, she must forgo purchasing two units of the second product, which is the same as saying that the opportunity cost of one unit of the second product is 1/2 unit of the first good. Taken together, this establishes the intercept points of 10 and 20 on the budget constraint line shown in Figure 6-5, and the budget constraint's slope (-1/2). We can derive that slope more formally, with basic algebra, by looking at the "rise over the run" using the two intercept points for this budget constraint line. Doing this shows that

$$\frac{\frac{I}{P_A}}{\frac{I}{P_B}} = \frac{P_B}{P_A} = \frac{5}{10},$$

where I represents income, P_A = the price of good A ($10), and P_B = the price of good B ($5).

A two-dimensional graph only allows us to look at two products at a time, so when using these models we will often assume that consumers spend all of their income on just two products. This is only done to keep the graphs simple; more products can easily be added by abandoning the graphs and expanding the equations that underlie them. For example, if a consumer buys four products instead of two, we know that the budget constraint is simply

$$(P_1 \cdot Q_1) + (P_2 \cdot Q_2) + (P_3 \cdot Q_3) + (P_4 \cdot Q_4) = I,$$

where P_{1-4} are the prices of the four goods, Q_{1-4} are the quantities of the four goods consumed, and I is the consumer's income. In other cases, it may be reasonable to think of the product shown on one axis of a two-dimensional graph as a specific good or service, and the "good" shown on the other axis as representing all other products the consumer buys and uses. Therefore, the usefulness and general power of the models are not, in practice, greatly affected by keeping them this simple.

On the most basic level, note that the budget constraint line gives us another way to demonstrate the ideas of scarcity and trade-offs. The consumer can buy and consume any combination of these two products on or inside the budget constraint line, but cannot attain any combination outside (above and to the right) of the constraint. At all points on or inside the constraint the choice of what combination of the two products to buy is entirely up to the consumer, but along the constraint line buying more of one product always requires giving up some units of the other product.

Figure 6-5
A Budget Constraint Line

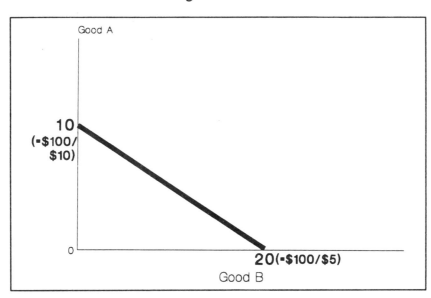

The consumer shown above has an income of $100 a week and buys only two goods, A and B. Good A sells for $10 a unit, Good B for $5 a unit. That identifies the budget constraint line shown above, which has a slope of -1/2 that is determined by the relative prices of the two goods. The consumer can buy any combination on or below the budget constraint line, but can not afford any combination represented by a point above it.

Changes in Income

When consumers' incomes increase or decrease, their budget constraint lines also shift. An increase in income will lead to a parallel, rightward shift of the budget constraint line, while a decrease in income leads to a parallel, leftward shift. The shifts must be parallel, because the relative prices of the goods shown on the axes which determine the slope of the budget constraint line have not changed. Therefore, the change in income affects only the position of the line and its intercepts, not its slope. This is shown in Figure 6-6.

Changes in Prices

Holding a consumer's income constant while changing the relative prices of the goods used to derive a budget constraint line will also cause that line to shift, but in a different way from the income shifts just shown. If the price of one good decreases, for example, a consumer will be able to buy more units of it over some time period, and the intercept point on that axis will move further away from the origin. The intercept for the other good does not change, of course, since its price has not changed. That is shown in Figure 6-7 (panel A), as is an increase in price for one of the two goods (in panel B), which leads to an inward shift of that intercept.

Figure 6-6
Shifts in Budget Constraint Lines

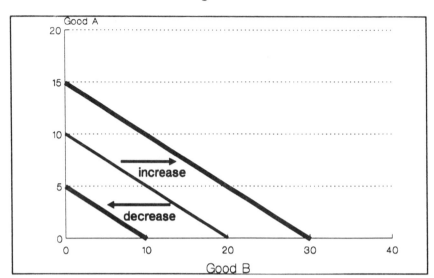

With the price of good A = $10 and the price of good B = $5, the shifts of the budget constraint lines shown above represent an increase in income from $100 to $150 a week (the rightward shift) and a decrease in income from $100 to $50 a week (the leftward shift). At all points on the highest line, the consumer spends $150 for these products; on the middle line, $100; and on the lowest line, $50.

If the prices of both products change simultaneously, the slope of the budget constraint line will change so long as the relative prices of the two products are changed (i.e., the value of the ratio of the two prices changes). This must happen, of course, whenever the price of one product increase and the other decreases (as shown in panel C of Figure 6-7).

But if the prices for two goods increase or decrease in equal proportions, leaving the relative price ratio unchanged, the budget constraint line will remain parallel to the original budget constraint line and shift inward or outward, respectively. Such changes reflect a change in the consumer's real income, or purchasing power, even though his or her nominal or money income has not changed. For example, if money income is fixed at $100 and all prices decrease 10 percent, the consumer can buy any combination of products that previously cost up to $110. So, in effect, the consumer's real income has increased 10 percent.

It is not surprising that, graphically, this kind of result looks exactly like the change in income discussed earlier, and shown in Figure 6-6. Real income was also changing in the situation shown there, since the consumer's money income was rising or falling while the prices of the products purchased remained constant.

Figure 6-7
Shifts in Relative Prices and Budget Constraint Lines

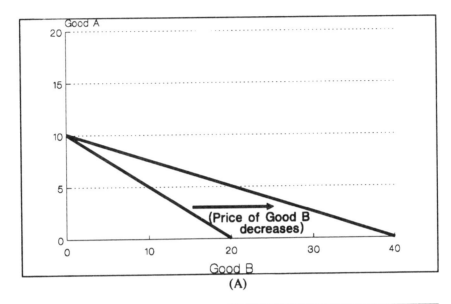

(A)

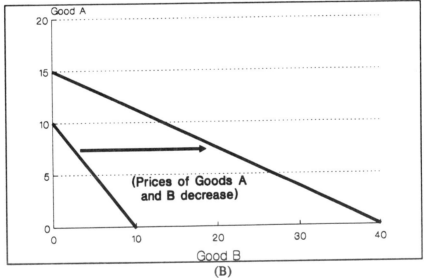

(B)

182

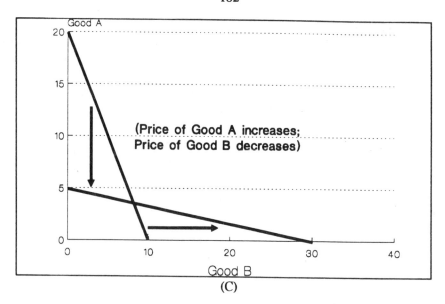

(Price of Good A increases;
Price of Good B decreases)

Good B

(C)

When relative prices change, the opportunity cost of consuming one good instead of another is changed. This occurs whenever one price changes and the other is constant, as shown in the top graph (panel A), or when both prices change in different proportions as shown in the middle graph (panel B), or when prices for the two goods change in different directions as shown in the bottom graph (panel C). All of these changes affect the slope of the budget constraint line.

Indifference Curves

Consumers can't afford to buy all the goods and services they want, but they can afford to buy some of them. Their personal tastes and preferences allow them to compare different combinations or 'bundles' of products, and rank any one bundle as inferior, superior, or equal to another bundle. Bundles that provide equal satisfaction are said to lie on a consumer's indifference curve for those products, and the notions of rational behavior and utility maximization allow economists to identify several basic properties of these indifference curves. Combining those curves with budget constraint lines establishes a unique, equilibrium level of purchases for products, that is determined by a consumer's preferences and income, and by the prices for those goods.

Characteristics of Indifference Curves

To escape the idea that people use precise, quantitative measures of utility as they try to maximize the satisfaction they derive by consuming a variety of goods and services, during the first half of this century economists Vilfredo Pareto and Nobel laureate Sir John Hicks began to argue that consumers more typically compare different combinations of products they might consume, and rank those "bundles" as superior, inferior, or equal in terms of providing satisfaction or utility. This focus on ordinal rather than cardinal measures of utility led to the development of *INDIFFERENCE CURVES*, such as those shown in Figure 6-8.

An indifference curve is a line drawn through all of the points on a graph that show the different combinations of two products which will leave a consumer equally satisfied. At any point on a given indifference curve, then, a consumer's total level of satisfaction is fixed at some constant level. It doesn't matter to the consumer where on that curve he or she is, or in other words the consumer is completely indifferent about moving to any point on the same curve.

Higher (up and to the right) indifference curves represent a higher level of total satisfaction than lower (down and to the left) indifference curves, so the consumer is certainly not indifferent about what indifference curve he or she is on. Our behavioral assumptions are that consumers try to maximize their total satisfaction and, since both products shown on the axes are defined as "goods," that the consumer feels better off any time more of both goods are attainable. So, for example, consuming 10 hamburgers and five movies a month must provide a higher level of satisfaction than consuming only four hamburgers and one movie a month *if* a consumer likes hamburgers and likes going to movies.

Consumers are free to trade off purchases of some units of one good for compensating units of another good in whatever ratios they find in line with their personal preferences. But because it violates our notion of economic goods and rational behavior to say that any point with more of both goods is not preferred to any point with fewer units of **both products**, we also know that indifference curves will be negatively sloped (since consumers must give up some units of one good as they acquire more units of another good in order to hold total utility constant), and that indifference curves cannot intersect (see Figure 6-9). The smooth, convex ("bowed-in" toward the origin) shape of indifference curves occurs as a result of a more technical and somewhat complex hypothesis, which is explained in the next section.

Figure 6-8
An Indifference Curve

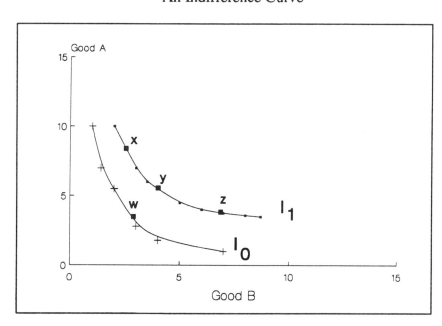

In the graph shown above, points x, y, and z provide this consumer with equal levels of total satisfaction, and so must lie on the same indifference curve, labeled I_1. At point w the consumer has less of both goods A and B than at point y, so w must lie on a lower indifference curve, I_0, and give the consumer less satisfaction than any point on I_1.

The Marginal Rate of Substitution

Suppose you derive pleasure from just two goods, gourmet food and stylish clothing. We could derive an indifference curve for you by starting you with some level of both goods and then finding out the minimum number of units of clothes you would require to make you willing to give up one unit of food, how many units of clothes you would require to give up another unit of food, and so on. The amount of one product a consumer will give up to get a unit of another product, *holding total utility constant*, is known as the *MARGINAL RATE OF SUBSTITUTION* (MRS).

The MRS is always derived from a negative relationship between the two products graphed on an indifference curve, for the same reason that the indifference curves have a negative slope: the consumer must trade some of one good to get more of the other while staying on the same indifference curve. (If the amount of both goods consumed increased, he or she would move to a higher indifference curve.) However, economists customarily express MRS as a positive number, measuring the relative quantity of one product that is given up to acquire a unit of the other good. This can easily be accomplished by multiplying the expression relating the trade-off between the two goods by -1, so algebraically in this case

$$MRS = -\frac{\Delta F}{\Delta C}$$

This equation is read "the marginal rate of substitution is equal to -1 times the change in food divided by the change in clothing."

Figure 6-9
Indifference Curves Cannot Intersect

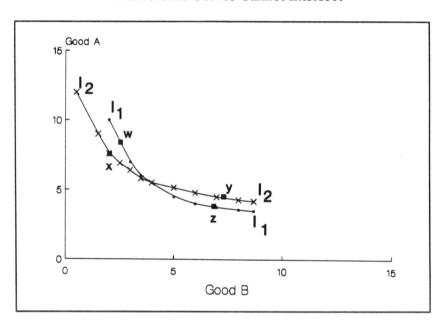

Point w in the graph shown above offers more of both goods A and B than point x, so it must lie on a higher (preferred) indifference curve. But point y, which is on the same indifference curve as point x, offers more of both goods than point z, which is on the same indifference curve as point w. It is logically inconsistent for the same consumer to prefer w to x, be indifferent between x and y, and then prefer y to z. Since this intransitivity violates the assumption that consumers always prefer more of a good to less, we know that indifference curves for rational consumers cannot intersect.

What is most important for you to see here is that the MRS changes as we move along an indifference curve. Specifically, the MRS is determined by the slope of the indifference curve at any given point, and depends on the amounts of the two products being consumed at that point. For example, if you have a lot of food and very little clothing, as shown at point a in Figure 6-10, you will require a lot more food to make you willing to give up a unit of clothing (holding total satisfaction constant). That is the same as saying that, at this point, you will give up a lot of food to get just a little more clothing. But moving down and to the right along the indifference curve, to the range where you have more equal amounts of food and clothing (as at points b and c in Figure 6-10), you will normally be willing to trade a more equal number of units of one product for the other, again given the constraint that your level of total utility or satisfaction remains fixed. And at point d, where you have a lot of clothing and very little food, you will require many additional units of clothing to keep you equally satisfied if you must give up one unit of food. So you see that total satisfaction depends both on the absolute levels *and* on the relative mix of the two products consumed.

Formalizing this typical pattern of consumers' willingness to trade one good for another gives us the assumption of a *DIMINISHING MARGINAL RATE OF SUBSTITUTION*. That is, in most cases, the rate at which a person is just willing to trade good Y for good X decreases as the amount of good X the person has increases and the amount of good Y decreases. Thus, as we move down along the indifference curve in Figure 6-10, the MRS of food for clothing decreases (since more and more clothing is required to get the consumer to give up a unit of food) as the amount food being consumed decreases and the amount of clothing being consumed increases. Graphically, this is reflected by the indifference curve becoming flatter as we move simultaneously down along the food axis and rightward along the clothing axis.

<hr>

Figure 6-10
The Diminishing Marginal Rate of Substitution

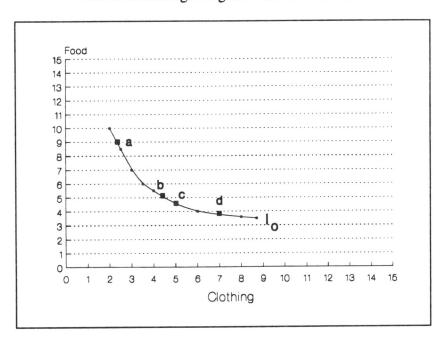

At different points on an indifference curve, the amount of one good that a consumer is willing to forgo to acquire an additional unit of the other good will vary. Moving down and right along the curve shown above, the consumer will agree to sacrifice less and less food for an additional unit of clothing, as the amount of food he or she has decreases and the amount of clothing already being consumed increases. For example, between points a and b, the consumer will give up four units of food to get one unit of clothing; but between points c and d, an additional unit of clothing is only worth about one-half unit of food to this individual.

<hr>

Utilitarian Vs. Indifference Curve Models of Consumer Choice

Now that you have reviewed the basic characteristics of indifference curves and budget constraint lines, we can bring these two fundamental components of consumer choice together into a unified and complete model of rational, optimizing behavior. You may already feel that indifference curves are more abstract, and certainly no more realistic, than the quantitative measures of marginal and total utility that we abandoned so quickly in the first sections of this chapter, and in some respects that is true. But these models don't assume that consumers sit around drawing indifference curves the way the earlier models assumed that consumers could determine and use numerical measures of utility.

Instead, indifference curve analysis assumes only that consumers decide whether one combination of products is preferred to, equal to, or inferior to other combinations of goods they might consume, and that they know the prices of these products and their own income constraints reasonably well. If consumers do, in fact, consider these factors carefully in making many of their purchases (particularly their routine, often-repeated purchases and the occasional "big-ticket" buys), economists can expect the more elaborate apparatus of indifference curve analysis to better predict a wide range of choices made by households and individuals, and the effects of several kinds of public policies on consumers' economic welfare.

Equilibrium and Utility Maximization

A nice thing happened when economists wanted to combine graphs of indifference curves and budget constraint lines. Since both curves are drawn on the same axes, one set of curves can easily be superimposed on the other, as in Figure 6-11. The result is that, given some budget constraint line *and* a diminishing marginal rate of substitution which causes indifference curves to be bowed in to the origin, a unique equilibrium point (labeled E) occurs at the combination of products that maximizes the consumer's level of satisfaction, on indifference curve I_2.

Other indifference curves (such as I_1) are attainable to this consumer, but offer less utility to the consumer or household. Still other indifference curves (such as I_3) represent a higher level of satisfaction for the consumer, but are not attainable given the consumer's current income and the product prices that establish the budget constraint line. In this model of consumer choice, a tangency point rather than an intersection of two lines indicates the equilibrium solution for our decision maker. The intersection points shown on I_1 are, in fact, inferior solutions where the consumer is spending too much on one good and not enough on the other. Similarly, any point inside the budget constraint line represents forgone utility that the consumer could capture by increasing his or her consumption of both goods.

Study Figure 6-11 carefully -- be sure you understand why the curves shown there look the way they do and why point E, rather than points A, B or C, is this consumer's optimal consumption mix and level for these two goods. Concentrate on what consumers are trying to do, where the constraints they face in doing this come from, and what the typical pattern of deriving satisfaction from the consumption of different products is. If you don't follow any part of this, review the earlier sections in this chapter or talk with your instructor before going on to the next section.

Figure 6-11
Equilibrium Consumption Levels

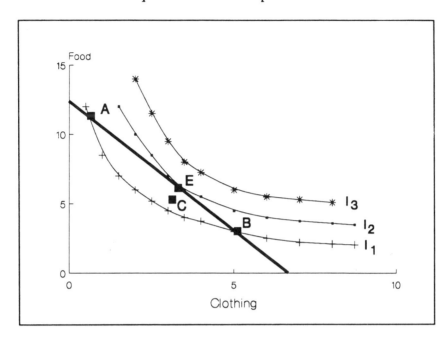

At point E, this consumer maximizes total utility (on I_2) subject to the budget constraint imposed by a limited income and positive prices for these scarce goods. Points A, B, and C lie on lower indifference curves, while the indifference curve labeled I_3 is unattainable. At point A the consumer is consuming too much food and not enough clothing, and increases utility by moving along the budget constraint line to point E. At point B, too much clothing and not enough food is consumed. At point E, the slope of the indifference curve equals the slope of the budget constraint line. From this, and from the conclusion that the consumer is maximizing utility, we know that

$$\frac{MU_{food}}{P_{food}} = \frac{MU_{clothing}}{P_{clothing}}$$

Applications and Extensions of Consumer Choice Models

Indifference curve models can be used to derive a consumer's demand curve for a product by showing a change in the product's price and the corresponding change in the quantity of the product demanded. This quantity change can then be separated into two component parts: the substitution effect and the income effect. The substitution effect always leads consumers to buy less of a product as its relative price increases. However, the income effect will decrease consumption as price increases only for normal goods, not inferior goods. Still, since the substitution effect is almost always, if not literally always, larger than the income effect, price increases for inferior goods regularly lead to a decrease in the overall quantity demanded. The rare (perhaps non-existent) exception is the Giffen good, for which the income effect overwhelms the substitution effect.

Deriving an Individual's Demand Curve

To use indifference curve analysis to derive an individual's demand curve for some product, start by thinking about exactly what we have to show: a change in the quantity of some good or service demanded that results from a change in its price. That shouldn't be hard, since you have already seen how to use a budget constraint line to represent a change in the price of a product. Figure 6-12 shows a decrease in the price of sunglasses, and a corresponding increase in the quantity of sunglasses that this consumer will buy. That's really all you need to derive two points on the demand curve for sunglasses, since you know that $P_1 > P_2$ and can see that, in this case, $Q_{d1} < Q_{d2}$. By showing many changes in price instead of just one, we could identify the entire demand curve; but the key point of an inverse relationship between price and quantity demanded has been shown with just one price change.

With a little experimentation you can see that, depending on where you draw the tangency points for the two indifference curves and budget constraint lines that are used to show the change in the price of sunglasses, it is theoretically possible to have the quantity demanded remain unchanged after the price of sunglasses changes (i.e., demand would be perfectly price inelastic in that range), or even to have the quantity demanded increase as a result of a price increase (indicating a Giffen good). Ultimately, as discussed in Chapters 1 and 3, the law of demand is an empirically based assertion, supported by: 1) the substitution effect of a price change for all products, 2) by the law of diminishing marginal utility for most products, and 3) by the income effect of price changes for normal goods. We looked at the diminishing marginal utility link to the law of demand earlier in this chapter. Using indifference curve analysis, we can now examine the income and substitution effects of a price change more carefully.

Figure 6-12
Indifference Curve Analysis and the Law of Demand

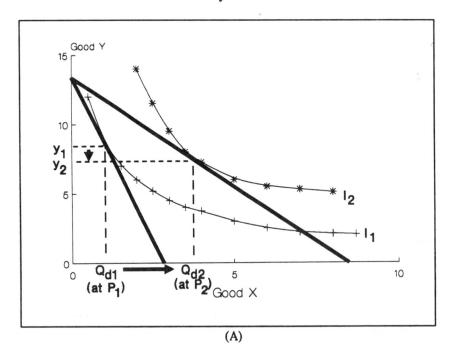

(A)

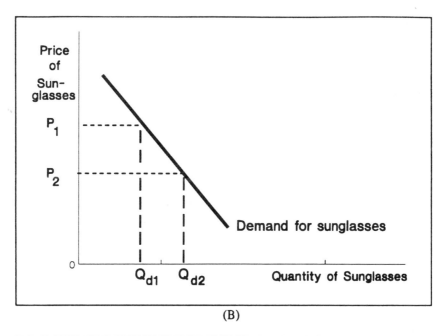

(B)

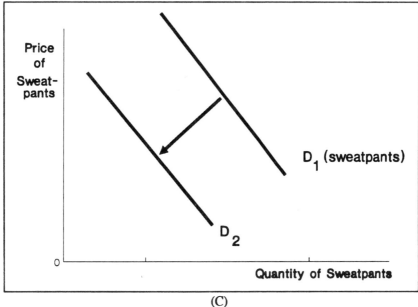

(C)

As the price of sunglasses falls from P_1 to P_2, the indifference curve model in panel (A) shows this consumer increasing the amount of sunglasses consumed from Q_{d1} to Q_{d2}. That leads to a downward-sloping demand curve for sunglasses, as shown in panel (B).

In panel (A), again, note that the quantity of sweatpants purchased also changes when the price of sunglasses changes, even though the price of sweatpants does not change. That means the demand curve for sweatpants has shifted -- in this case decreased -- since the quantity of sweatpants purchased at the same price has decreased. The decrease in the demand for sweatpants is shown in panel (C).

Separating Income and Substitution Effects

Recall that the substitution effect refers to the change in the quantity of a product demanded that occurs when its relative price changes. That means that even if we hold a consumer's income constant, a change in the price of a product leads to a change in the quantity demanded because it is now more or less expensive than some substitute products, which the consumer could use to satisfy the same general wants and provide utility. On the other hand, the income effect of a price change means that the consumer will clearly move to a higher or lower indifference curve as a result of the increase or decrease in real income that the price change causes. In 1915, Eugene Slutsky[3] suggested a way to separate out these two components of a price change, which can be illustrated with indifference curve analysis (shown in Figure 6-13).

Slutsky's method allows economists to calculate these measures using price and consumption levels that are empirically observed. In fact, it's not particularly difficult to establish what levels of the affected products some consumers were buying before and after a price change, and from that to know how much to adjust their income to allow them to be able to just afford their original consumption levels at the new price ratio. If such adjustments were made, it would then be easy to compare a consumer's final mix of purchases -- those made after adjusting for the income effect -- to the two bundles observed earlier. So, even though these graphical models are highly abstract, they are thoroughly compatible with concrete and measurable indicators of consumer behavior. To further illustrate their "real-world" relevance, we use these models to look at some additional aspects of demand and consumer behavior in the final section of this chapter, and then, in Case Study #8, apply them to an important and longstanding public policy issue.

Normal, Inferior, and Giffen Goods

Figure 6-13 depicts income and substitution effects associated with a decrease in the price of a normal good. How can we know that? Simply because the income effect associated with the price decrease is positive, which meets the definition of a normal good that we provided in Chapter 1. The price decrease makes this consumer wealthier in real terms, and as a result of this income effect the quantity of the product he or she purchases increases.

In Figure 6-14, we use indifference curves and a change in income (represented by the parallel shift in the budget constraint line) to demonstrate the notion of an inferior good -- the demand for good X falls as a result of the increase in income. Then, in Figure 6-15, we demonstrate that the income effect associated with a decrease in price for an inferior good will be negative, partially offsetting the substitution effect associated with a price change for the good in question.

---

[3]"On the Theory of the Budget of the Consumer," reprinted (in translation) in Kenneth E. Boulding and George J. Stigler, eds., *AEA Readings in Price Theory*, Chicago: Richard D. Irwin, Inc., 1952.

Figure 6-13
Income and Substitution Effects Revisited

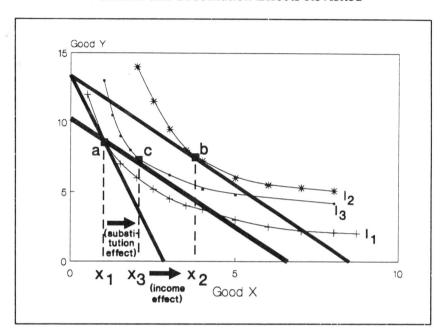

A decrease in the price of good X allows a consumer to attain a higher level of satisfaction by moving from an original equilibrium position, point a, to a higher indifference curve, at point b. If we take away enough income from the consumer so that he or she can just afford to purchase the original bundle of goods (point a), this shifts the consumer to a final budget constraint line passing through point a but parallel to the new budget constraint line that was observed after the change in the price of good X. In other words, even though we take away some income, we allow the consumer to buy goods X and Y at the new price ratio. Given the change in relative prices, the consumer will not stay at point a, but instead will move to point c. There, he or she will still be better off than at point a, though not as well off as he or she would be if we did not take away this income.

The increase in the quantity of good X demanded represented by the movement from point a to point c (shown as X_1 to X_3 on the X axis) represents the substitution effect, which is caused solely by the change in the relative price of goods X and Y. The movement from point c to point b (shown as the distance between X_3 and X_2 on the X axis) represents the increase in the quantity of good X demanded due to the positive income effect associated with the decrease in the price of good X.

Figure 6-14
Inferior and Normal Goods

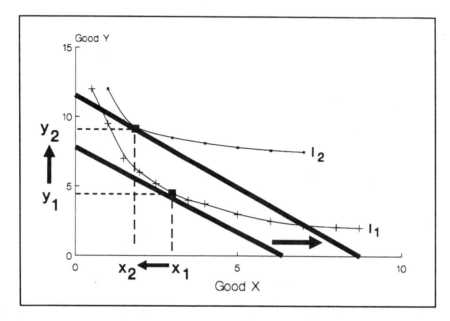

The increase in income shown in the graph above results in a decrease in the demand for good X and an increase in the demand for good Y. The prices of these goods haven't changed, but the increase in income leads to a decrease in the quantity of X purchased (from x_1 to x_2) and an increase in the quantity of Y purchased (from y_1 to y_2). From this we know that good X is an inferior good, and good Y is a normal good.

Figure 6-15
Income and Substitution Effects for an Inferior Good

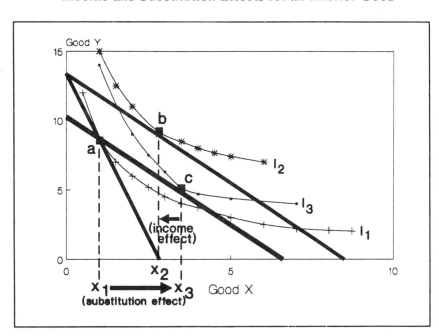

Using the same procedures described in Figure 6-13, the substitution and income effects for a decrease in the price of good X are shown in the graph above. The movement from point a to point c is the substitution effect, which occurs because of the change in the relative price of goods X and Y. The movement from point c to point b is the income effect associated with the decrease in the price of good X. Here, however, because X is an inferior good, the income effect partially offsets the substitution effect.

If a negative income effect is so large that it more than offsets the substitution effect, as shown in Figure 6-16, the result is that strangest of all products, the Giffen good, which exhibits a positive relationship between price and quantity demanded. There is no undisputed empirical evidence of a Giffen good actually occurring in human history after the *ceteris paribus* assumption has been met, but it is nevertheless interesting to establish how the income and substitution effects for such a product would have to be related for this kind of product to exist.

The discussion in this chapter thus far has been exclusively theoretical, but remember that policy makers are often put in the position of establishing laws and administrative guidelines even in situations in which there is (and perhaps can be) no laboratory or empirical evidence about the consequences of their actions. In such cases, theoretical evidence can be especially helpful in making public as well as private consumption decisions, and in setting up programs that implement those decisions. And as we noted in our discussion of the procedures used to separate substitution and income effects, theoretical models such as indifference curve analysis frequently lead to measurable and testable predictions or explanations of individuals' behavior in the face of changing economic conditions, including their income level and the prices of the things they buy. Those ideas are developed further in the following case study.

194

Figure 6-16
Income and Substitution Effects for a Giffen Good

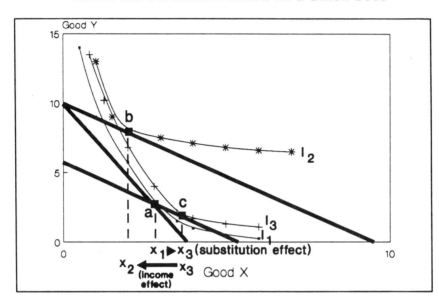

A Giffen good has income and substitution effects that work in the same direction as those for an inferior good, as shown in Figure 6-15. But the income effect for a Giffen good is so large that it more than offsets the substitution effect, resulting in a positive (direct) relationship between price and quantity demanded. In the graph above, for example, a decrease in the price of good X leads to a net *decrease* in the amount of X consumed by this individual, from X_1 to X_2.

Case Study #9#8
Food Stamps vs. Cash Transfers vs. Food-Price Subsidies

In Chapter 4 you saw that economists usually view direct cash payments to producers who are deemed worthy of government assistance programs (for whatever reasons) as more efficient than such hidden subsidies as price supports, production or import quotas, etc. Here, we will analyze the economic effectiveness of three alternative types of *consumer* assistance programs -- food stamps, food-price subsidies, and direct cash transfers -- that can be used to assist low-income families. There is considerable humanitarian support for the goals of such programs among the general public, politicians from both major parties, and professional economists as well. There is also a fairly strong consensus among economists concerning the general features and structure of such programs that will be most effective for the government *and* for the recipients of these benefits. While people (including economists) often disagree on questions concerning the optimal level of these assistance programs, that's another question. Here, let's see whether a food stamp, food-price subsidy, or direct cash transfer program would help low-income families most on a per dollar basis.

A food *PRICE-SUBSIDY PROGRAM* for consumers is, as you might suspect, quite different from a food subsidy program for producers, such as those you saw in Chapter 4. In particular, to help consumers with a subsidy program the government must lower the price of food, not raise it. Though such programs haven't been widely used in the United States, in practice they might well be easier to administer than something like the food stamp bureaucracy. Eligible families might submit their receipts for approved food items directly to the government and receive a cash reimbursement for some proportion of their expenditures. Or, they might receive an identification card to present to grocers who elected to participate in the program, and the grocers would then collect some portion of the food bill from the consumer and submit the rest of the bill (plus a handling fee) to the government for reimbursement.

As shown in Figure 6-17, this kind of subsidy would simply change the price of food relative to all other products the consumer might buy, increasing the amount of food low-income families could purchase by whatever proportion the government set in its program. This would lead those consumers to increase the amount of food consumed[4] and allow them to reach a higher indifference curve. Depending on the price elasticity of the demand for food, as reflected in consumers' total food expenditures, the quantity of non-food products purchased could rise or fall. If total spending for food increases (indicating elastic demand in this price range), non-food spending must decrease, and vice versa. Food producers will clearly have economic incentives to support this kind of consumer subsidy; in fact, such a program could help to eliminate the surpluses that have resulted from the price floors for American farm products that the federal government enforced over the past 50 years. Non-food producers would also gain sales from this program if the demand for food is price inelastic (which is quite possible), and so would probably support it unless the additional taxes they paid to finance the program more than offset those benefits.

Figure 6-17
Consumer Price Subsidies vs. Direct Income Assistance

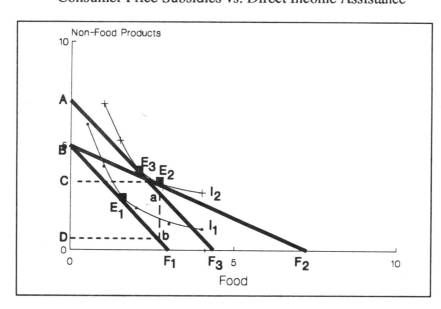

A food price subsidy provided by the government to low-income families shifts a consumer's budget constraint line from BF_1 to BF_2 in the graph above, and increases the consumer's total utility by allowing a move from point E_1 to point E_2, on a higher indifference curve.

Constructing the hypothetical budget constraint line labeled AF_3, which uses the presubsidy price ratio and is just tangent to the higher indifference curve, identifies the minimum amount of income (ab) that would be required to make the consumer just as well off as he or she is with the price subsidy. That amount is less than the amount the government must spend to pay for the price subsidy (the distance from E_2 to point b, which is equal to CD on the vertical axis).

---

[4]Unless, that is, food is a Giffen good for low-income families, which is not suggested by empirical evidence.

But asking what the cheapest way is for the government to make a low-income consumer as well off as he or she is after the food-price subsidy radically changes the focus of this problem. To answer this question, we will assume that relative prices remain as they were before the subsidy, and then shift out to a new budget constraint line that is parallel to the presubsidy constraint, until it is tangent to the same higher indifference curve that the food-price subsidy allowed the consumer to reach. That means the vertical distance labeled ab in Figure 6-17 represents the purchasing power, or income, required to make the consumer as well off as the subsidy did.

Is that more or less than the cost of the subsidy to the government? It is clearly less, since the cost of the food-price subsidy is the vertical distance between point E_2 and the consumer's original budget constraint line, which is equal to the distance shown as CD on the non-food axis. AB is smaller than CD in this example, and always will be with indifference curves that are convex to the origin. (The vertical distance AB is equal to the distance labeled ab directly under point E_2, since points a and b are exactly the same vertical distance apart and lie on the same parallel lines as points A and B. Given the bowed-in shape of indifference curves, point E_2 will always be further above the original budget constraint than the parallel budget constraint line constructed to measure the minimum required size of the direct cash transfer.)

From this, we can conclude that the direct cash transfer program could make recipients just as well off as a food-price subsidy at a lower cost to taxpayers. Non-food producers would definitely experience increased sales to low-income families as a result of the cash transfer program, because there is no substitution effect caused by a decrease in the relative price of food. Food producers will still enjoy some gains in sales from the income transfers, assuming that food is a normal good; but they will not benefit from increases as large as those that would be prompted by the food-price subsidies, because of the absence of the substitution effect.

Are direct cash transfers also preferred to a *VOUCHER SYSTEM*, such as the current food stamp program? For some families they are, and for other families cash transfers are just as effective. To see why look at Figure 6-18, where food stamps lead to a "kinked" budget constraint line. Without food stamps, a family's budget constraint is shown as AB. Then, with vouchers that can only be spent on food, but which do not change the price of food or other products the family consumes, the budget constraint becomes ACDE. Why? Since food-stamp recipients must pay some fraction of the value of the food stamps they receive -- say $100 for coupons that will buy $150 worth of food -- part of the original budget constraint line does not change. At most, for example, the family can still spend a maximum of OA for non-food items, and the range AC shows that if the family chooses to buy so many non-food items that it can not afford the food stamps, it will stay on its original budget constraint schedule. But, if it reduces its non-food expenditures sufficiently to buy the food stamps, its effective income *in this range* shifts out to segment DE.

Consumers whose preferences are such that their indifference curve is tangent within segment AC of the budget constraint line may not be helped by the food stamp program, but clearly would be by a direct cash transfer of $50, which would shift the *entire* budget constraint line outward and to the right. Consumers whose indifference curves are tangent to a point on segment DE will be just as well off with the food stamp vouchers as they would be with the cash transfer. Finally, as shown by comparing indifference curves I_2 and I_3, a consumer with a tangency point directly at point D could be better off with the cash transfer than with the food stamps.

Given this general, though somewhat qualified, superiority of cash transfers to food stamp vouchers, why are food stamps more commonly used? Partly, no doubt, because food producers are more interested in supporting food stamps than general cash transfers. Perhaps more fundamental, though, is a deep-seated distrust many taxpayers and politicians have about low-income families' and individuals' abilities to spend the cash transfers wisely, which really means the way these taxpayers and politicians would like them to spend it. That argument may make some sense if we consider a person whose income is low because of chronic problems such as alcoholism or drug addiction. But it is far more troubling if we think of a poor family that wants to cut back sharply on its spending on food to buy more reliable cars or better appliances, housing, or education, which often represent the means to break what many observers have described as the vicious circle of poverty. Vouchers for education or other products that entail external benefits, which economists often support, are one thing. Vouchers for food are, perhaps, something else again -- especially if you believe most low-income families can decide how to spend their income on food and other products more wisely than policy makers in Washington can decide that for them.

Figure 6-18
Cash Transfers vs. Food Stamp Vouchers

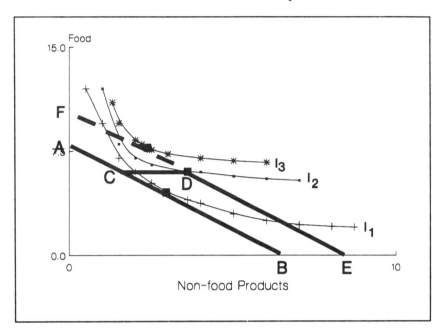

The shift in the budget constraint line from AB to ACDE represents the qualified increase in income provided by food stamps. A family whose indifference curve is tangent to the new budget constraint schedule at point D or on segment AC would be able to reach a higher indifference curve, I_3, if the government provided a direct cash transfer equal in dollar value to the food stamp subsidy. That would extend the budget constraint to FE, including the dashed line DF. For families with an indifference curve tangent along segment DE, the food-stamp and cash-transfer programs are equally effective.

Chapter Summary

1) Individuals and households derive satisfaction, or *UTILITY*, by consuming scarce goods and services. *MARGINAL UTILITY* is the satisfaction gained or lost by consuming one more or one less unit of a product. The *TOTAL UTILITY* derived from the consumption of a product is equal to the sum of the marginal utilities associated with each unit of the product consumed.

2) If all products were subject to the law of diminishing marginal utility and consumers could easily and accurately use precise quantitative measures of the marginal utility they derive from consuming each of the products they use, it would be easy to establish that the law of demand is firmly grounded in the process of utility maximization and rational consumer choice. However, because these assumptions are both extreme and limiting, economists have developed the more general functions used in *INDIFFERENCE CURVE* analysis to study the process of consumer choice that underlies market demand schedules.

3) Taking the total area under the demand curve up to the level of output being consumed provides a dollar measure of the value consumers place on the total utility they derive from this consumption. This measure of economic value in use may well be greater than an estimate of the market value of this level of output --

measured by multiplying the market price for the product times the quantity consumed -- because value in use also includes the area of consumer surplus.

4) To maximize the total utility derived from the consumption of two goods, A and B, consumers must set

$$\frac{MU_A}{P_A} = \frac{MU_B}{P_B}$$

This suggests that when the price of a product changes, the resulting change in the quantity of the product demanded, and therefore the price elasticity of demand for this product, will depend on how quickly the marginal, not total, utility for the product changes as the level of consumption is adjusted.

5) Indifference curve analysis is built around *BUDGET CONSTRAINT LINES* and indifference curves. The former reflect a consumer's income and the relative prices of the products he or she consumes. The latter depict the different combinations of two goods that will provide a consumer with equal levels of total utility.

6) Changes in income and product prices result in shifts in budget constraint lines. Changes in the quantity of products consumed result in either shifts to higher or lower indifference curves, or movements along the same indifference curve, depending on whether the consumer's total utility increases, decreases, or remains constant.

7) Indifference curves are negatively sloped, bowed in (convex) toward the origin, and cannot intersect. The negative slope and non-intersection characteristics result from assuming that products the consumer views as goods are shown on the axes, and that consumers will prefer more of these good to less. The bowed-in shape of indifference curves reflects the assumption of a *DIMINISHING MARGINAL RATE OF SUBSTITUTION* between the two goods.

8) The *MARGINAL RATE OF SUBSTITUTION (MRS)* between two goods is the measure of how much of one product the consumer would be willing to give up to acquire one more unit of the other product, holding total utility constant. The MRS is therefore determined by moving along an indifference curve, and reflects the slope of that curve at those consumption levels for the two products. We assume that if a consumer already has a lot of one good and not much of the other, he or she will require a lot more of the already abundant good to be willing to forgo another unit of the product that is being consumed in relatively small quantities.

9) Consumers maximize utility subject to their budget constraints at the consumption level where an indifference curve is just tangent to the budget constraint line. At any other point on the budget constraint, the consumer is using too much of one good and not enough of the other. At points inside the budget constraint line, total utility can be increased by consuming more of both goods. Indifference curves that lie entirely above the budget constraint line represent even higher levels of satisfaction, but are currently unattainable.

10) Indifference curve analysis can be used to derive an individual's demand curve for a product by showing a change in the price of one good through a shift in the budget constraint line, and the resulting change in the quantity of the product demanded as the consumer moves to a new equilibrium position on a different indifference curve.

11) Indifference curve analysis can be used to separate the income and substitution effects associated with a change in the price of a product. Doing this confirms that these effects are reinforcing for normal goods; offsetting, with the substitution effect dominating, for inferior goods; and offsetting, with the income effect dominating, for Giffen goods.

12) (Case Study #8) Indifference curve analysis has been used to evaluate the comparative effectiveness of different kinds of government assistance programs to low-income families. Economists usually favor direct cash transfers as the most cost-efficient way of providing such assistance, and favor vouchers tied to purchases of specific products over subsidies that change the relative price of food or other products these families purchase.

Review and Discussion Questions

1) Do you derive satisfaction from activities that do not involve the consumption of goods and services? If so, can you still express some kind of relationship between the marginal and total utilities associated with your participation in these activities?

2) Using the procedures presented in our discussion of Table 6-1, what kind of demand schedule would you observe for a good that is characterized by increasing marginal utility over the entire range of output levels an individual can afford to consume?

3) Use Figure 6-3 to describe at least one circumstance under which Nero would have financially gained by burning Rome. What are the estimates of value in use and value in exchange as shown in this graph, before and after the fire?

4) The marginal utility schedules for the two individuals shown in Figure 6-4 are given below. Show that total utility from their consumption of this product is equal before and after the changes in quantity demanded shown in Figure 6-4.

Consumer #1		Consumer #2	
Units Consumed	Marginal Utility	Units Consumed	Marginal Utility
1	20	1	54
2	19	2	37
3	18	3	25
4	17	4	10.2
5	16	5	4.8
6	15	6	4.4
7	14	7	4.3
8	12	8	4.2
9	11	9	4.1
10	10	10	4

5) Estimate your spending on two non-complementary goods -- e.g., fast food and magazines, or soft drinks and gasoline -- for a week or two. Pick products that you will typically buy several units of over this time period. Using the average price you pay for these products and the total amount you spend for them, construct a budget constraint line. Then, as carefully and honestly as you can, try to draw your own indifference curve for these products that would be tangent to this budget constraint line. From this, do you think your actual spending decisions maximized your utility? Explain.

6) Using the schedules developed in question #5, above, show how a 50% increase or decrease in the price of one product would affect your consumption of both products.

7) Show how a positively sloped indifference curve violates the assumption that consumers prefer "more to less" of the goods shown on these axes.

8) Draw an indifference curve that violates the assumption of a diminishing marginal rate of substitution. Explain carefully how the schedule you draw violates this assumption.

9)   At point A in Figure 6-11, is $\dfrac{MU_f}{P_f}$ greater than, equal to, or less than $\dfrac{MU_c}{P_c}$?

10) Based on the indifference curve analysis you studied in this chapter, is the law of demand theoretically or empirically based? Using the schedules you developed in question #6, above, plot two points on your demand curve for the product which you showed experiencing a price change.

11) Given a decrease in the price of Good A, how will income and substitution effects influence the quantity of the product a consumer demands if she views it as a) a normal good, b) an inferior good, and C) a Giffen good?

12) (Case Study #8) After reading the case study, what general mix of price subsidies, food-stamp vouchers, and direct income transfers do you favor as a means of assisting low-income families? Why? How do the public choice issues discussed in Chapter 5 come into play in setting public policies in these areas?

Chapter 7
Short-run Production and Costs

In This Chapter...

we begin our investigation of key factors that lie behind supply schedules, and several other features of business behavior. Specifically, we describe how firms establish the cost of producing different quantities of output, based on their short-run production schedules and prices for inputs. Together with competitive forces, which are studied in later chapters, these production costs strongly influence a firm's decisions concerning how much output to produce and offer for sale at different prices.

Production Schedules

To derive its supply schedule, a firm must first consider its best available production technology. That is, it must find how to produce different levels of output using the fewest scarce resources. In this section, we consider short-run situations in which the firm uses one variable input and at least one fixed input. The total, marginal, and average product schedules that are found under that setting all reflect the law of diminishing marginal returns, which was briefly introduced in Chapter 1. Production schedules with two variable inputs are discussed in Chapter 8, and long-run production decisions are presented in Chapter 10.

Total Product

Just as patterns of rational consumer choice underlie the law of demand, the processes of production and competition underlie the law of supply. Defining these two terms suggests quite clearly why this is so: *PRODUCTION* is simply using economic resources to make goods and services for consumers, or for other businesses and organizations. *COMPETITION* is any action intended to promote one party's interests over another's, whenever two or more individuals or organizations are attempting to acquire the same scarce resources. Producers compete with other producers trying to sell similar or identical products; consumers compete with other consumers trying to buy similar or identical products. Producers deciding what quantity of output to supply at various prices must be concerned both with the costs of their own production activities, and with the output levels they expect their competitors to produce and sell.

Different features of production and competition are incorporated into economic models that try to explain and predict market supply forces, and the behavior of individual firms and industries. Economists use the term *FIRM* to describe any kind of business organization, including corporations, partnerships and sole proprietorships. An *INDUSTRY* is any group of firms producing identical, or highly similar, products.

Some economists' work on production and supply issues focuses on literally fundamental and often debated questions, such as why firms exist at all, and what they try to maximize. Those questions are introduced in Case Study #10, at the end of this chapter, and considered further in several later chapters. Other questions about the roles firms play in the United States and other modern economies are more down to earth, and at least partly empirical in nature. For example, in Case Study #9 we show how economists approach the question of whether *PROFITS* earned by U.S. firms, and in particular by the largest industrial firms, are unreasonably high.

But all of these discussions build on the key facts and relationships presented in the body of this chapter. In particular, we know that all firms are in the business of producing goods or services. They do this using productive resources that must be purchased or leased in some broad sense, entailing different kinds of costs. And in the short run, a firm's cost schedules are tied to its production schedules in a predictable, and even determinate, way.

Understanding this will soon help you see how firms reach basic supply decisions -- deciding what output levels to produce when facing different prices for their products -- although those results cannot be fully presented until you have looked at the process of competition as well as issues of production and cost. You must also understand the differences in the ways economists and accountants (who prepare the "raw data" on these concepts) define and measure profits and costs. Those differences are explained later in this chapter.

But the first point for you to see is that the costs of producing different levels of outputs depend on input prices and production technologies. To establish that point, we must look at several basic economic relationships, beginning with a production schedule that is similar to the one you saw briefly in Chapter 1.

Figure 7-1 illustrates a typical short-run *TOTAL PRODUCT SCHEDULE* for a firm, which shows how many units of a good or service a firm can produce by using different quantities of a variable input and some level of a fixed input or inputs. The table in Figure 7-1 is a short-run production schedule because at least one input (in this case capital) is fixed. The specific values on the total product schedule are, once again, easiest to explain by considering the marginal contribution of each unit of the variable input, in this case labor.

Marginal Product

As you saw in Chapter 1, marginal product schedules show the change in total output associated with a one-unit change in the variable input. So, for example, the marginal product of the fifth worker shows how much more will be produced when five workers are hired rather than four. The formula for the marginal product of labor is, therefore:

$$MP_L = \frac{\Delta TP}{\Delta L}$$

Read this equation as "the marginal product of labor equals the change in total product divided by the change in the number of units of labor employed." Figure 7-2 shows a marginal product schedule in tabular and graphic form.

This marginal product schedule is consistent with the law of diminishing marginal returns, which you first encountered in Chapter 1. Here, however, marginal product rises for a time (through the third worker) before it declines. That often happens in the initial range of production schedules, as the advantages of specialization and the division of labor outweigh the effects of spreading the fixed input across a larger number of workers, or whatever the variable input may be. (If your "product" is a unique person, such as a movie star or a scientific or engineering genius, even labor may represent a fixed input, while capital goods such as movie cameras, computers or laboratories are variable inputs.) Eventually, however, as each variable input has less and less of the fixed input to work with, diminishing returns set in and the marginal product of the variable input decreases. Marginal product may even become negative at some point, if the variable inputs are so crowded in relation to the fixed input that they get in each others' way and reduce total production. Of course, no sensible employer will voluntarily pay to employ that many units of the variable input. For that reason, the range in which marginal product is negative is often described as an uneconomic region of the production schedule.

Figure 7-1
The Total Product Schedule

Units of Capital (for Other Fixed Inputs)	Units of Labor (or Other Variable Inputs)	Total Product (Q)
10	0	0
10	1	10
10	2	25
10	3	45
10	4	60
10	5	70
10	6	75
10	7	77
10	8	77
10	9	75
10	10	70

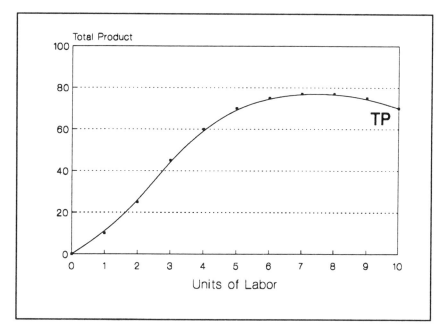

The total product graph above shows the relationship between a variable input, labor, and the quantity of a good or service produced in a given period of time. The presence of a fixed input, in this example capital, indicates that this is a short-run production schedule. In the long run, a firm has enough time to change the level of all inputs.

Figure 7-2
The Marginal Product Schedule

Units of Labor	Total Product	Marginal Product of Labor
0	0	--
1	10	10
2	25	15
3	45	20
4	60	15
5	70	10
6	75	5
7	77	2
8	77	0
9	75	-2
10	70	-5

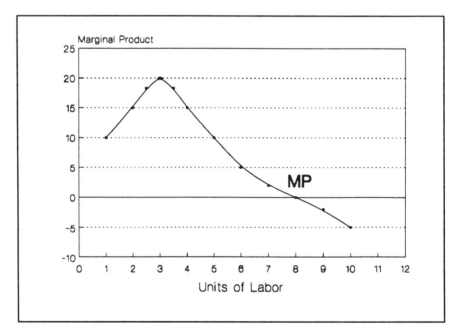

From the total product schedule shown in Figure 7-1 and repeated here, a marginal product schedule is derived that shows how much total product changes when one more or one less unit of a variable input is employed. Total product for any employment level is therefore the sum of the marginal product values for each of those units. For example, if five units of labor are hired, total product is equal to the sum of the marginal product values for the first five workers.

It is important for you to note here exactly how the marginal and total product schedules are linked together. As long as the marginal product of labor is increasing (through the third worker), total product increases at an increasing rate. While the marginal product is positive but decreasing (from the third to the eighth worker), total product still increases, but at a decreasing rate. When marginal product falls to zero (at the eighth worker), the total product schedule "flattens out" at its maximum level. And when marginal product becomes negative (beginning with the ninth worker), total product begins to fall. This is reviewed graphically in Figure 7-3.

Figure 7-3
The Relationship Between Total and Marginal Product

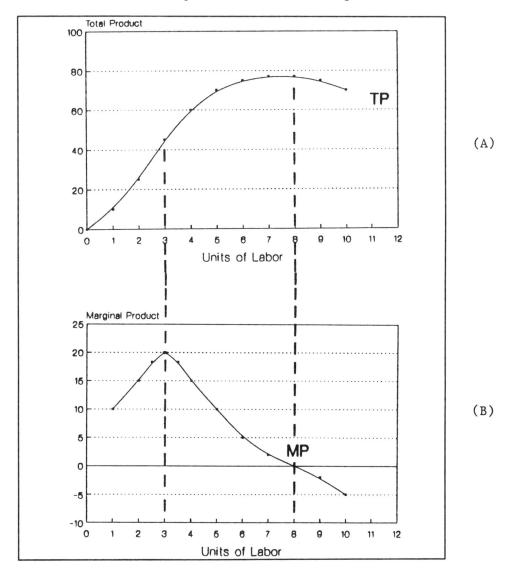

The total product schedule shown in Figure 7-1 is shown again here (top panel), together with the marginal product of labor curve (lower panel) that leads to the total product curve.

As up to three units of labor are employed, marginal product increases and total product increases at an increasing rate. When more than three but fewer than eight units of labor are employed, the marginal product of labor is positive but decreasing, so total product rises at a decreasing rate. When more than eight workers are hired, total product falls because the marginal product of labor becomes negative. We will not show this last, uneconomic, region of the production schedule again, since firms will not knowingly and voluntarily pay to hire these resources.

Average Product

You've probably been calculating averages in math classes since the sixth grade, so this particular production schedule won't come as any great surprise. The *AVERAGE PRODUCT* of labor, or of any other variable input, is found simply by dividing total product by the number of units of the variable input used to produce it. For example, when 5 workers are hired and 70 units of output are produced, the average product of the 5 workers is 14 units of output. So, using labor as the variable input, the formula for average product is:

$$AP = \frac{TP}{L}$$

A more subtle and important relationship in economics is the direct linkage between marginal and average product schedules. Here, and for any other marginal and average schedules discussed in later chapters, the key point to note is that an average value rises whenever the marginal value is greater than the average, and falls whenever the marginal is lower than the average. To see why, let's look at a mildly exaggerated example.

Suppose we calculate the average height of students in your economics class, which turns out to be 5'8". Then, suppose one more student walks into the classroom, and we recalculate the average. This time it is 6'10". Assuming the calculations were done correctly, what do we know about this "marginal" student who increases the average height so much? We know the basketball team probably has a new player, because this person is, to say the least, extremely tall. But the key point is that the average class height increased because the marginal height was greater than the average. If one of the munchkins from *The Wizard of Oz* had walked in instead, the marginal value would have been less than the average, and as a result the average would have decreased.

Figure 7-4 shows this relationship between marginal and average values graphically, in terms of the marginal and average products of units of labor. In fact, the total product curve first shown in Figure 7-1, the marginal product curve first shown in Figure 7-2, and the average product shown in this figure are all directly related. Given the numerical values for any one of these curves, it is an easy matter to derive the other schedules in this family of production curves, as suggested in the table included in Figure 7-4. In the following sections, we will use these production curves to derive the related group of cost curves that firms can use in calculating profits and in determining their supply decisions.

In terms of general patterns of increasing or decreasing values, remember that all of these short-run schedules are driven by the law of diminishing marginal returns, which results because at least one input in the production process is fixed.

Cost Schedules

Given information on input prices, it is a simple matter to convert production schedules into cost schedules and curves. The simplest case, which is presented here, is to assume that a firm or industry's hiring levels are small enough, relative to the total markets for its inputs, to have no effect on the input prices. Under that setting, and using the production functions from the first section of this chapter, it will be clear that the general shapes of short-run total cost, marginal cost, average total cost, and average variable cost curves are also determined by the law of diminishing marginal returns.

Total, Variable, and Fixed Costs

How much will it cost a firm to produce a specific level of output in the short run? Given the production technologies and schedules we discussed above, that all depends on what the firm must pay for the inputs -- fixed and variable -- it uses in undertaking that production. In this chapter, we will make the simplifying assumption (which is true for many firms) that the price of those inputs is not affected by whatever level the firm chooses to purchase or hire. In other words, the overall markets for labor, capital, and other inputs are too large to be significantly affected by this one firm. We will look at cases where this assumption does not hold true in Chapter 15.

Figure 7-4
A Family of Production Schedules

Labor	Total Product	Marginal Product	Average Product
0	0	--	--
1	10	10	10
2	25	15	12.5
3	45	20	15
4	60	15	15
5	70	10	14
6	75	5	12.5
7	77	2	11

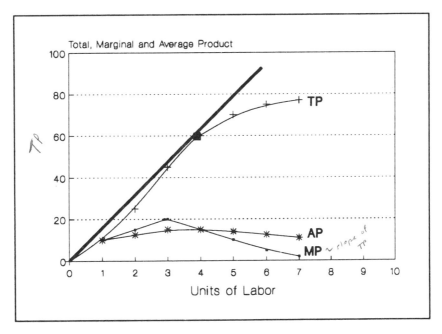

The average product schedule rises as long as marginal product is greater than average product, and falls when marginal product is less than average product. Therefore, marginal product must cut through the average product curve at its maximum point, as shown in the table and graph above. Note too that at this output level a straight line from the origin is just tangent to the total product schedule. The slope of such a ray from the origin to the total product schedule indicates the average contribution of each input unit used to produce that level of output -- i.e., the average rate of rise over run from the origin to the point on the total product schedule. The slopes of such rays increase over the range where 0-4 workers are employed, and decline beyond that point. The slope is therefore maximized when this ray is tangent (from above) to the TP curve, in this case when four workers are hired.

208

For now, suppose that the price for each unit of labor that a firm hires is $10 a unit (for the relevant time period in the production schedule first shown in Figure 7-1 -- which might be an hour, day or week, etc.). Then, if we say that the firm must pay $25 for its fixed input(s) over this same time period, we find the *TOTAL COST (TC)* schedule for these output levels that is shown in Figure 7-5.

Figure 7-5
The Total Cost Schedule

Capital	Labor	Total Product	Fixed Cost (Cost of Capital) +	Variable Cost (Cost of Labor) =	Total Cost
10	0	0	$25	$ 0	$25
10	1	10	25	10	35
10	2	25	25	20	45
10	3	45	25	30	55
10	4	60	25	40	65
10	5	70	25	50	75
10	6	75	25	60	85
10	7	77	25	70	95

TC = FC + VC

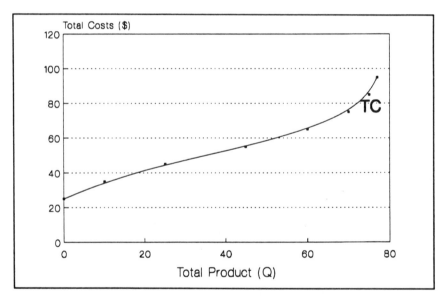

The total cost graph plots the total cost and total product (i.e., output) columns shown in the table above. It is assumed that the firm pays $25 for its fixed capital input in this time period, regardless of the output level it chooses to produce. It pays $10 for each unit of labor it chooses to employ. Total cost is equal to the sum of fixed cost and variable cost, and increases as output rises because the firm must hire more units of the variable input to increase production levels.

You can also see from the information provided in Figure 7-5 that total cost (TC) can be easily broken down into two smaller categories, fixed costs (FC) and variable costs (VC). In other words, algebraically,

$$TC = FC + VC$$

FIXED COSTS are those that do not vary as the output or production level is increased or decreased. *VARIABLE COSTS* are those that do change with the level of output; in the short run they always rise as output levels are increased. In fact, since fixed costs are a constant value, if we subtract fixed cost from total cost we find that the variable cost curve looks just like the total cost curve, but begins and remains at a lower level. The vertical distance between the two curves is, of course, determined by the amount of a firm's fixed costs. This is shown in Figure 7-6.

Figure 7-6
Total, Variable, and Fixed Costs

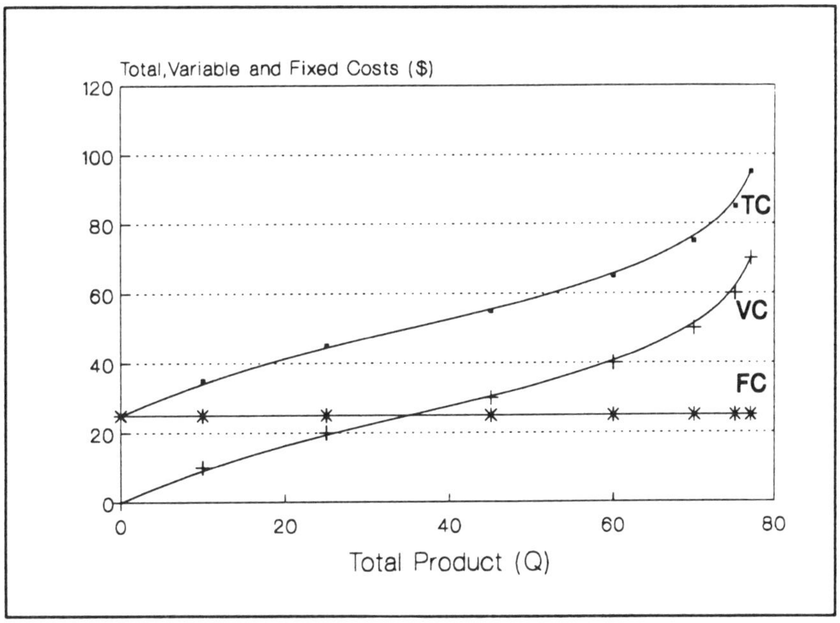

Subtracting a constant value representing fixed cost (FC) from total cost (TC) provides a schedule for variable cost (VC) that is parallel to and below the total cost schedule. Here, as in Figure 7-5, fixed cost is assumed to be $25; variable and total costs both rise as the level of output is increased by hiring more units of variable inputs.

Marginal Cost

The change in total cost associated with a one-unit change in the level of total output is known as the *MARGINAL COST* of production. Algebraically this means

$$MC = \frac{\Delta TC}{\Delta Q}$$

Marginal cost values can't be determined precisely from the tabular data in Figure 7-5, since the changes in output associated with hiring one more or one less unit of labor are greater than one unit of final product. However, we can get an approximate value for marginal cost by dividing the change in total cost by the change in the number of units produced. And more precisely, we can use the total cost graph to derive marginal cost, by taking the change in total cost for each additional unit of output. That is, in fact, simply the slope of the total cost schedule as we increase or decrease output by one unit. Plotting those values give us the graph of the marginal cost schedule shown in Figure 7-7. Over the initial range in which total cost increases at a decreasing rate, marginal cost is positive but declining. Then, when total cost begins to increase at an increasing rate, marginal cost is positive and rising.

Figure 7-7
Marginal Cost

Labor	Total Product	Total Cost	Marginal Cost $= \frac{\Delta TC}{\Delta TP} = \frac{\Delta TC}{\Delta Q}$
0	0	$25	$ ----
1	10	35	1.00
2	25	45	.67
3	45	55	.50
4	60	65	.67
5	70	75	1.00
6	75	85	2.00

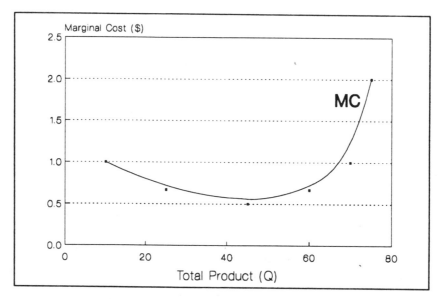

The table above shows a numerical *approximation* of marginal cost, found by dividing the change in total cost by the change in the number of units of total product while moving down each row of the table. More precisely, by examining the slope of the short-run total cost schedule (shown in Figures 7-5 and 7-6), we know that initially marginal cost is positive but decreasing, over the output range in which total cost rises at a decreasing rate. At higher levels of output, total cost begins to increase at an increasing rate, which means that marginal cost is positive and increasing. The approximations of marginal cost shown in the table above also confirm that pattern.

AVERAGE FIXED COST (AFC) is equal to fixed cost divided by the total level of output, and since fixed cost is a constant value, AFC becomes smaller and smaller as output is increased. *AVERAGE VARIABLE COST (AVC)* and *AVERAGE TOTAL COST (ATC)* are "U-shaped" curves that decrease as long as marginal cost lies below them, and rise once marginal cost cuts through their minimum values. Summarizing the algebraic expressions for these schedules, we have

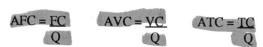

$$AFC = \frac{FC}{Q} \qquad AVC = \frac{VC}{Q} \qquad ATC = \frac{TC}{Q}$$

Numerical and graphical examples of these schedules are presented in Figure 7-8.

Figure 7-8
Average and Marginal Cost Schedules ✳ *Important* ✳

Total Product	Fixed Cost	Variable Cost	Total Cost	AFC	AVC	ATC
0	$25	$ 0	$25	$ ---	$ ---	$ ---
10	25	10	35	2.50	1.00	3.50
25	25	20	45	1.00	.80	1.80
45	25	30	55	.56	.67	1.22
60	25	40	65	.42	.67	1.08
70	25	50	75	.36	.71	1.07
75	25	60	85	.33	.80	1.13

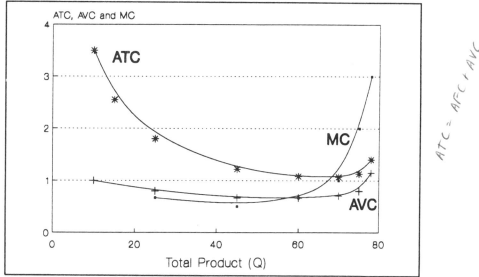

ATC = AFC + AVC

Dividing the fixed cost, variable cost, and total cost schedules developed in Figures 7-5 and 7-6 by the level of output results in the average fixed cost, average variable cost, and average total cost schedules and graphs shown above. Average total cost (ATC) is equal to average fixed cost (AFC) + average variable cost (AVC), allowing for slight rounding errors. The AVC *and* ATC lines must fall as long as marginal cost (MC) lies below them, but rise after MC passes through their minimum points and lies above them. AVC becomes ever closer to ATC as the output level increases, because AFC always declines as output is increased.

Graphically Linking Production and Cost Schedules

To drive home the point that both short-run production and cost curves are primarily influenced by the law of diminishing returns, in this section we juxtapose the total product and total cost curves, the marginal product and marginal cost curves, and the average product and average variable cost curves.

Total Product and Total Cost

We will now formalize the relationships between various production and cost schedules, which you may have already begun to see, beginning with the total product and total cost curves. Each of these two schedules is really an inverted image of the other because both schedules are driven by the same economic force, the law of diminishing marginal returns.

When total product rises at an increasing rate, total costs *must* rise at a decreasing rate. In this range, a firm gets more additional output each time it hires one more worker, even though it doesn't have to pay any more to hire the second or third worker than it did to hire the first. Although total costs are rising as the firm hires more workers to increase output, *on a per unit basis* output costs initially fall because the average productivity of the first few workers increases as more workers are hired.

Increases in the marginal product of labor over this range result from specialization and the division of labor, not from differences in workers' effort or skills that would lead to differences in their wages. Similarly, it is the law of diminishing returns, not lesser skill and enthusiasm of employees, that eventually causes productivity to fall as output is increased, so long as at least one factor of production is fixed.

After entering the range of diminishing returns, total product increases at a decreasing rate; therefore, total cost increases at an increasing rate. Each additional unit of output that the firm produces in this range requires more labor, and therefore costs more to produce, than the previous unit of output. To summarize, then, the total cost schedule looks the way it does because the total product schedule looks the way it does, which is to say *because* of diminishing returns. This is shown in Figure 7-9.

Marginal Product and Marginal Cost

The marginal product and marginal cost curves tell exactly the same story about the relationship between production and cost functions that you have just seen in reviewing the total product and total cost schedules. Of course, since we can derive marginal schedules from totals, or *vice versa*, that's not surprising. But it should help you visualize and remember these key relationships to note, explicitly, that marginal costs are falling when (actually *because*) marginal product is rising. This is, as you have already seen, the range of increasing returns to the variable input. But once diminishing returns set in, marginal product decreases and marginal cost increases. Therefore, marginal product and marginal cost schedules are also inverted images of each other, as shown in Figure 7-10.

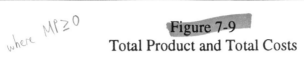

Figure 7-9

Total Product and Total Costs

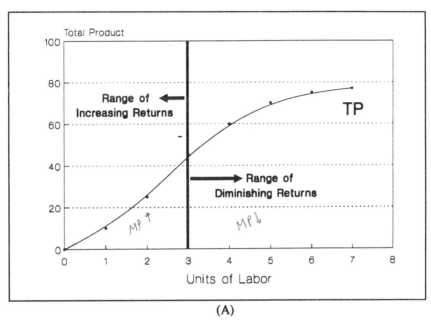

(A)

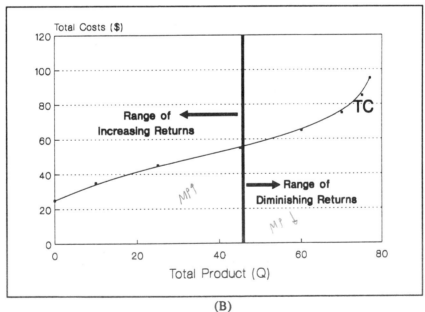

(B)

The total product curve shown in panel (A) reproduces the schedule developed in Figure 7-1; panel (B) reproduces the total cost curve derived in Figure 7-5. Before diminishing returns set in total product increases at an increasing rate, so total costs rise at a decreasing rate. After diminishing returns are encountered total product rises at a decreasing rate, which causes total cost to rise at an increasing rate. Note that the diminishing returns begin at the same level of output (TP = 45) on both graphs.

Figure 7-10
Marginal Product and Marginal Cost

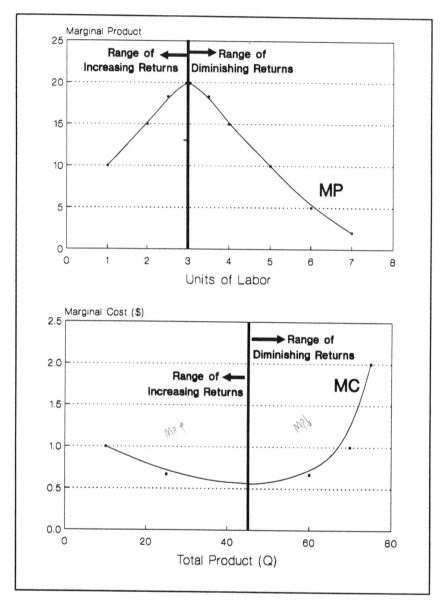

The marginal product and marginal cost curves shown above were first presented in Figures 7-2 and 7-7, respectively. Viewing the two graphs together, you can see that the level of total output where marginal product begins to decrease (equal to the *sum* of the marginal products for the first three units of labor) is the same level of output at which marginal cost begins to increase. At that point, diminishing marginal returns set in.

Average Product and Average Variable Cost

The short-run average product and average variable cost schedules are, once again, inverted images of each other; and both are driven by diminishing marginal returns. As you saw earlier, the average total cost schedule has the same general "U-shape" as average variable cost, again because of diminishing returns. The minimum point on the average total cost schedule will, however, occur at a somewhat higher level of output than the minimum point on the average variable cost curve (or the maximum point on the average product schedule), because it is influenced by fixed as well as variable costs. This is shown in Figure 7-11.

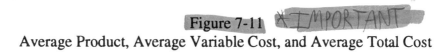

Figure 7-11   ✗ IMPORTANT

Average Product, Average Variable Cost, and Average Total Cost

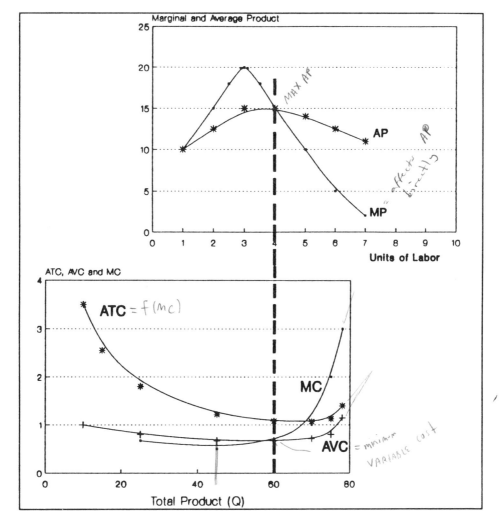

The relationship between marginal product and average product shown panel (A) was developed in Figure 7-4; the family of cost curves shown in panel (B) was presented in Figure 7-8. Note here that the minimum point on the average variable cost schedule occurs at the same level of total output as the maximum point on the average product curve, since the shape and position of both curves is determined by the law of diminishing returns (plus, for cost curves, the assumption of fixed prices for inputs). The minimum point on the average total cost schedule occurs at a somewhat higher level of total output due to the influence of average fixed cost, which declines as output increases even in the range of diminishing returns.

Costs ? / input (C.E.L.L.)

profits

216

You can once again see the relationships between the marginal and average values for both production and cost schedules in this Figure, which were discussed and shown earlier. The role of diminishing marginal returns is easiest to see in the two curves showing the marginal product and marginal cost values; but of course we can derive both total and average schedules from those respective marginal curves, or *vice versa*. The key point to see, in other words, is that diminishing returns literally shapes all of these schedules and graphs.

Special Features of Economic Costs

While you have seen the general relationships that influence basic cost schedules in the last two sections, you probably do not know that economists' definition of cost is different, in several respects, from that used by accountants, businesses, and most other people. In particular, economists focus on the general idea of opportunity costs, which include implicit as well as explicit costs; but they also point out that historical or 'sunk' costs are irrelevant in making decisions about the current best use of economic resources. Their different understanding of cost also leads them to distinguish between two types of profits -- normal profits and economic profits. Most surprisingly, at least to some, economists consider normal profits as a cost of staying in business, and a return for accepting risks.

Explicit vs. Implicit Costs

(accounting)

If you want to hurt economists' feelings, remind them of the joke that defines economists as the one group of people who don't have enough personality to be accountants.

Actually, economists and accountants do have many things in common, including a keen interest in firms' production costs and the impact of those costs on profits. Most of the business data economists work with is, in fact, originally compiled by accountants who follow the "standard accounting practices" referred to in every corporate annual report. But economists sometimes revise that data, or look at it from a different perspective than accountants do, because the economic meaning and function of profits and costs are not always the same as they are in accounting.

The distinction between explicit and implicit costs is one such case. *EXPLICIT COSTS* are those which a person or business pays out directly, usually after receiving some kind of statement or invoice. Expenditures for raw materials, workers, or the repayment of loans are all examples of explicit costs.

IMPLICIT COSTS, on the other hand, are those incurred by business owners even though they don't receive a written bill for some resource, and may never write out a check or transfer cash to cover these cost. The standard example of an implicit cost is a business owner -- say a farmer -- who leaves a paying job to run the new business. We'll assume the annual salary in the original job is $20,000. So, at the end of the first year of farming, after paying all explicit costs for seed grain, fertilizer, etc., suppose there is $30,000 "left over." Is that residual money all profit? An economist would say no, counting the $20,000 that could have been earned working for someone else as an implicit cost of running the farm.

Any business owner's time and labor has an opportunity cost -- in this case the $20,000 that could have been earned working for someone else or, more generally, the highest forgone alternative use of this person's time at a comparable level of risk. Therefore, profits in this example are really $10,000, assuming that any other implicit costs have already been subtracted from revenues. And, if the farmer's former employer offered a large enough raise in his or her old job, say to $35,000, the farmer would now be facing an economic loss in continuing to work as a farmer. On the other hand, if someone offered our farmer $100,000 a year to work in a life-threatening job, such as being the human cannon ball in a traveling circus, we would have to adjust that salary to compensate for the higher risk involved to make it truly comparable to the income earned by running the farm.

Sunk Costs

In some cases, accountants see costs where economists don't. We will present a highly stylized example of such a situation here, but don't dismiss it lightly on that account. This idea has an important role in several upcoming chapters (starting with Chapter 9), which discuss output decisions made by firms operating in different kinds of markets. It is also important for consumers to understand the idea of sunk costs, in terms of knowing what costs *not* to consider in making good economic decisions. To begin to see why these costs are so eminently irrelevant in making both production and purchasing decisions, consider the following example.

Suppose an automobile firm pays $1 million for a machine that is custom made to stamp out unique hood ornaments for a new luxury car. Assume too that the machine can't be moved or modified to do anything else, so it has no alternative use. Now, if no one buys these luxury cars, but a market for the hood ornaments does develop and brings in $200,000 a year more than the cost of all other resources used to make them (e.g., labor and raw materials), should the firm do that? Using accounting costs the company's managers might say no, if the average cost for this machine is $250,000 a year based on a useful life of, say, four years. The firm's economist will say yes, however, because the real cost of using the machine is zero, and the $1 million that has already been paid for the machine is a *SUNK COST*.

The firm wouldn't pay $1 million to buy another such machine to make these ornaments, since it only expects to recover $800,000 over its four-year life. But it has already paid for this machine, and it can't re-sell it or use it to make other things, so it will be better off getting $800,000 than nothing. We'll assume the economist convinces the firm to make the ornaments and gets a raise, and the managers who were misled by using accounting costs are fired because of their bad economics. Remember, we told you it was a stylized story. It does have a moral, however: *sunk costs do not change present or future costs, so they should be ignored in making current decisions about how to use economic resources.*

Economic vs. Accounting Costs

Economists consider both explicit and implicit costs in determining how profitable a firm or specific business project really is. Many accountants have also recognized the value of considering implicit costs in some settings, such as our example of the farmer who formerly worked for someone else. Based solely on financial considerations, neither good economists nor good accountants would advise you to leave your current job to start a new business unless it appeared that the opportunity cost of your forgone salary was going to be fully covered.

In other situations, however, accountants do not, or in some cases cannot, use implicit costs the way economists do. Forgone earnings aren't, for example, an allowable cost of business in calculating profits for tax purposes, or in preparing a corporate annual report. And when implicit costs can't be measured precisely, accountants are more likely than economists to ignore them altogether. On the other hand, tax laws and accounting conventions may lead accountants to treat depreciation costs on a piece of equipment with no alternative use as a business expense, despite the discussion of sunk costs in the previous section. The perspectives of these two disciplines, while usually complementary, can be markedly different on some points.

Economists and accountants disagree most profoundly in their treatment of costs and profits when economists insist on treating some level of profits as a *cost* of doing business. Admittedly, that sounds a little strange when you first hear it. But before you side with the accountants on this point, consider the economists' reasoning.

Normal Profits as an Economic Cost $= (Explicit + Implicit)\ cost$

The resources that are used to run a business during any period of time could be used to do other things. For example, a business owner can always sell the business and put the proceeds in federally insured savings accounts or certificates of deposit, or buy government Treasury bonds. All of these financial instruments are *relatively* risk free -- which is to say much less risky than running most, if not all, businesses -- and they all provide an annual return expressed as some rate of interest. That interest rate represents an opportunity cost for business owners, unless they have other alternatives that would return even more after adjusting for different levels of risk. In any case, if business owners don't expect to earn profits high enough to cover these opportunity costs on very safe investments, at least in most years, they will not risk their resources in these business enterprises.

Accordingly, economists define *NORMAL PROFITS* as the profit level that is just high enough to induce business owners to leave their resources in their current use, without attracting any new net investment in this kind of firm by others. In businesses that are relatively stable and risk-free, such as many grocery chains, local banks, and utility companies, normal profits may be only slightly higher than what the business owners could earn by putting their funds in Treasury bonds or other relatively safe investments. In riskier businesses, such as movie studios, gold mines, start-up firms looking for high-tech breakthroughs, or those engaged in illegal operations, owners must realistically expect low earnings in some years, and even occasional losses. Therefore, they will not invest in such firms unless they expect their *average* annual returns to be higher than those earned by the grocery stores, regional banks and other less-risky businesses. That means normal profits will be higher in riskier industries, on average, to compensate for the expected wider variance in annual performance.

Economists define *EXCESS* or *ECONOMIC PROFITS* as any return greater than normal profits. In the short run, these higher rates of profits signal producers to shift more resources into businesses that provide certain goods and services. In the long run, however, excess profits in an industry can signify that there are barriers to effective competition in those product markets. These theoretical and public policy topics are covered in several later chapters. But you have now seen enough about production, costs, and profits to consider some important questions that concern the owners, managers, employees, and customers of privately owned firms in a market-oriented economy. Several such questions are discussed in the following two case studies.

Case Study #9
The Fortune 500 and Obscene Profits

Every few years, a large corporation or public opinion research group will ask a randomly selected group of people what level of profits American businesses typically earn. The responses always range from lows of 10-15 percent to highs of as much as 50-100 percent, with the average response somewhere between 25 and 40 percent. Most people answering or reading about these surveys don't pay much attention to the question that naturally occurs to economists -- 25-40 percent of what? -- because this is usually presented and reacted to as an emotional issue.

Actually what seems to upset some people most about corporate profits isn't percentage measures, but rather news stories reporting that some large firms have earned hundreds of millions of dollars of profits during the last year, or even part of a year. If these profits are earned by oil companies when fuel prices are rising rapidly or while severe rationing programs are in place, or by manufacturing companies that are closing some of their older factories and laying off long-time employees, public charges of greed, corporate irresponsibility, and obscene profits are never long in coming. Then, in response, some businesses will launch their own public relations campaigns to explain that their profits really aren't as high as people think they are. A few years ago, for example, Texaco commercials featured comedian Bob Hope explaining that oil company profits, like profits for U.S. manufacturing firms in general, averaged about 4 percent for each dollar in sales -- less than you earn on savings accounts at commercial banks. Economists are generally unimpressed with both sides of this particular debate.

When economists look at profits they first see returns for taking risks, which provide incentives to businesses to produce the things that consumers want to buy at the lowest possible cost (i.e., using the fewest possible scarce resources). High profits earned by some firms encourage other producers to enter those industries, or to adopt more effective production technologies. These incentives promote greater competition among firms, which benefits consumers by holding down prices and raising product quality.

From an economic perspective, then, in evaluating whether profits are in fact obscene or made the old-fashioned way, by firms *earning* them, we want to compare profits to some base measure of what the owners of these firms are risking. Some businesses organizations (such as Texaco) suggest using *PROFITS AS A RETURN ON SALES* (revenues) to do this. However, economists prefer to look at profit as a *RETURN ON STOCKHOLDERS' EQUITY*, a lesser-known measure of what stockholders are currently investing or risking in a firm.

When a company *originally* sells ownership shares of common stock to raise financial capital, usually through special institutions known as investment banks, those funds represent the stockholders' initial equity claims against the firm's assets. Similarly, homeowner's equity refers to the part of the value of his or her home that a homeowner has paid for, that is not offset by claims a bank, mortgage company, or other creditor may have against the property.

Note that stockholders' equity is not affected by later sales of stock on what most people refer to as the stock market, because that is a secondary market where one person who owns previously issued stock sells to another person who wants to buy stock. The company which has its stock traded on the New York or American Stock Exchange does not receive the proceeds from those sales, the person who sells the stock does (less a stockbroker's commission for handling the transaction).

But stockholders' equity in a firm *is* affected when the firm incurs losses that lower its equity value, just as a fire would lower the equity a person has in a house that was not fully insured. And conversely, if a firm earns profits and reinvests some of those dollars in the business, it increases stockholders' equity because the dollars that were reinvested were, in fact, the stockholders' funds. To use our homeowner analogy again, this is equivalent to adding to the value of a house by paying for some kind of improvement or expansion of the property, such as a new kitchen or bedroom.

While claims that profits as a return on sales average only four or five percent are quite accurate in an accounting sense, from an economic standpoint this is not a relevant measure of the function of profits -- as a return on risk-taking -- because sales dollars are often not related to business risk in any meaningful way. Consider, for example, a grocery selling canned peas. On average, it earns only one cent of profit on every dollar's worth of peas it sells. Then it uses 99 cents of that sales dollar to go out and buy more peas, which are again sold for a dollar. Over the fiscal year, the grocery repeats this process thousands of times; and at the end of the year it might have sold $100,000 worth of canned peas, earning profits of $1,000 on those sales. But at no time during the year did the grocery risk $100,000 in canned peas. Instead, it turned over its inventory of peas many times, marking up the goods sold by about one percent each time through the process. This is, in fact, what profit as a return on sales measures -- markups over a firm's costs.

In firms that turn their inventories over several times a year, such as grocery stores, it is not at all uncommon to find low markups. But firms that sell a relatively small number of more expensive products each year, such as commercial jets or railroad locomotives, are likely to have higher markups. The return on sales measure of profits varies widely from industry to industry in exactly that way.

The *average* return on sales is just what Bob Hope said it was, four to five percent; but since this doesn't reflect a return on risk, it doesn't provide a good economic measure of profits for all firms. Consequently, firms in industries where the return on sales is relatively low aren't led by higher return on sales figures in other industries to exit their current industry and enter those. It is true, however, that if you are comparing firms *within the same industry*, perhaps in deciding what company's stock you want to buy, for example, the return on sales measure can give you useful information on markups and other aspects of a firm's operating efficiency.

Most importantly, differences in the rate of return on stockholders' equity are related to risk taking, and do signal profit opportunities to investors and firms. High returns lead to additional resources in those markets, and low returns lead to the exit of firms or resources engaged in those production activities. The easiest way to show that is with data on the average returns on sales and stockholders' equity for all U.S. corporations.

Figure 7-12 shows these measures over the past 30 years, together with the interest rates on 10-year Treasury bonds paid over the same period. Comparing profit measures to comparatively risk-free returns on Treasury bonds is in line with the discussion of normal profits as a cost of doing business, provided earlier in this chapter. And you can see in Figure 7-12 that there is a fairly clear relationship between profits as a percentage of stockholders' equity and the rate of return on relatively low-risk government bonds. The return on equity measure is not drastically higher than the return on the Treasury bond -- this measure of profits normally ranges from 10-15 percent, while the interest rates usually fluctuate in the 6-12 percent range. And both of these series track toward the high end of their respective ranges during years of high inflation, and toward the lower end of their ranges when inflation is least severe.

Figure 7-12
Corporate Profits in the U.S. Economy

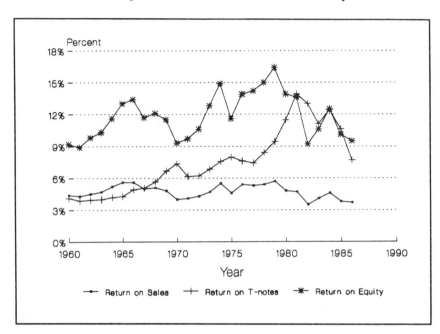

The bottom data series above shows after-tax profits as a return on sales for U.S. corporations. The top series shows after-tax profits as a return on stockholders' equity. The middle series shows, for purposes of comparison, interest rates on 10-year U.S. Treasury bonds. If corporations did not usually earn more with their resources than they could by buying Treasury bonds, they would usually shut down. That is, in fact, another way of showing that profits expressed as a return on sales are not good economic measures of profits for different kinds of businesses.

Source: 1988 *Economic Report of the President.*

You may wonder whether these average profit measures are disproportionately influenced by the large number of relatively small corporations in the U.S. economy. Put differently, are these profit measures much higher for the nation's largest corporations? Not really. As shown in Figure 7-13, average profit measures for *Fortune* magazine's annual list of the 500 largest industrial firms in the U.S. are extremely close to the returns earned by all corporations.

Can it be said, then, based on this data, that most large and small corporations in the United States face competition that is intense enough to hold their profits down to normal profit levels, by keeping prices in line with costs and requiring the use of efficient production techniques? Again, not really, at least based solely on this information. In fact, this is a question which evokes significant disagreement among microeconomists. Some claim that large corporations are so insulated from competition that they do not have to hold their costs down carefully to stay in business, and choose instead to increase salaries, staffs, and other perks at stockholders' expense. But many others argue that competition from U.S. and international firms, and the threat of hostile takeovers and buyouts, do guarantee effective competition -- limiting both corporate profits and management's ability to ignore stockholders' interests.

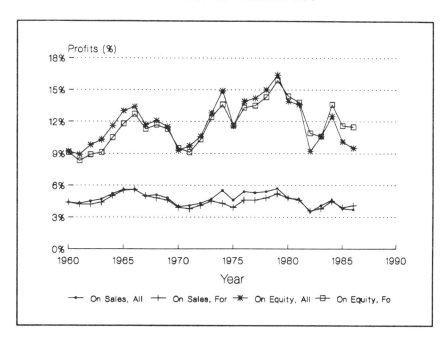

Figure 7-13
Profits for the "Fortune 500"

The top two lines in this graph report median levels of profits as a return on stockholder's equity for the Fortune 500 industrial firms and all U.S. corporations. (Half of the companies included in each series earned profits higher than the median level; half earned lower profits.) The bottom two lines show median levels of profits as a return on sales for the same two groups of firms.

Both pairs of data series show that median profits for the largest 500 industrial corporations in the United States are generally in line with average profits earned by all U.S. corporations. These data also tend to trend together over time, suggesting that they are influenced by the same general factors and economic conditions.

Sources: 1988 *Economic Report of the President* and annual issues of *Fortune* magazine's "Fortune 500" list.

We will return to these issues in later chapters. Here, we want to be sure you understand what profits are, how they are measured and reported, and how high they typically are in the United States. Those are important and interesting topics in their own right, which underlie many of the later discussions in this book on the effective degree of competition in the U. S. economy.

Case Study #10
Competing Theories of the Firm

When Adam Smith wrote what became the first major textbook on economics, in 1776, he discussed two very different kinds of firms. One group included the local butcher, baker, and cobbler shops that thrived at that time, and led many to describe Smith's England as a nation of shopkeepers. These firms were almost always *SOLE PROPRIETORSHIPS*, owned and managed by one person who was individually liable for any debts incurred by the business and who also received all of the profits it earned.

The other kind of businesses Smith discussed, scathingly, were state-chartered monopolies that held an exclusive license to engage in a particular kind of business, or to conduct all trade in a particular area. The largest such company in Smith's time was the British East India Company, which had the royal franchise to carry on the trade between Britain and the spice-rich countries of the East Indies. Such monopolies were usually granted in exchange for payments to the Royal treasury, which was chronically low on funds in this pre-income tax era. Often, though, other kinds of influence, including side payments to ministers in positions of authority, were used to supplement or replace the payments to the Treasury, and guarantee these exclusive rights.

In considering both types of firms -- the shopkeepers and the government-created monopolies -- Smith explained most of their behavior in the marketplace by assuming that owners wanted to maximize profits. That basic assumption was, almost exclusively, what economists used to analyze decisions by firms and predict their behavior for almost 200 years. Even today, it is a key assumption in most such models of firm behavior. With this simplifying assumption, economists are still often able to derive predictions that are detailed enough for the purposes of their studies, and to analyze current public policy questions.

But there can be problems with this one-dimensional way of analyzing firms. For example, treating a small, family-owned restaurant the same way as General Motors doesn't help us explain how and why these firms are different. Why, in other words, are some kinds of businesses (such as law firms) usually organized as sole proprietorships or *PARTNERSHIPS*, while other kinds of firms are usually *CORPORATIONS*. One reason is that owners of sole proprietorships and partnerships are personally responsible for all debts of the business (and receive all of its profits), while stockholders of corporations risk only what they have invested in the firm, even if it declares bankruptcy. These limited liability provisions are undoubtedly attractive to stockholders, but in exchange they give up much of the control of the firm to corporate officers and a board of directors, who are usually selected by the firm's top corporate officers. What do the stockholders stand to lose from this loss of control, if anything?

Similar questions arise which involve more routine features of firms operating in different industries. For example, different kinds of management hierarchies and worker and management compensation packages often appear to be systematically linked to the kind of products firms produce. That is, the technology of producing and selling certain products seems to make certain types of pay and management schemes more effective for these companies. The same factors may also influence managers' objectives for the firm, including how large they would like to see the firm become, and how much they are willing to trade off profits, at least in the short term, to accomplish that growth.

Findings from this line of reasoning provide more details for economists' general body of theory on the decisions firms make internally, not just decisions about how many units of a product to produce and sell in the market at different price levels. And as this is done, the firm becomes less of a mysterious and unexplored "black box" in economic theory, no longer a generic entity that is simply assumed to buy inputs, produce outputs, and maximize profits.

The reasons for this new investigation into the workings of firms are not hard to see. By the 1920s, prominent economists and lawyers were writing about the separation of ownership and control that came with the expanded role of publically held corporations. They anticipated, correctly, that the mass production, capital-intensive methods pioneered by Henry Ford and others would make this kind of corporation increasingly important in the twentieth century, and that the managers of these firms could have some latitude to promote their own interests over those of the stockholders.

This concern led, later, to several *MANAGERIAL THEORIES OF THE FIRM*. In these theories, some economists argued that corporate managers often improve their own salaries, fringe benefits, job security, and reputations by maximizing sales or "market share" instead of profits. Other economists suggested that the managers could best meet these personal goals by maximizing corporate growth, employment, or even expenses. There is, of course, nothing wrong with seeing which of these assumptions provides the best predictions for various firms and industries, and using them accordingly. But from a more narrowly theoretical perspective, all of these single-measure maximization objectives are problematic because they fail to explain why the structure of a particular firm or industry makes it more likely to adopt one of these objectives, or some mix of them.

The most promising work that has begun to provide such explanations has been pioneered by Ronald Coase (the same man who developed the Coase Theorum discussed in Case Study #7) and Oliver Williamson. Over 50 years ago, Coase noted that a key reason why business firms evolve is to lower the transactions costs of production, distribution, and sales. Put simply, he argued that firms can be seen largely as a set of long-term employment agreements, and that an employer hires workers when it becomes too expensive to establish detailed contracts with other firms or sub-contractors who will agree to do a specific task for a set price. Coase believed that a firm's full-time employees agree to provide a certain level of effort in return for some level of compensation. The firm then decides what specific jobs employees will do (subject to agreements with the employees, any applicable union contracts, and labor laws or regulations), without having to negotiate a separate contract for each new task or assignment.

Firms will still choose to continue to use some outside contractors to do specific tasks when it is easy (i.e., not costly) to write such contracts, in part because this does not tie the employer to the same kind of long-term relationship and obligations that it faces with its employees. A firm will also hire outside contractors to do highly specialized tasks when it is too expensive either to train its own workers to do those jobs or to hire workers who are skilled in these tasks on a full-time basis. But hiring employees of its own gives a firm the flexibility to determine what they will do and how long they will do it, without having to write a new contract every time business conditions or production tasks change.

Williamson greatly expanded on this notion of transactions costs as a reason for the existence of firms, to deal with problems of *INCOMPLETE CONTRACTING* and *CREDIBLE COMMITMENTS*. In later chapters, we consider several factors that lead to the problems Williamson sees as lying behind the particular structures adopted by different kinds of firms, as well as the establishment of other kinds of private institutions found in virtually all market economies. Here, a few examples are sufficient to illustrate his general points.

First, consider how shareholders can know whether the corporate officers and board of directors, who supposedly work for them, are doing a good job. That's a more difficult problem in some businesses than in others because of differences in *MONITORING COSTS*. Shareholders in a steel company, for example, can easily determine how much steel the company produced in a given year, what it cost to produce that quantity of steel, how much steel the company sold last year, and how those figures compare to other steel companies. But in a pharmaceutical company that does extensive research on new drugs, managers have much more discretion in choosing what projects to pursue, and comparisons with other research companies are harder to make because they often are doing research on different kinds of drugs or products. Because most new drugs are designed to be unique in some respects, it is far more difficult for shareholders to determine whether expenditures for manager "perks" have been hidden in the costs of the firm's research projects. This will, economists predict, lead shareholders of the drug research firm to design contracts for managers and directors that tie more of their compensation to the value of the firm's earnings or stock prices, or both. And because executives of steel companies have less latitude and are easier to monitor, we would expect more of their payments to be in the form of a base salary. When they do a poor job it is easier for stockholders to discover that and to get rid of them.

In another vein, consider firms that sign contracts with resource owners who can then "hold them up" after the contract is signed. A professional athlete who signs a long-term contract and then decides to withhold some or all services unless he gets more money is one such example. Another is a skyscraper owner who refuses to pay rent to the person who owns the land the skyscraper is built on, knowing that the landowner can no longer use the land for any other purpose. Here, the landowner and the professional sports team do have legal remedies, but those remedies are expensive and time consuming. And once again, the two cases are somewhat different, due to differing monitoring and *ENFORCEMENT COSTS*. Great athletes can often collect their current salary *and* pressure owners to trade them or give them a raise by playing less effectively than they are capable of playing. Owners can complain or even sue the athlete who does this, but that is inevitably a difficult thing to prove in court -- one of the first such suits we know of was brought against baseball player Dave Parker by the Pittsburgh Pirates, after they traded him to another team. The Pirates claimed that Parker's performance was impaired by a drug problem, and sought damages from him based on the difference between an expected performance level and what Parker actually did on the field during the last years he was under contract with the Pirates.

In some of these cases, again, such problems can be at least partly remedied in ways that affect the structure, management, and compensation programs of a firm. Landowners may insist that building developers buy their property, or provide substantial advance payments or escrows, or "cut them in" for a share of the skyscraper's earnings. Owners of professional sports teams can name some superstars as player-managers, build performance-incentive bonuses into the players' contracts, and offer contracts for fewer years.

In general terms, these cases illustrate the near or sometimes literal impossibility of anticipating and allowing for all contingencies in a contract. However, the particular structures adopted by firms will, to some extent, be designed to promote desired performance - i.e., insure a credible commitment -- from employees, managers and other business associates, even in the face of unexpected conditions. What is required to do that varies from firm to firm and from industry to industry. But some general factors are also important -- such as firms' reputations for dealing with customers, workers, and stockholders -- as are other factors that are usually considered non-economic. Along these lines, economists Armen Alchian and Susan Woodward have noted that

> We believe it is important to recognize the forces of ethics, etiquette, and "proper, correct, reasonable, moral, etc." standards of conduct in controlling business relationships.
>
> ...A remote auto repair shop servicing an unlucky traveler whose car's fanbelt has unexpectedly failed might charge far more than the cost of replacing the belt, in order to extract almost the total value of an emergency repair to the unfortunate driver -- the value of the service to a customer in dire straights. Or, imagine an ambulance operator or a doctor charging a price reflecting the value of emergency service to a critically injured person. Not without reason is such behavior condemned. It is wicked and reprobate, and it's inefficient.
>
> If such opportunistic expropriation were expected by travelers, they would travel less, or take expensive safety precautions to avoid expropriation. The avoidance costs would exceed the true cost of providing the emergency service, so that society would incur greater costs if people did not behave "responsibly, fairly, conscientiously and ethically." Whatever the emotive language, "decent" behavior saves resources and enables greater welfare.[1]

The new research on the theory of the firm offers many new insights, and even more questions, to supplement the traditional models and questions economists have asked about businesses and business managers. We will consider several of these new issues in later chapters, after we discuss the traditional models in the next few chapters. The focus in the traditional models is on market and industry-level issues of price and output decisions, building on the standard assumption that firms seek to maximize profits. While you may be inclined to dismiss those models as too simplistic or naively theoretical in orientation, based on what you have read here, that would be a mistake.

As you work through the traditional models, remember that the level of analysis and the questions addressed there are different, in many ways, from what you have read about here. Remember, too, as you saw in Chapter 2, that which set of models you use depends on the kinds of questions you are asking, and the degree of detail you can effectively incorporate into your models. And while the new studies sometimes revise, as well as supplement, the traditional models, the assumption of profit maximization is by no means dead or without its uses. After all, private firms that don't earn sufficient levels of profits don't stay around very long, at least not as the same firm and under the same management. And managers of firms that must maintain "acceptable" levels of profits to stay in business may well find it important to know how to maximize profits, even if that's not precisely what they do all of the time. The bottom line is that both the traditional and new models of the firm are useful and important, in large part because they usually address different, although related, kinds of issues and problems.

Chapter Summary

1) The short-run *TOTAL PRODUCT* schedule shows the relationship between the number of units of variable inputs employed and the quantity of output produced. Because of the law of diminishing marginal returns,

---

[1]"The Firm is Dead; Long Live the Firm," *Journal of Economic Literature*, 26, March 1988, p. 77.

while total product may initially increase at an increasing rate as more units of the variable input are employed, it must eventually rise at a decreasing rate.

2)   The *MARGINAL PRODUCT* of a variable input measures the change in total product associated with the use of one more, or one less, unit of the variable input. As long as marginal product is positive, the total product schedule is increasing. The law of diminishing marginal returns implies that marginal product will eventually decline as more units of the variable input are employed.

3)   The *AVERAGE PRODUCT* of a variable input is found by dividing total product by the number of units of the variable input that are being employed. Average product rises as long as marginal product is greater than average product, and falls once marginal product becomes less than average product.

4)   The *TOTAL COST* schedule shows how much it costs to produce different levels of output, and may be broken down into fixed and variable cost schedules. *FIXED COSTS* are the payments to factors of production that must be used in a constant quantity during the short run. *VARIABLE COSTS* are payments for resources that can be employed in different quantities even in the short run. Fixed costs do not vary as the level of output changes, variable costs do.

5)   *MARGINAL COST* measures the change in total cost associated with a one-unit change in the level of output produced. When marginal cost is positive but decreasing, i.e., in the range of increasing marginal returns, total cost rises at a decreasing rate. In the range of diminishing returns, marginal cost is positive and increasing, so total cost rises at an increasing rate.

6)   Average total, variable, or fixed costs are found by dividing total cost, variable cost, and fixed cost by the number of units of output produced. *AVERAGE FIXED COST* always declines as the level of output increases. *AVERAGE TOTAL COST* and *AVERAGE VARIABLE COST* decline as long as marginal cost is lower than these respective schedules, and increase after marginal costs rise to a level higher than the average cost values. In other words, short-run average total cost and average variable cost schedules are "U-shaped." They initially fall as output increases, but eventually increase due to rising marginal cost values, which occur because of diminishing marginal returns in production.

7)   Assuming fixed input prices, marginal cost falls over the range of output where marginal product is rising, and rises when marginal product begins to fall. Total product and total cost graphs, and average product and average variable cost graphs are, similarly, inverse images of each other. All of these schedules are driven by the law of diminishing marginal returns.

8)   Most production costs, such as payments for raw materials and other resources, are *EXPLICIT COSTS* which require direct monetary payments; but others are not. While accountants must sometimes ignore *IMPLICIT COSTS* faced by individuals and *FIRMS*, which do not entail direct expenditures of money, economists see implicit costs as no less a cost of doing business than explicit costs.

9)   *SUNK COSTS* are historically incurred charges that are not affected by changes in current or future levels of output, and therefore have no bearing on decisions made by firms or individuals concerning the best present uses of economic resources.

10) Some level of *PROFITS* is required to induce business owners to leave resources in their current uses, as compensation for the risk they incur through these investments. *NORMAL PROFITS* are the profit level that is just high enough to do this, without attracting any new net investment to these areas. Normal profits are an economic cost of staying in business, even though accountants do not treat them as costs.

226

11) The level of profits that represents normal profits varies somewhat from *INDUSTRY* to industry, since the *PRODUCTION* of some products is inherently riskier than others. Normal profits are higher in riskier industries. Any profits greater than normal profits are *ECONOMIC OR EXCESS PROFITS*.

12) The economic role of profits is to signal producers what products consumers want to see produced in greater quantities, and to compensate successful and efficient producers for the risks they incur in using scarce resources to produce these products. Losses are equally important in discouraging inefficient or undesirable production.

13) (Case Study #9) In discussing whether business profits are too high or too low, economists compare those returns to what business owners could receive by investing in relatively risk-free financial instruments, such as government-insured savings accounts or Treasury bonds. They also focus on profit measures that view profits as a return for risk-taking, not as a return on sales or other measures of a business' size. Historical evidence on profits earned by the largest U.S. firm offers some evidence on the effective level of *COMPETITION* these firms face, but that evidence is not conclusive in addressing such topics.

14) (Case Study #10) Economists have traditionally relied on the simple assumption of profit maximization to predict how firms will respond to different economic forces. However, some economists now look at differences in the kinds of products firms produce, and the kinds of resources they must use to produce these goods and services, to explain why certain kinds of *CORPORATIONS* are organized and managed the way they are. Profit maximization assumptions are still useful in addressing many questions -- particularly market or industry-wide adjustments in product price and output levels -- but the new theories of the firm are most promising in looking at intra-firm decisions. The impacts of transactions costs and *INCOMPLETE CONTRACTING* are especially important in these new theories.

Review and Discussion Questions

1) Suppose a firm that pays all of its workers the legal minimum wage can determine which job applicants will be the most reliable and industrious employees. As it increases output in the short run by hiring more workers, will its ability to distinguish better employees offset or reinforce the law of diminishing marginal returns?

2) From the marginal product of labor schedule given below, calculate the total product schedule and identify the output and employment levels at which diminishing returns set in.

Units of Capital	Units of Labor	Marginal Product of Labor
100	0	--
100	1	50
100	2	80
100	3	100
100	4	90
100	5	70
100	6	40
100	7	5
100	8	-5
100	9	-15

3) From the tables in question #2, above, and those calculated in your answer to that question, calculate the average product of labor schedule, and graph it to show the relationship between the average and marginal product of labor.

4) Assuming that the capital input shown in question #2, above, is paid $1,000, and each unit of labor receives $120 in the relevant time period in which this production occurs, calculate a total cost schedule for this production process, and show graphically how it can be separated into its fixed cost and variable cost components.

5) Use the total cost schedule you derived in the previous question, and the related data you determined in previous questions, to determine at what output level marginal cost reaches its minimum.

6) Calculate the average fixed cost, average variable cost, and average total cost schedules associated with the cost schedules you developed in question #4. Show graphically how they are related to the marginal cost schedule for this production process, which you considered in the previous question.

7) Over what employment and output ranges in the data you developed above, in questions 2-6, are marginal product and marginal cost increasing and decreasing, respectively. In what ranges are total product and total cost increasing at an increasing rate, and increasing at a decreasing rate, respectively.

8) What are your major explicit and implicit costs of attending college, or of taking your economics class? How would you report the costs of these activities if you were turning them in as a homework assignment for an accounting class?

9) Which of the following two statements is consistent with economists' understanding of the notion of sunk costs?

   a) "We've invested too much in this project to give up on it now."
   b) "Don't throw good money after bad."

10) Suppose you read 10 annual reports released last year by large U.S. corporations, and find that eight of the companies report profits, and two losses. Of the profitable firms, three are planning major expansions in their current product lines to face growing competition from other firms, three foresee a stable continuation of "business as usual" over the next decade, and two are phasing out current product lines to begin production of new goods and services. From this description, how many firms appear to be earning: a) normal profits, and b) economic profits? How many are incurring economic losses?

11) Would you rather own stock in a company in which economists would say normal profits have to be a relatively high rate of return, or low? Why? What does this tell us about these firms, and about you?

12) How do government taxes and subsidies for some businesses affect the economic role of profits in signalling producers what goods and services to make and sell? Are these government programs ever justifiable on economic grounds? Explain. Are all existing tax and subsidy programs likely to be justified on purely economic grounds? Explain.

13) (Case Study #9) What reported profit measures in a corporate annual report would you examine to help you answer questions #10 and 11, above?

14) (Case Study #10) From the perspective of a worker, does regular employment with a firm lower any major transactions costs compared to working on a "free-lance" basis, in effect as a private contractor? Explain.

Chapter 8
Business Decisions on Least-Cost Production

In This Chapter...

we consider production situations in which two variable inputs can be employed, not just one as in the examples presented in Chapter 7. A key reason for doing this is to stress the importance of the relative prices of substitutable inputs, rather than the absolute price level for a single productive resource. The tools we develop here also allow us to look ahead to long-run cost schedules and issues, which are formally developed in Chapter 10.

Cost Minimization and Profit Maximization

Businesses hire engineers to find different ways of producing products using as few inputs as possible, in a technological sense. But market prices for inputs also send signals to engineers and economists, which affect their optimal mix of inputs from a bottom-line perspective: cost minimization and profit maximization.

Total Revenue Minus Total Cost, Revisited

A firm that is trying to maximize profits faces several key decisions. It must choose what products to produce and sell, determine what quantity of output to produce, and decide how to make and market these goods and services. The questions of what products to produce and what specific quantities of output to produce to maximize profits will be discussed in later chapters. Here, you will see how another part of the firm's profit maximization problem is addressed -- minimizing the costs of producing any chosen output level when firms can adjust the mix of inputs they use in reaction to changes in the prices of these inputs.

As you saw in Chapter 7, the most effective way to use inputs to produce outputs depends in part on the technologically determined relationship known as a production function, which specifies how much output can be produced from a given quantity of productive resources. But when more than one variable input can be used to produce a product, the firm must also weigh the relative prices of those inputs. In such cases, the firm's position is analogous to that of consumers who derive satisfaction from the consumption of two or more goods. Those consumers' purchases of goods and services are affected both by the satisfaction they derive from additional units of the products *and* by the prices they must pay for them.

For a firm to maximize profits, it *must* minimize the costs of producing whatever output level it chooses to produce. Since profits are equal to total revenues minus total costs, the higher the total cost for a given volume and value of sales, the lower the profits. This discussion takes the product quality levels that the firm chooses to maintain as a given. In fact, the issue of product quality can be defined broadly as part of the question of what product to produce, since a Rolls Royce is in many ways a different product than a Hyundai. Therefore, when economists talk about *COST MINIMIZATION* they usually aren't referring to the kind of cost-cutting that occurs when a firm reduces the quantity or quality of its output. Instead, at a given level of output and product quality, cost minimization is seen as a necessary, but not sufficient, condition of profit maximization. That requires eliminating wasteful practices in the production process, and substituting less expensive inputs for more expensive ones whenever that can be done without reducing quality.

Isocosts

Firms establish spending plans, or budgets, that reflect both the output level they choose to produce and the relative prices of the inputs they employ. Changes in the total level of spending shift the entire graph economists use to represent these budgets, known as an isocost line, while changes in the relative price of inputs change the slope of the isocost line.

Production Budgets and Resource Prices

Like households, firms face budget constraints that are directly affected by the prices of the things they buy. What firms buy are, of course, the inputs they use to produce goods and services -- i.e., land, labor, capital, and entrepreneurship. Graphically, we can easily show a cost or production budget based on any two of these inputs; but economists usually choose to depict capital and labor because they are the most general and, typically, most important inputs. These graphs, such as the one shown in Figure 8-1, are known as *ISOCOST* lines.

Figure 8-1
Isocosts

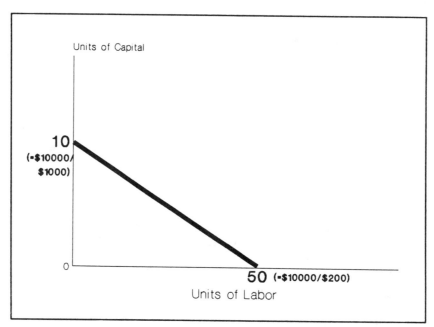

At any point on the same isocost line, a firm spends the same total amount of money for inputs, even though at each point it employs a different mix of the two variable inputs that are used to derive the schedule. Here, it is assumed that the firm spends $10,000 a week on capital and labor. The initial rental price of a unit of capital for one week is assumed to be $1,000, while the weekly wage for a unit of labor is assumed to be $200. Thus, the intercept for the capital axis is 10 units, the intercept for the labor axis is 50 units, and the slope of the isocost line is -1/5.

At different points on the same isocost line, a firm spends the same total amount of money, but employs different combinations of the two inputs identified on the axes. The Greek word iso means same or equal, as in an isosceles triangle in which two of the three line segments have the same length. Isocost lines show, therefore, all the different combinations of two inputs that can be purchased for the same cost.

Changes in Production Budgets and Resource Prices

When a firm decides to spend more to purchase inputs, to produce a higher level of output, it shifts to a higher, but parallel, isocost schedule, as shown in Figure 8-2. The same kind of shift occurs if there is a proportional decrease in the price of inputs while the firm maintains its dollar level of expenditures. In either case, more inputs are purchased while the slope of the isocost is unchanged, since the relative prices of the inputs are not changed. Conversely, a proportionate increase in input prices will move the firm to a lower, though still parallel, isocost schedule (also shown in Figure 8-2). This is graphically equivalent to a decision by the firm to spend less on productive resources when the prices of the resources are unchanged.

Figure 8-2
Changes in Real Levels of Spending for Inputs

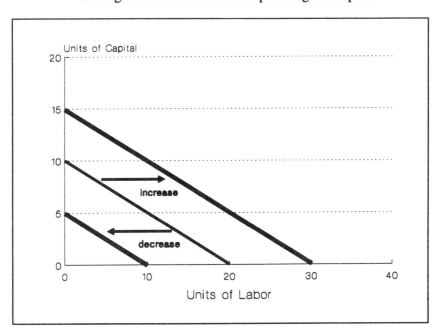

When input prices are fixed, spending more for inputs to increase output moves a firm to a higher isocost schedule (i.e., shifts the schedule to the right). However, that same kind of shift will occur if a firm holds its dollar expenditures for inputs constant while the input prices are decreasing in equal proportions.

A leftward shift of an isocost line shows the effect of a decrease in the level of spending for inputs when input prices are constant, or a constant level of dollar spending at a time when input prices are rising at an equal rate.

If the relative prices change for the two inputs shown on an isocost schedule, the slope of the isocost must also increase or decrease. This happens whenever one input price changes and the other input price stays constant. It also occurs when the prices move in opposite directions, or when they both increase or decrease, but at unequal rates. This is reviewed in the series of graphs shown in Figure 8-3.

Figure 8-3
Changes in the Relative Prices of Inputs

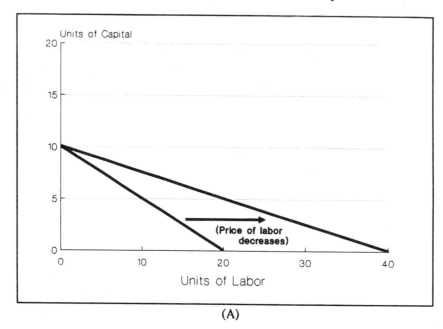

(A)

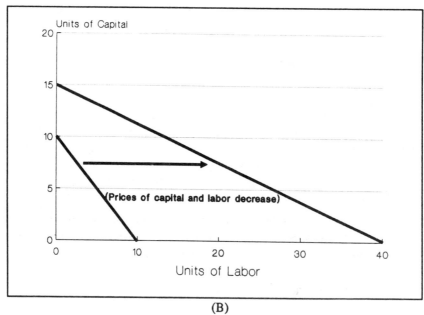

(B)

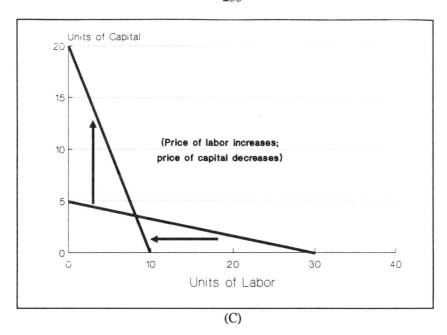

(C)

In each of the three graphs above, we assume that a firm spends the same amount of dollars to purchase inputs before and after the shifts in the isocost lines. However, the top graph (panel A) depicts a change in the slope of the isocost line which results from a decrease in the price of labor while the price of capital is constant. The middle graph (panel B) shows the prices for both inputs decreasing; but the price of labor falls relatively more than the price of capital, so the slope of the isocost still changes. In the bottom graph (panel C), the price of capital decreases while the price of labor increases. This is all analagous to the effects of changes in output prices on consumers' budget constraint lines, shown earlier in Figure 6-7.

Isoquants

Firms hire inputs to produce output, and the rate at which they can transfer inputs into output is determined by the technological relationships that establish their production functions. Most production functions exhibit several general properties, which economists represent graphically in isoquant curves. The feasible mix of inputs -- i.e., the degree to which one input can be substituted for another -- is also established in the production function. Combining that information with the data on the relative prices of inputs, discussed in the previous section, economists and business managers can determine the most cost effective way to produce different levels of output using more than one variable input.

General Characteristics of Isoquant Schedules

Naturally, firms purchasing factors of production aren't just interested in what they spend on inputs; they also care about how much additional production they get from each unit of input they hire. If hiring one more unit of capital increases output five times as much as hiring an additional unit of labor, but only costs twice as much, then capital is a "better buy." In equilibrium, therefore, firms will hire capital and labor at levels where

234

$$\frac{MP_K}{P_K} = \frac{MP_L}{P_L}$$

(As in earlier chapters, MP_K and MP_L represent the marginal product of capital and labor, respectively, while P_K and P_L are the prices of these inputs.) If the equality shown above does not hold, the firm is not minimizing the costs of producing whatever level of output it has chosen to make. It should hire more of the inputs that provide it with the greater output per dollar, at the margin, and fewer units of the other input.

We will look at this formulation of equilibrium conditions for hiring inputs in greater detail in Chapter 14. Here, we will use the isocost schedules developed above with a related kind of production measure, known as an *ISOQUANT* curve, to see how a firm can identify the optimal mix of two inputs that should be used to produce a given level of output at the lowest possible cost. Isoquant means, literally, same quantity; and isoquant schedules show the different combinations of two inputs that can be used to produce the same quantity of output. More specifically, an isoquant shows different combinations of the *minimum* quantities of two inputs a firm can use to produce a constant level of output, because we assume that inputs are being used as efficiently as possible from the standpoint of production technology.

To identify the *economically* efficient mix of inputs, we will put isoquant and isocost schedules together in the same graph. In other words, we will consider production and cost issues together, just as businesses do on a regular, if not daily, basis. But first, there are some basic points about isoquants you must understand. The isoquants shown in Figure 8-4 exhibit four typical characteristics:

1) Isoquants are negatively sloped;
2) Higher (up and to the right) isoquants represent a higher level of output;
3) Isoquants do not intersect; and
4) Isoquants are convex, or "bowed-in" toward the origin.

Be sure you understand the significance of these characteristics and, as discussed below, why they each occur. Note also that these characteristics are, in many respects, very similar to those of the indifference curves discussed in Chapter 6. Indifference curves were also negatively sloped, bowed-in toward the origin and non-intersecting. But that happens for different reasons, since isoquants deal with production, not consumption, decisions.

Considering the first characteristic listed above, for example, the negative slope of isoquants reflects the fact that capital and labor are, to some degree, substitutes in the production process. If a firm reduces the number of units of labor inputs it is using, total output can only be maintained if it uses more capital. That establishes an inverse, or negative, relationship between changes in the quantities of the two inputs, holding output (total product) constant. That negative slope holds regardless of what two inputs are used to drive the isoquant -- remember, we are only using capital and labor here as the most general examples of such inputs.

The second characteristic of isoquants is simply that higher (up and to the right) curves represent a higher level of output than lower isoquants. That's easy to see in Figure 8-4, simply by noting that each point on a higher schedule always represents the use of more of both inputs than some of the points on all lower isoquants. Using more of both inputs will, naturally, lead to greater levels of output.

The third characteristic listed above notes that it is logically inconsistent to show two isoquants intersecting. To do so would suggest that, in some ranges, fewer resources would produce relatively higher levels of output, and more inputs would produce fewer units of output. That logical inconsistency is demonstrated in Figure 8-5.

The final characteristic of isoquants is their convex, "bowed-in" shape. This results from a more subtle and complex relationship, which is discussed in the following section. If you studied indifference curves in Chapter 6, however, you will once again note an obvious parallel between the rationale for their convex shape and that of the isoquants. The key distinction here, again, is to see the relationship shown on an isoquant curve in terms of production, not consumption.

Figure 8-4
Isoquants

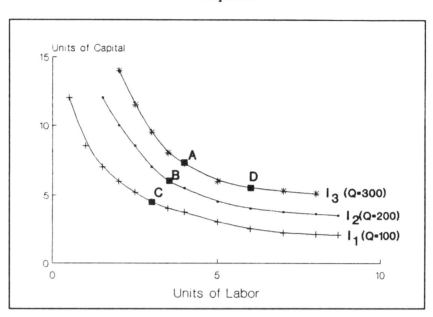

At each point on a given isoquant (e.g., points A and D on I_3) total output is constant. Moving along a particular isoquant, we can read from the axes the various combinations of two inputs that can be used to produce that quantity of output. When fewer units of either input are employed, output can be held constant only by using more of the other input, which accounts for the negative slope of an isoquant curve.

Higher (up and to the right) isoquants show higher levels of output -- i.e., output at any point on I_3 is greater than at any point on I_2. Confirming that, note that at point A on I_3, more capital *and* labor is used to produce output than at point B on I_2, or point C on I_1.

The Marginal Rate of Technical Substitution

In moving from one point to another along an isoquant, the level of output, or total product, does not change. But the amounts of the two variable inputs used to produce this output do change. Less capital might be used, for example, but that will require the use of more labor to maintain the same level of output. Now suppose we continue to reduce the amount of capital used in the production process, one unit at a time. Typically, as we do this, it becomes more and more difficult to go on substituting labor for capital. That is, the marginal product of each unit of capital that is given up becomes increasingly greater, while the marginal product of each unit of labor that is substituted for the units of capital becomes increasingly smaller.

Figure 8-5
Isoquants Cannot Intersect

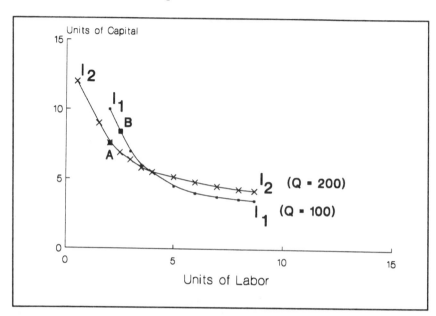

Suppose the isoquant labeled I_1 represents a total output of 100 units, while I_2 represents 200 units. If I_1 and I_2 intersect, as shown, then at point A on I_2 it takes fewer units of both inputs to produce 200 units of output than it does to produce 100 units of output at point B on I_1. That violates the assumption that inputs are being used at peak production efficiency, and so to avoid such violations of the assumption of technological effeciency, isoquants cannot intersect.

The number of units of one input required to substitute for one unit of another input, holding the level of output constant, is known as the *MARGINAL RATE OF TECHNICAL SUBSTITUTION (MRTS)*. (Its consumption counterpart is the marginal rate of substitution or MRS, that was introduced in Chapter 6.) Algebraically, MRTS is equal to the slope of an isoquant at any given point. In the isoquant graphs shown in this chapter, this is given by the change in capital inputs divided by the change in labor inputs as we move along the isoquant, or

$$MRTS = -\frac{\Delta K}{\Delta L}$$

As with the MRS, we will express the MRTS as a positive number, even though the change in one input is always positive, and the other negative. Since we know isoquants are negatively sloped, the sign isn't really the issue -- the absolute size of the MRTS is. We can emphasize that by doing away with the minus sign, as shown above -- multiplying the ratio of the changes in the two inputs by -1 to make the MRTS a positive number.

The idea that it typically takes more and more units of one input to substitute for a second input, as the amount of the second input is steadily decreased, is known as the principle of the *DIMINISHING MARGINAL RATE OF TECHNICAL SUBSTITUTION*. While this idea sounds consistent with the law of diminishing marginal returns, it is actually based on a different kind of relationship. Diminishing returns occur because at least one input is fixed, while another input is increasing. The diminishing MRTS occurs as one input is decreased while the other is increased, so *both* inputs are variable. But the input that is increased is not a perfect substitute for the input that is decreased -- particularly when relatively few units of the first input are left to work with.

Graphically, the diminishing MRTS means that the slope of the isoquant will be different at each point on the schedule, and that isoquants will have a "bowed-in" appearance. In more precise and technical terms, isoquants are convex to the origin. This is shown in Figure 8-6.

Figure 8-6
The Diminishing Marginal Rate of Technical Substitution

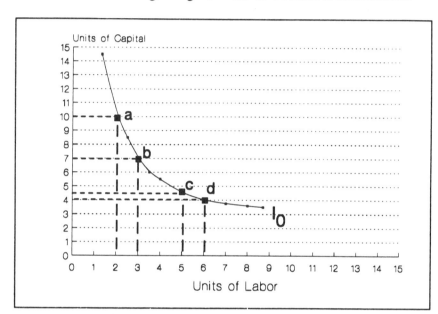

At different points on an isoquant, the amount of one input required to substitute for a unit of the other input, holding output constant, varies. Specifically, moving down and right along the curve shown above, it takes more and more units of labor to hold output constant as we give up successive units of capital. For example, between points A and B, one additional unit of labor can offset a reduction of three units in the amount of capital the firm employs. But between points C and D, an additional unit of labor can only offset approximately one-half unit of capital. With fewer and fewer units of capital to work with, the producer finds it more and more difficult to substitute labor for capital.

Equilibrium Points and Cost Minimization

Since isoquants and isocost schedules are drawn using the same variables on their axes, they can easily be combined in a single graph, as in Figure 8-7. Note that the tangency points in that figure result from the negative slopes of the two kinds of schedules, and from the bowed-in shape of the isoquants that occurs because of the diminishing MRTS. What significance do these tangency points hold, and how much can we make of them?

The tangency point between an isoquant and an isocost indicates the least-cost combination of variable inputs that can be used to produce the level of output represented by the isoquant, given current prices for the inputs. No greater level of output can be achieved at this cost (i.e., the firm cannot reach a higher isoquant at this expenditure level for inputs), and any lesser output level can be produced using fewer inputs (i.e., on a lower isocost schedule). The tangency point between an isoquant and isocost schedule is therefore one possible equilibrium point -- a firm will move to this point *if* this is the output level it chooses to produce and *if* the firm minimizes the costs of producing these products. At these tangency points, the rate at which the firm can substitute capital and labor in its production process -- as shown by the slope of the isoquant -- is equal to the rate at which the inputs trade in the marketplace -- as shown by the slope of the isocost. This is another indication of the economic efficiency that is achieved *only* at these tangency points.

Figure 8-7
Least-Cost Production at Different Output Levels

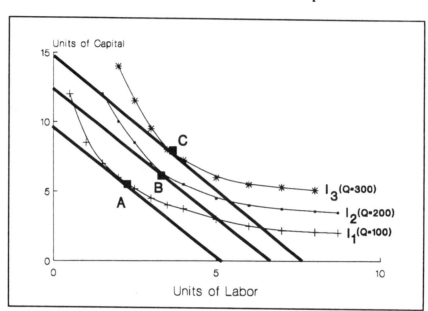

Given the input prices reflected by the isocost schedules shown above, and the technologically efficient alternatives for producing a product as shown by the isoquants, a firm can determine the least-cost method of producing various output levels. For example, the optimal mix of capital and labor to produce 100 units of output is at point A; the optimal mix to produce 200 units at point B; and the optimal mix to produce 300 units at point C. We can't tell which output quantity the firm will choose to produce from this information -- it may be more profitable to produce 100 units than 300 units, or *vice versa*. But we do know the optimal production mix of inputs can change if the isocost and/or isoquant curves change.

However, this analysis doesn't tell us what specific level of output the firm will want to produce, because we don't know anything about the revenue side of the firm's operations. So, even if we assume that the firm wants to maximize profits, and use the simple notion that profits are equal to total revenues minus total costs, we have no way to specify which of the least-cost tangency points the firm will try to reach. That's a major difference between isoquant/isocost analysis and the indifference-curve/utility-maximization analysis covered in Chapter 6 -- consumers try to maximize utility as an end in itself; firms may practice cost minimization for a given level of output, but only to achieve some other goal.

What can be shown directly, as in Figure 8-8, is the economic inefficiency of producing at any point other than one of these tangencies. When that happens, too many units of one input are used, and not enough units of the other input. Put differently, more units of output could be produced at the current expenditure level for inputs; or the current output could be produced at a lower cost.

Figure 8-8
Failing to Minimize Production Costs

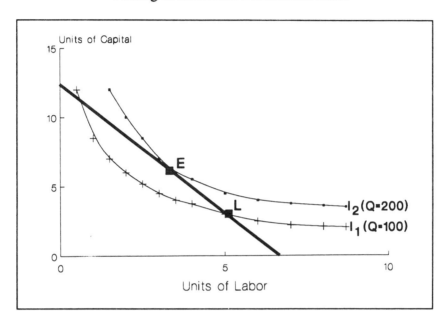

At a given expenditure level, represented by the isocost schedule in this figure, firms that are not minimizing production costs produce less output than they could. For example, suppose this is a "political patronage" office in which managers try to keep employment levels high (at point L rather than point E). To do this, managers must accept a decrease in output from I_2 (200 units) to I_1 (100 units). And at point L,

$$\frac{MP_K}{P_K} > \frac{MP_L}{P_L}$$

so while this may be a wise political choice, it doesn't minimize the costs of producing the I_1 output level.

A firm's interest in minimizing costs, and economists' interest in being able to model and predict such behavior, should become even more apparent to you in the next few chapters, as we develop more complete models that identify a firm's optimal level of output. But there are other features of firms' behavior which we can examine here, using isoquants and isocosts. Most of these topics, considered in the following section and case study, revolve around the fact that outputs can be produced in different ways -- meaning different inputs are, to some degree, substitutes for each other.

Some Applications and Extensions of Isocost and Isoquant Analysis

Isoquants and isocosts can be used to identify the substitution and output effects associated with a change in the price of a variable input, in the context of short-run production and hiring decisions. Or, assuming all of a firm's inputs are variable, isoquants and isocosts can be used to analyze long-run expansion paths or the long-run cost schedules for a firm.

Changes in Input Prices

Suppose that a firm using variable units of capital and labor to produce its product is faced with an increase in the price of labor. How will it react? Isoquant and isocost curves can help us answer that deceptively simple question, with considerable precision and detail.

As shown in Figure 8-9, the firm facing an increase in the price of labor has to make several choices. For convenience, we will assume that it limits output and hiring decisions to either the original production level (I_1), or the level it could produce by maintaining its initial level of spending for inputs and reducing its output (to point B on I_2).

Figure 8-9
Output and/or Hiring Changes Resulting From a Higher Input Price

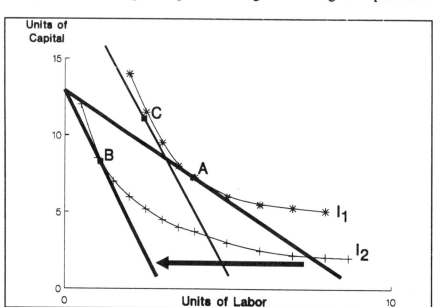

A sharp increase in the price of labor is shown by the leftward shift of the isocost schedule in the graph above. If the firm decides to hold its spending for inputs at current levels, its output level will fall from I_1 to I_2, or from point A to point B. On the other hand, if the firm decides to maintain its current output level, it will move from point A to point C along I_1, by substituting units of capital for the now more-expensive units of labor. The isocost line that is tangent to I_1 at point C reflects the new relative prices of capital and labor and, of course, a higher level of total spending for inputs by this firm.

Of course, a firm may choose to operate at other output levels; and indeed, the higher labor costs might even lead it to shut down entirely. Those decisions depend, once again, on the firm's revenues as well as on its production and cost levels. But by assuming here, only temporarily, that the final choice will be either on I_1 or I_2, we can identify additional choice patterns related to a firm's optimal mix of inputs.

Output and Substitution Effects

When a change in the price of an input leads to a change in the level of output a firm decides to produce and offer for sale, that is known as an *OUTPUT EFFECT*. You saw these effects earlier, in Chapter 3, from a different perspective, when resource prices were included as one of the general determinants of supply. Here, you should also recognize that output effects influence a firm's decisions about hiring all variable inputs, not just the input which experienced the price change. For these other inputs, output effects offset, partly or entirely, the substitution effects that are caused by a change in the relative prices of the inputs.

Let's discuss some examples of these forces at work, which are shown graphically in Figure 8-10. First, consider a case in which an increase in the price of labor leads not only to a positive substitution effect for capital, but also to some decrease in the output level that the firm produces. That output effect clearly tends to decrease the amount of labor *and* capital that the firm will use, so the substitution and output effects have offsetting impacts on the firm's demand for capital. Whether the demand for capital increases or decreases depends on which effect -- substitution or output -- is quantitatively larger.

When the price of labor falls, the substitution effect will reduce the amount of capital a firm wants to employ. But the output effect will be positive because the lower price for labor will normally increase the total quantity of the product the firm chooses to make, and that tends to increase its demand for capital. Again, whether the output or substitution effect will be greater is an open and empirical question that varies from case to case.

Considering the output and substitution effects for the input which experiences a price change, we find that they are typically reinforcing. For example, an increase in the price of labor will lead to a decrease in the quantity of labor demanded, because of both the substitution *and* the output effects. A decrease in the price of labor will lead to an increase in the quantity of labor demanded, again because of both the substitution and output effects.

Figure 8-10
Output and Substitution Effects

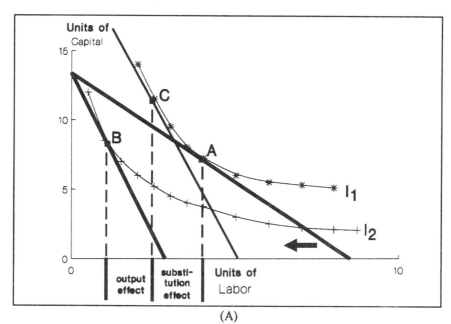

(A)

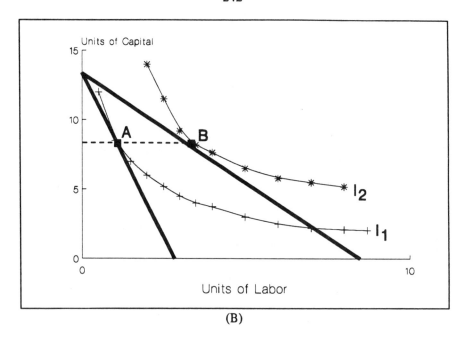

(B)

In the graph shown in panel (A), a firm is assumed to reduce its output level (moving from point A to point B) when faced with an increase in the price of labor. At the new price ratio, if the firm produced its original level of output (on I_1 at point C), the change in the quantity of labor demanded in moving from point A to point C represents the substitution effect of the price change. The rest of the decrease in the quantity of labor hired (from point C to point B) is due to the output effect. Note that this panel is essentially the same graph shown in Figure 8-9.

In the graph shown in panel (B), a decrease in the price of labor is assumed to lead to an increase in the firm's output level from I_1 to I_2 (point A to point B). Whether the firm's demand for capital increases, decreases, or remains the same depends on the relative size of the substitution and output effects. Here, the demand for capital is shown as remaining constant.

The Long Run: A Look Ahead

In Chapter 1, we defined the long run as a period of time long enough for a firm to vary all of its inputs; or, in other words, there are no fixed inputs. Clearly, isoquants and isocosts can be used to show long-run situations, since both inputs shown on the axes of these schedules can vary. In fact, in the earlier sections of this chapter, only the assumption that at least one input not shown explicitly on these axes was fixed allowed us to use these graphs to investigate short-run production and cost issues when the firm has two variable inputs.

Now, if we assume that a firm uses only capital and labor, or that all its inputs are variable, we can use isoquant and isocost analysis to look ahead to the long-run issues that are developed in greater detail, using other analytical tools, in Chapter 10. In Figure 8-11, we first trace out the *EXPANSION PATH* of tangency points (labeled A-C) that a firm will follow *if* it increases its long-run level of output, assuming that the relative prices of capital and labor do not change. Some production technologies lead to a relatively greater use of capital as output is increased, others to a greater use of labor. Such *CAPITAL-INTENSIVE* and *LABOR-INTENSIVE* growth patterns can have, as you might suspect, important effects on both long-run employment patterns and the incomes received by those who supply these factors to firms. We will have more to say on those issues in later chapters.

Figure 8-11
Expansion Paths

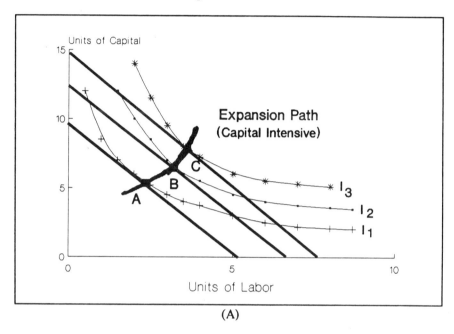

(A)

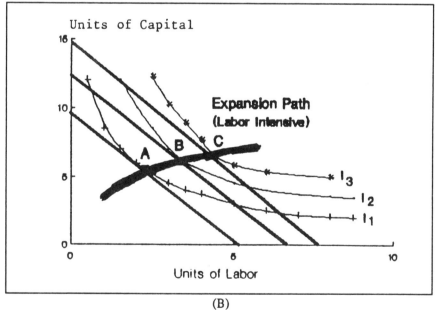

(B)

Holding input prices constant and plotting out the most efficient means of producing successively higher levels of output, as shown by the tangency points of these isoquant and isocost schedules, shows a firm's expansion path. The first graph (panel A) depicts a firm that faces a capital-intensive expansion path, in which relatively more capital than labor is used as the output level is increased. The second graph (panel B) shows a firm that has a labor-intensive expansion path -- it is more cost efficient for this firm to increase the relative amount of labor employed as its output level rises.

Given the input prices used to draw the isocost schedules in Figure 8-11, the output levels indicated by the isoquants, and the further assumption that these are the only inputs a firm uses, we can also construct long-run total cost and average total cost curves by multiplying the number of inputs used times their price, and plotting the total or average total cost at each level of output. Examples of this procedure are shown in Figure 8-12. In the first set of graphs (panels A-C) average total cost (ATC) is constant as output increases; in the second set of graphs (panels D-F) ATC rises at higher output levels; and in the third set (panels G-I), ATC falls as output rises. The fourth set of graphs (panels J-L), show a combination of the earlier three situations, where average total costs initially fall as output rises, then enter a range where ATC is constant as output increases, and finally ATC rises with still further increases in total product, or quantity. Note that these different kinds of linkages between costs and output level are determined by the production technology assumed to exist in these ranges, as reflected by the different patterns shown in the isoquant schedules.

Remember that the schedules shown in these last two figures are long-run relationships where all inputs are variable, not short-run schedules that are subject to the law of diminishing marginal returns. Our primary discussion of these long-run schedules is presented later, in Chapter 10. However, many uses of isoquant and isocost analysis involve short-run analysis that focuses on the substitutability of inputs and their relative prices. Some economists have used these tools to look at questions involving different kinds of production and inputs, at times in rather surprising areas. Case Study 11 summarizes one such study.

Figure 8-12
Deriving Long-run Cost Curves from Isoquant and Isocost Schedules

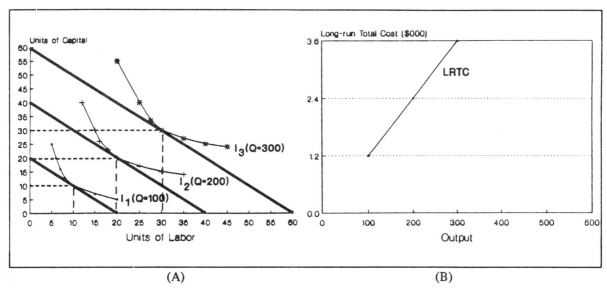

(A)   (B)

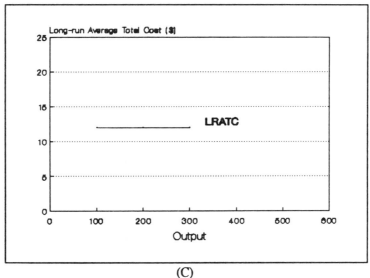

(C)

In panel (A), equal increases in the levels of all inputs lead to proportionate increases in output. Assuming that the firm uses only capital and labor, as shown, and that the prices of these inputs do not change, the firm's long-run total cost schedule will be linear and positively sloped (panel B), while its long-run average total cost schedule will be perfectly flat over these output ranges (panel C).

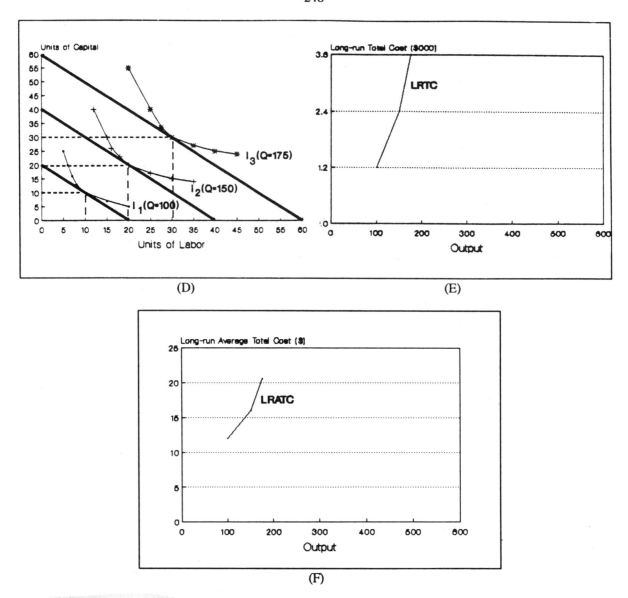

(D)

(E)

(F)

In panel (D), increasing all of the firm's inputs by an equal percentage leads to a less than proportionate increase in output. Therefore, the firm's long-run total costs increase at an increasing rate as output is increased (panel E), and its long-run average total cost curve is also upward sloping (panel F).

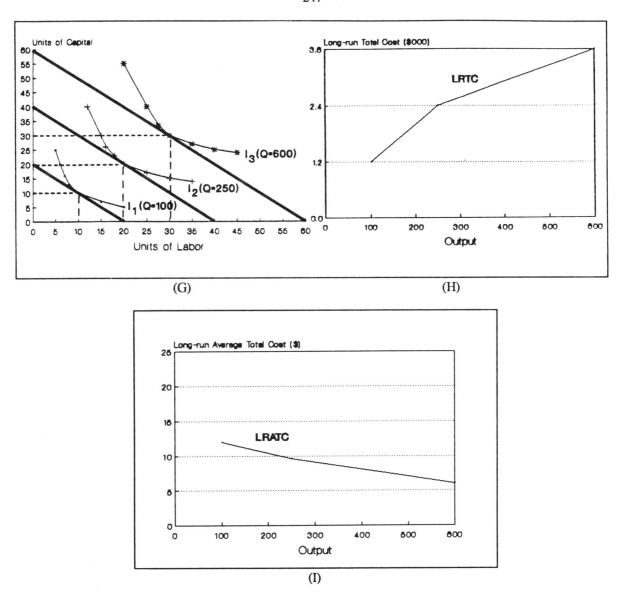

(G)

(H)

(I)

In panel (H), long-run total costs rise as output increases, but at a decreasing rate. Therefore, long-run total costs are positive but decreasing (in panel I). This occurs because the firm experiences a more than proportionate increase in output when it hires more of all of its inputs in some equal proportion (panel G).

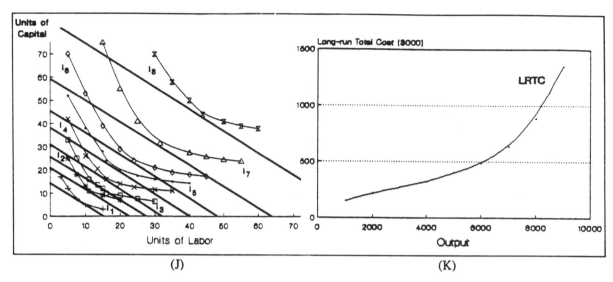

(J)

(K)

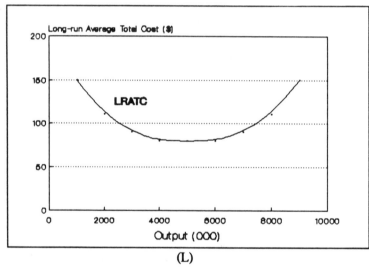

(L)

The last three graphs (panels J-L) show that, over different ranges of output, the same firm may experience all of the production and cost relationships shown in the first three sets of graphs. In panel (J), however, $I_1 = 1000$ units of output and each subsequent isoquant shows an increase in output of 1000 units. This firm initially experiences falling long-run average total costs (panel L). But as output increases it then enters a range where these costs are constant and, finally, at still higher output levels, these costs begin to rise. These three ranges of long-run production and cost schedules are discussed at greater length in Chapter 10.

Case Study #11
Isoquants and Professional Baseball Managers

Think of professional baseball teams as firms, with managers who try to maximize the number of games the teams win each season. Winning games attracts fans to the ballpark, who buy tickets, beer, hot dogs, peanuts, and souvenirs, all of which contributes to a team's financial success. But the managers of these teams normally don't worry about many of the financial aspects of running the business side of their teams (in some cases, they would be woefully unprepared to do so) -- their job is just to win as many games as they can, given the players they have to work with.

Fortunately for baseball managers, players, and economists, baseball is a simple game. In fact, studies have shown that there are just two major inputs that win games. The first is offense, which basically means hitting the ball when the other team pitches it to you. The second is defense, which primarily involves getting players who can pitch so well that the other team can't hit the ball. Fielding the ball can also be important on defense, but the quality of fielding across major league teams is relatively consistent. Fielding errors usually account for between two percent and three percent of the fielding "chances" a team has over the season. Hitting and pitching performances vary much more, and are usually responsible for most of the differences in won-loss records for different teams.

Economist Gerald Scully[1] found that the statistically most effective measures of hitting and pitching are, respectively, team slugging averages (total bases divided by times at bat) and team strike-out-to-walk ratios. Better known measures, such as batting averages and pitchers' won-loss records, aren't complete in some senses (e.g., in batting averages a single counts as much as a home run), or aren't true measures of hitting or pitching per se (again, for example, won-loss ratios depend on pitching *and* hitting, not just on a pitcher's performance). Using the slugging and walk/strike-out measures, then, Scully and Philip Porter[2] estimated "frontier unit" isoquants for each of the major leagues over a twenty-year period, which were used as measures of the maximum number of wins a team could achieve given its personnel in a given year.

The shape of the frontier unit isoquants, such as the one shown in Figure 8-13, is the familiar "bowed-in" curve you have seen throughout this chapter, and reflects the degree to which hitting and pitching can be substituted to win ballgames. However, the frontier unit isoquant has been constructed to adjust for differences in playing talent across teams, so that the schedule shows "unit wins" that could be achieved with a team's personnel *if* the manager can get the team to perform up to its potential. Therefore, the manager's effectiveness is judged by how close he comes to his team's predicted number of wins, given the team hitting and pitching he has to work with. If all managers were perfectly efficient, they would get their teams on this "frontier" isoquant. But in fact, no manager is likely to be perfect -- baseball isn't *that* simple. Instead, some managers are likely to be more efficient than others.

Who were the best managers in baseball according to Porter and Scully? Over the period they studied (1961-1980), Earl Weaver of the Baltimore Orioles had an efficiency rating of 98.7 percent. (These were good days for the Orioles, before their record consecutive loss streak of 1988 and jokes that they, like Michael Jackson, wore gloves on one hand for no apparent reason.) Sparky Anderson, who managed the Cincinnati Reds and the Detroit Tigers, was second with a rating of 96.1 percent. Billy Martin, of the Twins, Tigers, A's, Rangers and (eventually) five times with the Yankees, was tenth with a 91.2 percent rating. Some other managers had ratings lower than 80 percent, which perhaps isn't surprising given all of the things a manager can do that affect a team's performance -- such as setting the team roster and starting line-ups, selecting starting pitchers and setting their rotation, making player substitutions during a game, positioning the defense, maintaining morale, and (especially during spring training) teaching and conditioning the players.

---

[1] "Pay and Performance in Major League Baseball," *American Economic Review*, December 1974, pp. 915-31.
[2] "Measuring Managerial Efficiency: The Case of Baseball," *Southern Economic Journal*, January 1982, pp. 642-50.

Figure 8-13
A "Frontier Unit" Isoquant for Professional Baseball Teams

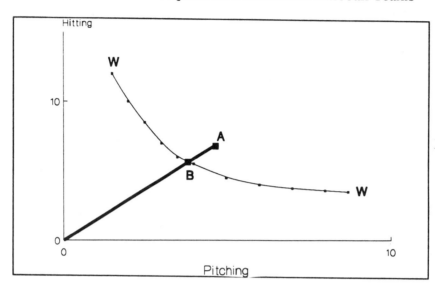

This special kind of isoquant is similar to those you saw earlier in the chapter, in that the inputs are, to some degree, substitutable. That leads to the typical, bowed-in shape of the schedule; this frontier indicates the minimum amounts of hitting and pitching teams require to win a given percentage of their games, assuming that managers use those inputs at maximum efficiency. So, in this case, a team that isn't run at peak efficiency will use more inputs to achieve a certain percentage of wins than a team that is run more efficiently. For example, a team at point A has a mix of hitting and pitching identified by the straight line drawn from the origin to this point, but it is predicted that they could win the same number of games they do with fewer inputs, at point B. Efficiently managed teams will be on this frontier unit isoquant; inefficiently managed teams are at points lying off of the isoquant, with the degree of inefficiency measured by the distance from the isoquant.

Porter and Scully estimated that Weaver's managerial efficiency added about $675,000 to the Orioles' annual revenues, measured in 1969 dollars. That estimate is fairly close to the values Scully had estimated in other studies for superstar baseball players like the Dodgers' Hall-of-Fame pitcher, Sandy Koufax. Managerial salaries typically aren't as high as those for superstar players, but in recent years there have been signs that many teams are recognizing, financially and in other ways, the value of good managers and coaches. This seems to be true in all professional sports, not just baseball. In 1987, for example, the New York Knicks wanted to hire an assistant coach from the Boston Celtics as their head coach, but the Celtics held a long-term contract and would only release the assistant for a first-round draft choice. This is clear evidence that coaches are, increasingly, recognized as valuable team assets in their own right.

Chapter Summary

1) To maximize profits a firm must minimize the cost of producing whatever level of output it decides to make and offer for sale, while also maintaining the level of product quality it has chosen to offer.

2) An *ISOCOST* line shows the different combinations of two inputs a firm can buy for some fixed level of expenditure, given the relative prices of the two inputs. Changes in these prices or in the level of the firm's expenditures for inputs lead to shifts in the isocost schedule.

3) *ISOQUANTS* show the different combinations of two inputs a firm can use to produce a fixed level of output, assuming that all inputs are used as efficiently as possible from a production standpoint. Typically, isoquants are negatively sloped, bowed-in toward the origin, and do not intersect. The negative slope shows that the inputs are substitutable in the production process, and the bowed-in shape further refines this relationship by suggesting that the substitutability of inputs is subject to the *DIMINISHING MARGINAL RATE OF TECHNOLOGICAL SUBSTITUTION (MRTS)*. Intersecting isoquants violate the assumption that all inputs are used at their maximum level of production efficiency.

4) The MRTS between two inputs is the measure of how many units of one input are required to maintain a constant level of output when one unit of the other input is removed from the production process. The MRTS is therefore determined by moving along an isoquant schedule, and reflects the slope of that curve at the different hiring rates for the two inputs. We assume that the inputs are imperfectly substitutable, which means that as we give up successive units of one input it takes an increasing amount of the second input to hold output constant. The assumption of a diminishing MRTS is based on the relationship between two variable inputs, not between variable and fixed inputs.

5) Tangency points between isoquant and isocost schedules indicate the least-cost combinations of two variable inputs that can be used to produce given quantities of output. At these points, we know that

$$\frac{MP_A}{P_A} = \frac{MP_B}{P_B}$$

where A and B are inputs. However, we can not determine from the information in these schedules which isocost line and output level the firm will choose to use, even if we assume the firm wants to maximize its profits. That is a key difference between these schedules and the indifference curves and budget constraint lines considered in Chapter 6.

6) Changes in the price of an input lead to *OUTPUT* and *SUBSTITUTION EFFECTS* that affect all of the inputs a firm uses, not just the one input which experienced the price change. Isoquant and isocost schedules can be used to distinguish between the output and substitution effects *if* we know how a firm adjusts its production levels in response to the new relative prices.

7) Isoquant and isocost schedules can also be used to illustrate a firm's long-run behavior, since both inputs used to derive these schedules are variable. Holding input prices constant, and plotting the points a firm will choose to operate at if it increases output, shows the long-run *EXPANSION PATH* for the firm. Technological considerations may make such growth either *CAPITAL or LABOR INTENSIVE*.

8) Isoquant and isocost schedules can be used to derive a firm's long-run total cost and average total cost schedules. The firm's technological opportunities, reflected in its isoquant schedules as output is increased, may cause it to face rising, constant, or falling average total costs in the long run.

9) (Case Study #11) Managers of professional baseball teams have the job of getting the most output (wins) from their player inputs (in particular, hitting and pitching). Studies indicate that some managers are much more effective than others, and that they can contribute as much to a team's financial success as a superstar player.

Review and Discussion Questions

1) Under what reasonable circumstances might a firm fail to minimize the costs of producing a given level of output?

2) On a single graph, draw the isocost schedules associated with the following cases:

Case #	Price of Capital	Price of Labor	Total Firm Expenditures for Capital and Labor
1	$10	$10	$100
2	10	5	100
3	5	5	100
4	5	5	50

3) Can isoquants be positively sloped? Explain.

4) Draw a negatively sloped isoquant that violates the assumption of a diminishing MRTS. Explain carefully how the schedule you draw violates this assumption.

5) In Figure 8-8, assuming total output and input prices are held constant, identify a point where

$$\frac{MP_K}{P_K} < \frac{MP_L}{P_L}$$

and another point where

$$\frac{MP_K}{P_K} = \frac{MP_L}{P_L}$$

6) In Figure 8-9, how do we know that the isocost that is tangent to I_1 at point C represents a higher level of total expenditures for inputs than the firm's original isocost schedule, which is tangent to I_1 at point A? How could we identify the output and substitution effects for this firm if it decided to maintain production at I_1 after the increase in the price of labor, instead of reducing output to I_2?

7) Draw an expansion path for a firm that is capital and labor neutral.

8) Based on the schedules shown in Figure 8-12, and the relevant material presented in Chapter 6, explain the relationships between long-run total product, long-run total cost, long-run average total cost, and long-run marginal cost.

9) (Case Study #11) If we accept the estimate of Earl Weaver's value to the Baltimore Orioles provided by Porter and Scully, what is the maximum salary he could expect from the team? What would determine the minimum salary he would accept? How is that maximum salary related to his efficiency as a manager?

Chapter 9
Perfect Competition: The Efficient Ideal

In This Chapter...

we present the basic models of perfectly competitive industries and firms -- developing total, average, and marginal revenue schedules, and combining them with the cost schedules developed in Chapter 7. With this information, the profit maximizing level of output and supply schedule for a competitive firm is determined. And, although the assumptions that are used to develop these models of perfect competition are not fully met in any existing industry, the competitive ideal also establishes several important criteria that are regularly used in assessing the effective degree of competition and economic efficiency in U.S. and international markets.

Market Structures and Economic Efficiency: An Introduction

Some people enjoy competition "just for the thrill of it," others don't. Most economists approve of active competition among producers on the supply side of the market, and among consumers on the demand side, because this results in an efficient use of scarce resources and, consequently, the ability to satisfy more of people's wants.

The models of perfectly competitive industries and firms developed in this chapter are idealized constructs, designed to focus on price competition among large numbers of relatively small firms which sell identical products. Other kinds of competition and industry structures are certainly possible and, in fact, more often seen in modern, industrialized economies. But some of the characteristics of pure competition are met in major U.S. industries even today.

The formal case for the linkage between market structures and measures of economic efficiency is presented in this chapter and in the next four, which cover different models of imperfect competition. The term *MARKET STRUCTURE* refers to the set of characteristics in an industry that establishes both the kind of competition that takes place there and the extent of that competition. These characteristics include the number of firms in an industry, the relative ease or expense other firms face in entering the industry, and the feasible degree of product and price differentiation among competing firms.

In Chapters 11-13, the market structures known as monopoly, monopolistic competition, and oligopoly are introduced, by assuming that industries are characterized by fewer firms, higher barriers to entry, or greater product and price differentiation than what is assumed in the models of perfect competition presented in this chapter. These different characteristics lead, in turn, to different price, production, and profit outcomes. Those outcomes are related directly to the supply and demand models developed in previous chapters, and to several important public policy issues, including the federal and state antitrust laws and enforcement programs that attempt to maintain and strengthen competition in U.S. markets.

Characteristics of Perfectly Competitive Firms

Just as competitive games are built around a set of rules that treat individuals or teams equally, in terms of providing them with an opportunity to play and win the games, economists are most confident in supporting an idealized kind of competition that would occur if firms operated in industries with four special characteristics or rules. Their models of perfect competition are based on the following assumptions:

1) *All firms and consumers in the industry are price takers;*
2) *Firms can easily enter or exit the industry;*
3) *Firms produce identical products; and*
4) *Firms and consumers have complete information about product price, quality, and availability.*

Price Takers

The most basic characteristic of *PERFECT COMPETITION* is that the output level of any individual firm is a small and insignificant part of the total market output of its product. This is assumed to be true even at firms' maximum or minimum output levels, and the key consequence of this characteristic is that no action the firm takes in increasing or decreasing output will have any effect on the market price for its product. In other words, the firm is a *PRICE TAKER*, and can sell as much or as little as it chooses at the market price, as shown in Figure 9-1.

Figure 9-1
The Competitive Firm Faces a Market-Determined Price

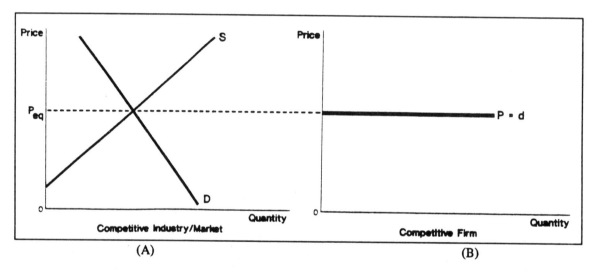

(A)   (B)

The equilibrium price (P_{eq}) of a product produced by a perfectly competitive firm is established by market supply and demand forces, as shown in panel (A). An individual firm in this industry can sell as many units as it chooses at that price, as shown in panel (B). In other words, the market-determined price establishes the firm's horizontal demand schedule, and that price (P) is equal to the firm's demand curve (d).

If a perfectly competitive firm tries to charge more for its product, consumers simply buy from any one of the many other firms selling the same product at the market price. A competitive firm could charge a lower price than its competitors, of course; but that's pointless (in other words, stupid) since the firm can already sell as much as it wants to at the market price. There are several industries in which this pricing patterns is, in fact, regularly seen. For example, farmers can find out what prices they can get for their crops by reading the financial sections of major newspapers, or displays on blackboards or video terminals at most of the grain elevators and other storage sites for farm products located all around the country.

Individual buyers are also assumed to be price takers in competitive markets, purchasing quantities that are small enough, relative to the total market output, to have no impact on price. Again, we often observe this characteristic in many important markets. Buyers of farm products, including groceries, are one example. And individuals who want to buy or sell stocks, mutual funds, or savings instruments such as certificates of deposits are typically price takers, who are told by their banks, brokers, or in financial reports what prices they must pay, or can receive, for these "paper assets."

The price-taking characteristic means that perfectly competitive markets are extremely impersonal in many respects: farmers often don't know who will eventually buy and consume their crops, and people who buy and sell stocks usually never know who is ultimately on the other side of their deals. The point is, of course, that they don't need to know that -- what they care about are the market prices that indicate the relative scarcity of the products they are buying or selling, and their own judgments about whether those prices are likely to rise or fall in the future.

One warning is in order here before considering the other three assumptions made in models of perfect competition: don't think that, because of the price-taking characteristic, agricultural and financial markets in the United States or any other country must be perfectly competitive. In U.S. agricultural markets, for example, extensive government involvement in setting price floors, protective tariffs, and quotas are clearly not features of perfect competition. How well the stock market fits the description of a competitive market is considered in the case study at the end of this chapter.

Easy Entry and Exit

The second key characteristic of a perfectly competitive industry is that firms can begin producing a product, or cease producing it, without incurring large start-up or shut-down costs. The effect of *ENTRY* into the industry by a significant number of new firms, or expansion by existing firms, or some combination of both, is to shift the industry supply curve to the right. That lowers the market price for a product, *ceteris paribus*, as shown in the panel (A) of Figure 9-2. *EXIT* (or decreases in production levels) by a significant number of firms shifts the industry supply curve to the left, and raises the market price for the product. This is shown in panel (B) of Figure 9-2. Any change in the market price will, of course, change the price at which firms in a competitive industry must sell their output. Examples of such shifts are, once again, easy to find. In one such case, as more farmers began to grow soybeans over the past 20-30 years, the market supply of this crop increased dramatically. That led to lower prices for soybeans in years when demand was unchanged, or increased less than supply. And when the market price for soybeans fell, every soybean farmer faced that lower price. They could, of course, stop growing soybeans and exit this market. But no single farmer's action was large enough to significantly affect the market supply curve, or the market price.

There is a very strong relationship between the ease of entry and exit in an industry and the effective level of competition in the production of goods and services offered by that industry, which we discuss throughout the next four chapters. In simple, common sense terms, however, you should already be able to see the basis for that connection. When entry and exit is easy, economic profits or losses will, respectively, serve to draw new firms to an industry or drive some existing firms away. The general result of that process is to reward firms that efficiently produce the kinds of products consumers want to buy, as you saw in Chapter 7. High costs of entry and exit restrict firms' ability to respond to these signals.

Homogeneous Products

The word homogeneous is derived from a Greek word that translates, literally, as "same kind." Perfectly competitive firms must produce identical or *HOMOGENEOUS PRODUCTS* which are, in consumers' eyes, perfect substitutes. Using agricultural products and financial securities as examples once again, when you've seen one bushel of corn (at least with kernels of a certain size, moisture content, and cleanliness, reflected in the grading standards for such products), you've pretty much seen them all. Similarly, a hundred shares of AT&T common stock is just like every other hundred shares of AT&T, regardless of who owns, buys, or sells it.

Figure 9-2
Entry and Exit in a Competitive Industry

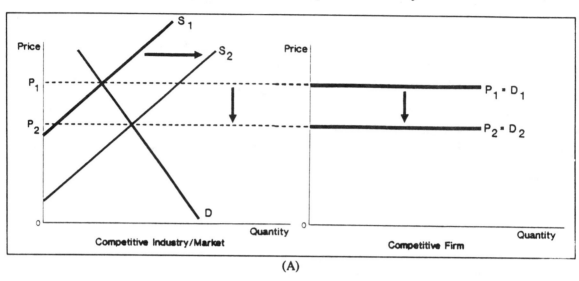

(A)

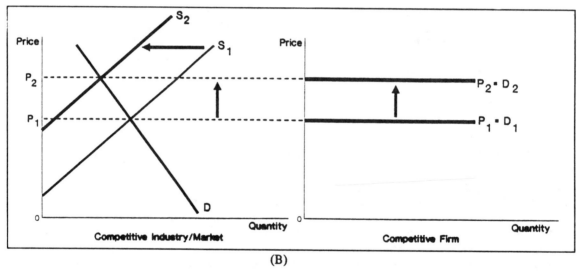

(B)

In the two graphs shown in panel (A), entry into a competitive industry causes the industry supply curve to increase. The resulting decrease in the market price for this product means that individual firms in the industry must now sell their products at the new, lower, price (P_2). In panel (B), exit from the industry leads to a decrease in supply and an increase in price. The firms that continue to produce this product will receive a higher price (P_2) when they sell their output.

Not all homogeneous products are produced by perfectly competitive firms, however. Steel, copper, glass, and other industrial materials tend to be produced by very large firms that make and sell a significant part of the output of their respective industries. In such cases, the capital costs of building and operating huge factories often makes entry into, and exit from, the industry both difficult and expensive.

As you will see more formally in Chapter 12, *HETEROGENEOUS PRODUCTS* are differentiated in terms of physical or design features, or by other seller characteristics such as warranty and return policies. These products may be close, but are not perfect, substitutes in the eyes of consumers. A major consequence of these real or perceived quality differences is that the products will not sell for identical prices, so the firms that sell them are no longer price takers.

Complete Information

In perfectly competitive markets, we assume that all consumers and producers have complete information about product quality, availability, and price. This includes firms' information about the productive resources they use to produce goods and services. In effect, that means we are assuming that all of this information is a free, noneconomic good. But as you saw in Chapter 1, economists recognize that information *is* scarce, and commands a positive price. Why make such a counter-factual assumption here, then? Partly because the models of perfect competition were developed before economists established the notion of scarce information as a central part of their theories. Primarily, though, this is done because it is still useful to determine what will occur when information is complete and costless, and then see how those results are changed by relaxing those unrealistic assumptions.

From the discussion of the four assumptions used in models of perfect competition, you can probably tell that no real industries are made up of firms that exhibit all of these characteristics, although a few markets are close on some counts. What happens when firms don't have these features is discussed in the next several chapters. However, it is at least as important for you to understand this chapter in depth than it is for you to learn the material in the later chapters, despite the fact that those chapters deal with cases that are frequently more realistic. The reason for this is simply that the models of perfect competition developed here help to establish the standards economists use to evaluate both theoretical and empirical measures of a firm's economic efficiency, and measures of the degree of control a firm may exercise over its own industry. In fact, apart from the chapters on basic supply and demand models, many economists view this as the most important chapter you will study in a first course on microeconomics.

Revenue Schedules For Competitive Firms

The basic characteristics of competitive industries and firms give rise to a particular set of revenue schedules, which we introduce here and then combine with the cost schedules developed in Chapter 7. This allows us to determine the equilibrium conditions for a perfectly competitive firm in the last section of the chapter, and to establish basic measures of economic efficiency from those equilibrium conditions.

Demand/Average Revenue Schedules for Competitive Firms and Industries

The demand curve facing the perfectly competitive *firm* is the horizontal line at the market determined price level. The *industry* demand curve for both perfectly and imperfectly competitive firms is simply the market demand curve you have seen and worked with in earlier chapters. This was shown in Figure 9-1, and is shown again with some additional labels in Figure 9-3. The new labels indicate that demand schedules are also average revenue schedules. And remember, as shown in Chapter 4, that because the competitive firm's demand curve is a horizontal line, it must be perfectly price elastic. These points deserve a bit more explanation and discussion.

Recall that total revenue (TR) is equal to the price (P) of the output units sold times the quantity (Q) sold, or TR = P(Q). AVERAGE REVENUE is, of course, equal to total revenue divided by the quantity sold, so substituting we have AR = TR/Q = $\frac{P(Q)}{Q}$ = P. Price represents the amount of revenue received by the firm *per unit* sold, and we read the price received at any given quantity of sales directly off of the demand schedule. In the particular case of the perfectly competitive firm, it is even easier to see that demand must equal average revenue, since price and average revenue are constant at the market-determined level, and that price level *is* the firm's demand curve.

Apart from recalling the geometry that tells you that horizontal demand schedules are perfectly elastic, which you saw in Chapter 4, you can see now in fuller detail why and how that is so. Even an infinitesimal increase in price by a firm facing this kind of demand curve will result in sales dropping to zero, because consumers can easily buy identical products from other firms at the market price. Therefore, expressing the percentage change in quantity demanded over the percentage change in price, we get a value that approaches infinity as the change in price is made smaller and smaller but the change in quantity demanded remains very large (or total, in the sense that the firm loses all of its sales).

Figure 9-3
Competitive Firms Face Perfectly Elastic Demand/Average Revenue Schedules

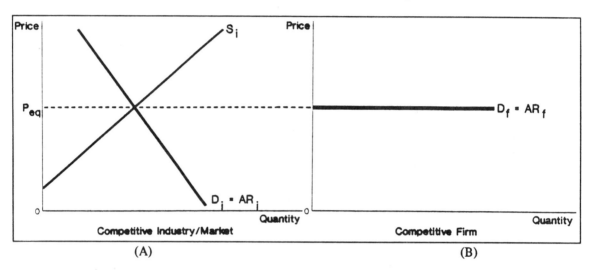

(A)   (B)

The competitive *industry's* demand curve (D_i), shown in panel (A), exhibits different price elasticities at each point on the schedule. The demand curve facing the competitive *firm* (D_f), shown in panel (B), is infinitely price elastic, because the firm would lose all of its sales if it attempted *any* price increase, even a very small one. Both demand curves are also average revenue schedules -- for the industry (AR_i) and firm (AR_f), respectively.

Total and Marginal Revenue Schedules for Competitive Firms

Since a competitive firm can sell as many units of its product as it chooses at the market price, its total revenue schedule will be linear and positively sloped. In other words, since TR = P(Q), and P is a set value for competitive firms, total revenue will increase by the value P each time the firm sells an additional unit of output. Stated that way, it is clear that the competitive firm's marginal revenue schedule, which shows the revenue it receives by selling one more unit of output, is equal to the market price of the product it sells. As you will see in Chapters 11-13, this is not the case for imperfectly competitive firms.

When the market price for a product produced by competitive firms changes, all of the firms' revenue schedules will also shift. That occurs because, as you have seen earlier, the firms' demand schedules will shift when changes in supply and/or demand at the industry level cause the market price of the product the firms produce to change. These shifts in a competitive firm's family of revenue curves are shown in Figure 9-4.

Figure 9-4
Total and Marginal Revenue Schedules for Competitive Firms

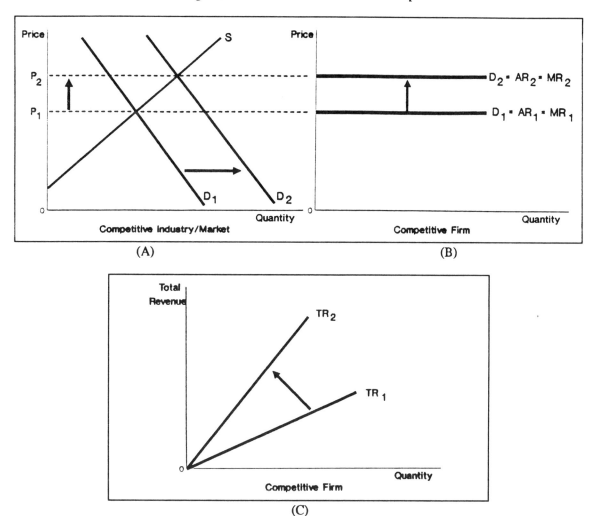

An increase in demand for the product produced by a competitive industry is shown as a rightward shift in the industry demand curve in panel (A). This results in an increase in the market price for the product (panel B), which means that the competitive firms' demand curve (which is also its average and marginal revenue schedule) will shift up. A firm's total revenue schedule is found by multiplying the number of units it can sell by the price it receives for the products. So, as shown in panel (C), an increase in the market price for the product will also increase the competitive firm's total revenue schedule.

Combining Revenue and Cost Schedules

Now we can combine the revenue curves developed above with the cost curves derived in Chapter 7. By finding the level of output at which total revenue exceeds total cost by the greatest amount, we can also determine the output level the firm will choose to produce in order to maximize profits. This is shown in Figure 9-5, first using total revenue and total cost curves, and then using average cost and average revenue curves.

In both of the figures shown there, the output levels shown maximize a firm's profits; but the techniques used to identify these output levels use geometric rather than economic logic and intuition. The following section begins by reviewing a more important and economically oriented procedure that also establishes the profit maximizing level of output. This is, in fact, the procedure we will use from this point on to identify profit maximizing output levels for *any* kind of firm, including those that are not perfectly competitive.

Equilibrium Conditions in Competitive Markets

Short-run profit maximization in all types of industries occurs at the output level at which marginal revenue equals marginal cost. Knowing this, the short-run supply schedule for a competitive firm can be shown to be its marginal cost curve at all points above the minimum point on its average variable cost curve, which represents the firm's shutdown point. After allowing for entry and exit, equilibrium in a competitive industry occurs where price equals marginal cost and minimum average total cost, and representative firms earn only normal profits. This indicates an optimal degree of productive and allocative efficiency in the industry.

Marginal Revenue = Marginal Cost: The Golden Rule of Profit Maximization

Suppose you find someone who is willing to give you a perfectly good $20 bill every time you give them $1. Based purely on economic considerations, should you make those trades? Of course, since you take in more than you pay out each time. But tomorrow, suppose the same person comes back to trade again, and now is only willing to give you $10 for every dollar you give them. Again, strictly as a financial proposition, should you do it? Or instead, should you refuse because you are only getting half as much for each dollar as you did yesterday? Naturally, you should do it. In fact, you will continue to trade up to the point where the person offers you one dollar or less for each dollar you want to trade. At that point, it's not to your advantage to trade any longer. The goose has stopped laying golden eggs.

The economic moral of this little fable is that firms maximize profits by producing and selling products using the same rule you were using in this example: they add to their profits (or lose less, if we are discussing an unprofitable firm) by producing and selling additional products as long as marginal revenue exceeds marginal cost. If selling a product brings in 20 additional dollars in revenues and only adds $1 to costs, that's good business. Spending $19 to bring in $20 isn't as great a deal, but the additional $1 in profits (or $1 less in losses) is still worth having. This is illustrated in Figure 9-6.

The marginal revenue and marginal cost schedules shown in Figure 9-6 don't give us enough information to know whether that firm is maximizing profits or minimizing losses. To determine this, we have to know whether *total revenue* is greater or less than *total cost* or, equivalently, whether *average revenue* is greater or less than *average total cost*. That kind of information is shown in Figure 9-5 and also, numerically, in Table 9-1. In both of these cases, however, firms are shown earning profits. So you may wonder why any firm that is losing money would continue to stay in business, even if you happen to know that in any given year many firms that are losing money continue to produce goods and services -- including some Fortune 500 firms. In turns out that even highly competitive firms, which can get out of their current line of business very easily, may be acting rationally by continuing to operate at a loss in the short run. That is the subject of the following section.

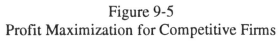

Figure 9-5
Profit Maximization for Competitive Firms

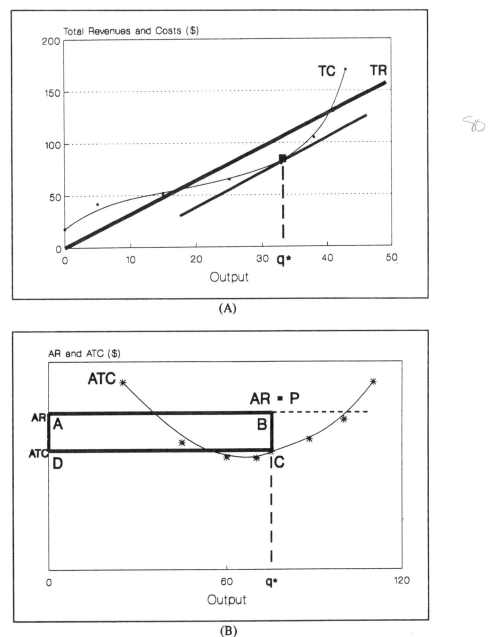

(A)

(B)

In panel (A), the total revenue schedule for a competitive firm, shown earlier in Figure 9-4, has been superimposed on the total cost schedule developed in Figure 7-5. Economic profits are maximized at output level q*, where total revenues exceed total costs by the greatest amount. This level of output is found by constructing a tangent to the total cost schedule that is parallel to the total revenue schedule. Moving to either higher or lower

262

output levels, the total cost curve draws closer to the total revenue schedule and reduces the level of profits, eventually exceeding revenues and thus depicting a range of output levels where the firm will incur losses.

In panel (B), the average revenue (AR) or demand schedule for the competitive firm, presented earlier in Figure 9-3, is shown with the average total cost (ATC) schedule developed in Figure 7-8. The firm earns average economic profits equal to the difference between AR and ATC for each unit of output it sells, so its total economic profits are equal to that vertical distance times the horizontal distance which reflects its output level. This total area is shown above as the rectangle labeled ABCD. By maximizing the area of this rectangle, which is done here at q*, the firm will maximize its profits.

Figure 9-6
Setting MR = MC: Economists' Golden Rule

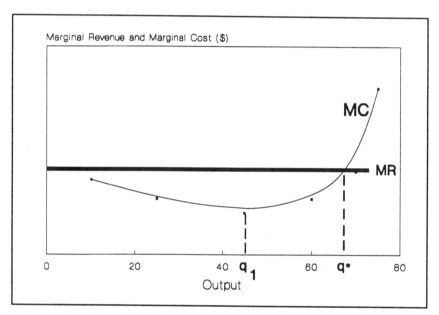

To maximize profits or minimize losses, a firm should choose the output level at which marginal revenue (MR) is equal to marginal cost (MC). As long as MR > MC, the firm will earn more profits or lose less by increasing output. When MR < MC, it costs the firm more to make its last unit of output than it receives by selling it, so it should reduce its output level to q*. Note that firms will not maximize the difference between MR and MC, at q_1. Firms net the most money on a single transaction at q_1, but can increase *total* profits by selling additional units as long as MR > MC.

The MR = MC rule for profit maximization or loss minimization applies to all kinds of firms. However, the particular MR schedule shown above is for a competitive firm, as developed in Figure 9-4. The MC schedule is taken from Figure 7-7.

Table 9-1
A Numerical Example of Profit Maximization By a Competitive Firm

Price/ Average Revenue	Output	Total Revenue	Marginal Revenue	Fixed Costs	Variable Costs	Total Costs	Marginal Costs	Economic Profit Or Loss
$10	0	$ 0	$ --	$15	$ 0	$ 15	$ --	$-15
10	1	10	10	15	5	20	5	-10
10	2	20	10	15	7	22	2	-2
10	3	30	10	15	11	26	4	+4
10	4	40	10	15	17	32	6	+8
10	5	50	10	15	27	42	10	+8
10	6	60	10	15	42	57	15	+3
10	7	70	10	15	64	79	22	-9
10	8	80	10	15	96	111	32	-31

Using hypothetical data that is consistent with the cost and revenue schedules developed earlier in this chapter and in Chapter 7, you can see that the profit maximizing firm will increase output up to the point where MR = MC (shown above at the output level of 5 units), but no further. Using discrete data as in the table, if this firm can only produce and sell whole units of output it will be equally well off producing either 4 or 5 units, in terms of profit maximization. Using continuous data, as in Figure 9-7, shows that firms have a financial incentive to produce all of the way up to the point where MR = MC.

The Shutdown Point and Short-Run Supply Schedules

Figure 9-7 shows a competitive firm that is incurring losses in the short run. We know the firm is losing money because the demand/average revenue schedule is lower than the average total cost curve at all levels of output. And we know this is a short-run situation because only part of the firm's costs are variable. (Note that average variable costs are less than average total cost, and remember that ATC = AVC + AFC.) As you saw in Chapter 7, the difference between average total cost and average variable cost at any level of output is average fixed cost. So, given that, the question is whether this firm will be better off shutting down, or continuing to operate at a loss. The answer is that, in the short run, this firm is going to lose some money whether it shuts down or continues to operate. Therefore, it will try to decide which way it loses less. If the firm shuts down, it still has to pay its fixed costs; if it continues to operate, it may lose more, less, or the same amount. With the costs and revenues curve shown in Figure 9-7, it will lose less by continuing to produce and sell its product. So, in this case, it will choose to operate in the hope that it will be able to lower its costs in the future, or experience an increase in demand and product price. If that doesn't happen, eventually the firm will go out of business.

The key thing to see in this short-run situation is that, by continuing to produce, the firm recovers all of its variable costs *plus* some, though not all, of its fixed costs. It must pay its fixed costs regardless of whether it operates or not, so those costs are effectively irrelevant in its decision on whether or not to stay in business. The real question is, therefore, can it cover anything more than its variable costs? If so, it should continue to produce. If it can't, it should shut down and cut its losses. The point at which a competitive firm will just cover all of its variable costs is, in fact, the point at which its marginal cost curve cuts through its average variable cost curve. At any market price below this level the firm will shut down, so this is known as the firm's *SHUTDOWN POINT*.

Figure 9-7
Minimizing Losses

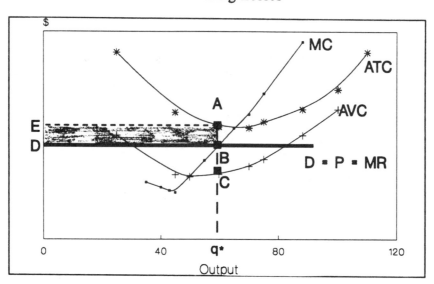

Financially, the best possible output level for the firm is at q*, where MR = MC. There, if it chooses to operate, it will lose an amount equal to AB on each unit it produces and sells. But, if it shuts down, it must pay its fixed costs, which have an average value of AC at this level of output. Since AB is less than AC, the firm will continue to produce in the short run, and face total economic losses equal to the area labeled ABDE.

At any price above the shutdown point, the firm produces where MR = MC to minimize losses or (at prices that are higher than the firm's average total costs) to maximize profits. As shown in Figure 9-8, this means that the marginal cost curve at all points above its intersection with the AVC schedule is the competitive firm's short-run supply schedule. In other words, it shows how much the firm will produce and sell at all different prices above the shutdown point.

Economic Profits, Entry and Exit, and P = Minimum ATC

Suppose many firms in a competitive industry are operating at a loss in the short run and that, over time, it becomes clear they will not be able to lower their costs or expect an increase in the market demand for the product they produce. Eventually, some firms' owners will shut down operations and move their resources out of the production of this good or service into some other endeavor. As shown earlier, in Figure 9-2, the effect of this exit is to decrease the *industry* supply curve, which leads to a higher market price and demand schedule for the remaining *firms* in this industry, even though the market demand curve does not change.

Figure 9-8
The Competitive Firm's Shutdown Point and Short-Run Supply Schedule

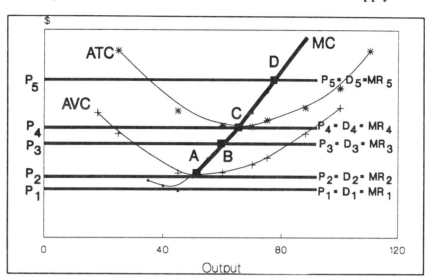

At all prices above P_2, the firm will produce where MR = MC. So, at P_3 it will produce at point B, at P_4 it will produce at point C, and at P_5 it will produce at point D. Note that all of these points lie directly on the firm's marginal cost curve, demonstrating that at all prices above point A the MC curve is the firm's short-run supply schedule. At point A, the firm is technically indifferent between shutting down and continuing to produce, based only on its short-run financial considerations. At any point below point A (i.e., at any price lower than P_2), the firm will minimize its losses by shutting down.

A related kind of adjustment process is shown in Figure 9-9; but in this case we see entry into the market, which occurs when competitive firms earn short-run economic profits. Recall from Chapter 7 that economic profits are payments that exceed the opportunity costs of the resources invested by firms. Or put differently, since economists count normal profits as a cost of doing business and include them in total cost and average total cost schedules, economic profits are earned whenever revenues exceed these cost measures. Since we also assume that entry into a competitive industry is easy and relatively inexpensive, economic profits will quickly lure new firms into an industry. That shifts the industry supply curve to the right, lowering the market price for products produced by these firms. Once again, the firms' demand curves shift even though the market demand curve is constant.

266

Figure 9-9
Economic Profits Cause Entry Into Competitive Markets

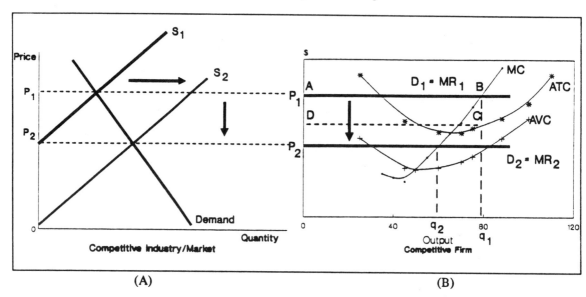

(A)   (B)

Initially in the pair of graphs shown above, the market supply schedule is S_1 and the price taken by competitive firms is P_1. Firms with these cost and revenue schedules will produce where MR = MC, at q_1, and earn both normal *and* economic profits (shown as area ABCD). This will attract new firms into the industry, shifting the industry supply schedule to the right (to S_2) and lowering the market price for the product (to P_2). Since this price is below the firms' ATC schedule, there will eventually be some exit from the industry. That will move the industry supply schedule back toward S_1, and market price back toward P_1, but not all of the way back if resource owners are learning from these adjustments. The eventual equilibrium position for the industry, given this level of industry demand and a representative firm's production costs, is shown in Figure 9-10.

Equilibrium in a competitive industry occurs when the price a firm takes (i.e., its demand and average revenue schedule) is tangent to the firm's average total cost curve, as shown in Figure 9-10. At any higher price firms will earn economic profits, so entry will occur; at any lower price firms will not earn normal profits, so exit will occur.

Competitive firms achieve two kinds of *PRODUCTIVE EFFICIENCY*. First, they always produce whatever output level they choose to produce at the lowest possible cost. Second, in equilibrium, they also produce the particular level of output at which production costs are lowest, q* in Figure 9-10. In fact, competitive firms have little choice in these matters -- they effectively have no margin for error in choosing the right output level and the right production technology. Because entry into their industries is so easy, if they don't meet both of these efficiency criteria they won't earn normal profits, and will be driven out of business by other firms that do.

As significant as this idea of productive efficiency is, perfectly competitive firms also achieve an even broader measure of efficiency, which we discuss in the final section of this chapter.

267

Figure 9-10
Equilibrium for a Competitive Firm

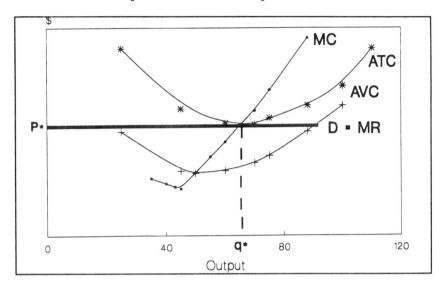

In equilibrium, competitive firms produce where MR = MC and earn normal, but not economic, profits. This occurs when price (p*) is equal to the minimum point of the firm's average total cost schedule, which indicates an optimal degree of efficiency in production. Price is also equal to marginal cost, which indicates the optimal allocation of scarce resources.

P = MC and the Optimal Allocation of Scarce Resources

Notice in Figure 9-10 that, after entry and exit has occurred, competitive firms reach an equilibrium where P = AR = MR = MC = minimum ATC, and the firm is earning only normal profits. We have already explained why P = AR = MR for a competitive firm, why MR = MC is the profit maximizing or loss minimizing level of output for any producing firm, and the significance of the P = minimum ATC result. Now, more importantly, you must understand the significance of the P = MC outcome which, as you will see over the next few chapters, occurs as a routine outcome *only* in competitive industries.

Remember that price is a measure of what consumers must give up to acquire a unit of a product, and that consumers will buy a given product so long as they value additional units of the product more than they value what they must give up in order to buy them. Many consumers may enjoy substantial amounts of consumer surplus when they buy their first few units of a product at its market price but, at the margin, the last unit of the product that is purchased only provides sufficient satisfaction to justify the price that the consumer had to pay. In other words, no consumer surplus was obtained from that particular unit, and the market price measured its full value to the consumer.

The marginal cost of producing that last unit of output measures the economic value of the resources the firm used to produce that product, in terms of the other things those resources could have been used to make. If production had stopped at a lower level of output where P > MC, at points such as q_1 in Figure 9-11, consumers would value additional units of this product (measured by the prices they are willing and able to pay) more than the value of the resources required to produce this additional output (measured by the marginal cost or supply schedule shown in this figure). If production moved beyond the point where P = MC (e.g., at q_2), the cost of producing the last units of output would exceed the value consumers place on the last units of the product that are produced (i.e., P < MC). Only where P = MC is there an optimal degree of *ALLOCATIVE EFFICIENCY*.

268

Figure 9-11
P = MC and the Optimal Allocation of Resources

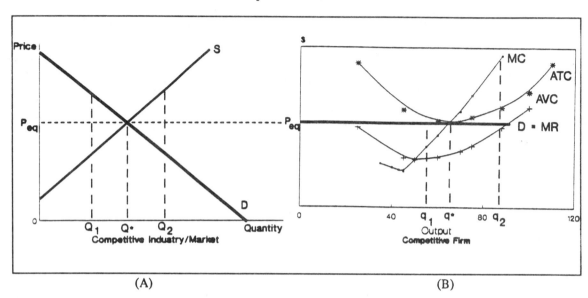

(A)   (B)

The graph in panel (A) shows the market demand and supply schedules in a competitive industry. That supply schedule is, as explained in Chapter 1, found by horizontally summing up the supply schedules of individual firms in the industry. The graph in panel (B) depicts a representative firm in this industry.

At the equilibrium level of output, shown as Q* and q* in the two graphs, there is an optimal allocation of resources because P = MC. Note that if output was held below this level, say at Q_1 and q_1, firms would not be maximizing profits and, at the industry level, both producer *and* consumer surplus would be reduced. Most importantly, at those levels consumers value additional units of the product more than they value other things that could be made with these resources, since P > MC.

At output levels that are too high, shown as Q_2 and q_2 in the two graphs, firms also fail to maximize profits. But again, most significantly, at those levels the value of other goods and services that could have been produced with these resources (measured by MC) exceeds the price consumers are willing and able to pay for the last units of this output.

When P > MC, economists say there is an underallocation of resources to the production of the product in question, because marginal units of output are valued more than the resources required to produce them. If P < MC, however, the marginal output is not valued as much as the inputs used to produce it, in terms of the other things that the inputs could have been used to produce. So, in these cases, we say that there is an overallocation of resources to this industry or product. That means, of course, that when P = MC there is neither an overallocation or underallocation of resources. Or, stated in a more affirmative way, economists say that the allocation of scarce resources is optimal. That's a strong sounding statement for economists to make, and in fact it is made with several underlying assumptions and qualifications.

Specifically, in making this claim for perfectly competitive markets economists assume that price and marginal cost figures accurately reflect the true costs and benefits to all consumers and producers that are affected by the production and consumption of a product. That means that they assume there are no significant externalities associated with the product, as discussed in Chapter 5, on either the supply or demand side of the market. Even more broadly, they assume that efficiency in the allocation process is to be judged by market criteria, which means that all of the dollar signals provided by consumers and producers are taken as equal -- a dollar spent for atom bombs or caviar is counted no differently from a dollar spent to buy soup for a soup kitchen or heat in an orphanage, and dollars spent by the foolish or the criminally insane count just as much as dollars spent by the wise and the saintly.

As discussed in Chapter 2, this kind of methodological individualism is very democratic in an economic sense: one dollar equals one vote, and everyone's dollars count the same. But, by the same token, that requires us to recognize one additional qualification in saying that P = MC signals an optimal allocation of resources. Specifically, such statements are made in the context of a given pattern of income distribution, since shifts in family incomes will lead to changes in market demand for many products, which in turn will affect production and hiring decisions made by many firms. Factors affecting the distribution of income are largely economic in nature, as you will see in Chapters 15 and 16. But as you almost certainly recognize already, they are also shaped by public policies and the political climate in a nation. Minimum wage laws, public assistance programs for low-income families, tariffs, quotas, and tax policies all have an impact on the spending and resource hiring patterns observed in private markets, whether or not those markets are competitive.

The efficiency standards derived from the models of perfect competition developed in this chapter are very important in discussions on many such public policies. By achieving these efficiency outcomes the economic problem of scarcity is lessened, in the sense of producing the greatest market value of output from the limited resources that are at our disposal. Historically, that stress on efficiency and production has been the major force in the rise of the middle classes in industrialized nations, not just the rise of a few rich and powerful families. But at the same time, public policies which stress security and equality in the political and economic spheres have also contributed to personal welfare in these nations.

Mainstream economists have never suggested that perfect competition represents a complete world view, even in an ideal, purely theoretical, framework. Many of the policy issues mentioned here will be considered in later chapters, as modifications to the workings of a system of competitive markets. And other policies are intended as remedies for problems that develop when markets are not, or in some cases cannot be, perfectly competitive. That issue is introduced in the next chapter.

Case Study #12
The Stock Market and the Efficient Markets Hypothesis

The popular image of Wall Street, and in particular the two large stock exchanges in New York's financial district (the New York and American Stock Exchanges) is a kind of legal battlefield or playground for the wealthy, tainted by the unscrupulous dealings of powerful traders exploiting "insider" information. This image is promoted in fictional treatments as diverse as movies like *Wall Street* and *Trading Places*, and Broadway musicals like *How Now Dow Jones* and *How To Succeed In Business Without Really Trying*. At times, investigations and convictions of those who have violated the regulations of the Securities and Exchange Commission support this view -- Ivan Boesky's case is one of the most publicized recent examples. But in general, and in sharp opposition to these popular images, economists view financial markets such as the stock exchange as examples of extremely efficient, and in many respects very competitive, markets. The factual evidence supporting this efficient market view of the stock market is both extensive and, in some respects, subtle. We will consider some of that basic evidence here.

Companies that are listed on the major stock exchanges typically have millions of shares of common stock outstanding, and that stock is owned by literally thousands of stockholders. Over a hundred million shares of stock are traded in the United States every weekday, and prices for many well known stocks change every few minutes, if not every few seconds. Very large companies, like General Electric, Eastman Kodak, and Gulf Oil, have more than 100,000 stockowners; and AT&T and General Motors have more than a million. However, some institutional investors own substantial portions (a few percent or more) of some listed companies. These institutional investors include mutual funds (like the Dreyfus and Vanguard Funds, or others operated by most of the large brokerage houses) and pension programs for large groups of unionized or non-unionized employees (one of the largest of these is TIAA-CREF, a plan originally set up by Andrew Carnegie for college professors and administrators). Corporate raiders and takeover artists, such as T. Boone Pickens and Carl Icahn, have also acquired major holdings in large companies like Unocal, Disney, TWA, and Texaco. And some of the (relatively) smaller companies listed on the major stock exchanges are controlled and managed by the families which started or built up the companies. For example, the Steinfeld family currently manages and controls the Shelby Williams company, which makes much of the furniture purchased by large hotels and restaurant chains around the country. It is not unusual for such companies to become listed on "over-the-counter" markets, and eventually on the large national exchanges, as they sell stock to raise the financial capital required to expand their business. But, over time, the founding family's role in these business often declines, or ends abruptly when the company is sold. The classic example of this pattern is the Ford Motor Company, which was run by Henry Ford and his children (including Edsel) for more than four decades. Now, of course, Ford is a more typical enterprise, publicly owned and managed by employees who are not related to the Ford family.

This background information suggests that there is a high degree of competition on the stock market, but probably not perfect competition for the stocks of all companies, because some individuals or groups do hold large blocks of stocks. In those cases, buying and selling decisions made by major stockholders can have an impact on the market prices for these securities. In fact, even if the large stockholders only buy or sell a relatively small number of their shares, that may trigger rumors and reactions by other traders. Still, the stock market probably comes as close as we get in the United States to a competitive market that is large, highly visible and national in scope.

It is an even better example of a market that is a well organized, carefully studied, extensively documented, and widely forecast. A wealth of information on the stock market goes out every day on news broadcasts, through the financial press (in particular, through well known publications such as *The Wall Street Journal*, *Forbes*, *Fortune*, and *Business Week*), in more expensive investors' newsletters and "hot tip" services, and from an international industry of brokerage and research firms. Finance and economics professors write hundreds of articles a year on investment and risk-minimization strategies that can be used on the stock market; and those who publish the most promising studies are frequently hired by brokerage houses or large banks as consultants or full-time employees, to try out their ivory-tower ideas in the trading pits.

Given this degree of information gathering, and modern communications facilities that transmit new information globally in a matter of seconds, some scholars developed what has come to be known as the *EFFICIENT MARKETS HYPOTHESIS*. Those who accept this idea, including many prominent economists, claim that the prices of products traded on such efficient markets (including major stocks, bonds, commodities, and futures options on these products) almost immediately reflect all publically-known information that has an impact on the value of those products. Stated this way, the theory sounds somewhat bland and innocuous; but it offers several surprising and important predictions, which have been used to test the theory. For example, if current prices really do signal everything that is known about a security (except, of course, by those with "inside information," who are legally prohibited from making trades to profit from this knowledge), then on average anyone should be able to pick a group of stocks *at random*[1] that will perform as well as the stocks recommended by professional stock researchers and brokerage houses. In fact, to the extent that they save on brokerage commissions by doing this, they should do a little better than those who pay for these services. To dramatize this, proponents of the idea sometimes choose a portfolio by throwing darts at lists of stocks, blindfolded, or have children or monkeys throw the darts for them. Local newscasters love these stunts, but you can see why full-service brokers and the "hot tip" newsletters often argue against the validity of the efficient-markets hypothesis. If it became widely known and accepted as true, the demand for their services would fall as many investors began to purchase no-load mutual funds, or individual securities from discount brokers who do not offer research services and buy/sell recommendations.

So what do the empirical tests of the efficient market theory of the stock market show? The results are generally favorable to the theory, but mixed in enough respects to keep the issue alive. For example, over periods

---

[1]The classic book on this idea is Burton G. Malkiel's *A Random Walk Down Wall Street*, first published in 1973, and re-issued in several later editions (New York: W. W. Norton & Co.).

of several years or longer, the dartboard approach usually does work as well as the *average* return earned by buying the recommended lists from the major brokerage houses. In other words, the recommended lists don't consistently outperform the average return for all stocks listed on the exchange. Of course in any given year about half of the lists outperform the market average, and about half are below it -- that's what makes the average an average. Over longer periods of time, few research services are able to outperform the market, and those that do typically do so by very small amounts. A monitoring service run by *Forbes* columnist Mark Hulbert found, for example, that only a dozen or so of the 100 portfolios recommended by investment newsletters were able to "beat the market" from 1980-88, and even those by not much.[2] The large, institutional investors had about the same record.

Several popular "rules of thumb" used by some prominent investors and advisors have also been shown to give results that are, at best, only in line with the average performance of the market over the long run. (One such rule, in vogue with some investors for a time, is to buy a stock after its price has risen for two consecutive days, and sell if it falls three days in a row.) Most impressive, perhaps, are studies that tried to determine how quickly you would have to execute buy and sell orders to consistently gain from public releases of information that would be expected to affect certain stock prices. Some results indicate that you have about thirty *seconds* to act before the information is incorporated into the stock prices -- and that's efficient by almost anyone's standards.

But some recent research has also uncovered a few anomalies, which is to say evidence that runs contrary to the predictions of the efficient market theory. For example, stocks of smaller companies seem to rise faster than the market average *early in the month of January*. No one knows why this happens so regularly, or why buyers haven't recognized this and begun purchasing these stocks in earlier months, until the January performance of these stocks comes back in line with that of other stocks.

Many people have argued that an even greater challenge to the efficient market theory comes in the occasional periods of extreme market volatility. Volatility is, of course, a well known part of the stock market's behavior, as shown in Figure 9-12. The best known examples of big crashes on the stock market are "Black Tuesday" (October 28, 1929), which some writers claim precipitated the Great Depression, and much more recently "Black Monday" (October 19, 1987). Black Monday is actually the greater challenge to the efficient market theory, since it was larger in size and occurred after the reforms and limits to stock speculation that were enacted after the 1929 crash, and in an era of modern trading and communications technology. Therefore, we will look at a few facts and theories pertaining to this second great and inglorious episode on Wall Street.

By all standard measures, except the number of brokers and investors who jumped out of office windows in New York's financial district, "Black Monday" was a much darker day than "Black Tuesday." It came after a long and dramatic rise in stock prices (more than 200 percent in inflation-adjusted terms over a five-year period), which peaked in August of 1987. But on Black Monday the Dow-Jones industrials fell more than 500 points -- a 23.2 percent decline in the value of these stocks, which was almost double the 12.8 percent fall on Black Tuesday that occurred more than 60 years earlier. The market value of U.S. securities (including those that are not in the Dow Jones index) fell by some $500 billion on Black Monday alone, and there were many more declines shortly before and after this one-day performance. So, if the stock market is really so efficient, how can something like that happen so suddenly and unexpectedly? In other words, how could stock prices get so far out of line before or after the crash, depending on which price level you think was "right"? Why wasn't the decline better anticipated and more spread out?

The answers to those questions depend in large part on who you choose to believe. But we do have a fairly good record of the events leading up to Black Monday, which analysts must somehow incorporate into their explanations.

---

[2]Reported in Susan Lee, "Efficient Market Theory Lives!," *Wall Street Journal*, May 6, 1988, p. 16.

Figure 9-12
Volatility in Common Stock Prices, Or Why Every Bull and Bear Has Its Days

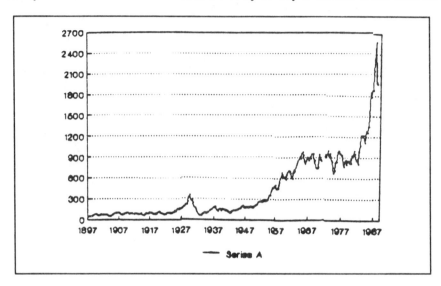

Over the long run stock prices trend with the growth of the national economy, but they are also subject to more frequent and extreme fluctuations. This occurs because of uncertainty about the future performance of the economy *and* speculation about the actions other buyers and sellers in the market will take which, in the short-run, are affected by psychological and political events (such as President Eisenhower's heart attack in the 1950s) as well as purely economic factors.

The "price" plotted here is the well known Dow-Jones industrial index. This index is a weighted average of prices for 30 common stocks (since 1928 -- originally the index included fewer stocks) of "blue chip" U.S. corporations. The blue chips are large, relatively safe and stable firms, and the data points shown are closing values for the Dow Jones industrials on the final business day in the months of January, April, July and October.

In October of 1987, many investors were concerned about the prospects of a recession, higher interest rates, or a combined effect in which higher interest rates might lead to a recession. Such concerns were supported by the knowledge that the economy had already surpassed the longest length of time for continuous peacetime growth and expansion in the post-WWII period, so many investors felt the country was "due" for a recession. It also appeared that the Federal Reserve Bank was pursuing policies designed to raise interest rates, slowly and gradually, which is bad news for businesses (because that affects their cost of investing) and, therefore, the stock market. Then, more dramatically and proximate to the crash, a series of unfavorable developments occurred.

For example, on Tuesday, October 13, Democrats controlling the House Ways and Means Committee agreed to support legislation making corporate takeovers less attractive. Such takeovers had, in part, stimulated the rise in stock values in the previous five years. Then, on Wednesday, October 14, data on the U.S. trade deficit was released which was worse than had been anticipated by most market analysts. That pushed interest rates up faster and the market fell by almost 100 points. On Thursday, October 15, one of the nation's largest banks raised its prime interest rate, and Treasury Secretary James Baker announced (to West Germany, in particular) that he was prepared to let the dollar fall further against foreign currencies. That was taken as a sign that interest rates would have to increase even more in the future, and the market fell another 57 points. On the Friday before Black Monday, Iranian gunboats attacked a U.S.-flagged oil tanker in the Persian Gulf, and general pessimism on interest rates, economic growth, and corporate profits continued. The market fell another 108 points. Over the following weekend the news continued along these lines, and when foreign stock exchanges opened while it was still Sunday night in New York, U.S. stocks listed on those exchanges began to fall rapidly.

When the New York exchanges opened on Black Monday, the general fall in prices was fast and furious. Computerized, "program trading" accounts that were set to sell large blocks of securities when prices for stocks and related futures contracts fell by such levels kicked in. And investors who had bought stocks on margin (by giving their brokers as little as half of the purchase price for stocks, and using the stocks themselves as security on these loans as long as the prices for the securities stayed high enough to cover this amount) had to sell or come up with more cash to cover their weakened positions. Trading in hundreds of stocks was suspended when the specialists on the exchanges who are charged with maintaining an orderly market in individual stocks used up their cash reserves, and banks refused to provide them with loans to maintain financial liquidity. Many individual investors couldn't get through to their brokers because of busy telephone lines, and many orders that were received couldn't be executed that day. On the nightly news that Monday, television journalists with little or no training in economics raised the spectre of another Great Depression in reports running from 15 seconds to 15 minutes in length. Over the next several weeks, a few economists and "prophets of gloom" who had written about an imminent economic collapse sold thousands of books and appeared on television talkshows to say they told us so.

Fortunately for the average economist and investor, things didn't turn out so badly over the next few weeks and months. Interest rates fell a little, as did the trade deficit, and the dollar leveled off against most other currencies. The national economy continued to grow (which led some economists to dust off the old line that the stock market has successfully predicted nine of the last five recessions). By the end of 1987, in fact, the market had recovered sufficiently to exceed its level at the beginning of the year by a comfortable margin, although it was still several hundred points below its August highpoint.

Proponents of the efficient markets hypothesis claim that all of this is consistent with the actions one would expect rational investors to take as such information becomes known and economic trends unfold. Opponents say it more closely resembles the speculative excesses and mob psychology seen in periods of financial panics and manias. Some of these writers claim that the market was only turned around as a result of extraordinary actions taken by the Federal Reserve System in re-establishing liquidity and access to cash for specialists and other traders, or by a small group of banks and traders who may have secretly manipulated key futures contracts on stock indexes that are traded on the Chicago Board of Trade. As it turns out, you will probably have to decide for yourself between these different explanations, or on how to blend them together, at least until those who analyze such episodes have better data from more such crashes to work with.

It does appear more likely that, as as Robert Schiller[3] and other economists have argued, the efficient market idea is more powerful and less prone to volatile swings in price levels when we consider a few, closely related stocks (such as those for firms in the same industry), rather than the overall market level as reflected in index values like the Dow Jones Industrials or the Standard and Poor 500. It may also be true that markets operate more rationally and efficiently in times of relative stability than they do in times of sudden and dramatic change. Ultimately, of course, this depends on how individual buyers and sellers in the market act under such conditions. After all, a market is only as efficient and rational as the people who trade in it.

Chapter Summary

1) Economists have identified several different levels of competition among buyers and sellers, ranging from the abstract notion of *PERFECT COMPETITION* presented in this chapter to several varieties of *IMPERFECT COMPETITION* and monopoly, which are considered in later chapters.

2) Perfectly competitive industries are characterized by price taking buyers and sellers with complete information on product price, quality, and availability. Firms in these industries produce *HOMOGENEOUS PRODUCTS*, and can easily exit or enter the industry. Such industries may not actually exist, at least in

---

[3]For a non-technical discussion of Schiller's work and the academic debate over the efficient markets hypothesis, see Gary Hector, "What Makes Stock Prices Move?," *Fortune*, October 10, 1988, pp. 69-76.

industrialized countries. However, economic models of such industries can be used to establish important efficiency criteria for real industries and competitive practices, and some U.S. firms and industries do meet several of these assumptions.

3) Buyers and sellers are *PRICE TAKERS* if their actions are such a small part of the overall activity in a market that they have no effect on product prices. In these cases, firms can buy or sell as much as they want at the market-determined price. That means this price simultaneously represents the firms' demand, *AVERAGE REVENUE*, and marginal revenue schedules. We know, therefore, that competitive firms' demand curves are perfectly price elastic, even though this is not true of the overall industry/market demand curves for the products they produce.

4) *ENTRY* by a large number of firms into a competitive market and industry will increase market supply, thus lowering the market price that represents the demand and marginal revenue schedules for the firms in this industry. *EXIT* from the market by a large number of firms decreases the industry supply curve and raises the market price, *ceteris paribus*.

5) Competitive firms must maximize profits or they will be driven out of business by firms that do. Firms maximize profits by producing where the positive difference between total revenue and total cost is greatest. This will always be at the output level at which marginal revenue (and therefore price, for perfectly competitive firms) is equal to marginal cost.

6) In the short run, a firm that can sell products at a price high enough to cover all of its variable costs and any part of its fixed costs will lose less money by producing than by shutting down. If it cannot cover all of its variable costs, however, it should stop producing. Therefore, since competitive firms that produce will operate where price equals marginal cost, their short-run supply schedule will be the marginal cost curve at all points greater than the minimum point on the average variable cost curve (the *SHUTDOWN POINT*).

7) Easy entry and exit in perfectly competitive industries means that firms reach an equilibrium position at which they earn only normal profits, and price equals both marginal cost and the minimum level of average total costs. This indicates that competitive firms achieve both *PRODUCTIVE AND ALLOCATIVE EFFICIENCY*. In other words, there is an optimal allocation of scarce resources assuming that no significant externalities exist, that we take the current pattern of income distribution as a given, and count each dollar spent in this and other markets as equally important.

8) (Case Study #12) The stock market is probably the best, though not a perfect, example of a competitive market in the United States that is large, highly visible, and national in scope. It is certainly extremely efficient in routine periods and, according to some analysts, perhaps so even during periods of great volatility, such as "Black Monday" of 1987 and "Black Tuesday" of 1929.

Review and Discussion Questions

1) Who do you believe benefits most from competition among a) producers, b) consumers, and c) employees and other resource owners? Why? In terms of the five general economic goals discussed in Chapter 2, which are most likely to be achieved under a system of perfect competition, and which are least likely?

2) If individual farmers in the U.S. are price takers, what characteristics of perfect competition are not met in this industry?

3) How much control over price would you say the following firms have: a) a new and used car dealership; b) a steel company; c) a physician; d) large and small banks; e) fast-food restaurants; and f) a television station

and network? Does the horizontal demand curve facing a perfectly competitive firm invalidate the law of demand?

4) List some recent examples of firms entering and exiting markets at both the local and national levels. Did you think of more examples of local or national firms? Which of the examples you listed would you say operated in the most competitive industries, and which in the least competitive?

5) Why might the rule of setting marginal revenue equal to marginal cost be easier for a firm to implement than trying to look at the difference between total revenue and total cost? Which of these two procedures, if either, do you think firms really use on a daily operating basis? If a firm produces at a level where total revenues and total costs are equal, is it earning profits? Will it continue to produce if this is the best it can do?

6) As nearly as possible, given the following data for a purely competitive firm, identify its shutdown point, its short-run supply schedule over the output ranges that are shown, and the output levels at which it could earn economic profits.

Total Product	Average Variable Cost	Average Total Cost	Marginal Cost
0	$00.00	----	----
1	90.00	$250.00	$ 90.00
2	82.50	162.50	75.00
3	78.33	131.67	70.00
4	78.25	118.25	78.00
5	81.40	113.40	94.00
6	88.67	115.33	125.00

7) Using the data from question #6, above, construct a graph that shows a competitive firm in equilibrium, earning only normal profits. (Hint: the equilibrium level of output may not be precisely at one of the integer values shown in the table.) How can you show, using your graph, that the firm is meeting the criteria for productive and allocative efficiency, as discussed in the text.

8) (Case Study #12) Describe how the stock market might work if it was a very inefficient market. Would that be a good development for brokers and authors of "hot tip" newsletters? For individual and institutional investors? Could this condition continue over time? If so, how?

Chapter 10
Long-Run Cost Schedules, Minimum Efficient Scale,
and the Level of Competition

In This Chapter...

the production and cost models developed in earlier chapters are extended to deal with cases in which all of a firm's inputs are variable and the law of diminishing returns does not hold. In this setting, firms may face average total cost schedules that rise, fall, or remain constant as the output level is increased. Economists have identified several factors that lead to these differences in long-run cost schedules, but can not predict reliably what kind of long-run cost curve a given firm or industry will face. That can only be established conclusively through empirical research. Similarly, only through "real world" observations can it be shown whether the long-run cost and demand curves facing a firm are conducive to a competitive market structure, or likely to lead to some type of imperfectly competitive market structure.

Long-Run Costs and Economies or Diseconomies of Scale

Economies of scale are present when a firm's long-run average total cost (LRATC) curve falls as its output level increases. Diseconomies of scale lead to a rising LRATC curve, while constant economies of scale are indicated by a horizontal segment of this curve. Production technologies, managerial efficiencies or inefficiencies, and changes in input prices that are related to changes in the firm's output level are the major factors that generate economies, diseconomies, or constant economies of scale. Those factors are important, since differences in firms' LRATC curves related to the size of a firm's operations have a significant effect both on how the firm chooses to operate and the overall level of competition in an industry made up of such firms.

Long-Run Cost Schedules

In driving home the importance of distinguishing between the long run and the short run, Lord Keynes once summed things up by noting "In the long run, we are all dead." Fortunately, we can be a little less morbid on this point, and show why both short-run and long-run considerations are important to business executives and to policy makers. We will begin that discussion in this chapter, and expand it in several later chapters.

The key difference between the short run and the long run is that all inputs are assumed to be variable in the long run, while at least one input is fixed in the short run. The most important result of that difference is an obvious one, at least to economists: When no inputs are fixed the law of diminishing returns is no longer relevant, and neither are the short-run cost schedules which were derived from that basic relationship (in Chapter 7). So what do we have left to work with in the long run? Or what can we develop to use in place of those short-run cost schedules?

Actual production must be done in a real facility using some capital resources, so to say that such inputs are variable is really to say that the time horizon is long enough for a firm to change the level of these and all other inputs. For example, in the long run a firm has time to design, build, or acquire whatever size factory, stock of capital equipment, or amount of land it chooses to use in achieving its production goals, not just vary the amount of labor it hires.

Each possible mix of inputs offers the firm a production schedule and a set of cost curves that are, in fact, a standard set of short-run cost curves *once a specific plant is built and treated as a fixed input.* So in estimating

278

LONG-RUN COST SCHEDULES, a firm is really looking at a set of alternative short-run cost schedules that show the best way of producing any output level the firm wants to produce. In this context, best means minimizing the cost of producing different levels of output. Therefore, long-run total cost and average total cost schedules identify the least-cost method of producing different output levels when firms are free to use any mix of inputs.

Specifically, this means that the *LONG-RUN AVERAGE TOTAL COST (LRATC)* curve will be derived from a series of short-run average total cost schedules, each of which assumes a different level of capital usage and productive capacity. Not surprisingly, some plant sizes are more efficient in producing certain output levels than others, as shown in Figure 10-1. The long-run average total cost curve connects points from a series of short-run average total cost curves, to show the least-cost production methods and plant sizes that the firm would use to produce different levels of output. It is therefore an envelope curve, with the envelope containing all of the short-run average total cost curves the firm would face in building production facilities of different sizes, designed to produce different levels of output.

Figure 10-1
The Long-Run Average Total Cost Schedule

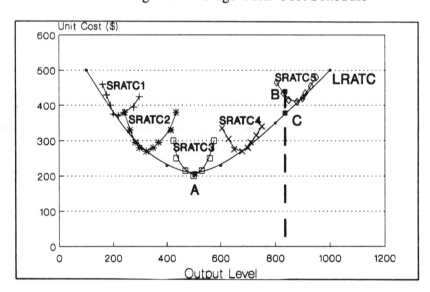

Long-run curves are relevant when firms have time to choose any level of capital and all other inputs. Once a firm builds and operates a particular plant and equipment base, however, it will work off of the short-run schedule associated with that plant size as long as that facility is a fixed input. Here, the curves labeled SRATC 1, 3, and 5 are short-run cost curves associated with a relatively small, medium, and large-scale plant, respectively. The LRATC is derived from these short-run cost curves (and others) by connecting all of the points representing the least-cost means of producing a given level of output. Point A is thus a point on both a short-run and long-run ATC curve. Point B is on a short-run ATC curve but *not* on the long-run LRATC curve, because point C offers a lower-cost way to produce the same amount of output when the firm has enough time to build a different size plant (a little smaller than the plant associated with SRATC5).

The particular shape of the long-run average total cost curve shown in Figure 10-1 is chosen as a matter of convenience and illustration. It is not necessary, for theoretical reasons, that LRATC curves have the same "U-shape" as the short-run ATC and AVC curves derived in Chapter 7, and then used in the short-run models of perfect competition in Chapter 9. In fact, in the following section you will see that economic theory does not preclude long-run average cost schedules that exhibit strictly positive, negative, or zero slopes, or the U-shape that combines all three of these features. The shape of *long-run* average total cost schedules for different kinds of firms can only be established through empirically based observations and calculations, not by economic theories and laws. However, the factors that generally influence the shape and slope of long-run cost schedules can be identified, as well as their broad economic consequences.

Economies of Scale and Increasing Returns to Scale

How many times have you bought the large, "economy size" of a product to get a better deal, or heard that mass producing a product will substantially lower its costs. Students often find the law of diminishing returns surprising and confusing just because they have heard that large volumes of output are cheaper to produce (on a per unit basis) so many times. In the long run, bigger can be cheaper; but it isn't always or, in fact, even usually that way. Yet when it is, the results can be dramatic.

In pre-industrial eras, for example, guns, fine fabrics, glassware, mechanical toys, and even most fruits and vegetables were all luxury goods that were hand-made or grown exclusively for the rich and powerful. In the last few centuries much of the progress made in producing these goods for mass markets was based on technological and scientific breakthroughs that created entirely new products and production methods. But some of it was also due to expanding the *level* of output in these industries.

When unit production costs are lowered as the level of output is increased we say a firm is operating in a range of *ECONOMIES OF SCALE*. In such ranges, *LONG-RUN MARGINAL COSTS (LRMC)* lie below the long-run average total cost curve, as shown in Figure 10-2. Sometimes these economies occur because firms can purchase large quantities of inputs at lower prices than small quantities of the same inputs. But that begs the basic question of why it is ever less expensive to produce and sell large quantities of any product, including inputs, than small quantities.

Figure 10-2
Economies of Scale

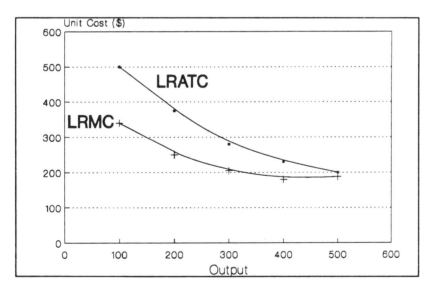

Over the range of output levels shown above, using hypothetical data, this firm experiences economies of scale. With the freedom to vary all inputs, the firm is able to reduce average production costs as it increases output. Long-run marginal costs are, therefore, always below the long-run average total cost curve. Many firms enjoy economies of scale over some range of production, but very few experience economies of scale over all feasible output levels.

The more revealing cases of economies of scale are those in which falling per unit costs occur directly because production methods for the firm's output are more efficient at higher output levels. In those cases, economists say that a firm experiences *INCREASING RETURNS TO SCALE*, because increases in the use of *all* inputs lead to a more-than-proportionate increase in the level of output. For example, suppose a 10 percent increase in all inputs leads to a more than 10 percent increase in output. Assuming input prices are constant, that means per unit production costs will fall as the firm produces more output.

At this point, you should be asking "What causes increasing returns to scale?" Usually, the cause is one of three things, or some combination of these factors: 1) increased specialization and division of labor, 2) more effective use of indivisible inputs, and 3) technical efficiencies. We will consider each of these factors in turn.

Larger output levels and the corresponding growth in the number of resources a firm employs often create additional opportunities for specialization and the division of labor. For example, when a firm is very small a single manager may spend part of his or her time as a bookkeeper, part as a personnel manager and safety director, part as a production supervisor or troubleshooter, and part as a sales consultant. With sales and output growth more managers are hired, and each can spend more time in fewer, but more focused, activities. The same kind of thing happens with skilled and unskilled production workers, and the use of specialized tools and machinery. Costs are lowered whenever doing one small part of a job is more efficient than producing an entire product, or a relatively large part of the product. As a result, at least up to a point, the benefits from specialization can help a firm lower its production costs by increasing the productivity of managers, workers, and capital resources.

The second general source of increasing returns to scale is the greater opportunity to use *INDIVISIBLE INPUTS*, which must be acquired in relatively large and expensive units. For example, some machines that substitute for labor (or for less complex machinery) produce large quantities of output in short periods of time, but are costly to purchase or lease. One example is the machines that rapidly insert corks in bottles of wine. Small vineyards that produce low levels of output rarely buy such machines because they would sit around, unused, most of the time. So these firms use hand labor or smaller, slower, and less expensive corking machines. But as a winery expands the larger and more expensive machines often become a profitable investment, because the firm can use the equipment more often and more intensively, and because the expense is offset by sufficient decreases in expenditures for other resources, such as labor.

Expanded use of indivisible resources can result in increasing returns to scale, but there is often a high degree of "lumpiness" in these resources' impact on a firm's production and cost schedules. In other words, a firm either uses these lumpy inputs that produce so efficiently, or it doesn't. If holding unit production costs down by using them makes the difference between staying in business or failing, the firm must either sell a large volume of output or shut down. For such businesses, there are no middle-of-the-road solutions or production levels. Instead, they must attain what physicists might describe as a "critical mass" of production and sales.

Note also that an indivisible input might be a specialized kind of worker -- not just machinery. For example, insurance companies have to find large enough markets to cover the cost of their actuaries; and nuclear power plants must serve markets large enough to pay for the services of highly specialized engineers.

The third major factor which can promote increasing returns to scale is called *TECHNICAL EFFICIENCY*, and does apply only to capital resources like machinery and other physical facilities, not to labor or other inputs. Certain characteristics of capital inputs sometimes make it less expensive to build and use large structures rather than small ones. For example, the laws of geometry dictate that a large pipeline, tanker ship, or any other physical cylinder that is used to store or transport liquids, gases, or "flowable" solids such as grain and sand, will require less construction material to handle a given volume of product than two smaller cylinders used to handle the same amount. Remember, the opening on a 16"-diameter pipe is larger than the sum of the openings on two 8"-diameter pipes, because that area is found by multiplying *pi* times the *squared* radius of the opening. The formula for the surface area of a cylinder, which is more complex and not so well known, offers a related kind of technical efficiency, and indicates the savings in construction materials even more directly. But you should also recognize that the cost of engines, pumps, or other parts used with cylinder-shaped equipment may rise faster than the costs of construction materials decrease, resulting in an economic limit on the maximum size of such vessels. Those limits are, in fact, a subject for the following section.

Diseconomies of Scale and Decreasing Returns to Scale

With economies of scale, bigger *is* better in terms of minimizing the average cost of producing a unit of a product. Why, then, if many products are characterized by such economies over some range of output, don't these savings and efficiencies from bigness go on forever? In some cases physical limits develop, for example in fueling or cooling large engines, or in the ability of building materials to withstand stresses once a building becomes too high or a bridge span becomes too long. But more often, economists find human and organizational limits to the effective size of different kinds of organizations, including firms, labor unions, and government agencies.

As any organization becomes very large it is increasingly difficult to coordinate all the information about the various facets of its operations. Top managers know less about their employees, fewer details concerning the operation of different departments, and less and less about the specialized personnel and operational functions that evolve as employment and output levels are increased. That makes it more difficult and expensive to collect the information needed to develop strategies that will achieve the goals of the organization.

It also becomes difficult to implement policies efficiently once they are developed. Frequently, more and more layers of middle-managers must be put in place to deal with these problems; in short, bureaucracy sets in and unit production costs go up. Government agencies are a particularly visible example of this problem because federal, state, and urban government has become so large in the twentieth century, with branches and departments that are often larger than most private firms or unions. But the private sector, too -- including both "big business" and "big labor" -- is by no means immune to bureaucratic arrangements, or to the coordination and information problems associated with operating on a larger scale. So bigger is not always better, either in business or in other pursuits.

When *DISECONOMIES OF SCALE* are directly related to production inefficiencies that arise at higher levels of output, and not to financial considerations such as rising input prices, we refer to this phenomenon as *DECREASING RETURNS TO SCALE*. Technically, decreasing returns to scale exist when an increase in all inputs leads to a less-than-proportionate increase in output. For example, hiring 20 percent more inputs might lead to only a 10 percent increase in the level of goods and services produced. With constant input prices, the result of these decreasing returns to scale are that average total costs rise, as shown in Figure 10-3. And, of course, as you saw in Chapter 7, when average costs are rising the marginal cost schedule must lie above the average cost curve.

Economists describe the kind of long-run cost schedule shown in Figure 10-3 as exhibiting diseconomies of scale or increasing costs; either phrase implies the same thing. The equivalency of these terms simply reinforces a relationship you have seen several times now -- what happens in the physical production process and in input markets determines what will happen to a firm's costs.

Constant Economies of Scale and Returns to Scale

The LRATC curve in Figure 10-4 shows a firm that experiences economies of scale over the output range from 0 to Q_1, and diseconomies of scale at all output levels greater than Q_2. Between Q_1 and Q_2, however, long-run average costs are constant. That means no significant economies or diseconomies of scale are at work in this range, or that they are both present but offsetting. This condition is described, not surprisingly, as *CONSTANT ECONOMIES OF SCALE*. If input prices are fixed and firms produce over this range of output using the same mix of capital, labor and other inputs, this also indicates the presence of *CONSTANT RETURNS TO SCALE*. That is, an increase in all inputs leads to an exactly proportional increase in output.

Figure 10-3
Diseconomies of Scale

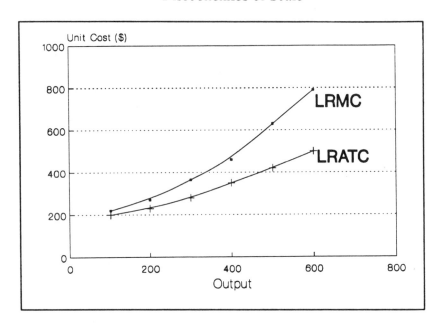

The firm depicted here experiences diseconomies of scale. Even with the freedom to vary all inputs, the firm faces higher average production costs as it increases production levels. Long-run marginal costs are, therefore, always above the long-run average total cost curve. Diseconomies of scale set in for many firms at relatively high output levels, due to the increased complexity of managing a very large operation.

Though not shown in Figure 10-4, between Q_1 and Q_2 long-run marginal costs must be equal to long-run average total costs. As shown in Chapters 7 and 9, average costs rise only when they are pulled up by marginal costs that are higher than average, and fall only when they are pulled down by marginal costs that are lower than average costs. Therefore, when average costs remain constant over some range of output, marginal costs must equal average costs.

Empirical studies indicate that many firms do produce in a range of constant economies of scale, although at low output levels manufacturing firms often experience economies of scale (see Case Study #13, at the end of this chapter). That results in an "L-shaped" long-run average total cost schedule, where the L is laid down on its long side and positioned so: ⌊____. This general shape suggests that production costs will be lower if firms can sell enough output to move through an initial range of decreasing long-run average costs, into a more extensive range of constant economies of scale.

Empirical evidence of firms producing in a range of diseconomies of scale is somewhat rare, because firms will usually find it in their own best interest to reduce output levels when unit costs rise as they grow larger, assuming there is a range of economies of scale or constant economies of scale at lower output levels. However, there have been recent and highly publicized examples of large firms "downsizing" their plants and narrowing the range of products they produce -- including "blue chip" firms in the American automobile and steel industries -- in part to lower unit production costs.

Figure 10-4
Constant Economies of Scale and U-Shaped LRATC Curves

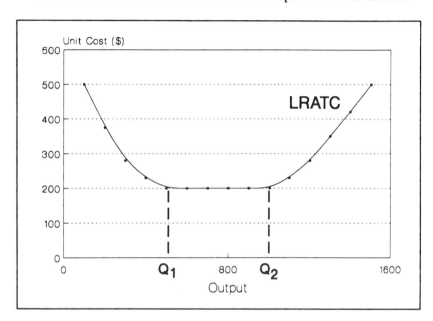

The long-run average total cost curve will be U-shaped if, as shown above, a firm first experiences economies of scale (up to Q_1), then constant economies of scale (from Q_1 to Q_2), and finally diseconomies of scale (beyond Q_2). While firms are more likely to encounter economies of scale at relatively low output levels and diseconomies of scale when production is relatively high, it is not established by economic theory that all firms or any one firm will, in fact, be subject to either or both of these effects. The shape of a firm's long-run average total cost schedule depends on the specific technological characteristics associated with the production of the firm's product(s), and the prices of the inputs it uses. The general shape and specific values on the schedule can only be established with any degree of precision by empirical studies, or by careful engineering and factor-price estimates.

As you will see, decreasing returns to scale and diseconomies of scale can help to maintain a competitive structure in an industry, while increasing returns to scale and economies of scale can lead to imperfectly competitive market structures, and sometimes even to monopolies. Therefore, returns to scale and economies of scale are crucial issues in debates on public policies designed to maintain an effective degree of competition in major U.S. industries, not merely technical concerns for corporate production engineers and cost accountants. The linkage between the cost-minimizing scale of production and the degree of competition within an industry is introduced in the later sections of this chapter, and underlies much of the discussion of the next three chapters. That means, of course, that you should study it very carefully. But first we will complete our study of perfectly competitive industries, now seen operating in the long run.

Long-run Economic Efficiency: The Competitive Ideal Revisited

If the economies of scale in an industry allow a perfectly competitive market structure to evolve, firms will produce where price is equal to long-run marginal cost and minimum average total cost. In other words, the optimal degree of productive and allocative efficiency is achieved in the long-run as well as in the short run.

However, the possibility of substantial economies of scale and constant economies of scale can lead to long-run industry supply curves that look very different from short-run supply curves, and contribute to the evolution of imperfectly competitive industries and markets.

Minimizing LRATC

Suppose a perfectly competitive firm faces the long-run average total cost schedule shown in Figure 10-5, and with a price of P_1 is operating at either q_1 or q_3 -- i.e., at a point that is not the lowest point on the LRATC curve. Even though the firm is maximizing profits and producing efficiently *given the size of its current factory and other capital inputs* (as indicated by short-run average total cost schedules 1 and 3), at these output levels it has not reached its final, long-run equilibrium. The assumption of easy entry and exit guarantees that this firm, or other firms that can produce identical products, or both, will move quickly to the plant size indicated by the short-run cost schedule tangent to the LRATC schedule at q_2. How this happens depends on whether we start from q_1 or q_3.

Figure 10-5
Economies of Scale and Long-Run Equilibrium for the Competitive Firm

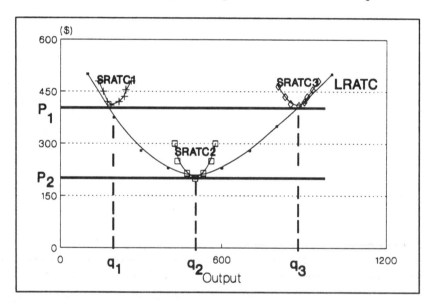

Short-run average total cost curves 1, 2, and 3 are used to derive the LRATC schedule as explained in Figure 10-1. Each set of short-run cost curves represents different plant sizes and productive capacities.

The competitive firm shown here faces a smooth, U-shaped LRATC curve that exhibits both economies and diseconomies of scale. At high prices (such as P_1 and above), firms operating relatively large ($SRATC_3$) or small ($SRATC_1$) plants may earn normal and even economic profits. But firms currently in or out of the perfectly competitive industry will soon build more efficient, low-cost plants ($SRATC_2$), to earn the highest possible profits. This entry will drive price down, to P_2. Firms will then survive only if they produce q_2 units of output, at the minimum points of both the $SRATC_2$ and LRATC curves. Firms operating any other plant size or at any other output level will be forced to exit the industry.

If the firm is initially at q_1, taking a market price of P_1, it or other firms can earn economic profits by expanding output and moving to a plant size associated with any short-run cost schedule that is tangent to LRATC at a level below P_1. This increased output at the industry level will, as you saw in Figure 9-2, cause the market price of this product to fall towards P_2. In fact, as long as the price is greater than P_2, new firms will enter the market and output will expand. Eventually, to remain in business, each firm must move to a point where P_2 = MR = MC (short run and long run) = minimum LRATC (and $SRATC_2$).

A firm initially operating at q_3 will be forced to reduce its plant size or exit the industry, even though the overall industry will experience *net* entry as long as the market price for this product is greater than the minimum point on the LRATC schedule. As the market price falls, the firm producing at q_3 will find itself in an untenable position. It can avoid losses only by operating a smaller plant or by leaving the industry.

If the price in this market falls below P_2 more firms will exit, shifting the industry supply curve to the left and raising the price toward or above P_2. These adjustments will continue until the long-run equilibrium is restored, exactly at P_2. Cost schedules in a perfectly competitive industry do not shift as a result of this entry and exit, *ceteris paribus*. Instead, entry and exit establishes a high degree of price flexibility which the firms can not manipulate, and producers are relentlessly driven to a point where productive and allocative efficiency are fully achieved. It's a wonderful ideal in the long run, as in the short-run models developed in Chapter 9. But, once again, this market structure is more imaginary than realistic, and these efficiency outcomes are most important in providing criteria to use in evaluating firms from other, less ideal, market structures.

Economies of Scale and the Level of Competition

As you saw in Chapter 9, perfect competition can exist when an industry is composed of a large number of relatively small firms, each producing an insignificant part of total industry output. But extensive economies of scale and increasing returns to scale imply that large firms can produce output at a lower unit cost than small firms. That can lead to imperfect competition: industries populated by fewer, relatively large firms, or in extreme cases by only one firm that supplies all the output in a given market. Imperfect competition that is caused by economies of scale presents an important policy trade-off in trying to achieve the efficiencies associated with competitive markets and those associated with the cost savings achieved by large-scale, mass-production enterprises.

This tradeoff does not occur, however, every time increasing returns to scale exist over some, but not all, of a firm's feasible output range. If scale economies are quickly exhausted and replaced by constant economies or diseconomies of scale, there may still be room for a large number of *relatively* small firms in the industry. That happens, in fact, whenever demand for the product produced by these firms is very large relative to any firm's output level. Modern agriculture is, once again, a good example of such a situation: while it is inefficient to operate a cattle ranch or grain farm smaller than several hundred acres, at least as a primary source of income, consumers purchase so much grain and livestock each year that even very large farms of many thousand acres have no real impact on the market prices of these products.

Long-Run Supply Curves, Increasing and Decreasing Costs, and Economies of Scale

To complete this analysis of perfectly competitive firms and industries, we will compare their long-run and short-run supply curves. To begin, note that in both the short run and long run firms will maximize profits by setting marginal revenue equal to marginal cost. Knowing that allows us to derive the schedules shown in Figure 10-6. In panel A of that figure, the firm's long-run supply (LRS) curve is equal to its marginal cost schedule at all points above the long-run average *total* cost schedule. In some ways, that's not so different from the short-run schedule developed in Chapter 9. True, short-run supply was identified there by the marginal cost curve at all points greater than average *variable* costs, but remember that in the long run all costs are variable. Therefore, in the long run, the firm must shut down if it does not cover its total or, as shown here, average total costs.

286

Panel B in Figure 10-6 shows that the long-run supply schedule is more elastic than the short-run schedule for a competitive industry. Both of these schedules are found by horizontally summing the supply schedules for individual firms, as you saw in Chapter 1, but for the long-run schedule we must also add the output that will be produced by firms that enter the market when price rises above the breakeven point. Recall too that allowing time for sellers to respond to price changes is the most important determinant of price elasticity of supply. That affects both firms currently in the industry and those that enter in response to price increases. Taken together, then, industry supply must be more elastic in the long run than in the short run.

Figure 10-6
Long-Run Supply Curves for Competitive Firms and Industries

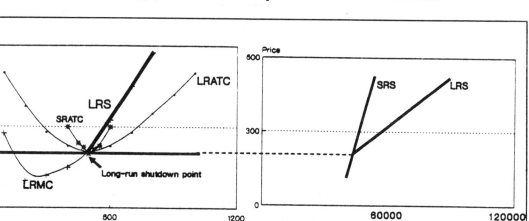

(A)   (B)

Panel (A) shows the competitive *firm's* long-run supply curve and shutdown point. The firm will produce along its long-run marginal cost schedule at all prices equal to or greater than its long-run minimum average total cost (P_1 and above), and shut down at any lower price.

Panel (B) compares the competitive *industry's* short-run and long-run supply schedules. The short-run schedule begins at a lower price because firms may operate even if they do not cover their total costs in the short run. The long-run schedule is more elastic because entry by new firms increases quantity supplied at prices that provide economic profits to firms currently in the industry, and because existing firms can increase output more in reaction to higher prices when they are given more time to adjust.

The precise shape, and even the sign of the slope, of a long-run supply curve for a competitive industry is determined by the level of costs facing the industry as it increases or decreases output. As you have seen, that will be influenced by the economies or diseconomies of scale the industry encounters as output levels are increased or decreased, and by the effect (if any) that changes in an industry's level of output have on the prices of the inputs it uses. We will assume here that input prices are not changing for other reasons, and that the level of technology is fixed. But it should be clear that changes in these factors cause the long-run supply curve for an industry to shift -- i.e., increase or decrease -- depending on the direction of the change in resource prices, or technological improvements.

287

An industry that produces under conditions of constant economies of scale, and which can hire as many or as few inputs as it likes without affecting their prices, will face a perfectly elastic (i.e., horizontal) long-run supply curve, as shown in Figure 10-7. Industries which exhibit such long-run supply curves are known, not surprisingly, as *CONSTANT-COST INDUSTRIES*. These industries tend to share many characteristics with the examples of competitive industries you have seen before. In particular, industries which purchase small quantities of resources, relative to the overall market for these inputs, can employ many more or many fewer resources with little or no influence on their prices. For example, the amount of labor, capital, and plastics used in the frisbee and hula hoop industries is so small that frisbee and hula hoop output could quadruple or fall to nearly zero from year to year (as it occasionally has) without affecting those input prices.

Figure 10-7
Long-Run Supply in a Constant-Cost Industry

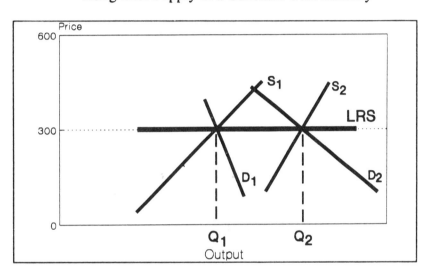

Demand for the product produced by this industry is shown increasing over time, from D_1 to D_2. That would increase price along (short-run) S_1, but assuming the industry: 1) is competitive, 2) produces under conditions of constant returns to scale, and 3) can employ more (or fewer) inputs without affecting their prices, that will lead to entry by new firms and increase supply from S_1 to S_2. The equilibrium price at both Q_1 and Q_2 is identical, and this gives us two points on the industry's long-run supply curve. Under these conditions, the long-run supply curve will be horizontal.

An *INCREASING-COST INDUSTRY* experiences higher costs as it increases output levels in the long run. That may occur because the firm encounters decreasing returns to scale in the production process for its own output, or because its input prices rise as it buys more of them to produce larger quantities of goods or services. Clearly, industries which employ a major portion of some input are most likely to encounter rising input prices as they expand output. Examples include the automobile industry's purchases of steel and tires; or a large university located in a relatively small town hiring secretaries and other hourly employees; or, at the national level, the federal government, which hired over 5 million workers (military and civilian) in 1989. An industry that employs inputs produced by firms that face diseconomies of scale may also experience rising input prices as it uses more resources to produce more output. But whatever the underlying cause, an increasing-cost industry will exhibit an upward sloping long-run supply curve, as shown in Figure 10-8. Producing more products in such industries always entails higher unit costs, so higher levels of output will be made available by producers only if the price they receive rises enough to cover their increased costs.

288

Figure 10-8
Long-Run Supply in an Increasing-Cost Industry

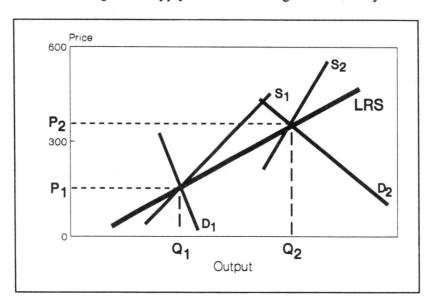

As in Figure 10-7, demand for the product produced by the industry shown here increases over time, from D_1 to D_2, encouraging entry by firms as price increases along (short-run) S_1. But now the expansion in output results in higher unit costs, due to decreasing returns to scale, rising input prices, or both. Over time, entry by new firms causes supply to increase from S_1 to S_2, but the equilibrium price and quantity after entry (P_2, Q_2), are higher than the original equilibrium price and quantity (P_1, Q_1). From these two points on the industry's long-run supply curve, we identify a positively sloped schedule.

Finally we come to the rarest (and strangest) of the three cost scenarios -- which some economists claim does not occur at all in reality unless there are improvements in production technologies -- the *DECREASING-COST INDUSTRY*. For long-run production costs to fall as output levels increase, holding technology constant, an industry must either enjoy increasing returns to scale in production that persist over large ranges of output, or face falling input prices as it employs more inputs. If that does happen the result is the counter-intuitive enigma that has tripped up many students in principles of economics courses, the downward sloping long-run supply curve (Figure 10-9).

In Chapter 17, you will see that at least one key input, labor, normally is *not* available at lower prices when employed in greater quantities at the market level. This limits the cases in which we are likely to find decreasing-cost industries to those which are not labor-intensive. And in fact, since labor costs often rise as major industries expand their hiring, this can offset increasing returns to scale in production activities and cost advantages in purchasing larger quantities of other inputs, which again helps to explain why downward-sloping long-run supply curves are so rare. Still, such industries are at least theoretically possible, so beware in choosing your answers on exam questions. Utility companies providing services in local and regional markets are most often cited as possible examples of these industries, as discussed in the section on natural monopolies presented later in this chapter.

Figure 10-9
Long-Run Supply in a Decreasing-Cost Industry

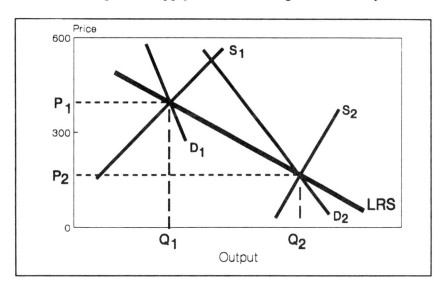

As in Figures 10-7 and 10-8, demand for the product produced by the industry shown here increases over time, from D_1 to D_2. Once again, price initially increases along (short-run) S_1, which encourages entry by new firms and shifts the supply curve from S_1 to S_2. But firms now face falling unit costs due to increasing returns to scale, falling input prices, or both, so the equilibrium price after entry, P_2, at output level Q_2, will be lower than the original equilibrium price, P_1, at output Q_1. From the two equilibrium points we identify a negatively-sloped long-run supply curve for the industry. This phenomenon is at best rarely observed, and some economists claim that it never occurs if there are no changes in production technologies.

Diseconomies of scale and long-run increasing costs encourage production in the setting of relatively small, competitive firms, where such firms are more efficient in holding down production costs. Constant returns and costs are compatible with industries made up of either large or small firms, because production in either kind of firm can be equally cost efficient. However, economies of scale and decreasing costs across sufficiently large output levels promote industries that are very unlike economists' models of perfect competition. This creates important policy issues in the areas of antitrust law, regulation, and enforcement activities, which are introduced in the following section and discussed in greater detail throughout the next three chapters.

Minimum Efficient Scale, Concentration Ratios, and the Efficiency Dilemma of Natural Monopolies

The lowest level of output at which a firm achieves all significant economies of scale is defined as its minimum efficient scale (MES). When MES is small relative to the overall level of sales in an industry, it is feasible for a large number of firms to compete in the market, each producing at the MES level of output. However, when MES is large relative to current output levels for a product, some form of imperfect competition is likely to result. In the most extreme case, the least-cost way to provide the output in a market is to have only one firm -- a natural monopoly -- produce it. In that situation, it is literally impossible to achieve all of the efficiency and zero-profit outcomes found in models of perfectly competition, regardless of whether the natural monopoly is publically or privately owned, and regulated or not. Similar kinds of productive and allocative inefficiencies are also observed in less extreme forms of imperfect competition than natural monopolies, which are indicated in very broad terms by high industry concentration ratios.

Minimum Efficient Scale

Imperfect competition occurs when individual firms produce and sell a significant part of the output in a market, and thus have a direct effect on market prices for these products. That can happen if economies of scale make it impossible for a large number of firms to produce a product, because the level of demand is too low for many firms to sell the volume of output required to achieve all significant economies of scale. For example, consumers have neither the inclination nor the funds to buy enough cars to support several hundred automobile companies as large as General Motors, or even several dozen. Consequently, the model of perfect competition is often not a good model to use in explaining or predicting events in the automobile industry.

Economists have estimated the lowest level of output at which firms in various industries can achieve all major economies of scale in production. This point is known as the industry's *MINIMUM EFFICIENT SCALE (MES)*, and illustrated in Figure 10-10. The basic policy issues raised by economists' studies on MES are: 1) just how competitive are markets in industrial nations like the United States; and 2) how active should the government be in maintaining or increasing that level of competition? F. M. Scherer, one of the leading economists who has conducted such studies and gathered together results from other important studies on MES, concluded in an often-quoted paper that, in the United States, "national market concentration in most industries appears to be much higher than it needs to be for leading firms to take advantage of all but slight residual scale economies."[1]

Some economists, judges, and policy makers have concluded from this analysis, and other similar studies, that legal actions can and should be used to break up many large U.S. firms. They believe that would increase competition in some markets, or at least keep existing firms from becoming much larger through mergers with, or takeovers of, firms producing competing products. But other economists and interested observers stridently disagree with these conclusions. For example, economist John S. McGee made the case for a *laissez faire* approach to these public policy issues in responding to Scherer's remarks:

> I see little reason to spend much more time estimating optimum plant or firm sizes.... When property and markets are at work, and consumers are permitted to choose what and from whom to buy, it is...a trivial matter what the facts of technical economies are, or what economists and engineers have to say about them. Consumers will choose products and firms that offer what is, to their tastes, the best deal. Consumers will make the trade-offs between prices and product qualities. The prices they pay for the qualities they buy are signals to anyone who would do better by them. Such economies as there are will assert themselves, and no one need be concerned how large or small they are.[2]

As you may have guessed, McGee has not convinced Scherer and many other economists that his lack of concern with these measures of MES is appropriate. In fact, the debate signaled by this exchange between Scherer and McGee is one of the longest standing and most significant areas of disagreement in microeconomics witnessed over the past 30-50 years. You will be assessing many points in this debate for yourself as you work through the remaining sections in this chapter, and in the next three chapters on market structures and industrial organization.

---

[1] "Economies of Scale and Industrial Concentration," in H. J. Goldschmid, *et al.*, eds., *Industrial Concentration: The New Learning*. Boston: Little, Brown and Co., 1974, p. 54.

[2] "Commentary," in Goldschmid *et al.*, p. 104.

Figure 10-10
Minimum Efficient Scale

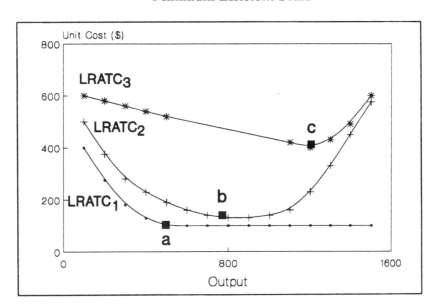

On the three long-run average total cost curves shown above, minimum efficient scale occurs at the points labeled a, b and c. At these points firms are just large enough to realize all significant economies of scale, and there are no important cost savings to be gained simply by growing larger. Whether any of these firms would operate in a competitive industry at the MES level of output depends on the number and size of other firms in the industry. If the level of market demand for the products produced by these firms is small relative to the MES level of output for a typical firm, a large number of equal-sized firms can not survive and sustain perfect competition in the industry.

Concentration Ratios

One simple measure of the level of competition among existing firms in an industry is the N-*FIRM CONCENTRATION RATIO*, which expresses the percentage of sales or production accounted for by the largest n firms in the industry. So, for example, if the largest four firms accounted for 25 percent of sales and output, and the four next-largest firms had an additional 15 percent of the business, we would say that the four-firm concentration ratio in this industry was 25 percent, and the eight-firm concentration ratio is 40 percent (25 percent + 15 percent). Table 10-1 reports concentration ratios for selected major industries in the United States, and you can see that some of those measures are indeed high. The picture of U.S. industries they present is certainly not close, on many counts, to the strict assumptions of perfect competition which were presented in Chapter 9.

On the other hand, there are several problems in using just these ratios to judge how competitive and efficient an industry is. First, they consider only U.S. firms, and ignore the effect of competition from foreign firms. As you probably know, international competition has become much more important in the past few decades. For example, U.S. manufacturers of steel, household appliances, computers, textiles, shoes, automobiles, and industrial equipment (such as bulldozers) have been particularly beset by competition from foreign firms, to the delight of consumers of these products who are looking for lower prices and/or higher quality.

A second limitation of concentration ratios concerns industries in which markets tend to be local or regional, such as the pre-mixed concrete that is delivered to construction sites in huge mixer trucks. In these cases, national concentration ratios overstate the effective level of competition facing any individual consumer of these products, who might only have one or two sellers to choose from as a practical matter of delivery costs.

Table 10-1
Concentration Ratios in Selected U.S. Industries, 1982

Industry	4-Firm Concentration Ratio(%)
Hard Surface Floor Coverings	99
Motor Vehicles and Car Bodies	92
Electric Lamps	91
Cereal Breakfast Foods	86
Photographic Equipment	74
Rubber Tires and Inner Tubes	66
Aircraft	64
Primary Aluminum	64
Phonograph Records and Pre-recorded Tapes	61
Soaps and Other Detergents	60
Cookies and Crackers	59
Metal Cans	50
Radio and TV Sets	49
Blast Furnaces and Steel Mills	42
Motors and Generators	36
Ship Building and Repairs	35
Musical Instruments	33
Petroleum Refining	28
Pharmaceutical Preparations	26
Mens' and Boys' Suits and Coats	25
Mobile Homes	24
Canned Fruits and Vegetables	21
Periodicals	20
Wood Household Furniture	16
Womens' Dresses	6
Concrete	6

Source: U.S. Department of Commerce, "Concentration Ratios in Manufacturing," *1982 Census of Manufacturers*, MC82-S7, April 1986.

A third limitation in using concentration rates as general indicators of the level of competition is that, in some cases, competition among a few large but equal-sized firms can lead to relatively competitive and efficient results. This can be especially true in terms of lowering production costs if there are substantial scale economies associated with high production levels. On the other hand, if there is collusion on pricing and output decisions among firms in a highly concentrated industry, there will be even less competition than the concentration ratio suggests.

Finally in this short list of problems with concentration ratios as a general measure of competition, you should recognize that competition across industries is, in some cases, as important as intra-industry competition. Competition across industries occurs regularly, whenever products produced by industries with different government industry-classification codes (used to calculate the concentration ratios) sell goods and services that are reasonably close substitutes. For example, entertainment products such as movies compete with entertainment products produced in other industries, such as television programs and sporting goods. Because of this, defining a firm's close competitors is often a key part of legal cases under the antitrust laws, and outcomes can literally turn on questions such as whether waxed paper and paper bags are close substitutes for cellophane wrap.

All things considered, the information provided by n-firm concentration ratios for different industries is almost always interesting, but not always crucially important, in public policy discussions on the effective degree of competition in the United States and global economies. Studying broad changes in the overall pattern of concentration ratios in the United States, such as those shown in Tables 10-2 and 10-3, may be more reliable and helpful than examining ratios for particular industries. The general picture that emerges from these tables is, in fact, that there has been no major or sustained trend toward either greater or lesser concentration in the United States economy over the last century. But the reasons for that lack of a trend are complex and often controversial, involving production technologies and (dis)economies of scale, competitive behavior among national and international firms, and antitrust policies and enforcement efforts at the state and national levels. These issues are considered at length throughout the next several chapters.

Table 10-2
Distribution of 4-Firm Concentration Ratios, 1982

4-Firm Concentration Ratio (%)	Number of Industries
90-100	7
80-89	11
70-79	20
60-69	34
50-59	49
40-49	72
30-39	77
20-29	86
10-19	65
0- 9	21
	442

Using a "4-digit" classification code to assign U.S. manufacturing firms to different industries, the Department of Commerce report on "Concentration Ratios in Manufacturing" from the *1982 Census of Manufacturers* (published in 1986) reported the overall distribution of industrial concentration shown above.

Table 10-3
Concentration in U.S. Manufacturing, 1895-1977 (Selected Years)

Year(s)	% of Manufacturing Production in Industries With 4-Firm Concentration Ratio > 50%	% of All Production by 100 Largest Manufacturing Firms
1895-1904	33	Not Available
1947	24	23
1954	30	30
1958	30	32
1972	29	33
1977	Not Available	34

While the portion of total manufacturing output produced in relatively concentrated U.S. industries and by the largest industrial firms does change somewhat from year to year, these data show no long-term trend to substantially higher or lower levels of concentration.

Sources: G. Warren Nutter, *The Extent of Enterprise Monopoly in the United States, 1899-1930* (Chicago: University. of Chicago Press, 1951), pp. 35-48, 112-50; F. M. Scherer, *Industrial Market Structure and Economic Performance* (Boston: Houghton Mifflin, 1980), pp. 68-69; "Concentration Ratios in Manufacturing," from the *1977 Census of Manufacturing*, U.S. Department of Commerce, MC77-SR-9.

The last measure of industrial concentration we will discuss here is the statistic most widely used today by the U.S. Justice Department in determining whether to allow or oppose mergers between two firms in the same industry. Known as the *HERFINDAHL INDEX* (named, as you might suspect, for an economist, Orris Herfindahl), this index is calculated by adding together the *squared* value of the market shares of firms in an industry (again determined by their percentage of industry sales or output), and indicates greater industry concentration when there are a few very large firms in the industry. For example, consider two hypothetical industries that are each made up of only three firms. In the first industry, suppose one firm has a market share of 90 percent (or, in calculating the index, .9), while the other two firms each produce five percent of the total output (.05). Adding the squares of these values gives us a Herfindahl index of 0.8150 (.81 + .0025 + .0025). If the second hypothetical industry has three equal-sized firms, its Herfindahl index will be 0.33 (.11 + .11 + .11). A monopoly that produced all of the output in an industry would, obviously, have an index of 1.0. For purposes of illustration, Table 10-4 below shows the real data used to construct a Herfindahl index of 0.2525 for U.S. auto sales (including those by foreign producers) in 1984.

Table 10-4
Herfindahl Index for U.S. Auto Sales, 1984

Firms	Unit Sales	Market Share
General Motors	4,600,512	0.4432
Ford	1,979,317	0.1907
Chrysler	1,078,716	0.1039
Toyota	557,982	0.0538
Honda	508,420	0.0490
Nissan (Datsun)	485,298	0.0468
American Motors	202,570	0.0195
Volkswagen	177,322	0.0171
Mazda	169,666	0.0163
Subaru	157,383	0.0152
Volvo	97,915	0.0094
Mercedes Benz	76,051	0.0073
Audi	70,220	0.0068
BMW	68,650	0.0066
Mitsubishi	39,768	0.0038
Saab	32,768	0.0032
Peugeot	19,406	0.0019
Porsche	18,550	0.0018
Jaguar	18,044	0.0017
Isuzu	17,233	0.0017
Alfa Romeo	3,702	0.0004
Ferrari	568	0.00005
Fiat	391	0.00004
Lancia	21	0.000002

Herfindahl Index = 0.2525

Source: *1985 Ward's Automotive Yearbook*

We don't yet have as many studies tracing out historical trends in Herfindahl indexes as we do for the more traditional n-firm concentration ratios. But in one such study Raymond Vernon constructed Herfindahl indexes for world competition in four industries: automobiles, petroleum, aluminum smelting, and pulp and paper production.[3] To his expressed surprise, Vernon found sharp declines in all four of these measures over the 1950-1970 period (in each case from initial values of around .2 down to around .1 or below). But there are, in fact, several reasons for not viewing such trends as surprising. When industrialized nations rebuilt their economies after World War II, it was widely recognized that competition in markets for manufactured goods would increase. Global banking services and cheaper forms of transportation, communications, and information processing also developed over this same period, strengthening the trend toward increased competition. Direct competition between U.S. producers in these and other industries may have declined as measured both by the Herfindahl index and n-firm concentration ratios over some or all of these years, but in the global marketplace competition was clearly heating up.

It is also important to note that the Herfindahl index is subject to many of the same problems as n-firm concentration ratios. For example, given that economies of scale lead to an industry structure with a few large

---

[3]"Competition Policy Toward Multinational Corporations," *American Economic Review*, May 1974.

firms, it may still be true that such firms produce the industry output at lower costs, and sell it at lower prices, than would be the case if the industry was legally "broken up" to achieve a lower Herfindahl index. Once again, this is more likely to be true if products sold by firms classified in other industries are reasonably close substitutes for those produced in the concentrated industry.

Models of different kinds of imperfectly competitive industries are developed in the following section and in the next three chapters, to address many of these issues more fully than the simple concentration measures presented here. Even in cases where conclusive answers to questions on production efficiency and direct competition on the basis of product price can not be established, these models give us a better means of predicting the actions firms in such industries are likely to take, and the problems those actions may present for consumers and policy makers.

In broadest terms, models of perfect competition look at competition among the many; but now it is time to begin our study of competition among the few, starting with the case that inspired one of the world's most popular and enduring board games, monopoly.

Natural Monopolies

In the most extreme case of imperfect competition, a firm enjoys such pronounced cost advantages that it can produce the total market output of a good or service at a lower cost than would be possible if any greater number of firms -- even two -- attempted to supply this output. Such a firm is known as a *NATURAL MONOPOLY*.

Classic examples of natural monopolies are public utilities -- such as local telephone, electric, gas, and water companies. While there are many of these companies nationally, in any given neighborhood there is only one gas, telephone, or water company which consumers can contact to deliver these products to their home. Why only one of each kind of company, given the efficiency advantages of competition among many small firms?

Common sense and basic economics tell you that it would be prohibitively expensive to serve each home and business with even two sets of telephone and electric wires, sewage and water pipes, or natural gas lines. Technological change may, of course, undo these economies of scale in the future. In fact, recent studies have suggested that generating electricity and drilling for natural gas, as opposed to local delivery of such products, is often not characterized by natural monopoly. Similarly, long-distance telephone services are no longer characterized by natural monopolies, although local telephone services still are -- which explains the motivation behind the Justice Department's case to force AT&T to divest the "Baby Bell" regional telephone companies in 1983. But direct competition between small utility companies providing identical services at the local level still fails, because it is simply too costly to support even two such companies.

A natural monopoly faces economies of scale over most, if not all, of the output range that is demanded in the markets for such products. In the case of local public utilities, the sources of those economies are clear to see. The utilities incur very high fixed costs in providing a basic distribution, switching, or pumping network, but then face very low marginal costs in terms of "hooking up" or serving one more customer in an area where the central distribution network is already in place. When this happens, as shown in Figure 10-11, economists and public officials face a dilemma in trying to devise regulatory schemes setting price and output levels that allow these firms to achieve the productive *and* allocative efficiency measures that are associated with perfectly competitive firms.

Not all monopolies are natural monopolies, as you will see in the following chapter; but all kinds of monopolies typically fail to achieve these competitive criteria. As a result, government policies can sometimes be used to adjust outcomes in imperfectly competitive markets, to more closely achieve at least some of these efficiency standards. But there are practical as well as theoretical impediments and costs to such policy actions. For example, it is difficult and expensive for public officials to develop accurate data on firms' demand and cost schedules, let alone forecast future values for such variables, even in constantly regulated industries like natural monopolies. One reason for this is that pricing schemes which allow utilities to earn a set rate of return over their costs establish incentives for firms to pad their costs with larger staffs, bigger offices, etc. Regulated companies also seek an approved rate of return that is comparable to those earned by firms with similar levels of costs and capital investments -- even though the economic risks faced by the regulated companies are significantly lower if they face less competition from other firms producing identical products, or close substitutes.

Figure 10-11
A Natural Monopoly and the Efficiency Dilemma

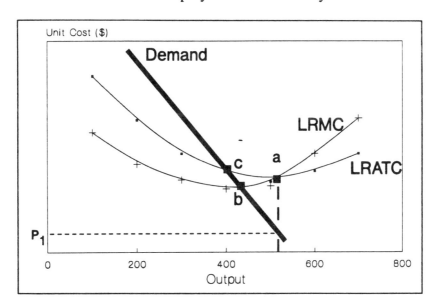

Given the market demand for a product and cost schedules for a producer shown above, the least expensive way to produce any output levels that consumers are willing and able to buy is to have that output produced by only one firm, a natural monopoly. Note that it is literally impossible for this firm, or a public regulatory group that is empowered to set this firm's price and output levels, to find a price where the firm covers its costs and simultaneously achieves the competitive standards of productive and allocative efficiency. At point a, where MC = minimum ATC, the firm incurs losses because, based on the position of the demand curve, it can only sell that output by charging a price of P_1. If a decision is made to set P = MC at point b, where the demand curve and marginal cost curve intersect, the firm again incurs losses. If price is set equal to ATC at point c, where the demand curve intersects the ATC curve, the firm earns normal profits but produces where P > MC and minimum ATC. No point allows the firm to earn only normal profits and produce where P = MC = minimum ATC, whether the firm operates privately, or is subject to public regulation, or is publically owned and operated.

In some areas, government agencies at the local, state, or federal level directly own and operate utility companies -- typically with local water, bus, or subway services, but occasionally with local or regional electric companies. That might seem to make it politically easier to follow the allocatively efficient practice, suggested by economist Harold Hotelling in the 1930s, to set P = MC and subsidize the losses of a natural monopoly with public tax dollars. But even then it is difficult to determine what part of the operating costs facing these firms is an inevitable part of providing these products, and what part reflects inherent political inefficiencies, such as building and maintaining unprofitable bus or subway routes to neighborhoods that have enough votes or other political clout to insure that the subsidy dollars benefit their areas.

Judging the relative effectiveness of direct public ownership of utilities versus private ownership subject to public regulations often comes down to a choice between the expected efficiency of a public regulatory commission compared to that of public officials employed directly as production and service managers. Unfortunately, but not surprisingly, both of these groups face perverse economic incentives. Regulatory commissions *and* publically managed utilities have often become political steppingstones for ambitious persons interested in higher office. (A notable example of this was Louisiana's populist "Kingfish," Huey Long, who challenged Franklin Rossevelt for control of the Democratic party in the 1930s.) These jobs are also career steppingstones for those interested in lucrative management positions with other utility companies, or in post-regulatory careers as consultants for several utility companies. And of course managers of publically and privately-owned utilities are susceptible to the allure of large, plush offices, or the prospects of a safe and steady job with little risk, or both. As Nobel-laureate economist George Stigler argues, we are safest in assuming that these public and private officials will be, on average, just as open to these temptations (and others) as the rest of us. Neither saints nor sinners have been shown to be overrepresented among public utility regulators or executives.

In several ways, the dilemmas posed by natural monopolies are more intractable and pervasive than the problems we will discuss in broader models of imperfect competition, presented in the next four chapters. But much of what you have already learned here will carry over to those scenarios. For example, as with natural monopolies, we will evaluate the performance and economic efficiency of firms presented in the later models of imperfect competition using the criteria developed from the models of perfect competition in Chapter 9, and in this chapter.

It is also important to note that, even in facing intractable dilemmas such as natural monopolies, economists keep looking for innovative ways to make the best of a difficult situation. For example, William Baumol and other economists have recently promoted the idea of regulating the maximum prices natural monopolies can charge, rather than their cost or profit levels. That way, although there will still arguments about what those prices should be, largely based on cost and profit data, the firm's incentives to minimize costs and produce efficiently are reestablished once their price has been set through the regulatory process.

Case Study #13
Empirical Estimates of Long-Run Cost Schedules and
Minimum Efficient Scale

One of the first rigorous attempts to empirically estimate the overall relationship between output and cost levels at the firm or industry level was published by economist Joel Dean in 1941.[4] Dean found a basically linear relationship between *total* costs and output levels in a hosiery mill, over an output range of 4,000 dozen to 48,000 dozen pairs of hose per production period. That suggested flat, rather than U-shaped, marginal and average total cost schedules, and set off a rush by other economists to estimate production costs in different kinds of firms and industries. Several different methods of measuring and estimating these costs were developed; but some economists challenged the feasibility and usefulness of conducting such studies, given what is known about accounting data on costs and profits, and the behavior of firms in different market settings.

The purpose of this case study is not to suggest a resolution for all parts of these debates, which are still ongoing in the research literature, but to review the three principal methods that have been used to provide direct statistical measures and estimates of "real-world" cost functions -- time-series, cross sectional, and engineering studies[5] -- and to summarize the findings from some of the more important studies. We also review related estimates of minimum efficient scale in several different U.S. industries.

Dean's investigation of the hosiery mill was a *TIME-SERIES STUDY* of how cost levels varied as the output level at a particular factory changed. Time-series studies collect data for a period of months, years, or even decades; and because of that they are especially useful and reliable in some respects. For example, by collecting data from a particular factory or firm, few theoretical estimates of what would happen to costs if output levels and/or input prices changed are necessary. Instead, the data collected are analyzed to show what really did happen to production costs when these variables changed. Furthermore, by maintaining a narrow focus on one

---

[4]"Statistical Cost Functions of a Hosiery Mill," *Studies in Business Administration*, Volume 14, No. 3, University of Chicago Press.

[5]A fourth procedure, developed in a seminal article by George Stigler published in 1958, identifies what size firms in an industry are gaining market share, and what size firms are losing market share, or being driven out of business. "Surviving" firms are assumed to be more efficient than firms that are losing market share, and with this "survivor principle" investigators indirectly derive evidence about ranges of economies or diseconomies of scale.

299

firm or plant, the data are usually based on highly similar, if not identical, accounting procedures used to measure different categories of costs. Studies that use data from many different firms face much more severe problems on this count.

But time-series studies face serious problems, too. In particular, it is often too expensive for researchers to follow a firm's cost data over periods of time that are long enough to classify as the long run, at least in major manufacturing industries where capital inputs are frequently fixed for periods of five to 10 years, or even longer. Moreover, when a study does use cost data collected over several years, they must be adjusted to account for any inflation or deflation that has occurred in this period of time. Fortunately, such adjustments are *relatively* easy and straightforward to make. More problematic, though, and common to all kinds of statistical studies on cost schedules, is the need to convert data from a firm's accounting records into categories that are more compatible with economic analysis. For example, as you saw in Chapter 7, economists prefer to treat some level of normal profits as a cost of doing business, while accountants do not. And even more frequently troublesome is getting good estimates of the current value of a firm's plant and capital equipment, which are often carried on accounting records at historical and tax-depreciated levels that have little relationship to their true economic worth.

Some of these problems, but not all, are avoided in *CROSS-SECTION STUDIES* that collect data on output and cost levels from several different plants or firms in an industry at the same point in time. Data can often be collected from production facilities with very different output levels, and then it may be far less expensive to investigate economies of scale and returns to scale with cross-section studies than with time-series methods. Also, cross-section studies usually don't face serious problems in adjusting for inflation. However, they do face greater problems in using accounting data from many different firms, which often use different accounting practices and reporting measures.

The final procedure that has been extensively used by economists trying to estimate long-run cost schedules is known as an *ENGINEERING STUDY*. In this approach, economists rely on interviews or surveys of engineers who are designing or operating factories to collect data on the minimum cost of producing different output levels. In some cases (particularly in estimates of building new factories), this approach can reduce the problems with interpreting accounting data. But on the other hand, engineering estimates are often closely tied to current input prices, and especially sensitive to changes in their relative values. Furthermore, as with all survey and interview work, engineering studies are open to questions about the representative nature of the group of firms or engineers selected for inclusion in a study, and within that group to any bias in results that is linked to the interviewees' decisions to respond (or not) to the investigators' questions.

None of the empirical methods of estimating economies of scale is easy to implement or free from problems of data collection and interpretation. For that reason, it is reassuring when estimates from two or more of the different kinds of studies are available, particularly when results are reinforcing rather than contradictory. With that background, take a few minutes to look over Table 10-5, which presents selected findings from some key early studies on long-run cost schedules in various U.S. firms and industries. Two time-series studies are reported first, then a group of cross-section studies, and finally a group of engineering studies.

Except in what were identified as special cases in the main body of this chapter (such as natural monopolies), the findings reported in Table 10-5 generally suggest that industrial firms have to produce some minimum level of output to realize economies of scale that are present through initial production ranges, but then find that these economies are exhausted, and enter a reasonably broad range of constant economies of scale. That once again raises the question of how large the level of minimum efficient scale (MES) is relative to the market level of output for various industrial products. That is an explicitly empirical question which many economists have studied, and results from some of the early work in this vein are summarized in Table 10-6.

Table 10-5
Statistical Estimates of Long-Run Cost Schedules

Industry Group	Results
I. Time-Series Studies	
Electricity	Substantial economies of scale
Airlines	Constant economies of scale
II. Cross-Section Studies	
Retail Shoe Stores	U-shaped LRATC schedule
Shipping	Economies of scale in hauling, but not handling
Cement	Substantial economies of scale
Electricity	Substantial economies of scale; but constant average administrative costs
Airlines	Constant economies of scale
Trash Collection	Considerable economies of scale in cities of up to 20,000 residents
Railways	Mixed results -- one study finds no significant economies of scale from general expansion; another finds increasing LRATC in eastern states, but decreasing LRATC in southern and western states
III. Engineering and Questionnaire Studies	
Manufacturing	Economies of scale, up to plant capacity levels
Metals	Economies of scale to 80,000 pounds/month, then constant constant returns
Cement	Substantial economies of scale

Sources: Adapted from Edwin Mansfield's *Microeconomics: Theory and Applications*, 6th ed., New York: W. W. Norton & Co., 1988, pp. 224-25.

Recall F. M. Scherer's claim, discussed earlier in this chapter, that firms seem to grow larger than is required in order to achieve all significant scale advantages. Scherer based his statement largely on data like that reported in Table 10-6. Comparing the number of U.S. firms actually operating in these industries to the estimates of the maximum number of MES-sized firms that could have been sustained by the level of market sales for these products, Scherer's claim holds up. But the issue is somewhat more complicated than that procedure suggests.

For example, looking at international as well as domestic competition modifies the outlook considerably, as we illustrated in the Herfindahl index for the automobile industry that was presented in Table 10-4. That adjustment makes many U.S. industries look less concentrated; but other factors work in the opposite direction. To wit -- if some products are produced and sold in local or regional markets, rather than in national markets, concentration may be a more severe problem than the data in Table 10-6 suggest. As noted earlier, pre-mixed concrete is a good example of a product that is effectively produced and sold in local, or at best regional markets. So is food served by restaurants and catering services.

Table 10-6
Empirical Estimates of Minimum Efficient Scale

Industry	MES as a % of U.S. Output	Maximum Number of MES-Sized Firms/Plants Compatible With Market Output/Sales Levels
I. Studies Based on 1967 National Output Levels		
Cigarettes	6.6	15
Paints, Varnishes, and Lacquers	ˍ1.4	71
Shoes (Nonrubber)	0.2	500
Household Refrigerators and Freezers	14.1	7
Beer Brewing	3.4	29
Broad-woven Cotton and Synthetic Fabrics	.2	500
Glass Containers	1.5	67
Cement	1.7	59
Steel (Integrated Wide-strip Works)	2.6	38
Ball and Roller Bearings	1.4	71
Storage Batteries	1.9	53
II. Studies Based on 1947 National Output Levels		
Flour Milling	.3	333
Canned Fruits and Vegetables	.4	250
Distilled Liquors	1.5	67
Farm Machinery	1.3	77
Diversified Meat Packing	2.3	43
Gypsum Plaster and Plasterboard	2.5	40
Soap and Detergents	5.0	20
Automobiles	7.5	13
Fountain Pens	7.5	13
Copper Refining	10.0	10

Sources: For data in section I., F. M. Scherer, "Economies of Scale and Industrial Concentration," in H. Goldschmid, H. Mann, and J. Weston, eds., *Industrial Concentration: The New Learning*, Boston: Little, Brown and Co., 1974, p. 26. See also L. Weiss, "Optimal Plant Size and the Extent of Suboptimal Capacity," in R. Masson and P. Qualls, eds., *Essays in Honor of Joe S. Bain*, Cambridge, Mass.: Ballinger, 1976. For data in section II., J. Bain, "Economies of Scale, Concentration, and the Conditions of Free Entry in Twenty Manufacturing Industries," *American Economic Review*, March 1954, pp. 15-39; and also Bain's *Barriers to New Competition*, Cambridge, Mass.: Harvard University Press, 1956, pp. 71-86. All estimates are based on engineering studies and assume that markets for these products are national in scope.

Perhaps most importantly, the economy has undergone several important changes since these early studies on economies of scale and MES were conducted and economists began their ongoing debate about the effective degree of competition in the United States and other industrialized nations. In the last 10-15 years, as the U.S. economy has adjusted to heightened levels of international competition in many important markets, and as the importance of the service has increased in both the U.S. and world economies, economists have used increasingly sophisticated statistical tools to look for evidence of economies or diseconomies of scale in a wide variety of enterprises, and built on those findings to update the debate on the nature and extent of competition. Consider, for example, the following sample of such studies, grouped by broad product types:[6]

Food Products. U.S. corn farms of 500-1,000 acres were shown to be more efficient than smaller farms, while tea farms in Sri Lanka were most efficient in sizes of 300-400 hectares. Flour milling and fluid milk companies were found to be most cost efficient with 100-250 employees, while cheese companies had L-shaped cost curves that flattened out at employee levels greater than 100. Supermarkets in England exhibited economies of scale that were most pronounced for smaller firms, but which leveled out into constant economies for larger stores, and showed slight diseconomies of scale for the very largest firms. Production costs appear to decline in breweries as output levels rise, especially among relatively small operations.

Consumer Services. Independent banks were found to face U-shaped cost curves, while multi-bank holding companies faced constant economies of scale. Credit unions more often and consistently experience economies of scale. Insurance companies experience economies of scale in their demand for cash balances, which are used in investment ventures (after paying off policy claims). Pension programs for state and

---

[6]S. C. Cooke and W. B. Sundquist, "Cost Efficiency in U.S. Corn Production," *American Journal of Agricultural Economics*, November 1989; J. Roberts, "A Microeconomic Analysis of Tea Production Using a Separable Restricted Profit Function," *Journal of Agricultural Economics*, May 1989; C. R. MacPhee and R. D. Peterson, "The Economies of Scale Revisited: Comparing Census Costs, Engineering Estimates and the Survivor Technique," *Quarterly Journal of Business and Economics*, Spring 1990; R. P. Tilley and R. Hecks, "Economies of Scale in Supermarkets," *Journal of Industrial Economics*, November 1970; A. J. Chalk, "Competition in the Brewing Industry," *Managerial and Decision Economics*, March 1988; N. Rangan et. al., "Production Costs for Consolidated Multibank Holding Companies Compared to One-Bank Organizational Forms," *Journal of Economics and Business*, November 1989; C. Lawrence, "Banking Costs, Generalized Functional Forms, and Estimation of Economies of Scale and Scope," *Journal of Money, Credit and Banking*, August 1989; T. Kohers and D. Mullis, "An Update on Economies of Scale in Credit Unions," *Applied Economics*, December 1988; J. F. Outreville, "The Long-run and Short-run Demand for Cash Balances: The Case of Insurance Companies," *Quarterly Review of Economics and Business*, Winter 1988; R. Pope, "Economies of Scale in Large State and Municipal Retirement Systems," *Public Budgeting and Finance*, Autumn 1986; E. Cohn, S. Rhine and M. Santos, "Institutions of Higher Education as Multiproduct Firms," *Review of Economics and Statistics*, May 1989; J. R. Hough, "A Note on Economies of Scale in Schools," *Applied Economics*, February 1985; D. F. Vitaliano, "On the Estimation of Hospital Cost Functions," *Journal of Health Economics*, December 1987; N. L. McKay, "An Econometric Analysis of Cost and Scale Economies in the Nursing Home Industry," *Journal of Human Resources*, Winter 1988; J. A. Nelson, "Household Economies of Scale in Consumption," *Econometrica*, November 1988; A. O. Guyaponge and K. Gyimah-Brempong, "Factor Substitution, Price Elasticity of Factor Demand and Returns to Scale in Police Protection," *Southern Economic Journal*, April 1988; L. G. Thomas, "Advertising in Consumer Goods Industries: Durability, Economies of Scale, and Heterogeneity," *Journal of Law and Economics*, April 1989; T. E. Keeler, "Scale Economies in the U.S. Trucking Industry," *Journal of Law and Economics*, October 1989; J. M. Thomas and S. J. Callan, "Constant Returns to Scale in the Post-Deregulatory Period: The Case of Specialized Motor Carriers," *Logistics and Transportation Review*, September 1989; D. W. Caves, L. R. Christensen and M. W. Tretheway, "Economics of Density Versus Economies of Scale: Why Trunk and Local Service Airline Costs Differ," *Rand Journal of Economics*, Winter 1984; A. M. Pagano and C. E. McKnight, "Economies of Scale in the Taxicab Industry," *Journal of Transport Economics and Policy*, September 1983; G. J. Shoesmith, "Economies of Scope and Scale in Petroleum Refining," *Applied Economics*, December 1988; A. C. Krautmann and J. L. Solow, "Economies of Scale in Nuclear Power Generation," *Southern Economic Journal*, July 1988; J. F. Hennart, "Upstream Vertical Integration in the Aluminum and Tin Industries," *Journal of Economic Behavior and Organization*, April 1988.

municipal workers also exhibited economies of scale in investing their funds. Private universities were found to experience economies of scale in most operations, while public universities have typically exhausted scale advantages in undergraduate teaching, but not in graduate teaching and research. Elementary schools in the United Kingdom and Canada, and secondary schools in the United States have all been reported to enjoy cost savings through economies of scale. Similarly, hospitals are often found to face significant economies of scale; and one study of nursing homes in Texas found that these operations were not capturing all available economies of scale. Private households appear to gain directly from economies of scale in making several kinds of expenditures, especially for shelter. However, police protection services in Michigan exhibited no significant scale economies, and advertising for consumer goods (such as cigarettes, soaps, toothpaste and soft drinks) was found to operate in the range of decreasing returns to scale.

Transportation. Numerous studies have been conducted on the U.S. trucking industry, and as a group report very mixed results. There does seem to be a pattern of greater economies of scale for small trucking firms than for large firms, and it appears that economies of scale may have become more pronounced after the deregulation of the industry in the early 1980s. On the other hand, in some specialized segments of the trucking industry (such as carriers of household goods), constant returns and unit costs were observed. Commercial airlines have shown greater cost sensitivity to traffic density patterns and average lengths of flights than to economies of scale. Taxi companies exhibit U-shaped cost curves, with an optimal size of about 75 thousand fares a year.

Energy and primary metals. One study found oil refineries to have U-shaped cost curves, and be most efficient at operating levels of about 400 million barrels a day. Nuclear power plants with single reactors were found to be producing in a range of decreasing returns to scale, but dual-reactor plants enjoyed increasing returns to scale over much wider ranges of output. Scale economies were found in the aluminum and tin industries when firms practiced "upstream vertical integration" (e.g., by processing and refining their own raw materials).

Using the concepts of long-run cost schedules and returns to scale, a richer and more detailed picture of market structures in the U.S. and other industrialized nations can be drawn, and the analytical models economists develop can be held up to the "stylized" empirical facts on production and cost economies presented in this chapter. But the empirical findings themselves clearly are not sufficient to help us understand why firms in different kinds of imperfectly competitive markets compete the way they do, and what might be done to make them more economically efficient *given* such constraints as economies of scale and high levels of MES. Those topics are considered in much greater detail in the following three chapters.

Chapter Summary

1) A firm's production is carried out with a given set of capital inputs at any specific point in time, but in the long run firms can vary the size of that capital and all other inputs. Therefore, *LONG-RUN COST CURVES* show the least-cost means of producing any chosen level of output by identifying the most efficient mix of inputs, including the optimal level of capital resources. The *LONG-RUN AVERAGE TOTAL COST* curve is an envelope curve, found by connecting the least-cost points from a series of short-run average total cost curves, which are each based on a particular level of capital usage and output scale.

2) *INCREASING RETURNS TO SCALE* in production occur when an increase in all inputs leads to a more-than-proportional increase in output. Such returns may occur because higher output levels provide greater opportunities for specialization and the division of labor; or for substitution of inputs (particularly *INDIVISIBLE INPUTS* which must be used in relatively large, "lumpy" units); or *TECHNICAL EFFICIENCIES* involving capital inputs. *ECONOMIES OF SCALE* describe decreasing long-run average

total costs as output levels are increased, which will occur if a firm experiences increasing returns to scale in production or if its input prices fall as it increases purchases of inputs to expand its output.

3) *DECREASING RETURNS TO SCALE* occur when an increase in all inputs leads to a less-than-proportional increase in output. This typically occurs when firms grow so large that it becomes more difficult and expensive to manage the flow of information to and from workers, managers, and key policy makers in the organization. *DISECONOMIES OF SCALE* describe increasing long-run average total costs as output levels are increased, which occur if a firm experiences decreasing returns to scale in production or if a firm's input prices rise as it increases purchases of inputs to expand its output.

4) *CONSTANT RETURNS TO SCALE* occur when long-run average total costs are level as production levels rise and fall. Assuming that input prices are unchanged, they occur in the absence of either economies or diseconomies of scale, or when these two forces are offsetting.

5) A perfectly competitive firm has not reached its long-run equilibrium until it produces at the minimum point on its long-run average total cost schedule. At any higher point and market price, *ceteris paribus*, firms will earn economic profits, leading to entry by new firms that lowers the product price and drives firms to the plant size at which P = long-run MC and minimum LRATC. At any price lower than this level some firms will exit the industry, until the market price again rises to equal LRATC.

6) *LONG-RUN SUPPLY CURVES* for competitive firms are equal to their long-run marginal cost curves at all points greater than minimum LRATC. At the industry level, the competitive long-run supply curve is more elastic than the short-run supply curve due to entry by other firms and greater production responses to price changes by existing firms. However, long-run supply begins at a higher price than the short-run supply curve because all costs are variable in the long run, and firms must cover LRATC or shut down.

7) Long-run supply curves in *INCREASING, DECREASING, AND CONSTANT-COST INDUSTRIES* will be, respectively, upward sloping, downward sloping, and horizontal.

8) *MINIMUM EFFICIENT SCALE (MES)* refers to the lowest output level at which a firm realizes all significant economies of scale and other cost savings in producing a product. When MES is small relative to the market level of output for a product, it is possible to observe an industry that is highly competitive. But when MES is relatively large, some form of imperfect competition is likely to prevail. How nearly existing U.S. firms come to producing at the level of MES, and behaving as economists' models of perfect competition predict, is a subject of considerable debate.

9) Several measures have been developed to measure industry concentration. Traditional *N-FIRM CONCENTRATION RATIOS* indicate the percentage of sales or output accounted for by the largest four, eight, 16, or 32 firms in an industry. *HERFINDAHL INDEXES* add up the squared value of the sales or output of all major firms in an industry, which gives more weight to the effect of one or two very large firms in an industry. None of these relatively simple measures have shown a long-run trend toward greater concentration in the U.S. manufacturing sector over this century, but some individual industries have become more concentrated, at least at the domestic level.

10) Economies of scale over all relevant output levels are not compatible with the model of perfect competition, because production costs will be lower for very large firms which are not price takers. In the extreme case of a *NATURAL MONOPOLY*, it is impossible for the firm to earn economic or normal profits and simultaneously produce where P = MC and minimum ATC. This presents a dilemma to regulators when such firms are legally chartered as monopolies to achieve scale-related savings in production costs, but subject to regulatory control of price and output levels.

11) (Case Study #13) Many U.S. industries initially experience economies of scale at relatively low output levels, but most seem to face constant long-run costs over wide ranges of output. Only a few empirical studies of different industries have found evidence of substantial diseconomies of scale; but we would not expect to find firms operating in these ranges if viable production alternatives are open to them. There is some evidence that firms and industries with constant long-run average total costs tend to operate at considerably higher levels of output than would be required to achieve minimum efficient scale.

Review and Discussion Questions

1) Suppose, for technological reasons, it was only possible for a firm to build and operate the three plants associated with $SRATC_1$, $SRATC_2$, and $SRATC_3$, in the graph below. Identify this firm's long-run average total cost curve.

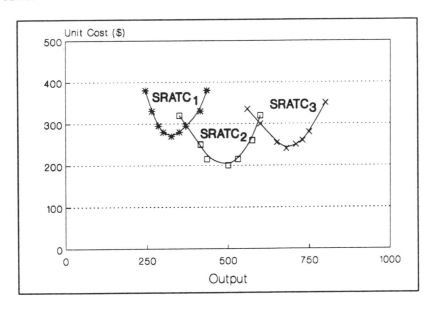

2) What might cause input prices to fall as a firm employs more units of these resources? Can economies and diseconomies of scale occur even when resource prices are constant?

3) List as many examples as you can of firms (at the local or national level) which have "downsized" in recent years. Was there any evidence that such steps were taken because of problems associated with diseconomies of scale? (Check recent copies of the *Wall Street Journal*, *Business Week*, or entries in the *Business Periodicals Index* to find such stories.)

4) If all firms and industries were characterized by constant returns to scale, would private businesses and executives of those firms face any major incentives to increase their size? Explain.

5) In Figure 10-5, in what sense do both economic and normal profits encourage the firm to produce at q_2?

6) Could the long-run supply curve for a natural monopoly be its long-run marginal cost curve? Why or why not? If no entry or exit into an industry that is not a natural monopoly is feasible, will the industry's long-run supply schedule be more or less elastic than its short-run supply schedule?

7) Draw the long-run supply curves for the three industries shown below, and identify whether each industry faces increasing, decreasing, or constant costs over the long-run.

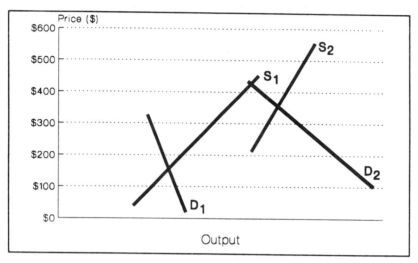

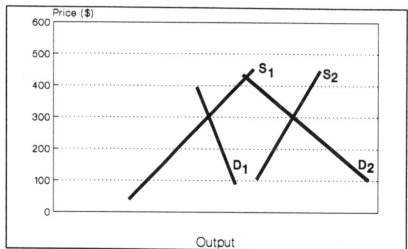

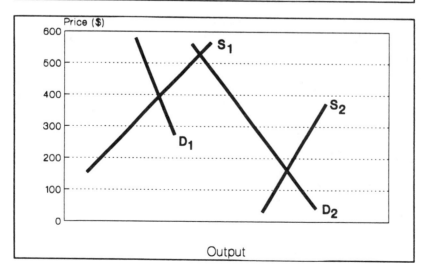

8) Identify the output level on each of the three following long-run total cost schedules where a firm achieves minimum efficient scale. If, at the current price level for the product produced by this firm, the *industry* output level is 1,000 product units a year, which of the three cost schedules shown are most and least compatible with a competitive market structure? Which of these cost schedules, if any, suggest that a firm might be a natural monopoly, again assuming an annual output level of 1,000 units? Over what output ranges on these cost schedules do you observe economies or diseconomies of scale.

Output	$LRTC_1$	$LRTC_2$	$LRTC_3$
25	$ 250	$ 250	$ 400
50	400	600	700
100	700	1,400	1,200
250	1,500	4,000	2,500
500	2,500	9,000	6,000
1,000	4,000	20,000	14,000
2,000	6,000	44,000	32,000
4,000	8,000	96,000	72,000

9) Suppose the Department of Justice adopts, as rules of thumb, cutoff levels using the Herfindahl index and 4-firm concentration ratios, above which it will oppose mergers between any of the largest 10 firms in an industry. Specifically, let those levels be .5 and 50, respectively. Is it possible for the Herfindahl index to be greater than .5 while the concentration ratio is less than 50 percent, or *vice versa*? Explain your answer. Can both measures ever equal 1.0 (100 percent)? Why or why not?

10) Suppose you have the authority to regulate the privately-owned natural monopoly shown in Figure 10-11. What price and output level would you set, and what other policies (if any) would you use to satisfy the firm's constituents (including consumers, employees, managers, and stockholders)? Explain why you would choose to use these policies, and discuss their strengths and weaknesses.

11) (Case Study #13) Does the empirical evidence presented in this case study lead you to support the position advocated by F. M. Scherer or by John S. McGee, as presented in the chapter? Why or why not? Was your thinking on this issue affected by your review of the empirical evidence? If so, how?

Chapter 11
Monopoly

In This Chapter...

we consider markets in which products are sold by a single seller, a monopoly. As you might suspect, such firms do not follow the price-taking behavior exhibited by perfectly competitive firms, and can often earn higher profits than competitive firms facing the same production costs and market demand for their products. We begin our discussion by examining the key characteristics of monopolies, and the conditions that make it possible for monopolies, or firms with some degree of monopoly power, to emerge in some markets. Then we develop models to show the results of a monopolistic market structure, in terms of a firms' pricing and production behavior, its profits, and broader measures of economic efficiency. The special issues of predatory pricing and monopolies' effects on technological progress are considered in two case studies at the end of the chapter.

Characteristics of Monopolies

A monopoly attempts to choose the price and quantity combination on the industry demand curve which will maximize profits. It faces the industry demand curve because it is the only producer of a good or service in its market. A pure monopoly is also protected from competition with firms selling the same product by high barriers to entry, such as legal restrictions on producing a good or service, economies of scale in the production or distribution of the product, brand loyalty on the part of consumers, and perhaps even the firm's reputation for engaging in predatory pricing practices. Monopolies face very different kinds of total revenue, average revenue, and marginal revenue curves from those associated with perfectly competitive firms, because of the basic differences in the characteristics of these two kinds of firms.

Price-Seeking Firms

A pure *MONOPOLY* -- from the Greek words mono and polis, meaning "one seller" -- is a single firm that produces all of the market output of a good or service. By definition, then, a monopoly faces the total market demand curve for the good or service it sells, as shown graphically in Figure 11-1. From that curve, it is clear that a monopoly can not sell any level of output it chooses at one, set price, like perfectly competitive firms. Instead, to increase sales a monopolist must move along its demand curve by lowering its price. And to receive a higher price for its product it must move up along its demand curve by reducing its output and sales levels. In short, a monopoly has to look for the particular price (and the corresponding level of output) that maximizes its profits. Monopolies are therefore considered *PRICE SEEKERS*, not price takers like the perfectly competitive firms introduced in Chapter 9.

Any firm that is not such a small part of the total market for its product that its output has no effect on product price is said to: 1) have some degree of monopoly power; 2) operate in an imperfectly competitive market structure; and 3) be a price seeker which faces a downward-sloping demand curve. Monopolies are the most extreme, "pure case" of imperfect competition, and so represent a good starting point for our study of these firms. But they are certainly not the only kind of imperfect competition, and not even the most common kind observed in today's industrial economies, as you will see in the next few chapters.

Figure 11-1
Monopolies as Price Seekers

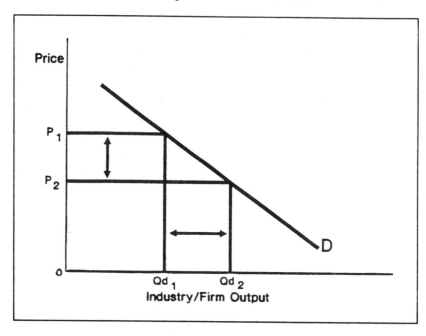

A monopoly faces the downward-sloping industry demand curve for its products because it is, by definition, the only seller of those products in its market area. In other words, the firm *is* the industry in this market. Consumers buy a greater quantity of a monopolist's products when prices for its product are decreased, and a smaller quantity when prices are increased. So monopolies and all other firms that face downward-sloping demand curves must try to find the one price and quantity combination on their demand curves where profits are maximized.

Barriers to Entry

Why do monopolies, and firms with some degree of monopoly power, arise? Or put differently, why aren't all firms perfectly competitive? Competitive firms can quickly and inexpensively enter and exit their industries. But in pure monopoly, various kinds of *BARRIERS TO ENTRY* make entry into an industry so expensive that it is, for all practical purposes, prohibited. The most important barriers to entry economists have identified can be grouped together in four major categories: legal restrictions, economies of scale, brand loyalties, and predatory pricing practices.

Legal restrictions refer to the laws and regulations that prohibit entry into some markets, and make it very costly to enter others. Classic examples of outright prohibitions to entry are patent and copyright laws which give inventors, authors, or their agents (usually companies) exclusive rights to produce or sell the products they created. Other kinds of legal prohibitions aren't, however, tied to the invention, creation, or discovery of new products. For example, the United States Postal service is protected from competition in its highly profitable first-class letter service. There is little doubt that, at least in some metropolitan areas, private companies could provide such services profitably, and at lower postage rates than the Post Office currently charges. But individuals who try to open such services are quickly forced out of business by federal agencies and the courts. (However, competition from private companies delivering packages and providing premium, "express mail" services has been allowed in recent years. And no one tries to compete directly with the Post Office in delivering fourth-class "junk mail," because rates on those materials are too low to be profitable. In fact, earnings from first-class letters are used to subsidize fourth-class mail, in part because the direct-mail industry lobbies very hard to keep those subsidies in place.)

Laws requiring licenses to work in certain occupations also make entry into some kinds of businesses and jobs more difficult and expensive. These regulations are often imposed by state and local governments. For example, physicians, pharmacists, and attorneys in all 50 states face stiff certification procedures before they are allowed to practice; and many states require licensing for plumbers, building contractors, architects, teachers, barbers and cosmetologists, chauffeurs, cab drivers (and often taxicabs themselves), restaurants, mechanics, masseurs, etc.

In some of these cases there are sound reasons for these legal impediments to entry. For example, virtually all economists support some system of patent and copyright laws because they clearly establish and define the property rights for creative work. Those property rights encourage more people to develop their new ideas, and thereby speed the flow of both technological and artistic work. However, there are also costs associated with any such restrictions, because the legal barriers mean that only "authorized" copies of novels or performances of plays will be permitted, and that only licensed doctors, lawyers, and pharmacists may sell their services to consumers. These supply restrictions establish some degree of monopoly power for the authorized sellers in each of these cases -- effectively decreasing supply of that particular product at least in the short run and, thereby, increasing the prices for these products that consumers will pay. In some cases these costs exceed the benefits associated with the legal restrictions.

Several economists argue, for example, that the time when a federal postal service was essential (because of poor transportation and communications networks and unsettled and even lawless areas in the country) has long passed in the United States and most industrialized nations. They also question the need for government licensing of attorneys, mechanics, teachers, etc. After all, market forces serve to reward the best workers in these professions, and penalize or even eliminate the incompetent. Nor is it uncommon for private organizations of professional workers to certify the qualifications of their members, thereby reducing or eliminating the need for government quality standards and enforcement action. While these private certifications can also become an expensive barrier to entry for workers just entering a new profession, in some cases they are more helpful to consumers than cumbersome government certification programs, and less expensive. But economists are often derided for putting this much faith in the market process, particularly in cases like those where some economists have argued (in all seriousness) that it is unnecessary to license even brain surgeons.

The key thing for you to see at this point is simply that legal restrictions often reduce the level of competition in certain markets, and to recognize the possible trade-offs associated with such policies.

Economies of scale can establish barriers to entry and, in extreme cases, lead to cases of natural monopolies, as you saw in the last chapter. If producers must build large factories to hold down unit production costs, that makes it expensive and difficult for new firms to enter such markets (e.g., think of the automobile and oil refining industries). And when minimum efficient scale (MES) is large relative to overall output levels in a market, the barrier to entry is especially pronounced. If entry by a new, large firm does occur in such cases, that will sharply increase competition in that industry for a time and quite possibly result in some firms facing short-term losses, or even exiting the industry in the long run. In summary, then, when MES is large relative to the output levels in a market, monopolies or some other form of imperfect competition are likely to emerge.

BRAND LOYALTY is another kind of barrier to entry, although it often works in conjunction with the barriers presented by economies of scale and minimum efficient scale, as shown in Figure 11-2. In effect, when consumers have a strong preference to buy a familiar brand of some product, producers who consider competing in their market by offering a new brand face high costs in convincing consumers that the new product is a satisfactory substitute, which meets or exceeds standards for the well known products. The new products have to sell at price levels consumers will accept, and in some cases producers must also build up a network of retailers and service facilities to distribute the new products and provide warranty and repair services. Proving that the new product is as good as existing brands sold at comparable prices, and that it can be purchased and serviced as conveniently as the old brands, is a very expensive proposition in markets for many kinds of products.

An example of firms facing those these difficulties was provided by the telephone companies which offered long-distance services for the first time after the legal break-up of the AT&T system in the early 1980s. Competing companies, especially GTE and MCI, advertised heavily to inform consumers about the new choices in this market, claiming that their services were as good or better than those provided by AT&T, and available at

312

lower prices. In response, AT&T countered with ads that stressed the risks consumers and businesses were taking by chosing a fledgling long-distance system, and the importance of the "standard" services AT&T had provided for years, which some of the new companies were not yet offering. The result was that many more consumers chose AT&T than the new, competing services in a national "sign-up" period that was part of the settlement in which AT&T divested itself of local-service telephone companies such as Pacific Bell, Bell South, and Ameritech.

Figure 11-2
Brand Loyalty and Advertising Costs as a Barrier to Entry

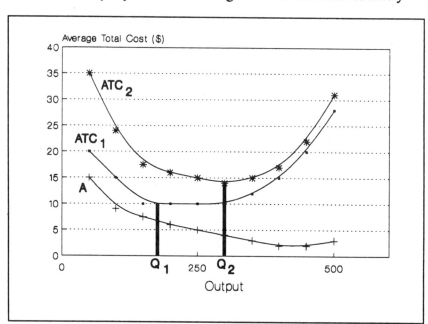

ATC_1 represents a firm's average total costs excluding advertising, and suggests the MES level shown as Q_1. But suppose this firm is trying to enter a monopolistic industry in which customers exhibit brand loyalty to existing products. The firm estimates that it can adequately offset that loyalty with an advertising campaign that will have the average costs shown in schedule A. Therefore, its overall cost schedule is found by adding schedules A and ATC_1 at each level of output, which results in the schedule ATC_2. On that higher schedule, MES occurs at output level Q_2, a greater volume and one that is more expensive to produce than Q_1 on ATC_1. So brand loyalty and advertising costs increase barriers to entry in this market.

   This example suggests that brand loyalty was a significant advantage for AT&T, which the new rivals had to face and try to offset. It also illustrates that there are quite logical reasons for companies to promote brand loyalty for their own products, and attack brand loyalties for their competitors' products. But note too that product reputations are important and useful to consumers, as well as producers, because consumers can know with greater certainty what they are getting when they purchase a certain brand of product. We consider these last points in greater detail in later chapters. Here you should see that, despite those benefits, brand loyalties also represent significant barriers to entry in some industries, including telephone services, computer equipment, soft drinks, canned foods and cereals, soaps, and alcoholic beverages.
   PREDATORY PRICING is said to occur if a large firm in an industry tries to drive out smaller firms by temporarily cutting its prices to levels below its own (and the smaller firms') average total costs, thus incurring economic losses. Supposedly, the large firm does this because it has sufficient reserves to withstand these losses

313

longer than the small firms can, or because it can use earnings from one area of its operations to offset the losses it incurrs in the particular areas where the small firms are trying to compete with it. Once the small competitors are driven out of business, the large firm supposedly buys up the assets of these ex-rivals at bargain prices, and raises its prices to levels that result in economic profits that are even higher than they were before the competition was eliminated. Firms thinking about entering this industry will come to expect this response and be reluctant to compete in it, even though the existing firm earns higher than normal profits. In this way, allegedly, an effective barrier to entry is established.

But predatory pricing is, by far, the most controversial barrier to entry that economists discuss. The controversy centers around the question of whether predatory pricing would ever be the most effective method for large firms to eliminate competition from smaller, competing firms. In legal circles there is somewhat less debate on this point; and in fact several firms have been convicted and fined for supposedly engaging in these practices. Nevertheless, while some economists are adamant in claiming that predatory pricing has often been observed in the past, and can regularly occur now or in the future, other economists are equally sure that it rarely has, and that it will never be a major problem. The latter group of economists claims that it is simply too expensive for a firm to practice predatory pricing, given alternative ways of precluding entry and eliminating competition, such as buying up the stock or assets of the entering firm, or merging with competing firms where that is legally allowed. This topic is the subject of one of the extended case studies at the end of this chapter, and is also related to the discussions on limit pricing and antitrust policy you will see in Chapter 13.

Inter-Product and Foreign Competition

While downward sloping demand curves and barriers to entry are characteristics of firms with at least some degree of monopoly power, at this point we must point out that some firms and markets that look like monopolies on first glance may, in fact, be very competitive. For example, you might be inclined to claim that all industries with high domestic concentration ratios and Herfindahl indexes, as presented in Chapter 10, are monopolies or near-monopolies. But consider two basic reasons why these empirical measures of monopoly power have to be refined, and very carefully used, before it can be established that such an industry is indeed a monopoly, or near-monopoly. The first reason involves competition from products that are reasonably close substitutes for those which are made and sold by the firm that is claimed to be a monopoly. The second reason involves the production of identical products *or* close substitutes by foreign producers.

The issue of domestic firms producing products that are close substitutes was dramatized in one of the most famous antitrust cases in U.S. history. In 1947, the Justice Department sued the duPont company for "...monopolizing, attempting to monopolize and conspiring to monopolize" the cellophane market in the United States. At that time, duPont produced about 75% of the cellophane sold in the United States; had historically charged several times more for a given quantity of cellophane than other wrapping materials, such as aluminum foil; and according to economists George W. Stocking and Willard F. Mueller, "thought cellophane had unique qualities and...adopted a strategy designed to prevent competition from any other producer, in short, to protect its monopoly. It also priced cellophane from the outset to yield monopoly revenue."[1] But in 1956, the U.S. Supreme Court handed down a split decision, ruling that "cellophane's interchangeability with other materials...suffices to make it part of [the] flexible packaging market," and that the "great sensitivity of customers in the flexible packaging markets to price or quality changes...[prevents] duPont from possessing monopoly control over price."[2]

In other words, the Court didn't buy Stocking and Mueller's conclusion that duPont had achieved a true monopoly position, and ruled that cross price elasticities of demand (the Court used that very term) were high enough to determine that there was no relevant cellophane market, but rather a broader "flexible packaging market" in which cellophane was only one of many close substitutes. A concentration ratio or Herfindahl index that looked only at cellophane production or sales missed that point. And even if duPont had controlled 100% of U.S. cellophane output, the court decision meant that before concluding any company had successfully monopolized a market to earn excess profits it had to be determined whether enough close substitutes were

[1]"The Cellophane Case and the New Competition," *American Economic Review*, 45, March, 1955, p. 54.
[2]U.S. vs. E.I. duPont de Nemours Company, 351 U.S. 377, 1956.

available to prevent the company from enjoying a true monopoly position. Our point here is not to re-judge the merits of the cellophane case, only to show that the possible presence of close substitutes must be considered before it can be established that a monopoly exists in some market.

The same general problem occurs if concentration ratios and Herfindahl indexes are calculated to measure sales and output levels for only domestic producers in markets where a substantial part of the business is going to foreign firms. You have already seen an example of this in the context of imperfect competition, though not pure monopoly, in the calculation of a Herfindahl index shown in Table 10-4. If we counted only domestic companies in that example, it would appear that the United States automotive industry was more nearly monopolized than in fact it is. The same is true in many other industries. When foreign-supplied products account for a major share of U.S. markets, that increases the level of competition in the supply of these goods, which in turn exerts pressure on both domestic and foreign producers to hold prices down, keep product quality up, and respond quickly to changes in consumer preferences.

Strictly in terms of judging the effective level of competition in a market, it makes no difference whether companies are foreign or domestically owned. However, data collected by various public and private agencies often include only domestic companies, and public perceptions of competition in some markets sometimes seem to be based only on U.S. firms, which may be older and more established sellers in these markets, and more familiar to consumers.

Proving the existence of a pure monopoly is, for all of these reasons, probably as difficult and unlikely as proving the existence of an industry that meets all of the assumptions of perfect competition. But it would be a serious mistake to ignore the models developed in this chapter, just as it would to ignore the basic competitive models in Chapter 9. Models of monopoly show us, with considerable precision, what would happen in an industry if a firm did succeed in eliminating its competition, erecting high barriers to entry, and avoiding public regulation as a natural monopoly. And that is precisely what every company and every individual who wants to maximize profits and income would most like to do! (That is, become the only company selling oil, cars, or wonder drugs; or the only person who can write and sing a hit song, execute spectacular ballet steps, or hit 1,000 home runs in a major league career.) We can evaluate the level of monopoly power in a market by seeing how close firms come to the outcomes predicted by the models of pure monopoly. And even more importantly, if they begin to approach these results we can use these models to predict, more accurately than we can with other models of perfect or imperfect competition, how they will react to changes in demand or cost factors. That is, in fact, precisely what the rest of this chapter is about.

The Monopolist's Revenue Schedules

You saw in Figure 11-1 that the monopolist's demand curve *is* the industry or market demand curve for the product it sells. You also should remember from Chapter 9 that a firm's demand curve (which shows the prices at which it can sell different amounts of output) is its average revenue schedule (because total revenue equals price times quantity, and average revenue is simply total revenue divided by quantity, or $AR = TR/Q = PQ/Q = P$). So given a monopolist's demand curve, we can easily derive the monopolist's total and marginal revenue schedules, as shown in Table 11-1. The schedules are then shown graphically, in continuous form, in Figures 11-3 and 11-4.

Table 11-1
Average, Total, and Marginal Revenue Schedules for a Monopolist

Price/Average Revenue	Quantity Demanded	Total Revenue	Marginal Revenue
$10	0	$ 0	$--
9	1	9	9
8	2	16	7
7	3	21	5
6	4	24	3
5	5	25	1
4	6	24	-1
3	7	21	-3
2	8	16	-5
1	9	9	-7
0	10	0	-9

The first two columns here show points on the demand curve for a monopolist -- i.e., the quantities of its product consumers are willing and able to buy at different prices. The monopolist faces the industry demand curve, and must lower price to increase the number of units it sells. Note that its total revenues -- P(Q) -- first rise, then reach a maximum and fall back to 0. Marginal revenue -- the change in total revenue when one more (or one less) unit of output is sold -- is positive as long as total revenue is rising, and negative whenever total revenue is falling. But a monopolist's marginal revenue always falls as the firm lowers price to sell more output. In fact, with the linear demand curve shown here marginal revenue falls off exactly twice as fast as the demand (average revenue) schedule. That is, each $1 decrease in price lowers marginal revenue by $2.

Because a monopolist must lower price to increase the quantity of a good or service it sells, its marginal revenue curve is not equal to price (or average revenue), as it was for competitive firms which could sell any quantity they chose at the market price. In fact, for a typical monopolist, and for any firm with some degree of monopoly which faces a downward-sloping demand curve, marginal revenue falls off faster than the demand curve because the firm has to lower its price on all of the units it sells, including those it was selling before at a higher price. This is what results in the area labeled "revenue loss" in Figure 11-3, and the marginal revenue curve that lies below the demand curve in Figure 11-4.

This process often sounds strange to students taking their first course in economics, but if you think about it a minute you will see that it is, in fact, the kind of behavior you usually see in the marketplace. And you can even identify several reasons why this is so. For example, in your lifetime you have lived through many cases of falling prices for different products, such as gasoline, computer equipment, televisions, stereo equipment, and interest rates charged by banks and other kinds of financial service companies on different kinds of loans. In all of these instances, when prices fell they fell for all people who made new purchases in these markets, including many who would have been willing and able to buy the products at the old, higher, prices.

316

Figure 11-3
Graphically Deriving a Monopolist's Marginal Revenue Schedule

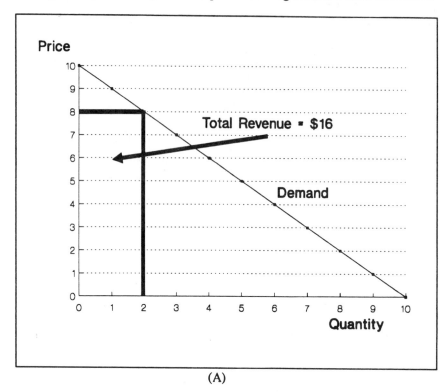

(A)

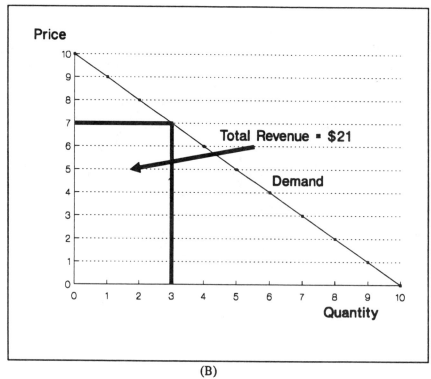

(B)

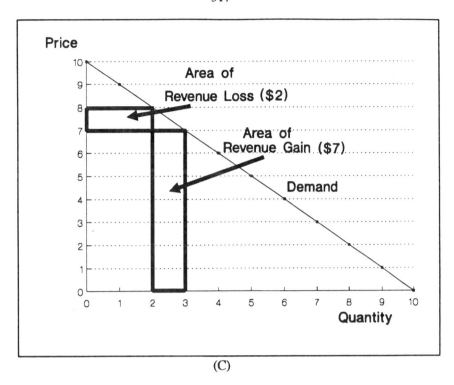

(C)

To sell more output, a monopolist lowers its price. In panels (A) and (B), the total revenue of selling 2 and 3 units of output at prices of $8 and $7, respectively, is shown to be $16 and $21. This corresponds to the values shown in Table 11-1.

When this firm lowers price from $8 to $7, its marginal revenue will therefore represent the net effect of selling one more unit of output, but receiving a lower price for each unit sold than it did before. As shown in panel (C), it gains revenues equal to the area of the vertical rectangle in the graph, but loses revenues equal to the area of the horizontal rectangle. On net, as shown in the fourth column of Table 11-1, the firm's marginal revenue from selling the 3rd unit of output is +$5. You can confirm that value by calculating the area of the two rectangles in panel (C) ($7 in revenue gains, $2 in revenue losses).

Figure 11-4
The Monopolist's Total, Average, and Marginal Revenue Schedules,
and Price Elasticity of Demand Revisited

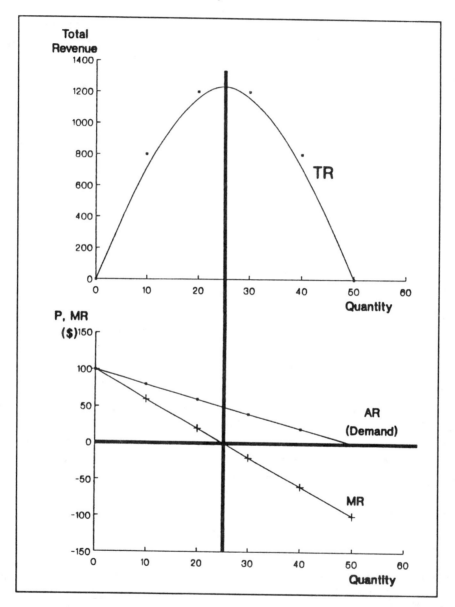

This graph depicts a typical total revenue (TR) schedule for a monopolist, and shows the same pattern as those shown in Table 11-1. With linear demand curves like the one used there, note that marginal revenue (MR) falls off exactly twice as fast as demand (i.e., average revenue -- AR) and is equal to zero when TR is maximized. From the total revenue test for price elasticity of demand, developed in Chapter 4, we know that this demand schedule is elastic in all ranges where marginal revenue is positive; inelastic whenever marginal revenue is negative; and unitary elastic when marginal revenue is 0.

So when a monopoly decides to increase revenues by lowering price (which happens as long as it is in the price elastic range of its demand schedule), the price decrease is typically offered to all buyers. And it's actually easy to see why that is so. If the monopolist tries to lower price for some customers but not others, those they sell to at low prices can quickly realize a profit by selling the products to the customers the monopoly still tries to charge a higher price. In effect, the monopolist would create its own competitors by selling to some customers at lower prices than others. And as a practical matter, it is also difficult for most monopolists to know which of their customers are willing and able to pay a higher price, and which are not. The firm also stands to lose a considerable amount of customer loyalty if it tries to enforce such policies, not to mention legal actions for price discrimination -- a topic we cover in a later section of this chapter. The key point here is that, except in some very unusual circumstances which we will discuss at the end of this chapter, monopolists and other kinds of firms must uniformly implement price changes for all customers.

That leads us back to the conclusion you have already seen: When a monopolist or any firm facing a downward-sloping demand curve raises and lowers prices for all of its customers, and potential customers, the marginal revenue schedule will lie below the demand curve, and fall off at a faster rate.

With these revenue schedules for the typical monopolist in hand, you are ready to see how such a firm finds its profit maximizing price and output levels. To do that, in the next section we use the same cost schedules that were developed in Chapter 7, and used to study perfectly competitive firms in Chapter 9. With both cost and revenue schedules incorporated into our model of pure monopoly, it is then a simple matter to identify the short-run and long-run equilibrium position for the monopolist, and to compare these monopoly results with those derived for competitive firms.

The Monopolist in Equilibrium

For monopolists and all other kinds of firms, the golden rule of profit maximization is to produce the level of output at which marginal revenue equals marginal cost, and charge the applies if a monopolist finds itself in a loss minimization situation, so long as it covers all of its average variable costs in the short run, and all of its average total costs in the long run (just as with perfectly competitive firms). Barriers to entry allow some monopolies to earn both short-run and long-run economic profits, by restricting output and charging higher prices than competitive firms would if they faced identical cost curves and market levels of demand for their products. Using the P = MC and P = minATC criteria developed in Chapter 9, economists argue that monopolies exhibit allocative and productive inefficiencies, and specifically that they underallocate scarce resources to the production of the goods and services they sell.

Profit Maximization: MR = MC

The rule the monopolist uses to find the output level which will maximize its profits, given these revenue and cost schedules, is exactly the same rule used by a perfectly competitive firm: it sets marginal revenue equal to marginal cost. At any other output level, one of two things will happen: 1) if the firm sees that marginal revenue is greater than marginal cost, that will be a clear signal that it can increase total profits (or reduce losses) by increasing its output level; but 2) if marginal cost is greater than marginal revenue, it is equally clear that profits will increase (or losses decrease) if the firm reduces its output level. Figure 11-5 shows a monopolist earning economic profits equal to the shaded area labeled ABCD, selling the profit-maximizing level of output labeled Q*, at which MR = MC. If you don't have a firm grasp of why this is the profit maximizing level of output for any kind of firm, go back now and re-read the discussion associated with Figure 9-6.

Once the monopolist has established its most profitable level of output, it will charge the highest price that consumers are willing and able to pay for that quantity of products. In Figure 11-5, to find the profit-maximizing price simply start at the intersection point of marginal revenue and marginal cost and go up vertically to the demand curve (at point B), then horizontally over to the price axis (point A). Even if firms don't have precise knowledge or statistical estimates of their demand, revenue, and cost schedules to work with (although some do,

Figure 11-5
A Profit-Maximizing Monopolist

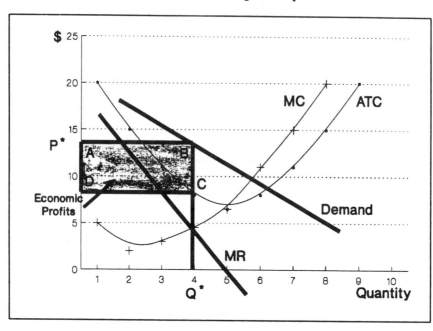

This monopolist is assumed to operate with cost curves exactly like those facing the competitive firms studied in the last two chapters. Although the monopolist faces a downward-sloping demand curve, and a separate marginal revenue curve that lies below its demand curve, it still maximizes profits by setting MR = MC, which calls for producing Q* units of output. The monopolist then sets price P* -- the price associated with output level Q* on its demand curve -- and earns economic profits identified by the shaded area labelled ABCD. Because of high barriers to entry, this will be both the firm's short-run and long-run equilibrium position, *ceteris paribus*.

---

and particularly the large firms that might be expected to behave most like monopolists), if they successfully maximize profits through a simple process of trial and error this is where they will end up, so long as these schedules do not shift.

Be careful not to fall into the trap of thinking that a profit-maximizing monopolist can make a profit charging any price it chooses. In fact, just because a firm is a monopolist doesn't mean that it is guaranteed to make a profit. For example, you can have your own monopoly as a blacksmith in many towns in the United States today, if you want to try to make a living at it. But except in areas where horseback riding is popular with Yuppies or ranchers, your profits, if any, will be slim. Figure 11-6 demonstrates that some products are just not in sufficient demand, given the costs of producing them, to offer even a monopolist the opportunity to earn economic or even normal profits. As you can see, the graph in this figure shows a monopolist which would continue to operate in the short run because it is covering all of its variable and some of its fixed costs (which are represented by the distance between ATC and AVC). But unless costs fall or demand increases, even the monopolist will eventually have to leave this market.

The situation shown in Figure 11-6 is, however, far less interesting to economists than the one in Figure 11-5. After all, who cares much about monopolists that can't earn enough profits to stay in business (except, of course, for the owners and employees of a monopoly that comes to this end). Instead, most people care about how high a successful monopolist's profits are, how long they are expected to continue, and what kinds of problems monopolies entail for an economy.

Figure 11-6
A Monopolist Minimizing Short-Run Losses

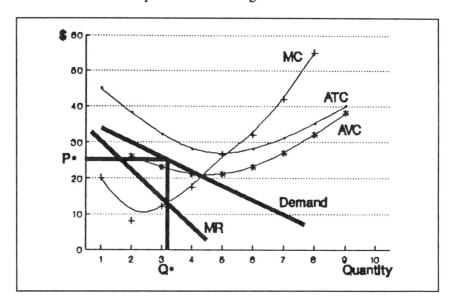

This monopoly's profit-maximizing or loss-minimizing level of output is found, as always, by setting MR = MC. At that level, this firm finds that it covers all variable and some fixed costs, so like a perfectly competitive firm in the same situation it will lose less by continuing to operate than by shutting down in the short run. But in the long-run it will have to exit this industry unless demand increases or costs decrease sufficiently to allow the firm to earn at least normal profits.

How high the economic profits earned by monopolists will be varies from case to case, and is determined by the relative position of the firm's revenues (i.e., its demand curve) and costs. Some monopolies would literally be worth a fortune to their owners while others, as in the blacksmith example, would be worth little or nothing at all. How long a monopoly's economic profits will continue -- if in fact any are earned in the first place -- depends on the effectiveness of the monopolist's barriers to entry.

If those barriers are sufficiently low the monopoly will not operate alone in the industry very long. Other firms will enter and the industry will become an oligopoly or some other form of imperfect competition, described by the models in the next two chapters.

If the barriers effectively disappear, allowing many firms to eventually produce and sell the same product, the industry will become perfectly competitive, as described by the models already covered in Chapter 9.

But in the extreme case where barriers to entry are so successful that they deter all other firms, we have the case of pure monopoly. Then, as shown in Figure 11-5, the simple but powerful outcome is that the firm's long-run equilibrium position is the same as its short-run equilibrium, assuming that demand and cost factors are otherwise unchanged in all significant respects.

The extent to which the pure monopoly outcome is bad news for an economy is discussed in the following section on the measures of productive and allocative inefficiency associated with monopoly power, and in the case study on "Dynamic Competition Through Technological Change" at the end of the chapter.

Productive Inefficiency and Allocative Inefficiency

The basic model of a monopoly earning economic profits illustrates three different outcomes that trouble most economists who are concerned about the efficient allocation of scarce resources. That model was shown in

Figure 11-5, *assuming* that the cost curves facing the monopoly are the same as those that firms would face if, somehow, the monopoly could be broken up into a perfectly competitive industry. In the Figure, note that:

a) At the profit-maximizing level of output, the price the monopolist receives is greater than the average cost of producing the quantity of output it makes and sells -- or P > ATC.

b) At this level of output, price is also greater than the minimum possible level of average total cost -- or P > minATC. And

c) Price is also greater than the marginal cost of producing the firm's last unit of output -- or P > MC.

Let's discuss the significance of each of these three inequalities in turn.

First, P > ATC is just another way of saying that the firm is earning economic profits, which only troubles economists part of the time -- specifically, in the long run. In the short run, economic profits in both perfectly competitive and imperfectly competitive markets tell producers that consumers want more of a product, and that they are willing and able to pay for it at levels that will cover all of the firm's economic costs of producing it. So in this sense economic profits serve both as a signal of what consumers are eager to buy and as an incentive to promote the reallocation of resources into the production of those products. That's all to the good if we assume, as economists typically do, that individual consumers are the best judges of what is in their own best interests. But in the long run economic profits indicate the presence of barriers to entry, which restrict the flow of more resources into the production of these products. Therefore, in the long run, P > ATC is a sign of monopoly power, which normally means that other kinds of inefficiencies are present as well.

Specifically, productive inefficiency is signaled by the P > minATC inequality. To see this, note that in Figure 11-5 if output is increased beyond the equilibrium level where MR = MC, per unit production costs continue to fall, at least for a time. In other words, average production costs (ATC) aren't at the lowest *possible* level at the monopolist's equilibrium output level, and the monopoly might even be able to increase production to the level at which they are and still earn economic profits. The monopolist chooses not to do this, however, simply because it isn't in the firm's own economic interests to do so. Its profits are decreased, not maximized, by moving to the higher output levels. Once the monopolist goes beyond the point where MR = MC and spends more to produce each additional unit of output than it takes in by selling it, its average revenue falls off faster than its average total costs.

The most serious charge against monopolies is that they lead to an inefficient allocation of an economic system's scarce resources. This is most clearly indicated, in equilibrium, by the P > MC inequality. What this means is that for the last unit of output a monopolist makes and sells, where MR = MC, consumers value this product (as measured by P) more than they value the next-best use of the resources that are used to make the product (as measured by MC). Consumers, as well as economists and policymakers who accept consumers as the best judges of what they do or do not value, would like to see additional resources used to produce more units of this product. But a typical monopolist that maximizes profits will stop short of the P = MC level, so we say there is an underallocation of resources to this market. That simply means that to produce out to the point where P = MC more units of this product would have to be produced, and more resources used to produce them.[3]

This underallocation result holds true not only in cases of pure monopoly, including the public utilities discussed in the section on natural monopolies in Chapter 10, but also in oligopolies and other kinds of imperfectly competitive firms discussed in later chapters, which produce such major products as automobiles, airplanes, oil, and stylish clothing. The firms that produce these products, and many others, often limit output levels and produce where P > MC. They can therefore be said to be allocatively inefficient, based on this criterion.

---

[3]To sharpen your understanding of this discussion on optimal resource allocation, and to contrast the monopoly outcome to results in markets that are perfectly competitive, review the discussion of resource under- and overallocation associated with the existence of externalities in Chapter 5, and the discussion of the P = MC result in Chapter 9.

However, if you conclude from this discussion that competitive firms are run by angels and public-spirited benefactors, while monopolies and other firms that are imperfectly competitive are run by greedy capitalist pigs, you are still missing some basic points in the analysis. We address that point more directly in the following section, by reviewing some of the major similarities of, and differences between, competitive and monopolistic firms.

Comparing Monopoly and Perfect Competition

The characteristics and outcomes associated with basic economic models of monopoly and perfect competition are summarized in Table 11-2. Those results primarily indicate differences between the two kinds of firms, but an important thing to keep in mind as you compare those entries is that both models were based on the behavioral assumption that firms -- whether they are perfectly competitive or perfect monopolies -- try to maximize profits. Whether profit maximization itself is morally good, bad, or indifferent, is not addressed in the models. Instead, profit maximization is simply an assumption that allows economists to predict how both kinds of firms will respond to changes in prices, production costs, and other economic variables. And that's an assumption that has stood the test of time in economic analysis, in terms of yielding predictions and explanations of firms' behavior which usually conform to the real-world behavior of the firms.

Table 11-2
Comparing Monopolies and Perfectly Competitive Firms

	Allocative Efficiency	Productive Efficiency	Economic Profits Possible	Revenue Schedules	Profit Maximization Rule
Perfect Competition	P = MC	P = min ATC	SR, yes; LR, no	P = MR	MR = MC
Monopoly	P > MC	P > min ATC	SR, yes; LR, yes	P > MR	MR = MC

Monopolies and perfectly competitive firms have some characteristics in common, and some that are different. Both maximize profits by producing the level of output at which MR = MC. But the competitive firm is a price taker, and faces a horizontal demand curve equal to the market price for its product that is also its marginal revenue curve. A monopolist, on the other hand, faces the downward-sloping industry demand curve and a marginal revenue curve that lies below its demand curve. It seeks the highest price on its demand curve at which it can sell the profit-maximizing level of output.

While both kinds of firms may earn economic profits in the short run, that leads to entry by new firms in competitive markets which continues until, in the long run, firms earn only normal profits. In monopolies, barriers to entry prohibit that response, and therefore economic profits may continue even in the long run. Competitive firms meet the criteria for productive and allocative efficiency since P = minATC and P = MC, respectively. Typical monopolies will produce where P > minATC and P > MC, even though to maximize profits they must minimize the costs of producing the output level they do produce. A monopolist's inefficiency stems from the nature of the demand and marginal revenue schedules it faces -- which lead it to restrict output to increase price -- not because the firm has no interest in holding down its production costs.

In fact, strictly in terms of economic effects, it's not necessary to address loaded questions about the ethics of profit maximization because, under the assumption, both a thoroughly evil man and a saint running either a competitive firm or a monopoly would behave the same way in terms of pricing and output decisions, given identical market conditions. In other words, with identical cost and *industry* demand curves, anyone running a monopoly would set a higher price and lower output level to maximize profits than they would if the same industry was composed of perfectly competitive firms taking the market price as a given. In both kinds of market structures demand curves, cost curves, and the level of competition *all* serve to constrain or direct the behavior of firms. But other things being equal, more competition benefits consumers in terms of lower prices and efficient, low-cost production -- as well as more mundane aspects of customer service. For example, to paraphrase Adam Smith once again, a butcher in a competitive market has more reason to be pleasant to customers after having an argument with his or her spouse than a butcher who owns a monopoly in some remote town.

In terms of basic questions on price and output levels, the fundamental point for you to remember is that even though monopolists are price seekers, they are still seeking and moving toward one particular price, which is determined by the demand, marginal revenue, and cost curves the firm faces. Of course, given the choice and a serious interest in earning more money, you would naturally prefer to be a monopolist in some market rather than one of many competitive firms selling the same product. That would offer you the chance to earn economic profits in both the short run and the long run, and relieve you from the daily pressure of direct competition.

But even monopolists face many operating constraints. In particular, to maximize profits a monopolist must minimize the cost of producing its equilibrium output level (i.e., keep costs at a point on the ATC curve, though not at minATC), and follow the dictates of marginal analysis as rigorously as competitive firms.

For the most part we will be focusing on the ways in which competitive firms and imperfectly competitive firms are different. But it is also important to remember how the firms are similar, particularly in terms of the assumed motivation of the firms' owners. The different outcomes in the different market structures are a function of the different circumstances the owners find themselves facing, not basic differences in the makeup of the owners themselves.

An Illustrative Curiosity: The Monopolist's Missing Supply Curve

We will now consider a theoretical point that, though not of earth-shattering importance in its own right, helps to clarify several aspects of monopoly behavior *and* the appropriate use of graphical analysis in economics. The conclusion from this exercise often surprises students, which is okay; and then confuses them, which is not. The conclusion is that monopolists have no supply curve. The best way to avoid the confusion is to read all of this section before looking at the graph in Figure 11-7.

In the models of perfect competition covered in Chapter 9, as the price facing a competitive firm changes, firms move along their marginal cost schedule (at all prices greater than minAVC) to find a new level of output to sell. Each different price leads to a different level of output, or quantity supplied, and that relationship turns out to be coincident with the part of the firm's marginal cost schedule lying above the AVC curve.

Unfortunately, that's not the case with a monopoly (nor with any imperfectly competitive firms) for several reasons. First, as you have already seen in Figure 11-4, the monopolist produces where P > MC, so we know that the firm's MC schedule is *not* simultaneously its supply curve along any range of output, as it was for perfectly competitive firms. In other words, we can't take a price and look at the corresponding point on the MC schedule to find the output level that the monopoly will produce at that price. Next, it is quite possible for two different price levels to be associated with the same level of output, or quantity supplied, for the monopolist. This is shown in Figure 11-7, but before you look at that graph recognize that when two prices can lead a firm to supply the same quantity of output, that destroys the notion of *any* unique correspondence between price and quantity supplied, and along with it any hope economists had of finding a unique, graphable, supply curve.

In effect, while a monopolist can know its cost and revenue schedules just as competitive firms do, changes in monopolists' revenue schedules can affect the slope as well the position of these curves, and that is not true for competitive firms. (This is also illustrated in Figure 11-7.) For monopolies, therefore, some demand shifts may cause the firm to continue producing the same level of output as before, but charge a different price. That could never happen with a perfectly competitive firm, where the short-run supply schedule was well behaved and clearly defined. The fact that it can happen in a monopoly means we can't plot out a distinct set of points to identify that firm's supply curve.

Now you can look at Figure 11-7, and after studying it say that you are among that small fraternity of people who know that monopolists' have no supply curve. But there are still many other aspects of this market structure to understand, which are even more important in terms of public policy considerations involving price and output levels, and the quality of service consumers enjoy in the marketplace.

Figure 11-7
The Monopolist Has No Supply Schedule

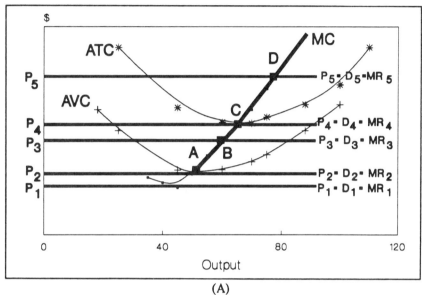

(A)

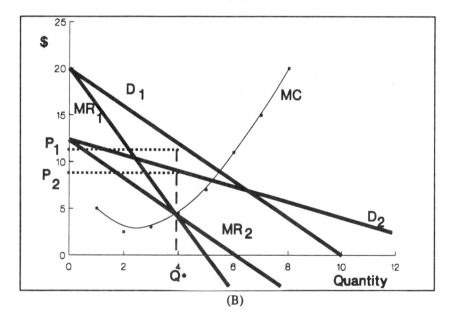

(B)

In panel (A) we show, as we did earlier in Figure 9-8, that as the price = demand = marginal revenue curve facing a perfectly competitive firm changes, the firm will supply the quantity indicated on its marginal cost curve at all prices above the minimum point on the average variable cost curve. This establishes the firm's short-run supply curve -- which shows a unique correspondence between price and quantity supplied.

No such correspondence exists for a monopoly, or other imperfectly competitive firms that face downward-sloping demand and marginal revenue curves. In panel (B), note that for both of the two demand curves shown the equilibrium level of output is Q*. However, on D_1 the monopolist charges P_1 for this level of output, and on D_2 the firm charges P_2. Thus, there is no unique set of price and quantity supplied coordinates that we can use to plot out a supply schedule for this kind of firm.

Public Policy Issues Concerning Monopolies

Apart from general concerns about productive and allocative efficiency, and an underallocation of scarce resources to certain markets, monopolies are also associated with several kinds of specific problems that may call for public policy actions and remedies. These problems include: 1) the reallocation of economic welfare from areas of consumer surplus to producer surplus; 2) the creation of areas of pure deadweight loss; 3) the separation of management and ownership functions in large corporations, which leads to a principal-agent problem and further concerns about the efficiency standard that will be maintained in these companies; and, 4) under special circumstances, different degrees of price discrimination -- or charging different prices to different customers for the same product, even when the production costs of supplying those customers are identical.

Deadweight Loss Revisited

The social costs of resource misallocations arising from monopolies are most clearly represented by the kind of graph shown in Figure 11-8. The major point to understand from this graph is the concept of a deadweight loss, which you first encountered in Chapter 4. Compared to a perfectly competitive firm facing identical cost schedules, a profit-maximizing monopolist will restrict output in order to command a higher price for its product. This results in both a loss of economic welfare -- shown as the shaded area of deadweight loss labeled ABC -- and a reallocation of welfare from consumer surplus to producer surplus -- shown as the shaded area labeled DEAF.

Economists have tried to estimate the dollar value of the deadweight loss that occurs because of the existence of monopoly power among all kinds of imperfectly competitive firms in the U.S. economy. Those studies are summarized later, in Chapter 13, after you have reviewed models of other kinds of firms that exercise some degree of monopoly power. For now, just be sure you remember clearly what deadweight loss is -- a decrease in consumer surplus that is not offset by a gain in producer surplus, or a decrease in producer surplus that is not offset by a gain in consumer surplus -- and why monopolies create deadweight losses, through the underallocation of resources indicated by the P > MC result. Recognize too that if the amount of deadweight loss associated with monopoly power is thought to be very high, that represents clear support for considering the use of anti-trust laws and regulations to prevent or break up monopolies. Whether or not such policies should be adopted and enforced depends, of course, on whether the benefits of doing so are expected to outweigh the costs.

Figure 11-8 can also be used to demonstrate that, contrary to complaints by some journalists and social critics, if a monopolist is maximizing profits in a short-run equilibrium position it will *not* experience an increase in total revenues by raising its price. How do we know that? Because we know that: 1) profits are maximized where MR = MC, 2) MC is > 0 over all ranges of output, 3) when MR is > 0 a firm is operating in the price elastic segment of its demand curve, and 4) by setting MR = MC where MC > 0, the typical monopolist must be operating in the elastic range of demand. That means that if the monopolist raises its price above the equilibrium level, *ceteris paribus*, quantity demanded will fall off enough to lower the firm's total revenues. Once again, this shows that the demand curve is a constraint facing the monopolist, as well as all other kinds of firms. It also means that some of the popular horror stories about monopolies are not true, and thus not a proper concern for the Antitrust Division of the Department of Justice. But others may be.

Figure 11-8
Monopolies, Deadweight Loss, and Price Elasticity in Equilibrium

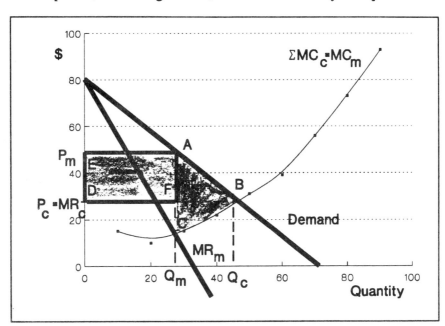

In a perfectly competitive industry market price is set at the level where the industry demand curve is intersected by the industry supply curve. That supply curve is found by horizontally summing up the supply curves for all firms in the industry, which are their marginal cost curves at all values greater than average variable costs. Therefore, the competitive industry's supply curve is labeled ΣMC_c in this graph. Given the market demand curve shown above, the competitive market price will be P_c, which establishes the demand and marginal revenue curves for all firms in the industry. In equilibrium, the competitive output level is Q_c.

If this industry is monopolized without affecting the level of industry demand or production costs, the monopoly will face a marginal revenue curve (MR_m) that lies below its demand curve. So even if its marginal cost curve (MC_m) is identical to the competitive supply curve found by adding up the marginal cost schedules of the competitive firms, as shown above, the monopoly will choose to produce a smaller output level (Q_m) and charge a higher price (P_m) than the competitive industry. The reduction in output captures some area that was formerly consumer surplus as producer surplus for the monopolists (the shaded area DEAF), but also lowers total welfare by an area of deadweight loss (ABC).

Monopoly Power and the Separation of Ownership and Control

In 1929, 11% of U.S. nonfinancial corporations were privately owned, or controlled by majority ownership in which an individual and/or his or her immediate family controlled more than half of a company's stock, and could therefore direct the company's policies by electing at least a majority of the firm's Board of Directors. About 23%

of nonfinancial corporations at that time were run by an individual or family that owned less than 50% of a company's stock, but still had enough influence to effectively control the Board of Directors.[4]

By 1963, only 3% of these corporations were privately or "majority" owned, while the portion of companies run through "minority control" fell off to 9%. The vast majority of firms (83.5%) were subject to "management control,"[5] which means that corporate officers are able to obtain enough shareholders' proxies to elect a majority of the Board of Directors. The Board of Directors then approves such things as investment and operating plans proposed by the corporate officers, salary and benefit packages for the corporate officers, and even the appointment of the corporate officers themselves. This arrangement is simply a logical consequence of the fact that, for large corporations with thousands of stockholders, it is very rare for any one stockholder, or small group of stockholders, to own enough stock to believe that their votes will have any significant effect in choosing a Board of Directors or on other company issues. In practice, therefore, most shareholders simply sign proxies authorizing the incumbent corporate officers or Board of Directors to cast their votes, or don't bother to vote at all.

This separation of corporate ownership (the stockholders) and control (the managers, and the Board of Directors appointed by the managers) is very similar to some of the public choice problems discussed in Chapter 5, but now seen operating in the private rather than the public sector. In fact, both of these problems are representative of what can happen when economic "principals" (the shareholders, voters, or other groups whose interests are ultimately at stake) employ or elect "agents" (Senators, corporate directors, attorneys, etc.) to represent them, and discover that the agents' best interests are not always the same as their own.

This issue presents a notoriously difficult problem to control for in studies that evaluate the efficiency of very large firms, and how actively corporate officers pursue their own rather than stockholders' interests. The basic problem in preparing such estimates is that actions which satisfy the vanity and interests of the executives/agents -- such as increasing a company's sales levels and corporate officers' support staffs, salaries, or benefit packages -- can sometimes also be consistent with the goal of profit maximization for a firm, at least in the long run if not in the short run. It's not always easy to tell when they are, and when they aren't.

There are, however, other factors that put clear limits on the degree to which corporate officers and directors can ignore stockholders' interests. Competition from firms in the same industry and the prospect of entry by new competitors (foreign and domestic) rank high on this list. Perhaps the most dramatic examples of such effects in recent decades have been the successful entry of foreign producers and products in the U.S. automobile and consumer electronics industries. The threat of such competition in other industries, and of hostile takeovers by competing domestic or foreign competitors, has literally made headlines in recent years, and brought new kinds of incentives, discipline, and behavior to the corporate world. Many economists and financial analysts argue that just knowing people such as T. Boone Pickens and Carl Ichan are always on the lookout for firms that can be organized or run more profitably keeps many managers of large companies "on their toes." But other scholars and business leaders worry about the effect some anti-takeover measures may have on companies' efficiency, profits, and stock values -- measures such as "golden parachutes" which provide current managers with lucrative retirement or severance benefits if a hostile takeover occurs, or large acquisitions of corporate debt to make a company less appealing as a takeover target.

Several kinds of economic models have been developed to explore the consequences of managerial goals that either replace or modify the profit-maximizing goal you have studied thus far. The best known of these models were developed by William J. Baumol, and compare equilibrium results for firms that maximize market share (i.e., sales or total revenues), or market share subject to some minimum-profit constraint, to those for firms that maximize profits. A simple version of this kind of model is shown in Figure 11-9.

As you saw in Chapter 2, whether economists choose to work with profit-maximizing, sales-maximizing, or managerial and behavioral models of a firm depends on several factors, including what is known about the firm or industry under study, the kinds of questions the models will be asked to address, the costs and benefits of using and testing these models, and ultimately how well the models predict the behavior of firms and industries at different times and under various conditions.

---

[4] A. A. Berle, Jr. and G. C. Means, *The Modern Corporation and Private Property*, New York: Macmillan, Inc., 1932, p. 115.

[5] R. J. Larner, *Management Control and the Large Corporation*, New York: Dunellen Publishing, 1970, p. 12.

329

Finally, in the last section in this chapter, we will consider the policy issues associated with price discrimination. These are the unusual but sometimes important cases in which imperfectly competitive firms are able to charge different customers different prices for identical goods or services, and make those price differences stick.

Figure 11-9
Maximizing Revenues From Sales With a Profit Constraint

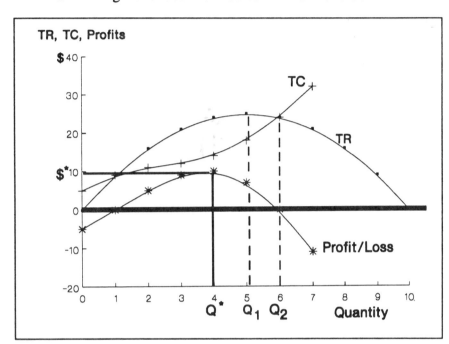

A standard total revenue schedule for a monopolist (as developed in Figure 11-4) and a total cost schedule (as developed in Figure 7-5) are shown above. The profit-maximizing level of output occurs where the positive difference between these two curves is greatest, at Q*. In fact, we can construct a schedule of economic profits at all output levels, as shown, to show again that maximum profits, labeled $*, are earned at Q*.

If the firm chooses to maximize its sales revenues instead of profits, perhaps to deter entry by new firms or because of managerial preferences and pay incentives, it would produce at Q_1 where profits would be lower than at Q* (and perhaps even negative for some firms, at least in the short run). Alternatively, the firm's managers might decide to maximize the quantity of output sold subject to some minimum-profit constraint, which they judge will satisfy stockholders and deter attempts at hostile takeovers. Suppose that minimum profit level is set at the level of normal profits (i.e., $0 of economic profit). Then the maximum level of sales consistent with that profit constraint occurs at Q_2. It is theoretically plausible that, in some cases, revenue or sales maximization strategies will increase long-run profits but decrease short-run profits. Whether or not that will occur cannot be determined from this basic model.

Price Discrimination

Many of the services you buy can never be re-sold, especially services like health care; riding a plane, boat, or bus; watching a play or first-run movie at a theatre; or a non-transferable membership in a health club or social fraternity. Goods that can not be resold are much less common, but think about blood transfusions and artificial or transplanted organs that are, literally, incorporated into consumers. Once the consumer who buys these "products" is gone, so are these goods.

If it also turns out that:

1) different individuals or groups of people will pay different prices for this special kind of good or service,
2) producers can easily tell what different consumers are willing to pay, and
3) producers can make and sell the products sold to these different customers at identical costs,

then *PRICE DISCRIMINATION* can be practiced. This will only happen when barriers to entry limit the amount of competition in these markets. Otherwise, new firms would enter to sell to the customers who were paying the higher price, and prices would fall to the level where only normal profits are earned. Price discrimination doesn't happen often, as this rather severe list of pre-conditions is meant to imply; but it sometimes does. Before we review some examples and models of this phenomenon, be sure you understand its formal definition and the circumstances that must exist for it to develop and endure. To review, then, price discrimination occurs *only* when companies with some degree of monopoly power sell identical products to different consumers at different prices, even though the costs of producing and delivering these products to the different consumers do not vary.

Examples of price discrimination can include such things as a doctor charging a rich patient (who may have an all-inclusive medical insurance policy) more than a poor patient (who may have little or no insurance) for performing the same operation in the same hospital. Or consider a movie theatre chain that owns all of the theatres in an area (which happens to be true in Lafayette, Indiana, and many other small cities) charging students less than non-students, or charging less to see a 1:30 show than a 3:30 show. Or think about hotels and large restaurant chains that offer "senior citizen discounts," and airlines that set up "super-saver" fares that are designed to charge business passengers more than families using the same flights to go on a two-week vacation.

Remember, however, that if there are cost differences in providing these products to the different groups of customers, a two-tiered (or more) pricing structure is not necessarily price discrimination. For example, public utilities typically charge large industrial and business customers lower rates for electricity, water, and natural gas than residential customers. But that's largely because it costs far less to build and maintain a distribution system to carry a large volume of product to one location, like a factory or high-rise office building, than it does to deliver the same amount of product, divided up into much smaller units, to thousands of individual homes.

Firms which can engage in price discrimination do so because it is profitable, as we show graphically in Figure 11-10. The pricing structure shown there, in which the market is divided into two discrete groups of customers and two different prices are charged for the same product, is called *THIRD-DEGREE PRICE DISCRIMINATION*. This is the simplest form of price discrimination, but it clearly demonstrates two of the key requirements for price discrimination to occur. Namely, it shows that firms practicing price discrimination must be able to: 1) separate their market into different two groups of customers with different demand characteristics -- in particular different price elasticities of demand; and 2) keep the customers who pay a lower price from reselling to those who pay more.

If those conditions are met, the monopolist maximizes profits by setting two different prices because there are now different marginal revenue schedules associated with each of the demand curves representing the different groups of customers. Calling the marginal revenue curves for those groups MR_1 and MR_2, as in Figure 11-10, the monopolist will add up those schedules to find its total marginal revenue curve. This is the amount it takes in from increased sales when it lowers price for both groups of customers -- and the firm obviously values those additional dollars, wherever they come from. The firm's profits are therefore maximized by setting this combined marginal revenue equal to the marginal cost of producing additional units of output to sell, at the overall output level shown as Q*.

Part of this total output is sold to each of the two groups, with the precise amount determined from the MR curve for each group. Additional units will be sold in each part of the market so long as the marginal revenue obtained is greater than or equal to the marginal cost of producing Q*, because doing so always adds to profits or decreases losses, as you have seen before. In equilibrium, therefore, $MR_1 = MR_2 = MC$ of producing the unit of

331

output labeled Q*. Prices for the two groups of consumers are set at the points on D_1 and D_2 associated with MR_1 and MR_2 -- or P_1 and P_2, respectively.

Doing that shows, not surprisingly, that the group of customers which is less sensitive to price increases (with demand curve D_2) will pay a higher price for the product than the group that is more sensitive to price changes. In fact, that's how the firm increases its profits through price discrimination -- by charging more to the less-sensitive group, and then selling more units to the group that is more price sensitive by charging them a somewhat lower price. But none of this will work if the price-sensitive group of customers can buy from the monopoly at P_1 and resell to the price-insensitive group for a price below P_2 but above P_1. If they can, the monopolist simply creates its own competitors by selling some of its output at the lower price in the first place, and the effect of that competition is to gradually eliminate the price difference (and therefore the price discrimination). When third-degree price discrimination can occur, however, note that for both groups of consumers the monopoly still produces where P > MC and P > minATC. In other words, there is still allocative and productive inefficiency present in this situation.

Figure 11-10
A Monopolist Practicing Third-Degree Price Discrimination

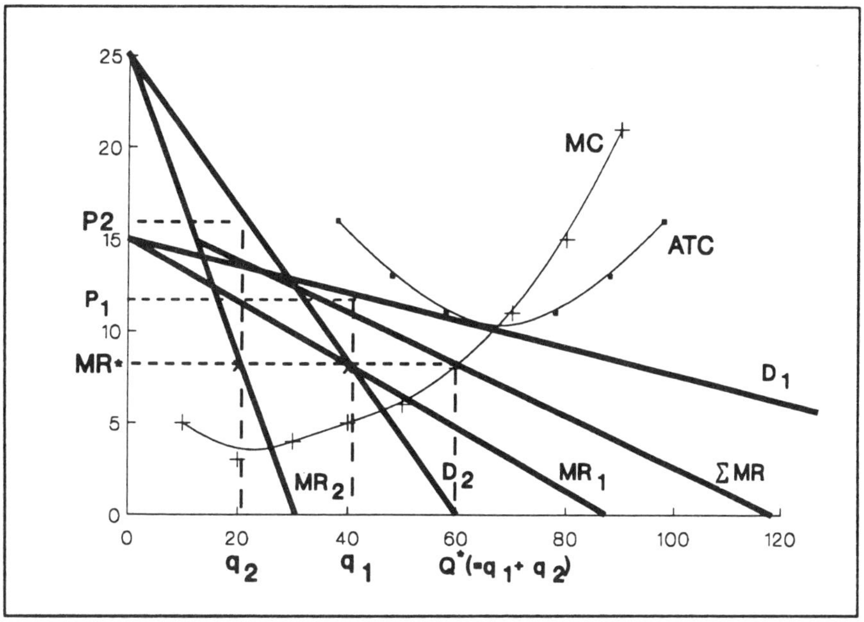

This monopolist finds that one group of its customers (shown as D_1) is more sensitive to price changes for its product than another group of customers (shown as D_2). If reselling between these groups is impossible, and it is easy for the firm to distinguish between the two groups (e.g., by defining the first group as people who have a membership card in the American Association of Retired Persons), it will maximize profits by horizontally summing MR_1 and MR_2, as shown, and finding the level of ΣMR that is equal to MC (shown as MR*). Then, the firm will sell q_1 and q_2 at P_1 and P_2, respectively, because these output and price levels are associated with the points on MR_1 and MR_2 that are equal to MR*. Note that $Q* = q_1 + q_2$, and that P_1 and P_2 are both greater than ATC at output level Q*.

332

The most extreme form of price discrimination is known as *FIRST-DEGREE PRICE DISCRIMINATION* or, as it is sometimes called, perfect price discrimination. In this setting, as shown in Figure 11-11, the firm is assumed to be able to precisely determine the maximum amount each of its customers is willing and able to pay, then charge that amount (which may well be a different price for every customer). Once again, we must also assume the product can not be resold. Taking these assumptions together, it is a severe challenge to the creativity of textbook authors to come up with a plausible example of this kind of situation -- our best shot is a doctor specializing in the treatment of a very rare condition, who has access to detailed information on his or her patients' income, wealth, and insurance coverage. (Ideally, the doctor would even have invented a new kind of thermometer to put in patients' wallets, which would quickly read out the maximum amount the patient is willing and able to pay for these services.)

Figure 11-11
A Monopolist Practicing First-Degree Price Discrimination

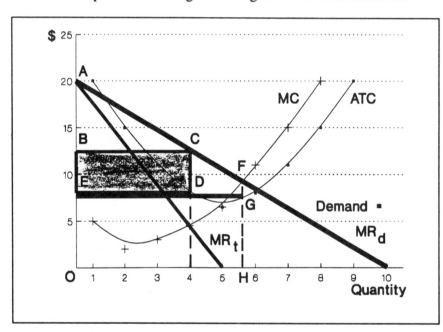

This firm charges the maximum price each customer is willing and able to pay for a unit of its output. That means the firm's demand curve is also its marginal revenue schedule (MR_d), because it takes in the price it charges to sell an additional unit of output but does *not* lower prices for those who are willing and able to pay a higher price. The firm will maximize profits by expanding production out to the level where P = MR = MC.

Without price discrimination the firm's profits are equal to the shaded area BCDE, found by using the typical, single-price marginal revenue schedule labeled MR_t. With perfect price discrimination, the firm adds as profits the areas ABC and CFGD (since total revenues = 0AFH, total costs = 0EGH, and economic profits = EAFG). Without price discrimination consumer surplus is equal to area ABC; with first-degree price discrimination there is no consumer surplus.

But there are two key reasons to be interested in such an unusual situation. First, it illustrates a drastic reallocation of welfare, because *all* consumer surplus in this market is captured by the producer. That happens literally by definition -- since each consumer pays the maximum amount her or she is willing to pay for each unit of the product consumed, there is no consumer surplus. Second, and even more surprisingly, this firm will now

produce out to the level where P = MC, satisfying economists' condition for allocative efficiency. Indeed, such a firm would produce the same level of output as a competitive firm if industry demand and cost schedules were identical, where MC = MR for the monopolist and ΣMC (industry supply) = D for the competitive industry, so there would clearly be no underallocation of resources in this market even though it is monopolized.

Any complaints economists, consumers, or policy makers make about first-degree price discrimination will, therefore, relate to distributional questions concerning levels of profits and consumer surplus, rather than allocative efficiency. That's important to understand because, even in cases of second and third-degree price discrimination[6], which are more realistic and frequently observed in the real world, output levels are usually higher than they would be under ordinary monopoly conditions (i.e., with no price discrimination), while at the same time some redistribution of welfare from consumer surplus to producer surplus occurs. The higher output levels with price discrimination result from the lower prices and higher sales volumes achieved in market segments where demand is relatively more price elastic. Those increases in production somewhat moderate the problem of resource underallocation in monopolies that do not practice price discrimination; but that improvement comes with the corresponding cost (to buyers) of decreases in consumer surplus.

As you come to the end of this chapter remember that it is normally better to be a monopoly -- even one that isn't able to engage in price discrimination -- than to have to buy from one. But remember, too, if you do get the chance to be a monopolist someday, to make sure it is in a market where demand is strong, barriers to entry are high, and there are few close substitutes for your product. Because just being a monopoly that seeks for the best price for its product, rather than taking a market price as a given, isn't enough to guarantee a life of wealth and luxury.

Case Study #14
Predatory Pricing -- Fact or Fiction

In Phillip Massinger's *A New Way to Pay Old Debts*, written in the middle of the 17th century, the wealthy and malicious villain of the play, Sir Giles Overreach, threatens to ruin one of his poor neighbors by tearing down fences, destroying his crops and herds, and ruining his reputation and credit standing. Overreach recognizes that he may be legally liable for these actions. But he also knows that the legal process moves slowly and expensively, particularly in civil matters. So Overreach expects to financially destroy the neighbor long before any final legal remedy will be available. The process may be costly for Overreach as well as for the poor neighbor, but the wealthy villain expects to survive and then buy the neighbor's property at a depressed price.

This isn't precisely the idea of predatory pricing mentioned earlier in the chapter, where we referred to a firm with monopoly power lowering the price of its product to drive out smaller firms. But Massinger's plot indicates clearly that the idea of predatory pricing is very old and well established in the popular conception of what monopolies are, and what they do. Indeed, it is part of the modern layperson's folklore of economic understanding.

The U. S. legal record actually tells a similar story. Several firms have been accused and sometimes convicted of engaging in predatory pricing, which is illegal under the anti-trust laws you will study in Chapter 13. The most famous case[7] involving charges of predatory pricing was decided in 1911, with judgment brought against the Standard Oil Company which was owned by John D. Rockerfeller -- a "robber barron" or "captain of industry," depending on your interpretation of economic history and political ideology. While the idea of predatory pricing wasn't new at that time, the public's view of a predatory giant like the Standard Oil Company was. The firm was one of a handfull of large new monopolies, or monopoly "trusts," ruthlessly efficient both in terms of business

[6]*SECOND-DEGREE PRICE DISCRIMINATION* occurs when a firm charges different prices for its product based on different purchase volumes (e.g., by offering bulk-purchase discounts) that do not reflect differences in the producer's costs. These pricing schemes are discussed in more advanced textbooks, including Hal R. Varian's *Intermediate Microeconomics: A Modern Approach*, 2nd ed., New York: Norton & Co., 1990.
[7]Standard Oil Co. of New Jersey v. United States, 221, U.S. 1, 1911.

methods and scientific research on future products. In the early part of this century the company seemed invincible to many observers.

Standard was accused of lowering prices below its costs in some local markets to eliminate competition there, while covering these losses with profits made in other regions. The company was, in fact, found guilty of violating U.S. antitrust laws, and this successful prosecution was largely responsible for later laws passed explicitly to prohibit predatory pricing practices.

Then, in 1953, Aaron Director of the University of Chicago Law School suggested to economist John S. McGee that he suspected Standard Oil had not practiced predatory pricing, because doing so would not have been the most profitable way for it to eliminate the smaller firms. He also thought someone should go back and analyze the data to see what really had happened.

McGee was, in his own words, "astounded" by this suggestion, and agreed to investigate against his better judgment "for, like everyone else, I knew full well what Standard had really done." But in a report published in 1958, McGee concluded that while Standard had, in fact, practiced price discrimination -- charging different prices in different markets to maximize profits, based on different demand characteristics in these regional markets -- it had not practiced predatory pricing by setting prices below its costs.[8] According to McGee, the facts in this case confirmed Director's prediction and logical arguments. The same logic and analysis have since convinced many other economists and lawyers (including Robert Bork, the controversial Reagan nominee to the Supreme Court whose appointment was not confirmed by the Senate in 1988) that predatory pricing rarely, if ever, is in a monopolist's best interest.

McGee pointed out that to practice predatory pricing a firm must already have achieved a position with considerable monopoly power. So the idea of predatory pricing itself can not explain how a firm attains a monopoly position in the first place. His study showed that Standard Oil achieved its dominant place in the petroleum industry through more than a hundred acquisitions and buyouts of other firms, before it was in a position to be able to engage in predatory pricing. Specifically, the company had begun operating with a literally insignificant part of the total market, and as late as 1870 controlled only 10% of the nation's petroleum refining business.

There are, McGee pointed out, also clear advantages in using acquisitions and mergers to maintain or strengthen monopoly power in a market, rather than using predatory pricing. In particular, if there are profits or other economic benefits to be had by combining two or more firms, buyouts and mergers are a logical way to accomplish this because the gains can be used to make both those who buy a firm *and* those who sell it better off, or to make both parties in a merger wealthier. Conversely, predatory pricing imposes losses on both firms, at least in the short run.

McGee also pointed out that the losses imposed by predatory pricing are not equally shared. A large, powerful firm that practices predatory pricing must, in fact, be willing to endure much larger losses than its intended victim(s). Why? Mainly because the monopoly sets its "too-low" price on a much greater volume of sales than the firm(s) it has targeted for elimination. Around the time of the Supreme Court decision in the Standard Oil case, for example, Standard controlled about 75% of the refining market. Assuming its pre-unit production costs were equal to those of its competitors, it thus stood to lose three times more from a given price cut than its competitors would if they matched Standard's price cuts. On the other hand, if Standard's costs were lower than those of the smaller, targeted firms (suggesting economies of scale), that would be a more basic cause and concern for monopoly power than predatory pricing practices. And if Standard's costs were higher than the targeted firms, its losses from predatory pricing practices would be that much greater again than theirs.

A large firm which attempts to eliminate competitors through predatory pricing must also be able to sustain its low prices and high losses as long as the facilities of the competitors are capable of producing its product. That may be a very long time, because the competing firms have several ways to extend their life. For example, they may be able to shut down their facilities and lose only their fixed costs, but still get back into business quickly if the large firm raises prices above their level of average variable costs. Or, the targeted firms may minimize losses by not matching the large firm's price decreases entirely. If that is possible, the competitors will lose less than

---

[8]"Predatory Price Cutting: The Standard Oil (N. J.) Case," *The Journal of Law and Economics*, October 1958, pp. 137-69.

their fixed costs unless the predatory pricer lowers its price even more to take away more customers, and in the process loses even more money itself. The competing firms also have the option of selling their assets to firms other than the predatory pricer, which will extend or renew the competitive threat with new sponsors, and a new bankroll. Things can clearly get expensive for the predatory pricer.

Through an outright purchase or merger, on the other hand, a large firm considering predatory pricing can probably get these same assets by paying only their market value, or just slightly more. It thereby begins earning monopoly levels of profits sooner, and avoids a number of other problems. For example, it doesn't run down the value of its own resources, and those of the firms it hopes to acquire, in a period of overproduction brought about by the increased volume of consumption and sales that results from the lower, predatory prices. It furthermore avoids customers' (and their political representatives') outrage from "price shock" when prices are raised from the below-cost, predatory level, back to the level that maximizes monopoly profits. And it also makes employees out of those who work for the competing firm, who may otherwise have the skills to start a new, competing firm if they are left unemployed by the predatory-pricing policy.

Several findings emerge from this analysis: 1) Unless the predatory firm has significant barriers to entry in place, its monopoly position is not secure; 2) if the only barrier to entry a firm has is a reputation for predatory pricing, a monopoly position may well cost it more to maintain than it can ever expect to recover; and 3) predatory pricing is only one way of eliminating competition while alternative options are, at least in many cases, likely to be far less expensive. That is the gist of McGee and Director's arguments against the idea of predatory pricing.

But now for the other side of the story. Evidence does exist that predatory pricing has been used to destroy competition, or at least reduce it, in several markets. Historical examples have proven easier to document than current examples, but that's not surprising since predatory pricing has been illegal through nearly all of this century in the United States, and documents detailing the use of the tactic would be carefully obscured or hidden away by any executives who engaged in those activities. For example, some firms are likely to explain "special" low prices as an attempt to help low-income consumers, and not draw attention to the long-run profitability or anti-competitive effects of such policies. Other firms may claim that market conditions *require* them to operate at a loss in the short-run, and that their price is at least greater than their average variable costs, conforming to the predictions of economic theory in such settings.

Looking at one of the clearest historical examples of predatory pricing, we can turn to an 1885 document from the Hankow Shipping Conference. This Conference was a cartel of ship owners that fixed rates on freight shipped between China and the United Kingdom, and adopted the following policy toward rivals who attempted to enter their market:

> ...(I)f any non-Conference steamer should proceed to Hankow to load independently, any necessary number of Conference steamers should be sent at the same time to Hankow to underbid the freight which the independent shipowners might offer, without any regard to whether the freight they should bid would be remunerative or not.[9]

Why, anyone who is familiar with McGee and Director's arguments must ask, would this cartel have practiced predatory pricing? Ignorance is one possibility, and should not be dismissed out of hand in this case. Perhaps the Hankow Conference members simply didn't know that there were better ways to eliminate this competition since, after all, they couldn't have read McGee's article. But other economists have argued that the structure of the cartel made such predatory policies more attractive to the cartel members because: 1) losses were shared among the cartel members, so each member was more willing to accept the cost of predatory pricing policies; 2) any gains from acquiring or merging with a competing firm would also be shared by all cartel members, so no one firm had the same incentives to arrange those deals and thereby eliminate the interest in predatory pricing; 3) basic cost considerations may have made it impossible for the cartel to buy up all of the independent shippers who might

---

[9]Quoted in B. S. Yamey, "Predatory Price Cutting: Notes and Comments," *The Journal of Law and Economics*, 15 April 1972, p. 139.

have chosen to enter this market; and 4) given the earlier three reasons, the most effective policy was to lock up this highly profitable market and encourage the independent shippers to look to other, more easily entered, markets.

The idea that monopolistic firms or groups of firms engage in predatory pricing in some special cases depends crucially on whether the practice represents an effective barrier to entry that persuades potential entrants to compete somewhere else, or at least to enter on a much smaller scale than they otherwise would. This *strategic* effect is very difficult to document empirically both because, as noted earlier, predatory pricing is illegal, and because the effect of such a policy is, when successful, predicted to be felt by *potential* entrants in a market, who may never actually enter it or even be known to be considering entry.

IBM and Anheuser-Busch are, however, two firms that some economists, Department of Justice lawyers, and (especially) competing firms have accused of practicing predatory pricing in recent decades.[10] Earlier incidents involving the American Tobacco Co. and duPont have also been labeled as predatory pricing episodes by some economists, although they are often quick to point out that such policies appeared to be exceptional cases, not standard practice.[11]

Overall, then, the topic of predatory pricing still plays an active role in discussions of economic theory and public policy, though that role is both more controversial and limited than it was four decades ago. The idea has, perhaps, a more interesting history than future, at least in works by professional economists. But its place in the minds of people who like to complain about monopoly power while watching the nightly news, or relaxing at their neighborhood bar, is still secure. And that also makes the topic appropriate for introductory courses in microeconomics.

Case Study #15
Dynamic Competition Through Technological Change[12]

Joseph Schumpeter, the "perennial gale of creative destruction" economist you first met in Chapter 3, got off many more provocative and insightful lines in his famous book, *Capitalism, Socialism and Democracy*, first published in the 1940s. The particular idea we want to consider here is his claim that, despite the various inefficiencies described in this chapter, monopolies have been responsible for more technological progress and greater improvements in living standards than competitive firms. Schumpeter criticized economists who simply infer that because equilibrium outcomes at fixed points in time show that monopolies are less efficient than competitive firms, they must also be less efficient in a dynamic, long-run sense. In his view, the most significant kind of long-run competition often involves one monopoly or oligopoly being replaced by another that provides a substitute, but basically new, product. For example, the system of canal transportation in the United States and other nations which were industrializing in the 19th century was replaced by the railroad industry, which was itself weakened by the development of the automobile and truck industries, which in turn were weakened by emergence of commercial airlines. None of these industries was perfectly competitive -- and in fact, they were all characterized in their heydays by a high degree of monopoly power. Schumpeter argued that

> As soon as we go into details and inquire into the individual items in which progress was most conspicuous, the trail leads not to the doors of the firms that work under conditions of comparatively free competition but precisely to the doors of the large concerns...and a shocking suspicion dawns upon us that big business may have had more to do with creating that standard of life than with keeping it down.[13]

---

[10]See D. F. Greer's *Industrial Organization and Public Policy*, 2nd ed., New York: Macmillan, 1984, pp. 198-99, 316-20.

[11]See W. L. Baldwin, *Market Power, Competition, and Antitrust Policy*, Homewood, Ill.: Irwin, 1987, pp. 205-08.

[12]This case study is adapted from the much more extensive discussion in Chapter 12 of Baldwin's *Market Power, Competition, and Antitrust Policy.*

[13]*Capitalism, Socialism, and Democracy*, 3rd ed., New York: Harper and Row, 1950, p. 82.

337

Schumpeter was clearly right in arguing that technological progress has been a major factor in the economic development of industrialized nations over the past two-and-a-half centuries. This has been well documented in definitive studies on the sources of economic growth and development published by Edward Denison and other economists over the past 25 years (see Case Study #19, at the end of Chapter 15, for a summary of these reports). But Schumpeter was less clearly right about the link between large concerns and technological innovation and discovery, at least thus far in this century. That is the issue we will review here.

Table 11-3 summarizes the relationship between firm size, measured by employment levels, and spending for research and development (R&D) programs by U.S. companies. From this table, you can see that about 90% of the firms engaged in these programs have fewer than 1,000 employees, but that over 70% of the total spending on these activities is accounted for by the very largest firms -- those with 25,000 or more employees. Schumpeter's hypothesis is, then, clearly not totally wanting for empirical support.

Table 11-3
U.S. Companies with R&D Programs, 1981

# of Employees	# of Firms With R&D Programs	R&D Spending ($ Millions)		
		Private $	Federal Grant $	Total $
< 1,000	12,500*	$ 2,038	$ 484	$ 2,522
1,000-4,999	839	2,702	511	3,213
5,00-9,999	218	1,866	559	2,425
10,000-24,999	211	5,685	1,253	6,938
≥ 25,000	141	23,071	13,661	36,732
Total	13,909	$35,362	$16,468	$51,830

Far more small firms engage in R&D work than large firms, but the large firms spend far more on the projects than the small firms. This does not show, however, where major technological breakthroughs are usually made. Nor does it show that firms consistently spend more for R&D as they get larger. Those issues are considered in later tables and discussion.

*Estimated by the Bureau of the Census from a 1981 survey of firms with fewer than 1,000 employees.

Source: National Science Foundation, *Research and Development in Industry*, 1981, Washington, D.C.: U.S. Government Printing Office, 1984, pp. 12, 15, 20, 24.

But the evidence is not totally in Schumpeter's favor, either. For example, Table 11-4 shows by looking only at the 20 largest firms in various industries (which includes most of the firms with 25,000 or more employees) that there is no clear evidence that the largest of these firms spend proportionately more than the relatively smaller firms in this group. In other words, a certain amount of size and market power may be conducive to R&D activities, but outright monopolization of an industry is neither required for, nor necessarily beneficial to, this work. In fact, one major study on this issue concluded that while "a slight amount" of concentration is conducive to technological change, "further increases in concentration do not seem to be associated with more rapid rates of technological advance. In part, this may be due to less competitive pressure and fewer independent loci for decision making."[14]

[14]E. Mansfield, J. Rapoport, A. Romeo, E. Villani, S. Wagner, and F. Husic, *The Production and Application of New Technologies*, New York: W. W. Norton, 1977, p. 16.

Table 11-4
R&D Spending as a Percentage of Net Sales, by Industry Group
(includes only manufacturing firms engaging in R&D activities)

Industry Group	Firm Size	
	8 Largest	Next 12 Firms
Food and Kindred Products	0.3%	0.3%
Textiles and Apparel	0.3	0.5
Lumber, Wood Products, and Furniture	1.0	0.9
Paper and Allied Products	1.2	1.2
Industrial Chemicals	3.0	3.2
Drugs and Medicines	5.5	7.7
Other Chemicals	2.2	2.1
Petroleum Refining and Related	0.7	0.4
Rubber Products	2.1	1.9
Stone, Clay, and Glass Products	2.1	0.7
Ferrous Metals and Products	0.5	0.7
Nonferrous Metals and Products	0.6	1.0
Fabricated Metal Products	1.4	1.1
Office, Computing, and Accounting Machines	10.4	10.1
Other Machinery, Except Electrical	3.5	1.8
Radio and TV Receiving Equipment	2.6	2.3
Communication Equipment	6.3	4.1
Electronic Components	5.8	7.3
Other Electrical Equipment	3.0	2.6
Motor Vehicles and Motor Vehicle Equipment	4.2	1.0
Other Transportation Equipment	0.2	0.6
Aircraft and Missiles	4.6	3.4
Professional and Scientific Instruments	7.7	5.4
Other Manufacturing	0.4	0.9
Total	1.8%	3.0%

The eight largest firms in these industries spend, on average, a lower percentage of their net sales on R&D work than the next 12 largest firms in the same industries (1.8 vs. 3.0%, respectively). This is not consistent with Schumpeter's theory of innovation and firm size.

Source: National Science Foundation, *Research and Development in Industry*, 1981, Washington, D.C.: U.S. Government Printing Office, 1984, p. 31.

Table 11-4 also indicates that a disproportionate amount of R&D spending is concentrated in a small group of industries. Only 10 of the 24 industries listed (industrial chemicals, drugs and medicines, office computing, other machinery [both electric and non-electric], communication equipment, electronics, motor vehicles, aircraft and professional equipment) spend 3% or more of net sales for R&D, among either the largest eight or next-largest 12 firms in the industry. Only five industries spend 5% or more in either set of firms. Some of this concentration in R&D activity is explained by a few very large firms that are known, worldwide and historically, for their scientific research and technological innovations -- firms like IBM, AT&T, Kodak, and General Electric. But all firms in these "high-tech" industries, regardless of size, are likely to be characterized by above-average R&D

expenditures.[15] While this does not support Schumpeter's conclusion linking firm size to technological progress in all cases, it may be consistent with his general view that the concentrated industries of one era tend to maintain their dominant position until they are supplanted by a new generation of large firms which then build up and control a new technology.

But even that conclusion is in doubt, based on studies that have investigated what kinds of firms were responsible for certain technological breakthroughs. Perhaps the most widely quoted conclusion from a study on the linkage between firm size and technological innovation is from a 1958 study of 61 important inventions made in Great Britain and the United States in the first half of this century. In this report, it was found that

> More than one-half of the cases can be ranked as individual invention in the sense that much of the pioneering work was carried through...without the backing of research institutions and usually with limited resources and assistance or, where the inventors were employed in institutions, these institutions were, as in the case of universities, of such a kind that the individuals were autonomous, free to follow their own ideas without hindrance.
> ...Even where inventions have arisen in the research laboratories of firms, the team responsible for it seems often to have been quite small.[16]

On the other hand, this same report noted that marketing and product development activities, as opposed to invention per se, were often expensive and might require the resources of a large corporation.

Another British study, published in 1957, studied 152 firms that were engaged in R&D work and concluded that, while there were some advantages to firm size in conducting industrial research, the scientific base of the products produced by an industry and related technological opportunities for product improvement were the primary determinants of R&D spending.[17]

Edwin Mansfield concluded in 1968, after conducting numerous case studies and surveys of American industries (including iron and steel, petroleum refining, bituminous coal, chemicals and electronics), that

> Contrary to the allegations of...Schumpeter...there is little or no evidence that industrial giants are needed in all or even most industries to insure rapid technological change and rapid utilization of new techniques.... There seem to be considerable advantages in a diversity of firm sizes, no single firm size being optimal in this respect.[18]

Fredrich Scherer, using Federal Trade Commission data collected in the mid-1970s, estimated the responsiveness of R&D spending and the number of patents filed to differences in firm size, and the number of patents filed relative to differences in firms' levels of R&D spending. These "elasticity" measures, published in 1984, are reported in Table 11-5. Given these results, Scherer concluded that the evidence "tilts on the side of supporting the Schumpeterian hypothesis that [firm] size is conducive to the vigorous conduct of R&D," but also that it "leans weakly against the Schumpeterian conjecture that the largest sellers are especially fecund sources of patented inventions."[19] The results linking R&D spending levels to patents suggest that there are no uniform economies of scale to R&D spending across the full range of the largest U.S. manufacturing firms.

[15]See R. Nelson, M. Peck and E. Kalachek, *Technology, Economic Growth and Public Policy*, Washington, D.C.: Brookings Institution, 1967, p. 67.
[16]J. Jewkes, D. Sawyers and R. Stillerman, *The Sources of Invention*, London: Macmillan, 1958, pp. 82, 88.
[17]C. F. Carter and B. R. Williams, *Industry and Technology Progress*, London: Oxford University Press.
[18]*The Economics of Technological Change*, New York: W. W. Norton, p. 217.
[19]*Innovation and Growth: Schumpeterian Perspectives*, Cambridge, Mass.: MIT Press, 1984, pp. 234-35.

Table 11-5
Differences in Firm Size, R&D Spending and Patents Received

	Number of Industries	Percentage of Total
I. Firm Size and R&D Spending		
Constant Returns (Large and small firms spend effectively equal % of revenues on R&D)	140	71.4%
Increasing Returns (Large firms spend a higher % of revenues on R&D)		
1) At all sales levels	29	
2) Only for very large firms	11	
TOTAL	40	20.4
Diminishing Returns (Small firms spend a higher % of revenues on R&D than larger firms)	16	8.2
II. Firm Size and Patents Received (In industries where 5 or more firms received patents)		
Constant Returns	91	73.4
Increasing Returns		
1) At all sales levels	9	
2) Only for very large firms	5	
TOTAL	14	11.3
Diminishing Returns		
1) At all sales levels	18	
2) Only for very large firms	1	
TOTAL	19	15.3
III. R&D Spending Levels and Patents Received		
Constant Returns	74	59.7
Increasing Returns		
1) At all R&D spending levels	16	
2) Only at very high R&D spending levels	3	
TOTAL	19	15.3
Diminishing Returns		
1) At all R&D spending levels	30	
2) Only at very high R&D spending levels	1	
TOTAL	31	25.0

Source: Fredrich Scherer, *Innovation and Growth: Schumpeterian Perspectives*, Cambridge, Mass.: MIT Press, 1984, pp. 233-35.

Of course in some specific industries all of Schumpeter's theories may hold. And if, in the future, research becomes more expensive and closely tied to the use of large quantities of capital which embodies "state-of-the-art" technologies, his theories may even be confirmed as more general findings. At the present time, however, Schumpeter's claims about the relationship between technological progress and firm size or market concentration have not held up strongly enough to ease most economists' concerns about resource misallocations and other specific kinds of inefficiencies associated with the existence of monopoly power.

Chapter Summary

1) A pure *MONOPOLY* is the sole producer of a good or service. It is a *PRICE SEEKER* because it faces the industry demand curve for its product, and must therefore reduce its price to increase the number of units it sells. Enduring monopolies are characterized by high *BARRIERS TO ENTRY*, such as legal restrictions, economies of scale, *BRAND LOYALTIES*, and (perhaps) *PREDATORY PRICING* practices.

2) Domestic concentration ratios may overstate the degree of monopoly power enjoyed by the producer(s) of a given product due to competition from products that are close substitutes, or from foreign firms selling identical products. Not all monopolies are profitable or long-lived; those that are typically produce products with few close substitutes, and for which demand is strong.

3) The typical monopolist's marginal revenue schedule falls off faster than its demand curve, because price decreases benefit consumers who were already paying a higher price as well as those who only buy when prices are lowered. Like a perfectly competitive firm, however, the monopolist's profit maximizing equilibrium occurs at the output level where MR = MC. Since this occurs where MR > 0, we know that the monopolist will operate at a point on its demand curve that is price elastic.

4) If barriers to entry are sufficiently high, the monopolist's long-run and short-run equilibrium positions will be identical, *ceteris paribus*. Since a typical monopolist operates where P > MC and P > minATC, and can earn long-run economic profits, it does not satisfy the criteria for either allocative or productive efficiency. In fact, there is an underallocation of scarce resources to products produced by these firms, a deadweight loss in welfare resulting from this restriction of output, and a reallocation of consumer surplus to producer surplus (compared to results in a competitive market facing the same industry demand and cost schedules).

5) A monopolist has no unique supply schedule, because demand shifts can result in it choosing to produce the same level of output at more than one price.

6) Firms with extensive monopoly power are usually large, publically-owned corporations. These firms often have so many stockholders that their officers, and the Board of Directors which they nominate and usually elect by voting stockholders' proxies, exercise far more control over these firms' actions than the companies' legal owners (i.e., the stockholders). This raises serious questions about the officers' commitment to cost minimization and profit maximization, because their interests are not identical to those of the stockholders. These issues have been explored using models that incorporate managerial preferences and behavior, but factors limiting the range of managerial discretion in such matters have also been identified.

7) *PRICE DISCRIMINATION* is the practice of charging different customers different prices for identical products, when there is no difference in the cost of providing the good or service. It can occur only when: a) different customers exhibit different demand characteristics for a product, b) the firm can effectively classify customers into two or more groups according to their willingness and ability to pay, c) those who purchase the product at a lower price can not profitably resell it to those who are charged more, and d) a firm selling such a product has at least some protection from competition by other firms selling identical products

or close substitutes. While not a common practice, when price discrimination does occur some or all consumer surplus is captured by producers, as producer surplus. At the same time, the underallocation of resources normally associated with monopolistic firms will be reduced as the overall level of output is increased.

8) (Case Study #14) Predatory pricing occurs when a firm with monopoly power temporarily lowers prices below its costs, in order to drive out competing firms. There are some historical examples of predatory pricing behavior; but many economists have argued, and shown in some of the most famous cases of alleged predatory pricing, that the procedure is too expensive to be widely used, especially in light of other means available to firms that want to eliminate current competition. Some economists now argue that the most important use of predatory pricing is strategic, in that it deters competition from firms that might consider entering a market in the future.

9) (Case Study #15) Some prominent economists have argued that large firms in highly concentrated industries are more often the source of technological innovation and long-run improvements in living standards than small, competitive firms. The available empirical evidence on this topic offers only weak support for this hypothesis, however, particularly in terms of the relationship between firm size and the development of new, patented products or industrial processes.

Review and Discussion Questions

1) a) Do high barriers to entry guarantee a firm economic profits in the short-run and the long-run? b) Can firms operating in industries where barriers to entry are low ever face downward-sloping demand curves? c) What do you think are the major barriers to entry in each of the following industries or occupations: automobiles, commercial aviation, local restaurants, university professorships, and the Presidency of the United States?

2) What are the major sources of competition for the following companies and products: Chevrolets, soft drinks, McDonald's hamburgers, a local electric company, and Sears?

3) Suppose a farmer discovers the Fountain of Youth really does exist on one of her fields, but it only works if people drink a glass of water directly from the fountain -- shipping or bottling the water destroys its "powers." If the farmer's marginal costs of supplying this water are effectively 0, show graphically how much water she should sell, and what price she should charge, to maximize profits. Is demand elastic at that price?

4) Would a "single-price" monopolist (i.e., one that does not practice price discrimination) ever choose to produce where $P < MC$ or $P < minATC$, in the short run or in the long run?

5) If the monopolist's demand curve effectively constrains its pricing decisions, why doesn't its supply curve do the same thing?

6) Will a monopoly owned and operated by one person, or by one family, have more or less incentive to maximize profits and minimize costs than a large corporation with thousands of stockholders, no one of whom controls as much as 1% of the voting shares of stock in the company?

7) a) Do any consumers benefit from predatory pricing? b) Why is it legal for a firm to charge different prices when costs vary from customer to customer, but not revenues (due to different demand characteristics)? c) Are demand levels and elasticity considered when firms which do not engage in price discrimination set their prices?

343

8) (Case Study #14) a) As a consumer, would you prefer that a firm maintain its monopoly position through predatory pricing or by other means, such as mergers and buyouts? b) Which of these practices would you prefer if you owned a small company trying to compete with the dominant (near-monopoly) firm? c) Which practice would you prefer if you owned stock in the firm that is in a position to consider using predatory pricing policies?

9) (Case Study #15) List what you believe are the five most important technological advances of the past century, and try to determine whether the major products using those technologies were invented, *and* nationally marketed or developed, primarily by small, competitive firms, or by large firms that might be expected to have a substantial degree of monopoly power. Are your conclusions consistent with the Schumpeterian hypothesis discussed in this case study?

344

Chapter 12
Monopolistic Competition

> ## In This Chapter...
>
> and the next chapter, on oligopoly, we introduce models of imperfect competition in industries with more than one firm. In monopolistic competition, a large number of relatively small firms sell differentiated, heterogeneous products. In oligopolies, a few large firms face the strategic question of how best to compete, or to cooperate, to maximize profits. In each of these market structures firms have some degree of market power, but not always for the same reasons and certainly not with the same results. Still, the characteristics we assume to exist for firms in both of these market structures are more realistic than those we used in presenting the models of perfect competition and perfect monopoly. In fact, monopolistic competition models are frequently used to explain or predict the behavior of firms in the retail trade industry, or firms engaged in different forms of nonprice competition.

Characteristics of Monopolistically Competitive Firms

Monopolistically competitive firms and industries share some characteristics with perfect competition: firms are relatively small, and entry into and exit from the industry is relatively easy and inexpensive. But in one key respect monopolistic competition is like monopoly: firms face downward sloping demand and marginal revenue curves because they sell differentiated products. A monopolistically competitive firm's products are made at least slightly different from those sold by competing firms by direct physical or styling differences, by different ancillary products and support services provided by sellers, or by perceived differences in product quality that are strengthened (or even established) through advertising.

Easy Entry and Exit

The stores where most college students spend most their money are neither perfectly competitive nor perfect monopolies. When you buy groceries, clothing, books, or meals in fast-food restaurants, or when you rent an apartment, you usually deal with fairly small businesses. They are small, that is, in terms of their physical size, employment levels, and the overall level of resources that would be required to open and run a similar kind of business if you thought there was enough demand in your community to support another such establishment.

While it's true that you and your friends probably couldn't afford a franchise from one of the leading hamburger chains like McDonalds or Burger King even by pooling your funds -- at least at this point in your careers -- you probably could start a "no name" hamburger stand if you wanted to make that your part-time or full-time work for a few years. Or you could make and deliver sandwiches to students living on or around campus (as former Vice President Hubert Humphrey and his wife did when he was a graduate student). And there are, of course, many people in your community who can afford to pay the franchise fees to the big restaurant chains *if* they think that's where the best financial opportunities are.

All of this suggests that entering this kind of industry is not a terribly difficult or expensive thing to do, at least compared to most business ventures. Nor is it particularly difficult to sell a successful business of this kind when the owner decides to leave that industry -- for example, if you decide to sell your "no name" hamburger stand when you graduate.

The barriers to entry and exit facing hamburger or retail clothing and bookstore businesses are certainly much less substantial than barriers to entry in starting new manufacturing companies to produce and sell cars, steel, electricity, or pharmaceuticals. And of course, as you saw in the last chapter, barriers to entry are important in terms of restricting competition and providing sellers with some degree of latitude in setting profitable price and output levels. So the lack of major barriers to entry in small businesses such as those engaged in retail trade will also be important in determining the kind of economic outcomes we see in those markets. But those outcomes are also affected by other industry characteristics.

Differentiated Products

In terms of the costs of entry and exit, you have just seen that firms in the market structure economists label *MONOPOLISTIC COMPETITION* are much more like competitive firms than monopolies. But the phrase monopolistic competition implies a market structure that combines characteristics of both perfect competition and monopoly, so the next logical step is to see in what ways these firms are more like monopolies than competitive firms.

Until this point, we have dealt only with firms that were assumed to produce homogeneous, or identical, products. The characteristic of monopolistic competition that makes firms in these industries partly like monopolies is that their products are, at least in terms of consumers' perceptions, *DIFFERENTIATED* or heterogeneous. And to the extent that consumers see the product a firm sells as different from those sold by other firms, that makes the firm effectively unique, and more like a monopolist.

But the extent of that differentiation is limited in monopolistic competition by the availability of close (though not identical) substitutes. For example, the clothes sold at one store may be slightly different from those sold in other stores in terms of styling and fashion, even though the materials and quality of workmanship are much the same. And the services offered by the stores that sell these products -- including such things as "free" alterations, no-questions-asked return policies, and complimentary gift wrapping -- are often very much alike, but still a little different in each store. Similarly, in the fast-food business broiled hamburgers taste a little different from grilled hamburgers, but not so much for us to think of them as being in different markets.

Producers in these markets frequently compete by *ADVERTISING* to stress differences in price *or* nonprice factors, or both, of the goods and services they sell. In fact, they may try very hard to make the overall package of prices and services they offer seem distinct and different from what is sold by competitors, even if those differences are very difficult to measure or observe in terms of physical characteristics. For example, beer and soft drink consumers are often unable to identify their favorite brands of these products in blind taste tests, and audiophiles are similarly often unable to hear the performance differences they pay for in expensive stereo equipment. Nevertheless, much of the advertising for these products stresses these "quality differences," and some consumers are adamantly loyal to one brand of product or another in these markets.

Whether these perceived product differences are real or largely imagined, they definitely will affect the demand and revenue curves for firms that sell these goods and services.

Demand and Marginal Revenue Schedules in Monopolistic Competition

A demand and marginal revenue schedule for a monopolistically competitive firm are shown in Figure 12-1. Because a monopolistically competitive firm is seen as offering a slightly different product, or mix of products and customer services, it can not sell more or less output without affecting the price it receives for those products. To increase sales the firm must lower its price, which implies a marginal revenue schedule that lies below, and falls off faster than, its demand curve. This is exactly what you saw in the models of monopoly presented in Chapter 11. However, demand is likely to be more price elastic under monopolistic competition than pure monopoly, *ceteris paribus*, due to the large number of firms in the monopolistically competitive industry which are selling products that are close substitutes.

Figure 12-1
Demand and Marginal Revenue Schedules in Monopolistic Competition

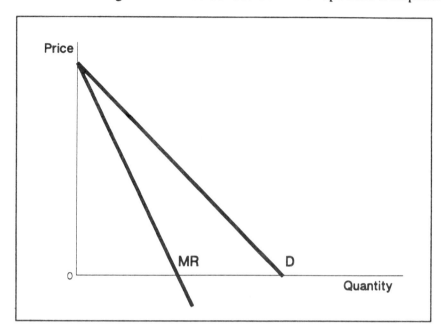

Product differentiation results in downward-sloping demand and marginal revenue schedules in monopolistic competition.

Also, remember that entry and exit are easy and commonplace in this market structure. When firms enter and exit a monopolistically competitive industry the demand and marginal revenue curves for a firm that was already selling in this market, or which remains in the market after other firms leave, will decrease or increase, respectively, as shown in Figure 12-2. At any given point in time, and with a certain level of customer spending in one of these markets, when new firms selling similar products enter the industry, existing firms will notice a drop in their sales at all possible price levels -- i.e., their demand and marginal revenue schedules will shift to the left. On the other hand, if competing firms leave the industry, the remaining firms will experience an increase in their business, which is to say their demand and marginal revenue schedules shift rightward.

Taken together the assumptions of easy entry and exit, production by a large number of relatively small firms, differentiated products, and nonprice competition, make up the basic characteristics of monopolistic competition. That name for this kind of industry was first used by the economist Edward Chamberlin in the early 1930s. Both Chamberlin and the British economist Joan Robinson independently worked out the basic models presented in this chapter during the years of the Great Depression. At that time there was widespread interest in trying to develop a better understanding of imperfect competition involving more than one firm, and in linking that analysis to the economic problems of that turbulent period.

Today, the models of monopolistic competition are used in somewhat more limited ways by economists, primarily to look at firms engaged in retail trade or engaging in nonprice competition, or both. The models of oligopoly that you will study in Chapter 13 are now more often used to address microeconomic problems and policy issues involving production and competition among large firms selling in more concentrated industries. But models that deal with the economics of retail trade and nonprice competition are useful in their own right, even in the basic sense of understanding the economic world that surrounds you every day. Models of monopolistic competition are, therefore, still a major part of the contemporary literature on imperfect competition, though perhaps not as large a part today as Chamberlin and Robinson might have expected them to be.

348

With that general background and basic understanding of demand and marginal revenue schedules in monopolistic competition, it is a simple matter to re-introduce the cost schedules used in the last few chapters, and with them to identify the profit and efficiency outcomes for this market structure.

Figure 12-2
Entry, Exit, and Demand Shifts in Monopolistic Competition

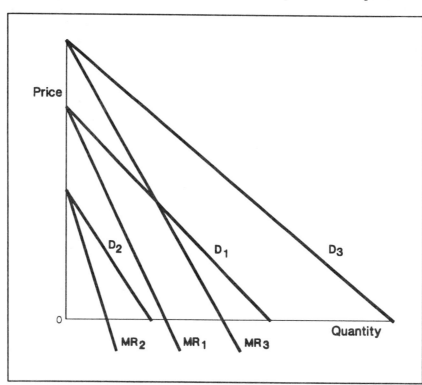

Entry by competing firms in a monopolistically competitive industry will reduce the level of sales at all price levels for existing firms, as shown by the shift from D_1 and MR_1 to D_2 and MR_2. Exit by competing firms results in increased demand and marginal revenue schedules for remaining firms in the industry, as shown by the shift from D_1 and MR_1 to D_3 and MR_3.

Equilibrium Conditions in Monopolistic Competition

As in all market structures, the golden rule of profit maximization in monopolistic competition is for firms to produce where marginal revenue equals marginal cost. Easy entry and exit in the industry guarantee that firms will only earn normal profits in the long run. However, because firms face downward-sloping demand and marginal revenue curves, in equilibrium they produce where price is greater than marginal cost, and above the minimum point on their average total cost curve.

Profit Maximization: MR = MC (Again)

A monopolistically competitive firm will maximize profits or minimize losses at the output level where marginal revenue equals marginal cost (MR = MC), just as monopolies and perfectly competitive firms did, and for the same reasons. Remember, if a firm stops producing where MR > MC it would take in more revenue by producing and selling an additional unit of output than the cost of producing and selling it. In other words, its profits will rise or losses will fall if the firm does produce and sell the next unit of output in this range of production (so long as price is above the shutdown-level and covers average variable costs, as you saw in Chapters 9 and 11). Conversely, when MR < MC a firm will make higher profits or lose less by reducing output to the level where MR = MC. That's because it's just not good business to make and sell an additional unit of your product for less than it costs you to make and sell it.

With this profit-maximizing rule in hand once again look at the graphs in Figure 12-3, where the standard set of cost curves used in both the perfect competition and monopoly chapters are combined with the demand and marginal revenue schedules for a monopolistically competitive firm. In part (A) of this graph, a monopolistically competitive firm is shown earning economic profits; in part (B), the same kind of firm is shown incurring losses. You may be surprised to note that these graphs appear identical to the basic profit-maximizing and loss-minimizing graphs shown in the last chapter, for a perfect monopoly. But what makes the analysis different for monopolistic competition is that entry and exit costs are relatively low in this market structure, while they were prohibitively high in the model of perfect monopoly.

A monopolistically competitive firm in a long-run equilibrium position is shown in Figure 12-4. Unlike a pure monopoly, in the long run it produces where P = ATC and earns *only* normal profits, just as perfectly competitive firms did in long-run equilibrium. That means, as we first explained in Chapter 7, that given the level of economic risks inherent in producing its product, the monopolistically competitive firm earns just enough to cover all of its economic costs and keep it producing in this industry. But these profits are not high enough to attract entry by any new firms. A monopolistically competitive firm will, in fact, produce the level of output which maximizes its profits at the lowest possible cost, at a point directly on its ATC curve. That raises the next question and topic for discussion: Are monopolistically competitive firms economically efficient, both in terms of productive efficiency and allocative efficiency?

Allocative Inefficiency: P > MC

In monopolistic competition, firms always produce a level of output where P > MC. As you have already seen in our discussion of perfect competition and perfect monopoly, what that means to economists is that consumers value the last unit of output produced by the firm -- indicated by the price they are willing and able to pay for this product -- more than they value the next best use of the resources used to produce the product -- as measured by MC. This suggests that there is an underallocation of resources to the production of this product, just as in the case of pure monopoly. However, unlike some monopolies, monopolistically competitive firms don't even have the wherewithal to expand production to the level where P = MC; if they tried to produce at that price and output level they would incur losses and eventually have to go out of business. To see that, suppose the firm produced where its demand and marginal cost curves intersect, and charged the price associated with that level of output on its demand curve. As you can see in Figure 12-4, that intersection point and price is below the firm's ATC curve, so the firm would incur losses.

350

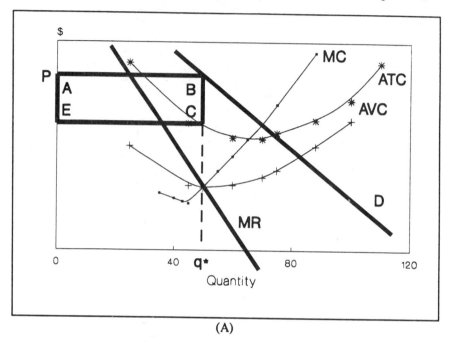

Figure 12-3
Profit and Loss Positions for Firms in Monopolistic Competition

(A)

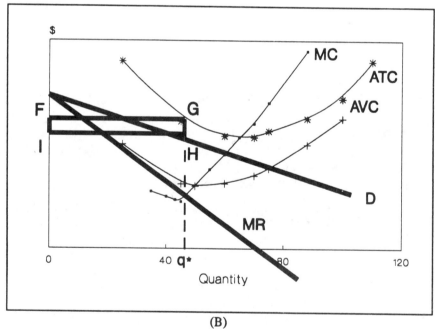

(B)

In panel (A), a monopolistically competitive firm maximizes profits by producing where MR = MC, and earns economic profits equal to the area ABCE. In panel (B) the firm minimizes short-run losses (area FGHI) by producing at q*. Easy entry and exit in this industry structure will eventually eliminate the profits or losses. In the profits case entry and expansion by competing firms would shift the firm's demand and marginal revenue schedules to the left until economic profits are eliminated. In the loss case exit by some firms would cause demand for products sold by remaining firms in the industry to increase, and those exits will continue as long as firms incur losses.

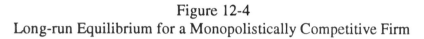

Figure 12-4
Long-run Equilibrium for a Monopolistically Competitive Firm

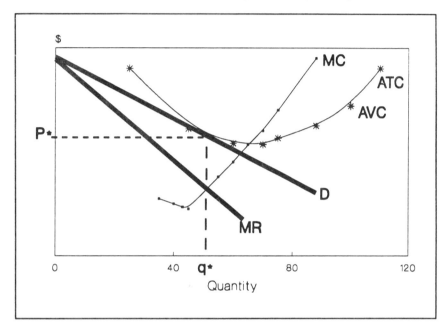

In long-run equilibrium, a monopolistically competitive firm produces where MR = MC and P = ATC. The firm's demand curve will be tangent to its ATC schedule at this level of output, because any other level results in economic profits or losses that lead to entry into or exit from the industry, indicating that the market is not in long-run equilibrium. Note too that P > MC and minATC, so the equilibrium outcome is neither productively nor allocatively efficient.

If monopolistically competitive firms were somehow transformed into perfectly competitive firms without affecting their cost schedules, they would become allocatively efficient by producing where P (and MR) = MC. But what would have to happen to make a monopolistically competitive firm perfectly competitive? In short, it would require eliminating product differentiation and forcing the industry to supply a homogeneous product, thereby eliminating the monopolistic features of the industry. That would result in a horizontal demand and marginal revenue schedule for each firm in the industry, since each firm would be so small as to have no significant effect on market price and output levels. Is that an outcome we want to promote through public policy measures, such as antitrust laws and regulations limiting advertising and other means of product differentiation, in order to achieve the P = MC criterion of allocative efficiency? Perhaps not, if there is also value to variety in product form, style, and substance, both in the everyday purchases of ordinary consumers and more elite events (such as the annual Academy Awards programs, where a big part of the show is seeing what each star is wearing). We will return to the general issue of diversity vs. efficiency after reviewing the productive efficiency outcome in monopolistic competition.

Productive Inefficiency: P > minATC

In long-run equilibrium a monopolistically competitive firm produces where P = ATC, but not at the very lowest point on the ATC schedule (where MC = ATC), which is where perfectly competitive firms produced. Clearly, the only way a firm's demand curve can be tangent to the lowest point of a U-shaped ATC schedule is if its demand curve is horizontal, which means that it must be infinitely price elastic. But once again, that will happen only if we eliminate product differentiation and have all firms sell homogeneous goods and services.

The assumption of easy entry and exit in a monopolistically competitive industry does mean that we can guarantee cost-minimizing behavior at the equilibrium level of output, unlike the result we found with pure monopolies. Although profit maximization requires cost-effective production at the equilibrium level of output in all market structures, including perfect monopoly, cost minimization is literally a matter of survival in both perfect competition and monopolistic competition. These firms have no cushion of economic profits that might allow them to put some of the returns from the business into unnecessarily high manager salaries or "perks," or to indulge in the luxury of relaxing a little about what the competition and market conditions in general are doing. Managers of monopolistically competitive firms have to be as efficient in operating their business as managers of perfectly competitive firms, or else they will soon be looking for new work. Productive inefficiency exists in monopolistic competition strictly because of the product differentiation, demand-side characteristics of the industry, not because of any inherent incentive or principal-agent problems for managers, employees, or storeowners.

The equilibrium outcomes for monopolistically competitive firms are compared with the same outcomes for perfectly competitive and monopolistic firms in Table 12-1. But that's not the end of the story for monopolistic competition, because we have still have the issue of trade-offs between these technical measures of economic efficiency (which are no less important for being technical) and product variety and differentiation. That discussion is in turn related to the sometimes controversial issues associated with the economics of advertising, which are discussed in the case study at the end of this chapter.

Table 12-1
Comparing Perfect Competition, Monopoly, and Monopolistic Competition

	Allocative Efficiency	Productive Efficiency	Economic Profits Possible	Revenue Schedules	Profit Maximization Rule
Perfect Competition	P = MC	P = minATC	SR, yes; LR, no	P = MR	MR = MC
Monopoly	P > MC	P > ATC	SR, yes; LR, yes	P > MR	MR = MC
Monopolistic Competition	P > MC	P > minATC, but = ATC	SR, yes; LR, no	P > MR	MR = MC

The Debate on Monopolistic Competition

In monopolistic competition consumers benefit from the variety provided through product differentiation but lose in terms of the standard measures of productive and allocative efficiency. That tradeoff has spawned one of the loudest and most enduring debates in microeconomics, on the real value of diversity and product differentiation in general, and the economics of advertising in particular.

Product Diversity vs. Excess Capacity

According to William Cowper, variety is the spice of life. At least for some products, consumers and producers seem to agree with him. Automobiles come in dozens of models that offer different combinations of performance, comfort, economy, dependability, and style or "image." Record and book stores pre-sort their products into many different categories for us, knowing that some customers specialize in one or two of those fields, while others have more eclectic tastes and buy from many different areas. In part, then, variety in production is supported by consumers interested in expressing their own tastes, which naturally differ from person to person. But in other cases consumers express an internal, personal demand for diversity -- choosing to eat Chinese food and see a horror movie one night, Mexican food and a comedy the next. What does economics have to say about all of this, beyond the basic model of monopolistic competition which provides the general framework for much of this discussion?

A monopolistically competitive producer who is considering how much to differentiate his or her product must carefully weigh the costs and benefits involved. The more different the product is, the more monopolistic control the producer may have (at least in the short run, before entry by competing firms), since there won't be as many close substitutes to compete against. But by exactly the same token, a highly differentiated product is itself a poorer substitute for the products sold by other firms in an industry, and extreme differentiation moves a firm out of the central part of the markets for those products. In some cases, additional differentiation provides enough benefits in the form of monopolizing a specialized part of the market to make this worth while. In other cases, it is more profitable for a monopolistically competitive firm to limit the differentiation, and keep its products more like those in the main part of the market.

In the final analysis, how much differentiation we observe in the marketplace depends on how widely dispersed consumer preferences for different characteristics in some product group are. If they are tightly focused on certain core characteristics, producers will find it more expensive to give up this large segment of the market by changing the mix of their products' characteristics significantly. So, for example, action movies always involve certain stock elements: chase scenes, fights, diabolical villains with oversized henchmen, and dialogue featuring "in-your-face" humor. When customer preferences are more diverse across individuals, or when variety itself is highly prized by individual consumers, products will accordingly tend to be more varied. A good example of this level of consumer sophistication can usually be found by reading the short description of the current on and off-Broadway plays in each week's issue of *The New Yorker* magazine.

Of course production costs associated with product differentiation are also relevant to this discussion. The less expensive it is to offer differentiated products, the more variety we would expect to see, *ceteris paribus*. Many technological breakthroughs in recent years have made new kinds of product diversification possible, including such "high tech" breakthroughs as gene splicing and biological engineering that have made new strains of plants and even animals available to producers and consumers. On the other hand, pronounced economies of scale can sometimes make it quite costly to implement separate production methods required to offer extensive product differentiation. That is why passenger vans are usually customized at specialty shops rather than in large automobile factories, and why they cost significantly more than standard vans.

Until recently, many economists argued that the higher costs and lower output levels associated with product differentiation represented a clear, net loss to an economy whenever monopolistic competition supplanted perfect competition. But today, using more sophisticated models that capture more of the gains associated with product variety and differentiation, economists are more reluctant to pronounce either of these market structures as uniformly superior to the other. Instead, the trade-off between variety and higher costs is explicitly recognized, including distributional effects if only some consumers like the greater variety but others don't. That simply means that consumers who prefer standardized and rather plain products will lose by paying higher prices to cover higher production costs if market pressures lead all major firms in the industry to compete on the basis of product differentiation. The consumers who prefer the wider range of choices will, of course, gain. Exactly this kind of change was seen in the early decades of the U.S. auto industry when Henry Ford, who sold Model-Ts in any color "as long as it's black," finally had to give in and meet the competition from other companies (especially General Motors) which sold more brands and models of cars, in more colors, and with more optional equipment.

Competition by Location

In 1929, economist Harold Hotelling published a pioneering study that looked at how firms in a certain market area might compete in terms of where they chose to locate their businesses. To take a very simple example, think of a small, one-road town, where consumers' homes are evenly spaced along that road. Suppose that a business, say a grocery or furniture store, is located exactly at the mid-point of that road (point A on the line below). Say too that consumers at this store must pay delivery costs which are proportional to the distance their houses are from the store.

If another store offering identical goods and facing identical costs wants to enter this market, where would it try to locate? If it feels that it must have equal access to all of the customers in this town to stay in business, it will obviously locate across the street or right next to the existing business (at point B). If a third store of this kind enters the market under these circumstances, it too will want to locate near these first two stores (as shown by point C). Think of this the next time you see several gas stations grouped together on different corners of a busy intersection.

Where to Build a Business: A First Scenario

Business Location: _____BAC_____
Household Location: x x x x x x x x x x x x x x x x

These very simple results can change radically if we assume customers are not uniformly distributed along this road, or if still more firms believe there is enough business to support additional firms in this market. Clearly, firms will cluster where customers cluster in the first case. But if there is sufficient business in this market to support at least several firms, it will eventually be worthwhile for one or more of them to locate some distance away from the "central business district."

Firms that locate in outlying locations may well charge a higher price for their products, which customers won't hesitate to pay if there are offsetting savings on the transportation costs they must pay by shopping "downtown." So in effect, the outlying firms have established a limited kind of location monopoly, at least until firms enter near them to compete in this local market. As the overall market area grows and the town's population and wealth increases, this process may repeat itself many times.

In the last thirty years, economists have begun to use these models of *SPATIAL COMPETITION* to study nonprice competition involving other kinds of product differentiation, such as different physical or aesthetic characteristics among similar kinds of products. For example, we can think of standard automobiles such as Chevrolets, Fords, and Hondas as being the middle points on a line similar to the one in the diagram shown earlier, but which looks at competition in the new car industry with inexpensive cars like Yugos on one far end of the line, and luxury automobiles like Rolls Royces on the other end. Actually, of course, the larger car companies often make many different models of cars themselves, to sell in different parts of the automobile market. But clearly Yugos don't really compete with BMWs or Jaguars in a very direct sense, even though they are all cars. So the idea of space in models of spatial competition can be used to refer to "product space" based on various characteristics of different brands of a good or service, not just geographic distances.

On the original issue of spatial competition in terms of geography and distance, remember that the three most important factors in buying real estate are always "location, location, and location." But in broader terms that is true largely because time, convenience, and transportation costs can be significant nonprice determinants of where people choose to live, work, and shop.

There have always been moral as well as economic critics of market production oriented to the satisfaction of style, comfort, and a desire for novelty. Many observers complain that some of these marketed differences in product quality are only imagined, not real. Others go so far as to distinguish between rational and irrational preferences for product differences, where product differentiation that satisfies rational preferences are counted as increasing social welfare, while differentiation aimed at satisfying irrational preferences does not. The problem with this line of thinking is, of course, trying to agree on what kind of and how much differentiation is rational, and what is not. Typically, the only way economists have to determine what preferences consumers have is to look at the products they choose in the marketplace, and that makes any distinction between rational and irrational preferences meaningless, in purely economic terms, when such questions refer only to what characteristics of a product consumers like and dislike.

Nonprice Competition: A Quick Summary

When products sold by firms in the same industry are perceived to be heterogeneous, firms may compete in any or all of the following ways: a) by offering their products at lower prices; b) by improving product quality (real or perceived); c) by offering free or low-cost support services, such as repairs and alterations; d) by offering a wider range of ancillary features or products that complement their basic product; and e) by advertising to stress these differences and the desirability of their own product.

The forms of nonprice competition just listed as items b)-e) have become more prevalent over the last century, as products and business structures alike have become more complex and specialized. Communications networks and modern marketing techniques have offered firms more ways to attract customers, and more ways to package their products and the "deals" they offer buyers. A century ago, mail-order catalogs with black-and-white pictures and basic information on prices were state of the art business practice; and most catalogs came from stores that sold everything from cosmetics to houses to farming equipment. Today, the choices for businesses and consumers alike are greatly expanded, and there are many more ways to catch buyers' eyes. Catalogs are still one popular marketing tool among retailers, of course; but they tend to be much more glamorous and specialized than they were in earlier decades.

In the most general terms, monopolistically competitive firms use product differentiation to reduce the impact of competitive actions taken by other firms -- whether those actions involve price or nonprice competition.

Case Study #16
The Economics of Advertising

When a firm advertises it has two basic goals: to increase the demand for its product(s), and to make that demand less sensitive to price changes -- i.e., less price elastic. It tries to do that with two district parts of its advertisements: 1) by providing information about product price, availability, and features; and 2) through "persuasion" of either a subtle or an overt nature.

Beyond this basic agreement about the goals of advertising, however, there are serious disagreements among prominent economists about the real effectiveness of the advertising that firms do. Some agree with John Kenneth Galbraith that advertising is so powerful that it allows large corporations to create the demand for most of the products they chose to produce, and in the process set up a general social structure that is dependent on keeping people perpetually unsatisfied and acquisitive. According to Galbraith, "The firm must take every feasible step to see that what it decides to produce is wanted by the consumer at a remunerative price. ...It must replace the market with planning."[1] Galbraith also claims that the means for this control is readily at hand -- although it is not inexpensive or to be handled cavalierly:

The management of the private consumer is a task of no slight sophistication; the cost is considerable, and it uses some of the most expert and specialized talent to be found anywhere in the planning system.

---

[1]*The New Industrial State*, Boston: Houghton Mifflin, 1967, p. 24.

Its most obvious instrument is advertising. And the uniquely powerful instrument of advertising is television which allows of persuasive communication with virtually every user of goods and services with no minimum requirement in effort, literacy or intelligence.[2]

That doesn't paint a very flattering picture of advertising *or* consumers. And in one of his earliest books Galbraith was even more blunt and colorful in describing his judgment on how American consumers have gone down a primrose path:

The family which takes its mauve and cerise, air-conditioned, power-steered, and power-braked automobile out for a tour passes through cities that are badly paved, made hideous by litter, blighted buildings, [and] billboards.... They pass on to a countryside that has been rendered largely invisible by commercial art.... They picnic on exquisitely packaged food from a portable icebox by a polluted stream and...spend the night at a park which is a menace to the public health and morals. Just before dozing off on an air mattress, beneath a nylon tent, amid the stench of dying refuse, they may reflect vaguely on the curious unevenness of their blessings. Is this, indeed, the American genius?[3]

By making advertising such an important part of his overall system of social and economic domination by big business, big labor unions, big government, technical experts, and bureaucracy, Galbraith may have done more than any other economist and social critic to make advertising a controversial issue in the popular press and the professional economics literature. (The one possible exception is Vance Packard, who created a furor with his book on subliminal advertising and thought-control techniques, *The Hidden Persuaders*.)

Strident responses to Galbraith have been filed by numerous conservative economists, some of whom refuse to accept Galbraith as a serious economist even though he is a former President of the American Economic Association. But perhaps the strongest challenge to Galbraith's arguments on advertising and the effectiveness of corporate planning were posed by Robert Solow, a not-so-conservative Nobel laureate from M.I.T. Solow is best known for his theoretical models of economic growth, but in one of his rare pieces for general audiences he wrote that

Galbraith's story that the industrial firm has 'planned' itself into complete insulation from the vagaries of the market is an exaggeration, so much so that it smacks of the put-on. ...I should think a case could be made that much advertising serves only to cancel other advertising.

If Hertz and Avis were each to reduce their advertising expenditures by half...what would happen to the total car rental business? Galbraith presumably believes it would shrink. People would walk more, and spend their money instead on the still-advertised deodorants. But suppose...that all advertising were reduced.... Galbraith believes that in the absence of persuasion...total consumer spending would fall. Pending some evidence, I am not inclined to take this popular doctrine very seriously.[4]

Another large issue in this debate concerns the side-benefits (or costs, depending on which side of the argument you take) of having profit-oriented newspapers, radio and television stations, and entire mass-media networks, largely supported by advertising revenues. Several decades ago economists such as Nicholas Kaldor, who had little else good to say about advertising, were at least willing to concede that it brought the benefit of lower prices for magazines and newspapers which carry news, practical information and educational material to the public. But with the growing importance of commercial television and arguments about the falling quality of both television programs *and* the magazines and newspapers that cater to generations raised on television programs supported by corporate commercials, even that benefit is now routinely questioned.

The available facts and research findings on advertising and its effects aren't extensive and compelling enough to settle all of these arguments conclusively, or to change the mind of anyone who has formed strong opinions on

---

[2]*Economics and the Public Purpose*, New York: Mentor, 1973, p. 133.
[3]*The Affluent Society*, Boston: Houghton Mifflin, 1958, pp. 199-200.
[4]"The New Industrial State or Son of Affluence," *The Public Interest*, Fall 1967, pp. 104-05.

these issues. But there is enough evidence to inform many aspects of the debate, and perhaps even to influence those who approach the topic with an open mind:[5]

- Advertising expenditures by all U.S. companies currently represent about 2% of aggregate national income, a figure that has grown slowly over the past several decades. This is considerably higher than what is found in many other countries, especially in socialist economies and developing nations.

- Some kinds of products are much more heavily advertised than others -- for example, TV soap operas are called that because they have been sponsored so long by companies like Proctor and Gamble, which sell soaps, detergents, toothpastes, deodorants, and nail polishes. These companies targeted their advertising to the predominantly female audiences of afternoon TV in the 1950s and 60s, and spent heavily to make their brand names known and trusted by those viewers.

- In some markets, heavily advertised brands sell for considerably more than unadvertised products which are physically identical. In other markets, studies have found that legal prohibitions or restrictions on advertising resulted in less competition and higher prices. For example, a 1972 study found that prices for eyeglasses were higher in areas where advertising was restricted than in areas where it was not, and a 1984 study found that fees for exams by optometrists were 45% lower, on average, in cities that allowed these health-care providers to advertise in media other than the Yellow Pages.[6]

- Advertising by retailers is much more likely to include information on prices than advertising by manufacturers. And there are clear incentives to spend more on advertising for products which offer higher profits on incremental sales (i.e., where the difference between price and marginal costs are greatest). That suggests that firms with high degrees of market power are likely to be big advertisers, *ceteris paribus*, and that is almost certainly part of the reason behind the extensive campaigns by the major beer and soft drink companies. Of course, one company's advertising for these products can be largely offset by a competing firm's ad campaign, so decisions on advertising expenditures depend largely on what strategies rivals are expected to undertake. It is also possible that existing firms advertise heavily in order to keep new firms from entering the market, as discussed in Chapter 11.

- In general, a new product will be advertised heavily, especially if it is radically unlike existing products on the market. The same is true for products which most consumers find difficult to evaluate accurately in terms of quality and reliability, such as house paints, automobile tires, and over-the-counter drugs. Reputations for safety and effectiveness will be particularly valuable for such products, and in these cases it is appropriate to think of advertising as a kind of investment providing a long-term stream of future benefits instead of a simple cost of producing and selling current output.

It has proven to be very difficult to determine the effect of advertising expenditures on consumer spending levels, because firms' decisions to advertise are influenced by many factors other than responses in consumer spending. There is, however, a fairly large body of evidence that indicates firms use percentage-of-sales rules to

---

[5]The summary that follows is adapted from Richard Schmalensee, "Advertising," in *The New Palgrave: A Dictionary of Economics*, J. Eatwell, M. Milgate, and P. Newman, eds., London: The Macmillan Press Ltd., 1987, Vol. 1, pp. 34-36.
[6]Lee Benham, "The Effects of Advertising on the Price of Eyeglasses," *Journal of Law & Economics*, October 1972, pp. 337-52; and John E. Kwoka, Jr., "Advertising and the Price and Quality of Optometric Services," *American Economic Review*, March 1984, pp. 211-16.

set the general level of their advertising budgets, with some variations related to more aggressive campaigns that attempt to change a firm's levels of sales and market share. Several important studies have concluded tentatively, but consistently, that advertising is generally not a major factor in determining sales levels in an industry, and that advertising typically follows cyclical changes in sales, rather than leading them.

Economists have also studied the positive correlation between advertising expenditures and high rates of industry concentration -- that is, the fact that advertising is more prevalent and extensive in highly concentrated industries. Early work in this area suggested that firms' market shares may be less stable in markets characterized by heavy advertising, and that price elasticity of demand may be lower in these markets. But those results may also be a function of basic product characteristics in these markets, so those findings are still open to question.

Industries with high advertising-to-sales ratios typically have higher profit measures (at least in terms of accounting profits). That relationship is regularly cited by critics of advertising, but may also be due to using accounting data that treats advertising expenditures as an ordinary expense instead of an investment. Or, it may simply reflect the relationship between higher profit margins and the returns to advertising, noted above, which may be caused by many factors other than expenditures for advertising.

To summarize, while microeconomics isn't known for its controversies, at least compared to macroeconomics, the debate over advertising is clearly one of them in matters grand and small. As Richard Schmalensee writes,

> Advertising has been controversial, probably more so than its importance would justify, at least since the emergence of the mass media in the last century.
>
> ...Since advertising does provide some information, one must specify how information would be provided if advertising were banned. In principle an omniscient bureaucrat can provide information to perfectly rational consumers optimally, so that a properly administered advertising ban can do no harm.
>
> [But] in practice, bureaucrats are far from omniscient, and the way in which information is presented to consumers affects the extent to which they retain and use it. Advertisers have every incentive to present information effectively, though they rarely have any incentive to present all information that might affect decisions. Advertising, like democracy, is terrible in principle but better than any known alternative in practice.
>
> ...In general the literature offers no support for a presumption that market-determined advertising levels are socially optimal. But it also fails to provide any workable scheme for regulating those levels in the public interest. (p. 35)

Chapter Summary

1) *MONOPOLISTIC COMPETITION* is characterized by easy entry and exit of firms and *PRODUCT DIFFERENTIATION* through *NONPRICE COMPETITION* such as *ADVERTISING*, product design and styling changes, business location, and customer services such as return and exchange policies or "free" gift wrapping.

2) A key result of product differentiation is that firms in monopolistically competitive industries do not sell products that are perfect substitutes for products sold by other firms in the industry, although the products are highly similar. This means that each firm will face downward-sloping demand and marginal revenue schedules, and must lower product prices to increase sales.

3) When a new firm enters a monopolistically competitive industry, the demand and marginal revenue schedules for existing firms will shift leftward, *ceteris paribus*, as a result of this increased level of competition. When some firms in this kind of market structure exit, demand and marginal revenue schedules for remaining firms will shift outward and to the right.

4) Firms in monopolistically competitive industries may earn short-run economic profits or incur losses; but in the long run, because entry and exit is relatively quick and inexpensive, they will earn normal profits -- no more, no less.

5) In equilibrium, monopolistically competitive firms produce where P > MC and minATC. Therefore, they exhibit allocative and productive inefficiency, despite easy entry and exit in the industry, because of product variety and differentiation. Whether the benefits of this diversity and variety are greater than the costs of the inefficiency is a matter of long-standing debate among microeconomists, particularly since at least some of that variety is accomplished by influencing consumers' perceptions of similar or even identical products through persuasive advertising.

6) The economists who developed the early models of monopolistic competition were seeking a very general kind of theory to address issues of imperfect competition involving more than one or two firms. Today, other kinds of models are typically used to study questions involving industries with a small number of relatively large firms and restricted entry. But the models of monopolistic competition are still an important set of theories because they address some kinds of markets, and nonprice competition, quite effectively.

7) (Case Study #16) Some economists claim that advertising allows firms to create and increase the demand for their products. Other economists counter that most advertising simply counteracts the claims made in the advertisements of competing firms. Empirically, many "stylized facts" about advertising have been established over the past several decades, including: a) there is usually more advertising for consumer products with high "mark-ups" than those with low mark-ups; b) in some markets, but not all, advertised products tend to sell for higher prices than unadvertised products; c) retailers are more likely to advertise product price information than manufacturers; d) new products, and those which consumers are not able to evaluate by simple inspection for quality and safety features, are more likely to be advertised than other kinds of products; e) firms often set their advertising budgets using simple rules, such as a fixed percentage of sales revenues; f) advertising expenditures are usually not a major factor in determining industry sales levels, but there is a positive correlation between industry concentration and advertising expenditures, and g) industries with high advertising-to-sales ratios tend to earn high levels of accounting profits.

Review and Discussion Questions

1) In tabular form, list the different characteristics (not equilibrium outcomes, as shown in Table 12-1) of firms operating in the market structures we have labeled monopolistic competition, perfect competition, and monopoly. Include such factors as ease of entry, types of product and competition, and the shape of demand and revenue schedules.

2) If product differentiation in monopolistic competition only results in normal profits for firms in the industry, why do they continue to do it? At the industry level, is product differentiation required to have a downward-sloping demand curve?

3) At the firm and industry levels, compare and contrast the effects of entry and exit in perfect competition and in monopolistic competition.

4) Given your choice, and strictly in terms of financial rewards, would you prefer to own and operate a perfectly competitive firm or a monopolistically competitive firm?

5) How would you measure the degree of allocative inefficiency, productive inefficiency, and excess capacity for a monopolistically competitive firm? How would you measure the benefits of product differentiation and variety provided by the same firm, or its overall industry?

6) How does one monopolistically competitive firm view a competing firm in the same industry, and deal with its actions? Does that suggest a weakness in this theory's ability to explain and predict the behavior of firms in industries where barriers to entry are high and competition is among a few, very large firms?

7) (Case Study #16) Write a one-page essay taking the pro or con position on the following proposition: Resolved -- that mass media advertising (including television, radio, newspapers, and magazines) shall henceforth be limited to plain, black-and-white pictures; lists of product characteristics or ingredients (such as those on current labels for food products); and information on suggested retail prices.

Chapter 13
Oligopoly

In This Chapter...

we analyze oligopolies, industries populated by a few large firms. The hallmark of oligopoly is a direct interdependence between these firms. In fact, there are so many different ways that these firms can compete and affect each others' operations that there is no single model of the equilibrium situation in oligopoly, as there was for firms in perfect competition, monopoly, and monopolistic competition. However, there is enough consistency in results across the different models of oligopoly to draw some basic conclusions about productive efficiency, allocative efficiency, and the possibility of earning long-run economic profits in this market structure.

Those conclusions are developed in this chapter, and the major U.S. antitrust laws passed to deal with the undesirable effects of imperfect competition -- and oligopoly in particular -- are also described. Mergers, which have frequently been used to establish oligopolies in industries that were formerly less concentrated, are discussed in the Case Study at the end of the chapter.

Characteristics of Oligopolies

Oligopolistic firms sell a large part of the total industry output of the goods and services they produce. Therefore, other things being equal, they must lower price to sell more, so their marginal revenue curves lie below their demand curves. In that respect oligopoly and monopoly are very similar. However, because there are more than one of these large firms in an oligopoly there can be competition between the firms, or collusion among them. In either case there is a high degree of interdependence, and each firm's actions affect the other firms in the industry. There are also high barriers to entry, and less price flexibility than is observed in less concentrated market structures.

Interdependence and Economic Models of Competition Among the Few

Most large U.S. corporations, such as those included in the Fortune 500 list of the nation's largest manufacturing firms, are not monopolies. But neither are they small, competitive firms, of either the perfectly or mnopolistically competitive variety. Instead, these business giants compete against a few other large corporations which produce identical or slightly differentiated products. Their market structure is known as *OLIGOPOLY*, which translates literally as "few sellers."

Each of the large sellers in an oligopoly is very aware of who its competitors are and keeps close tabs on what they are doing -- with good reason. Firms in these industries affect their own market position, but also those of their competitors, whenever price, output, advertising, or other major operational changes are made. In turn, they are affected by changes made by their competitors. This interdependence is the single most important and distinguishing characteristic of oligopoly, and is reflected in all of the different models of this market structure which economists have developed.

The notion of interdependence among competing firms also moves us squarely into the realm of *STRATEGIC BEHAVIOR*, which means that both the actions and reactions of competitors and, in some cases, collaborators must be explicitly considered. In this sense, oligopoly models share several key features with the war games that military tacticians play. In particular, winning (or even survival) in these settings often depends not only on a firm or a nation's own strength, but also on its relative strength as compared to other "players."

The fundamental problem that the characteristic of strategic interdependence creates for anyone looking for a single, definitive model of oligopoly is that the interdependence among oligopolistic firms can, and does, take many different forms. For example, in some industries a dominant firm may establish itself and effectively compel much smaller firms to follow its pricing and output decisions. In others, firms currently in the industry may be primarily concerned with preventing entry into the industry by new firms -- that is, they try to affect, and are themselves affected by, the behavior of firms that aren't even in their industry at the present time. In still other cases, firms in an oligopoly may assume their competitors will set price and output at specific levels, but then revise those assumptions and their own behavior as they learn more about their rivals' actions and reactions. And at the international level, where contractual agreements setting prices and sharing sales among firms in the same industry are legal, or at least effectively beyond the enforcement powers of the U.S. Department of Justice, firms in some industries must decide when it is in their best interest to join and cooperate with such a cartel, when it is more advantageous to join the cartel but then cheat on their collusive agreement, and when it is best to remain entirely outside of the cartel's formal agreements even though they will still be affected by its policies.

We present models based on each of these possible forms of interdependence in this chapter, and develop some general conclusions on oligopoly that hold in all of these cases. But remember that there are other ways the interdependence among firms in an oligopoly may manifest itself, which means that other forms of oligopoly which are not presented here can arise in some industries, or at different times.

Barriers to Entry

Apart from interdependence, the major characteristic of an oligopoly is high barriers to entry in the industry. While these barriers are not assumed to be so high as to permanently prevent all entry, as in the extreme case of perfect monopoly, they are high enough to restrict or delay it, making entry a very expensive proposition. The major forms these barriers may take are the same kinds discussed in Chapter 11 for monopolies -- most notably economies of scale, legal restrictions such as patents and copyrights, and strong brand loyalties supported by extensive advertising campaigns. In oligopolies, however, the economies of scale are not so extensive or long-lasting to lead to natural monopolies. Nor are the other barriers of entry completely impenetrable. For example, patents and copyrights may make it impossible for competitors to produce identical products, but not to develop and produce close substitutes. And brand loyalties are not so strong to keep consumers from considering a switch to a competing brand, especially when price or other product features make it more attractive to do so.

In comparing barriers to entry in monopolies and oligopolies, then, everything comes down to a matter of differences in degree. But those differences are sufficiently great to lead to very different kinds of market structures.

"Sticky" Prices

Many economists argue that another characteristic of oligopoly is that prices in these industries rise and fall less often than they do in either perfect competition or monopoly. As you have already seen in the basic models of those market structures, whenever marginal cost or marginal revenue schedules shift, we predict a corresponding rise or fall in price. But according to the "sticky price" argument, in oligopolies large firms are often fearful of disrupting the delicate, strategic balance that has been achieved in the industry, so they don't change their price and risk retaliation from their large, powerful competitors if changes in their costs and revenues are relatively small. They especially want to avoid "price wars," such as those that have occasionally broken out among the major airlines in recent years.

Other economists have suggested that in oligopolies extensive production, marketing, and sales networks make changing prices itself a very costly activity -- either in the direct costs associated with printing, distributing, and implementing new price lists used by sales agents and customers, or by losing customers to firms which hold prices constant. Note that to argue that these cost factors will lead to less frequent price changes in oligopolies than in other market structures, it must also be argued that those costs are higher in oligopolies than in competitive, and perhaps even monopolistic, industries. That argument is plausible, at least in some respects. For example, certainly in the two examples of highly competitive markets we used in earlier chapters, agriculture and

363

the stock market, price changes are made and nationally disseminated with great frequency and at little or no cost to individual buyers and sellers of these products.

The basic idea that making price changes can be a costly activity has been widely accepted by economists, and incorporated into a variety of models addressing many kinds of topics. But the claim that these costs are more pronounced among concentrated industries, and among oligopolies in particular, is subject to considerable debate. Assertions that oligopolies are reluctant to lower prices for fear of setting off ruinous price wars, or to raise prices because their competitors will hold their prices steady to draw more customers, are especially open to dispute.[1]

For our purposes, Table 13-1 adequately summarizes the current evidence on this debate. Firms in concentrated industries do seem to change their prices less frequently than firms in highly competitive industries, but the linkage between the degree of concentration and price rigidity is not a simple and direct one. Nor are the reasons for that linkage fully understood by economists, either as a microeconomic issue involving different market structures, or as a macroeconomic topic affecting the overall price level and rate of inflation. As you might suspect, this is an active area of study and investigation for many economists.

Table 13-1
Price Flexibility And Industry Concentration Measures

Industry Concentration Level	4-Firm Concentration Ratio (1982, %)	Degree of Price Flexibility, 1960-83 (100 = Competitive Index)
High (Motor vehicles, tobacco, non-ferrous metals)	79	38
Moderate (Paper, stone, clay, glass, chemicals)	42	25
Low (Apparel, printing, furniture)	26	14
Perfectly Competitive (Corn and wheat farming)	~.01	100

The frequency of price changes is shown here as a percentage of price changes in industries with four-firm concentration ratios of about .01 percent -- that is, compared to very competitive industries made up of small firms. Industries that are more concentrated exhibit less price flexibility, but increasing degrees of concentration do not uniformly lead to less price flexibility. Note that the most concentrated group of industries changed prices more often than the moderate and low-concentration groups of industries.

Source: Paul A. Samuelson and William D. Nordhaus, *Microeconomics*, New York: McGraw-Hill, Inc., 1989, p. 260.

[1] Current textbooks on industrial organization, such as Stephen Martin's *Industrial Economics* (New York: Macmillan, 1988), review the theoretical and empirical research on these questions.

364

Models of Oligopoly Behavior

Although there is no one best model of oligopoly because of the different ways firms in this market structure can interact, many of the most important and commonly observed forms of interdependence in oligopolies have been analyzed. The models presented in the following section are examples from that group, and deal with the cases of cartels, price leadership by dominant and barometric firms, limit-entry pricing, and duopolies. The models all yield consistent findings on several issues that are of great interest to economists and policymakers, including optimal price, output and profit levels in oligopolies, compared to those observed in other market structures.

Cartels: Collude, Cheat, and Repeat the Process

The production of electrical equipment, crude oil, diamonds, rubber, tea, and several metals and minerals have been, at one time or another, largely under the control of international cartels. A cartel is a group of firms acting together to reduce competition in an industry, and cooperating to set prices and divide up production, sales, and profits in their industry. Obviously, to accomplish those objectives, the firms in the cartel must control all, or at least a major part of, the production of a good or service.

Today, the most visible and important cartel is OPEC, the Organization of Petroleum Exporting Countries. Since the early 1970s, the members of OPEC have been keenly interested in how they should act to maximize the overall level of profits earned by their cartel. And in trying to increase those profits, they have developed a deep appreciation of basic economic models and ideas. So much so that, a few years ago, a cartoon in *The New Yorker* magazine showed an oil minister from the Middle East talking with a Western businessman in the back of a limousine, saying "As Adam Smith so eloquently stated...."

Consumers and policymakers from nations that aren't members of OPEC also have a serious interest in the decisions made by the cartel, since those decisions affect the prices they pay for crude oil and petroleum-based products, as well as short-run inflation and unemployment rates all over the world. The major oil-consuming nations and firms have even tried to develop better models of OPEC's position themselves, and to use those models to find ways to counter the cartel's economic power. So once again this is a case where economic models aren't just academic exercises in abstract theory; instead, they directly affect economic well being in most parts of the world.

Fortunately, the starting point for the cartel model is fairly simple, and based on a model you have already seen. That's because a cartel controlling 100% of the production of a good is -- if it can keep all of its members in line and behaving in a way that will maximize the overall industry level of profits -- just like a monopolist that produces its product in several different plants. That is shown in Figure 13-1, a graph virtually identical to the basic monopoly model presented in Chapter 11. The only real difference in this Figure is that the marginal cost schedule has a summation sign in front of it, indicating that a cartel (or a multi-plant monopolist) must add up the marginal cost schedules of its different producing units to determine what the additional costs of increasing its output level will be. To minimize production costs, a cartel will use its lowest-cost facilities first, and only bring on the higher-cost units if demand is strong enough to charge prices that will cover those costs. Profit maximization *for the industry* will occur, as usual, at the output level where marginal revenue intersects this marginal cost schedule. The area of economic profits in this graph is equal to the difference between price and average total cost (shown here as P_c and AC on the vertical axis, respectively) times the level of output.

How the cartel divides its profits among members is a matter of constant discussion and negotiation within the cartel. The least-cost providers who undertake more of the production (in order to maximize profits) will, clearly, argue for some direct relationship between member firm's production levels and profits. But to set output and price at their monopoly levels, all members can gain by having the higher-cost producers cut back on the amount of product they would otherwise produce and sell. If they don't cut back, the industry level of output will be higher, and the price for the cartel's product will be lower. That decreases the industry's profits by moving beyond

365

the MR = ΣMC level of output in Figure 13-1. For that reason, even the highest-cost producer in the cartel has some bargaining power in negotiating for its share of the industry profits.

Figure 13-1
A Cartel Maximizing Industry Profits

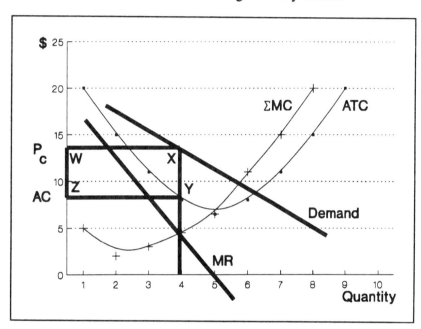

To maximize the total level of profits earned in the *industry*, a cartel will set MR = ΣMC. In that way, production costs are minimized by using the most efficient (i.e., low-cost) factories or other production sites. The result will be a cartel price level of P_c, and economic profits equal to area WXYZ. The effect of perfect collusion in this industry is exactly equivalent to what we would observe in a multi-plant monopolist if the monopolist faced identical cost, demand, and marginal revenue schedules.

But in fact, the threat of firms in the cartel expanding their output beyond their assigned quotas turns out to be a more general and even more serious problem for the cartel than the division of profits among its members. That's because each member in the cartel has strong economic incentives to cheat on the collusive agreement, even though the agreement by individual members to restrict price and output levels is what pulls the industry profits up to the monopoly level in the first place. We show this situation for an individual firm in Figure 13-2 where, for purposes of illustration, we assume the firm is one of 10 member firms in a cartel, all of which have identical cost schedules and are assigned one-tenth of the total cartel output and profits. These assumptions simplify the presentation, but are not required to observe the kind of result we describe below.

You can see in Figure 13-2 that once a member firm receives its production and profit quotas from the cartel, it can increase its own profits by moving out to the point where its own MR and MC schedules intersect. It does that by secretly selling more than its alloted quota, and that requires lowering the price it charges for those "extra" units. The price must be lowered because two kinds of new customers come to the cheating firms in a cartel. The first group are those who are at a point low enough on the industry demand curve that they would not buy at the cartel price, but will buy at the lower, cheating price. The second group are those who were buying at the cartel price already, but from some other firm. Attracting either kind of customer increases the cheating firm's short-run

366

economic profits, but also creates long-run problems which make it difficult for the cheating to go undetected by other firms in the cartel. For example, the first group of customers might resell the products it buys from the cheating firms, charging a price greater than the cheating price but less than the cartel price. That would clearly attract the attention and displeasure of all of the firms in the industry, and would not be a tenable situation in the long run. (Recall the stringent requirements for practicing successful price discrimination, discussed in Chapter 11.) Losing the second group of customers to cheating firms can also alert other cartel members that something is rotten in the cartel. That may lead to greater policing and enforcement efforts in the cartel, or to a faster break up of the cartel as other firms begin cheating too, in self-defense.

Figure 13-2
The Cartel Member's Dilemma: To Cheat or Not to Cheat

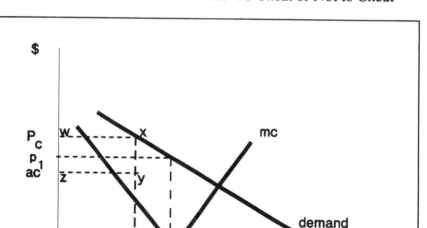

This cartel member is assigned output level q_0 and a level of economic profits equal to area wxyz, assuming its average costs are ac. For convenience, we have assumed here that this profit area is 1/10 of area WXYZ in Figure 13-1. The firm is expected to sell its allotment of output at the cartel price P_c, which maximizes total profits earned by the cartel. But note that the *firm* can increase its own profits by secretly selling additional units of output at lower prices, up to the point where its mr = mc, at price p_1 and quantity q_1.

George Stigler, a Nobel-laureate economist, developed a numerical example to illustrate the power of these long-term limits on cheating, which also suggests some ways for cheating firms to cheat more successfully. Let p equal the probability of a rival firm learning about a secret price cut offered by a cheating firm. Then 1-p is the probability that a rival does not hear about a price cut, and $(1-p)^n$ is the probability that all n rivals in the cartel will not learn about the price cut. That means that $1-(1-p)^n$ is the probability that at least one rival firm *will* discover the price cut. Even if p is as small as .01, when n = 100 the likelihood of getting caught is 63.4%; and when n = 1000 that probability increases to 99.996%. If discovery is related to the number of customers to whom the cheating firm offers a lower price, the smart thing for it to do is offer the price cuts to a few large customers, thus minimizing the chances of detection. But the cheating can still be uncovered if rival firms get lucky and discover physical evidence of cheating, or if they become suspicious when they lose an unusual number of their largest customers.

In broad terms, the inherent problem with cartel stability is that all of the firms in the cartel face incentives to cheat, and as more firms cheat on the collusive agreement the cartel moves further away from monopoly-equivalent price and output levels. More specifically, cheating lowers product price and expands output, moving the industry closer to a competitive position. If that happens long enough, or is done by enough firms in the cartel, it will clearly pay the firms to re-establish the cartel price and output agreement, and again earn monopoly profits for the overall industry. But once that is done, the incentives for individual firms to cheat are also put in place again, so this collude-cheat-collude cycle may be repeated several times. And typically each time through the cycle it becomes harder for the cartel to re-establish the trust among firms that is required for effective collusion.

Not surprisingly, then, most cartels eventually fail, either because they break up from within, or because of increased production by non-member firms and producers of substitute products (which is encouraged the more the cartel succeeds in maintaining pricing discipline within the cartel). However, a cartel's life can be extended if better ways of monitoring and enforcing compliance within the cartel are put into place, if there are fewer members in the cartel to begin with, and if there are fewer producers of the product who remain outside the cartel.[2] And, of course, a cartel will be stronger if there are few close substitutes for its product -- i.e., if the price elasticity of demand for its product is low -- or if demand for the cartel's product is growing, so that firms won't see their sales fall even if there is some cheating in the cartel.

But cartels aren't the only form of oligopolistic interdependence or, over the long run, even the major form. The limited nature of that impact stems from their own inherent instabilities, the unusual circumstances that must prevail for a relatively small number of firms to control enough of the output in a market to make a cartel feasible, and the legal and economic countermeasures that cartel customers (and their governments) can adopt. The oligopoly models we discuss in the following sections typically get less media attention than cartels, but they can be every bit as significant in national and international markets for some products.

Price Leadership: Barometric and Dominant Firms

In some oligopolies, one firm is regularly the first firm to announce price changes, with other firms in the industry soon following suit. This practice is known as *PRICE LEADERSHIP*, and is most often described in one of two forms. In cases where the price leader is about the same size as most other firms in the industry, the leader is considered a *BAROMETRIC FIRM*, which means that it faces cost and revenue schedules that are representative of those the other firms in the industry face. A barometric price leader may simply be a little faster in recognizing and responding to changes in market conditions than the "following" firms, or just become the recognized price leader by tacit agreement of the other firms in the industry. The International Paper Company, which accounted for less than 15% of the U.S. market share in this industry during the mid-1970s, was sometimes cited as a barometric price leader in this period.

Barometric price leadership is an interesting thing for economists and industry analysts to observe, and can certainly be used to predict short-term actions of other firms in the industry. But frankly, economists don't have very good models to explain how and why an otherwise typical firm in an oligopoly will come to be recognized as a price leader; and the economic significance of this kind of interdependence is quite limited. The more important case of price leadership, particularly in terms of public policy issues, involves the dominant-firm model of oligopoly. And in this case, the economic theory and evidence is much stronger.

A *DOMINANT FIRM* is, as the name suggests, much larger and more powerful than other firms in the industry. In fact, the smaller firms in this kind of industry form a kind of competitive fringe, and must follow the dominant

---

[2]If you haven't read it already, you may want to read Case Study #4 at the end of Chapter 3 to learn more about the history of OPEC, and the reasons for its unusual success and longevity.

368

firm's price leadership or risk being targeted for reprisals, and perhaps even being taken over, by the dominant firm. In the 1940s and 50s, Alcoa and IBM were often considered dominant-firm price leaders in the aluminum and mainframe computer industries, respectively.

The theoretical model of dominant-firm price leadership is shown in Figure 13-3, where D is the industry demand curve; S_{cf} is the quantity that all of the small, competitive fringe, firms in the industry will produce and sell at all possible prices; and d, mr, and mc are the dominant firm's demand, marginal revenue, and marginal cost schedules, respectively. The dominant firm maximizes profits by setting mr = mc, as usual, producing quantity q_d and charging price p_d. The competitive fringe firms take that price as a given -- a constraint of doing business in this industry -- and produce q_c level of output. The total quantity sold at this price will be Q, which is equal to $q_d + q_c$ -- that is, to the combined output of the dominant and smaller firms in the industry.

Figure 13-3
The Dominant-Firm Model of Oligopoly

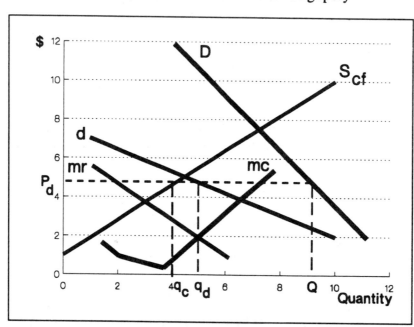

Given the market or industry level of demand for its product, D, and the supply schedule for the competitive fringe of small firms operating in its industry, S_{cf}, a dominant firm can identify its own demand curve, d, by horizontally subtracting the quantity on S_{cf} from the quantity on D at all possible prices. The quantities remaining indicate how much consumers will purchase from it at all prices, and from this schedule the firm can also identify its marginal revenue schedule, mr. Given its marginal cost schedule, mc, it will maximize profits at the output level q_d, where mr = mc, assuming the price (p_d) at that output level is greater than its average costs. The total industry output will be Q, which is equal to $q_d + q_c$, where q_c is the amount the competitive fringe will produce and sell once the dominant firm has set this price in the market. (In this graph, q_d is 5, and q_c -- the combined output produced by all of the competitive fringe firms -- is 4, so Q = 9.)

Most of this should be familiar from earlier models you have seen. The only new problem here is to determine the position of the dominant firm's demand curve, d. The dominant firm does that by estimating how much the group of smaller, competitive firms in the industry can produce at each price, and subtracting that quantity from the total level of industry output that consumers will purchase at those prices.

Notice that the dominant firm, like a successful cartel, will produce where price is greater than marginal cost, and can continue to earn economic profits in the long run because of high barriers to entry (at least for firms aspiring to its position in the industry). That means the dominant firm produces where price is greater than average total costs, so neither of the criteria for productive and allocative efficiency, as described in Chapters 9-12, are met. Those outcomes also hold in the models of oligopolistic behavior presented in the following two sections.

Limit-Entry Pricing and Residual Demand Curves

When the firms in an oligopoly set a price and output level, their profits are maximized by producing where marginal revenue equals marginal cost. At the industry level, this means a certain segment of the demand for the products sold by these firms is met, as shown in Figure 13-4. But also note there that a considerable portion of the demand curve awaits any other producer who can enter the market and profitably produce units of output at lower prices -- this is the segment labeled as *RESIDUAL DEMAND* in part A of the figure, which begins at a price of $20.

That segment of the demand curve has been replotted in part B of Figure 13-4, along with the average total cost schedule for what we will assume is the firm most likely to enter this industry. In other words, all other firms that might enter face even higher costs. If the most-likely entrant's ATC schedule is anywhere tangent to or below the residual demand curve, it can profitably enter this market. Then, the resulting increase in the industry output level will put downward pressure on prices, and lower the profits for the firms already producing this product.

Figure 13-4
Limit-Entry Pricing

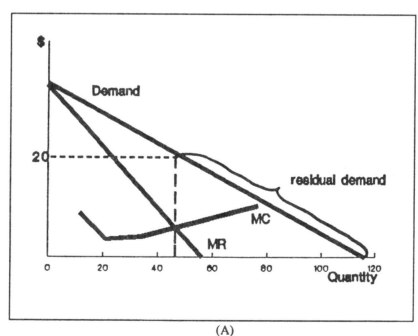

(A)

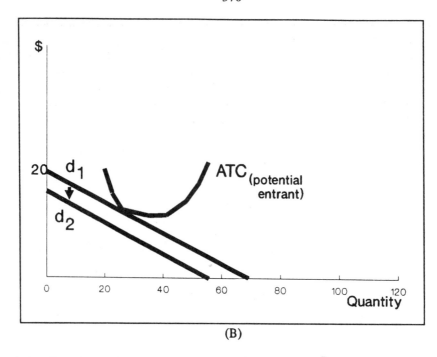

(B)

In panel (A), existing firms in an oligopoly are initially producing where MR = MC, and charging a price of $20. This leaves the segment of the demand curve below $20 for potential entrants in this market, who will be willing to enter if their ATC schedule is at least tangent to this residual demand curve d_1, as shown in panel (B). In that panel, we have simply redrawn this residual demand curve from the data in the first panel, starting at a price of $20 and taking total quantities from panel (A) *minus* the current production level of the existing firms.

Entry by the new firms would increase output and lower price and profits for the existing firms in this industry, so to prevent the entry they may decide to forgo some short-run profits and set a price < $20. That leaves a smaller segment of residual demand for the potential entrants, as shown by the downward shift from d_1 to d_2 in panel B.

Given this lower level of demand and the cost schedule shown above, potential rivals will now find that it is unprofitable to enter this market. The existing firms have sacrificed some profits in the short run in order to deter entry and keep their profits higher in the long run.

To avoid this, before the entry by the new firm takes place, the existing firms may find it more profitable *in the long run* to lower price just enough to shift the residual curve downward -- now starting at a price < $20, as shown on schedule d_2 in part B of Figure 13-4. That will prevent entry in the market, but note well that this is the only case we have encountered where a firm will produce *beyond* the point where short-run marginal revenue equals marginal cost. Once again, however, this model of oligopoly shows that in equilibrium firms can earn long-run economic profits, and produce where P > ATC and > MC.

Cournot Duopolies and Reaction Functions

The last major model of oligopoly we will present here was actually the first formal model of competition among a small number of firms developed by an economist. Augustin Cournot, a Frenchman who wrote in the first half of the 19th century, developed this model to explore the interdependence between two firms which produced all of the output in an industry. This form of oligopoly is known as *DUOPOLY* (which translates as two sellers), and is most important today because it illustrates most simply the idea of a *REACTION FUNCTION* for firms in an oligopoly setting. That function most directly formalizes the idea of interdependence in this market structure.

In the simplest version of Cournot's model, he assumed that two firms sell a product which can only be produced from natural resources at one site, and that this resource is freely available to both firms -- i.e., at $0 marginal cost. (Cournot described firms selling a special mineral water which they took from a free-flowing spring. The stream flowed only on property which the two producers owned, and customers brought their own buckets or other containers to carry the water away.)

If one of the two Cournot firms gets into business before the other, it behaves like a monopolist because it does not know that the other firm will soon be able to sell the same product. It will, therefore, sell the monopoly level of output where marginal revenue equals marginal cost, as shown in panel (A) of Figure 13-5. Since MC = 0 in this example, the firm will produce where MR = 0, too, at an output level of 500, and set the corresponding price, P_1. Given the linear demand curve labeled AB, this output will be exactly half of that which would occur if the good were to be given away to consumers (in other words, where P = MC = 0, at an output level of 1000).

When the second firm finds that it can sell this product, too, it sees that there is unsatisfied demand for this product in the range labeled CB. Using the terminology of the limit-entry model presented earlier, this is the residual demand curve given an output level of 500 buckets of water a day for the first firm. On that basis, the second firm would decide to produce 250 additional units of water a day, as shown in panel B of Figure 13-5. That moves the two-firm industry further down the industry demand curve, to price P_2 and a total output of 750 units. Already this is different from the perfect monopoly solution, at a lower price and higher output level; but the process doesn't stop there.

Surely, Cournot wrote, the first firm will now recognize its original mistake in thinking that no other firm could produce its product. And assume that it now believes the second firm will continue to produce 250 units of output a day, no matter how much the first firm decides to produce. That means the first firm now faces the residual demand curve DB, as shown in panel A of Figure 13-5. And from that, it will decide to maximize profits by producing one-half of the 750 units for which there is still positive demand. We therefore add its new output of 375 to the second firm's current output of 250, to find that the new industry output will be 625.

But the second firm will soon recognize the first firm has changed its output, and calculate its new residual demand curve (625 units are not satisfied by the first firm's output) and its optimal level of output (half of 625, or 312.5, which makes the total industry output 687.5). By now, undoubtedly, you are wondering how long this process of adjustment and re-adjustment will go on. The answer is: until each competing firm actually produces, and continues to produce, the amount the other firm expects it to produce.

The easiest way to see that, and to use this model to understand an important and general characteristic of oligopolies, is to understand the reaction functions for these two Cournot firms shown in Figure 13-6. A reaction function shows what one firm is going to do when another firm in its industry takes some action. In Cournot's example, we see how much the first firm will produce when the second firm produces various levels of output, and *vice versa*. Note that the points we saw in the discussion of Figure 13-5, above -- 500 units for the first firm when the second firm produces 0, and 375 when the second firm sells 250; and for the second firm, 250 units when the first firm produces 500, and 312.5 when the first firm produces 375 -- are all shown here, too. More importantly, there is a unique point, labeled d in this graph, at which each firm produces 333 1/3 units, for a total industry output of 666 2/3 units. Only at this point does each firm produce, and continue to produce, the level of output that the other firm assumes it will. Therefore, once the firms converge to this point the industry will be in equilibrium, and remain there as long as demand and production costs for the product are unchanged.

Figure 13-5
Production and Price Decisions in a Cournot Duopoly

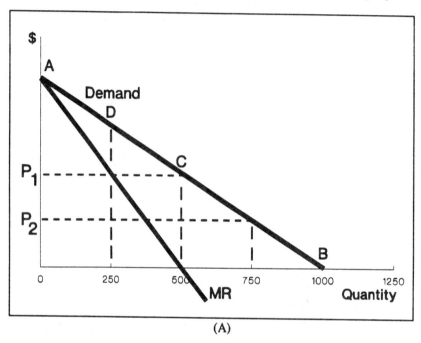

(A)

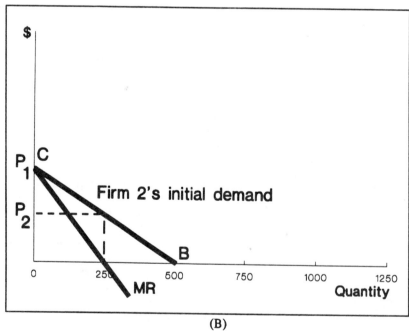

(B)

The industry demand curve AB in the panel (A) faces both producers in a Cournot duopoly, where marginal and average costs are assumed to be 0 at all output levels. If one firm begins producing before the other, it will maximize profits by producing where MR = MC, which occurs at an output level of 500 and allows the firm to charge P_1. That leaves the range CB of the demand curve for the second producer to work with, which we have

373

re-plotted with an associated MR schedule in panel (B). The second firm will now produce where its MR = MC, and add its production of 250 units to the first firm's output of 500. Industry output increases to 750 and price falls to P$_2$, which naturally lowers profits for the first firm. But if that firm now assumes that the second firm will continue to produce 250 units of output, the first firm now faces a residual demand curve of DB, as shown in panel (A). It will therefore set a new price and output level accordingly, and that once again affects the second firm's position. This adjustment process by both firms will continue until each firm produces the amount of output the other firm assumes it is going to produce. That equilibrium position is identified in Figure 13-6, by constructing the firms' reaction functions.

Figure 13-6
Reaction Functions for a Cournot Duopoly

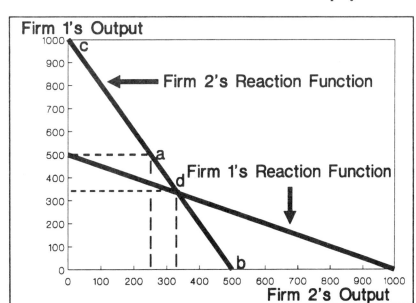

From Figure 13-5, we know that Firm 2 in this Cournot duopoly will produce 250 units of output when Firm 1 produces an output level of 500 (point a). We can also see here that Firm 2 will produce 500 units if Firm 1 produces 0 (point b), and 0 units if Firm 1 produces 1000 (point c). We plot these and other output points for Firm 2, to see how it reacts to any output level Firm 1 chooses to produce. Then we do the same thing for Firm 1, as shown above.

There is only one point on both of these reaction functions at which each firm produces the amount the other firm expects it to, and continues to produce that amount after the other firm establishes its output level. The Cournot firms will be driven to that equilibrium position, where each firm produces 333 1/3 units of output, so total output for this two-firm industry will be 666 2/3. The price for that output level will be taken from the industry demand curve shown in panel (A) of Figure 13-5, and it is clear that from consumers' perspective this is a better result (a higher output and lower price) than perfect monopoly, but not as good as the competitive result where price would equal marginal cost (in this case 0), and output would be maximized.

This result is intuitively sensible in several key respects: First, each firm faces the same cost and demand schedules, and sells a homogeneous product, so it is not surprising that they end up producing the same amount. Second, the final industry output is greater than the monopoly level of 500, but only 2/3 of what the perfectly competitive output would be (where P = MC). Finally, the equilibrium price for this product is lower than the monopoly price, but higher than the competitive price. So in this case imperfect competition -- even among only two firms -- turns out to be much better for consumers than no competition at all.

The basic Cournot model demonstrates clearly that oligopolies must take into account what other firms in the industry are doing. In practice, real-world reaction functions for oligopolistic firms can be expected to be much more complex and sophisticated than this, particularly in *anticipating* how rival firms are likely to react to competitors' changes in price, output, or other factors, and not just assuming that the competitors will continue doing whatever they are doing now. But that goes further than we need to go here. For now, use the Cournot model to see how the inherent interdependence in oligopoly (represented most formally in these reaction functions) makes this market structure fundamentally different from the models of perfect competition, monopoly, and monopolistic competition covered in earlier chapters.

Most basically, the extensive interdependence in oligopoly makes it impossible to establish one, definitive model for firms in this industry. As we noted earlier, there are as many different models of oligopoly as there are different varieties of interdependence among these large, potentially powerful firms. But at the same time, notice that in the models of cartels, dominant firms, limit-entry pricing, and Cournot duopolies, certain characteristics and outcomes were always encountered. Those common features, and the reasons for their presence in these and virtually all other oligopoly models that have been developed by economists, are the subject of the last major section of this chapter. They are also a major part of the basis for the extensive and uniquely American body of antitrust legislation, which is reviewed in the following section as well.

Efficiency Outcomes in Oligopoly, and U.S. Antitrust Laws

Barriers to entry in oligopolies make it possible for firms to earn long-run economic profits, and to produce at levels where price is greater than both marginal cost and average total costs. This indicates the presence of both allocative and productive inefficiency, but empirical estimates of the actual dollar value of the efficiency losses due to imperfectly competitive market structures in the U.S. economy are surprisingly small. Still, those effects can obviously be substantial in individual industries, and the overall effects might well be larger if several major antitrust laws had not been passed and enforced over the last century.

Productive and Allocative Efficiency in Oligopolies

Because oligopolistic firms produce a substantial portion of the overall level of output in their industry, they affect the price of the product they sell as they increase or decrease their level of output. To sell more products, given its current level of demand, an oligopolist must lower its price. That is just another way of saying these firms face downward-sloping demand curves, which means they also face marginal revenue schedules that lie below their demand curves.

Profit maximization typically occurs at the output level where MR = MC, and even in the limit-entry model where this is not true the firm will charge a price that is greater than MC because of the downward sloping and separated demand and marginal revenue schedules. Oligopolies do not, therefore, meet the P = MC criterion for allocative efficiency. Instead, the P > MC outcome indicates that consumers value the last unit of output produced by an oligopoly more than they value the best alternative use of the resources used to produce it. So once again, we can say that imperfect competition leads to an underallocation of resources to these markets.

Consumers would like to see these firms use more inputs to produce more of these products, and sell them at lower prices. The firms could do that up to a point and still earn economic or at least normal profits, but they won't -- because their profits are maximized at the point where MR = MC. In short, by restricting output they command a higher price and higher profits than they would if the industry were more competitive, *ceteris paribus*.

The presence of economic profits, and in particular long-run economic profits, means that a firm is producing where P > ATC. Therefore, oligopolies also fail to meet the competitive criterion for productive efficiency. The basic long-run source of this failure is, of course, the same as that we identified for monopolies: high barriers to entry. Without those barriers, short-run economic profits would lead to increased production and competition, and firms in this industry would be driven to a long-run position where P = ATC. (But they still might not be driven to the point where P = minATC, as we saw in Chapter 12, if product differentiation led to a monopolistically competitive market structure.)

   Table 13-2 compares the four market structures described in Chapters 9-13. This is the final and most complete version of this table you will see. It demonstrates most clearly why economists are strong supporters of competitive market organizations, at least as long as small firms can produce at unit costs that are as low as those achieved by larger firms. No other mechanism so quickly or reliably achieves productive and allocative efficiency with so little central direction and bureaucracy, automatically taking into account the unique circumstances of individual producers and the preferences and budgets of individual consumers.

Table 13-2
Comparing Perfect Competition, Monopoly, Monopolistic Competition and Oligopoly

	Allocative Efficiency	Productive Efficiency	Economic Profits Possible	Revenue Schedules	Profit Maximization Rule
Perfect Competition	P = MC	P = minATC	SR, yes; LR, no	P = MR	MR = MC
Monopoly	P > MC	P > ATC	SR, yes; LR, yes	P > MR	MR = MC
Monopolistic Competition	P > MC	P = ATC, but > minATC	SR, yes; LR, no	P > MR	MR = MC
Oligopoly	P > MC	P > MC ATC	SR, yes; LR, yes	P > MR	MR = MC*

* Except for the limit-entry pricing model.

   This is not to say that the government can not design and enforce policies to strengthen and maintain competition in some markets. But in many respects that public policy legislation and regulation is driven by the fact that consumers will usually be better off when they can purchase goods and services from competitive firms; and producers will usually be better off if they can somehow establish the position of selling their products in imperfectly competitive markets. This is the basic moral of the material you have covered in Chapters 9-13.

   Note too that making a once-monopolistic or oligopolistic market more competitive will, other things being equal, result in higher levels of output at all possible price levels. That shows that, together with the production and cost models developed in Chapters 7 and 8, the degree of competition among the producers of a product underlies the basic supply curves you have studied from the very beginning of this course, just as the consumer choice process developed in Chapter 6 lies behind the demand curves for consumer goods and services.

Statistical Estimates of Efficiency Losses From Imperfect Competition

   The theoretical analysis of oligopoly and other forms of imperfect competition has demonstrated the loss of economic efficiency in each of these market structures. In this section we will briefly review the empirical evidence on how much the inefficiency from all forms of imperfectly competitive product markets -- monopoly, monopolistic competition, and oligopoly -- costs the United States economy each year. We refer to this aggregate measure of imperfect competition as the degree of monopoly power in the economy, which is meant to suggest that oligopolies and monopolistically competitive firms have limited degrees of monopoly power, though of course not as much as a pure monopolist.

The seminal study on the dollar value of the impact of imperfect competition in the United States economy was published in 1954, by Arnold Harberger of the University of Chicago.[3] He concluded that the total welfare loss from monopoly power in the manufacturing sector was equivalent to about .1 percent (that is, one one-thousandth) of the total amount of income generated in the national economy each year. Many economists at that time were surprised by that small value, and several criticized the procedures and data that Harberger used. Some of these critics, as well as others who were Harberger's supporters, conducted new studies using different approaches and information to test his results. Many came up with similar estimates of welfare loss but a few later studies found much higher costs -- ranging from four to seven percent of national income. Those studies were themselves then criticized on several points, and their estimates judged to be "almost certainly exaggerated," so the best current estimates are that the true costs lie "somewhere between 0.5 and 2 percent."[4]

Why would these effects be so small? Several reasons make the findings easier to understand. First, many U.S. industries are relatively competitive, especially when competition from foreign firms is considered. Second, many imperfectly competitive firms are subject to government regulation, which is designed to limit their ability to exercise their monopoly power. Finally, as demonstrated in graphs showing the area of deadweight loss for imperfectly competitive firms (such as Figure 11-8) welfare losses are likely to be a relatively small part of the total sales volume for these firms. Suppose, for example, that monopoly power exists in sectors that generate 20% of national income each year, and that the welfare loss for these firms averages 10%. The total welfare loss for the nation each year would then equal .1 times .2, or only 2% of national income.

But recognize that inefficiencies of 1-2% of national income are not trivial -- in dollar terms, the current value is some $57-114 billion. And remember too that monopolies *redistribute* welfare from consumer surplus to producer surplus, as well as imposing deadweight loss and productive inefficiencies. The estimates from Harberger and others don't justify ignoring monopoly power as a public policy issue; they simply suggest a sense of perspective in considering these problems, relative to other economic problems.

Antitrust Legislation

The first major U.S. antitrust law was the Sherman Act of 1890, passed long before economists had developed any careful empirical estimates of the costs of monopoly power to the nation's economy. In fact, rather than reflecting an organized effort by economists to promote such legislation, this law was enacted at a time of great *public* concern over the large trusts that had developed in key industries -- most notably railroads, steel, banking, and oil. Those concerns, and outright fears, were heightened by authors and journalists of the time, including political cartoonists such as Thomas Nast.

The Sherman act made it illegal to "monopolize, or attempt to monopolize, or combine or conspire...to monopolize," or to act "in restraint of trade." But nothing was said in this legislation about specific business practices that were to be considered illegal -- that was left to the courts to decide. And the only practice that the courts consistently held to be illegal was price fixing. The first major decision on price fixing came in 1897, and many later cases were required to establish that this practice was illegal under virtually any circumstances. Some of these legal precedents are even of fairly recent vintage. For example, one of the latest cases involved American Airlines and Braniff International setting prices on fares out of the Dallas-Fort Worth airport in 1982.

Other business practices that can have anticompetitive effects, including mergers and buyouts of competing firms, or of suppliers and distributors, are still judicially reviewed against the rather vague standard of actions that

[3]"Monopoly and Resource Allocation," *American Economic Review*, 44 (May 1954), pp. 77-87.

[4] This assessment, and an excellent survey of this debate and research literature, is provided in F. M. Scherer and David Ross, *Industrial Market Structure and Economic Performance*, 3rd ed. (Boston: Houghton Mifflin, 1990), pp. 661-67.

"unreasonably" reduce competition. That phrase in antitrust policy dates back to a landmark case against the U.S. Steel Company in 1920, in which it was decided that even though this company controlled about 60% of the U.S. manufacturing capacity to produce steel, size alone was not an offense under the law. Instead, the precedent established was to use the "rule of reason" to determine whether or not companies had acted to monopolize their industry and restrain trade. And in many respects that procedure is still operative today. For example, many economists consider a 1982 decision to dismiss a Justice Department case against IBM -- with the finding that the case was entirely without merit -- a direct reconfirmation of the rule of reason.

Additional laws have been passed, however, to made certain kinds of business practices other than price fixing illegal. The Clayton Antitrust Act, passed in 1914, prohibits price discrimination; and the Robinson-Patman Act of 1936 amended that Act to strengthen those prohibitions if the effect of price discrimination is to substantially lessen competition (another vague standard, at least in practical and legal terms), or to create a monopoly. The Celler-Kefauver Amendment to the Clayton Act, passed in 1950, prohibits several additional practices, including: 1) "tying agreements," which require customers to buy other products sold by a producer when they buy one product from that firm; 2) acquisition of competing firms' stock or assests if the effect is to reduce competition; and 3) appointing members of the board of directors from competing firms to the same boards in or out of that industry (a popular practice for a time, known as interlocking directorates). The Federal Trade Commission Act of 1914 makes deceptive business practices illegal, including untruthful or unsubstantiated advertising claims.

This set of antitrust laws and enforcement activities in the United States is quite different from those of most other industrialized nations, putting much more emphasis on, and faith in, the idea of competition between firms selling identical or very similar products. In other nations, large companies are often given more latitude in sharing information about pricing and production plans; and in some countries that cooperation is encouraged and even supported as a part of government planning and coordination programs. Recently, increased foreign competition has led the Department of Justice to show greater flexibility in allowing joint ventures between U.S. firms in the same industry, and even between U.S. and foreign firms. For example, in the early 1990s several joint ventures between firms in the troubled U.S. automobile industry and foreign producers were initiated -- including projects involving Ford and Mazda, and Chrysler and Fiat, Renault, and Mitsubishi.

There are long-standing and intense debates among some economists, and many policy makers, about whether there is currently too little or too much antitrust enforcement to allow U.S. firms to compete effectively in the global marketplace. One part of that debate involves the fact that not all laws and regulations passed in the name of maintaining competition have, in practice, had that desired effect. For example, the Miller-Tydings Resale Price Maintenance Act of 1937, and over 40 similar state laws passed after extensive lobbying efforts by retailers' associations (and especially pharmacists), inhibited the expansion of discount stores and direct price competition by establishing what were known as "fair trade" items. By law, these products could not be sold for less than the manufacturer's suggested retail price. But by and large these laws have now been rescinded, or made ineffective by discount stores exploiting loopholes in the laws, as well as court judgments decreeing all or part of the laws invalid.

Despite those predictable problems with abuse by powerful special interest groups, nearly all American economists agree that the government does have a role to play in maintaining competition, and that antitrust laws are a necessary part of that function. That in itself is testimony to their concern about the adverse effects on productive and allocative efficiency that are associated with all forms of imperfect competition, and in practice especially with oligopoly (since perfect monopolies are so rare, unless they are extensively regulated, and monopolistically competitive firms are small and limited in their power and profitability).

Case Study #17
The Urge to Merge[5]

Mergers are business combinations or takeovers involving two or more firms which, after the merger, act as one, larger firm. Combinations of two or more firms which produce identical or very similar products are known as *HORIZONTAL MERGERS* (one recent example was the merger between US Air and Piedmont Airline). When a firm that produces a good or service is combined with another firm that uses that product as an input in its production activities, that is known as a *VERTICAL MERGER* (for example, if a shoe company buys up a firm that makes the leather or chemicals it uses in making shoes). *CONGLOMORATE MERGERS* are those in which two firms which produce unrelated products are brought together under some common management structure (for example, if a meat packing company merges with a company that makes perfumes).

Mergers have been one of the most important ways in which once-competitive industries have become more concentrated over the past century. Therefore, in this case study we offer a brief history of recent merger activity among large U.S. firms, but do not focus on the details of any specific merger, actual or proposed. The questions we will be asking are: When have the greatest numbers of mergers taken place in the United States, and why? What kinds of merger were taking place in these periods, and why? And what polices at the Justice Department have influenced merger activity in recent years, and affect it today in particular?

Economic historians and specialists in the area of industrial organization often point to four "waves" of merger activity during the past 100 years. The first two periods of extensive merger activity ran from about 1883-1904 and from 1918-1929. In both of these periods the combinations of large corporations were predominantly horizontal mergers. In fact, the first period was the time of "trust building" among American industrial and financial companies which led, as you saw earlier, to the passage of the first key pieces of U.S. anti-trust legislation.

Politicians like President Theodore Roosevelt built their careers on populist campaigns of "trust-busting" in this era, and writers like Frank Norris made theirs with fictional and journalistic pieces like *The Octopus*, which featured big businesses as the inexorable and often oppressive agents of change and progress, crushing many individuals and families in the process.[6] From an economic standpoint, however, what was driving the merger activity of these periods was the rapid development of truly national markets, resulting from technological advances in transportation and communications. Specifically, coast-to-coast railroads and telegraph and telephone lines, along with the settlement of the Western frontier, encouraged the development of larger markets, and of much larger firms to serve those markets.

During the second wave of horizontal mergers, national antitrust legislation was already "on the books," and instead of dozens of firms merging or being bought up to form one large, powerful trust, there were more often cases where two or three firms were merged to form a large firm in a fairly concentrated industry. As George Stigler has described these two periods, the first saw mergers for the purpose of forming monopolies, the second for the formation of oligopolies.[7]

---

[5] Adapted from Stephen Martin, *Industrial Economics: Economic Analysis and Public Policy*, New York: Macmillan, 1988.

[6] Here's a passage from *The Octopus*, to give you a flavor of Norris' outlook:

You are dealing with forces, young man, when you speak of Wheat and Railroads, not with men. There is the Wheat, the supply. It must be carried to feed the People. There is the demand. The Wheat is one force, the Railroad, another, and there is the law that governs them -- supply and demand. Men have only little to do in the whole business. Complications may arise, conditions that bear hard on the individual -- crush him maybe -- but the Wheat will be carried to feed the people as inevitably as it will grow. (Cambridge, Mass.: Riverside Press, 1958, p. 395 -- first published in 1901.)

[7] "Monopoly and Oligopoly by Merger," *American Economic Review*, 40, May 1950, pp. 23-34.

The third wave of extensive merger activity in the United States occurred from the late 1960s through the early 1970s. In this period, almost 80% of the large mergers were conglomerate mergers, in which firms tried to diversify their activities to spread the risk of shifts in industry supply and demand curves, spread the fixed costs of managing their organizations over more component firms, and build up multinational "corporate empires" to enhance profits or managerial egos, or both. The empirical evidence on the profitability of conglomerate mergers is mixed, at best. Many studies suggest that these combinations are less profitable, particularly in terms of returns to stockholders, than other businesses of similar size. Conglomerates also appear to have negligible effects on concentration levels in markets for specific products, which is not surprising since the conglomerate is, effectively, a combination of firms operating in different markets. There is some evidence that conglomerate structures lead to a kind of managerial trade-off, with improved performance in long-term planning and investments (due to the existence of larger and more specialized staffs to study these issues), but poorer performance in monitoring, evaluating, and strengthening current divisions of the conglomerate in the short-run.

The last major period of merger activity in the United States occurred in the mid-1980s. In 1985, for example, 29 corporate acquisitions valued at $1 billion or more took place, the largest being General Electric's $6.3 billion purchase of RCA. Interestingly, many of these mergers arose as the conglomorates built up in the 1960s sold some of their subsidiaries. Many of the divesting conglomerates effectively narrowed their market focus, often by selling some of their units to firms that were already major players in the markets in which the divested units were competing. Proceeds from these divestitures were then frequently used to expand holdings in the markets where the conglomerate believed it was strongest. So, for example, in this period Gulf & Western Industries sold 147 of its divisions, but acquired 10 others.

Increased competition from foreign firms contributed to the pressure on many firms which led to this most recent round of merger activity, but so did changing guidelines and enforcement standards for mergers at the Department of Justice under the Reagan administration.

The Justice Department maintains guidelines on which mergers it will permit under the provisions of current antitrust legislation and regulations, and which mergers it will attempt to block -- through legal prosecution if necessary. It tries to permit those mergers which allow firms to take advantage of economies of scale and lower production costs, or otherwise improve the effective level of competition between producers -- both domestic and international -- in the marketplace. Mergers that reduce the number of key competitors without promoting these benefits to a sufficient degree will, ideally, be prohibited. Unfortunately, it's often not clear what the overall effects of a given merger will be until it is too late to change the decision to allow or forbid the combination. In retrospect, some mergers that are allowed probably shouldn't be, and some that are forestalled probably should be permitted.

The Justice Department issued written guidelines for corporate mergers in 1968, 1982, and 1984. The 1968 standards for horizontal mergers are shown in Table 13-3. These standards closely followed the legal decisions handed down in the major cases tried under the Clayton Act in earlier years and, as shown, varied depending on whether or not the four-firm concentration ratio of sales in an industry was 75% or higher.

The 1968 guidelines also called for challenging mergers of firms with more than 2% market shares in markets and industries where concentration ratios were rising, and provided for exceptions when a merger would enable firms that would otherwise go out of business to survive. Vertical mergers were challenged between firms selling 10% or more of an input product and firms buying six percent or more of that resource, unless the merger erected no significant barriers to entry for other firms that might decide to produce this input. (Other percentage guidelines triggering challenges to vertical mergers were also specified.) Conglomerate mergers could be challenged if they forestalled potential entry into a market, or created unreasonable advertising or reciprocity advantages among units owned by the same conglomerate. Tradeoffs between scale economies and increased market power resulting from mergers were typically resolved in favor of limiting market power, by challenging the mergers in court, if necessary.

Table 13-3
1968 Department of Justice Standards for Challenging Horizontal Mergers

Acquiring Firm's Market Share	Acquired Firm's Market Share
4%	4% or more
10%	2% or more
15%	1% or more

Less Concentrated Industries (4-Firm Concentration Ratio < 75%)

Acquiring Firm's Market Share	Acquired Firm's Market Share
5%	5% or more
10%	4% or more
15%	3% or more
20%	2% or more

These entries show the cutoff points established for federal challenges of horizontal mergers in 1968. Combinations between firms smaller than those listed were not opposed; those between larger firms usually were, unless the mergers were judged necessary to keep the firms in business.

Source: Department of Justice, *Merger Guidelines*, May 30, 1968.

The 1982 standards modified and extended the 1968 standards in several respects. First, much more attention was given to the issue of defining a firm's relevant market by geographical area and cross-product competition. A "5% substitutability rule" was adopted, under which the Department considered all of the firms to which customers would turn if a product's price was raised 5% as being part of the relevant market in defining a firms' competitors. In practice, however, much like the earlier standards, that list of competitors was derived by considering buyers' and sellers' perceptions, design similarities across products, transportation costs, and historical price movements and purchase patterns.

In considering horizontal mergers, the 1982 standards also substitute Herfindahl indexes for the 4-firm concentration ratios used in the 1968 standards. We explained Herfindahl indexes earlier, in Chapter 10, although the Justice Department standards modify these indexes to express the simple percentage terms in ranges from 0 to 10,000, instead of the basic 0-to-1 range we described earlier.[8]

The 1982 guidelines classify industries with a Department of Justice Herfindahl value of 1,000 or less as unconcentrated, those with values between 1,000 and 1,800 as moderately concentrated, and those with values of 1,800 or more as highly concentrated. The guidelines for challenging mergers generally call for contesting a combination when this index rises by 50 or more points in highly concentrated industries, although 50-100 point increases may be accepted if it is found that entry into the industry, firm conduct and performance, and other factors, are not adversely affected. In moderately concentrated industries, increases of 100 points or more are challenged.

The concern over vertical mergers was generally deemphasized in these guidelines, because such mergers do not directly affect concentration ratios in the production or sales of any given product. However, vertical and

---

[8]The conversion to this new scale is easy -- just multiply by 10,000. For example, in a market with 10 equal-sized firms, the measure you saw in Chapter 10 was $10(.1)^2 = .1$. The Justice Department measure will be $.1(10,000)$, or 1,000. Similarly, a perfect monopoly has a Herfindahl index of 1, or in Department of Justice values 1 x 10,000 = 10,000.)

conglomorate mergers may still be challenged if the Justice Department feels that they raise barriers to entry in a market that is already highly concentrated, eliminate potential competitors, or make collusion easier and more likely. Exceptions to the guidelines for all mergers are explicitly allowed in cases of failing firms or improved efficiency (i.e., economies of scale and improved operation), as in the 1968 guidelines. But those exceptions are still seen as rare cases.

The 1984 guidelines are basically modifications of the 1982 guidelines, particularly in clarifying that more than the simple Herfindahl indexes given above will be considered in deciding whether or not to challenge a proposed merger. Nevertheless, the same numerical guidelines are maintained. The major new development in the 1984 guidelines is a greater willingness to consider efficiency gains resulting from mergers, suggesting that some combinations which would otherwise be challenged can be approved on these grounds. These efficiencies may include such factors as "achieving economies of scale, better integration of production facilities, plant specialization, [and] lower transportation costs...." Most generally, mergers are only to be opposed when they are likely to result in a "significant danger to competition."[9]

Under these standards more mergers occurred in the mid-1980s, in large part because the Department of Justice was less likely to challenge companies that wanted to merge through both friendly and hostile takeovers. The new standards represent, in various degrees, the more conservative administration and political climate in Washington during the 1980s; the perceived need to allow U.S. firms to compete more aggressively with foreign firms through mergers and a freer regulatory climate; and finally, a greater willingness to consider the efficiency gains that may be attained through mergers, which other nations have allowed on a larger scale than the United States in recent decades.

In earlier centuries, before technologies associated with increasing returns to scale became so prevalent, competition and efficiency always went hand in hand. Today they still usually do, but only up to a point. Future public policies on mergers and other anti-competitive corporate activities are likely to reflect these increasingly complex relationships, based on the U.S. position as a global producer, consumer, and competitor.

Chapter Summary

1) Oligopolies are industries populated by a relatively small number of very large firms, which are highly interdependent and protected from additional competition with other firms by high barriers to entry. Prices change less often in imperfectly competitive markets than they do in highly competitive situations, and some economists claim that prices are particularly "sticky" in oligopolies.

2) The high level of interdependence in oligopolies makes it impossible to develop a single, representative model of this market structure. Instead, different models must be used to capture the different forms of interdependence which may evolve.

3) Cartels, which are illegal in the United States, occur when a group of competing firms with market power agree to restrict output and set a common price, in order to increase industry-wide profits. Total cooperation and control over production of a product by a cartel is identical to the result for a multi-plant monopolist. However, individual members in cartels always have an economic incentive to cheat on the collusive agreement, by secretly selling more than their alloted quota at a price below the cartel price. This leads to an inherent instability in cartels, and an often-observed pattern of collusion-cheating-collusion, etc.

4) Price-leading firms evolve in some oligopolies, sometimes as representative "barometers" in their industry, and also in cases where one very large firm dominates a number of smaller firms selling identical or very similar products.

[9]Department of Justice, 1984 *Merger Guidelines*, pp. 35-36.

5) If existing firms in an oligopoly can prevent future entry by lowering price and expanding output beyond the short-run profit-maximizing level, it may pay them to do so in order to decrease the residual demand available to potential entrants. This is a rare exception to the MR = MC "golden rule" of profit maximization.

6) Oligopolistic firms tend to develop explicit or implicit "reaction functions," which identify their responses to competitors' changes in price and output levels. An early model of these functions was developed in Augustin Cournot's theory of duopoly, in which equilibrium price and output levels fall between the monopolistic and competitive levels.

7) As a general result, oligopolies do not meet competitive criteria for productive and allocative efficiency, due to high barriers to entry and because these firms face downward-sloping demand curves. They will therefore affect economic welfare adversely, unless those losses are offset by cost savings associated with economies of scale.

8) (Case Study #17) Mergers served as a major means of building up concentration levels in U.S. industries over the past century. Public policies such as antitrust laws have been developed to limit the number of vertical, conglomerate, and particularly horizontal mergers. Changes in these policies and other economic conditions help to explain the timing and nature of the four major "waves" of mergers in U.S. history.

Review and Discussion Questions

1) Which characteristics of oligopolies are likely to promote price rigidity, and which to promote price flexibility?

2) What is the best model of oligopoly among those presented in the chapter? Why do you consider it to be better than the other models?

3) Why is it easier to establish and maintain a cartel in the diamond market than, say, in the automobile industry?

4) Why are the non-dominant firms in the price-leadership model developed in this chapter price takers? How would you show an increase or decrease in the strength of the dominant firm, *ceteris paribus*?

5) Will a limit-entry oligopoly try to operate where *long-run* MR = MC? Explain.

6) In what sense are the reaction functions developed for Cournot duopolies naive?

7) Given identical U-shaped average total cost curves, will oligopolies or monopolies more nearly achieve an optimal degree of productive and allocative efficiency?

8) (Case Study #17) Does the statistical evidence on the effects of monopoly power in the U.S. economy, presented in this chapter, suggest to you that the merger guidelines adopted by the Department of Justice in the 1980s were too severe or too lax? Explain your answer.

Chapter 14
New Topics in the Study of Industrial Organization

In This Chapter..

we extend the production, cost, and market structure models presented in the last seven chapters, examining three approaches featured prominently in recent work by economists studying how firms interact among themselves and with their customers in different competitive settings. The three approaches are known as: 1) the economics of information, 2) game theory, and 3) the theory of contestable markets. Although essentially independent, each of these approaches can be used to extend the more traditional models developed in Chapters 7-13, and are sometimes used together. In fact, along with material covered in some of the following chapters, these approaches are what largely distinguish the microeconomic analysis of the last 30 years from studies of similar issues and problems in earlier decades and centuries. That doesn't make the material in previous chapters incorrect or less important in any practical sense; but the new approaches have raised important new questions and issues to study, and offer additional answers for both old and new questions concerning how firms interact and compete.

The Economics of Information

Information is costly to acquire, update, and store in an organized way, so consumers must decide how much to spend on information that can help them buy products they find most satisfying, at the lowest possible price. It will pay them to spend more time searching for this kind of information for some products than for others; and in many cases, some consumers in a market area will be better informed than others. Because it is often expensive for producers to find out what prices their competitors are charging, and because producers recognize that some consumers do not shop around for the lowest possible price for many kinds of products, we often observe identical products selling for different prices at different stores. This is a major modification to the basic market structure models presented in Chapters 11-13, and other important issues arise when we consider situations where buyers and sellers have different amounts of information about the products they are buying and selling -- i.e., when information is asymmetric.

Information and the Rule of One Product, One Price

The basic market structure models developed to study price, output, and efficincy issues in Chapters 9-13, which as a group form the traditional core of material in economists' study of industrial organization and competition, are generally alike in one key conclusion: They almost always indicate that identical products will be traded at a single price in a given market area. The two exceptions to this rule that were presented in these earlier chapters were price discrimination and, in the model of monopolistic competition, cases where an identical shirt or pair of pants might be sold for two or more different prices if other customer services -- such as free delivery, gift wrapping, or liberal return and guarantee policies -- are different at different stores. But those are rather narrow and limited exceptions: Price discrimination only occurs when firms with some degree of monopoly power sell identical products which consumers can't resell at different prices, so it can be argued that these firms are really selling their products in different markets. And in monopolistic competition, differences in the ancillary goods or services provided suggest that the total bundle of goods and services consumers are buying is different, and would therefore be expected to command different prices.

Neither of these exceptions to the rule of one price are true exceptions, then, and neither explains situations in which two or more stores or firms in the same city sell an identical, resellable product (such as a certain size and brand of soft drink) for different prices. But you probably know of, or could easily find, stores where identical clothing, food, books, gasoline, and auto parts are sold for different prices, with no important differences in ancillary services. That raises an important question: Can economists explain those price differences for identical products without abandoning the key findings of the market structure models presented in earlier chapters?

They can, although it entails some important qualifications concerning the circumstances under which the earlier models will apply to real world pricing patterns. To see how that all works out, first consider Table 14-1, which is based on two studies that collected information on product prices in New Orleans and Boston about 15 years ago. Then, as today, even in stores that offered similar kinds of consumer services, prices for identical products (including the same brands of products, in some cases) varied considerably. Of course some price differences occur when one store puts an item on sale to try to attract more customers while other stores put different products on sale, or don't have a sale at all. But many of the price variations shown in Table 14-1 are more persistent than that, and some are essentially permanent. In short, some stores almost always have lower prices for certain products than other stores -- even other stores that offer identical non-price services to consumers.

Information turns out to be a key reason for those enduring price differences, including information about such general factors as the availability of products and close substitutes, and the likelihood of recent or upcoming price changes at different stores. But most fundamentally, it depends on the information consumers have about the prices charged for a given product at different stores, and the information producers have about the kinds of customers who are most likely to buy their products at higher or lower prices. Therefore, to understand these price differences, we will first examine the effect of information on prices from the perspective of consumers, and then from the perspective of producers.

Information and Consumers

In making their consumption purchases, people face a two-step decision process -- first they decide what they want to buy, then they decide how many resources to devote to the task of *SEARCH*, or looking for lower prices and other product features. Search is a costly activity that always requires time, and often other valuable resources as well.

For example, you can sometimes telephone sellers to get price information on their products, especially if you know exactly what brand and model you want to buy, with what optional features. But for many products, such as cars, you aren't likely to learn a seller's lowest price unless you personally go out to the dealers, to convince them you are a serious buyer who is likely to be swayed by a lower price. You may not even know exactly what product model and options you want, at least for some goods, until you go out and shop around first hand. That means you have to give up time, as well as money for gas and shoeleather, and perhaps car-ratings services or price guides that tell you about dealer costs on different models. Worst of all, you have to meet an unending stream of car salesmen -- people who will claim to be your close friend after knowing you five minutes, but then try to extract as much consumer surplus from you as they can. Fortunately, not all products require that much search for information about product price, quality, and optional features. But that in turn raises the question of why people devote more search time and resources to some purchases than others.

Table 14-1
Price Differences for Selected Products

New Orleans

Product	(1) Number of Sellers	(2) Average Price($)	(3) Dollar Measure of Price Dispersion	(4) Percentage Measure of Price Dispersion
Cameras (expensive)	7	$540.20	$17.68	3.27
Hair Spray	9	2.47	.11	4.47
Drill	9	15.03	.63	4.60
Paint (gallon)	10	8.43	.44	5.19
Hand cream	8	1.60	.09	5.63
Aspirin	9	1.30	.08	5.84
Deodorant	9	1.36	.10	7.01
Contact Lens Solution	8	2.34	.17	7.27
Razor Blades	8	2.46	.18	7.42
Cameras (inexpensive)	10	34.70	2.59	7.48
Black & White TV	14	159.40	12.02	7.54
Washing Machine	6	275.40	23.04	8.36
Mattress	13	97.05	11.74	12.09
Wrench	10	5.58	.72	12.83
Molded Chair	11	16.35	2.58	15.81
Flash Bulbs	9	1.84	.32	17.29
Lettuce	9	.37	.07	18.24
Lemons (dozen)	7	1.06	.22	21.08
Thermometer	9	1.44	.30	21.15
Toaster	7	14.55	3.68	25.40
Batteries	8	.16	.41	26.21
Carob Powder	14	1.77	.61	34.50
Contraceptives	7	1.13	.47	41.38

Boston

Product	Number of Sellers	Average Price($)	Dollar Measure	Percentage Measure
Bicycle	7	144.77	6.34	4.38
Paint (gallon)	22	8.19	.58	7.08
File Cabinet	15	109.45	9.03	8.25
Beer (case)	11	7.47	.65	8.70
Camera	15	329.12	29.78	9.05
Flying Lesson (hour)	9	29.67	4.15	13.99
Outboard Boat Motor	15	602.87	104.89	17.40
Auto Tune-up	15	39.57	7.27	18.37
Dental (teeth cleaning)	13	16.85	3.76	22.31
Car Towing (5 miles)	10	14.04	3.57	25.43
Styling Brush	12	4.33	2.01	46.42
Horoscope Charting	4	30.00	16.83	56.10

The average prices shown in column 2 are for a particular quantity, quality, and, where possible, brand of a product, which was sold at the number of stores indicated in the column 1. Column 3 reports a dollar measure of how much prices for these products varied from store to store (in statistical terms, the standard deviation for the average price shown in column 2). Column 4 measures the price variations in percentage terms, dividing column 3 by column 2. That allows us to compare price variations for products with high and low prices, and serves as the basis for much of the analysis of why some products exhibit more price variation than others.

Sources: For New Orleans prices, John A. Carlson and Donn R. Pescatrice, "Persistent Price Distributions," *Journal of Economics and Business*, Fall 1980, pp. 21-28. For Boston prices, John W. Pratt, David A. Wise and Richard Zeckhauser, "Price Differences in Almost Competitive Markets," *Quarterly Journal of Economics*, May 1979, pp.189-211.

In a pathbreaking article published in 1961, George Stigler identified four factors which influence the average amount of search consumers choose to expend in making a purchase:

1) The share of the consumer's budget used to purchase a good or service. The greater the share of the budget, the greater the potential savings from search will be, and hence the greater the amount of search.

2) The number of past purchases of the product, both for an individual consumer and all consumers of the good or service. As long as past prices are useful indicators of present pricing patterns in a market, the larger the fraction of experienced buyers in the market is, the greater the effective amount of past search that is represented in the market, and the more sellers have to price their goods and services under the assumption that buyers will know what the prices are that they and other sellers offer.

3) The number of past sellers of the product that are present in the market. Once again, as long as a seller's past prices are useful indicators of present prices, the greater the fraction of repeat sellers in the market, and the greater the amount of accumulated search consumers have.

4) The geographical size of a market. The larger the geographical area, the higher the cost of the search. And, of course, when search is more costly, people will engage in less of it, *ceteris paribus*.[1]

These same factors affect the amount of price variation that will endure in a market -- such as the variations shown earlier, in Table 14-1 -- because products that consumers compare carefully on the basis of price will tend to sell with only small price dispersions. In other words, if it doesn't pay a relatively large number of consumers to shop around and compare prices for a product, we would expect to find it sold for a wider range of prices. But if a product is one that most consumers buy carefully, after extensive search, we expect price differences to be smaller, other things being equal.

More specifically, considering the first of Stigler's four propositions, a key, testable prediction of his theory of information and search is that there will normally be less variation in prices of products that consumers spend a lot of their income on than for products that account for a smaller share of their budgets. For example, automobliles are much more expensive than washing machines, so Stigler would predict less variance in prices for automobiles than in prices for washing machines, as long as the other factors he notes are not substantially different for these two products. Is that sort of prediction confirmed or rejected by the data shown in Table 14-1?

Using the New Orleans prices for the products which consumers typically purchase in single units (drills, TVs, washing machines, mattresses, wrenches, molded chairs, thermometers, toasters, and cameras), in order to preserve a better estimate of the products' average prices, Carlson and Pescatrice calculated a statistical measure of the relationship between average price and price dispersion, or variance. They found a positive, relatively

---

[1]"The Economics of Information," *Journal of Political Economy*, June 1961, pp. 213-225.

strong,[2] and statistically significant correlation between these measures, which supports Stigler's prediction and theory. A clear example of this support is the case of expensive and inexpensive cameras where, in percentage terms, the variance in prices for inexpensive cameras is more than twice as great as the variance in prices for the more expensive cameras.

Less formally (since statistical tests are not used to evaluate this conclusion), the higher level of price dispersion in the Boston area, where a larger number of stores were surveyed from a larger market area, is also consistent with Stigler's theory. So too was the finding by the authors of that study that products sold in stores that rarely engage in direct price advertising have greater price dispersions -- for example, carob powder is typically sold in health food stores. In such cases, higher search costs due to the absence of price advertising apparently contribute to greater price variance.

But in both the New Orleans and Boston data shown in Table 14-1, there are examples that seem to conflict with Stigler's theory. For example, toasters were ten times as expensive as thermometers in the New Orleans data, but the prices for toasters varied more. In Boston, outboard boat motors were much more expensive than bicycles, but there was more variance in the prices for the motors. There is no compelling evidence to suggest that the toasters and boat motors represent a significantly smaller part of consumers' budgets than the thermometers and bicycles, respectively, so Stigler's first proposition would suggest that the higher priced items would not exhibit greater price dispersion. Why did they, and does that invalidate at least part of Stigler's theory?

Carlson and Pescatrice tried to explain some of these cases by focusing on differences across buyers and sellers, not just the average level of search costs across products. Some of the products they studied were, in fact, especially chosen to illustrate those differences.

We will discuss the differences among sellers in the following section. Here, the relevant question is how consumers of various products differ in ways that can lead to a wider distribution of prices for certain products.

To answer that, first consider the data in Table 14-1 on batteries, thermometers, and the flashbulbs that were required to take indoor pictures with most cameras and film when these studies were conducted. Some consumers of these products (and others products like them) are likely to want the products urgently, and not spend a lot of time searching for lower prices. For example, think of a tourist staying in New Orleans for the first time on a short vacation, whose camera batteries run down or who suddenly comes down with a low-grade fever. She isn't likely to spend much time looking around for low prices on batteries or a thermometer, or for flashbulbs either if she runs out of them.

Saving a little money by searching for lower prices for these products is usually worth less to tourists than to residents, who will purchase the same products many times in this particular market area. So the residents will often choose to search more than tourists, and end up buying these products at different stores than the tourists do. But even a resident who is mildly ill, or about to host a surprise party, or escorting out-of-town guests through the French Quarter in New Orleans will want a thermometer, camera batteries, or flashbulbs more urgently than residents who are not. Under those conditions, therefore, they may well choose to search less than they normally do, and less than most other residents purchasing the same products on the same day.

Because search costs for such products are effectively higher for some consumers than others, Carlson and Pescatrice expected to find more variance in those prices than for products such as hair spray, hand cream, deodorant, and razor blades which, they argued, were "purchased repeatedly [and] without great urgency most of the time." That was, in fact, the general pattern of price dispersions they found. The price variations for several of the products which some consumers would buy with a sense of urgency or duress had several times the amount of variance as the more routine, repeat-purchase group of goods.

Carlson and Pescatrice expected to find many products with higher average prices than thermometers selling for a wider range of prices. After they did, as a refinement and extension of Stigler's propositions, they asked: If it is true that prices for washing machines vary more than prices for automobiles, "is it because [the] cost of searching for washing machines relative to purchase prices is so much higher than for automobiles or is it because of the greater heterogeneity of those relative search costs for washing machines?" Clearly if those relative search costs differ among consumers for some kinds of products, there will be greater variance in the time and effort consumers devote to search, and therefore a wider dispersion of prices for those products. That is one basic

---

[2]The rank-order correlation measure was .66 on a 0-1 scale, where 1 is the highest possible degree of correlation.

extension of Stigler's seminal article on the economics of information; and there have been other, more complex, developments by other writers.

For example, if a buyer knows the approximate distribution of prices for some product, and faces a constant cost of collecting an additional price in his or her search process, it has been shown that the combined costs of purchasing the product and searching for lower prices can be minimized by setting a *RESERVATION PRICE*, and then searching until a price that low, or lower, is found.[3] A reservation price is defined as the maximum price a consumer is willing to pay for an additional unit of a product; and in the context of this kind of search strategy, that is also the price at which the expected marginal benefit of additional search is equal to its expected marginal cost. The bottom line is that consumers engaged in a price search will purchase a product at a price that is equal to or less than their reservation price, but continue to search when a they face a seller who charges a price that is above their reservation price.

To tie that back to Stigler's original four propositions, note that consumers who have purchased a certain kind of product in the past -- even in another market area -- have some information on price distributions for the product, which will usually make it easier for them to set a realistic reservation price. The same thing is true if sellers advertise price information extensively -- consumers begin their search with more information, or at least can get that information at a low cost. But in purchasing an expensive new product that is not widely advertised, or not sold in a competitive market where products and prices are at least very similar, search costs are likely to be high. In part, they are high because consumers must try to determine sensible reservation prices for the new good or service. (Think of the search costs many consumers paid in deciding which brand and model of a personal computer to buy in the early 1980s, when most consumers of these products were purchasing their first PC.)

Information and Producers

Now consider the preceding discussion on information and search costs from the perspective of a producer rather than a consumer, and try to figure out how to make some money from it. As a seller of some product, you know that some consumers have more information than others, that some engage in more price search than others, and that this means you can sell some of your products at higher or lower prices than your competitors will charge for identical items. You should also realize that the opportunity cost of an hour of search time is normally higher for high-income consumers than for low-income consumers, because they have to give up work or leisure time to engage in search. There are profit opportunities in this knowledge, and the shrewd businessowner will take advantage of that to earn higher profits or just stay in business, depending on how competitive his or her marketplace is.

What soon occurs to business owners is that if their store is situated where many customers want products urgently, or do not engage in extensive price search for other reasons, it will pay to charge higher prices. For example, a pharmacy located in a large hotel serving out-of-town business travelers, or a high fashion art gallery located in a popular tourist or resort area such as Sausalito or Hilton Head Island, will probably charge more for some items than stores selling the same products in a staid and stable suburb of Lincoln, Nebraska.

In effect, heterogeneity among consumers leads to heterogeneity among producers. Stores will specialize to some degree, especially in large cities, by serving either the penny-pinching, comparison-shopper group which searches out low-price bargains, or in serving the "urgent-wants" group of customers who don't have the interest in, or time for, extensive price search.

This tendency for stores to "segment" the market even for identical products, depending on the kind of customers they expect to serve, is reinforced by cost differences facing the sellers. For example, it's easy to see why clothing stores along the exclusive, high rent, shopping area in Chicago known as "the Miracle Mile" will often have to charge higher prices for a particular item than a store in Fargo, North Dakota, which happens to carry the same product. To stay in business, the Chicago store must cover its higher operating costs. The only real question they face is whether enough Miracle-Mile shoppers want these products from stores in this fashionable location to make it profitable to carry them. And the ultimate business consequences of these purchasing decisions by consumers are that some products are only sold in places like the Miracle Mile; other

---

[3]See M. H. DeGroot, *Optimal Statistical Decisions*, New York: McGraw-Hill, 1970.

389

products aren't sold there at all; and some are sold both there and in more commonplace settings, but usually not for the same price.

Information and Shopping for Credit

From May 1984 to May 1985, the Federal Reserve System prepared lists of annual percentage rates of interest (APRs) charged by local banks, savings institutions, credit unions, finance companies, and mortgage bankers in three cities: Akron, Ohio; Rochester, New York; and Sacramento, California. Rates for first and second-mortgage loans, new-car loans and personal loans were collected monthly and published in area newspapers. Results were also distributed to other local media, libraries, community organizations, and selected government agencies. In all three regions during the project period there were no binding price ceilings on these types of loans, a large number of firms were competing for this loan business, and the socioeconomic characteristics of the communities were judged to be similar and broadly representative of most U.S. communities.[4]

Telephone surveys were conducted in each city to collect information on credit use and shopping patterns for the 12 months preceding the distribution of this information, and again at the end of the project, to determine any changes in behavior resulting from the regular publication of this information. Findings from the test cities were also compared to nationwide surveys of other consumers.

In brief, the conclusions of the study were that increasing the availability of this information increased competition in two of the three markets, as measured by lower interest rates and a narrower dispersion of rates for first mortgages, and a narrower dispersion (but not average level) of rates on new-car loans. Personal loans were apparently not affected by the program, which is not particularly surprising since first mortgages and new-car loans typically account for a much larger portion of an average consumer's budget.

Interestingly, the researchers were also able to determine that while the availability of this information did not affect the likelihood that a given consumer would shop around for credit, it appeared to have improved the efficiency of those who did.

Whether such information collection and dissemination programs are themselves cost effective is not clear based solely on these results. For one thing, consumers and producers might behave differently if they knew the rate reports were permanent in their market area, rather than a one-year demonstration project. But what is clearly suggested is that the benefits of such programs are likely to be greater for some kinds of loans than others, and perhaps in some cities more than others, depending on the degree of competition in these markets and perhaps even the economic and demographic characteristics of the consumers who live there.

Information and search costs also help to explain why national franchise "chains" will develop for some products, such as hotels and fast food, where small, local firms selling the same goods and services can enter the market at reasonably comparable cost levels in all respects except their regional or national reputation. For example, there may be an independent drive-in that local consumers judge to be far superior to the national hamburger chains, or an independent hotel in a popular vacation city that regular visitors to the city prefer to national hotel chains such as Holiday Inn or Howard Johnson's. But many first- or second-time visitors to a city will not know about these local businesses, while they do know that they can get reliable quality in a known price range by taking their business to the franchise operations of the regional or national chains. In doing this they give up the chance to find something especially good and different, but also avoid (or at least greatly reduce) the chance of being stuck with something especially bad or overpriced.

Finally, from the perspective of producers, the level of competition in an industry and market area is, like operating costs, another constraint firms must consider in setting their prices. That is, of course, exactly what you saw in Chapters 9-13. But competition affects not only the level of average prices, it also acts on the degree of variance around those averages. Referring to Table 14-1 one last time, Carlson and Pescatrice found that prices

---

[4]The report was published by the Board of Governors of the Federal Reserve System in Washington, D.C., in March 1987, and is titled *Annual Percentage Rate Demonstration Project.*

for basic food items, such as lettuce and lemons, exhibited virtually no variance among stores in the highly centralized French Market area of New Orleans. In that locale, many sellers competed in stalls that were literally operating side-by-side, so competition was keen and search costs were extremely low. There were, however, much wider differences in prices for the same products when observations from suburban groceries, which are separated more both geographically and demographically (in terms of types of customers served), were added to the data base.

Remember that factors other than limited information can explain why prices for identical products vary, including tie-ins with other services provided to buyers by different sellers, and different supply and demand levels in different market areas. But within most markets information costs help to refine and extend the picture of market structures and competition presented in Chapters 9-13. That complicates and qualifies the findings from those basic models to some extent; but in studying some questions the costs of doing that are offset by the greater degree of detail and precision that is obtained when the problem of limited information is explicitly recognized.

Asymmetric Information

In this section we consider a special kind of information problem that is particularly important in a somewhat narrower range of market settings than the very general issues presented above. When this kind of information problem does occur, however, the effects on price, output, and employment levels can be substantial.

The issue of *ASYMMETRIC INFORMATION* arises when the amount of information different consumers and/or producers have about a particular product or market is unequal, in many cases because the costs of obtaining that information are different for different parties. Note that this doesn't assume that any producer or consumer is perfectly informed -- only that some are better informed than others.

There are many important and regularly occuring "real world" examples of assymetric information. For instance, business owners and managers often know better than their labor force what the current profitability of the enterprise is, and what its business prospects are over the next few years. On the other hand, production workers often know how diligently they are working far better than their supervisors and the business managers, and know which particular workers are doing a better job than others. The managers might get that information by monitoring workers carefully, but that can be an expensive proposition in its own right. All of these information issues in the labor market setting can affect employment levels, the terms of employment, compensation policies, and contract provisions between firms and unions if there is a collective bargaining agreement in force. These examples are considered in greater detail as a part of our discussion of labor markets, in Chapters 15 and 16.

Here, to see how asymmetric information can affect the workings of a product market, we will discuss an example reported by Kenneth Hendricks and Robert H. Porter, dealing with federal auctions of offshore oil leases.[5] The auctions they studied were for plots of land off the Louisiana and Texas coastlines conducted between 1954 and 1969, with prices adjusted to correct for the effects of inflation during these years. The auctions were conducted using sealed bids -- at a stated time all bids received by the government were opened, and drilling rights awarded to the highest bidder.

Hendricks and Porter compared the results of auctions of plots that were located next to tracts leased out in previous auctions and where oil had been discovered, called "drainage sales," to those where no adjacent tracts had been leased in earlier auctions and only seismic test data were available, known as "wildcat sales". They expected to find that firms which had drilled on tracts adjacent to the drainage plots had better information about the likelihood of discovering oil than the other bidders. (Before you read on, think for a minute about how you might try to prove or refute that prediction. What data would you try to collect and report?)

[5]"An Empirical Study of an Auction with Asymmetric Information," *American Economic Review*, December 1988, pp. 865-883.

Hendricks and Porter found that the percentage of drainage tracts drilled and the fraction of these tracts on which producers were successful in discovering oil and natural gas were much higher than the corresponding figures for wildcat tracts. Moreover, the average winning bid and level of net profits was higher on the drainage leases. These data are shown in Table 14-2.

Table 14-2
Bidding and Profit Statistics for Oil Leases on Wildcat and Drainage Tracts

	Wildcat	Drainage
Number of Tracts	1056	144
Number of Tracts Drilled	748	124
Number of Productive Tracts	385	86
Average Winning Bid ($)	2.67	5.76
(s.d. of wining bids) ($)	.18	1.07
Average Net Profits ($)	1.22	4.63
(s.d. of average net profits) ($)	.50	1.59
Average Tract Value ($)	5.27	13.51
(s.d. of average tract value) ($)	.64	2.84
Average Number of Bidders	3.46	2.73

s.d. = standard deviation; dollar values are in millions.

Wildcat tracts are not located next to any site where drilling has already discovered oil and gas; drainage tracts are. The additional information available on drainage tracts improves the ability to predict whether new discoveries will be found, and if so in what quantities. However, firms that have drilled on tracts that are adjacent to a drainage tract are likely to have more information on its value than other firms. This affects the bidding pattern in the federal auctions of these drilling rights, and the profits that firms earn from exploration and drilling.

Source: Hendricks and Porter, p. 866.

The data on improved discovery rates on the drainage tracts do not, per se, demonstrate that there was asymmetric information across the bidding firms. Public records on discoveries, estimates of "proven reserves" and the amount of production from existing wells may allow all firms to make better estimates of the potential for finding oil on drainage tracts. But Hendricks and Potter also found that

the average value of drainage tracts was more than twice the average value of wildcat tracts. Yet there was less competition, and profit was roughly four times higher on drainage tracts than on wildcat tracts. ...The government captured 77 percent of the value of the wildcat tracts [through the lease auctions], but only 66 percent of the value of the drainage tracts. Thus, even though drainage tracts were lower risk investments and yielded a significantly higher rate of return, firms were less likely to participate in these auctions. What can explain these facts? (pp.865-866)

Firms that have been drilling on a neighboring tract may develop better information on a drainage tract than other firms, for example by taking core samples while drilling. On wildcat tracts this isn't true, and information will be symmetric (i.e., equal among bidders) if we assume that the competing firms are equally proficient in using seismic surveys.

Therefore, neighboring firms may have a considerable advantage in bidding against non-neighboring firms on drainage tracts. In fact, if the neighboring firms bid what they think a drainage tract is worth, less only a normal rate of profit, competing firms will only win the auctions if they are overly optimistic about the field's potential value, and so on average they will incur losses on such "winning" bids. (Economists who study this phenomenon in auctions describe it as "the *WINNER'S CURSE.*")

This suggests that non-neighboring firms are likely to be especially cautious in their bids for such tracts, given their relative disadvantage in acquiring information. That caution, together with collusion and other imperfectly competitive practices which you studied in Chapters 11-13, can make it possible for the neighboring firms to obtain the rights for many of these drainage tracts on particularly profitable terms.

Additional data from the bidding and profitability records on these tracts support that hypothesis. The number of non-neighbor bids on the drainage tracts was more than twice as great as the number of bids from neighboring firms, but the neighboring firms won well over half of these auctions in which they bid at all. That is clear evidence of cautious bidding by the non-neighboring firms. And when neighboring firms didn't bid on a drainage tract, the non-neighboring firms that "won" these auctions wound up with, on average, significant losses on these plots -- a clear winner's curse situation. When neighboring firms bid for drainage tracts but lost the auction, the winning non-neighboring firms did earn positive profits. But their overall record on the drainage tracts was approximately zero profits. There are, apparently, strong information advantages in being a neighboring firm.

There was also some evidence of collusion and cooperation reported in this study. In particular, two-thirds of the drainage-field bids in this data set were cases for which two or more firms neighbored the tracts being auctioned. With active competition between the multiple neighboring firms in these auctions, most of the excess profits from such tracts would have been bid away by the neighboring firms which had reasonably equal information. Instead, on average, the profits on these tracts were as high as the overall average on all drainage tracts. It appears that the multiple neighbors may have formed bidding consortiums on these plots (which are legal in this market), or cooperated in more sinister ways. In the event, only 17 of the 74 multiple-neighbor tracts received bids from more than one neighboring firm.

This serves very nicely as a conclusion to the section on the economics of information, because it demonstrates the importance of information, and combines it with the kind of behavior predicted by the basic models of market structures presented earlier, such as cartel models. That shows that the traditional policy issues of anti-trust and competition are still with us, but in what has been labeled "the information age" we now have to recognize that firms compete (and sometimes collude) on the basis of information as well as price and output levels. And as you saw in earlier sections of this chapter, information also affects our behavior as consumers, and thereby a wide range of other public policy issues.

Game Theory

Game theory is a system of modeling behavior by two or more 'players' in situations where each player's gains or losses depend on the actions of the other players in the game, as well as their own. These techniques have been used to analyze such diverse activities as the strategies used by chess players, political candidates, opposing armies, competing and/or cooperating firms, and firms negotiating with individual workers or unions about an employment contract.

General Features of Games and Strategic Behavior: Interdependence Revisited

Several classic models of oligopoly theory were presented in Chapter 13; but it was also pointed out there that, because firms in this kind of market structure must consider the actions and reactions of competing firms, there are an endless number of ways firms might interact in these strategic settings. Given more information about the nature of the particular markets facing these firms, however, and their positions relative to their competitors, it is still often possible to predict how firms in that particular setting are most likely to act. To do just that, over the last 40 years mathematicians, economists, and other social scientists have explored many different features of such strategic interaction using *GAME THEORY.*

There are three common features in most of the game theory models used in economics:

1) Players are able to make "moves" in the game by using some or all of the resources they control to implement one or more strategies.

2) Players try to achieve some objective, which is typically stated as a constrained maximization or minimization problem (e.g., maximizing profits or utility subject to some cost or budget constraint). And

3) Players move toward some equilibrium position, or one possible equilibrium position among two or more possible equilibria, by evaluating the expected payoffs of the different strategies they can pursue.

When players can cooperate to increase gains or decrease losses for all players in the game we say that they are in a *POSITIVE-SUM GAME* -- just as buyers and sellers can both gain through voluntary exchange, as you saw in Chapter 1. When one player's gains are exactly offset by another player's losses, as in poker or any of the house vs. player games in Las Vegas and Atlantic City casinos, these are zero-sum games. *NEGATIVE-SUM GAMES* make all players worse off or hurt losing players more than other players gain, as in the deadweight loss examples you have seen throughout this book, including most tariffs, price controls, and models of imperfect competition. We will explore the common features of game theory models, and several other features that vary across different types of games, by reviewing some of the most widely-used models that have been developed in recent years.

The Prisoner's Dilemma

The prisoner's dilemma is one of the oldest and most basic examples of game theory. It was originally developed and applied in areas outside of economics (including political science and criminology), but quickly adapted by economists to explore such issues as the breakdown of cartels and other cases in which competitors fail to maximize their combined profits.

The scenario for the prisoner's dilemma always goes something like this: Two suspects are picked up on suspicion of burglary or a similar crime, but there is not enough evidence to convict either suspect of this felony unless one suspect agrees to testify against the other. If neither suspect agrees to testify they will both be convicted of a minor offense, say loitering, and serve a one-month sentence. If they both confess, they will each receive a two-year sentence. But if one confesses and the other does not, the police agree to let the one who testifies go free, and the suspect who is convicted will get a four-year term. In other words, the police and prosecutor's office offer incentives for both suspects to confess, and even stronger incentives to make sure that at least one confesses. They interrogate the two suspects in separate rooms, and present their "deal" as it is described above. What will happen?

The prisoner's dilemma model shows that there are strong forces at work in this setting that lead to the outcome in which both suspects confess and go to jail for two years, even though they could both be free in just a month if they cooperated and refused to confess. How can that happen? Look at Table 14-3, which identifies the choices each suspect can make, and all of the possible combinations of those choices (both confess, neither confesses, or one confesses and one doesn't). This table is also called a *PAYOFF MATRIX*, because the outcomes of the choices made by the players are also shown (in terms of the jail sentences each player will receive depending on who confesses and who doesn't).

Suspect #1 is shown playing the columns of this matrix, and suspect #2 plays the rows. If we assume that the suspects haven't gone through this routine many times before, don't entirely trust each other, and that neither is in a position to intimidate the other through threats ("rat on me and my family will get your family"), each player in this game has a *DOMINANT STRATEGY*. That simply means that they are better off making one particular choice, regardless of what the other player does. For example, player # 1 sees that if #2 confesses and she doesn't, she will spend four years in jail instead of the two years she could get by also confessing. In short, if she expects player #2 to confess, so should she. On the other hand, if she thinks player #2 won't confess, she can go free by confessing, or spend a month in jail if she doesn't confess. Either way, she serves less time by confessing.

Table 14-3
The Prisoner's Dilemma

Suspect #1

		Confess	Don't Confess
		#1, 2 Years	#1, 4 Years
	Confess	#2, 2 Years	#2, Go Free
Suspect #2			
		#1, Go Free	#1, 1 Month
	Don't Confess	#2, 4 Years	#2, 1 Month

In this game, suspect #1 decides whether to confess or not, which determines whether the game ends in either the left or right column. Suspect #2 faces a similar choice, and determines whether the final "payoff" for the players will be in the top or bottom row. Given the possible combinations of jail terms shown here each player sees that, no matter what choice the other player makes, their own sentence will be minimized by confessing. But when both confess the game ends in the top-left cell of this matrix, and both players receive two-year sentences. By cooperating and not confessing, they could have served only one month.

But player #1 faces exactly the same choices, and he will be better off by confessing, too, no matter what he expects player #1 to do. That's the dilemma -- both players see the other player's options, and are still led to a result that neither likes as well as what they could get by cooperating and trusting each other. Watch for this the next time you see an interrogation scene in your favorite police show.

To see how the prisoner's dilemma game can be applied to a more obviously economic setting, consider two pricing strategies for the only two pizza restaurants in a small western town that is 50 miles away from any other pizza joints. In that setting these two firms have some market power, but their profits also depend on their own relative prices, as shown in Table 14-4. There we assume that if both firms charge an average price of $9 for a pizza, their monthly profits will both be $1,000. If they both charge $12, profits for both firms will increase to $1,500. But if one firm charges $12 while the other charges $9, more customers will go to the pizzeria selling the less expensive pizza, its profits will rise to $2,500, and the firm charging $12 will suffer losses of $1,000.

This is very much like the cartel model presented in Chapter 13, because the two firms could collude to raise prices and profits, but each firm also faces an incentive to cheat on the collusion and lower its own price. And in fact, just considering the current payoff matrix shown here, no matter what one firm thinks the other firm is going to charge it sees that it will earn higher profits by charging $9. Since both firms face the same payoffs and behave the same way, they forego the chance to raise their prices and profits together. So in this case, once again, consumers find that even competition between two firms is better than no competition at all.

Table 14-4
Pizzerias and the Prisoner's Dilemma

		Veno's	
		<u>Charge $9</u>	<u>Charge $12</u>
	<u>Charge $9</u>	Veno's, +1,000 Mario's, +1,000	Veno's, -$1,000 Mario's, +2,500
Mario's			
	<u>Charge $12</u>	Veno's, +2,500 Mario's, -1,000	Veno's +$1,500 Mario's, -$1,500

If Veno assumes that Mario will charge $9 for pizzas, Veno will earn more by charging $9 rather than $12. If he assumes that Mario is going to charge $12, once again Veno's profits will be higher by charging $9. So Veno charges $9 no matter what Mario charges, and *vice versa*.

Recognize, however, that this is an extremely simplified model in that we have assumed away a whole range of intermediate decisions (such as letting firms charge prices other than $9 or $12), or letting the firm's learn from their experience in playing this game over and over again for a period of months or years.[6] We will consider several more realistic (and therefore more complex) examples below, and find that this sometimes leads to very different results, in terms of firms' behavior. But in broader terms -- especially in seeing how game theory models work, and what they try to establish -- the important thing for you to see here is that even this basic model illustrates both the cooperation vs. competition dilemma that faces many firms in imperfectly competitive market structures, and the process firms use to find an equilibrium strategy. In fact, what we have generated in this model is known as a *NASH EQUILIBRIUM*, which means that each player's final choice in this game (charging $9) is optimal given the other player's strategy.[7]

Repeated Games

In most market settings, including real world cases of the pizzeria pricing problem presented above, the players in a strategic setting don't make "once-and-forever" decisions about pricing and other competitive policies. Instead, they are likely to compete again next week, next month, and next year, facing at least some of the same competitors they faced today. That in itself opens up new incentives to alter their strategies and behaviors, and new avenues to make those changes. For example, even if it is illegal for firms to directly talk with each other to set prices or exclusive territories in order to to increase and cooperatively share their group profits, over time the firms may learn enough about how their competitors react to strategies of other firms to establish higher prices and divide up markets through tacit collusion. This is an example of what economists call a *REPEATED GAME*, meaning that payoff schedules for more than one period must be calculated and considered before firms or other players can decide how to maximize their total, long-term gains.

For example, if firms in a repeated game are willing to signal their willingness to cooperate with other firms (say by raising their own prices, but only maintaining those prices if other firms also restrict output and raise their prices), the prisoner's dilemma can be resolved, at least for a time. This is analogous to saying that the two burglars in the original version of the prisoner's dilemma aren't newcomers to the police interrogation and

---

[6]You can see a fairly simple version of this model that does permit firms to charge different prices in Morton R. Davis' *Game Theory: A Nontechnical Introduction*, rev. ed., (New York: Basic Books, 1983), pp. 84-86.
[7]This concept is named for the mathematician John Nash, who developed it in a game theory context in 1951.

plea-bargaining game, but rather seasoned criminals who may even expect to be caught again in the future. In that case, they may have learned how to minimize their time in jail by developing a sense of "honor among thieves." Their cooperation may, however, still be based on self-interest rather than any sense of altruism, since they know that if they confess this time the other player may retaliate by confessing in future rounds, or by violent means. Moreover, if a criminal gets a reputation for confessing, he will find it difficult to get new partners, and discover that his partners always confess if they are caught, because he now has a reputation for confessing himself.

Experimental Evidence on the Prisoner's Dilemma in a Repeated Game

The following experiment/game was conducted at Princeton University in 1963 by James Greismer and Martin Shubik, and is described in Davis' *Game Theory* (pp. 130-133):

Two students simultaneously pick a number between 1 and 10. The student who picks the higher number receives nothing; the student who picks the lower number is paid that number of coins, dollars, or whatever unit is being used. If both players pick the same number, a coin is tossed to determine the winner. Payments are made by the experimenter, not the player who loses the bid. Each player is told what the other player bids in each round, after the payouts are made. Players are separated and not allowed to communicate in any other way throughout the game. Some pairs of players are told in advance how many rounds the game will run; others aren't.

The results of this game were very much like the pizzeria example of the prisoner's dilemma presented earlier, in Table 14-4. Instead of cooperating by always bidding 10, which maximizes the total payout to the players and gives them both a 50% chance of winning 10 units each round, almost all of the players competed by substantially lowering their bids. Such competitive strategies "won" most games, but the payouts were very small. A few pairs of players did find ways to cooperate -- typically by alternating bids of 9 and 10 units -- but interviews after the game revealed that this pattern was often interpreted by the other player as an attempt to lull them into a false sense of security.

There was not evidence of an "end-game effect" among players who were told how many rounds they would play. Once players adopted a competitive or cooperative strategy and had some success with it, they usually continued it even on what some of them knew was the last round. Cooperating players could often have gained more by lowering their bid to compete on the last round, but the payoffs were apparently too low (never more than $1 a round in this experiment) to lead them to reconsider and renege on the implicit agreements established in earlier rounds.

How would these results be affected if players were allowed to sit next to each other, or talk over the telephone, as they prepared their bids? Lower transaction costs, including the costs of monitoring the other player's bids and delivering threats of reprisals if cooperation is not maintained, should result in higher average payouts to the players. Face-to-face conferences might be even more effective than telephone conversations, particularly in eliminating reneging bids when players know they are in the last round of the game.

Computer simulations have shown that such *"TIT-FOR-TAT" STRATEGIES* are one of the most effective ways to deal with the prisoner's dilemma, given a repeated-game format. To play this kind of strategy you simply punish (compete with) those who didn't cooperate with you in the previous round, and reward (cooperate with) those who did. But of course that also depends on the repeated game running for at least two or more periods into the future, because even a repeated game can have different results in its last period, or last few periods. For example, if one of the two burglars arrested has a terminal disease and doesn't expect to live more than a month, he or she may well try to get free now even if it means ratting on the other burglar. Or if a pizzeria is to be sold to new owners next week, or go out of business entirely, it may well pay the current owners to try to capture whatever short-run profits they can by cheating on a previous arrangement with competing firms to raise prices. And as you saw in Chapter 13, the stability of any collusive agreement can be affected by the number of sellers and substitute products in the market, and other market conditions such as changes in demand for an industry's product.

Sequential Games

In the games we have considered to this point, players made their moves simultaneously. But that's not always the case in sports, business, or games of chance. Often a "first mover" has a significant advantage, as in chess or a company that gets its brand of a hot new product to the market before anyone else. In other situations it is an advantage to move last, after you have seen your competitors' "cards" or "moves." Either way, if the order of play matters this can often complicate things in an industry, and in game theory models of that industry's market. In particular, we still need a payoff matrix to identify the choices players in a game can make, but we also need a way to trace out the sequence of decisions (or sometimes of more than one possible sequence). A fairly simple version of a *SEQUENTIAL GAME* is shown in Table 14-5, where the payoff matrix and the *EXTENSIVE FORM* of the game is presented. The extensive form is just a complete representation of all of the possible moves a player or players in a game might make -- in Table 14-5, this is shown with a "tree diagram."

A scenario that might lie behind the payoff matrix and extensive form shown in Table 14-5 can help you see some of the nuances of this model. Suppose that in this market area Spuds is the high-volume producer of a regular beer; and Fido is a smaller, older brewery, with a local reputation for high quality but charging somewhat higher prices. The breweries for both companies have enough excess plant capacity to introduce one new Light or Dark label of beer, but not both. The payoff matrix shows that it is better to produce the same kind of new beer that the other brewery does -- in other words, the top left and bottom right cells of the matrix are both Nash equilibria. But it will be better for Spuds if that is the Light beer (which will undoubtedly have less taste and probably sell for a lower price than the Dark beer), and better for Fido if Dark beer is made. The outcome will therefore depend on which firm can get the new beer produced and to market first. If that turns out to be Fido, it produces the Dark beer and maximizes its profits.

To keep things simple, we will assume that Spuds will produce Dark beer too once it discovers that Fido has the first-mover advantage. That means it doesn't view itself as powerful enough to threaten and punish Fido by claiming that it will produce Light even if Fido produces Dark, as a variant of the predatory pricing schemes discussed in Chapter 11. (In this case that wouldn't work anyway, since Fido still makes profits producing Dark beer if Spuds makes Light. Both firms would remain profitable -- just less profitable than they could both be.) Nor will we allow the possibility of a side payment of, say, $3,000 a week, made by Spuds to Fido if Fido produces Light instead of Dark. Such payments would leave both Spuds and Fido with $5,000 in weekly profits -- better than they could do producing Dark. But these payments are illegal under U.S. antitrust legislation, and the current presidents of U.S. beer companies are often too irascible to cooperate with each other anyway.[8]

In many games it doesn't matter whether one player goes first or last. For example, in matching coins with a friend all that matters is whether the pair of you toss heads, tails, or one head and one tail, not which coin was tossed first. And people buying sofas probably don't care which company was the first to introduce a particular shade of blue fabric, once two or more companies have that color abailable. But when order does count, in terms of earning profits or surviving a fight (physical or economic), it is crucial for the players and those who want to predict the outcome of the game to understand the key role of the sequence of moves.

---

[8]If your interest in threats and side payments has been spurred, these and many other extensions of game theory models are discussed in Hal R. Varian's *Intermediate Microeconomics: A Modern Approach*, (New York: W.W. Norton & Co., 1987).

Table 14-5
Spuds vs. Fido: A Sequential Game in the Dogland Beer Industry

I. The Payoff Matrix

		Spuds Light Beer	Spuds Dark Beer
Fido	Light Beer	Spuds +$8,000 Fido +$2,000	Spuds +$7,000 Fido +$2,000
	Dark Beer	Spuds +$1,000 Fido +$1,000	Spuds +$4,000 Fido +$4,000

II. The Extensive Form of the Game, With Fido Moving First

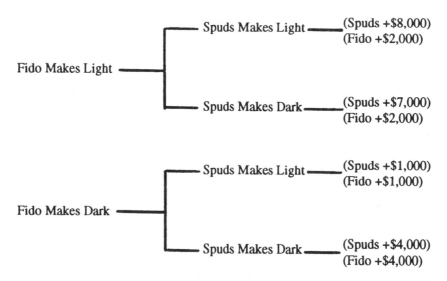

Looking only at the payoff matrix for this game, if Spuds makes Light beer Fido will make Light, too; but if Fido makes Dark beer Spuds will also choose to make Dark. Assuming it is impossible for the firms to produce both new beers (due to capacity constraints in producing or shelf-space constraints in selling the beers), which of the two possible solutions will occur is determined by which producer can get the new beer to the marketplace first. The decision tree schematic of the extensive form of the game shows that, if it has the first-mover advantage, Fido will limit Spuds' choices to the lower half of the tree diagram, where the higher profits in making Dark beer should be evident to Spuds.

Mixed Strategies

To conclude the section on game theory, we will briefly point out that many games and real-life situations call for a combination of strategies at various times, not a single strategy that is played over and over again. For example, in football the best teams have both a running and passing game, and try to cross up their opponents by occasionally running on an "obvious" passing play, and passing in a situation where teams normally run. In poker, the best players sometimes bluff and sometimes don't. In business settings firms employ such strategies as price cuts, advertising campaigns, extended warranties, and new product features in various combinations and at different times to lure more customers and outwit competitors.

MIXED STRATEGIES are best played by psychics who somehow know or usually guess right what the competition is going to do before they do it. Next best are people who learn more about their opponents than the opponents learn about them, largely through hard work and experience in their regular "games."[9] Finally, for more average mortals, mixed strategies can simply entail using various moves a pre-determined percentage of the time, but choosing when to use any particular move at random. Against your Saturday night poker group, for example, you may decide to bluff 25% of the time, and decide when to do that by flipping two dimes quietly in your hand, bluffing whenever you get two heads.

Game theory is an additional tool to use in analyzing the behavior of firms and other economic agents who are out to maximize their own satisfaction or financial position. It complements the models on market structures, supply and demand, and responses to economic incentives which we presented in earlier chapters, by incorporating strategic considerations involving rivals and/or collaborators in an explicit and highly flexible way. Frequently, however, the results from a game theory model only apply to the particular set of circumstances reflected in the specific form of the interdependence built into it -- so just as you saw in Chapter 13, different models are required to analyze different forms of strategic games, or for similar games played in different settings. But some results are more general in their usefulness. For example, when you use a mixed strategy for bluffing in poker and win, remember to occasionally let your opponents know -- "accidentally" if possible -- that you won by bluffing. That way they will be more likely to keep betting when you aren't bluffing, and you will win even more. Unless, of course, you come up against players who use mixed stategies even better than you do.

Contestable Markets

Both game theory and models incorporating the economics of information have now been widely used by economists for several decades. The formalized theory of contestable markets, which we review in this section, is newer and not nearly as well established. Some economists argue that it never will be, while others have begun to use it regularly and enthusiastically in their work.

We present the contestable markets material here in part because this controversy is a useful way for you to see how a new set of models and findings can make its way (or not) into the mainstream of economic analysis, and because several of the ideas from this literature are important and intuitively pleasing when seen as direct extensions of the traditional market structure models covered in Chapters 9-13. The ultimate verdict on these models, in terms of their widespread acceptance and use, is basically an empirical question that depends on how many important economic problems can be more fully or easily studied using this approach.

Characteristics of Contestable Markets

Over the past decade, a group of economists began to study cases where, they claimed, competition between a few, large firms might lead to outcomes that were as efficient as those in markets with competion between a large number of relatively small firms. They built up a set of models to explain why that might happen, focusing on situations in which it is easy for large firms to quickly enter and exit a market in which competitors are charging prices resulting in economic profits. This *POTENTIAL COMPETITION* results in *CONTESTABLE MARKETS*, and may be sufficient to insure that prices and profits will not be set above competitive levels -- even if the product turns out to be sold by a single supplier. Whether or not these contestable markets are at work in the U.S. economy, and if so, how widespread and significant they are, are the subjects of a considerable amount of debate among microeconomists.

---

[9] Recall the comment by former NFL coach, Bum Phillips, who offered a high but homespun compliment to opposing coach Don Schula: "He can take his'n [football players] and beat your'n, or he can take your'n and beat his'n.")

A market is said to be perfectly contestable if three conditions are met:

1) There is free entry and exit in the market.

2) Entering firms can produce at the same cost and output levels as existing firms, facing no competitive disadvantage in these respects.

3) Fixed costs in the industry are avoidable, not sunk, because they can be easily recovered by selling any resource or asset that carries a fixed cost. Furthermore, these assets can be bought or sold at identical prices by existing firms or potential competitors.

If these conditions hold, even a firm that is a natural monopoly will be limited by the threat of perfect competition to a price and output level which earns only normal profits, as shown in Figure 14-1. If the firm charges a higher price to try to earn economic profits, one or more of the its potential competitors will enter the market and charge a lower price, bidding away customers and profits. Competition quickly drives price down to the normal profit level and one firm will exit the industry; but because entry and exit is free the firm that exits (and any other potential competitors) maintain their threat to the firm that remains. The potential competition forces that firm to produce at prices no greater than those a copmetitive firm facing the same cost levels would charge.

Figure 14-1
Natural Monopoly in a Contestable Market

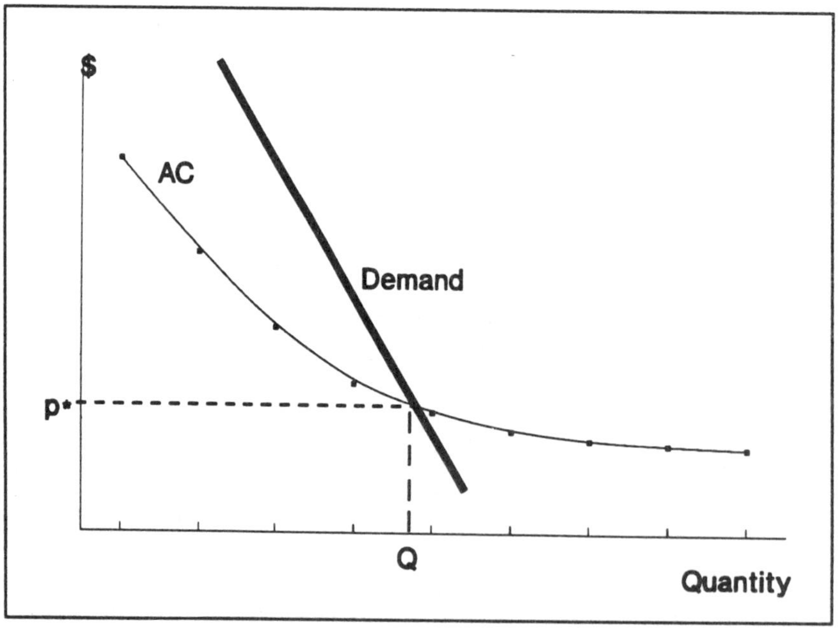

Under contestable markets, even an unregulated natural monopoly earns no more than the normal profit rate of return. In the graph above, such a firm must charge p* -- any higher price will lead to entry by a competitor that is not currently producing in this market. This price and output combination is productively efficient in the sense that the output level demanded is produced at the lowest possible price and cost which will keep the firm in business.

In effect, potential competitors stand ready to practice these *"HIT-AND-RUN" STRATEGIES* anytime the existing firm tries to charge a higher price, so the higher price never gets charged. The equilibrium position will be at the highest level of output and lowest level of price on the demand curve facing the natural monopolist which is consistent with the continued operation of the firm (assuming it does not receive subsidies from the government or some other patron). That level of output will be produced at the lowest feasible cost.

When contestable market assumptions are met in markets where production and cost schedules do not lead to natural monopolies, but several firms competing in what would otherwise be an imperfectly competitive market, the potential competition can actually lead to results that are identical to those that evolve in perfect competition. The exact size and number of the firms that will produce in such settings depends on the nature of the cost schedules these firms face, as shown in Figure 14-2.

The key result developed in these simple versions of the contestable markets model is that competitive efficiency can be achieved without government policy and regulation even in settings where only a small number of firms are currently producing. But while this is a theoretical possibility, critics of the contestable markets theory point out that very few industries appear to have the characteristics listed at the beginning of this section. However, as you have now seen several times, that apparent lack of realism doesn't necessarily mean that an economic model should be abandoned, or that its findings can not prove to be important on many practical matters.

Figure 14-2
Contestable Markets With Two Or More Producers

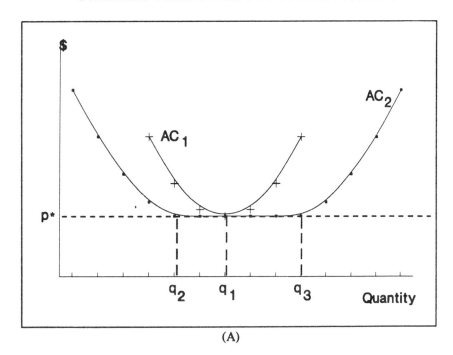

(A)

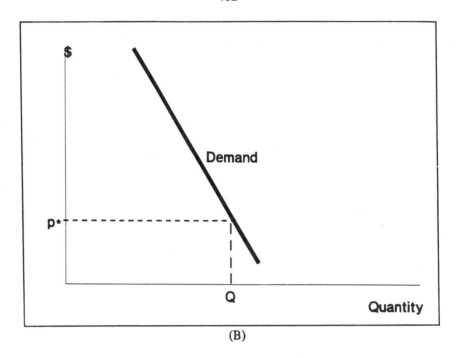

(B)

The first graph above shows two possible cost schedules facing individual firms operating in a contestable market that is not characterized by natural monopoly. AC_1 has the standard "u-shape" with a unique minimum point at output level q_1; AC_2 has an extensive range where production costs are minimized, between q_2 and q_3. The second graph shows the industry demand curve for the product produced by these firms. The threat of entry and hit-and-run tactics by potential competitors will force price down to p*, as indicated in both graphs. The industry level of output will be at Q.

The output level for individual firms will depend on the shape of their cost schedules. If costs are as shown on AC_1, firms will produce q_1. If they are as shown in AC_2 firms will produce between q_2 and q_3, and it is quite possible that firms of different size will operate in the same industry. In all of these cases, an optimal degree of allocative (P = MC) and productive (P = min AC) efficiency is attained, even though there may not be a large number of relatively small firms currently producing this product. Instead, the threat of potential competition is sufficient to lead to these results.

Economists who have developed and used the contestable markets model claim that, like perfect competition, it provides policymakers with a useful normative standard for efficiency outcomes, even in markets where its unrealistic assumptions are not met. They state:

Perfect contestability is not likely to be satisfied exactly by any real market. Yet it does provide a standard against which actual markets can be compared, no matter if the relevant production techniques and market demands dictate production by a single giant firm or by a multitude of independent enterprises. ...[It] is therefore an appropriate target for public policy.
[T]here are objective structural market conditions that can be examined to determine the relevance of contestability in practice. And where these conditions do not hold even approximately, actual industry configurations can, nevertheless, be usefully compared to those that would result if the markets were

structurally contestable. In sum, it is not arbitrary heroic assumptions, but the operation of the invisible hand in structurally contestable markets that leads to our results.[10]

They also claim that several major industries are sufficiently like the idealized version of a contestable market to make these models useful in analyzing and evaluating their actual behavior. Some sectors of the commercial airline industry and regional banking services are the most-often cited examples; and in both of those industries recent deregulation episodes did lead to a dramatic expansion in the level of these services provided to some areas, suggesting that potential competition may have been waiting in the wings in many localities.

Furthermore, at least some characteristics of competition in these markets are reasonably close to the assumptions of the contestable markets model. Think of an airline that already has landing rights and jetway gates in two cities, say Cleveland and Richmond, but does not currently operate flights between those cites, even though some other airline does. If the fares for current flights on this route are increased to levels that result in economic profits, the potential competitor can quickly begin to offer its own service, even if it plans to leave the market again when the first firm lowers its price to the competitive level.

Alfred Kahn, an unusually witty economist and former Chairman of the Civil Aeronautics Board during the Carter administration, once described airplanes as "marginal costs with wings." He used that description to suggest that an airline's fixed costs are not sunk, and that its hit and run tactics can be virtually as fast as an air strike. Similarly, when regulatory restraints are minimal, a bank that wants to open a branch in a nearby city will be only a little slower than the airline offering a new route. In fact, in many college towns banks set up temporary offices in trailers or tents when students return to campus for the fall semester, because they want to attract the new accounts. But are these characteristics sufficient to guarantee the outcomes predicted in the contestable markets models, or a reasonably close approximation of them? Only partly.

Empirical studies have been conducted to determine how contestable many industries, and the airline industry in particular, really are. The results conflict with the contestable markets theory in several ways. For example, profits on heavily travelled airline routes are apparently sensitive to the degree of market concentration on the routes -- meaning potential competition isn't keeping prices and profits at competitive levels -- and barriers in obtaining jetway gates at large airports and operating computerized reservation services do appear to restrict entry in many market areas.[11]

Many economists now view contestable market theory, when applied to settings where firms produce a single good or service, as a modest extension of the theory of perfect competition, rather than a fundamental challenge or revision of the theories of imperfect competiton. Others maintain a more favorable assessment, as noted earlier. But there is wider appreciation for the innovations offered in the theory when applied to settings where firms produce more than one product. That is the subject of the final section of this chapter.

Producing Multiple Outputs: Economies of Scope and Scale

Most large industrial firms produce more than one product, and in some cases find that the average production costs of making those goods are lower than they would be if the same products were produced separately, by different firms. In the contestable markets literature these cost savings are described as *ECONOMIES OF SCOPE*, in contrast to the concept of economies of scale which you studied in Chapters 8 and 10, using models of a firm producing a single product. With economies of scale, doubling all inputs leads to a more than proportional increase in output, so average production costs fall. With economies of scope, producing cars and trucks instead of just one or the other leads to financial savings or direct production advantages for these products, and that causes average costs to fall.

[10].William J. Baumol, John C. Panzar, and Robert D. Willig, *Contestable Markets and the Theory of Industry Structure*, rev. ed., San Diego: Harcourt Brace Jovanovich, 1988, pp. 35 and 45.

[11]One such study is Stephen A. Morrison and Clifford Winston's "Empirical Implications and Tests of the Contestability Hypothesis," *Journal of Law and Economics*, April 1987, pp. 53-66. A more general criticism of contestable markets theory (not limited to the airline industry) is offered in William G. Shepard's "`Contestability' vs. Competition," *American Economic Review*, September 1984, pp. 572-587.

These cost savings may come directly through the more efficient use of machinery, personnel, or other resources in the production process, or from advantages in buying raw materials in greater volume, or from greater administrative flexibility in being able to quickly shift production from one product to another as market conditions change. Empirical studies have found such savings in offering some combinations of financial services in both the banking and insurance industries, in providing certain combinations of medical services at hospitals, and in producing different models of cars and trucks and the automotive industry, as suggested above.

Along with technical advances in specifying and measuring cost functions to account for such economies, the contestable markets model has led to other conceptual insights building on the notion of economies of scope. For example, if economies of scope exist in competitive or contestable markets, we will certainly observe multiproduct firms. If there are no economies of scope, it will be possible to separate the production processes for the various goods and services. And in fact, if producing multiple products results in diseconomies of scope, competitive and contestable firms must function as single-product firms. Finally in this brief introduction to the idea of economies of scope, note that a multiproduct firm which does not experience economies of scope can not exist as a natural monopoly, because it would always be possible to separate the production processes for the multiple products and have two or more smaller firms produce them at an equal or lower average cost.

To summarize the broader body of theory and empirical work that has been done on the contestable markets hypothesis, the overall message has been for economists and policy makers not to look only at the number of firms now operating in an industry to judge its efficiency, and in particular not to regulate rates of return and average costs too tightly in natural monopoly markets that are contestable. That message has already had some direct, practical applications in the United States, especially in the recent deregulation efforts in the airline, banking, and telephone industies. For example, in 1989 Baumol and a colleague used these arguments to convince a federal judge to set a maximum price in the long-distance telephone market, and let a small number of competitors fight it out on the basis of lower prices, cost savings in production, and the quality of service. Compare these incentives to those established under traditional regulatory schemes, which provide a maximum rate of return over approved costs, and let utilities increase their profits only by increasing their approved costs. That's not to say that the contestable markets variation of utility regulation can work in all settings, but where it may it seems to be well worth considering.

And even if the uses of contestable market theory prove to be far more limited than its developers now expect them to be, these ideas and models offer a splendid current example of how economic theory and empirical knowledge are expanded over the years. It is seldom a quick or easy process, and fundamental new insights are, almost by definition, few and far between. But when they do come, they change the way academics, public officials, producers, and consumers look at the world.

Case Study #20 #18
Flexible Pricing Strategies: A Brief History[12]

All three of the sections in this chapter offered models that modify the simple models of price determination developed in Chapters 9-13, which stressed the golden rule for profit maximization, MR = MC, in both competitive and imperfectly competitive markets. Economists haven't been the only ones questioning how, in practice, firms in different market structures set prices and try to maximize profits if they don't have precise data on marginal revenues and marginal costs, or if it is too costly for them to change prices every time there are small changes in the demand for their products, or in the costs of producing them. In particular, product pricing is also a key topic of study in marketing courses; but the story told about pricing rules in those courses has often been sharply different from economists' MR = MC rule, even though most marketing professors understand the importance of that outcome for profit maximization. Until recent years, what the marketing professors were more likely to teach about were pricing strategies designed to meet some target rate of return. In large industries that most often meant to a system of gradual and predictable price changes, along the lines developed by Alfred P.

---

[12]This case study is adapted from a classic *Business Week* article on "Flexible Pricing" which was published in the December 12, 1977 issue. The article is often reprinted in business anthologies.

Sloan for General Motors in the 1920s. Under these strategies prices might sometimes be modified in light of competitive pressures, but not regularly or quickly.

From 1929-1945 there was little opportunity to practice Sloan's precepts under normal business conditions, because of the economic upheaval of the Great Depression and World War II. But for the next 25 years -- a time of rapid growth in the U.S. economy with limited competition from foreign producers of manufactured products -- annual price changes for most broad categories of products were relatively steady and modest through periods of rapid economic growth with only occasional recessions. Price changes averaged about 5% a year, and rarely fell below 0% or rose above 10%.

The major U.S. industrial firms did seem to gear pricing and other business decisions to long-run growth and earnings objectives. Some chief executives explicitly stated that they tried to smooth out price and earnings fluctuations, and meet high, steady targets. Citicorp, for example, set a goal of 15% annual growth in earnings. Several industries, such as chemical products, established long-term contracts which simply passed on cost increases from sellers to buyers. But that all began to change in the 1970s.

In that decade, the combination of double-digit inflation, even larger increases in energy and natural resource prices initiated by OPEC, wage and price controls under the Nixon administration, deregulation in the trucking and airline industries, new government safety and environmental regulations, and two especially severe recessions resulted in sharp reductions in price stability.

Firms still tried to pass their own higher costs on to consumers in these years, but often unsuccessfully. For example, in 1975 and 1976 price increases were announced, and then partly or entirely withdrawn, in the steel, paper, aluminum, and chemical industries. Weak demand, excess capacity among domestic firms, and increasingly stiff competition from foreign producers undercut those pricing policies. Firms began to abandon long-term contracts in favor of more flexible, but less predictable, arrangements. Prices were more frequently determined and reviewed on a product-by-product basis, carefully considering market conditions instead of using a standard cost-plus formula or other across-the-board rules. The automobile industry offers a clear example of those trends.

At General Motors (Sloan's own company), long-range profit targets were still used to guide pricing in broad terms, but executives also agreed that there was "a more sensitive effort to assess the competitive relationship of products and the costs of making them." Government safety and fuel-efficiency standards hit GM and other auto manufacturers on the cost side of this equation, while low-cost imports produced by Honda, Toyota, and Nissan took substantial market share from the United States producers -- 14.5% of the United States market from 1978 to 1988.[13] GM initially responded by lowering prices on subcompact models on the West Coast, where competition from the Japanese producers was stiffest. Then it began introducing more large-size car models, where profit margins were higher and consumers viewed the product quality and overall satisfaction from U.S. brands more positively. One result of this strategy was that the ratio for prices on the highest and lowest-priced cars produced by GM and other U.S. firms increased from 3-to-1 to 4-to-1, and then even higher. Another strategy adopted at this time was to equip cars in all size ranges with different combinations of optional features, to allow more flexible pricing even within a particular product line, and to target different groups of consumers within each of these sub-markets.

In other industries, price leadership practices based on targeted rates of returns became increasingly rare and more difficult to enforce among U.S. firms. *Business Week* cited foreign competition as a major reason for the abandonment of such policies in the steel, computer, glass container, and chemical industries.

The chairman of the Zenith Radio Corporation, John J. Nevin, indicated that Japanese competition in producing TV-sets had been particularly successful against Zenith in part because Zenith insisted on keeping prices up to protect profit margins. Eventually, like the automobile industry and others, in the face of this intense competition Zenith began looking for "niches" where specialized products could be sold at higher prices and profit margins, but pricing more aggressively (i.e., lower) in the larger markets for standard products.

A vice president for a data-processing company explained that "Because we can no longer depend on forward pricing, we try to find a proprietary enclave where our product has a unique application. This offers us a competitive alternative and helps protect our revenue stream from fluctuations." At U. S. Elevator Corp.,

---

[13]*Business Week*, "Detroit Tries to Rev Up" (June 12, 1989).

406

President George C. Tweed was also saying "we try to find something to sell where we have a unique edge. Then pricing isn't so traumatic." His company sought out jobs "nobody else wants," such as elevators on ships and in nuclear plants.

A classic example of a market niche pricing strategy in these years was the Hewlett-Packard company's approach to selling pocket calculators. It developed the special-feature, high-price calculator market, while Texas Instruments and several Japanese companies chose to produce simpler machines which sold for lower prices, but in greater volume.

Both Hewlett-Packard and Texas Instruments also helped to develop and popularize the use of "learning-curve" pricing in the United States, which involves steadily lowering prices for a product to sell it in greater volume over time. In part, this strategy may be based on achieving economies of scale; but more importantly, according to these companies, it recognizes that producers learn how to produce standard products faster and more efficiently over time (regardless of the level of output voulume), once production begins. Learning-curve pricing is often an aggressive policy, in that companies can decide to make a product based on sales estimates that assume prices will be lowered below the initial cost of production, even though no one presently knows how the necessary cost savings will be made. But even in 1977, according to Professor Steven Wainwight of the Harvard Business School, Japanese companies had already used this strategy for several years "in everything from steel, to textiles, to electronics."

Changing prices frequently and establishing different prices for a wide variety of options on a previously standardized product are costly activites, but the costs of these flexible pricing policies have been greatly reduced by the declining costs of computerization for both large and small companies. More generally, flexible pricing strategies may promote the survival and development of more small firms if they can claim niches for unique products that are not characterized by substantial economies of scale. But that is clearly not always the case. Offering a wide range of options on a mass produced product like automobiles suggests that large output levels are necessary to survive, and some observers correctly (but a little prematurely) predicted the end of American Motors in 1977. The failures and mergers of such companies would, of course, result in higher domestic concentration levels in many key manufacturing industries. Recognizing that, economist Hendrick Houthakker of Harvard University, and a member of President Nixon's Council of Economic Advisers, argued that the Justice Department would have to modify antitrust guidelines in several industries to allow U.S. firms to "achieve the economies of scale necessary to match the foreign competition."

Purely in terms of pricing strategies, the attention to flexible pricing in many U.S. industries has served to bring their competitive strategies, and the marketing professors' models of their pricing behavior, closer to economists' traditional models of profit-maximizing behavior. But at the same time, economists' recent work on such models and topics as the separation of corporate ownership and control, limit-entry pricing, imperfect information, and game theory have moved the economics profession closer to a world view where strategic pricing decisions by imperfectly competitive firms and a range of prices for identical products can occur, and may even be necessary for survival.

Chapter Summary

1) Because information about products and prices is costly to obtain, consumers must decide how many resources to devote to the process of searching out that information when they are going to make a purchase. The optimal amount of *SEARCH* varies for different products, and is influenced by such factors as: a) the portion of the consumer's budget that is allocated to expenditures for a good or service; b) the number of experienced buyers in the market for a product, who have useful price information from their previous purchases; c) the proportion of sellers who continue to sell a product over different time periods, and whose prices are positively correlated over time; d) the geographical size of the market; and e) the percentage of purchases made by consumers with "urgent wants" to be satisfied.

2) Products which consumers buy without searching extensively for low-price sellers will, *ceteris paribus*, be sold for a wider range of prices than those which do elicit careful search.

3) Because consumers are heterogeneous in terms of the amount of price search they expend in purchasing products, producers selling identical products will also specialize to serve different groups of consumers, and charge different prices. This tendency is reinforced when different kinds of sellers do business in stores that have different operating costs.

4) When buyers and/or sellers operate with *ASYMMETRIC INFORMATION*, price, output, and profit levels in a market are often affected. Typically, those with better information will fare better than those with less.

5) Models which try to determine the optimal "moves" available to two or more parties based on the expected outcomes of their combined decisions are known as *GAME THEORY*. Many such games can be solved to identify one or more *NASH-EQUILIBRIUM* positions, which are those in which each player moves optimally given the move(s) made by the other player or players.

6) Altering the number of periods a game is expected to run, or the order in which players make their moves, can affect the outcome of a game. These modifications are explored in what are known as *REPEATED AND SEQUENTIAL GAMES*, respectively. Games can also be characterized as *POSITIVE, NEGATIVE, OR ZERO-SUM GAMES*, depending on whether it is possible for all players to gain or lose as a result of playing the game, or if one player can gain only by making another player lose an equivalent amount.

7) The model of *CONTESTABLE MARKETS* stresses the role of potential competition in limiting price and profit levels for existing firms in an industry, theoretically even in cases where only one or a small number of firms are serving a market. A perfectly contestable market is characterized by free entry and exit, and the absence of any sunk costs (any fixed costs are assumed to be avoidable, by selling off assets that entail them at competitive prices). *POTENTIAL COMPETITORS* are also assumed to be able to produce at the same cost level as firms currently producing in an market.

8) In a perfectly contestable market, if a firm earns economic profits entry will occur quickly, and prices and profits will be driven down to the competitive level that is compatible with the continued existence of one or more firms in the industry. At that level, firms that entered while economic profits were earned may exit again, but the threat of these *"HIT-AND-RUN" STRATEGIES* means that production will continue at efficient price and output levels.

9) Firms that produce more than one product may experience *ECONOMIES OF SCOPE* as well as scale. In these settings too, production and price levels will be efficient if the market is perfectly competitive or contestable.

10) Advocates of the contestable market theory believe it is consistent with the characteristics and behavior observed in several important industries (such as commercial air travel) and provides important public policy criteria even in industries where it is not. Detractors of the theory regard it as, at best, a modest extension of the theory of perfect competition, not consistent with the empirical results from industries such as airlines or other supposedly close examples of the theory, but perhaps more useful in exploring cost relationships for multi-product firms.

11) (Case Study #20) Pricing strategies used by major U.S. industrial firms frequently call for some goal other than equating short-run marginal revenue and marginal cost. However, increased international competition and greater variability in other market forces have led to the adoption of flexible-pricing strategies over the last 20 years, which do focus more on determining the most profitable price for individual products, rather than across-the-board rules such as cost-plus or target price increases established for all of a firm's products.

Review and Discussion Questions

1) Rank the following list of products to show which you would expect to exhibit the greatest price variability (as a percent of the product's average price).

   a) beer
   b) car touring
   c) contact lens solution
   d) contraceptives
   e) file cabinets
   f) flying lessons
   g) hair spray
   h) horoscope charting
   i) lettuce

   Briefly state why you expect each product to exhibit relatively high or low price variance. Compare your rankings to the measures of price variance for these products shown in Table 14-1. Explain how your rankings are like the actual rankings, or not.

2) Would a wealthy consumer be likely to spend more or less time, and more or less money, engaging in price search than a low- or middle-income consumer, *ceteris paribus*? Why or why not?

3) Suppose laws are passed requiring all identical products to be sold for identical prices in all stores, nationwide. For example, manufactures might be required to set the legal retail price for the products they provide to retailers. Discuss the effects of such a law in terms of economic efficiency and welfare, and likely producer and consumer reactions to such a law.

4) Are buyers, sellers, or neither of the two likely to have more information in each of the following exchanges:

   a) A professional musician buys a new guitar at a music store.
   b) A patient with a brain tumor selects a neurosurgeon.
   c) A homemaker buys a loaf of bread.
   d) A teenager trades baseball cards received as Christmas presents with his four year old sister.
   e) A Martian asks you to trade dollars for some of his/her/its currency.
   f) An economist signs a contract to write her first textbook with a leading publishing house.

   How are information issues likely to affect these exchanges?

5) What are the Nash-equilibrium outcomes for the prisoner's dilemma game shown in Table 14-3, if the game is played by the following pairs of players?

   a) two altruists
   b) two sadists
   c) two masochists
   d) a sadist and a masochist
   e) a married couple

6) In Table 14-3, what happens if Puds moves first? Can Fido offer Puds a side payment which will improve both firms' position when Puds moves first?

7) How are the characteristics of a perfectly contestable market like, and unlike, those assumed in the models of perfect competition, monopoly, monopolistic competition, and oligopoly?

8) In Figure 14-2, how do we know that allocative efficiency is optimal?

9) Give examples of possible economies of scope for the following kinds of firms:

a) farms
b) steel mills
c) appliance manufacturers
d) fast food restaurants
e) grocery stores
f) elementary and high schools
g) universities

10) Briefly summarize the positions of the supporters and detractors of contestable markets theory. Which position do you find more convincing?

11) Are flexible-pricing schemes consistent with all of the basic market structures you have studied in this course? Why or why not?

Chapter 15
Competitive Markets for Factors of Production

In This Chapter...

we analyze how prices and employment levels are determined for the factors of production -- land, labor, capital and entrepreneurship -- when those factors are bought and sold in perfectly competitive markets. In the next chapter, we examine imperfectly competitive markets for these productive resources.

You have already seen several reasons why it is important to understand the operation of these factor markets: 1) firms care about outcomes in these markets because prices for these inputs affect their production costs and supply decisions; 2) these same prices largely determine income levels for individuals and households, and thereby set the budget constraints for their consumption, saving, and investment decisions; and 3) it is impossible to set factor prices that simultaneously give individuals high incomes and firms low production costs, so once again hard choices and trade-offs must be faced.

The Demand for Factors of Production

A firm's demand for factors of production is based on the demand for the products it uses the factors to produce, and on the marginal productivity of the factors of production. A perfectly competitive firm's factor demand is represented by the value of marginal product (VMP) curve, which is downward-sloping because of the law of diminishing returns. The firm hires units of an input along this curve, as long as VMP is greater than the price of the factor. The price elasticity of demand for a factor depends on the price elasticity of demand for the product the factor is used to produce, the availability of other inputs which can be used as substitute inputs, the share of total production costs represented by payments for this factor, and the price elasticity of supply for substitute inputs.

Derived Demand

Factor markets are especially important to you because that's where you have to earn a living, now or someday very soon. So begin this chapter by asking yourself, why would anybody hire you?

Firms don't acquire productive resources just to keep them sitting around. Land, labor, capital, and entrepreneurship are "hired" to produce some kind of good or service.[1] If the demand for a product purchased by consumers increases or decreases, so will the demand for the resources used to produce it. That makes it clear that the demand for any factor of production is a *DERIVED DEMAND* -- deriving from the demand for products the factor is used to produce. The demand for productive resources also depends on how much output each unit of the factor of production can produce, given the amount of inputs that a firm has already hired to produce its output. In other words, it depends on the factor's marginal product in a firm's production process.

---

[1]The word hired, of course, describes acquisitions of labor better than capital or the other factors production -- which are purchased or leased. But to stress how similar things are considered in using more or less of *any* kind of input, we will use the word hired in this general sense here, and in the following chapter.

Marginal Product and VMP

A competitive firm can sell all of the units of the goods or services it produces at the market price, as you saw in Chapter 9. That price can rise or fall over time, but we will initially assume that it remains fixed. We will also work with the short-run production schedules that producers face at any given point in time. That means the firm has one or more fixed inputs, and generates output by hiring units of a variable input to work with the fixed inputs.[2]

In most short-run production processes, capital and land are fixed inputs and labor is the variable input. Moreover, for most firms payments to labor constitute the largest expenditure for any factor of production. In fact, about three-fourths of U.S. national income is paid out each year as wages and salaries, while profit, rent, and interest payments make up the other fourth. For these reasons, labor is used as the primary example of a variable input throughout this chapter and the next.

Whenever land, capital, or entrepreneurship is a variable input, however, producers will decide how much of it to hire in essentially the same way they decide how much labor to hire. For example, nationally known entertainers are themselves fixed inputs in producing their "shows," but they can use airplanes and other kinds of transportation and communications services to increase the number of performances they give each year. Comedian Jay Leno is well known for doing just that, but so do other entertainers -- including professional sports teams. The demand for the entertainers' services affects their demand for those variable inputs, as does the productivity of these inputs in helping the entertainers schedule and offer more shows. So while non-labor inputs exhibit some special features which we will describe in later sections of this chapter, the important thing to see here is that, all things considered, the markets for the four factors of production are much more alike than different. Don't lose sight of that point, even though we use labor as the most general example of a variable input in short-run production processes.

In that setting, a perfectly competitive firm takes the price for its output from the marketplace, and can only change its production level by hiring different amounts of its variable inputs. These firms also accept the wage rate for the workers they hire as a given, since employment levels at competitive firms are too small to have any effect on those wages. In short, perfectly competitive firms are wage takers as well as price takers.

So what else does a perfectly competitive firm consider in deciding how much labor to hire at a given wage rate? Just one thing, really: how much each unit of a variable input increases the firm's revenues, by increasing the amount of product the firm has to sell.

Table 15-1 shows the calculations a competitive firm makes in determining how many units of labor, or other variable inputs, to hire. The first four columns are simply a production function like those you studied in Chapters 1 and 7, showing the output levels that are produced by adding units of the variable input to some fixed input. In this example, diminishing marginal returns set in when the third worker is hired, and continue thereafter as the fixed input is spread out more and more thinly over an increasing number of workers. Remember, this effect holds even if all the workers are equally well trained, skilled, and motivated. It occurs simply because there is less capital per unit of labor as more workers are hired, so the marginal product of labor must eventually fall.

The next-to-last column in Table 15-1 shows that the perfectly competitive firm is a price taker, as you saw in Chapter 9. We have assumed here that each "Thing" (a clever product name) the firm produces can be sold for $2, no matter how many or how few units this firm chooses to sell. The last column, then, shows the only thing you haven't seen in earlier chapters -- the *VALUE OF THE MARGINAL PRODUCT (VMP)* produced for the firm by each worker it hires. The VMP for each worker is equal to $2 times his or her respective marginal product -- i.e., $VMP = P(MP_L)$, or column 6 = column 4 x column 5. In simple English, VMP is the change in a perfectly competitive firm's total revenues associated with hiring one more unit of labor.

---

[2] As you saw in Chapter 8, long-run factor markets, in which both capital and labor inputs are variable, can be analyzed using isoquant and isocost models.

Table 15-1
Calculating the Value of Marginal Product (VMP) Schedule

(1) Units of Fixed Input (Capital)	(2) Units of Variable Input (Labor)	(3) Total Product	(4) Marginal Product of Labor	(5) Product Price	(6) Value of Marginal Product (VMP)
10	0	0	--	$2	$--
10	1	10	10	2	20
10	2	25	15	2	30
10	3	35	10	2	20
10	4	43	8	2	16
10	5	48	5	2	10
10	6	51	3	2	6
10	7	52	1	2	2
10	8	51	-1	2	-2

The VMP (value of marginal product) for units of labor, or any other variable input, is calculated by multiplying the marginal product of the input times the price of the product which it produces. For a perfectly competitive firm, VMP eventually declines due to diminishing marginal returns in the production process.

The VMP schedule turns out to be this firm's demand curve for labor because, for any given wage rate, w, the firm will hire more units as long as VMP is greater than w. The logic of that hiring rule is simple, and can be seen clearly in this table: each time the employer shown there pays a worker w and sells their marginal product for more than w, the employer comes out ahead. Therefore, to maximize profits (or minimize losses) the employer continues to hire so long as VMP > w. This is really just another application of the marginal benefit = marginal cost rule, but now put in the context and terminology of a perfectly competitive market for labor (or other variable inputs). And in fact, if the firm can hire workers for any increment of time, not just for "lumps" of 8-hour days or 40-hour weeks, it will hire right up to the point where VMP = w.

If the wage rate changes, a perfectly competitive firm will move up or down its VMP schedule in hiring workers, or along the curve that is plotted from that schedule, as shown in Figure 15-1. More precisely, it moves along the downward-sloping section of the curve, where diminishing returns have set in. It will never stop hiring in the upward-sloping section associated with increasing marginal returns because, if it pays to hire a worker with a VMP of $20 in this range, it will also pay to hire all additional workers until the VMP is $20 in the range of diminishing returns. In other words, note that between the $20 point in the range of increasing returns in Table 15-1 (when one worker is hired), and the $20 point in the range of diminishing returns (for three workers), VMP is always higher than $20. That means the firm will hire all of these workers if the wage rate is $20 or less, thereby moving into the range of diminishing returns. You have already seen this result in a different setting, because in Chapters 9-12 all of the firms we discussed except natural monopolies produced in the range of rising marginal costs. That is, as you saw in Chapter 7, the range of diminishing returns in any family of short-run cost curves.

If the demand for the final product an input produces should increase over time, that will increase the product price, *ceteris paribus*, and increase the demand for inputs used to produce that product. Put differently, the VMP for all units of those inputs will increase, because their marginal product stays the same while product price increases.

414

Figure 15-1
VMP and the Demand for a Factor of Production in Competitive Factor Markets

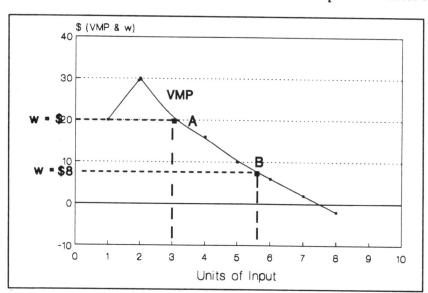

This VMP curve is plotted from the values in the last column of Table 15-1. Perfectly competitive firms are both wage and price takers, and hire more units of labor so long as the gain from hiring an additional worker (the VMP) exceeds the wage rate. To maximize profits or minimize losses, these firms hire up to the point where VMP = w. Therefore, if the wage rate changes, the firms move along the downward-sloping segments of their VMP schedules to determine optimal employment levels. For example, at a wage of $20 this firm will hire 3 workers, at point A. If the wage rate falls to $8 it will hire 5 full-time workers and a part-time 6th worker, at point B, but no more. In short, the negatively sloped segment of the VMP curve is a perfectly competitive firm's demand curve for labor.

If product price is fixed but the productivity of an input increases -- say as a result of better worker education and training (i.e., greater human capital), or technological improvements in capital goods, or because the amount of fixed inputs available for variable inputs to work with increases over time -- the VMP schedule for that input will again increase. But this kind of change also sets off a substitution effect for other inputs used in the production process. For example, as the productivity of farm equipment and chemicals improved throughout the last century, U.S. farmers substituted these inputs for agricultural labor to a remarkable degree.[3]

Decreases in factor productivity or in the demand for (and price of) the product a factor produces will just as clearly reduce the demand for a productive resource. These shifts in VMP -- the perfectly competitive firm's demand curve for a variable input -- are illustrated in Figure 15-2.

---

[3]Some students may recognize that improved factor productivity increases the supply curve for the product the factor makes, which will increase the equilibrium quantity of that product. If this increase in the quantity of the product that will be produced is sufficiently large, that output effect can entirely offset the substitution effect for the other inputs used by these firms. In U.S. agricultural markets, however, where supply and demand are both price inelastic, the supply increases led to relatively small increases in equilibrium output levels. Consequently, the number of farm workers employed fell sharply, even with some increases in demand for farm products due to rising U.S. and world populations.

Figure 15-2
Shifts in Factor Demand

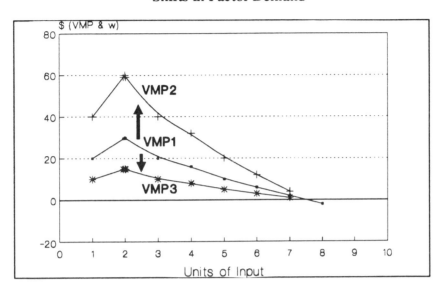

A doubling of the productivity of a factor of production would lead to higher values in column 4 of Table 15-1, which in turn would increase the values in column 6. This shifts the VMP curve upward from VMP$_1$ to VMP$_2$. A similar shift in the VMP curve results if demand for the product that labor is producing increases -- in this case causing the price for that product to double (as well as the values in columns 5 and 6 in Table 15-1). Decreases in labor productivity or in the demand for the product that labor is producing will, conversely, lead to downward shifts in VMP, toward VMP$_3$ (which is based on a 50% fall in marginal productivity *or* product price).

Price Elasticity of Demand for Labor and Other Inputs

For some kinds of labor and other productive resources, employment levels are quite sensitive to changes in their price. For others, they are not very sensitive at all. In short, price elasticity of demand varies for different productive resources, just as it does for different final goods and services, as you saw in Chapter 4.

One key influence on *FACTOR PRICE ELASTICITY OF DEMAND* is, in fact, the price elasticity of demand for the final product or products that the factor is used to produce. If consumers are very sensitive to price changes for a product, the firms that make it will be sensitive to even small changes in the prices of the factors of production they use. That's because higher factor payments (say wages) lead to a higher price for the product and, if demand for the product is price elastic, to a relatively large drop in sales. On the other hand, if people buy almost the same amount of a product when its price rises, then employers can pass on wage or other factor-price increases to customers while maintaining production levels close to what they were, and employing nearly as many inputs. This is another aspect of derived demand which all resource owners and employers must face: the price elasticity of demand for a factor varies directly with the price elasticity of demand for the products it produces.

Two other major determinants of the price elasticity of demand for a factor of production are similar to those we discussed as determinants of price elasticity of demand for final goods and services. They are: (1) the availability of close substitutes that can be used to produce the same goods and services, and (2) the proportion of the total costs of producing a product that is accounted for by payments to the given resource. If many close substitute inputs are available, then obviously the demand for a particular input will be relatively price elastic. And if a factor represents a relatively large part of the cost of producing a good or service, the demand for that factor is usually price elastic, *ceteris paribus*. Employers will be willing to give larger wage increases for labor that is difficult to replace in a production process (e.g., a superstar athlete whose play and personality draws many paying fans), or labor that represents a small part of their overall costs (e.g., ministers who preside at elaborate and very expensive weddings).

The price elasticity of demand for a given input will also be higher if the price elasticity of supply for other factors of production is high -- that is, if firms can expand their use of the other factors without driving up the prices for those inputs sharply. That makes it less expensive for producers to substitute those resources when the price of a given input increases, and the cheaper it is for firms to substitute the other resources, the more sensitive they will be to price increases for an input.

The Supply of Factors of Production

The supply of factors of production to perfectly competitive firms is perfectly price elastic, and set by the market price for a given input. At the market level, the supply of labor and entrepreneurial services is typically upward sloping, due to the higher opportunity cost of leisure time when payment rates to these factors increase. There is, however, an income effect associated with these higher rates, which leads many people to increase their demand for leisure.

The supply of land, or natural resources, is vertical. All payments for such resources represent economic rents, which are payments greater than the minimum amount required to make them available for use in a production process. The supply of capital resources is upward sloping because higher interest payments are required to make consumers give up the use of more resources today and defer consumption to future periods. That suggests a positive time premium for goods and services -- and therefore for money, which represents the ability to purchase goods or services. This positive time premium means that future expenditures and receipts must be discounted to find their present value.

The Supply of Labor and Entrepreneurship: Income and Substitution Effects

The quantity of labor and entrepreneurship available to prospective employers is, typically, directly related to the price paid to the owners of those resources. As the price increases, so (usually) does the quantity of the productive resource supplied. This relationship seems to be a matter of simple common sense. But in fact, two important concepts you have seen earlier -- the income and substitution effects -- underlie the relationship, as well as the occasional exceptions to it.

Higher payments for wages, salaries, and profits make it more expensive for individuals *not* to sell their time and energies to producers, because those higher payments make leisure time relatively more expensive. In other words, the opportunity cost of leisure has increased. A substitution effect occurs whenever relative prices change, and in this case the relative price of leisure has clearly gone up. That part of the increase in factor payments to labor and entrepreneurship will, therefore, always lead individuals to take less leisure and increase the number of hours worked, other things remaining unchanged.

But in this case it isn't reasonable to think that all other things remain unchanged. Recall that the payments made to factors of production are not only a direct cost of producing goods and services, but also the source of income for those who provide these resources to firms. As factor payments rise, the factor owners are receiving higher incomes. And if leisure is a normal good, as it appears to be for most people (at least in the income ranges that are achieved by most U.S. families), these higher incomes lead to an increase in the demand for leisure. Obviously, the only way to increase leisure time is to work less, so the income effect of higher wage or profit payments to individuals is to decrease the quantity of the labor or entrepreneurship they supply.

That leads to a basic question: Will the income effect of an increase in the factor payment entirely, or only partially, offset the substitution effect? Theoretically, it is possible for the income effect to dominate, leading to a *BACKWARD-BENDING FACTOR SUPPLY CURVE* such as the one shown in Figure 15-3.

417

Figure 15-3
The Supply of Labor and Entrepreneurship,
and the Possibility of Backward-Bending Supply Curves

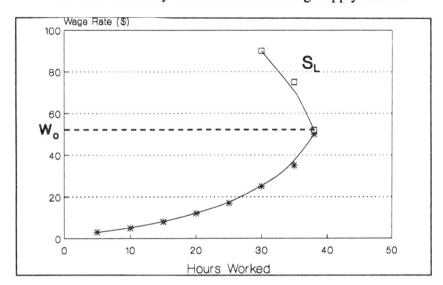

An individual's supply curve for labor or entrepreneurial services can be separated into two distinct ranges. On the upward-sloping segment of the curve, ab, which we observe for all factor-payment levels up to W_0, the substitution effect dominates the income effect. In this range, the individual responds to increased factor payments by working more hours, because of the higher opportunity cost of leisure time. In the negatively-sloped segment, bc, which begins at W_0 and continues for all higher rates of pay, the income effect dominates the substitution effect. Wage increases in this range will cause laborers to reduce hours worked, because their demand for leisure (assumed to be a normal good) is increasing. Workers who do not view leisure as a normal good will not have a backward-bending segment on their labor supply curve.

It is clear that there are some individual workers with backward-bending supply curves for their labor services. These are the people who quit their jobs after winning the lottery, or start taking more vacation days after they get a big raise. It is also true that, over this century, as wage rates have increased in real terms (i.e., adjusted for price-level changes), the average length of the work week for all workers has decreased. In 1909, the average work week for manufacturing workers was 51 hours; by 1990 that had fallen to 40.8 hours, and to 34.5 hours for all U.S. workers in the private sector excluding those in agriculture.[4] In effect, higher living standards were taken partly in the form of higher wages and incomes, and partly in the form of increased leisure.

Nevertheless, it is extremely rare to find negatively-sloped factor supply curves for the overall groups of workers in a particular labor *market*, because higher wages in one occupation or market area will attract workers from other occupations or areas. Accordingly, the market supply curves for labor we show henceforth will have a standard, upward slope.

---

[4]*Historical Statistics of the United States* and *Economic Indicators*, March 1991, both published by the U.S. Government Printing Office.

The Supply of Land: Economic Rents Revisited

In the markets for land (natural resources) and capital, the opportunity cost of leaving a resource unemployed clearly increases when the prices of these factors increase, just as in the markets for labor and entrepreneurship. But the issue of leisure time does not apply as it does in labor and entrepreneurial markets -- what does a machine or plot of ground care if it is used or left idle -- while other considerations become relatively much more important.

In a pure sense, land, by which economists mean all goods provided by nature which can be used to produce other goods and services, has the vertical and perfectly price inelastic supply curve shown in Figure 15-4. Nature has provided only so many of these goods, no matter how high or how low (including 0) their price. By definition, then, the supply of pure land can't be increased by human effort. Fields that are reclaimed from the sea as in Holland, and new forests that are grown by a logging or paper company to be "harvested" in 20 to 40 years, are indeed new inputs. But they are not classified as land because they weren't provided by nature. Instead, economists consider them new capital goods, created through long-term investments by producers. Those capital goods can certainly have a standard, positively sloped, supply curve; but pure land resources won't.

Figure 15-4
The Supply of Land (Natural Resources)

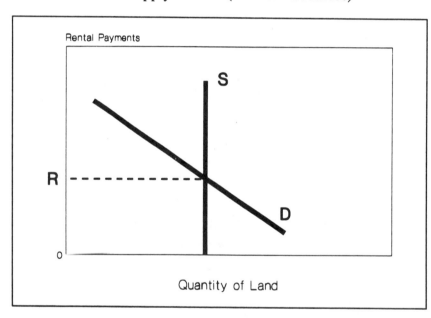

A resource that is provided by nature in some fixed quantity has a perfectly price-inelastic supply curve. For such a "pure" land resource, the quantity available for use is the same at a zero price, an infinite price, or any price in between. The price for such resources, R, depends (as always) on where the demand curve for them intersects the supply curve.

Uncultivated areas of land, virgin forests, and crude oil and mineral deposits are examples of such resources. However, when we include the other resources that may be required to find, transport, and prepare the land resources for sale to producers and consumers, the relevant supply curves for these products are no longer for pure land resources, but rather for inventories of refined resources. Those supply curves will have a standard (positive) slope.

There is, of course, an opportunity cost entailed in the decision to use a land resource in any one way -- specifically, the next best use that could have been made of it. But there is no opportunity cost involved in terms of reduced leisure time for these resources, so there won't be a backward-bending segment of these curves, either. What's left, in the absence of the standard, upward-slope of most supply curves, and the backward-bending segments observed for some labor resources, is the perfectly vertical supply curve for pure land resources.

Payments for the use of land are called *RENTS*, but the economic concept of rents is much broader than that statement implies. They key idea in economists' definition of rents is that they are payments over and bove the payment that would be required to keep a particular quantity of a resource available for use in a production process. Clearly, for the pure land resource shown in Figure 15-4 with perfectly inelastic supply, the same quantity of the resource will be supplied at any price, including zero. Therefore, *all* of the payment that is made for its use is economic rent, because the same amount of the resource will still be there, in the same form, even if it is paid nothing.

But what about a resource that has a standard, positively-sloped supply curve, as shown in Figure 15-5? This could even be the supply curve for labor resources, in the range where the substitution effect of wage increases dominates the income effect. Can any of the payments to this kind of resource be considered economic rent? Actually, yes. At all prices above the price required to first get some quantity of this resource to be made available in this factor market (point C in Figure 15-5), some units of the resource receive more than the minimum amount that is required to get them to supply the resource to this use. For example, at the price of $10, 50 units of labor are supplied; and the area ABC identifies payments over and above what would have been required to get all units before the 50th to work in this market. In Chapter 4, this area was called a producer surplus, which simply means that producer surplus is really another name for economic rents, and *vice versa*.

Figure 15-5
Producer Surplus and Economic Rents

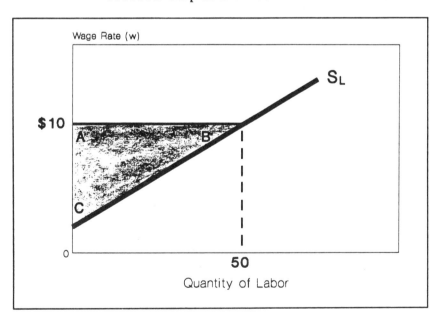

To get 50 units of labor in the factor market shown above, firms must pay a wage rate of $10. But that means all units of labor up to the 50th are paid more than the wage rate that is required to get them to work. The triangular area ABC represents their area of producer surplus, or economic rents. Wages paid to the last unit hired in this market, on points directly on the supply curve (such as point B) are transfer payments -- payments just high enough to entice this unit into this market, away from other uses.

Payments that don't provide any economic rent -- that are the minimum amount required to have the resource made available in a production process -- are the price and quantity points that lie directly on a standard, upward-sloping supply curve, such as point B in Figure 15-5. The 50th unit of labor won't be supplied in this use for a payment of less than $10, but will do something else instead (either in some other factor market, or in leisure and household activities outside of any factor market). A payment of $10 is just sufficient to make it worthwhile for this unit to forgo those alternative opportunities, and for that reason are called *TRANSFER PAYMENTS*. In simplest terms, they keep the resource from transferring out of this use and into its next-best alternative. Professional ballplayers who say that they would play for their teams even if they weren't paid to do it are saying, in effect, that anything they are paid to play their game is an economic rent. Most of them soon learn not to make such statements.

Sellers of productive resources naturally want to take in all of the rents they can, even if that means using political measures or union negotiations to increase their wages above their competitive alternatives. Economists describe such activities as *RENT-SEEKING* behavior, and often use the term in distinctly pejorative tones when rents are acquired through non-market or anti-competitive activities, such as favored tax treatment from a legislature, or collusion to form a cartel. (Think about it -- grants from the legislature and economic profits earned by cartels are, in fact, payments that exceed what the groups who receive them could earn in their next-best use of those resources. In other words, those payments are another form of economic rents.) Producers who hire or buy resources to use as inputs in their businesses are, of course, interested in trying to minimize the economic rents they pay.

In the competitive factor markets presented in this chapter, neither buyers nor sellers of inputs have any market power in setting wages, economic rents, or any other factor payments. That is not true, however, in the imperfectly competitive settings we will discuss in the next chapter.

The Supply of Capital Goods and Loanable Funds: Present vs. Future Opportunity Costs

Capital goods are intermediate goods, made to be used in producing other goods and services. Producing capital goods today entails the opportunity cost of reduced levels of current consumption, since the resources used to make the capital goods could have been used to make consumer goods. Therefore, in a general sense, the supply of capital resources depends on peoples' willingness to reduce their current consumption of goods and services, in order to finance the production of the products that will increase future output and consumption. Most people and businesses won't do that unless there is some financial incentive or other reward for going without things now.

For businesses, those incentives take the form of expected future profits. But for those who don't take the direct risks of a particular enterprise, and instead simply reduce their current consumption to make resources available for others to use in making capital investments, the payment is some form of interest. Businesses are net borrowers -- that is, as a group they borrow more than they save. Therefore, they depend on households to make resources available to finance their investment projects. In practice, this is accomplished through banks and other financial institutions, which serve as intermediaries between savers and borrowers.

Banks pay interest to those who make deposits in different kinds of savings accounts, then lend those funds out to borrowers at higher rates of interest. The "spread" between the rates banks charge to borrowers and pay to savers is the basic source of their own profits and, of course, of the revenues they use to pay their employees and the other factors of production which they use. But this spread is typically small, due to competition among banks and other firms that pay for deposits; so for now we will simply ignore it, and describe how the equilibrium rate of interest for a given kind of loan is set in the market for these savings and loanable funds. (To talk about "the" interest rate is, as you probably know, another simplification. Different rates are charged for different kinds of loans -- for example loans of different payback periods, or made to borrowers with different credit histories and financial security. But the general factors we describe below affect the rates for all different kinds of loans.)

The greater the rate of interest offered to savers, the greater the opportunity cost of *not* saving becomes. Because of that, the supply of loanable funds is upward sloping, as shown in Figure 15-6. What that really means is that, as the interest rate increases, more people are willing to reduce their current consumption, because they will receive more money in the future to buy the things they want then.

Looking quickly at the other side of this market, more funds will be demanded, and the number of capital investment projects undertaken will be increased, when interest rates decrease. That happens simply because, as the interest rate falls, the costs of borrowing to buy cars, houses, factories, and all other kinds of capital goods falls.

Not surprisingly, with an upward-sloping supply curve and a downward-sloping demand curve, an equilibrium interest rate and quantity of loanable funds are established. By now, this should be old hat to you. But there is one very special feature of this kind of market, which both suppliers and demanders of funds used for capital projects must face. That is the question of the *TIME VALUE OF MONEY*, or of the productive resources and final goods and services that money, in the form of loanable funds, is used to buy. The time value of these funds and resources is measured through the process of discounting, by calculating what are known as net present values.

Figure 15-6
The Loanable Funds Market

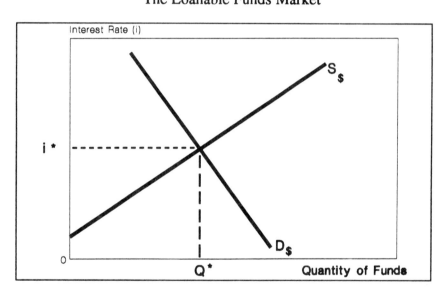

As interest rates rise, the quantity of loanable funds supplied increases and the quantity demanded decreases. Equilibrium is determined by the intersection of the supply and demand curves, as in other kinds of markets.

Discounting and Net Present Value

When you think about lending funds to others, three separate risk and cost factors are relevant to your decision. The first risk is the threat of inflation: What will happen to the prices of *all* goods and services between the time you lend out your funds and the time you are repaid. Obviously, if you think the inflation rate -- the average rate of increase for all prices -- is going to be 5% over the next year, from an investment standpoint it would be foolish for you to lend out funds over that period unless you receive at least a 5% interest payment over and above the principal sum you lend out.

The second risk you face is that whomever you lend the funds to may not repay them, for reasons ranging from death, illness, and business failure all the way to outright deception and fraud. Banks and other savings institutions spread these risks by forming risk "pools" made up of hundreds or thousands of borrowers who are judged to carry the same risk of loan default. The banks estimate the fees, or interest-rate premiums, required to offset the estimated number of loans that won't be repaid in each pool. Naturally, then, borrowers and investors who fall in the riskier loan pools will pay higher interest rates than those that are charged on safer loans.

The final and unavoidable cost you incur by lending out your savings is, as you saw earlier, giving up the use of those resources for the duration of the loan. You could have used those resources to increase your current consumption, or in alternative investments. Either way, giving up those uses imposes a real cost on lenders, which they must expect to recoup through the interest payments they receive.

With those three factors understood, it is easy to see why a sum of money that is to be paid to you at some time in the future (or that you will pay to someone else in the future) is worth less to you than that same sum would be if you received it or paid it out today. Inflation, default risk, and the real cost of reducing current consumption mean that money in your hand today is worth more than the promise of the same amount of money in the future. But at some premium, it will be worthwhile to trade that dollar today for more dollars in the future.

Calculating the present value of future payments is known as *DISCOUNTING*. For example, after considering all of the factors discussed above, if you decide you will only be willing to lend $100 today in exchange for the promise of $120 to be paid to you in exactly one year, your effective annual rate of discount is 20%. The higher that rate is, the more you value present income and wealth compared to future income and wealth. Conversely, someone who values a future payment of $1 exactly as much as a $1 payment today does not discount future income at all -- that is, their effective rate of discount is 0%.

Specifically, the *PRESENT VALUE* of an amount M to be paid in one year is calculated as

$$PV = \frac{M}{(1+i)} \qquad \text{(in one year)}$$

where i is the annual rate of discount, expressed in decimal form. Clearly, then, if i = 0%, the present value of any future payment is still equal to M. But as this discount factor increases, the value of the future payments fall. For example, if i = 10%, you value a dollar received or paid out one year from today as $1/1.1 = $.9091. But when that rate is 20%, you value a dollar to be paid one year from today only $1/1.2 = $.8333 -- more than 7 1/2 cents less than at a 10% rate. Another way of looking at this is to say that if the interest rate paid on your savings is 20%, you don't have to deposit as much today to have $100 in one year as you do when the interest rate is 10%. But recognize that the interest rate you are paid is greater than 0% precisely *because* of the risk and cost factors we have been discussing.

A positive rate of discount also means that the further in the future a dollar is to be paid, the less valuable it is today. In other words, if you value a dollar to be paid one year from now less than you do a current dollar, you will value a dollar to be paid two years from today even less than the dollar to be paid in one year. This inverse relationship between the value of money and time is given by the equation

$$PV = \frac{M}{(1+i)^t} \qquad \text{(in t years)}$$

where t is the number of years and M and i are defined as they in the last formula.

Using this formula, Table 15-2 shows the present value of $1000 over different periods of time, and at different interest rates. For example, the present value of $1,000 you will receive in 20 years is only $401.88 if the annual interest rate is 5%, and even less than that if the interest rate is higher. So when Jim Kelley, the pro football quarterback, signed a $40 million contract with a World Football League team when he first entered the pros, because those payments were to be made over a 20-year period the present value of his contract wasn't really $40 million, but less than $20 million. Poor guy.

Table 15-2
The Present Value of $1000

Annual Interest Rate (%)	Years to Payment				
	1	5	10	20	30
1	990.10	951.47	905.29	819.54	741.92
2	980.39	905.73	820.35	672.97	552.07
5	952.38	783.53	613.91	376.89	231.38
10	909.09	620.92	385.54	148.64	57.31
20	833.33	401.88	161.51	26.08	4.21

The present value of a future cash payment decreases as the interest rate rises (moving down in any column), and as the payment is pushed further into the future (moving to the right in any row).

Tables like Table 15-2, and the present value formula with which it is constructed, are routinely used by firms, governments, and individuals making long-run investment decisions. Those decisions require evaluations of such diverse things as the future costs and benefits of new factories, highways, and dams, and of buying a house or going to college. In other words, they are important whenever economic decisions deal with money to be paid or received in future years. And almost everyone, and every kind of organization, faces such questions sooner or later.

Because both future costs *and* benefits are encountered in virtually all of those cases, what we really want to calculate is the *NET PRESENT VALUE* of these various investments, which is simply the present value of the expected benefits minus the present value of the expected costs. Then, we can compare the value of the discounted benefits to the value of the discounted costs, and establish the overall rate of return on an investment, in percentage terms. Firms routinely compare these expected rates of return across all of their available investment opportunities, and will normally undertake the most profitable projects (on a risk-adjusted basis) first. But individuals and governments also make use of this procedure, since they engage in large investments in individual and social projects, respectively. For example, from the standpoint of pure economic efficiency in investments, we shouldn't pay the costs of building a highway, or of sending someone to college, if the rate of return is negative *or* lower than what we could earn on other investments with comparable risks.

Equilibrium Outcomes in Competitive Factor Markets

In equilibrium, perfectly competitive firms will maximize profits or minimize losses by hiring units of variable inputs up to the point where the factor's VMP is equal to the marginal factor cost (MFC). This is, of course, similar to the MR = MC result you saw in Chapters 9-13, and in more general terms to the marginal benefits = marginal costs rule for optimizing behavior by individuals, firms, and governmental agencies.

MFC = VMP

To review and extend the analysis of the previous section, let's step back and look at a graph of an overall factor market in a competitive setting. Panel (A) in Figure 15-7 shows a market supply and demand curve for a factor of production (in this case labor) interacting to set the equilibrium price (in this case the wage rate) for that input. These market curves are found by adding up (horizontally) the quantity of labor that each firm in the market will hire at each different wage rate, and the quantity of labor that individual workers in the market will supply at a given wage.

Figure 15-7
Equilibrium in a Competitive Factor Market

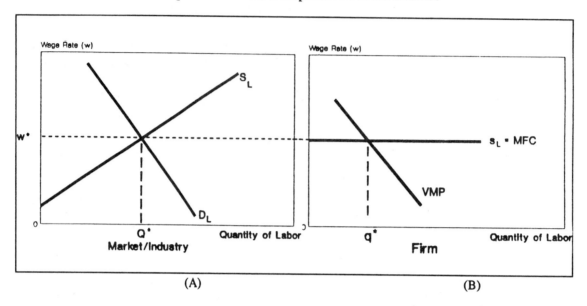

(A)   (B)

In a perfectly competitive labor market, the market demand curve is found by horizontally summing each firm's demand curve for a certain kind of worker (as derived in Figure 15-1). The market supply curve is the horizontal summation of individual workers' supply curves (developed in Figure 15-3). Typical market supply and demand schedules are shown in panel (A), resulting in equilibrium wage and employment levels of w* and Q*, respectively.

A competitive *firm* can hire as many workers as it wants at the market wage rate, but no workers will be willing to work for that firm at a lower wage rate. The firm's supply curve for labor is thus a horizontal line at the market wage rate (panel B). That wage rate is also the firm's cost of hiring additional workers, or its marginal factor cost. To maximize profits or minimize losses, perfectly competitive firms hire where VMP = MFC, at q*.

Panel (B) in this figure shows how the market price for labor (or any other factor) becomes the supply curve of that input for any individual firm that hires its productive resources in a competitive market. This is, in other words, how the firms act as wage takers in competitive factor markets. Because each firm is so small that it hires an insignificant part of the total quantity of labor (or other factors) hired in this market, it can hire as many workers as it wants at the market rate, just as it can sell all of its output at the market price. It must pay at least this wage rate or workers will simply go down the street and work for another competitive firm that does pay it. But there is also no point in the firm paying more than this wage, since it can get all of the workers it wants at this price. This shows clearly that the market price for an input is also the competitive firm's *MARGINAL FACTOR COST* of the input or, in plain English, what it has to pay out to hire one more unit of the resource.

The MFC curve intersects the perfectly competitive firm's VMP curve just as you saw earlier, in Figure 15-1, although we we didn't call the wage rate the MFC line at that point. The firm will hire, naturally, where these two curves intersect. Thus, we can re-state the hiring rule in this competitive setting (for labor and all other factors of production) as VMP = MFC. That emphasizes the parallels with the MR = MC output rule for firms in output markets, and with the more general marginal benefit = marginal cost rule used by consumers and government agencies in applying cost-benefit analysis to the economic decisions they must make. That's just one more way of showing that, in all areas of microeconomics, the notion of decision making at the margin is an essential feature of rational behavior.

Special Topics in Factor Market Analysis

To complete our review of competitive factor markets, in this section we examine three different topics that show how these markets work in 'the real world,' sometimes under conditions of unregulated price movements, and in others with legal price floors and ceilings. Specifically, we consider how compensating wage differentials are established across different labor markets, the effects of laws establishing minimum wages and maximum interest rates on consumer loans, and market returns on investments in human capital.

Compensating Wage Differentials

Why do doctors earn more, on average, than lawyers, secretaries, and carpenters? And why do doctors who work in Los Angeles or New York earn more than doctors in Indianapolis and Peoria? Even houses of equal size and quality cost more in some parts of the country than others, as well as downtown office space that is identical in appearance and size. Why? In this section, we will consider the question of how *relative* wages and other factor payments are set across various markets, not just in a single market for a particular kind of input.

But to think about different markets is, essentially, to already answer these questions in the basic way you saw even in the first chapter of this book. The fundamental thing to understand, once again, is that market-determined factor payments reflect and measure relative scarcity, just like market-determined prices for final goods and services. That scarcity is determined by the forces of supply and demand -- the two blades of the scissors all over again.

Resources that are very productive and contribute greatly to a firm's output and profitability will enjoy very strong demand. But at the same time, if such a resource is readily available -- say, for example, as general labor that requires comparatively little training and on-the-job experience -- then its supply may be high enough to keep the price of this resource relatively low. As always, it is the two forces together that determine the wage, salary, profit, interest rate, or rent that a resource commands in a factor market.

In practice, the supply of and demand for workers in a particular labor market are the results of decisions made by individual workers and firms. And a great many considerations enter into these decisions. For example, jobs characterized by unpleasant or dangerous working conditions typically attract a smaller supply of workers, so workers in those jobs receive a positive wage differential compared to workers with similar skills facing no such risks or unpleasant working conditions. Studies conducted in the United States, Great Britain, and Korea have found that jobs carry an annual premium ranging from $35 to $500 as the risk of being killed on the job goes up one death a year for every 10,000 workers. (To put this in perspective, in steel mills the approximate annual death rate is 1 in 10,000; in the logging industry, the fatality rate is about 10 times higher.) Although they vary considerably, these premiums suggest that if a firm with 1000 employees could implement safety programs which saved one worker's life every 10 years, it could reduce its annual wage bill by between $35,000 and $500,000.[5]

Wages also have to be higher, *ceteris paribus*, to offset the financial difficulties of the frequent or seasonal layoffs that occur in some industries. Conversely, relatively pleasant, intellectually satisfying, and very secure jobs sometimes pay less than jobs with lower skill requirements, simply because so many workers seek these jobs. Workers who live in particularly desirable geographical areas often receive lower wages because so many people are willing to pay a premium, in the form of lower wages, to live there. And of course workers in otherwise

[5]See Robert S. Smith's review article on "Compensating Wage Differentials and Public Policy," *Industrial and Labor Relations Review*, April 1979, pp. 339-52; and Ronald G. Ehrenberg and Smith's textbook on *Modern Labor Economics: Theory and Public Policy*, 4th ed., HarperCollins Publishers, 1991, pp. 274-77.

426

identical jobs frequently receive different wages based on cost-of-living differences in different regions of the country.

Wages, fringe benefits, working conditions, location, the social prestige of a particular occupation, and many other things go into an individual worker's utility schedule, and influence his or her decision about what kind of work to do, where to live, and what organization to work for. Economists don't assume that workers always take the highest-paying job, but rather that they take the job which, in conjunction with the many other circumstances of their lives, allows them to achieve the highest level of overall satisfaction.

The demand for any particular kind of worker is generally established by workers' productivity and the demand for the products a firm makes, as we showed earlier in this chapter. However, it is worth noting that certain firms will find other worker characteristics important, too, and try to attract workers who have them. For example, a company that finds it expensive to reduce the risk of injuries to its workers may try to attract single workers who are less risk-averse than most, perhaps by paying higher wages but offering lower insurance benefits. Conversely, a firm that finds absenteeism and turnover very costly may try to attract married workers who are more tied to a community -- in some cases such firms have adopted attendance bonuses that are paid to workers' spouses.

The result of all these supply and demand decisions are significant *WAGE DIFFERENTIALS* in different geographical areas and, as shown in Table 15-3, in different occupations.

Table 15-3
1987 Median U.S. Weekly Earnings of Full-Time Employees, by Occupation

Accountants and Auditors	515	Mail Carriers	487
Actors and Directors	429	Mechanical Engineers	722
Airline Pilots and Navigators	713	Mechnics and Repairers	424
Architects	720	Personnel and Training Specialists	507
Bakers	280	Photographers	356
Bank Tellers	290	Physicians	698
Bill and Account Collectors	315	Plumbers and Pipefitters	465
Butchers and Meat Cutters	326	Police Officers and Detectives	482
Caprenters	441	Private Guards and Police	266
Chemists (Except Biochemists)	631	Psychologists	483
Civil Engineers	664	Registered Nurses	482
Computer Programmers	543	Sales Representatives, Retail & Business Services	489
Construction Helpers	252	Sales Representatives, Retail & Personnel Services	222
Crane and Tower Operators	465	Secretaries	301
Farm Operators and Managers	275	Social Workers	413
Economists	635	Stock Clerks	285
Electrical Engineers	736	Taxicab Drivers and Chauffers	322
Electricians	471	Teachers, College and University	635
File Clerks	261	Teachers, Elementary Grades	462
Hairdressers and Cosmetologists	213	Teachers, Secondary Grades	503
Hotel Clerks	209	Telephone Operators	311
Lawyers	814	Tool and Die Makers	522
Librarians	452	Waiters and Waitresses	190
Maids and Housemen	198	Welders and Cutters	311

Source: Table B-31, *Labor Force Statistics Derived from the Current Population Survey, 1948-87*, U.S. Department of Labor, Bureau of Labor Statistics, August 1988, pp. 764-67.

427

Minimum Wage and Usury Laws: Price Controls in Factor Markets

As you saw in Chapter 4, people often aren't satisfied with prices that are based strictly on market measures of relative scarcity. Political leaders, in particular, may say "What a better world it would be if only this one little price for this one product was higher, or if this price for some other product were lower." Before long a law or regulation is adopted to change those prices, and everyone will supposedly live happily ever after.

The truth is that price controls typically create serious problems in factor markets, just as in product markets. In the competitive markets we are discussing in this chapter, those problems can be particularly severe. It may be that the benefits of some price controls are great enough to compensate for their costs, of course; but economists believe that is very unlikely. Let's look quickly at two examples of these price controls to see why. We will first examine an example of a price floor in labor markets, the minimum wage law, then a price ceiling in loanable funds markets, so-called "usury laws" on interest rates for consumer loans.

Minimum Wage Laws. A legal minimum wage is just that: the lowest wage that, by law, an employer may pay an employee. Obviously, a legal minimum wage that is set at or below the market wage will have no effect on wages or employment levels. But Figure 15-8 shows what happens in a competitive labor market when the minimum wage is set above the market wage. Some workers (Q_d) will continue to be employed at the now-higher wage, and will be better off; others ($Q^* - Q_d$) who were working at the market wage will now be unemployed, and worse off than they were. Still others who weren't trying to work at the lower market wage rate ($Q_s - Q^*$) will now look for work at the higher wage, but often won't find jobs and instead join the ranks of the unemployed.

Figure 15-8
The Minimum Wage in a Competitive Labor Market

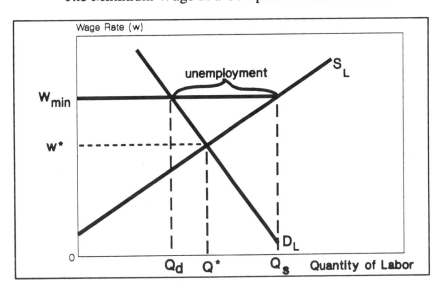

Initially, the competitive market wage and employment levels are w* and Q*. If a legal minimum wage higher than w* is imposed as shown, the result is a surplus of labor, since quantity supplied exceeds quantity demanded at w_{min}. Workers who want to work at this wage rate but cannot find jobs are added to official counts of unemployed workers. Workers who continue to work at the higher wage rate are better off than they were without the minimum wage law. Those who are laid off ($Q^* - Q_d$) are most clearly hurt by the law. A minimum wage imposed at or below w* would, obviously, have no effect.

So some workers will benefit from higher minimum wages, and some will lose. Will the gains outweigh the losses? That depends, of course, on the actual numbers involved each time the minimum wage is increased.

There is a wealth of historical evidence to consider on this question, however, and a longstanding debate over that evidence.

Many proponents of higher minimum wages point out that employment levels have increased after previous increases in the minimum wage, and argue from that evidence that no adverse effects on employment have resulted from the higher wages. But this ignores the fact that, because the U.S. economy was growing over time, the demand curve for labor was increasing even after the increases in the minimum wage. While this means that employment can increase while the minimum wage is rising, it doesn't mean that there is no cost associated with the wage increase. Instead, the increase in employment may be less than it would have been in the absence of the higher minimum wage.

Summarizing numerous studies on the effects of minimum wage laws in the United States over the past 40 years, and recent review articles on those studies, Ronald Ehrenberg and Robert Smith, two prominent labor economists at Cornell University, conclude that:

> a 10 percent increase in the minimum wage would reduce teenage employment by 1 to 3 percent and the employment of young adults (ages 20 to 24) by a somewhat smaller amount. There is no consensus...on the effects of minimum wage legislation on other adults, perhaps because far fewer adults are directly affected by the minimum wage (most have wages in excess of the minimum).[6]

The relative scarcity of labor, based on workers' productivity in contributing to the output produced and sold by firms and other organizations, is responsible for the level of the great majority of wage and salaries paid in the United States. Only a small percentage of workers at any given time is paid the minimum wage; and while many workers begin working at these wage rates, few do so for very long -- most develop valuable skills and experience on the job, or in educational programs. Minimum wage laws *may* have some role to play as a poverty relief measure, although most economists are skeptical about that given the negative effects on teenagers and young adults, who are exactly the workers many politicians claim they are trying to help with a higher minimum wage.

"Usury" Laws. Usury laws limit the interest rates banks and other financial organizations are allowed to charge on loans. They can conceivably apply to any and all types of loans, but they are usually applied to consumer loans -- such as credit card balances, installment purchases arranged through personal finance companies, and automobile loans. As our example of these laws, we will consider the effects of a cap on the allowable interest rates for bank credit cards -- such as Visa and Mastercard.

Suppose a family, call them the "Smiths," wants to buy a new washer and dryer. Many people don't finance their appliances on bank cards, of course, because they have access to cheaper credit and loans, or savings to draw on. But for reasons explained below, the Smith family is considering whether or not to buy the appliances, knowing they will have to pay the credit card interest rate if they do.

Let's say the Smiths currently have five young children and only one employed adult in the family. They recently bought a house and a used car, and the bank isn't willing to extend them more credit through secured loans that charge less interest than their credit card rate. (Besides, washers and dryers aren't as valuable as collateral on loans as cars and houses, because cars and houses are easier to resell, if necessary, in well established and generally stable markets.) The family has to decide whether it is worthwhile to apply for a credit card and charge the washer and dryer on the card. The bank has to decide whether or not to issue the credit card to the family, if they choose to apply.

William Dunkelberg and J. Stephenson[7] calculated how much a family could save by buying a washer and dryer, compared to doing the same amount of laundry in a laundromat (which entails transportation costs and giving up time that could be used in other ways, as well as feeding quarters into the laundromat's machines). They expressed these savings as a percentage of the average annual cost of purchasing and operating a washer and

---

[6] *Modern Labor Economics*, 4th ed., HarperCollins, 1991, p. 92.

[7] *Durable Goods Ownership and the Rate of Return*, National Commission on Consumer Finance Studies, Volume VI, U.S. GPO, 1974.

dryer, and found that those savings varied directly with the number of loads of laundry a household did each week:

Loads Per Week	1	2	3	4	5	6	7	8	9	10
Rate of Return(%)	10	12	15	17	22	29	34	41	46	54

Let's say, conservatively, that our hypothetical family, with two adults and five small children, does nine loads of laundry a week. It therefore pays them, if these numbers are correct, to finance a washer and dryer on a credit card even if they have to pay a 40% or 45% annual interest rate. Fortunately for them, the credit card rate is currently 22%, and a bank officer indicates that the bank is likely to issue them a card.

At the 22% rate, the bank is willing to take on the risk of unsecured loans to the Smith family -- up to the credit limit set for their bank card (say $1500, which many banks will offer even to college students and other relatively high-risk groups of borrowers). But suppose that, before the bank issues the card to the Smiths, the state legislature adopts a maximum interest rate of 18% on these cards after intense lobbying efforts by a self-styled "consumer action group." There is a long history of that kind of legislation and public complaint against high interest rates. In fact, the phrase "usury law" is based on biblical prohibitions of certain kinds of interest charges, and some religious and political leaders (including the early leaders of the Soviet Union) considered any interest charges as a spiritual or political sin.

But what happens to borrowers like the Smiths if these prohibitions are put in place, even in the apparently moderate fashion of limiting interest rates to 18%? The effects are shown in Figure 15-9.

Figure 15-9
Rationing Credit Under Usury Laws

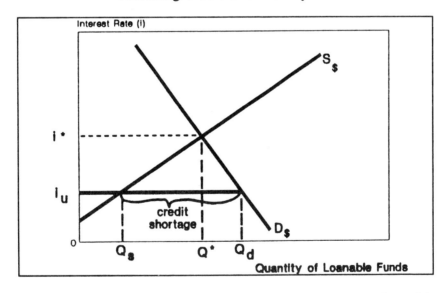

Initially, the equilibrium interest rate and quantity of funds borrowed and loaned are i* and Q*, respectively. A legal price ceiling, i_u, set below the market rate for this kind of loan, results in a shortage because the quantity of funds loaned out will decrease from Q* to Q_s, while the quantity of loans demanded will increase from Q* to Q_d. In that setting, lenders will ration out the loans they do make on a non-price (in this case non-interest-rate) basis. In particular, they are likely to make loans only to those who are the safest borrowers, in terms of their ability to repay the loans.

If banks must accept lower interest rates on the credit card accounts they issue, they will issue fewer of them. In particular, they will tighten credit standards and only issue cards to the people who are most likely to repay their loans. In general, that will not include large, low-income families like the Smiths, which have high debt-to-income ratios. So rather than lowering interest rates for all families, this usury law will eliminate the availability of this kind of credit for many families. (The Smith's may, however, rationally decide to turn to more expensive forms of credit, including illegal "loan shark" operations, as long as the rate doesn't exceed their rate of return on the appliances.) Other families -- those whose financial situation is strong enough to still qualify for the credit cards -- may benefit from the lower rates. But those probably weren't the families that the consumer-action groups which lobbied for the ususry law said they wanted to help.

The familiar moral of this story is: Good intentions without clear thinking and analysis rarely leads to good public policy on economic issues, and things can be even worse if politicians capitalize on favorable publicity that comes from adopting such price controls when journalists and voters don't understand the negative effects of such programs.

Human Capital

Figure 15-10 should be fairly reassuring to most college students. It suggests how much more, *on average*, people with various amounts of education earn than people with less education. Table 15-4 shows that a person's risk of unemployment falls as the amount of his or her education increases. Taken together, this means that there is a positive rate of return on investments in education for individuals who get these degrees and, perhaps, even to governments which subsidize education programs with tax revenues.

But some economists have pointed out that, beyond very basic and general skills such as reading and arithmetic, what people are taught in school is not what they use on the job, at least in many academic subject areas. They argue that the people who stay in school longer would, on average, be more productive than other workers even if they didn't go to school longer. What schooling really does, according to these economists, is *SIGNAL* or *SCREEN* more capable workers *for employers*.

Some schools, particularly at the college and graduate-school levels, may be prestigious enough to take only the very best applicants -- with "best" defined largely in terms of academic abilities, but to some extent also in terms of family wealth and social connections. These schools tend to graduate virtually every student who is accepted, but just attending that kind of school provides a signal to prospective employers.

Others schools screen students by accepting people with more varied abilities and backgrounds, but then assigning a wider range of grades based on competitive course performance, and perhaps even failing or driving off large numbers of weaker and less motivated students.

Both signaling and screening give employers valuable information about potential employees -- even if students haven't learned anything in school they will use on the job, and their productivity is no greater than it would have been if they hadn't gone to these schools.

As a public policy issue, government subsidies of education are economically sensible if education provides social benefits and a more productive labor force. But public funding is not appropriate if the gains from education are completely captured by individual employers and their employees who invested in education, or if there are less costly ways of identifying the most productive workers and increasing labor productivity.

From an individual worker's standpoint, however, it really doesn't matter why income goes up with additional education, or more on-the-job training, or anything else that makes you more valuable as a worker to an employer. All of these human capital decisions (which are distinct from consumption-oriented decisions to take academic courses just because you enjoy them) can be evaluated in terms of hard, cold cash. What does the education or training cost? What is the average rate of return to people who complete it? How do you adjust that average return if there is a larger (or smaller) risk that your own return will be less (or greater) than the average return? What are the discounted values for these costs and benefits? What interest rate do you use to discount those future sums of money? How much are the working conditions you will have in jobs that require more education worth to you? And so on.

431

Figure 15-10
The Economic Returns to Education

Total Money Earnings (Mean), Full-Time, Year-Round Male Workers, 1987

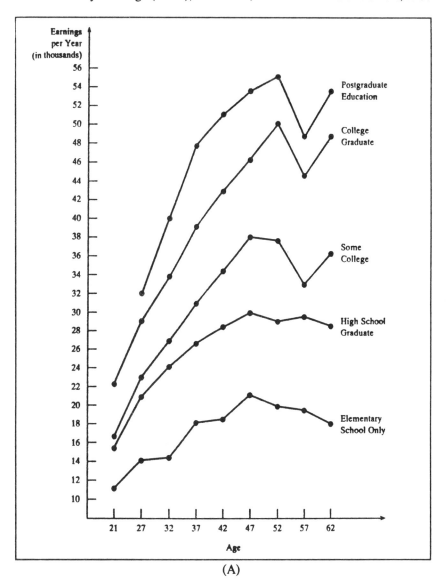

(A)

Total Money Earnings (Mean), Full-Time, Year-Round Female Workers, 1987

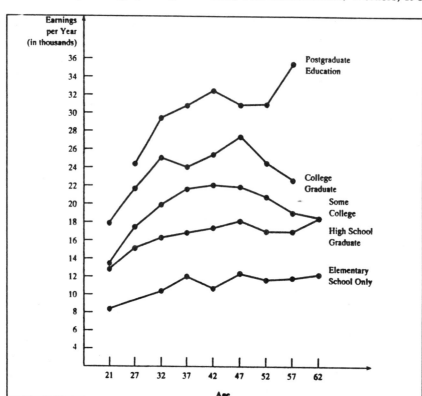

(B)

Workers with more education earn more, on average, than workers with less education. This is true both for male and female workers, and for adult workers of virtually any age. But because it is costly to acquire education, these gains represent a return on the investment workers make by accepting lower earnings in the present to go to school, with the expectation of higher future earnings. It is also true that some workers with little formal education earn more than many workers with more years of schooling. The differences in male and female earnings for workers with all levels of education are discussed in the next chapter.

Source: U.S. Bureau of the Census, *Money Income of Households, Families, and Persons in the United States: 1987*, Current Population Reports, Series P-60, No. 162, Table 36.

This is all very much like the decisions firms must make in undertaking their new investments. And of course individuals *are* acting as producers when they sell their own labor, or invest in it to improve its quality and productivity. In fact, for most people, this labor is their most valuable economic resource. Small wonder, then, that so many people do make such investments, particularly when the premium on mental skills and abilities is increasing, and the number of jobs that entail routine, manual labor is falling.

Table 15-4
Unemployment Rates for Persons Aged 25-64, March, Selected Years

		Educational Attainment			
Year	Overall	Less than 4 Years of High School	High School Graduate	1-3 Years of College	4 or More Years of of College
1987	5.7	11.1	6.3	4.5	2.3
1980	5.0	8.4	5.1	4.3	1.9
1970	3.3	4.6	2.9	2.9	1.3

Workers with more education are much less likely to be unemployed than workers who have not graduated from high school.

Source: *Labor Force Statistics Derived from the Current Population Survey, 1948-87*; U.S. Department of Labor, Bureau of Labor Statistics, Bulletin 2307, August 1988, p. 848.

These trends are not, however, inevitable and constant. For example, as the number of U.S. college graduates expanded rapidly in the 1970s due to the aging of the "baby boom" generation born from 1945-1960, the rate of return on a college education in the U.S. fell for several years. Still, as suggested in Figure 15-11 and by the growth in the percentage of Americans who have attended college since 1945, formal education has generally paid good dividends to graduates. Empirical estimates by labor economists suggest that the annual rate of return ranges from 5-15%, and many recent studies suggest returns in the 10-15% range. If you don't have a better investment opportunity (appropriately adjusted for the risks that are involved), and if the income you can earn without going to school longer isn't too high, school is the profitable place for you to be.

Case Study #19
The Slowdown in U.S. Productivity Growth, and Some International Comparisons

Labor *PRODUCTIVITY* is measured as the ratio output per unit of labor input -- e.g., as 30 loaves of bread per hour a baker works. For an individual worker, increasing productivity is the surest way to increase his or her wage. For the nation as a whole, increased productivity translates into more goods and services produced with the same inputs, which means that people have more to consume and that incomes and living standards are rising. Given this innate importance, and the fact that in the 1970s the rate of growth in U.S. labor productivity decreased dramatically, it is not surprising that the last 30 years have been a "golden age" for research on productivity. This case study is a brief review of that work.

Table 15-5 reports average annual growth rates in manufacturing productivity for four different time periods and 12 industrialized nations. Note that in all of these countries productivity growth was slower from 1973-79 than it was from 1960-73, and that (with only one exception) productivity growth was lower in the United States than in all the other countries in the first three time periods. The obvious question is, why did those things happen? The best answers economists can give to that question are based on findings such as those in Tables 15-6 and 15-7.

Table 15-5
Average Annual Growth Rates for Manufacturing Output per Man-Hour

Country	1950-60	1960-73	1973-79	1979-86
United States	2.0	3.2	1.4	3.1
Canada	3.8	4.5	2.1	1.4
Japan	9.5	10.3	5.5	5.6
Belgium	n.a.	6.9	6.2	5.3
Denmark	2.8	6.4	4.2	1.3
France	2.8	6.5	5.0	3.6
Germany	7.4	5.8	4.3	2.8
Italy	5.7	7.3	3.3	3.3
Netherlands	4.7	7.4	5.5	4.4[a]
Norway	3.4	4.3	2.1	1.9
Sweden	3.4	6.4	2.6	3.0
United Kingdom	2.1	4.3	1.1	4.4

[a] = 1979-85; n.a. = not available

Productivity growth decreased in most industrial nations after 1973, and was lower in the United States than most other industrialized nations from 1950-1979.

Source: Zvi Griliches, "Productivity Puzzles and R&D: Another Nonexplanation," *Journal of Economic Perspectives*, Fall 1988, p. 10. Griliches' source is a Bureau of Labor Statistics report, "International Comparisons of Manufacturing Productivity and Labor Cost Trends, 1986," U.S. Department of Labor publication 87-237.

The figures in Table 15-6 were developed by Edward Denison, in a series of classic studies on the sources of U.S. economic growth. The top set of numbers shows that much of the growth in total output for the U.S. economy occurred simply because, over time, the *quantity* of labor and capital inputs increased. The second group of numbers shows changes in the productivity of these factors, that translate into higher per capita incomes and output. Recognize, however, that the growth in the amount of capital inputs contributes to increases in labor productivity, by giving employees more factories and equipment to work with. Beyond that, Denison found that technological advances, economies of scale as enterprises and the overall economy grew larger, and improvements in labor quality -- such as those achieved through investments in human capital -- were they key factors in expanding the U.S. economy over most of the last century.

A recent study of productivity growth for thousands of categories of labor and capital confirmed the importance of the growth in the quantity of capital to U.S. economic growth and rising living standards, and in fact claimed that it is far more important than Denison and others have suggested, while the effects of increases in labor quality and other sources of productivity improvements were -- though positive -- much smaller.[8] Naturally, that suggests that policies designed to promote faster growth should stress increased capital investment.

[8] Dale Jorgenson, Frank Gollop, and Barbara Fraumeni, *Productivity and U.S. Economic Growth*, Cambridge, Mass.: Harvard University Press, 1987.

Table 15-6
Sources of Growth in U.S. National Income, 1929-1982

Source of Growth	Percent of Total Growth	
Input Quantity		51
Labor (Hours Worked)	32	
Capital	19	
Factor Productivity		49
Technological Advances	28	
Improved Quality of Labor	14	
Economies of Scale	9	
Improved Resource Allocation	8	
Legal-Social Environment	-1	
Other Factors	-8	

Source: Edward F. Denison, *Trends in American Economic Growth, 1929-1982*, (Washington: The Brookings Institution, 1985), p. 30. The first column does not sum to 100% due to rounding error. Denison's estimates are based on "real" values, meaning they have been adjusted for changes in price levels over this period.

Table 15-7 shows that productivity increases and decreases are not spread out evenly across different industries in the United States economy over time. Obviously, then, national productivity will increase more rapidly when a growing share of products is produced in sectors experiencing higher-than-average productivity increases, and *vice versa*. In fact, in the first half of this century, productivity growth was enhanced by the shift of jobs from agriculture to high productivity growth areas in manufacturing. But that trend could not continue forever, and is not a major factor in U.S. productivity growth today since agricultural jobs represent less than three percent of national employment.

Some of the drop-off in productivity growth through the 1970s, as reflected in Table 15-5, was due to a different kind of shift in employment: Manufacturing employment remained relatively constant as a percentage of total employment, but a growing proportion of national employment -- and output -- was found in service enterprises (including categories such as insurance and wholesale and retail trade, listed in Table 15-7). Historically, productivity increases have been relatively slow in the service sector, both because it has been more difficult to provide service workers with productivity-enhancing capital goods, and to measure productivity gains when they do occur.

Several other factors have been identified as at least partly responsible for the productivity slowdown of the 1970s. First and foremost are the rising energy prices of that period, initiated by the OPEC oil cartel. Increasing prices for this basic industrial input made some production methods inefficient almost overnight, requiring expensive and time-consuming adjustments. Shifts in product demand resulting from the higher relative prices of energy-intensive products, and the transfer of income from oil-consuming to oil-producing nations, also led to extensive structural adjustments in the economy.

Several studies found that the average quality of the labor force was dropping in the 1970s, as a result of more young workers taking jobs (the baby boomers were growing up) and an unprecedented number and percentage of women entering the labor force. These two groups, like all first-time workers, entered the job market with relatively little experience and few skills, compared to workers who had been in the labor force for some time. With a growing proportion of workers in this "first-job" category, average productivity levels were driven down.

Table 15-7
Productivity Growth in Major U.S. Business Sectors: Average Annual Rates

Sector	1949-66	1967-73	1974-85
All Private Industry	1.3	0.4	0.1
Agriculture, Forestry & Fisheries	-1.8	0.1	1.4
Mining	0.5	1.9	-4.3
Construction	1.7	-5.1	-1.1
Manufacturing	2.0	1.8	1.4
Transportation	1.0	1.6	0.1
Communication	2.7	3.0	2.3
Utilities	3.7	2.4	1.2
Wholesale Trade	0.8	0.8	-0.5
Retail Trade	0.6	-0.0	-0.4
Finance, Insurance, Etc.	-0.3	-0.9	-0.6
Services	-0.6	-0.2	0.1

Productivity is far from a constant factor across time or nations, as you saw in Table 15-5, or, as shown here, across different industry groups in the same country. When demand for goods produced by high productivity industries is growing rapidly, that tends to pull up the overall rate of productivity growth in a nation. Unfortunately, as the United States and many other nations discovered in the mid-1970s, the opposite statement is also true: rising demand for products produced in low productivity industries tends to slow the rate of productivity growth.

Source: Griliches, p. 11, whose source is Matthew D. Shapiro, "Measuring Market Power in U.S. Industry," National Bureau of Economic Research Working Paper No. 2212, 1987.

A final factor often cited as contributing to this period of low productivity growth is the adverse effect of government regulations on businesses. Rules dealing with environmental protection and employment practices (workplace safety and affirmative action programs, in particular) are most often cited in this context. No matter how great or small the overall social benefits of these programs, they usually increase firms' costs and reduce average output per worker. For example, workers that firms must hire to monitor and enforce the programs don't produce products for the firms, and so reduce productivity. The late 1960s and the 1970s were periods of rapid expansion of government regulation of business in the United States.

Let's now consider the second major issue raised at the beginning of this case study: Why did many other industrialized nations enjoy greater productivity growth than the United States in the 30-35 years after World War II?

For several decades after that war, the other industrialized nations were trying to rebuild their heavily damaged production base, and simply "catch up" to overall U.S. productivity *level*. To do that, they had to have productivity *growth* rates that were higher than those in the United States. Many of the countries did just that, as you saw earlier in Table 15-5. But that general pattern is not surprising to microeconomists, who expect to see investments flow to high-profit areas -- like countries that are rebuilding from periods of natural or manmade devastation, but still have a well educated and productive labor force, and quite possibly other natural and financial resources to draw on as well. Such circumstances present clear and relatively safe profit opportunities, because investors know what was profitable before the devastation took place. Investments quickly flow to those areas and productivity growth is, for some time, very high. In the period immediately following World War II, the recovery and growth of these industrial economies was also sped up by assistance programs funded by the United States, such as the Marshall plan.

Once these economies were rebuilt, they continued to enjoy advantages that helped them catch up with U.S. productivity levels, and exceed U.S. growth rates in productivity. Among the most important advantages were lower labor costs and the ability to import technology and management ideas that had been tested in the United States, without having to experiment and pay for ideas that didn't pan out. Still later, they began a full-blown competition in product innovation and research and development programs. And international differences in education and training programs, savings rates, and public tax and spending programs emerged, making some nations, including Japan, especially successful. But in a general sense, just as the United States had caught up with the established economies of Western Europe in the nineteenth century, the nations listed in Table 15-5 closed much of the gap in productivity and income levels by the late 1980s. A competitive and truly global economy had been reestablished.[9]

But that convergence of productivity and income levels doesn't extend to all nations. J. Bradford De Long recently criticized economists who accepted a simple and wide-ranging model of convergence, based only on data from countries which succeeded in becoming rich and industrially developed. He pointed out that Third World nations did not converge toward these levels, nor did countries like Spain, Portugal, Ireland, Argentina, and Chile, which were among the group of more developed nations in the late nineteenth century, but not successful in maintaining that position. De Long concluded that:

> The convergence of Japan and Western Europe toward U.S. standards of productivity in the years after World War II is an amazing achievement, and this does suggest that those present at the creation of the post-World War II international order did a very good job. But...the capability to assimilate industrial technology appears to be surprisingly hard to acquire, and it may be distressingly easy to lose.
>
> The forces making for 'convergence' even among industrial nations appear little stronger than the forces making for 'divergence.' The absence of convergence pushes us away from a belief that in the long-run technology transfer both is inevitable and is the key factor in economic growth. It pushes us away from the belief that even the nations of the now industrial West will have roughly equal standards of living in 2090 or 2190. And the absence of convergence even among nations relatively rich in 1870 forces us to take seriously arguments... that the relative income gap between rich and poor may tend to widen.[10]

Even where evidence shows that convergence is taking place -- among the U.S. states and the industrialized regions of Western Europe -- the rate of convergence tends to be very slow, about 2% a year.[11] If those historical rates hold in the future, the outlook is not very encouraging for today's less developed nations, including the regions and nations that were formerly part of the Soviet block, such as East Germany.

But while those findings may temper more optimistic estimates of future growth and convergence, they certainly aren't put forward as firm predications of future patterns. Economists have learned much about these forces in this century, but not nearly as much as there is still to be learned.

---

[9]See William J. Baumol's "Productivity Growth, Convergence and Welfare: What the Long-Run Data Show," *American Economic Review*, December 1986, pp. 1072-85. Also see Baumol's recent book, with Sue Anne Bately Blackman and Edward N. Wolff, *Productivity and American Leadership: The Long View*, Cambridge, Mass.: MIT Press, 1989.

[10]"Productivity Growth, Convergence, and Welfare: Comment," *American Economic Review*, December 1988, p. 1148.

[11]Robert J. Barro and Xavier Sala-I-Martin, "Convergence Across States and Regions," *Brookings Papers on Economic Activity*, Vol. 1, 1991, pp. 107-58.

438

Case Study #20
When to Cut a Forest

Apart from any value it takes on as a scenic area for humans, a wildlife preserve for animals, or a counteractant to the greenhouse effect, a forest can be thought of as a simple macro aggregation of individual trees. Suppose, for this case study, that the values forests have in those uses listed above are fully reflected in current lumber prices, as a result of the workings of private markets and government regulatory and tax policies. Given that assumption, the analysis that follows is relatively straightforward.

Most trees that are planted, cultivated, and harvested by commercial lumber and paper firms follow a predictable growth path, barring outside disturbances such as droughts, fires, floods, volcanic eruptions, and fungus and insect infestations. The trees tend to grow very rapidly in their early years, then the growth rate gradually slows down, as shown (hypothetically) in Figure 15-11. Growth is expressed there in percentage terms -- that is, in terms of how much more tree there is each year, compared to the amount of tree that was there a year ago.

Figure 15-11
When Do Trees Rate Better Than Bonds?

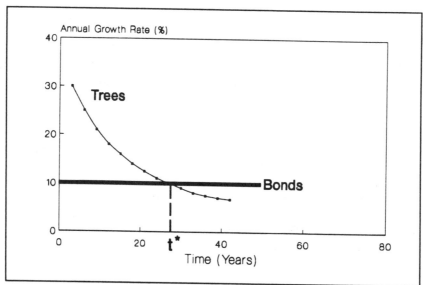

This graph is based on hypothetical data on growth rates for trees in a forest, and the interest rate on a bond, savings account, or other financial security. Given the annual rates of return on these assets as shown above, it will pay to plant and grow trees, and harvest them in year t*, when the trees are growing at the same rate as funds held in the financial securities.

Now suppose that you are in the lumber or paper business, and you have to decide when to most profitably harvest your organic resource. Two key factors enter your deliberation. First is your educated guess (since you are in this business) about where the price for your product is headed. Second is the growth rate of your product, *relative to the market rate of interest* you can get by investing the funds you would derive by cutting the forest and selling the timber products you make.

Again, for simplicity, we'll assume that you think the price of your product is going to stay the same. The question then becomes, simply, are you better off to harvest your forest now, or to let it keep growing for another year?

Under these assumptions, your decision isn't that difficult to make. If the marketable lumber in your forest is growing at 20% per year right now, and the interest rate you could get for investing the funds you will obtain if you cut the forest is only 10%, you would be foolish to cut the trees at this time. A year from now the re-invested funds will be worth 110% of what you invested; but the trees will be worth 120% of that amount if you let them grow, assuming you are right in predicting that prices for the tree products are going to stay the same. (There is more risk in holding trees as assets than investing in certain kinds of financial securities, of course; but we deal with that issue in other chapters.)

In general, the when-to-cut-a-forest problem is just a particular kind of present value problem. The future growth of the forest represents a source of future income which you have to discount, express as a rate of return, and compare to other investment opportunities. Then you can determine the best thing for you to do today.

It may be, for example, that you have some special investment opportunity which you think will pay you an annual return of 30%, while the forest is growing at 20%, and the interest rate on a relatively safe financial security is 10%. If you can't borrow funds to undertake the special investment, will you sell the trees and cut the forest? Yes and no. You *will* sell the trees to someone who is willing to pay more than 10% (but probably a little less than 20%); but the forest *won't* be cut, yet, unless you or someone else makes a mistake. At the *market* level, not just for you personally, it just doesn't pay to harvest the forest until its growth rate falls to the market interest rate, adjusted for the relative risk of holding the trees instead of cash, bonds, or other assets.

You probably didn't think about the price of trees, or decisions about when to cut them down, as being related to interest rates and the banking world before you took this course. But remember, by definition money is the kind of asset that can be used to purchase any other kind of resource or financial security. So not only with forests, but with any other specific kind of real asset, when the rate of return on the real asset drops below the interest rate that is available to those who hold money, bonds, and other paper securities, it pays to harvest or sell those real resources. (Unless, that is, you think those returns are only temporarily depressed, and are likely to rise in the future as the prices for the assets rise. Or, as in the case of art and antique collectables, when owning the assets also provides you direct non-monetary benefits -- that is, pleasure.)

If the rate of return on all kinds of real assets starts dropping, however, selling the assets to earn more on financial securities won't be a realistic option for long, because the rate of return on money and other financial assets will also drop. Why? Because the demand for funds to invest falls, while the supply of funds increases as long as investors try to sell real assets and put the funds into financial securities. Once again, this shows that microeconomic forces in investment markets are a key link to the performance of the macroeconomy.

Chapter Summary

1) The demand for a factor of production ultimately depends on the demand for the product it is used to produce, and how much each unit of the factor adds to the firm's total output. For a perfectly competitive firm, the demand curve for labor or any other factor is equal to the downward-sloping segment of the *VALUE OF MARGINAL PRODUCT (VMP)* curve for the input; VMP is found by multiplying product price times the marginal product of each unit of a variable input.

2) The price elasticity of demand for a factor of production is determined by the price elasticity of demand for the product it produces, the number of close substitutes that exist for the factor, the proportion of total production costs accounted for by the factor, and the price elasticity of supply of other (substitute) factors.

3) Market supply curves for factors of production are typically upward-sloping because the opportunity cost of not providing a productive resource to prospective employers increases as the factor payments (wages and salaries, rents, interest, and profits) rise. However, for individual workers who view leisure as a normal good

and demand more of it as their incomes rise, the income effect of a higher wage or salary may offset that substitution effect, leading to a backward-bending segment of their labor supply curve.

4) *RENTS* include payments to land or natural resources which are available in fixed supply. But economists also define rents as any payment above the minimum required to keep a factor employed in a production process. This kind of rental payment may be earned by factors other than land, including labor, and is effectively a producer surplus. *TRANSFER PAYMENTS* are the minimum factor payments that keep units of inputs employed in a production process.

5) A perfectly competitive firm will hire additional units of any factor of production as long as its VMP is greater than its price, or *MARGINAL FACTOR COST*. For example, additional labor will be hired until the firm reaches the point where VMP equals the wage rate. Competitive firms are a small enough part of the overall factor market that they can hire as many units of a productive resource as they want at the market rate of payment. Therefore, perfectly competitive firms are both price and wage takers.

6) Various kinds of jobs pay very different wage and salary rates, depending on the relative scarcity of a particular kind of worker which is determined by the supply of, and demand for, workers in those occupations. Skill requirements and many other job and worksite characteristics lead to these *COMPENSATING WAGE DIFFERENTIALS*.

7) Price controls in factor and financial markets lead to shortages and surplusses, just as in product markets.

8) The *PRESENT VALUE* of a sum of money to be paid or received at some future time is calculated by *DISCOUNTING* that sum by the expression $(1+i)^t$, where i is an appropriately chosen rate of interest and t is the number of time periods into the future that the money will be paid or received.

9) Business, government, and personal investments, including investments in *HUMAN CAPITAL*, all involve future costs and benefits. An expected rate of return on such investments is calculated by discounting these future receipts and outlays, and expressing the receipts as a percentage of the outlays. For most people, labor resources represent their most valuable economic asset, so they often make human capital investments in education and training.

10) (Case Study #19) Labor *PRODUCTIVITY* is a basic measure of output per labor hour, which ultimately determines individual and national income levels. Labor productivity has generally increased in the United States and other industrialized nations, but a period of much slower growth in these measures began in the 1970s.

11) (Case Study #20) The most profitable time to "harvest" a physical resource that is growing at some measurable rate is when that growth rate is equal to the market rate of interest on basic financial assets, like bonds and various savings securities. As long as the physical asset is growing faster than that rate, and its price is expected to remain constant (or rise), it should not be harvested.

Review and Discussion Questions

1) Construct two VMP schedules to show how a demand change that increases the price for a consumer product 50% will shift the VMP curve for a factor used to produce this product. Graph those two schedules, and show the shift caused by the increase in the price of the product the factor produces, *ceteris paribus*.

2) Prices for common stocks of electric utility companies are often described as "interest sensitive," and more specifically as inversely related to movements in interest rates. What, if anything, does this imply about the utilities' price elasticity of demand for capital equipment?

3) Will the supply curve for a "workaholic" ever be backward-bending? Why or why not?

4) For a "pure" land resource, what must happen to cause its price (i.e., its rental rate) to rise or fall? For a certain type of labor that is currently earning some economic rents, how will a shift in supply, or demand, *ceteris paribus*, affect the amount of those rents? Show this graphically.

5) If a competitive firm goes out of business, how will that affect the market price and employment levels for the productive resources it was hiring? If the market demand for a certain kind of labor increases, will that affect a competitive *firm's* supply of labor and the marginal factor cost curve for this labor? If so, how?

6) Pick three occupations from Table 15-3, and list as many factors as you can that explain the wage differentials among those three occupations. Then make a list of factors that explain why two workers with the same job, from any one of the three occupations, might have different wage or salary rates if one lived in San Francisco and the other in Glendive, Montana.

7) a) Do high-wage workers have any economic interest in supporting or opposing minimum wage laws, assuming competitive labor markets? (Hint: draw the market supply and demand curve for skilled workers, and think about how that might change if the minimum wage was increased sharply.)

   b) Show graphically how employment can grow after the adoption of a minimum wage if the demand for labor increases over time, but not as much as it would have without the minimum wage.

8) a) Which individuals in the following pairs of people are likely to have relatively higher or lower discount rates for future income and expenditures, *ceteris paribus*?

      1) a miser and a spendthrift
      2) a borrower and a lender
      3) you and your parents

   b) Calculate the present value of 10 annual payments of $100, with the first payment made today, when the interest rate is 8%, and again if the interest rate is 12%.

9) Would you attend college if you did not expect to earn higher wages with your degree? Would you take some of the courses you have taken even if they didn't raise your expected future income? Did what you learned in elementary school increase your future productivity as a worker? What about the subjects you studied in high school, and in college? Was there signaling or screening value in each of those schools? Did they all increase your human capital?

10) (Case Study #19) What factors can you identify which contributed to the rise in U.S productivity growth rates in the 1980s, compared to the 1970s, as shown in Table 15-5?

11) (Case Study #20) Graphically show how a change in the interest rate paid on financial securities, or a shift in the growth rate of the world's forests, would affect the optimal time to harvest a forest. Work from Figure 15-11.

Chapter 16
Imperfectly Competitive Markets for Factors of Production

In This Chapter...

we analyze markets for factors of production in which: 1) firms with some degree of monopoly power in selling their output hire productive resources, 2) firms buy enough inputs in a factor market to affect their prices and overall employment levels, and 3) workers organize to collectively negotiate terms of employment with companies, through labor unions. All of these situations can lead to different outcomes than those you saw in the previous chapter, on competitive factor markets.

Monopoly and Monopsony

Imperfect competition turned out to be a bad thing, in most cases, for consumers and businesses that purchase the products of firms with some degree of monopoly power. But what about the employees and owners of other inputs employed by monopolies or oligopolies, or by firms that have market power in hiring inputs? Are payments and employment levels for factors higher or lower in these firms? When production technologies are unchanged employment levels are lower, the last unit of a factor that is employed will receive a payment that is less than its VMP, and in some cases wages and other factor prices will be lower than they would be if the productive resources were hired by perfectly competitive firms.

MRP vs. VMP

Imperfectly competitive firms -- whether they be monopolists, oligopolists, or monopolistic competitors -- don't face the same kind of product demand curves that perfectly competitive firms do, as you saw in Chapters 9-13. And because the demand for a factor of production is derived from product demand, as you saw in the last chapter, the factor demand curve for competitive firms is different from the factor demand curves for imperfectly competitive firms.

Specifically, while a competitive firm can sell all of its output at the market price, the imperfectly competitive firm faces a downward-sloping demand curve for its product, and has to lower the price to sell more units. That's why the imperfectly competitive firm has a marginal revenue curve that lies below its demand curve, and it is also why this kind of firm will face a *MARGINAL REVENUE PRODUCT (MRP)* curve that lies below its value of marginal product (VMP) curve. Marginal revenue product is simply the amount a firm takes in by selling the output that an additional unit of input produces, or algebraically

$$MRP = \frac{\text{the change in total revenue}}{\text{one-unit change in factor employment}}$$

For a perfectly competitive firm price is equal to marginal revenue (P = MR). That means VMP = MRP for these firms, and the only reason the change in total revenue becomes smaller as more units of a variable input are hired is diminishing returns in the production process. But firms with any degree of monopoly power in the market for their output have MRP curves that decrease for two reasons: 1) diminishing returns, which affects their production processes just as it does those of perfectly competitive firms, and 2) lowering the price of their product in order to sell more units (i.e., P > MR).

It is easy to calculate the MRP schedule for a firm with monopoly power if we know its production and demand schedules, as shown in Table 16-1. (Note that this table uses the same production data you saw in Table 15-1, for a perfectly competitive firm.) And we can still calculate a VMP schedule for this kind of firm using the formula developed in Chapter 15: simply multiply product price times the marginal product of different units of the variable input. This is done in column 7 of Table 16-1 to show that -- for imperfectly competitive firms -- MRP (calculated in column 6) falls off faster than VMP. That is also clear when we plot these VMP and MRP schedules graphically, in Figure 16-1.

The key point of calculating these schedules and comparing them graphically is to show that the demand for labor and other variable inputs will be lower than the VMP curve for this kind of firm because it has to lower price to sell more units of output. It will hire additional units of an input as long the resulting increase in its revenues is greater than the increase in its costs. And clearly, the increases in revenues associated with hiring additional units of the input are shown, for a firm with monopoly power, by the MRP schedule, not the VMP schedule. (Look back at the earlier definition of MRP. Or just recognize that when the firm lowers price to sell more output, that decrease in price inevitably affects its revenues -- which is why its marginal revenue curve lies below its demand curve in the first place.) To summarize, then, the input demand curve for a firm with monopoly power will be the downward-sloping segment of its MRP curve, which lies below its VMP curve.

Table 16-1
Hiring Inputs When Firms Have Monopoly Power

(1) Variable Input (Labor)	(2) Total Product	(3) Marginal Product of Labor	(4) Product Price	(5) Total Revenue	(6) Marginal Revenue Product (MRP)	(7) Value of Marginal Product (VMP)
0	0	--	$5.00	$ ----	$ ----	$ ---
1	10	10	4.50	45.00	45.00	45.00
2	25	15	3.75	93.75	48.75	56.25
3	35	10	3.25	113.75	20.00	32.50
4	43	8	2.85	122.55	8.80	22.80
5	48	5	2.60	124.80	2.25	13.00
6	51	3	2.45	124.95	0.15	7.35
7	52	1	2.40	124.80	-0.15	2.40

The first three columns above are taken from Table 15-1, and show the same short-run production schedule used there to derive the factor demand curve for a perfectly competitive firm. But while that kind of firm can sell any level of output it produces at the market price, a firm with some degree of monopoly power must decrease price to sell higher levels of output. Its MRP schedule (column 6) shows how much total revenue changes when it hires additional units of the variable input and lowers product price to sell a greater quantity of output. The MRP schedule is the imperfectly competitive firm's factor demand schedule, because it shows the financial benefit to the firm of this additional employment and production. Note that the MRP values decrease faster than than VMP (column 7). VMP is found by multiplying product price times the marginal product of the variable input (column 4 times column 3).

445

Figure 16-1
MRP and VMP

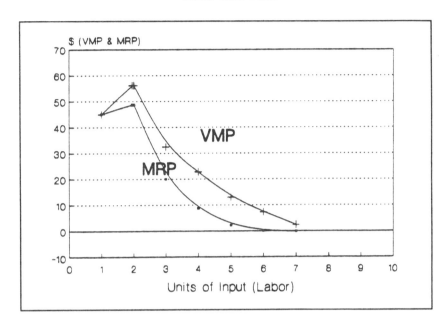

The VMP and MRP curves shown above are plotted from the values for these two schedules shown in Table 16-1. The imperfectly competitive firm's factor demand curve, the MRP schedule, lies below its VMP schedule, which is downward-sloping *only* because of the law of diminishing returns. The MRP curve is downward sloping due to the same rate of diminishing returns in the production process *and* because firms with monopoly power face downward-sloping product demand and marginal revenue schedules.

Wage and Employment Levels Under Monopoly

Since the downward-sloping section of the VMP curve is a perfectly competitive firm's demand curve for labor and other factors of production (as you saw in the last chapter), while the downward-sloping section of the MRP curve is an imperfectly competitive firm's factor demand curve and lies below its VMP curve, you can probably predict that things don't look so good for laborers or owners of other inputs that are hired by imperfectly competitive firms. In particular, if a firm enjoys some degree of monopoly power in selling its *output*, but hires its *inputs* in competitive factor markets, its employment level will be lower. But its factor prices will be exactly the same as those of perfectly competitive firms which hire the same kinds of inputs. That happens because a firm with monopoly power in an output market can still be a wage or rent or interest taker in factor markets. For example, a firm might be the major national producer of some exotic food delicacy, such as tabasco sauce, which can only be made from peppers that grow in a particular climate and area. But if that firm is only one of many equal-sized employers of agricultural and unskilled labor in this area, wage rates for its workers are not affected by how many, or how few, workers the tabasco firm hires. In a more common example, even offices of large manufacturing companies hire a very small percentage of the total number of entry-level secretaries and accountants employed in most large cities, and often pay the going wage rates for such services in those markets. The equilibrium wage and hiring levels for these kinds of firms are shown in Figure 16-2.

Figure 16-2
Monopolistic Employment Levels and "Exploitation"

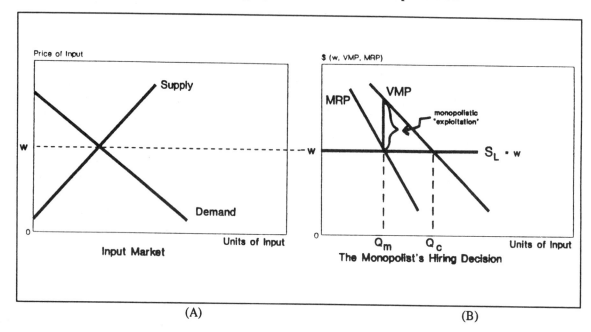

(A)   (B)

Firms with monopoly power in output markets but which hire inputs in competitive factor markets will pay the same input prices as perfectly competitive firms, based on the market supply and demand curves for the factors shown in panel (A). These firms will hire fewer inputs (Q_m, where w = MRP) than perfectly competitive firms do (Q_c, where w = VMP).

In a monopolistic factor market, the last worker hired is not paid his or her VMP. The difference between w and VMP at Q_m, shown in panel (B), is known as "monopolistic exploitation."

The labor supply curve S_L for this *firm*, shown in panel (B), is a horizontal line at the wage w established in the overall market for this kind of labor (panel A). The market wage rate is, therefore, still the same as it would be if this firm were perfectly competitive in both product and input markets. But the firm does hire fewer workers -- where MRP = w, rather than where VMP = w. And in an admittedly rather murky, philosophical sense, the firm can be said to "exploit" the workers it hires even though it pays the same wage rate as perfectly competitive firms, because the last worker hired is not paid his or her VMP, as was true in perfect competition. We still assume that all of these workers are equally skilled and productive, even to the point of being interchangeable in the production process, so it can also be said that all of the workers a firm hires are "exploited" when the last worker hired receives a wage that is less than his or her VMP. (Conversely, it can be argued that none of the workers in a perfectly competitive firm is "exploited," since the last worker is paid exactly his or her VMP, and the last worker is just as skilled and diligent as the other workers.)

"Exploited" is a politically loaded term, of course, as signalled by our use of quotation marks and the fact that the first economists to extensively discuss this issue were Marxists. But in strictly technical terms, economists of all persuasions define *MONOPOLISTIC EXPLOITATION* as the vertical distance between VMP and w at the equilibrium hiring level for a firm with monopoly power, shown in panel (B) of Figure 16-2 as Q_m. The difference in hiring levels for competitive firms (which hire where w = VMP) and firms with monopoly power (which hire where w = MRP) is shown in the same panel of this figure as the difference between Q_c and Q_m, a much more obvious disadvantage to the workers in this kind of factor market. Note that this finding is consistent with those presented in Chapters 11-13, where imperfectly competitive firms were shown to restrict output in order to charge higher prices than competitive firms, *ceteris paribus*. One result of restricting output is, clearly, to decrease the quantity of inputs these firms will hire.

Monopsony Power and Factor Supply

Monopoly power isn't the only kind of imperfect competition that is possible in a factor market. *MONOPSONY* occurs when a firm is such a large *buyer* of an input that its hiring levels have an impact on the market price of that input. Perfect monopsony occurs, therefore, if there is only one buyer of an input in a market. However, there is probably no "real world" example of perfect monopsony among the industrialized nations today, given the high degree of *FACTOR MOBILITY* in these countries.

Labor is probably the least-mobile factor (except, of course, for actual fields of land) given the complexity and many costs of re-locating a person, and especially a family. But in recent decades, unprecedented mobility has come to workers in the form of automobiles, state and national highway systems, and other forms of low-cost transportation including buses, trains, and subways. Communication and information networks on job openings have also increased labor mobility dramatically during this time. In short, the average geographic size of the labor market that workers face, and therefore the average number of firms that are potential employers of workers, has increased sharply. When workers have more firms to contact as potential employers, that clearly reduces a given firm's monopsony power; so, in more general terms, the more mobile labor and other resources are, the less monopsony power there will be in a factor market.

The best remaining examples of monopsony power in U.S. labor markets are probably the large military bases situated in remote areas where there is very little other reason for people to be, and perhaps regional hospitals that hire nurses in rural areas, or rural public school boards that hire teachers. A few decades ago, however, many mining towns in remote areas were "company owned and operated" (remember the song "Sixteen Tons"?), and sometimes the only feasible place many workers in these areas could be employed given the poor transportation facilities and limited educational opportunities available to those who wanted to get out of the mines. Sharecropping arrangements in depressed agricultural areas often worked much the same way.

When monopsony power does exist, firms weilding that power will face an upward-sloping supply curve for labor or other inputs. In fact, a perfect monopsonist faces the market supply curve of labor, just as a pure monopolist faces the market demand curve for its output. That means to hire more workers in its labor market a monopsonist has to increase the wage rate -- and increase it for all workers, not just the additional ones it wants to hire.

The wage rates for other workers must rise because we are still assuming all workers the firm hires for a particular job are equally skilled and motivated, and in even more practical terms because we can assume that workers know what other workers doing the same job are being paid. It is normally impossible for the firm to practice *WAGE DISCRIMINATION*, by paying different wages to different people doing the same job,[1] just as it is usually impossible for monopolists to practice price discrimination by charging different people different prices for the same product, as you saw in Chapter 11. Recent laws against such practices also make them more difficult and potentially costly to implement.

Because a monopsonist faces an upward-sloping factor-supply curve, its marginal factor cost (MFC) curve rises faster than the supply of labor curve, as shown in Table 16-2. (Recall that MFC is the change in the firm's total factor cost when it hires one more unit of an input.) Once again, this is a kind of logical "flip side" to the relationship between a monopolist's demand and marginal revenue schedules, which you first saw in Chapter 11.

Monopsonists also increase the economic rents they are paying to already-employed workers when they raise wage rates, just as monopolists increase consumer surplus when they lower prices to sell more output. That's not

---

[1] On the more specific issue of racial, ethnic, and gender discrimination, see Case Study #21 at the end of this chapter.)

why these firms raise wages or lower prices, of course -- it's just something that inevitably happens as these firms hire and sell more, respectively, based on a decision that expanding output will raise the firm's profits.

Table 16-2
Labor Supply and Marginal Factor Cost for a Monopsonist

(1) Units of Variable Input (Labor)	(2) Hourly Wage Rate	(3) Total Hourly Cost	(4) Marginal Factor Cost
0	$--	$--	$--
1	4	4	4
2	5	10	6
3	6	18	8
4	7	28	10
5	8	40	12
6	9	54	14
7	10	70	16
8	11	88	18

If a firm is the only, or even a major, employer in a particular factor market, it must increase wage rates or other factor payments when it wants to hire more inputs. This is shown in the first two columns above, and in the upward-sloping factor supply curve S_L in Figure 16-3. The firm pays these higher rates to all employed units of the factor, which results in the total factor costs shown in the third column (column 1 times column 2). Moreover, the firm's marginal factor cost -- the cost of increasing employment by one unit -- rises faster than the wage rate or other factor payment (compare columns 2 and 4).

Wage and Employment Levels Under Monopsony

A monopsonist will continue to hire workers until the marginal cost of hiring an additional worker (the MFC) equals the marginal benefit. If the monopsonist sells its output in competitive markets, that will be where MFC = VMP = MRP, at Q_{ms} in Figure 16-3. Note that the firm will not pay a wage equal to MFC at that employment level, since that wage (w_o) is higher than the wage rate it must pay to hire the number of workers it wants. The lowest possible wage rate required to hire Q_{ms} workers is found on the labor supply curve -- w_{ms}.

The equilibrium employment *and* wage levels for a monopsonist are lower than those we would observe if the factor market were perfectly competitive. Competitive firms would hire at the employment level and pay the wage rate determined by the intersection of the market supply and demand curves for labor, Q_c and w_c in Figure 16-3. The difference between the wage rate paid and the MRP for the last worker employed (at Q_{ms}) represents *MONOPSONISTIC EXPLOITATION*, an obvious parallel to the concept of monopolistic exploitation presented earlier. The same qualifications about the use of politically charged terms such as "exploitation" apply here, too, of course.

449

Figure 16-3
Monopsonistic Wage and Employment Levels, and "Exploitation"

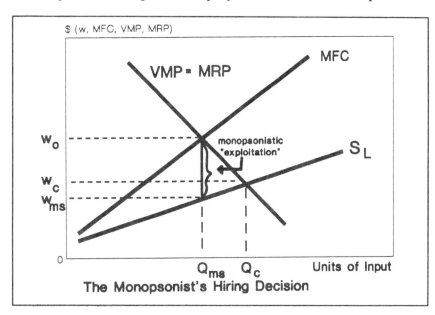

The Monopsonist's Hiring Decision

For a monopsonist which sells its output in a competitive market, the equilibrium employment level is where MFC = MRP = VMP, at Q_{ms}. The lowest wage that will secure that number of workers for the firm (on its labor supply curve) is w_{ms}. The difference between that wage rate and MRP for the last worker hired (w_o - w_{ms}) represents the level of monopsonistic exploitation. Q_c would be the hiring level if this labor market were perfectly competitive, and firms would pay the (higher) wage rate w_c, at which the demand curve for labor (VMP = MRP) and the supply curve for labor (S_L) intersect.

Monopsony and the Minimum Wage

Another interesting and illustrative curiosity in economic theory occurs if a minimum wage law is passed in a labor market characterized by a high degree of monopsony power: the minimum wage can actually lead to higher wages and employment levels simultaneously. What happens in these cases can be summarized in three steps.

First, the minimum wage w_{min} becomes the firm's new labor supply schedule out to the point on the original labor supply curve where wages are first higher than the minimum wage. (In Figure 16-4, the new supply curve is ABE.) That occurs simply because the firm can't, legally, hire workers at any lower wage than w_{min}; but it can hire all it wants at the minimum wage out to that point (point B). Beyond that level, to hire more workers the firm has to pay more than the minimum wage (on segment BE).

Second, the minimum wage also represents the firm's MFC curve out to the same point on the original labor supply curve, where wages become higher than the minimum wage. Until then, the monopsonist's extra cost of an additional worker is now constant and equal to the minimum wage, not rising. (The new MFC curve is ABCD.)

Finally, this new minimum-wage section of the MFC curve must be higher than the original monopsony wage w_1, and intersect the monopsonist's VMP/MRP schedule to the right of the original hiring level. This situation is shown graphically in Figure 16-4.

Figure 16-4
Minimum Wage Laws and a Monopsonist

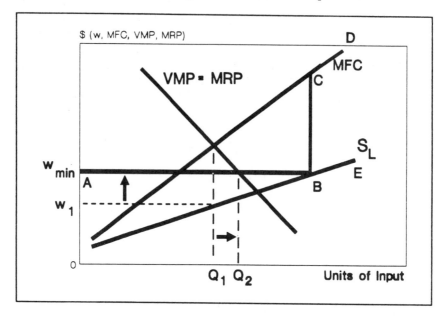

Unlike minimum wage laws in competitive labor markets (Figure 15-8), in monopsony markets such laws may result in both higher wages and employment levels. With a minimum wage imposed at w_{min}, the horizontal line AB becomes a segment of the firm's new labor supply curve, ABE. Line AB also becomes part of the monopsonist's MFC curve, because out to point B the cost of hiring one more worker is w_{min}. The entire, now "kinked" MFC curve becomes ABCD. Note that beyond point B, to attract more workers the firm must still increase wages above w_{min}.

Without the minimum wage, the firm would hire Q_1 workers (where MFC = VMP = MRP), and pay the corresponding wage rate, w_1, just as in Figure 16-3. But when the minimum wage is imposed as shown, the firm pays that higher wage and increases employment to Q_2 (where MRP = the new MFC). As long as it intersects the VMP/MRP curve to the right of point Q_1, a minimum wage higher than w_1 will increase employment levels in this labor market.

Supporters of minimum wage laws sometimes use this theoretical finding as an argument for adopting or increasing legislated minimum wages. Many economists are skeptical of those claims, however, for the simple reason that few labor markets in industrialized nations are dominated by one employer, or even a few large employers. As we noted earlier, the clear trend in recent decades has been for workers to have increased mobility, and that mobility sharply limits any firm's monopsony power (even in small rural towns where there is only one large employer, if there are other towns and employers within easy commuting distance).

In short, almost all economists see monopoly power as a much more widespread and troublesome problem than monopsony power. The model of monopsony developed in Figure 16-4 is as much an exercise to make sure you understand the curves and equilibrium conditions used there as it is a portrayal of a contemporary social issue, at least in industrialized nations.

Monopoly Plus Monopsony:
A Quick Review of Imperfectly Competitive Factor Markets

We haven't yet shown you the factor-market situation in which a monopolist is also a monopsonist -- the M & M model, if you like. But you have now seen all the component parts of such a model, which are brought together in Figure 16-5. Before looking at those graphs, however, make sure you have the right idea about what kind of employer would be both a monopolist and a monopsonist. The best example here is, once again, something from the public sector -- such as the army base in the remote rural town. The government certainly has monopoly power as an operator of an army (at least in politically stable nations); and if the base is sufficiently isolated, even the civilian workers in that area may have little choice in terms of working for anyone else. Therefore, such a firm will face disticnt and downward sloping VMP and MRP curves (with MRP < VMP), and distinct and upward sloping MFC and factor supply curves (with the MFC curve higher than the factor supply curve). With that understood, now turn to the comparison of the equilibrium situations in the four different kinds of factor markets, in Figure 16-5.

The competitive firm, the monopolist, the monopsonist, and the monopolist-monopsonist all hire at the employment level determined by the point where MRP = MFC. They pay the wage rate required to attract that level of employment, as determined by the supply curve S_L. But the differences between these four types of firms are also noteworthy. Both monopolists and monopsonists hire fewer workers than competitive firms, *ceteris paribus*, and both pay the last worker hired less than his or her VMP. Perfectly competitive firms don't engage in this kind of "exploitation," but not because the owners' motives are necessarily any more noble or altruistic. Instead, for these firms, what is compelling is that, since they represent such a small part of both their industry's product and input markets, their factor supply curve *is* their MFC curve (i.e., competitive firms are wage takers), and their VMP curve *is* their MRP curve (because perfectly competitive firms are price takers).

Unions and Collective Bargaining

Labor unions represent their members' interests in collectively bargaining for higher wages, better fringe benefits, and more desirable employment conditions generally. There are sometimes principal-agent problems in union officials pursuing their own interests rather than those of the union membership; but these officials are democratically elected, and must usually try to determine and follow workers' preferences in making trade-offs among wages, employment levels, fringe benefits, etc. Market forces, including the elasticity of demand for labor and other factors of production, establish sharp limits on the concessions unions can win from employers. But unions can influence those constraints over time through strategies designed to increase the demand for, or restrict the supply of, union labor. Studies suggest that those strategies have been successful in raising wages for union members some 10-20% higher than non-union workers. But whether that differential mainly reflects increased productivity, or supply restrictions that raise production costs and may even lower wages for non-union workers, is a matter of active debate among economists.

Bilateral Monopoly in the Labor Market

Labor unions have a long and colorful history which some scholars trace back to the medieval guilds of craft workers (such as bakers and goldsmiths), or even earlier. Modern unions developed for many reasons, and perform many different economic and social roles; but in this chapter we focus on their behavior as the recognized bargaining agent for their members. In that role, unions are concerned primarily with wage and employment levels, and to a lesser extent with fringe benefits (such as insurance, retirement, and vacation programs provided by firms to employees) and other workplace conditions (including job safety, and procedures for deciding promotions, job transfers, and disputes between individual workers and managers).

452

Figure 16-5
Wage and Employment Levels in Different Types of Labor Markets

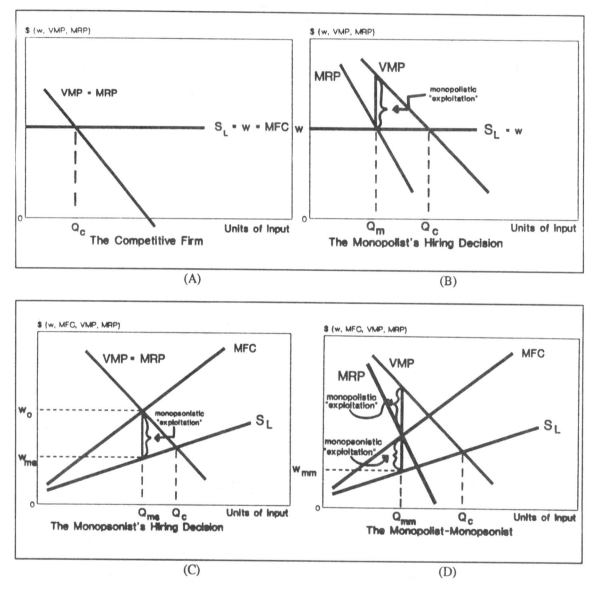

(A) (B)

(C) (D)

The basic factor market models for firms that are (a) perfectly competitive, (b) monopolistic, (c) monopsonistic, and (d) both monopolistic and monopsonistic, are shown here. The MRP curve represents the demand for labor (or other inputs) for each of these firms; and each firm hires up to the point where MFC = MRP to maximize profits or minimize losses. The competitive firm (a) hires Q_c and pays the going market wage. The monopolist (b) pays the market wage but hires fewer units (Q_m) of the factor. The monopsonist (c) and monopolist-monopsonist (d) pay lower wages and hire fewer workers than a perfectly competitive firm, *ceteris paribus*.

Unions deal with many different kinds of firms, including some that operate in highly competitive markets. But the modern era of unionism in the United States has most prominently featured negotiations between large, imperfectly competitive firms, and large, imperfectly competitive unions. So we begin our look at the economic effects of unions with an extreme example of imperfect competition: a pure monoposony which hires its workers from a union that has successfully organized all of the firm's employees. In other words, we have a monopoly buyer and a monopoly seller of labor. What happens then, in terms of wage and employment levels? That turns out to be a very good question, that can only be answered, "It depends." Figure 16-6 shows this economic version of the Mexican standoff or, as economist John Kenneth Galbraith describes it, "countervailing power."

Figure 16-6
Bilateral Monopoly in a Labor Market

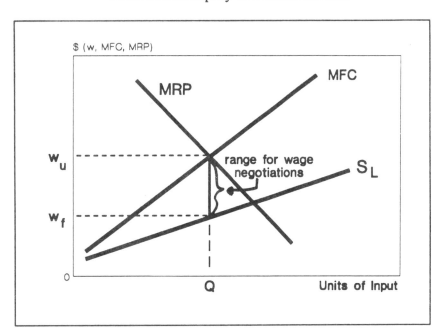

When a monopoly buyer faces a monopoly seller -- shown here in a labor market setting -- the outcome is indeterminate, a matter of relative bargaining power and skill. A monopsonist hiring at Q_0 (where MRP = MFP) wants to pay the wage rate shown as W_f, but a union seeks a contract paying W_u. The outcome is indeterminant unless we know the relative bargaining strength of the firm and the union.

The firm would like to hire at the employment level Q_0, where MFC = MRP, and pay the wage rate shown as w_f. The union, as you might suspect, strongly disagrees. It sees that the firm will maintain this employment level as long as it pays no more than MRP, so the union will try to achieve the wage rate w_u in the contract negotiations. That leaves a considerable range for negotiation, and this simple model can't tell us where in that range the wage will be set. It all depends on the relative bargaining power of the firm and the union, which is influenced by such factors as the their respective financial strength, overall business conditions in the industry and the national economy (including the unemployment rate), and the willingness of each side to accept a *STRIKE* as an alternative to signing a new contract. There is also the possibility that the union will be willing to trade off some of a wage increase from w_f toward w_u in exchange for employment of a larger number of workers (who are at least prospective, and perhaps even current, union members).

This *BILATERAL MONOPOLY* model of firm-union bargaining is, therefore, too simplistic to be useful in predicting the results of most cases of labor-management relations. Its primary usefulness here is in showing that a bargaining range for wage rates does exist in such factor markets.

Union Bargaining Preferences and Strategies

Unions' goals are to increase wages and fringe benefits for their members, to increase employment and membership levels, and to maintain an effective lobbying presence for union interests in Washington and the state legislatures. Obviously, there are often tradeoffs involved in trying to accomplish all of those goals simultaneously -- for example, raising wages will (except in some monopsony situations) lead firms to reduce the number of workers employed, *ceteris paribus*. Ultimately, that employment drop will translate into fewer union members. So union leaders face difficult choices in negotiating with firms, and in determining what policies will be popular enough with the union membership to keep them in office.

We also have to recognize that some union leaders, like some corporate executives and political leaders we have discussed in earlier chapters, become so well entrenched in their positions that serious principal-agent problems arise. In those cases, we have to consider when union actions are taken to benefit the personal interests of the union officials rather than those of the overall membership.

Several other variables influence which particular set of goals a union will pursue in an upcoming round of negotiations, and the likelihood that it will succeed in achieving those goals. Most generally, the elasticity of demand for labor determines how severe the trade-off between wage increases and employment losses will be, and also suggests something about the union's bargaining strength. If a firm's demand for labor is very price elastic, the firm is less likely to grant high wage concessions, more likely to be able to substitute other productive resources for labor, and will definitely lay off a relatively large number of workers if the union does succeed in negotiating a significant wage increase. Any way you look at it, that's not a bright outlook from the union's perspective.

Unemployment and profit levels in a given industry or labor market also play a part in determining how costly it will be for firms and unions to accept a strike, rather than sign a contract or at least continue to negotiate without a work stoppage. Ultimately, the costs and benefits of accepting a strike or accepting a new contract with given provisions on wages and other work rules must be estimated and compared by both unions and firms.

Some models of *UNION BARGAINING PREFERENCES*, based on historical observations and the fact that both higher employment *and* higher wage levels are viewed as desirable outcomes, suggest that unions will usually put more emphasis on seeking wage increases for current members in "good times," when demand for union labor is increasing and employment and membership levels are rising. But in times of falling demand the emphasis shifts to holding on to wage gains even in the face of some employment loss, particularly if the lay-offs and weak demand are expected to be temporary and short-run in nature. A simple graph of this pattern, developed by economist Alan M. Cartter, is shown in Figure 16-7.

Even more general, in some respects, is Nobel Laureate Sir John Hicks' model of bargaining (Figure 16-8), which can be used to predict or explain the length of a strike in a negotiating round where the size of the wage increase is the only major issue. The key forces at work in this model are the costs a strike impose on both employers and employees which, Hicks argued, can be expected to increase as the length of a strike increases. Therefore, both firms and unions will become more willing to compromise and settle a strike as it lengthens. Their "concession" and "resistance" curves -- based on the firm agreeing to higher wage increases and unions accepting lower wage increases -- will normally intersect after some period (and in most cases allow for settlements even before a strike begins). The intersection point identifies the amount of time the strike is expected to last.

Of course these models of the bargaining process are greatly simplified, and don't come close to incorporating the great number of issues involved in most contract negotiations, in some cases including personal characteristics of the leading individuals involved in the negotiations for the union and the company. And even granting that level of simplification, these models can not be used to predict or explain outcomes in particular cases until data on the economic circumstances of the organizations involved are collected and analyzed.

Figure 16-7
The Cartter Model of Union Bargaining Preferences

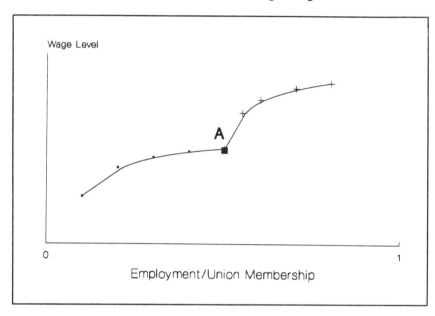

Beginning from the position shown at point A, in times of rising labor demand the union represented above prefers to pursue wage increases for existing members more aggressively than higher employment and membership levels. Therefore, moving to the right of point A, the union preference curve will have a relatively steep slope, where the rise represents increased wage payments and the run shows higher employment levels.

When the demand for labor falls, this union prefers employment cuts to wage concessions, particularly if the reductions are expected to be short-lived. That is, moving left from point A, the preference schedule is relatively flat. Of course, if the decrease in demand persists for a long period of time, the union may eventually decide its very survival depends on maintaining employment (and thereby union membership), so sharper wage concessions could then be observed

Still, the Cartter model is frequently a sensible representation and summary of union views -- when higher wages and increased employment levels are seen as the most desirable outcomes in a new contract. And the Hicks model emphasizes the idea that firms and unions will weigh the financial costs and benefits of accepting or rejecting a contract in deciding whether to take such a potentially dramatic action as a labor strike. The public, and particularly the press, frequently lose sight of these basic economic forces when strikes do occur. (That isn't all that often, actually, in terms of the total number of contracts negotiated each year. Some studies have found that more work time is lost to coffee breaks than to strikes in U.S. industry.)

456

Figure 16-8
The Hicks Model of Bargaining and Expected Strike Length

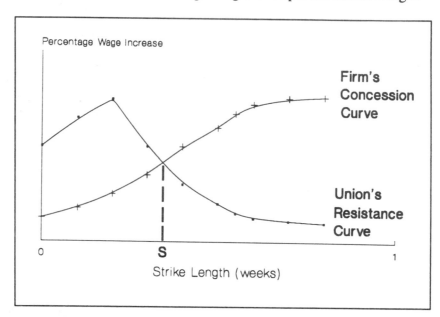

Suppose wage rates are the only major issue in a contract dispute. A firm may offer only a low wage increase if it thinks the union will accept it, either immediately or after a short strike. But the longer a strike continues the more customers and sales the firm will lose, meaning its costs of letting the strike continue will rise. So it will agree to higher wage concessions to avoid an even longer strike, as shown on the firm's concession curve.

For the union, the expectation that a short strike may win a higher wage concession may increase its members' initial determination to strike. But as the strike runs longer, lost wages deplete their financial resources and ability to continue the strike, and the threat of the firm hiring other workers or going out of business becomes more credible. Therefore, in time, the union will become willing to accept lower wage increases to avoid prolonging the strike. That results in the kind of union resistance curve shown above.

Plotting these curves together predicts the length of a strike. For example, if we have estimated these curves in an industry where contract negotiations are about to begin, we would predict a strike of S weeks. Up to that point, the firm is not willing to offer wage increases that are as high as the points on the union's resistance curve; but once that point is reached, there is no reason related to wages for the strike to continue. If the firm's concession curve is higher than the union's resistance curve on the vertical axis, with a strike length of 0 weeks, the parties will to settle with no strike at all.

Using basic supply and demand models, we can say more about the general strategies unions will use to improve their bargaining power, and wage and compensation levels in particular. Obviously wages for union members will be increased if the demand for their labor increases, or if the supply is decreased. And in fact, unions pursue several strategies that have just those effects. We will briefly consider four of them here: 1) increasing demand through training programs and by maintaining "hiring halls" of skilled workers; 2) restricting labor supply through formal licensing programs; 3) increasing the demand for union labor through legislation that requires the payment of union-scale wages on public-works jobs; and 4) increasing demand by supporting increases in legally established minimum wages.

1) <u>Training programs and hiring halls</u>. There are two basic kinds of unions, *CRAFT UNIONS* and *INDUSTRIAL UNIONS*. Craft unions organize workers with a particular skill, such as carpenters, electricians, and plumbers and pipefitters, regardless of where they work. Industrial unions organize all of the workers at a particular firm, such as General Motors or USX, regardless of what kind of job they do. In craft unions, it is common to find unions operating apprenticeship and training programs, and hiring halls where members report each day to be assigned to jobs that employers call in to the hall. In effect, this saves some firms from having to operate training programs on their own, allows them to hire skilled workers on a temporary basis if they don't have enough work to hire them permanently, and more generally to have easy access to skilled workers without entering into long-term employment contracts and benefit programs, as discussed earlier in Case Study #10. By lowering the firm's costs of finding and hiring these workers, and increasing their productivity through the training programs, the demand for this labor is increased. That increases wage or employment levels, or both, *ceteris paribus*; but when employers hire workers in this kind of arrangement there are clear, mutual benefits to workers and firms through a process of voluntary exchange.

2) <u>Licensing programs</u>. By lobbying for legal licensing requirements requiring lengthy training programs, unions and professional organizations (such as the American Medical Association or the American Bar Association) can sometimes artificially restrict the supply of workers in certain occupations. The result of such supply constraints is to increase wage rates and reduce the quantity of a service or skill available on the market -- a result analagous to a monopoly's practice of restricting output to increase prices and profits (even to the extent that unions, like monopolies, would like to sell more of its members' services at high wages if they could, but instead have to accept a lower quantity to get the higher price).

Many consumers and legislators, as well as members of the licensed professions, defend the use of extensive training requirements to eliminate quacks and frauds. In support of that position, we only have to note again that not everyone is willing to leave it to market forces to eliminate bad brain surgeons. But training requirements sponsored by unions, then enacted and enforced by government laws or regulations, frequently prove to be unreasonably restrictive in terms of any safety or quality considerations. In recent decades, for example, most states eliminated the effective distinction between barbers and cosmetologists, allowing cosmetologists to cut men's hair as well as women's. Barbers were formerly required to spend much more time in training than cosmetologists in many states, but few people (except old-line barbers, of course) noticed a decrease in the quality of men's haircuts when the higher licensing standards were eliminated.

3) <u>Legislation requiring union-scale wages</u>. The federal Davis-Bacon Act, and state or local versions of this legislation, require that "prevailing wages" must be paid to workers on government construction projects. By law or in practice, those prevailing wages are normally interpreted as union scale. Supporters of this legislation argue that it is necessary to keep contractors from cutting wages on these contracts, particularly the projects for highways, bridges, and large office buildings that are the lifeblood of many construction firms. Opponents argue that these laws drive up the costs of these projects at taxpayers' expense. In fact, even economists who strongly support collective bargaining and the importance of workers' rights to form and join unions generally take the side of the opponents. Clearly, such laws raise construction prices by increasing the costs of contractors who normally use non-union labor and pay lower wages. So the federal and the state versions of the Davis-Bacon act effectively reduce competition, and serve to increase the demand for union labor by driving up the price of non-union labor.

4) <u>Union support for higher minimum wages</u>. In recent decades, many of the nation's largest unions have steadfastly supported increases in the legal minimum wage even though few, if any, of their members are paid such low wages. Why? Many union officials claim, no doubt sincerely in some cases, that it is because of their social concern over living standards for low-income workers. But as you saw in Chapter 15, higher minimum wages often have a negative impact on many low-skilled workers, in the form of higher unemployment. And higher minimum wages benefit union members, and skilled workers in general, by raising the price of a substitute for skilled workers -- namely, unskilled workers. It is therefore a fair question

to ask how much unions would support higher minimum wages if they worked against their members' economic interests.

Empirical Evidence of Unions' Effects on Wage Levels

Literally dozens of studies have been conducted to determine how much, if at all, unions are able to raise wages for their members *vis-a-vis* non-union workers in comparable jobs. For many reasons, this is a very difficult thing to determine. For example, many people are surprised to learn that the percentage of U.S. workers who belong to unions is relatively small, and has been falling since the 1950s, as shown in Table 16-3. Furthermore, unionized workers tend to be concentrated in three kinds of occupations: manufacturing, where high levels of capital investment increase labor productivity and lead to relatively high wages even in the absence of unions; skilled craft trades, like carpentry and electrical work, where wages again tend to be high even without unions; and public-sector employment, where the absence of a "bottom-line" profit and loss statement combined with governmental taxing authority that is used (in part) to pay government employees' wages and salaries make it difficult to obtain precise measures of worker productivity, and establish the true level of demand for the goods and services these workers produce (as you saw in Chapter 5).

After statistically adjusting for these factors, as well as differences between union and non-union workers' levels of education and on-the-job experience, most studies suggest that union wages are 10-20 percent higher than those in identical non-union jobs. The 15% mid-point of this range is the most-often cited measure of this effect.[2] But even that is not the end of the story, and four additional complicating factors are often brought into this complex debate.

First is the point that fringe benefits for union workers tend to be higher than for non-union workers, so the 10-20 percent differential cited above may well understate the overall difference in total compensation for these two groups of workers. Second is the point that union employees may experience longer and more frequent periods of unemployment than non-union workers, and in particular they may accept some periods of unemployment waiting to take a union job (to get the higher compensation) instead of taking a non-union job. When that is the case, the wage and compensation differentials overstate the net advantage of union jobs over a worker's entire career.

The third point involves the question of whether unions have been able to increase the total amount of all wages paid in the economy -- to union *and* non-union members -- or instead have made union workers better off while making non-union workers worse off. That basically depends on whether the union wage advantages are achieved by increasing labor productivity and the overall demand for labor, or by restricting the supply of union workers, who are often highly skilled workers. If they primarily restrict supply, as shown in Figure 16-9, then the supply of non-union workers is likely to increase, lowering wages for non-union workers. There is some evidence that this may, in fact, be what has happened, because the long-run rate of growth in wage earnings has not risen significantly in periods when unions were relatively strongest. Nor did the overall share of income paid out as wages and salaries change dramatically during the last century.

But there is also some evidence that unions have increased productivity and labor demand by providing workers a "voice" in the workplace and bargaining process, even in cases where unions don't provide training programs and hiring halls. For example, one study found that union teachers are more productive in working with average-ability students than non-union teachers, even though teachers' unions provide very little of the training most teachers have and don't run hiring halls.[3] There is a vigorous debate about whether, and if so why, these positive

[2]See, for example, Richard Freeman and James Medoff's *What Do Unions Do?*, New York: Basic Books, 1984; H. Gregg Lewis' *Union Relative Wage Effects: A Survey*, Chicago: University of Chicago Press, 1986; Barry T. Hirsh and John T. Addison's *The Economic Analysis of Unions: New Approaches and Evidence*, Boston: Allen and Unwin, 1986; and Ehrenberg and Smith's summary, pp. 476-87.
[3]Randall Eberts and Joe Stone, *Unions and Public Schools: The Nonwage Effect of Collective Bargaining in American Education*, Lexington, Mass: D.C. Heath, 1984.

union-productivity differences exist in most unionized labor markets. In fact, this is the fourth and newest point in this debate over union wage differentials, and the last topic we will consider in the main body of this chapter.

Table 16-3
U.S. Union Membership, 1930-1988

Year	Membership (Thousands)	Percentage of Labor Force
1930	3,401	6.8
1934	3,088	5.9
1938	8,034	14.6
1942	10,380	17.2
1946	14,395	23.6
1950	14,300	23.1
1954	17,022	25.4
1958	17,029	24.2
1962	16,586	22.6
1966	17,940	22.7
1970	19,381	22.6
1974	20,119	21.7
1978	20,246	19.7
1982	19,763	17.9
1986	16,975	17.5
1988	17,002	16.8

Union membership jumped in the mid-1930s after passage of the Wagner Act, which provided a regular procedure for union certification votes under government supervision and guidelines. Membership grew again in the 1950s, while U.S. manufacturing was in a period of world dominance and in part because of the merger of the two largest, previously rival, organizations of national trade unions, the American Federation of Labor (AFL) and the Congress of Industrial Organizations (CIO). In the 1970s membership growth was revived as public employees were unionized on a widespread basis for the first time. Since then structural and demographic shifts in employment patterns -- particularly the growth of the service sector -- and increased competition from international and non-union firms, have led to sharp declines in the number of U.S. workers who are union members.

Sources: Ehrenberg and Smith, p. 446; and January issues of *Employment and Earnings*, published by the Bureau of Labor Statistics of the U.S. Department of Labor.

460

Figure 16-9
"Crowding" in Non-Union Occupations

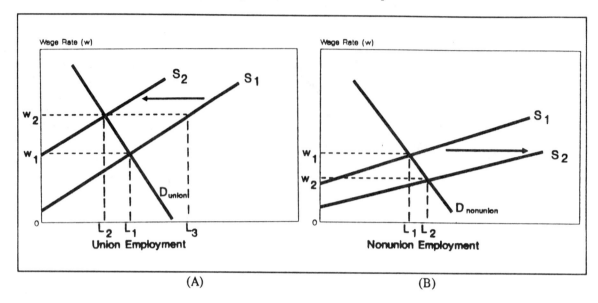

(A)   (B)

Restricting the supply of union labor (the shift from S_1 to S_2) will increase union wages from w_1 to w_2 in panel (A), but reduce employment from L_1 to L_2. As a result, some workers may wait to get a union job, as shown by the number of unemployed workers (L_3-L_2) at this wage rate.

Over time, some of these unemployed workers may move from union labor to non-union jobs, shifting the supply of nonunion labor from S_1 to S_2 in panel (B). That increase in supply will cause wages for non-union workers to fall, which further increases the observed wage differential between union and non-union jobs.

Richard Freeman and James Medoff have been the leading exponents of this idea of workers' "collective voice," used in the context of increasing labor productivity. They point to many studies in many different kinds of firms -- both manufacturing and service -- where productivity is higher in unionized firms, and identify several ways in which unions effectively assist *employers* as they represent the employees at a jobsite.

For example, if unions can reduce worker discontent by expressing it more forcefully to management, and by establishing "routine" procedures (such as seniority clauses) to determine promotions, entry into training programs, job transfers and reassignments, and even the choice of work shifts and vacation times, then when workers accept these procedures as reasonable and fair the turnover rates from worker resignations will be reduced. That reduces firms' training costs; and there is evidence that union employees quit their jobs less frequently than non-union workers (for several reasons, actually, including higher wage rates).

NO-STRIKE CLAUSES, found in virtually all U.S. collective bargaining contracts (but not in contracts from many other nations) also enhance productivity by guaranteeing firms that, during the term of the labor contract, workers will not walk off the job regardless of what local disputes or changes in the national economic environment arise. That provides firms a more stable labor force, and more predictable labor and training costs over the life of the contract. What U.S. firms give unions to get those no-strike clauses are *GRIEVANCE PROCEDURES*, which provide a step-by-step process to resolve disputes between the union and the firm, or between individual workers and their management supervisors, during the life of the contract.

Finally, unions may establish a clear means of collecting and forwarding workers' suggestions for changes in work rules and production methods, which can often improve efficiency at a firm. It is not unusual for workers using a particular piece of machinery or performing some task in a production process to discover a problem that the engineers who designed the equipment or the process have not anticipated. The trick is to get that information effectively presented and considered.

Many studies have been conducted to try to determine whether union workers are, *ceteris paribus*, more productive than their non-union counterparts. In general, it has been found that they are, sometimes by as much as 20-25%. But it is also clear that these productivity differences can diminish or disappear in times of deteriorating industrial relations practices in an industry, due either to dissent between unions and firms or to dissention in the union itself. Some economists also question the general findings of these productivity gains in unionized worksites, citing such offsetting factors as resistance to the adoption of new technologies and restrictive work rules, and pointing to some particular industries, such as construction, where it appears that unionization is associated with slower productivity growth over long periods of time.[4]

When union membership is associated with higher productivity, however, as it frequently appears to be, that explains how union and non-union firms can co-exist in the same industry, even when firms hiring union workers pay higher wages and benefits than non-union firms.

Case Study #21
The Economics of Discrimination[5]

A disproportionate share of poverty in the United States is concentrated among blacks, Hispanics, and females. Historically, these groups have been excluded from certain kinds of jobs, education, and membership in professional and social organizations. In some cases that exclusion was accomplished by "Jim Crow" laws, in others by custom and the social pressure of prejudice.

Apart from basic equity issues, there are clear economic costs associated with discriminatory laws and customs when they affect business decisions, and labor markets in particular. Not surprisingly, then, many economists have studied discrimination to identify its economic sources and consequences, and its current and historical impacts.

We will begin our review of that research with the basic, descriptive statistics on discrimination, and then see what researchers have learned about the causes of these patterns. Table 16-4 lists black-to-white income ratios from 1959-1986, for both male and female workers. It shows that these racial earnings differentials have narrowed over time for both males and females -- but much less, and much more slowly, for males than for females.

Table 16-5 lists female/male income ratios for full-time white workers in the United States. Again, the earnings differential shown there has narrowed somewhat over recent decades; but a sizeable gap still exists. Interestingly, these earnings differentials are much greater between married males and females (in households where spouses are present) than they are between single males and females: single females earn over 90% as much as single men. That strongly suggests that rearing children reduces women's earnings, a topic we consider at greater length below.

---

[4]See Ehrenberg and Smith, pp. 481-87 and 508-09.
[5]This case study is based largely on Chapter 14 in Ehrenberg and Smith's *Modern Labor Economics: Theory and Public Policy*.

Table 16-4
Black/White Earnings Ratios, by Gender

Year	Males	Females
1961	.66	.67
1965	.64	.71
1969	.66	.80
1973	.67	.85
1977	.69	.93
1981	.71	.90
1985	.69	.88
1987	.71	.91

These data are based on the median income for full-time, year-round workers, aged 14 or older prior to 1980, 15 or older thereafter.

Source: Adapted from Ehrenberg and Smith, p. 532, using June issues of the U.S. Bureau of the Census reports on *Money Income of Households, Families and Persons in the United States*, Consumer Income Series P-60.

Table 16-5
Female/Male Earnings Ratios

Year	Earnings Ratio
1964	.59
1967	.58
1970	.59
1973	.56
1977	.58
1980	.59
1983	.64
1986	.64
1987	.65

These ratios are based on median income for full-time, year-round, white workers.

Source: Ehrenberg and Smith, p. 536.

Table 16-6 shows 1983 black/white income ratios for males, and female/male income ratios for whites, in several broad occupational categories. Again, on average, in terms of these earnings it still pays to be a white male.

What economists want to know, of course, is why these differentials are the size they are, why they have changed in the ways they have over time, and what the overall costs of gender and racial discrimination are in an economic system. To help answer those questions, economists make a basic distinction between *CURRENT LABOR MARKET DISCRIMINATION*, which occurs when individuals doing the same job in the same kind of firm and community are paid different wages, and *PREMARKET DIFFERENCES* between workers of a given gender, or racial or ethnic background, in terms of education, training, or work experience. Both of these factors lead to earnings differentials; but the first represents a clear case of current discrimination, while the second means that workers from different groups will have different productivity in the labor market and so command different wages and salaries even if they work for employers who do not discriminate on the basis of gender, race, or ethnicity.

Table 16-6
Income Ratios by Race and Gender in Selected Occupational Categories, 1986

Occupational Category	Black Males to White Males	White Females to White Males
Professional Specialty	.76	.59
Executive and Managerial	.68	.59
Administrative Support (Including Clerical)	.82	.67
Technical and Sales	.69	.55
Service Occupations	.79	.55
Craft and Repair	.82	.72
Machine Operations and Laborers	.83	.63

These figures are based on mean earnings for full-time, year-round workers, aged 18 or over.

Source: *Money Income of Households, Families and Persons in the United States: 1986*, Consumer Income Series P-60, no. 159 (June 1988), Table 40.

That raises a basic question: Are earnings differentials based on pre-market differentials a form of discrimination? In a very current sense they aren't, but they certainly can be based on the effects of past discrimination.

For example, if you are a member of a group which expects to encounter discrimination when applying for managerial and professional jobs, you may rationally decide to invest less in your own education, training, and early job-market experience in such occupations, because those investments are costly and you know your opportunity to reach the top of such a career path is artificially restricted. Furthermore, if the public education that is provided to blacks or other minority groups is known to be inferior to that available to whites, the economic returns to that investment in human capital will also be lower, so the members of minority groups may rationally invest fewer resources in it.

Economists try to sort out the effects of these pre-market differences and current labor-market discrimination by looking at wage and income differentials across various groups of workers after statistically adjusting for worker characteristics related to productivity differences. Theoretically, any non-productivity pay differences that remain are a measure of current labor market discrimination.

Summarizing some of the key findings of this research:

1) Current labor market discrimination against black males was estimated to be approximately 10-15% of white males' earnings in the late 1960s; about 12% in the mid-1970s; and 6-17% in 1980 (depending on the age group of the workers) -- but the study on this latest time period (by Saul Hoffman and Charles Link) also found that among male college graduates blacks earned 10-18% more than whites. A broad estimate from these findings is that pre-market differences account for about half of the observed earnings differentials, and current discrimination the other half.

2) Full-time, year-round employees who are male Hispanics were estimated to earn 69% of what comparable white workers earned in 1984. Other studies suggest that most, if not all, of this differential may be attributable to language (English) proficiency, after controlling for other productivity-related measures.

3) A few recent studies have been conducted to investigate discrimination against Asians, who represent a small but growing percentage of the United States labor force. In 1980, Asian males earned about as much as white males in the United States on a per capita basis, while Asian women earned about 13% more than white women. After controlling for productivity differences, studies indicate no current labor market discrimination against workers of Chinese ancestry, slight (about 4%) discrimination against males of Japanese ancestry, and more (about 10-15%) against Filipino males.

4) About half of the earnings differentials between males and females of all races appear to be due to premarket differences, about a fourth to occupational segregation (i.e., predominantly "white male careers" or promotion paths), and about a fourth to various other kinds of current labor market discrimination.

All of the estimates of current labor market discrimination cited above may be somewhat high, given the inherent difficulties involved in measuring productivity characteristics across such large numbers of workers in all different kinds of occupations. To the extent that the variables used to capture productivity differences -- such as age, job experience, and education levels -- are incomplete and imperfect, the remaining wage differentials will not be entirely due to current labor market discrimination. Even so, it appears that there is a significant amount of discrimination present in labor markets today. That evidence supports calls for continuing, and perhaps even expanding, legal remedies for such abuses. But effective remedies also require some understanding of exactly why and where discrimination originates.

Labor economists have identified three major sources: employers, other employees, and customers. *EMPLOYER DISCRIMINATION* occurs when a business owner or manager has a preference for hiring workers of a certain gender or racial or ethnic type for all jobs, or for certain kinds of jobs. Workers from non-preferred groups will then either not be employed, assuming there are enough applicants at this firm to give the employer a choice of whom to hire, or they will only be hired if they agree to work for a lower wage than an equally productive worker from the employer's preferred group. Note that this is *not* profit-maximizing behavior on the part of the firm, because the employer doesn't hire up to the point where the unfavored workers' MRP is equal to the competitive wage rate for workers with this productivity, as shown in Figure 16-10. Therefore, discriminating employers will pay for their prejudice in the form of lower profits.

If a large number of employers choose to discriminate in certain occupations, the supply of labor in jobs open to the disfavored workers is increased, the supply of labor in jobs not open to them is decreased, and the result is a greater wage differential in these jobs than would otherwise be observed. The overall output in such an economy is also decreased in two ways. First, current production would be higher, and production costs decreased, if all workers who are qualified for more productive jobs were allowed to enter them. Second, over time, lower wages for workers who experience discrimination will lead them to invest less in training, education, and entry-level jobs that lead to managerial and professional occupations, so the future supply of labor in the nation will experience a decrease in quantity and (especially) quality.

EMPLOYEE DISCRIMINATION occurs when some workers refuse to take jobs with other workers of a certain gender, race, or ethnic background, or will consent to do so only if they receive a higher wage (which drives up employers' production costs). Conversely, they may agree to take a lower wage if they can work in a segregated workplace. Either way, they end up paying for this "privilege" in the form of lower wages or (in cases where they are able to command a higher wage to work in an integrated setting) lower employment levels than they would otherwise enjoy. Employers who are able to hire equally skilled non-discriminating workers will have a competitive advantage, assuming their goal is profit maximization.

CUSTOMER DISCRIMINATION occurs when consumers prefer to be served by workers of a certain gender, or racial or ethnic background, particularly in certain types of occupations. If this makes it more difficult for minority groups to enter certain prestige occupations, the result will be some degree of occupational segregation, which leads to decreased investment in education and training by minority workers as described above. But customers ultimately pay for these preferences in the form of higher prices for the exclusive services that result from the lower supply of labor to these occupations.

Figure 16-10
Employer Discrimination and Profit Maximization

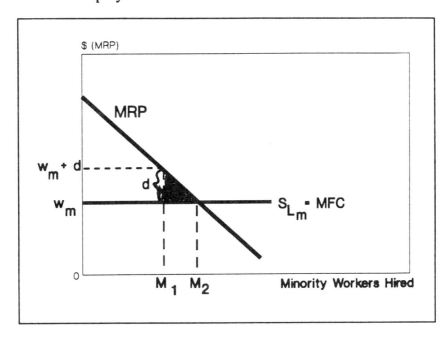

A non-discriminating employer hires minority and non-minority workers out to point (M_2), where their wage rate (W_m) and MFC is equal to their marginal revenue product, and in doing so maximizes profits or minimizes loses. A discriminating employer hires fewer minority workers (M_1), because he or she values their production less than that of non-minority workers. In effect, the minority workers must provide an "extra" level of output, shown above as d, before the discriminating employer will agree to pay them W_m. But the employer loses too, since MRP > MFC in the range from M_1 to M_2, and the employer gives up net revenues shown by the shaded triangle in this range. In short, the employer accepts lower profits or higher losses to indulge in his or her interest in discriminating against this group of workers.

The final kind of discrimination we will discuss is based on one of the most recent ideas developed in this application of labor economics, and one of the most controversial. *STATISTICAL DISCRIMINATION* refers to different pricing, pay, and promotion policies for customers or workers of a certain gender or racial or ethnic background, based on information about the *average* performance and behavior of their groups' characteristics (rather than the individual characteristics of persons who belong to the group). For example, suppose that a firm promotes fewer young women to key management positions because they know that, on average, more women than men will leave their jobs for some time to care for young children. Or suppose men are charged higher insurance premiums than women of the same age because, on average, they die younger.

There is clearly an equity issue here, in that an individual woman who is not going to leave her job to care for children, or an individual male who does not die at an early age, is financially penalized for being in a group where a large percentage of people do exhibit this costly (to employers or insurance companies) behavior. From a pure efficiency standpoint, statistical discrimination can also lead members of a group who are, on average, less likely to succeed in certain careers, to invest less in education and training for such jobs than they otherwise would.

Several recent laws and court rulings have made it illegal, or at least more difficult, to use these kind of statistical averages in awarding promotions in certain jobs, setting insurance premiums, or different annuity payments to men and women. The usefulness of the group averages as a signaling device has also decreased as the premarket differences between various groups has narrowed in several respects -- for example, more women are staying in the job market even while their children are young, and the female mortality rate from lung cancer has caught up with men's as more women have taken up smoking.

But of course by legally suppressing information on groups whenever it *is* accurate, the costs of doing business are increased. And ultimately those costs have to be paid in one way or another. In practice, female teens will likely find their rates for auto insurance rising, women will find their life insurance premiums going up, and men will find their annuity payments falling, in order to average out the costs that are, statistically, gender related. Similarly, company profits will fall, or product prices rise, or both, in order to cover the higher costs of paying, training, and promoting young male and female executives at equal rates, even though females are still, statistically, more likely than males to take time out of the job market while raising their children. Wealthy nations like the United States can certainly afford to eliminate some degree of statistical discrimination if they choose to do so, but not without paying significant costs.

That result is, at this point in this case study, hardly surprising. The clear message is that neither discrimination nor legal programs to end it are free.

Case Study #22
Efficiency Wages

Socialist Robert Owen and capitalist Henry Ford both raised eyebrows in their day by paying factory workers more than they could earn working for other employers. What is more, they both did this in successful businesses, and both found positive economic effects from the higher wages. Their employees stayed with them longer, and their employment offices were able to choose from a large number of applicants whenever they wanted to hire more workers. (Ford liked to hire and reward workers with the "right" character -- those who didn't drink or gamble.)

Perhaps Ford and Owen were ahead of their time in this respect; at least they were ahead of most economists, who have only recently begun to explore such practices. Economists now define an *EFFICIENCY WAGE* as the wage which maximizes a firm's profits by equating the marginal cost of hiring workers to the marginal benefits. That sounds standard enough, but they now interpret those costs and benefits more broadly than you have seen thus far in Chapters 15 and 16. Specifically, such factors as the lower training costs associated with lower quit-rates and turnover are considered, as well as the incentives that higher wages provide to employees to work harder than they otherwise would. "Shirking" or "goofing off" on a job that pays more than other jobs you can get is risky in terms of getting fired, which leads you to work harder to make sure you don't. Workers certainly benefit from the higher wage, but the firm benefits too from the greater effort and lower turnover.

Efficiency wages are more likely to be paid in some kinds of jobs and by some kinds of firms than others. In particular, a firm that spends a lot to train workers to do tasks that are specific to its production process will be more eager to keep turnover rates low and thereby reduce training costs. And if it is difficult to monitor workers' efforts in some kinds of jobs -- perhaps because output must be produced by a team of workers rather than people working alone, or because it is very expensive to check the quality of an employee's work after it is built into a complex product -- the higher wages will be especially important in preventing shirking.

Since higher, efficiency wages are attractive to workers for obvious reasons, and will lead some people who would not be willing to work at standard wages to enter the job market, another result they may have is to increase unemployment. In fact, many workers may experience periods of unemployment waiting to land an efficiency-wage job, which would contribute to the existence of some persistent, long-term unemployment, even in periods of nearly full employment in the national economy.

But recognize too that just because employers pay more than the average wage in a certain area or kind of job doesn't mean that they are paying efficiency wages. In the case of Henry Ford, specifically, there is evidence that he paid even more than the efficiency rate that would have maximized the Ford Motor Company's profits in these years. He did this, it appears, to satisfy his own paternalistic feelings toward his employees.[6]

Chapter Summary

1) Firms with monopoly power in output markets face downward-sloping *MARGINAL REVENUE PRODUCT (MRP)* schedules due to the law of diminishing returns *and* the firms' downward-sloping demand and marginal revenue schedules. As a result, even in factor markets where they are wage takers, these firms hire fewer workers than competitive firms, *ceteris paribus*, and pay the last worker hired less than his or her value of marginal product (VMP).

2) Monopsonists are firms that have market power as employers in input markets; only one or a few large employers hire workers and other inputs in such markets. These firms must increase wages or other factor payments to increase their hiring and output levels, so they face a marginal factor cost (MFC) curve that lies above their input supply curves. As a result, monopsonists hire fewer inputs than competitive firms, *ceteris paribus*, and pay the last worker hired a wage that is less than his or her MRP.

3) Under *MONOPSONY*, a minimum wage law can increase wage rates and employment levels simultaneously. This finding is not of widespread significance in an industrial nation like the United States, however, because high levels of *FACTOR MOBILITY* effectively limit the degree of monopsony power that firms can achieve.

4) *UNIONS* are organizations of workers which collectively bargain for better wages and working conditions. In settings where both firms and unions have some degree of market power (in extreme cases, this can be represented as *BILATERAL MONOPOLY*), there is a range for possible wage and/or employment outcomes. The specific wage and employment levels that are set in that range depend on the relative bargaining power of the firm and union involved in the negotiations.

5) In bargaining sessions union leaders and company executives must determine what outcomes they will pursue most aggressively, and what tradeoffs they are prepared to make among such variables as wages, employment levels, fringe benefits, and work rules. They must also weigh the costs of accepting a given set of contract provisions against the costs of a labor *STRIKE*. Some economists have represented these ideas using bargaining preference models, union resistance curves, and firm concession curves.

6) Unions try to increase wage rates for their members through various strategies which have the effect of increasing the demand for union labor or restricting its supply. Policies which increase demand by increasing workers' productivity are mutually beneficial to employers and employees. Policies which legislatively increase demand or restrict supply do not result in mutual gain through voluntary exchange, and are widely criticized by economists.

7) Available empirical evidence suggests that union workers receive wages that are 10-20% higher than nonunion workers in similar occupations, *ceteris paribus*. There is active debate among economists as to what part of this differential is due to higher productivity on the part of union members, and what part is due to supply restrictions that can increase wages for union workers while decreasing wages for nonunion workers.

---

[6] Daniel Raff and Lawrence Summers, "Did Henry Ford Pay Efficiency Wages," *Journal of Labor Economics*, October 1987, pp. S57-S86.

8) (Case Study #21) Women and members of some minorities receive wages lower than those paid to white males in similar jobs, *ceteris paribus*. They also bring, on average, lower levels of education, training, and experience to the labor market, particularly in many managerial and professional occupations. These *PREMARKET DIFFERENCES* widen the pay differentials associated with *CURRENT LABOR MARKET DISCRIMINATION* even further, and are themselves due in part to occupational segregation; unequal access to good schools; and *EMPLOYER, EMPLOYEE,* or *CUSTOMER DISCRIMINATION* -- all of which limit these workers' opportunities for advancement. Discrimination can benefit members of some groups at the expense of others; but it is generally not profit-maximizing behavior. Producers, workers, and consumers who engage in discrimination pay significant costs to indulge their prejudices. *STATISTICAL DISCRIMINATION* is more controversial, because eliminating it involves a trade-off in terms of equitable treatment to members of groups which, on average, do impose higher costs on employers or various kinds of firms (such as insurance companies).

9) (Case Study #22) *EFFICIENCY WAGES* are higher than wages workers can receive in other jobs, but still maximize profits for a firm by reducing turnover and training costs, and increasing workers' cost of shirking. While these productivity gains are desirable, efficiency wages may also be associated with somewhat higher levels of unemployment because workers are willing to remain unemployed longer to increase their chance of landing a job that pays efficiency wages.

Review and Discussion Questions

1) Given the choice, would you prefer to work for a perfectly competitive firm or a firm with some degree of monopoly power? List several factors that would influence your decision.

2) If a monopsonist could practice wage discrimination and pay each worker the minimum amount required to get him or her to work:

   a) what would be the relationship between the firm's MFC curve and its labor-supply schedule?
   b) how would the firm's wage and employment levels compare to those of a perfectly competitive firm, *ceteris paribus*?
   c) what level of monopsonistic exploitation would exist for the last worker employed by this firm?

3) Determine the wage and employment levels that result if a minimum wage is established which intersects a monopsonist's MRP curve to the left of employment level Q_1 in Figure 16-4.

4) Are unions in some sense the labor-equivalent of monopolies or oligopolies? Do you think they should be subject to prosecution under the antitrust laws discussed in Chapter 13? Why or why not?

5) How are the chances for achieving union objectives in a contract negotiation most likely to be affected by:

   a) very high or very low levels of unemployment among current union members?
   b) high levels of unemployment among non-union members?
   c) very high or very low profit levels at the firms where union members are employed?
   d) increased competition from foreign producers in markets that are heavily unionized?
   e) technological change (such as the widespread use of microcomputers) which makes it possible for more employees to work at home, or on a freelance basis?

6) Look up the term "featherbedding" in a dictionary, and describe it in terms of the union supply or demand-based strategies discussed in this chapter. Try to identify a current example of featherbedding.

469

7) Suppose all of the 10-20% average wage differential for union labor represented higher productivity on the part of these workers. How would that differential then be interpreted in terms of its overall impact on the economic problem of scarcity, and specifically in terms of the scarcity of labor?

8) (Case Study #21) Discuss the costs and benefits of a hypothetical legislation and enforcement program which could immediately result in the elimination of all earnings differentials associated with:

    a) current labor market discrimination.
    b) premarket differences between workers of different gender, race, or ethnicity.

9) (Case Study #22) How are "paternalistic" and "piece-rate" wages different in their motivations and effects from efficiency wages? How are they similar?

Chapter 17
General Equilibrium

In This Chapter...

we bring together many of the concepts and results developed in earlier chapters. The various parts of the economy -- households, firms, product markets, and factor markets -- are shown simultaneously, as an economic system. In that sense, this chapter is a natural bridge from the study of microeconomics to the study of macroeconomics, and to international questions involving the interaction of two or more economic systems. But a microeconomic view of general equilibrium analysis is important in and of itself, in terms of understanding the flow of resources from one market to another, how various markets and agents interact, and the often surprising effects of policies designed to adjust outcomes in a particular market on other sectors of the economy.

Market Interdependence

In your course on microeconomics, which is now nearly completed, we have discussed product markets and factor markets, markets for private goods and public goods, and policy issues and producer and consumer decisions in each of these settings -- but largely in isolation. In more formal terms, until now we have been working with PARTIAL EQUILIBRIUM ANALYSIS. But the real economic world doesn't stop working when only a partial equilibrium is established, so in the first section of this chapter we introduce the idea of GENERAL EQUILIBRIUM ANALYSIS, and consider how changes in particular markets spread across the entire economic system. As we do this, however, don't lose sight of the fact that general equilibrium analysis is ultimately built on the individual microeconomic foundations developed in earlier chapters.

A Wage and Price Control Example: Or Rube Goldberg Does Economic Policy

During World War II wages and prices were set by the federal government, both to restrict inflation in that time of massive public spending for the war effort, and to direct large quantities of strategic resources (such as metals, rubber, and petroleum) to military uses instead of private consumption. Many journalists, historians, and even economists claim that such war periods are the only times wage and price controls are generally accepted by the population and work reasonably well. But things don't really go all that smoothly even then. In one well documented case, price controls on corn in 1942-43 led to shortages of iron ore, livestock, industrial alcohol, rubber, petroleum shipments from the Gulf Coast, and casein (a product used to make many kinds of industrial adhesives). The price ceiling on U.S. corn did, however, benefit various Canadian, Caribbean, and Argentinian export industries. All of that sounds unlikely, to be sure; but here's what happened.

The price ceilings on corn led to a decrease in the quantity of corn produced, just as you would predict after reading Chapter 4. That meant less corn was available for dairy farms in the Northeast, and for cattle and hogs farms in the Midwest. These livestock farmers imported Canadian wheat to substitute for the corn (at a higher cost), but the corn shipments from Canada to U.S. farmers used up cargo space on Great Lakes freighters that had been carrying iron ore, which led to shortages in markets that used iron ore as an input. Furthermore, the wheat now used as feed had previously been used to produce industrial alcohol and rubber, so the available supplies of those products decreased, too.

The shortfalls in alcohol output were partially offset when alcohol producers substituted molasses for wheat as a raw material; however, the molasses had to be imported from the Caribbean, and that required freighter space that had previously been used to carry petroleum products up from Gulf ports. Similarly, hog farmers found that they could substitute skim milk for corn feed to some degree; but that depleted the supply of casein, because casein is produced from milk. When hog farmers started buying more milk, producers who used casein to make adhesives found they had to import more of it -- as it turned out from Argentina.

The price control on a single product, U.S. corn, led to all of these adjustments and problems[1].

The same kinds of problems still occur today in both economic and ecological systems, and frequently in both at the same time. For example, New Hampshire merchants recently complained that too little of the New England fishing business was coming their way due to a large local skunk population. The state government responded with a "skunk eradication program" and the fishing trade did increase, for about two years. Then the fish stopped biting and the fishing trade fell off sharply. After the fact it became clear that the skunks had held down the snapping turtle population, and with fewer skunks more turtles hatched and ate more fish[2]. That all goes to show that, in a general equilibrium perspective, it's not nice to fool with Mother Nature. Or in economic terms, it is virtually impossible to change one price, or one supply or demand schedule, without affecting several others.

The Circular Flow

The flow chart in Figure 17-1 is known as a *CIRCULAR-FLOW* diagram. It illustrates the links between the major decision-making units in a market economy, the categories of economic resources traded in product and factor markets, and the prices for those different types of resources. Households supply resources to firms and the government, and buy or receive goods and services from them. Firms sell goods and services to households and the government, but pay wages, salaries, rents, interest, and profits to households, and taxes and user fees to the government. The government collects taxes and other fees from households and firms, and provides goods, services, and income transfers, to them. Unlike business production, however, most government services and transfers are provided on some basis other than the fees (including taxes) an individual or family pays for them, given the economic roles of government discussed in Chapter 5.

Besides illustrating the interconnections and flows among these markets and sectors, the circular-flow diagram implies that the flows are constrained by a set of consistency requirements. One such requirement is that the resources sent to firms by households be sufficient to produce the final goods and services sent by firms to households and the government. Another is that the payments firms receive for these products must equal the factor payments they make to households, less what they pay to government in taxes and fees. Furthermore, the factor payments received by households from businesses and government, plus transfer payments received from the government, constitute the income households have available to spend on goods and services. That in turn equals what they spend, save, and pay in taxes.

A slightly different way to think of these constraints is simply that the value of inputs to a particular firm or sector of the economy must equal the value of its ouputs -- after all, the payments for those inputs come from the payments people make for those outputs. This general relationship between inputs and outputs can be broken down in greater detail, to see more about the different flows of resources in the economy.

[1] This episode was reported in the *Business Week* article "Corn for War" (October 23, 1943), and also discussed in Bela Gold's *Wartime Economic Planning in Agriculture* (New York: Columbia University Press, 1949).
[2] Susan W. Liebler, quoted in the *Wall Street Journal*, May 12, 1989, p. A10.

Figure 17-1
The Circular Flow of Spending and Income

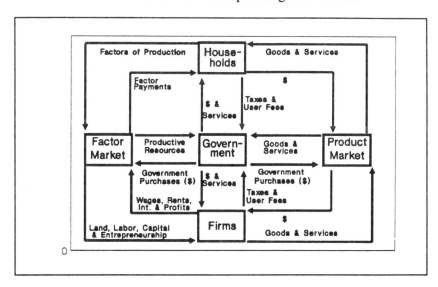

The outermost flow depicts the movement of land, labor, capital, and entrepreneurship from households to firms, which use these resources to produce the goods and services people consume. The inner, clockwise flow shows the monetary payments that are made for these outputs and inputs. Productive resources are exchanged in factor markets, final goods and services in product markets.

Government activities affect both households and firms, in both product and factor markets. The government produces some goods and services directly, and must hire resources to undertake that production. It also provides income transfers and services to households and firms. It finances its production and transfer activities through taxes and user fees, or through borrowing in financial markets (not shown directly in this chart).

Input-Output Analysis

An *INPUT-OUTPUT* table is used to show how the goods and services produced by the various industry groups in an economy over some time period (typically a year) are distributed to other industries for use as inputs in their own production processes, or to households where they are used as consumer goods. It also shows how various inputs are combined by these industry groups to produce their outputs. The table is, in effect, a matrix in which each industry group or sector appears twice, once as a consumer of products or productive resources, and once as a producer of them.

For example, the input-output table shown in Table 17-1 is a greatly simplified representation of a national economy, which uses hypothetical data. It is simplified in that it does not include financial markets, the government, the international trade sector, or specific product and industry entries. Still, it does capture the constraint of equal values for inputs and outputs, and the idea that a change in any one cell must lead to changes in one or more other cells in the table.

As an example, consider the entries for agriculture. Reading down the first column, we see that $200 billion of services and non-durable goods (such things as fertilizer, pesticides, and fuel products) went into agricultural production during the period covered by the table, as well as $100 billion dollars worth of durable goods (farm equipment, for example), and $450 billion worth of wages, salaries, rents, and profits paid out by this sector. In practice, some payments may also have been made for agricultural outputs (e.g., for seed grain or young animals that are raised and resold), but we have constructed this table so that only net values for each sector are shown.

Reading across the top row shows that services and non-durables manufacturing (such as the packaged-food industry and fast-food chains) purchased $350 billion of agricultural products as inputs; durables manufacturing purchased $250 billion; and households purchased the remaining $150 billion for direct consumption. The total value of the agricultural output sold ($750 billion, in the top row) equals the total value of inputs used to produce that output (as shown in the first column). The same thing applies to the two manufacturing categories; and similarly, the income payments made to households (the fourth row) must add up to the total household expenditures (the fourth column).

Detailed input-output tables for national economies have been constructed by a number of prominent economists, most notably Wassily Leontief, who pioneered the development and application of input-output analysis. Such tables may include hundreds of industries, along with entries for government and the foreign trade and financial sectors. With this wealth of detail, the tables can help economists study such things as: structural shifts in the economy, as some products become more important over time and others wither away; the effect of changes in one industry on other industries, and in factor markets; the long-term and far-reaching effects of public policy actions -- including the imposition of a tariff or excise tax on a particular product, or a general income tax on all factor payments; and the inherent difficulty of central planning in a large, complex economy, where administratively-determined price or output changes can set off hundreds of other changes that may require additional actions by a planning committee. Many of the insights from this analysis are derived from the internal consistency requirements in input and output results for an economic system, which stress the idea of general rather than partial equilibrium.

Table 17-1
An Input-Output Table
($ billions)

	Agriculture	Services & Non-Durables Manufacturing	Durables Manufacturing	Household Consumption	Total Output
Agriculture	---	350	250	150	750
Services & Non-Durables Manufacturing	200	---	400	900	1500
Durables Manufacturing	100	550	---	600	1250
Household Factors	450	600	600	---	
Total Inputs	750	1500	1250		3500

Each column shows the sources of the inputs to a given industry group, measured in dollar values. Each row shows where the output of a given industry group is used or consumed, again measured in dollar terms. Profits are treated as a payment to entrepreneurial inputs, so the total value of all inputs to an industry group must equal the total value of all outputs from it.

Today, economists more often develop quantitative analyses and predictions for these kinds of issues using large computer models of the national or world economy, which specify systems of simultaneous equations to show how products can be produced using various combinations of resources; the supply and demand functions for these various resources; how the income determined by the prices that are paid for these resources (and from government tax and transfer programs) will be spent; and the demand schedules for the products households buy with their incomes. In other words, these large-scale models are themselves general equilibrium systems which attempt to capture technological constraints, resource owners' decisions about how to use the factors of production they control, household consumption decisions, and public policy actions and interventions. Each of these individual decisions or constraints affects outcomes in other parts of the economic system, which is what the general equilibrium perspective is all about in broadest terms.

But general equilibrium models are also concerned with determining the economic efficiency of any set of institutional arrangements and incentives (that is, of economic systems); of the current set of prices, factor payments, taxes, and output levels in the system; and of changes in any of these variables. To see that, we must turn to the basic set of mathematical equations and graphs developed by economic theorists who work in the area of general equilibrium analysis.

Equilibrium Conditions Revisited, and Efficiency Measures Extended

In this section we briefly review the equilibrium conditions for consumers and producers in product and factor markets, then show how those individual equilibrium conditions must be linked together to establish a general equilibrium in an economic system of markets. That general equilibrium is shown to be Pareto efficient when markets are perfectly competitive if there are no market failures present in the system, and given whatever pattern of income distribution exists among the individuals in the economy. The presence of market failures means that perfect competition may not guarantee an efficient outcome. A different distribution of income will lead to a different set of price and output outcomes in these markets, which will also be Pareto efficient in the absence of market failures.

Consumer, Product-Market, and Factor-Market Equilibria

Economic decisions typically involve a process of constrained maximization. Consumers maximize total utility, or satisfaction, subject to the constraints of their limited budgets. Producers adjust output levels (and prices in imperfect competition) to maximize profits. Their actions are constrained by what consumers are willing and able to pay for their products, by what other producers can do to compete with their prices and products, and by what they must pay for the factors of production. There are equilibrium conditions for each of these decisions which we developed, separately, in earlier chapters. In general equilibrium, all of these conditions must be satisfied simultaneously. If any one condition is not met, adjustments across different product and factor markets will usually be necessary to achieve an efficient distribution of resources.

<u>Consumer equilibrium</u>. Consumers compare the satisfaction an additional unit of a good or service will provide for them to the price they must pay for that product, *and* with the level of satisfaction per dollar they can receive from all other products. So, in equilibrium,

$$\frac{MU_a}{P_a} = \frac{MU_b}{P_b} \dots = \frac{MU_n}{P_n} \qquad (1)$$

where a, b, ... n represent all the products the person consumes, MU is the marginal utility of the last unit of a product consumed, and P is the product's price. (So, for example, MU_a is the marginal utility of good a.) Note that if the satisfaction per dollar for the last unit of any product a consumer buys is greater than the same ratio for any other product, the consumer can increase his or her total utility by purchasing more of the former good, and less of the latter. With diminishing marginal utility and no "lumpiness" problems in buying products (for example, if consumers can buy any fraction of a product unit they want, not just integer units) that process smoothly returns the consumer to an equilibrium position and is consistent with typical, downward-sloping demand curves, as shown in Chapter 6.

Furthermore, for any two products we can rearrange the terms in this equation to show that

$$\frac{MU_a}{MU_b} = \frac{P_a}{P_b} \tag{2}$$

The first term in this equation, the ratio of the two marginal utilities, turns out to be equal to the marginal rate of substitution (MRS). Let's see why that is true.

In Chapter 6, you saw that the MRS is equal to the amount of one good a consumer is willing to give up for a compensating amount of the other good, such that the consumer's total utility remains unchanged. The marginal utility of a product is equal to the change in total utility produced by a small change in the quantity of the product consumed, divided by the change in the quantity consumed. Thus, for products a and b:

$$MU_a = \frac{\Delta U}{\Delta a} \quad \text{and} \quad MU_b = \frac{\Delta U}{\Delta b} \tag{3}$$

Substituting these two values into the left side of equation 2, the ΔU terms cancel out, and we are back to a Chapter 6 version of the expression for the MRS -- a ratio of the change in good a to the change in good b that holds total utility constant. This is shown in equation 4:

$$\frac{\frac{\Delta U}{\Delta a}}{\frac{\Delta U}{\Delta b}} = \frac{\Delta U}{\Delta a} \cdot \frac{\Delta b}{\Delta U} = \frac{\Delta b}{\Delta a} = MRS \tag{4}$$

Having now seen that the left-hand side of equation 2 is the MRS, we can see the real significance of that equation is to show that, in equilibrium, the ratio of consumers' trade-off in the satisfaction derived from the quantity of two goods consumed is equal to the ratio of the prices for the goods. In other words, people substitute units of these two goods in consumption uses (holding total satisfaction constant) at the same ratio the goods are exchanged in the marketplace (as shown by their relative price).

This equilibrium condition applies to all consumers in a market who face the same prices for products, which they always do in competitive markets and usually do in imperfect competition (the exceptions involve price discrimination, as you saw in Chapter 11, and price dispersions reflecting positive search costs, as shown in Chapter 14). Moreover, we know directly from equation 1 that when different consumers face the same product prices, marginal utilities for the last units of any product that any two or more people consume will be the same for these individuals, even though their total utility and the quantity of the product they consume may vary owing to differences in their preferences and incomes. As shown in Chapter 6, that means in equilibrium the slope of consumers' indifference curves (equal to the MRS) will be equal to the slope of the budget constraint line (which is determined by the relative prices of the two goods).

Factor-Market Equilibrium. Individuals also make supply decisions for the factors of production which they own and provide to employers. The employers who use these factors are, in turn, confronted with decisions about how many units of each input to hire or buy, given the prices of the inputs, the prices they receive for their own products, the technological constraints that determine how their outputs can be produced, and their estimates of the output levels that will maximize their profits. In producing a particular product, employers will hire factors to satisfy equilibrium conditions that are much like those facing consumers:

$$\frac{MP_1}{P_1} = \frac{MP_2}{P_2} \ldots = \frac{MP_n}{P_n} \tag{5}$$

where 1, 2, ... n are the various inputs a firm hires, MP is the marginal product of the last unit of an input hired, and P is an input price. What this condition means is that firms hire so that they obtain the same output per dollar from the last unit of every factor of production they use. If one input provides more output per dollar than others, the firm will hire more of it and less of other inputs. (In saying this we assume, as in Chapters 8 and 15 where this condition was first developed, that the firm continues to produce the same level of output, and "lumpiness" in purchasing inputs is not a problem.) These terms can also be rearranged to show that, in equilibrium,

$$\frac{MP_1}{MP_2} = \frac{P_1}{P_2} \qquad (6)$$

The left-hand term in this equation is equal to the marginal rate of technical substitution (MRTS), introduced in Chapter 8 as the change in one input required to offset the change in another input, holding total output constant. To show that, use the same procedure that we just used to show how the ratio of marginal utilities for two consumer goods is equal to the marginal rate of substitution. The marginal product of an input is the change in output (ΔQ) associated with a small change in the quantity of an input employed (letting i_1 indicate one input, and i_2 a second input):

$$MP_1 = \frac{\Delta Q}{\Delta i_1} \quad \text{and} \quad MP_2 = \frac{\Delta Q}{\Delta i_2} \qquad (7)$$

Substituting these two terms into the left side of equation 6, the ΔQ terms cancel out, and the remaining expression for MRTS is in the same form as that presented in Chapter 8 -- a change in one input divided by the change in another, such that total output is unchanged. This is shown in equation 8:

$$\frac{\frac{\Delta Q}{\Delta i_1}}{\frac{\Delta Q}{\Delta i_2}} = \frac{\Delta Q}{\Delta i_1} \cdot \frac{\Delta i_2}{\Delta Q} = \frac{\Delta i_2}{\Delta i_1} = MRTS \qquad (8)$$

Knowing that, the real importance of equation 6 is in showing that, in equilibrium, the ratio at which producers trade off inputs in their production processes is equal to the ratio of the prices for the inputs. In other words, producers substitute units of the inputs at the same ratio the inputs are exchanged in factor markets (as shown by their relative prices). This is another way of saying that, in equilibrium, the MRTS (which is the slope of the isocost curves that were developed in Chapter 8) equals the ratio of the inputs' prices . Otherwise, as shown most directly in equation 5, the firm is not minimizing the cost of producing a given level of output.

From Chapter 15, we also know that perfectly competitive firms hire an input out to the point where its value of marginal product (VMP) is equal to the input price. Taking labor inputs as our example, in equilibrium a perfectly competitive firm will hire more workers until

$$VMP = MP_L \, (P) = w \qquad (9)$$

where MP_L is the marginal product of labor, P is the price of the product the labor inputs are used to produce, and w is the wage rate for labor. Because all competitive firms face the same input and output prices, the marginal product of the last unit of an input being used to produce some output will be the same for *all* such firms that produce that output. (That is, since w and P in equation 9 are the same for these firms, MP_L must be the same, too.)

We are nearly ready to put these factor market outcomes together with the equilibrium conditions for consumer purchases developed earlier, to see the general equilibrium conditions for an economic system -- or at least a perfectly competitive system. First, however, we have to review the conditions for economic efficiency in output markets, to see how those conditions apply to the overall level of social production, not just production in a single market.

Output-Market Equilibrium. Allocative efficiency in the production of a particular product is achieved, as you saw in Chapters 9-13, when firms produce more of a product until the product's price is equal to the cost of producing the last unit of output produced and sold in the market. That is, P = MC. This outcome was routinely achieved in perfect competition, so in an economy where all industries are competitive we know that

$$\frac{P_a}{P_b} = \frac{MC_b}{MC_b} \qquad (10)$$

where a and b represent, once again, various products. Since competitive firms are price takers, firms producing the same product must take the same price. Therefore, the marginal costs for identical products made and sold by any two competitive firms must also be equal. That's important because marginal costs are based on the rate at which one good can be transformed into the other, by shifting resources from one production process to the other. We will explain that further in the following section, using the concepts of opportunity cost and a production possibilities frontier. But notice here how the linkage between production costs and product prices shown in equation 10 can be related back to the consumer equilibrium conditions shown in equation 2, because both equations have the same term for the ratio of product prices. That interconnection is a key part of general equilibrium analysis, which we will also return to shortly.

Production Possibilities Curves and the Marginal Rate of Transformation

A production possibilities frontier (PPF) is a curve that represents the various combinations of two outputs, or two broad categories of outputs, that a nation can produce in a given time period (say a year) using all available resources and the most efficient production technologies. In the PPF in Figure 17-2, at point A the nation produces only capital goods and at point F only consumer goods. Moving from A toward F to produce more consumer goods requires shifting resources away from the production of capital goods. Therefore, the opportunity cost of additional units of consumer goods is the forgone production of capital goods.

The production possibilities frontier in Figure 17-2 is "bowed out" from the origin, which suggests two important things: 1) productive resources are not perfectly substitutable in producing capital and consumer goods -- some are innately more productive in one use than they are in the other; and because of that 2) the opportunity cost of producing more units of either output increases as more units of that output are produced. This is shown in Table 17-2, in which we calculate the transformation rates of capital goods to consumer goods as the production point moves in steps from point A toward point F in Figure 17-2.

The *MARGINAL RATE OF TRANSFORMATION (MRT)* is the quantity of one product that must be given up to produce an additional unit of another product, given current production levels. So in Figure 17-2, at any point on the PPF the MRT is

the change in capital goods
the change in consumer goods

That is, of course, the slope of the PPF at any given point on the curve. The slope will always be negative, technically; but as you have seen before, when economists know a sign will always be positive or negative, they often concentrate on the absolute size of the relationship and express it in positive terms. To be mathematically correct, then, you can multiply this formula for MRT by -1 and make everything come out right.

Figure 17-2
The Production-Possibilities Frontier and Product Transformations

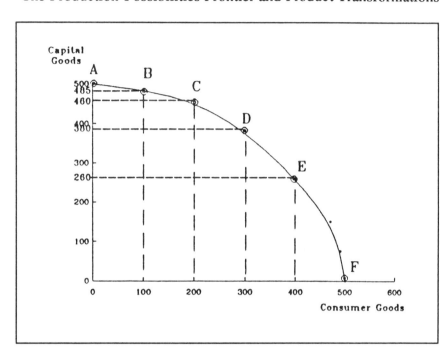

Full employment of all available resources and the use of technologically efficient production methods allows a nation to produce at any point on its production possibilities frontier (PPF), the curve ABCDEF. Inefficient production or unemployment leaves the economy inside its PPF schedule; points outside the PPF are currently unattainable.

Movement along a PPF implies transformation of some products into others, by shifting inputs from the production of one kind of output to the production of another. For example, moving from C to D in the graph above results in 100 additional units of consumer goods, but entails the cost of 80 units of capital goods.

Table 17-2
Transformation Rates and Increasing Costs

Production in Figure 17-2	Production Mix		Transformation Rate
	Capital Goods	Consumer Goods	
A	500	0	---
B	485	100	15/100 = .15
C	460	200	25/100 = .25
D	380	300	80/100 = .80
E	260	400	120/100 = 1.20
F	0	500	260/100 = 2.60

(In the table: 15 arrow between 500 and 485; 100 arrow to 100; 100 arrow to 15/100.)

Dividing the change in capital goods by the change in consumer goods, the real cost of increasing the level of consumer goods produced constantly rises, in terms of the units of capital goods forgone per unit of consumer good gained. For small changes this is defined as the marginal rate of transformation, and is equal -1 times to the slope of the production possibilities frontier at the point where a trade-off between the two outputs is being made. Even for the relatively large "steps" between the lettered points in Figure 17-2, it is clear that the real cost of producing additional consumer goods increases as the production mix moves from point A toward point F.

Because producing more of one good when resources are fully employed means producing less of something else, the MRT concept as we move along a PPF is essentially the idea of an opportunity cost. It is also, in real terms, a measure of the marginal cost of the last unit of either product produced. That is true because marginal cost is the dollar value of the resources used to produce an additional unit of output, and here we are evaluating those resources in terms of the real value of their most attractive alternative use -- the other product they could produce. In short, the marginal rate of transformation, marginal cost, and opportunity cost are all measures of the forgone production of some other product. And obviously, forgone production implies forgone consumption, which is the ultimate source of these opportunity costs.

What a nation produces largely determines what it has available for people who live in the nation to consume (entirely so if the nation doesn't trade with other nations), which brings us back to the linkage between production and consumption equilibria and related efficiency measures. Knowing all about an economy's production possibilities (which is clearly a more difficult thing to do in practice than a simple table or graph showing only two broad categories of goods suggests) still doesn't tell us what mix of products will be produced, or what mix people most want to see produced. Efficiency in pure production terms is achieved at *any* point on the PPF, in that all resources are fully employed in a technologically efficient manner. But allocative efficiency depends on producing the particular mix of outputs that people in the economy most prefer. To see that in the context of general equilibrium, we will next develop a measure of social consumption preferences.

Social Indifference Curves, Constrained Bliss, and the Impossibility Theorem

Curves I_1, I_2, and I_3 in Figure 17-3 are *SOCIAL INDIFFERENCE CURVES*, which each represent the combinations of two goods, or two groups of goods, which leave the people of a nation and economic system at some level of satisfaction. To show this in even more general terms than we used in Figure 17-2, we have replaced the consumer and capital goods labels on the axes of that graph with the generic "good a" and "good b" labels here.

Higher (up and to the right) indifference curves represent greater levels of satisfaction than lower curves; and the curves are "bowed-in" toward the origin because consumers typically don't view goods a and b as perfectly substitutable in providing satisfaction over all possible mixes of consumption bundles. For example, consider peoples' preferences for different combinations of food and clothing. If they already have a lot of food and not much clothing, they will normally not be willing to give up a unit of clothing unless they receive many more units of food. However, they would probably require less food to give up a unit of clothing if they had more clothing to begin with, and very little food. That means the ratio of the marginal utility of food to the marginal utility of clothing (the marginal rate of substitution, as noted above) declines as the amount of food the consumer has increases and the amount of clothing decreases.

Figure 17-3
Social Indifference Curves

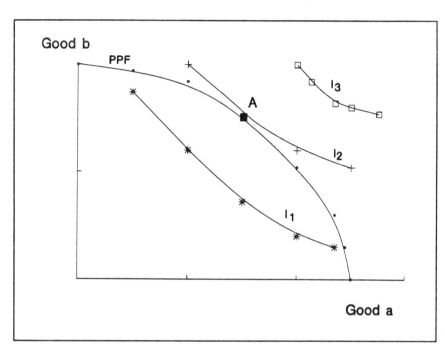

The social indifference curves labeled I_1-I_3 in the graph above represent levels of satisfaction derived from consumption of different combinations of the two goods shown on the axes. All points on a given indifference curve provide the same level of total satisfaction, but higher indifference curves (e.g., I_3) represent greater satisfaction than lower curves (e.g., I_1). Given this economy's production possibilities frontier (PPF), the highest level of satisfaction it can attain with just its own production is at point A, where I_2 is tangent to the PPF. I_3 is currently unattainable, and producing at any point on I_1 (even where it intersects the PPF) is inefficient, because it provides less than the highest possible level of satisfaction. Point A is, in fact, known as the point of constrained bliss.

The highest social indifference curve this economy can reach, based on its own production possibilities frontier, is I_2, which is just tangent to the PPF. Point A, the tangency point that lies on both I_2 and the PPF, is colorfully called the *POINT OF CONSTRAINED BLISS*. Higher indifference curves exist which this society would like to attain (such as I_3); but this is the maximum satisfaction the economy can achieve given its current resources and technology. Actually, we must assume here that these three social indifference curves are only a few such curves from the complete set of indifference curves for this society, and that the people of this nation could rank any point in this graph space as being preferred to, equal to, or inferior to any others. These are the same assumptions we made in Chapter 6, for an individual consumer's indifference curves, and together with the idea that the social indifference curves will be "bowed in" toward the origin they guarantee that a tangency point will exist to identify a unique point of constrained bliss. In truth, however, while these assumptions are generally reasonable for individual consumers, they are much more problematic when applyied to measures of social preferences. We will initially ignore those problems to complete our presentation of the basic general equilibrium model, but then consider the problems at some length and add some necessary qualifications to the general equilibrium results.

General Equilibrium Found

At the point where the social indifference curve is tangent to the production possibility frontier, the equilibrium conditions discussed earlier in the chapter will all prevail simultaneously in a perfectly competitive economy.

Some of these conditions are shown directly in Figure 17-4, where we have simply added a straight line with the slope determined by the relative prices of goods a and b at the unique level where this line will be tangent to both the PPF and the social indifference curve. In other words, at point A the marginal rate of substitution on the social indifference curve is equal to the price ratio for the two goods, as required for consumer equilibrium; and the marginal rate of transformation on the production possibility frontier is equal to the price ratio, as required for product market equilibrium. We could draw the price line higher or lower, of course, where it wouldn't be tangent to the PPF and this social indifference curve. But the economy can't consume on a higher line (outside the PPF); and to consume on any lower price line reduces the level of satisfaction achieved (to a lower social indifference curve). So given the PPF, the social preferences reflected in the indifference curves, and the price line, point A is the only point of general equilibrium. At that point, algebraically,

$$MRS = \frac{MU_a}{MU_b} = \frac{P_a}{P_b} = \frac{MC_a}{MC_b} = MRT \qquad (11)$$

which is just another way of saying that at point A the slope of the social indifference curve is equal to the slope of the price line, and both of those are equal to the slope of the PPF.

Part of the significance of these equalities was discussed earlier -- the rate that consumers trade off goods in deriving satisfaction is equal to the rate that the goods are traded in the market, and the rate of transforming the goods in production alternatives is also equal to that market rate of exchange for the goods. But what we add in equation 11 (and Figure 17-4) is the understanding that the rate of tradeoff in consumption, in providing consumers utility, is also equal to the transformation tradeoff in production. This direct link between equilibrium conditions for consumers *and* producers is the key part of general equilibrium analysis.[3]

This result shows that if consumer preferences for various goods change, that will directly change where producers will be in equilibrium, too. In other words, given the production technology and the availability of productive resources that determine where the PPF will be, in a perfectly competitive economy consumers will ultimately decide what is produced -- which is to say where on the PPF the economy will choose to be. This is sometimes called the principle of *CONSUMER SOVEREIGNTY* because consumers will get whatever they most want produced in this kind of economy, as measured by what they are willing and able to pay for different products.

---

[3]We also know that competitive firms will hire inputs up to the point where the ratio of their marginal products is equal to the ratio of the input prices, in order to maximize profits, minimize the costs of producing the output level and mix shown at point A, and just to stay in business. So, to repeat equation 5,

$$\frac{MP_1}{P_1} = \frac{MP_2}{P_2} \dots = \frac{MP_n}{P_n}$$

where 1 and 2 are, again, two different inputs. If this condition for efficiency in production didn't hold, the economy couldn't be at a point on its production possibilities frontier. We don't show that directly in Figure 17-4 or in equation 11; but it's there, or else we wouldn't be at point A in the first place.

Figure 17-4
General Equilibrium

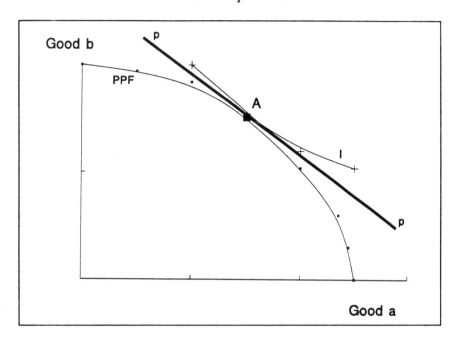

The relative prices for goods a and b determine the slope of line pp, and show the rate at which these two goods, or types of goods, are exchanged in the marketplace. In general equilibrium, a line with this slope will pass through point A just tangent to the PPF and the social indifference curve. At this point and with this price level, the marginal rate of substitution in consumption alternatives is equal to the price ratio *and* to the marginal rate of transformation in production alternatives. Furthermore, all resources are fully and efficiently employed; and in a competitive economy we know firms will pay a wage rate equal to the value of the marginal product of the last worker the firm hires.

An economy's general equilibrium position (point A in Figure 17-4) can change over time due to changes in preferences (i.e., the position of the social indifference curve), or in technology and the availability of resources (i.e., the position of the PPF). But when such changes occur in a perfectly competitive economy, prices will adjust quickly and the system will move to a new equilibrium, as shown in Figure 17-5.

Individuals' preferences and productive abilities play a key part in establishing the general equilibrium position for an economy in several respects. First, they play a large part in determining the quantity of resources (particularly labor) supplied to factor markets, which influences the position of the PPF. Second, they impact the rate of technological change and investment in capital goods through their willingness to save and invest, by postponing some consumption activities, as well as their creativity and persistence in searching for new knowledge and production technologies -- all of which affect the position and shape of the PPF. Finally, of course, consumer preferences establish the position and shape of social indifference curves, which together with the PPF determine the final position of the tangency point between these schedules.

Figure 17-5
Disequilibrium and Price Adjustments

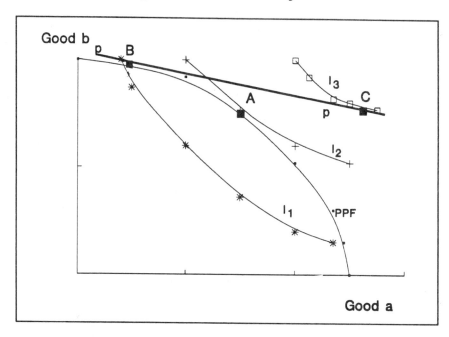

Suppose this economy was initially in general equilibrium at point B, but then consumer preferences changed so that they are now represented by the social indifference curves I_1, I_2, and I_3. At the old price ratio, shown by the line pp, consumers now want to consume more units of good a and fewer units of good b, ideally at point C on I_3. But I_3 is unattainable given the economy's production possibilities frontier, so a different equilibrium position evolves.

Specifically, the increased demand for good a causes its price to increase, while the price of good b falls due to decreased demand. A new equilibrium will be established at point A, with a price line for these two goods that goes through point A and is tangent to both the PPF and I_2, exactly as in Figure 17-4. That new price line will be steeper than pp as shown here, reflecting a higher relative price for good a and a lower relative price for good b. In fact, it will be the line pp shown in Figure 17-4.

The most severe way in which individual preferences affect these general equilibrium issues is, however, to make it impossible for anyone -- economists, political scientists, or any other group -- to find a reasonable way or decision rule (such as majority voting) to identify a consistent set of social preferences for an entire economy. That is, we can't ever precisely identify a unique set of social indifference curves for different combinations of goods and services, or different social policies. Reasonable here is formally defined by economists as accommodating all possible variations of individual preferences; collecting only indispensable information on preference orderings (without infringing on personal privacy by seeking details that are unrelated to preferences on social and economic issues); and satisfying a welfare criterion known as Pareto efficiency, which is discussed in the next section. The mathematical work which demonstrates the *IMPOSSIBILITY THEOREM* -- the idea that no method exists to identify social preferences while meeting these conditions of reasonableness -- was developed largely by Nobel laureate Kenneth Arrow, and included such insights as the intransitivity results that can occur in democratic elections, shown earlier in Chapter 5 (in Table 5-4).

Ironically, one case in which social indifference curves can be determined is when an economy and society are ruled by an omnipotent dictator. To maximize "social" welfare under that system, the dictator simply considers his or her own utility function. The same is true for the equally unlikely one-person, Robinson Crusoe economy (before Friday arrives), where an individual *is* the entire society. But such cases are considerably removed from the concerns of most real economies and policy makers. So the last question we will consider in this chapter is what general equilibrium analysis can say about government policy and economic efficiency without using the unknowable construct of a social indifference curve, or when an economy isn't perfectly competitive.

Perfect Competition and Pareto Efficiency in the Real World

Each of the conditions for general equilibrium that were discussed above, for consumers and firms in both output and factor markets, is met in an economy in which all industries are perfectly competitive. Every product price is equal to the marginal cost of producing the last unit of the product, firms hire more units of the factors of production until the factor price is equal to the value of the marginal product of the last unit of an input employed, and consumers maximize utility by equating the marginal utilities per dollar of the last unit of each product they consume. Furthermore, although the formal proof lies beyond the scope of this book, economists have shown that a set of prices always exists in a competitive system which leads to equilibrium in factor and output markets, no matter how large the system of products and markets, how many regional markets exist within the system, or how long the time lag between the production and sale of products. Two economists, Arrow and Gerard Debreu, have received Nobel prizes for their work on this body of proofs.

It is also clear that in a competitive system neither consumers nor producers will pass up the opportunity to increase their utility or profit, respectively, if they know of some opportunity to do so in the marketplace. In other words, if a better mix of consumption spending or production inputs is known, or a better level of output in their production activities, there is nothing in a purely competitive system to keep a producer or consumer from quickly adopting it. Doing so requires only voluntary exchanges in one market or another, and such exchanges are made whenever both parties in an exchange expect to improve their own welfare. That means that every known exchange that could make any person better off without making another person worse off will be made, and that meets the criterion known as *PARETO EFFICIENCY* (named for economist Vilfredo Pareto), which holds that any action is judged to improve equity and efficiency if it improves one person's welfare without reducing another's. Once all such exchanges have been made, general equilibrium is achieved in a perfectly competitive economy. From that point on, *ceteris paribus*, no change in production or consumption patterns can be made which makes someone better off without making someone else worse off.

By this particular normative standard, then, there appears to be small range for government intervention and public policy actions in a perfectly competitive economy. Adam Smith's invisible hand, discussed in Chapter 1 (in Case Study #2), appears to deliver this best of all possible economic worlds with only minor help -- and allowing for only minor interference -- from the various branches of government. Defending property rights and preventing fraud may help a competitive market system work more efficiently; but beyond that little government activity is required or tolerated. In short, a Pareto-efficient outcome seems to be achieved through a policy of *laissez faire*.

But of course most "real world" government policy, including economic policy, does not even attempt to work in just a Pareto-efficient framework. Instead, most policies are clearly expected to leave some people better off and others worse off, even as the laws and policies are being debated for possible enactment. Moreover, the notion that perfect competition will always be Pareto efficient is itself based on several assumptions which should be explicitly understood, and which sharply limit the idea that the role of government is of minor significance in a competitive economy.

Specifically, it must first be assumed that there are no cases of market failure, as defined in Chapter 5. Competitive markets can not deal with many problems involving public goods, and will often overallocate resources to markets characterized by external costs, and underallocate resources to those affected by external benefits.

The second assumption necessary for perfect competition to be Pareto efficient is that there be no substantial cost savings from producing in imperfectly competitive markets. Economies of scale make it inefficient to produce some goods in competitive industries, as shown in Chapters 10-13. And the existence of some imperfectly competitive industries introduces the possibility of "sticky" wage and price structures, which may thwart the efficiency of the competitive sectors in the economy, and of the overall system. Competitive markets can also be inefficient in cases where it is impossible to insure against some kinds or levels of risk, or to borrow against some kinds of assets (for example, human capital).

Finally, even in cases where a perfectly competitive system does achieve a Pareto-efficient equilibrium, that particular set of outcomes is dictated by the existing pattern of income distribution in the system. That affects the mix of outputs that are purchased and produced and, in turn, peoples' decisions about how many hours to devote to labor markets in the pursuit of higher incomes. If the pattern of income distribution is changed through the political process or some other shift in the allocation of endowments across households, a different equilibrium will result. That new equilibrium can be just as Pareto efficient as the first, and the initial distribution has no special normative justification just because it occurred first. In short, Pareto efficiency in perfect competition is not, in and of itself, an argument against the government's role in redistributing income.

In conclusion, then, general equilibrium analysis suggests that policy interventions designed to achieve a particular goal without disrupting the efficiency of an extensive system of private and reasonably competitive markets will face inherently difficult and complex problems. It does not, however, provide an ironclad or sweeping endorsement for a policy of strict *laissez faire*, in which there is no significant role for the public sector. Economists can only evaluate public policies from a careful and comprehensive cost-benefit standpoint, and recommend their acceptance so long as marginal benefits outweigh marginal costs.

Case Study #23
General Equilibrium Applications of Taxation, International Trade Policies, and Regulation[4]

General equilibrium studies on real-word issues are relatively new in the professional economics literature, and in some ways more time consuming and expensive to prepare than partial equilibrium studies. For both of these reasons, there aren't a great many examples of general equilibrium studies, applied to particular economic issues, for us to draw on at this time.

We can, however, briefly summarize work that has been done on three different topics from a general equilibrium perspective. In some cases, you will see that these studies extend or modify findings from partial equilibrium studies, because some of these topics were discussed in earlier chapters. All of these topics suggest the importance of general equilibrium studies in calculating the full value of impacts of different kinds of public policies -- i.e., in conducting cost-benefit analyses.

Taxation. General equilibrium models of taxation suggest that the tax system has a somewhat greater effect in redistributing income than researchers who have studied this issue using partial equilibrium techniques have reported. In particular, the general equilibrium studies find that tax systems in the United States and other nations are often more progressive than they initially appear. That happens in large part because the tax system lowers the pre-tax financial returns on assets that are not fully taxed, relative to those which are (for example, by lowering interest rates on tax-free municipal bonds, compared to taxable rates on corporate bonds). This lowers the after-tax returns high-income households can earn, and makes the distribution of income more equal than it would otherwise be.

---

[4]The general equilibrium taxation and trade results discussed here are reviewed by John B. Shoven and John Whalley, in "Applied General-Equilibrium Models of Taxation and International Trade: An Introduction and Survey," *Journal of Economic Literature*, September 1984, pp. 1007-51.

Perhaps even more striking in this literature are sharply higher estimates of deadweight losses from tax distortions than those reported in traditional, partial equilibrium studies. For example, one general equilibrium study suggested that the 1973 system of taxes and subsidies in the United Kingdom led to distortions which cost the nation 6-9% of its national income that year. Put differently, about a fourth of net revenues raised by the government were forgone because of the deadweight loss. Housing subsidies, excise taxes, and taxes on capital were identified as the major areas where these distortions occurred, which served to hurt upper-income families and benefit low-income families. In particular, the manufacturing sector of the national economy was particularly penalized, while housing was significantly subsidized.

In other studies, it has been shown that taxes on apartment buildings in some township areas in a metropolitan area will, in the long run, result in less building of new units in that area, and more building in surrounding townships or communities. But in time that affects relative rental prices in those areas, which again changes the economic returns earned by the owners of (and investors in) those units, as well as prices paid by renters.

In terms of analytical procedures notice how, in a general equilibrium framework, the study of tax incidence considers more than the direct amount of taxes paid by households in various income levels. Specifically, the effect of taxes on other market prices and production levels is explicitly considered and estimated, along with the feedback effects from those markets to the direct issue of how much after-tax income various households earn.

International Trade Policies. The European Common Market was formed in the 1950s to eliminate tariffs and quotas on most trade with other member nations. Great Britain immediately began debating whether to join the new organization or to maintain its traditional trade ties with the United States and British Commonwealth nations. Prominent economists estimated at that time that the efficiency gains that would accrue to Great Britain and other European Market nations from the new organization and mutual cooperation were relatively small. In fact, relative to national income in these countries, the gains were estimated at much less than 1%. The logic behind these estimates was simply that international trade constituted a small part of total economic activity in these nations, so removing the distortions of tariffs and quotas on that activity would have a minimal effect.

But recent studies using a general equilibrium perspective have estimated much larger gains from trade-barriers reductions in several cases, such as the 1986 free-trade treaty between the United States and Canada. In the new studies the larger gains that are expected to result from freer trade occur primarily because the greater volume of trade between nations will allow some industries (particularly in Canada, as it turns out) to achieve significant economies of scale.

Once again, the difference in this result comes from the explicit consideration of effects that go beyond the simple question of what will initially happen to price and trade levels if tariffs and quotas fall to zero. Long-term adjustments in the trading economies -- in this case decreases in long-run unit production costs in some industries -- lead to important secondary results.

Other studies adopting a general equilibrium framework have suggested that the long-term trade and production impacts of the energy shocks of the 1970s were probably less severe than thought at that time, and in fact relatively small in financial and output terms. Once again, that was because consumers and producers reacted to changes in these relative prices by consuming fewer petroleum-based products over time, while simulataneously increasing the production and consumption of a wide range of substitute products.

Regulation. Say regulation to an economist, and he or she will almost surely mention "unintended outcomes" in the next few sentences, because that's exactly what happens time and time again. For example: 1) Prohibition was supposed to eliminate drinking and promote temperance, but instead led to the rise of the bootleg liquor industry, speakeasies, and bathtub gin in the 1920s. 2) Regulating fares, cargos, and routes in the trucking industry in the 1960s and 1970s often resulted in empty trucks on return hauls, because truckers weren't allowed to carry whatever loads were available in areas where they had to deliver a shipment. That affected prices not just for trucking rates, but also for all of the products that trucks carried, or could have carried if rates had been lower. 3) Stiffer penalties and enforcement of drunk-driving laws in recent years have been shown to lead to an increase in the number of hit-and-run accidents in many areas, as drivers try to avoid the higher fines and longer time in jail for driving under the influence. And 4) stricter safety laws for drug testing increase the cost of developing new drugs, which reduces the number of pharmaceuticals that are discovered and brought to the market.

These unexpected and undesirable outcomes result in part because, as the general equilibrium perspective shows, it is often difficult to anticipate how a policy intervention in one market will affect outcomes in other markets.

In even more general terms, economists have also observed that, over time, regulatory agencies at all levels of government are often "captured" by the industries they are legally charged with regulating. By capture, economists mean that members of the regulatory body are often drawn from the regulated industry, or take a prominent position in the industry when their term on the regulatory agency is completed, or both. As a result, over time, regulatory agencies come to represent the interests of the companies which they regulate. And from a general equilibrium perspective, that is part of the overall outcome of regulation efforts we have to consider in evaluating their effectiveness.

Chapter Summary

1) *PARTIAL EQUILIBRIUM ANALYSIS* is concerned with adjustments in price, quantity, and other variables affecting a particular market. *GENERAL EQUILIBRIUM ANALYSIS* deals with similar adjustments over a large number of directly and indirectly related markets, from the perspective of an entire economic system.

2) Changes in one market often have surprising effects on other markets, including markets that may not appear to be directly related based on casual observation. Policies such as wage and price controls and environmental modifications have often lead to clear examples of these interconnections.

3) The linkages between the various decision-making sectors of an economic system, and between factor and product markets, are shown in a *CIRCULAR-FLOW DIAGRAM*. The same linkages and several consistency requirements in the production and consumption of various resources in different parts of an economy can be shown with an *INPUT-OUTPUT TABLE*.

4) The equilibrium conditions for consumers' purchasing decisions, firms' hiring decisions, and firms' pricing and output decisons -- which were each developed in earlier chapters -- must all be met simultaneously for a competitive market system to achieve general equilibrium.

5) The *MARGINAL RATE OF TRANSFORMATION (MRT)* is the amount by which one output must be reduced in order to release the resources required to produce an additional unit of another output. Graphically, this is the slope of a production-possibilities frontier (PPF) at any given point on the schedule. Moving in the same direction along a PPF that is bowed out from the origin, the cost of producing successive units of a good increases, as measured by the MRT.

6) A social indifference curve shows all of the combinations of two products which, when produced and consumed, leave the members of a society equally satisfied. The tangency point between a social indifference curve and the PPF for a society indicates its point of general equilibrium, assuming it can not bring in resources from other economies by trading. At this tangency point all of the society's resources are fully and efficiently employed, given the current state of technology and the prices for inputs established in factor markets. The marginal rate of substitution in consumption is equal to the marginal rate of transformation in production, and this point identifies the highest level of satisfaction the society can achieve at this time.

7) If a competitive economy is not in general equilibrium prices adjust until equilibrium is achieved, and until all known voluntary exchanges that make any individual better off without making someone else worse off are made. This result is *PARETO EFFICIENT*, and provides some support for the general policy of *laissez faire* because the overall effects of public policy actions are both difficult to predict from a general equilibrium perspective and likely to violate the standards of Pareto efficiency. In practice, however, there is a major economic role for government even in a basically competitive market system. That is because several kinds of problems typically impair the efficiency of such systems, including public goods, externalities, imperfect capital and insurance markets, economies of scale, and high concentration levels in at

least some markets. There is also often widespread public support for some level and form of income redistribution programs.

8) (Case Study #23) General equilibrium analysis has been widely used to study several economic issues and problems. Such studies have shown that: a) tax systems in some nations are probably more progressive than earlier studies indicated, because they affect rates of returns on assets purchased primarily by high-income families; b) the deadweight loss associated with tax distortions may be much larger than indicated in partial equilibrium studies; c) the gains from free trade may be greater than previously estimated, because of scale economies that are achieved through greater degrees of specialization and exchange; and d) government regulations often have unexpected and unintended consequences, because their effects are difficult to predict and control, including secondary effects in markets that are not directly regulated.

Review and Discussion Questions

1) Are models like those shown in Chapters 9-13, in which industry and firm decisions involving variables such as price and output levels are considered, partial or general equilibrium analysis models? Explain your answer.

2) In the general laws of supply and demand, presented in Chapter 3, what determinants of the level of supply and demand for a product are most directly related to the idea of general equilibrium analysis, and what key assumption is invoked to keep the basic models presented in that chapter in a partial equilibrium framework?

3) a) List the major groups of headings that would be required to have an input-output table, like the one shown in Table 17-1, incorporate all of the key sectors and markets shown in the circular flow diagram shown in Figure 17-1.

   b) In Table 17-1, increase the value in any cell by 10%. Then adjust other values in the table, as necessary, to re-establish the consistency requirements shown in an input-output table.

4) Suppose the conditions for consumer and product-market equilibria are being met in some system, but those for factor-market equilibrium are not. Verbally trace out how adjustments in that market would lead to adjustments in the other markets, in order for general equilibrium to be achieved.

5) Draw a production-possibilities frontier that shows: a) a constant marginal rate of transformation; and b) decreasing costs of producing successive units of either product.

6) Consider a social indifference curve that intersects a production-possibility frontier at two points. At those points, is the economy achieving: a) productive efficiency; and b) allocative efficiency? If both are not achieved, how does the economy have to adjust from each of the intersection points to reach its general equilibrium position?

7) Suppose the initial distribution of income in a society is achieved strictly through the operation of perfectly competitive factor markets. Does that constitute a normative argument against a governmental role in the area of income redistribution, or are there normative arguments for an active income redistribution role even under those conditions? If it is decided that the government will not redistribute income in a perfectly competitive system, is there any need for taxes or government? Explain your answer.

8) (Case Study #23) Select a current economic issue not discussed in this case study or in the body of this chapter, and discuss how some policy action might be used to address that issue or problem. Then identify as many possible direct and indirect consequences of that policy as you can, and indicate whether those consequences would support or weaken the intended results of the policy.

491

GLOSSARY

The chapter numbers shown in parentheses after each definition indicate where terms are first introduced and defined in the text. Most terms are used often again in later chapters, of course. And in some cases where a popular understanding of terms will suffice to allow a casual reference, formal definitions are postponed past the earliest uses of these terms, until the points where they are used more formally and extensively.

Absolute Advantage -- The ability to produce more units of a given product than some other producer, using the same quantity of resources. (Chapter 1)

Advertising -- The use of paid announcements to call attention to a product and to encourage customers to buy it by providing information on price, product characteristics, or availability, or by enticing consumers with such persuasive tactics as "bandwagon," "snob," "star endorsement" or "sex appeal" claims and special effects. (Chapter 12)

Allocative Efficiency -- The condition that is met when no reallocation of resources among production and consumption uses will increase economic welfare, given the existing distribution of income. In the absence of externalities, this condition is met when the market price of a product is equal to the marginal cost of producing the last unit of the product. Cf. productive efficiency. (Chapter 9)

Analytical Models -- Abstract and simplified representations of human behavior and institutions, designed to yield predictions about the consequences of changes in the variables incorporated into the model. Cf. descriptive models. (Chapter 2)

Arbitrator -- An impartial "third party" who is usually selected and paid by two parties involved in a dispute, and authorized to make a final decision which is binding on both parties. Cf. mediator. (Chapter 16)

Arc Elasticity -- A measure of the average responsiveness of the quantity of a product demanded or supplied to a change in the price of the product, or consumers' income, or the price of another good or service. Cf. mid-point formulas. (Chapter 4)

Asymmetric Information -- A situation in which one party involved in an economic exchange has more information about key economic variables -- such as prices, costs, profits, or labor effort -- than the other party or parties. (Chapter 14)

Average Fixed Costs (AFC) -- Fixed costs divided by the quantity of output produced (total product). (Chapter 7)

Average Product (AP) -- The quantity of output produced divided by the number of units of a variable input employed in the production process. (Chapter 7)

Average Revenue (AR) -- Total revenue divided by the quantity of goods or services sold. When a single price is charged for all products sold, average revenue equals the price that consumers pay for the output level, which is found on the demand curve for the product. (Chapter 4)

Average Total Costs (ATC) -- Total costs divided by the quantity of output produced (total product). (Chapter 7)

Average Variable Costs (AVC) -- Variable costs divided by the quantity of output produced (total product). (Chapter 7)

492

Backward-bending Labor Supply Curve -- A relatively unusual phenomenon in which, at sufficiently high factor price levels, the quantity of labor supplied will decrease as the wage rate increases. This indicates that the income effect of the increase in the wage rate is relatively greater than the substitution effect for these individuals, and that for them leisure is a normal good. (Chapter 15)

Barometric Price Leadership -- The pricing pattern in which a firm that is representative of most other firms in an industry in all key features comes to be recognized and established as the first firm to announce price changes for its product, with other firms in the industry soon following suit. (Chapter 13)

Barriers to Entry -- Factors that make it more costly to begin operating a new business in an established industry, or to work in a certain occupation. (Chapter 11)

Behavioral Models -- Analytical models which incorporate a high degree of detail concerning the motives, opportunities, and constraints facing individual decision-makers. The predictions of these models often can not be applied as widely as those derived from more abstract models. (Chapter 2)

Bilateral Monopoly -- A situation in which the only seller of a product or input must deal with the only buyer of the product or input. Equilibrium price and quantity levels are indeterminate in such a setting. (Chapter 16)

Bounded Rationality -- A class of behavioral models that takes into account the limits of knowledge and computational capacity in determining what actions will provide people the greatest satisfaction in their roles as consumers, producers, or voters. (Chapter 2)

Brand Loyalty -- Consumer preferences for a particular product sold by one firm, over substitute products produced by firms in the same industry. (Chapter 11)

Budget Constraint Line -- The graphical schedule that shows the different combinations of products a consumer or household can buy given a particular set of prices for those products and a fixed level of money income. (Chapter 6)

Business Cycles -- Fluctuations in the national levels of spending, output, employment, and prices around the average rate of long-term growth for each of these variables. (Chapter 2)

Capital -- Goods used to produce other goods and services; the financial returns to capital resources are some form of interest payments. (Chapter 1)

Capital-Intensive Growth -- Expansion in output that results in firms using relatively more capital and less labor (or other inputs) per unit of output produced. (Chapter 8)

Cartel -- An association of producers or sellers with the goal of attaining and exercising some degree of monopoly power in their market, in order to increase price and profit levels by restricting the quantity of the product they supply. (Chapter 3)

Causation -- A theoretically or empirically demonstrated relationship between two or more variables in which a change in one variable leads to a predictable change in another variable, or group of variables. (Chapter 2)

Ceteris Paribus -- Latin for "other things being equal." (Chapter 3)

Circular-flow Diagram -- A visual representation of the exchange of productive resources between households and firms in factor markets, and of final goods and services in output markets. These real flows of productive resources and final goods and services are matched by a monetary flow of factor payments and product sales revenues, respectively. The diagram can be expanded to include exchanges in financial markets, or those involving government and the international trade sector. (Chapter 16)

Coase Theorem -- The claim that, in the absence of significant transactions costs and with well defined property rights, voluntary exchange will lead to an optimal allocation of resources even in the presence of externalities. (Chapter 5)

Command Economy -- An economic system which relies primarily on central (i.e., government) planning to determine what goods and services will be produced, how they will be produced, and who will consume them. In some command economies, most capital resources are owned by the government. (Chapter 1)

Common Stock -- Ownership shares in corporations, carrying the right to vote for the company's board of directors and a residual claim to its profits and assets. (Chapter 7)

Commons -- Publicly owned resources with unrestricted access and use. (Chapter 5)

Comparative Advantage -- The ability to produce a good or service at a lower opportunity cost than some other producer. This is the economic basis for specialization by a productive resource or geographic region. (Chapter 1)

Competition -- Actions by two or more individuals or organizations attempting to acquire the same scarce resources. Consumers compete with other consumers to buy similar products; producers compete with other producers to sell similar products. (Chapter 7)

Complements -- Goods or services that are often consumed together (such as hamburgers, french fries, and catsup; or gasoline and automobiles). (Chapter 3)

Conglomerate Mergers -- Combinations or takeovers involving two or more firms which produce unrelated products. (Chapter 13)

Constant-cost Industries -- Industries in which per unit production costs of the most efficient sized firms do not change as the level of industry output varies. (Chapter 10)

Constant Economies of Scale -- A range of constant long-run average costs as a firm's output level changes. cf. economies and diseconomies of scale. (Chapter 10)

Constant Returns to Scale -- The condition that exists when a firm that increases or decreases all inputs experiences exactly proportional changes in output. Cf. increasing and decreasing returns to scale. (Chapter 10)

Consumer Surplus -- The difference between the monetary value consumers place on the satisfaction they derive from the consumption of some product in a given period of time and the monetary cost to them of acquiring these products. Cf. value in use and value in exchange. (Chapter 4)

Contestable Markets -- Any market where entry is easy, entering firms can produce at the same average cost as existing firms, and fixed costs are avoidable rather than sunk. The model is unlike perfect competition in prohibiting sunk costs and, more importantly, in stressing the competitive effects of potential competitors, even in settings where the number of actual producers is very small. (Chapter 14)

Copyrights -- The exclusive legal right to reproduce, publish, and sell the matter and form of a literary, musical, or artistic work. Usually granted for a fixed period of time (typically 50-75 years) from the work's first appearance. (Chapter 11)

Correlation -- A statistically determined linkage between two or more variables, in which changes in one variable are associated with changes in another variable or variables. Correlation does *not* establish a causal relationship between these variables. (Chapter 2)

Corporations -- Firms owned by stockholders who, under charters issued by some level of government, have their liability for actions and debts of the corporation limited to what they pay to buy stock in the firm. Cf. common stock, partnerships, and sole partnerships. (Chapter 7)

Cost Minimization -- Production methods that achieve a given output and quality level at the lowest possible cost; a prerequisite of profit maximization. (Chapter 8)

Cost-benefit Analysis -- The evaluation of current or proposed programs and policies by explicitly valuing the expected impacts of the plan, both positive and negative, in monetary terms, and then ranking that value against those for alternative proposals or uses of the resources required to implement the program. (Chapter 5)

Craft Unions -- Organizations of workers who practice a particular trade but work for many different employers, which attempt to improve wages, fringe benefits, and working conditions for their members. Cf. industrial union. (Chapter 16)

Credible Commitments -- Reliable assurances given explicitly in contracts, or implicitly through non-legal assurances, such as verbal statements and reputations, that certain, predictable actions will be taken in the future in dealing with customers, stockholders, employees, or others in the future. Cf. incomplete contracting. (Chapter 7)

Cross-price Elasticity of Demand -- A statistical measure of the responsiveness of the quantity demanded of a product to a change in the price of another good or service; calculated as the percentage change in the quantity demanded of that product, divided by the percentage change in the price of the second product. (Chapter 4)

Cross-section Studies -- Empirical studies that collect data from a relatively large number of units at a given period (or periods) of time. Cf. time-series studies. (Chapter 10)

Current Labor Market Discrimination -- Wage differentials for workers in identical jobs based on gender, race, or ethnic origins, rather than any differences in the workers' productivity. (Chapter 16)

Customer Discrimination -- The payment of different wages and salaries to workers who do identical jobs because of consumers' preferences to be served by, or avoid, workers of a certain gender, race, or ethnic background, at least in some types of jobs. (Chapter 16)

Deadweight Loss -- A loss of consumer and/or producer surplus caused by such factors as excise taxes, price ceilings, and monopoly power, which is not offset by any reallocation of revenues or other benefits to producers, consumers, or governmental units. (Chapter 4)

Decreasing Returns to Scale -- Less than proportional increases in output as all inputs are increased, resulting in increasing long-run unit costs if input prices are fixed. Cf. increasing and constant returns to scale. (Chapter 10)

Decreasing Cost Industries -- Industries in which unit production costs of the most efficient sized firms decrease as the level of industry output increases. (Chapter 10)

Deductive Models -- Predictions of behavior by individuals and institutions based on theoretical assumptions and the logically derived calculation of results based on those assumptions. Cf. inductive models. (Chapter 2)

Demand -- A schedule or graph of all possible prices for a product and the quantity of the product that consumers are willing and able to buy at each price during a given period of time. (Chapter 1)

Demographic Trends -- Consistent patterns of change in various measures of vital statistics (such as births, deaths, and marriages) for a nation's population. (Chapter 4)

Dependent Variables -- Quantities which change in value as a result of changes in the values for other, independent variables. (Chapter 2)

Derived Demand -- A schedule or graph showing the quantity of a productive resource a firm is willing to hire at each possible price for the resource; this demand is a function of the demand for the firm's product, which the resource will be used to produce, and the marginal product of each unit of the resource. (Chapter 14)

Descriptive Models -- Detailed and realistic representations of objects or relationships. These models usually do not yield predictions about the future values of variables, or explanations for the past and current values of variables. Cf. analytical models. (Chapter 2)

Diminishing Marginal Rate of Substitution -- The principle that, as a consumer consumes more and more of one product and less and less of another, holding total utility constant, he or she will only give up additional units of the first product in exchange for increasingly large amounts of the second product. (Chapter 6)

Diminishing Marginal Rate of Technical Substitution -- The principle that, holding output constant, the amount of of one input required to substitute for a second input will continually increase as successive units of the second input are given up. Cf. marginal rate of technical substitution. (Chapter 8)

Discount Rate -- The factor by which individuals or organizations reduce an amount of money to be paid or received at some time in the future, in order to express the present value of that sum. (Chapter 15)

Diseconomies of Scale -- A range of output along long-run cost schedules in which average costs rise as the output level is increased. Cf. economies and constant economies of scale. (Chapter 10)

Diversification -- Reducing risk by investing in more than one kind of risky asset; a kind of self-insurance which allows individuals or firms to earn a higher average return than they could by investing only in insured, relatively risk-free assets. (Chapter 7)

Divestiture -- Selling a subsidiary company or corporate unit for cash or other assets. (Chapter 13)

Dominant Firm Price Leadership -- A situation in which one very large firm controls most production and sales of a product, with the rest spread among a large number of relatively small firms. The dominant firm will consider the response of the smaller firms in the industry, but still has the power to select an overall price and output level for the industry. (Chapter 13)

Dominant Strategy -- In game theory, any action or "move" that will maximize one player's pay-off, regardless of what any other players choose to do. (Chapter 14)

Duopoly -- An extreme form of oligopoly, in which all production and sales of a product are controlled by just two firms. (Chapter 13)

Economic Efficiency -- Producing goods and services at the lowest possible cost, and at the optimal level of output. (Chapter 2)

Economic Freedom -- The right to acquire, hold, and dispose of economic resources through the process of voluntary exchange and in line with one's own interests and abilities. (Chapter 2)

Economic Growth -- A sustained increase over time in the real value of goods and services produced in a nation, often stated on a per capita basis. (Chapter 2 & 3)

Economic Incentives -- Monetary and non-monetary rewards that encourage such economic activities as work, consumption, saving, and investment. (Chapter 2)

Economic Incidence of a Tax -- Who ultimately bears the burden of a tax, often in the form of higher prices or lower wages, when sellers and employers are able to "pass on" a tax to consumers and employees. Cf. legal incidence of a tax. (Chapter 4)

Economic Justice -- Equity or fairness in the procedures used to exchange economic resources, and in the distribution of those resources. (Chapter 2)

Economic Profits -- Profits that exceed all opportunity costs a producer incurs -- i.e., any profits greater than normal profits. (Chapter 7)

Economic Security -- Protection from economic hazards such as poverty, unemployment, and inflation. (Chapter 2)

Economic Welfare -- A general measure of economic well-being and satisfaction, related to personal income and consumption levels. (Chapter 4)

Economics -- The study of how scarce resources with alternative uses can be used to satisfy human wants. (Chapter 1)

Economies of Scale -- A range of falling unit costs as a firm increases its output or production level when all inputs are variable -- that is, long-run average total costs are decreasing. Cf. diseconomies and constant economies of scale. (Chapter 10)

Economies of Scope -- Savings in a firm's average cost schedule achieved by producing some combination of two or more products, instead of having separate firms produce each good or service independently. (Chapter 14)

Efficiency Wages -- Wages higher than those a worker with given skills can earn in other jobs, but which still maximize profits for a firm by reducing turnover, training, and monitoring costs, and by encouraging higher levels of worker productivity. (Chapter 16)

Efficient Market Hypothesis -- The theory that some well organized markets -- particularly those where financial assets such as stocks, bonds, and futures contracts are traded regularly -- immediately incorporate all relevant information into the prices of the goods that are traded on these markets. Any "error" in these prices is, therefore, due to random forces; and there are no known forces at work that will cause the prices to change in a predictable direction. (Chapter 9)

Effluent Tax -- An excise tax, fee, or fine levied on a producer who engages in some form of pollution, assessed on the basis of the amount of pollution produced. (Chapter 5)

Embargo -- A collective action by producers to prohibit or limit sales of a product which they make, or by a government to prohibit or limit sales of a product that is made in territories under the government's control. (Chapter 3)

Eminent Domain -- The power of the state to take private property for public use, with due process and compensation provided to the owners. (Chapter 5)

Employee Discrimination -- The payment of different wages and salaries to workers who do identical jobs, because of co-workers' preferences to exclude members of a certain gender, race, or ethnic background. (Chapter 16)

Employer Discrimination -- The payment of different wages and salaries to workers who do identical jobs, because of owners' or managers' preferences to hire workers of a certain gender, race, or ethnic background. (Chapter 16)

Enforcement Costs -- A type of transaction cost incurred in requiring a party who enters a contract to fulfill that agreement. (Chapter 7)

Engineering Studies -- Studies of production costs which collect data by interviewing or surveying production officials (usually engineers, but sometimes accountants and other executives) about the costs of building and operating plants with different capacity levels. (Chapter 10)

Entrepreneurship -- Human risk-taking associated with the production of goods and services to satisfy wants; the financial returns to entrepreneurship are profits. (Chapter 1)

Entry -- Increased production in an industry at all possible price levels, which occurs because new firms begin to produce the product made in this industry. Cf. exit. (Chapter 9)

Equilibrium -- In economics, a balance between two or more variables. For example, at the equilibrium price, quantity supplied equals quantity demanded. (Chapter 1)

Excess Profits -- see **economic profits**. (Chapter 7)

Exchange -- Trading a good or service for another good or service, or for money. (Chapter 1)

Exchange Rates -- Prices of one nation's currency in terms of other nations' currencies -- i.e., the prices at which currencies from different countries can be bought or sold on world financial markets. (Chapter 3)

Excise Tax -- A tax on the sales of particular good or service. (Chapter 4)

Exclusion Principle -- The situation that exists for most goods and services (specifically, for private goods) in which producers are able to prevent those who do not purchase a product (or those who lawfully receive it from those who have purchased it) from using or consuming the product. (Chap 5)

Exit -- Decreased production in an industry at all possible price levels, which occurs because some firms stop producing the product that is made in this industry. Cf. entry. (Chapter 9)

Expansion Path -- The set of points where, with all inputs variable but input prices fixed, isoquants representing different levels of output are tangent to isocost schedules. This shows a firm's optimal input mix as it expands or contracts output, as long as the input prices are unchanged. (Chapter 8)

Explicit Costs -- Costs paid by transferring money or other financial assets to another party; actual expenditures. (Chapter 7)

Exports -- Goods and services sold to consumers or firms in another nation. (Chapter 3)

Extensive Forms -- In game theory, a complete representation of all possible combinations of moves all of the players in a game can make. (Chapter 14)

External (Spillover) Benefits -- Benefits associated with the production or consumption of a product but enjoyed by someone other than the producer or consumer. (Chapter 5)

External (Spillover) Costs -- Costs associated with the production or consumption of a product but paid by someone other than the producer or consumer. (Chapter 5)

Externalities -- Third-party effects associated with the production or consumption of various products. Cf. external benefits and external costs. (Chapter 5)

Factor Mobility -- The relative ease with which an input can relocate from one factor market to another, often by way of moving from one geographic area to another. (Chapter 16)

Factor of Production -- a productive resource, viz., land, labor, capital, or entrepreneurship. (Chapter 15)

Factor Price Elasticity -- A quantitative measure of the responsiveness of the quantity demanded or supplied for a productive resource to a change in its price; calculated as the percentage change in quantity demanded or supplied divided by the percentage change in the input's price. (Chapter 15)

Financial Capital -- Money and other "paper securities" (such as government or corporate bonds) that can be used to acquire real resources. Financial capital is not directly a productive resource, but it represents purchasing power over such resources. (Chapter 1)

Firms -- Any kind of business organization, including corporations, partnerships, and sole proprietorships. (Chapter 7)

First-degree Price Discrimination -- The form of price discrimination in which a seller is able to charge each buyer the maximum amount he or she is willing and able to pay for each unit of the product purchased. (Chapter 11)

Fixed Costs (FC) -- Production costs that do not change when a firm's level of output is increased or decreased. Cf. variable costs. (Chapter 7)

Fixed Input -- A productive resource that cannot be varied in quantity for some finite time period. (Chapter 1)

Free Rider -- Anyone who benefits from the production or consumption of a product without paying for it. Cf. external benefits and public goods. (Chapter 5)

Fringe Benefits -- Compensation other than wages and salaries paid for by employers and provided to workers, such as vacations, life and health insurance, paid holidays, and sick-leave. (Chapter 16)

Game Theory -- Models of strategic behavior, including moves and countermoves among individuals, firms, and/or other organizations. Often used by economists to analyze oligopolies. (Chapter 14)

General Equilibrium Analysis -- The study of significant adjustments made throughout an economic system, in all kinds of markets, in response to a change that affects supply or demand in any particular market. (Chapter 17)

General Law of Demand -- Price and quantity demanded are inversely related, holding constant such determinants of demand as income, the price of related products, consumer tastes and preferences, consumers' price expectations for the product in question, and the number of consumers in the market. (Chapter 3)

General Law of Supply -- Price and quantity supplied are directly related, holding constant such determinants of supply as the price of productive resources (inputs), technology, the price of other goods and services the supplier might produce, producers' price expectations for the product in question, and the number of sellers in the market. (Chapter 3)

Giffen Goods -- Goods for which quantity demanded increases as price increases, *ceteris paribus*. The existence of these goods is theoretically possible, because the income effect of a price change for a strongly inferior good may overwhelm the substitution effect. (Chapter 6)

Goods -- Tangible objects used to satisfy human wants. (Chapter 1)

Grievance Procedures -- A set of provisions, typically included in U.S. collective bargaining contracts, which specify the steps that will be used to resolve disputes between workers and management concerning work rules and other terms of the agreement during the contract period, usually culminating with binding arbitration. (Chapter 16)

Herfindahl Index -- A measure of industry concentration calculated by adding up the squared percentage of industry output or sales accounted for by each firm in the industry. (Chapter 10)

Heterogeneous Products -- Imperfect substitutes. Goods and services that are differentiated by physical or asthetic features, or by policies of sellers involving free returns, extended warranties, or other assurances to buyers. Cf. homogeneous products. (Chapter 9)

"Hit-and-run" Strategies -- A policy of quickly entering a market where economic profits are available, then exiting once those profits have been bid away. Not feasible when barriers to entry and exit are significant. (Chapter 14)

Homogeneous Products -- Perfect substitutes. Goods and services which are, from a consumer's perspective, identical in all significant physical and asthetic features, and in terms of sellers' policies in standing behind the products. Cf. heterogeneous products. (Chapter 9)

Horizontal Mergers -- Combinations or takeovers involving two, formerly competing firms that produced products traded in the same market. (Chapter 13)

Human Capital -- Innate or acquired human abilities that make a person more productive in producing goods or services. (Chapter 1)

Hypotheses -- Propositions linking two or more variables in a cause-and-effect statement, ultimately tested by comparing the hypotheses to empirical data that measure the same relationships. (Chapter 2)

Imperfect Competition -- A shorthand phrase used by economists to refer to all market structures except perfect competition. Cf. monopoly, monopolistic competition, and oligopoly. (Chapter 9)

Implicit Costs -- Costs faced by resource owners in the form of forgone earnings available from the best alternative use of the resources. These costs do not involve actual outlays of money; rather, they must be imputed. (Chapter 7)

Imports -- Goods and services purchased from producers in another nation. (Chapter 3)

Impossibility Theorem -- The principle that no system of rules or procedures can be designed which aggregates individual preferences into a clear, consistent, and complete schedule of social preferences. (Chapter 17)

Income -- Money received by a household from the sale or lease of its productive resources, or from savings loaned to others who use the funds to buy resources. Cf. wages and salaries, rent, profit, and interest. (Chapter 3)

Income Effect -- The change in the quantity of a good or service demanded when consumers are made wealthier or poorer, in real terms, by changes in the price of a product they consume -- even though their level of money income has not changed. Cf. substitution effect. (Chapter 1)

Income Elastic Demand -- A situation where, in percentage terms, a change in consumers' incomes leads to a larger response in the quantity of a product they demand. (Chapter 4)

Income Inelastic Demand -- A situation where, in percentage terms, a change in consumers' incomes leads to a smaller response in the quantity of a product they demand. (Chapter 4)

Income Elasticity of Demand -- A measure of the responsiveness of the quantity demanded of a product to a change in consumers' incomes. (Chapter 4)

Incomplete Contracting -- Relationships between two or more parties in which legally binding actions are explicitly specified for some conditions and contingencies, but other social or business conventions, including reputations of the parties who agree to the contracts, are implicitly relied on to guide actions when contingencies that are not specified arise. Cf. credible commitment. (Chapter 7)

Increasing Returns to Scale -- More than proportional increases in outputs when all inputs are increased, resulting in decreasing long-run unit costs if input prices are fixed. Cf. constant and decreasing returns to scale. (Chapter 10)

Increasing-cost Industries -- Industries in which unit production costs of the most efficient sized firms rise as the level of industry output increases. (Chapter 10)

Independent Variables -- Quantities which, when changing in value, cause changes in the values of other, dependent variables. (Chapter 2)

Indifference Curves -- A graphical schedule that shows all combinations of two products that provide the same level of total satisfaction to a consumer or household. (Chapter 6)

Indivisible Inputs -- Productive resources which must be purchased and used in relatively large and discrete units. (Chapter 10)

Inductive Models -- Predictions of behavior by individuals and institutions based on observed data and the study of current or past patterns in those data. Cf. deductive models. (Chapter 2)

Industrial Organization -- The study of pricing, output, and competitive strategies employed by firms operating in industries characterized by different levels of competition. (Chapter 9)

Industrial Unions -- Organizations of all workers in a particular industry, regardless of what trades they practice. Like craft unions, they represent their members in trying to improve wages, fringe benefits, and working conditions. (Chapter 15)

Industries -- A group of firms producing identical, or highly similar, products. (Chapter 7)

Inferior Goods -- Goods which experience a decrease in demand when consumers' incomes rise, and an increase in demand when incomes fall. Cf. normal goods. (Chapter 1)

Inflation -- A sustained increase in the average level of prices for all goods and services produced and consumed in a nation, holding product quality constant. (Chapter 3)

Inputs -- Another name for productive resources or factors of production; things used in a production process to make goods or provide services. (Chapter 3)

Input-output Table -- A tabular representation of production and consumption patterns in an economy, sector by sector, over some period of time. The total value of input payments for any sector in the table must equal the total value of the output of that sector. (Chapter 17)

Interest -- A monetary payment for the use of loanable funds or, in real terms, the price of capital resources. (Chapter 3)

Isocost -- A linear schedule that shows the different combinations of two inputs a firm can purchase for a given amount of money, holding input prices constant. (Chapter 8)

Isoquant -- A curve showing all efficient combinations of two inputs that can be used to produce a given level of output. (Chapter 8)

Labor -- All human effort except entrepreneurship directed at the production of goods and services; the financial payments for labor are wages and salaries. (Chapter 1)

Labor-Intensive Growth -- Expansion in output that results in a firm using relatively more labor and less capital (or other inputs) per unit of output produced. (Chapter 8)

Lags -- Time delays between a change in one variable and a resulting change in another variable, or another group of variables. (Chapter 2)

Land -- All natural resources that can be used to produce goods and services; the financial payment for land is rent. (Chapter 1)

Law of Demand -- Other things being equal, quantity demanded increases when the price of a good or service decreases, and *vice versa*. (Chapter 1)

Law of Diminishing Marginal Returns -- Total output increases at a decreasing rate as more and more variable inputs (productive resources) are combined with at least one fixed input. This occurs because, as more variable inputs are used, they each have less (on average) of the fixed input to work with. (Chapter 1)

Law of Diminishing Marginal Utility -- The generalization that total satisfaction from the consumption of a product will eventually increase at a decreasing rate (or perhaps even begin to decrease) as more and more units are consumed in a given period of time. In other words, the additional satisfaction from consuming each successive unit of a product eventually begins to decline. (Chapter 1)

Law of Supply -- Other things being equal, quantity supplied increases when the price of a good or service increases, and *vice versa*. (Chapter 1)

Legal Incidence of a Tax -- Who must legally collect a tax and send it in to the government -- often different from the economic incidence of the tax. (Chapter 4)

Long Run -- A production period of sufficient length so that no productive resources (inputs) are fixed in quantity. Like the short run, this length of time varies for different products and industries. Cf. short run. (Chapter 1)

Long-run Average Total Costs (LRATC) -- Total costs divided by the quantity of output when all inputs are variable. (Chapter 10)

Long-run Cost Schedules -- Schedules which show the minimum possible costs of producing various levels of output when all inputs are variable. (Chapter 10)

Long-run Marginal Costs (LRMC) -- The cost of producing an additional unit of output when all inputs are variable. (Chapter 10)

Macroeconomics -- The study of the causes and consequences of changes in such aggregate measures as national income, economic growth, and the rates of unemployment and inflation. (Chapter 2)

Managerial Theories of the Firm -- A class of economic models based on the assumption that managers maximize some aspect of their firms' performance other than profits, because they believe they such objectives will more effectively promote their own personal interests. (Chapter 7)

Marginal Analysis -- Weighing the incremental costs and benefits of an action or a change in circumstances. (Chapter 2)

Marginal Cost (MC) -- The change in total cost associated with a one-unit change in output (total product). (Chapter 7)

Marginal Factor Cost (MFC) -- The cost of hiring, buying, or leasing an additional unit of a productive resource, such as laborers, machines, or land. (Chapter 14)

Marginal Product (MP) -- The additional output obtained by employing one more unit of an input. (Chapter 1)

Marginal Rate of Substitution (MRS) -- The amount of one product a consumer or household will give up to attain an additional unit of another product, holding total utility constant. Cf. diminishing marginal rate of substitution. (Chapter 6)

Marginal Rate of Technical Substitution (MRTS) -- The number of additional units of one input required to hold output constant if a firm uses one less unit of another input. (Chapter 8)

Marginal Rate of Transformation (MRT) -- The quantity of one product which must be given up in order to provide the resources required to produce one additional unit of another good. Shown by the slope of the production possibilities frontier at any particular point on that curve. (Chapter 17)

Marginal Revenue (MR) -- The change in a firm's total revenue associated with the sale of one more or one less unit of its output. (Chapter 4)

Marginal Revenue Product (MRP) -- The dollar value of the additional sales a firm makes by selling the marginal product of the last unit of a variable input hired. In perfect competition, MRP is equal to the value of marginal product (VMP). The downward-sloping segment of the MRP curve is a firm's demand curve for a factor of production, in any kind of market structure. (Chapter 15)

Marginal Utility (MU) -- The change in total satisfaction that occurs when a consumer or household uses one more, or one less, unit of a product. Cf. law of diminishing marginal utility. (Chapter 6)

Market -- A geographic place or technological arrangement in which exchanges of goods or services are made. (Chapter 1)

Market Clearing Price -- The price at which quantity supplied is exactly equal to quantity demanded. Also known as equilibrium price. (Chapter 1)

Market Demand -- The sum of all individual demand curves or schedules for a good or service, showing all possible prices for a product and the quantities that these consumers are willing and able to buy at each price. (Chapter 1)

Market Economy -- An economic system which relies primarily on self-interested decisions by individuals and privately owned firms to decide what goods and services will be produced, how they will be produced, and who will consume them. Most productive resources are privately owned in market economies. (Chapter 1)

Market Failure -- The systematic overallocation or underallocation of resources that occurs in an unregulated market system when problems such as public goods, externalities, and imperfect competition are present. (Chapter 5)

Market Structures -- Economic models which examine firm and industry behavior under different levels of competition. Cf. perfect competition, monopoly, monopolistic competition, oligopoly, and monopsony. (Chapter 9)

Market Supply -- The sum of all individual supply curves or schedules for a good or service in a given market area, showing all possible prices for a product and the quantities producers are willing and able to sell at each price. (Chapter 1)

Mediator -- An impartial "third party" who is usually selected and paid by two parties involved in a dispute, to assist in factfinding and negotiation by making suggestions which neither party is required to accept. (Chapter 16)

Methodological Individualism -- A group of theories and models of human behavior based on the assumption that people rationally follow their own self-interest in their economic affairs, and that social or national welfare is determined by measuring the sum of all individuals' levels of satisfaction, income, or spending decisions. (Chapter 2)

Microeconomics -- The study of the economic actions of individual consumers, producers, families, firms, or, at the broadest level, a particular industry. (Chapter 2)

Mid-point Formulas -- Formulas used to calculate arc elasticities over a given range of output, which use the midpoints of two quantities, prices, or income levels. This avoids conflicting estimates from choosing different values of these variables as the base for determining percentage changes. (Chapter 4)

Minimum Efficient Scale (MES) -- The lowest production level at which a firm first realizes all significant cost savings associated with higher output levels. Also known as minimum optimal scale. (Chapter 10)

Minimum Wage -- A legal price floor for wages paid to workers. (Chapter 14)

Mixed Economy -- An economic system that combines some features of market, command, or traditional economies, or all three. (Chapter 1)

Mixed Strategies -- Alternating moves across two or more possible actions, to introduce the problem of uncertainty in the strategic decisions made by rivals. (Chapter 14)

Money -- Anything generally accepted as final payment for goods and services; a medium of exchange. (Chapter 1)

504

Monitoring Costs -- A type of transactions cost incurred in determining whether a party to an agreement has, in fact, satisfied the conditions of that agreement. (Chapter 7)

Monopolistic Competition -- A market structure characterized by a large number of relatively small firms, with easy entry and exit in the industry, but extensive product differentiation and nonprice competition. (Chapter 12)

Monopolistic Exploitation -- The difference between the value of marginal product (VMP) for the last worker hired by a firm and marginal factor cost (MFC) for that worker. (Chapter 16)

Monopoly -- A market structure in which one firm sells all of the output of a good or service for which there are no close substitutes, also characterized by high barriers to entry. (Chapter 11)

Monopsonistic Exploitation -- The difference between the marginal revenue product (MRP) and the wage rate that is paid to the last worker hired by a firm which faces an upward-sloping factor-supply curve. (Chapter 15)

Monopsony -- A labor market in which a small number of firms are the only available employers; in perfect monopsony, there is only one employer in the market. (Chapter 15)

n-Firm Concentration Ratios -- Measures of industry concentration calculated by adding up the percentage of sales or output levels accounted for by the largest n firms (usually, n = 4, 8, 16, or 32) in the industry. (Chapter 10)

Nash Equilibrium -- A situation in which two or more interdependent rivals have adopted the policies which maximize their economic position, given the policies adopted by the other rivals. (Chapter 14)

Natural Monopolies -- Industries in which the market level of output will be produced at the lowest possible cost by a single firm. These firms experience declining long-run average total costs as output levels are increased, at least over a major segment of the industry level of production. (Chapter 10)

Negative-sum Games -- Settings in which interactions between, or policies adopted by, two or more parties make all of the parties worse off. (Chapter 1)

Net Present Value -- For a given project or asset, the present value of all current and future revenues it provides, minus the present value of all current and future costs it entails. (Chapter 15)

No-strike Clauses -- An agreement frequently included in collective bargaining contracts, in which a union agrees not to call or support a strike by its own members during the term of the contract. (Chapter 15)

Non-exclusion Principle -- The idea that producers of public goods will be unable to prevent those who do not pay for their product from consuming it. Cf. external benefits and free riders. (Chapter 5)

Non-rival Consumption -- A property of some products whereby one person's use of them does not significantly reduce the quantity or the quality of the products remaining for others to use. Cf. public goods and quasi-public/private goods. (Chapter 5)

Nonprice Competition -- Attempting to increase a firm's profits, sales, or both, by engaging in product differentiation through advertising or product design changes, or by providing ancillary goods or services (such as easy credit policies, extended warranties, trading stamps, convenient store locations, courteous service, etc.) to customers. (Chapter 12)

Normal Goods -- Goods which experience an increase in demand when consumers' incomes rise, and a decrease in demand when income falls. Cf. inferior goods. (Chapter 1)

Normal Profits -- Profits that exactly cover the opportunity cost -- no more, no less -- associated with a business decision to use resources in a particular way; a rate of return just high enough to keep a firm engaged in its current line of business, without leading to net entry or exit in its industry. Cf. economic profits. (Chapter 7)

Normative Statements -- Statements involving personal value judgments concerning "what ought to be," rather than "what is, or will be." Cf. positive statements. (Chapter 1)

Occam's Razor -- The precept that, other things being equal, the simplest explanation should be preferred over more complicated ones. (Chapter 2)

Oligopoly -- A market structure in which a few large firms control the major part of production and sales for a given product, have a significant effect on market price and all other firms in the industry, and are protected by high barriers to entry. (Chapter 13)

Opportunity Cost -- What must be given up whenever a decision is made to use a resource in a particular way. Specifically, the value of the highest-ranked alternative use of the resource. (Chapter 1)

Organization of Petroleum Exporting Countries (OPEC) -- An oil cartel formed in 1960, that was able to sharply increase oil prices in the 1970s when it controlled about half of world crude oil production. (Chapter 3)

Overallocation of Resources -- Production of a product beyond the point where the social benefits of the last unit produced are greater than or equal to the social costs of producing that unit of output. Cf. external costs. (Chapter 5)

Output Effect -- Any change in the number of units of an input used by a firm that is brought about by the change in a firm's production level, after adjusting for any change in the number of units used resulting from a change in the relative prices of the inputs. Cf. substitution effect. (Chapter 8)

Pareto Efficiency (or Pareto Optimality) -- A state in which no change is possible that makes one person better off without making another person worse off. (Chapter 17)

Parity Programs -- Agricultural price support programs designed to maintain farmers' purchasing power, in real terms, at a level equal to that they enjoyed in some historical period. (Chapter 4)

Partial Equilibrium Analysis -- The study of adjustments in one market which equate supply and demand forces, without considering the effects of those adjustments in other markets, or the resulting "feed back" in the first market caused when other markets react to this initial change. (Chapter 17)

Partnerships -- A class of firms in which two or more owners are personally liable for all actions and debts of a business, and agree to share all expenses and profits in some specified proportion. (Chapter 7)

Patents -- The exclusive right to make, use, sell, or license an invention, usually awarded for a fixed period of time (typically 17 years in the United States). (Chapter 11)

Pay-off Matrix -- A table which shows the returns (gains and/or losses) that two or more "players" in a game-theory model will receive as a result of pursuing any particular action, when any other players in the game adopt any one of their own possible policies. (Chapter 14)

Perfect Competition -- An idealized market structure where no individual consumers or producers have a significant impact on product price; there are no effective barriers to entry and exit; products are homogeneous; and buyers and sellers have full information on product price, quality, and availability. (Chapter 9)

Point Elasticity -- A measure of the responsiveness of the quantity of a product demanded or supplied to an infinitesimal change in price. (Chapter 4)

Point of Constrained Bliss -- A point on the highest social indifference curve a society can reach, given its feasible production and exchange alternatives. If no trade with other economic systems is possible, this is the unique point at which the highest social difference curve an economy can reach is tangent to its production-possibilities frontiers. A point of constrained optimization. (Chapter 17)

Positive Statements -- An expression or theory dealing with what is, or what will be, rather than value judgments based on ethical claims about what should be. (Chapter 2)

Positive-sum Games -- Transactions in which all parties in an exchange are made better off. (Chapter 1)

Potential Competition -- A particular form of interdependence in which firms currently producing a product are constrained in setting price and output levels by the threat of entry by firms not currently in their market. (Chapter 14)

Predatory Pricing -- Attempts to monopolize a market by driving out smaller firms, or forestalling entry by potential competitors, through a policy of temporarily setting price at a below-cost level to impose losses on all firms in the industry. (Chapter 11)

Preferences -- An indication of consumers' rankings of different combinations of two or more products, relative to other combinations. Cf. tastes. (Chapter 3)

Premarket Differences -- Productivity differences across different groups of workers which lead to wage differentials, and may be at least partly determined by historically unequal opportunities for education, promotions, and access to certain types of careers. (Chapter 16)

Present Value -- The amount of money you would be willing to accept today as equivalent to a given sum of money to be paid or received at a specified future date. (Chapter 15)

Price -- The monetary cost of buying a good or service, or the monetary income received from selling a good or service. (Chapter 1)

Price Ceilings -- Legally imposed and enforced maximum prices, which lead to shortages and related resource allocation problems. (Chapter 4)

Price Discrimination -- Charging different prices for different units of identical products, in response to differences in customers' demand for the good or service (in particular, in their price elasticity of demand), and *not* to differences in the producer's cost of providing these products. (Chapter 11)

Price Elasticity of Demand -- A measure of the responsiveness of quantity demanded to a change in price, with both changes expressed in percentage terms and the resulting elasticity coefficient reported as a non-negative number. (Chapter 4)

Price Elasticity of Supply -- A measure of the responsiveness of quantity supplied to a change in price, with both changes expressed in percentage terms. (Chapter 4)

Price Elastic Supply or Demand -- A situation where, in percentage terms, a change in product price leads to a larger response in the quantity of a product consumers demand or producers supply. (Chapter 4)

507

Price Expectations -- Beliefs about the future prices for individual products, or groups of products. (Chapter 3)

Price Floors -- Legally imposed and enforced minimum prices, which lead to surpluses and related resource allocation problems. (Chapter 4)

Price Inelastic Supply or Demand -- A situation where, in percentage terms, a change in product price leads to a smaller response in the quantity of a product consumers demand or producers supply. (Chapter 4)

Price Seekers -- Imperfectly competitive firms which face downward-sloping demand curves, and must lower price to increase the quantity of their products demanded. (Chapter 11)

Price-subsidy Programs -- Government assistance policies which effectively decrease the price consumers must pay for some products, or increase the price producers receive for selling a product. (Chapters 4 and 6)

Price Takers -- Perfectly competitive firms which, because they represent such a small part of the overall market for a product, can sell (buy) as much or as little of a product (input) as they like without affecting its price. They take market-determined prices as givens, beyond their control. (Chapter 9)

Principal-agent Problems -- Incentive problems which result when one party hires or elects another to represent them in economic or political dealings, and the agent's interests are not exactly the same as those of the principal(s) whom they represent. (Chapter 5)

Private Goods -- Goods that are rival in consumption and not subject to the non-exclusion principle. Cf. public goods and quasi-public or quasi-private goods. (Chapter 5)

Producer Surplus -- The difference between the minimum monetary amount producers require to make them willing to supply a certain output level of their product over some period of time, and the amount that they actually receive for that level of output. Cf. economic rents. (Chapter 4)

Product Differentiation -- Real or perceived differences in characteristics of substitutable goods and services, including quality, styling, and other features associated with nonprice competition in imperfectly competitive market structures. As a result of product differentiation, consumers may view such products as close, but not perfect, substitutes. (Chapter 12)

Production -- Using economic resources to make or provide goods and services to consumers. (Chapter 7)

Production Controls -- Government imposed output limits (i.e., quotas), typically designed to set minimum output levels in command economies or maximum output levels for products which are supported by price floors and government purchasing programs in market-based economies. (Chapter 4)

Production Possibilities Frontier -- A schedule or graph of alternative combinations of commodities that can be produced if all available resources are used at maximum efficiency. (Chapter 1)

Productive Efficiency -- Using least-cost production methods for whatever level of output a firm chooses to produce and, ideally, producing a level of output where average total costs are minimized. (Chapter 9)

Productive Resources -- See Factor of Production. (Chapter 1)

Productivity -- For any productive resource, a measure of output per unit of input. (Chapter 15)

Products -- Goods or services. (Chapter 1)

Profits -- Total revenues minus total costs. Cf. normal profits and economic profits. (Chapter 7)

Public Choice Theory -- The assumption that voters, politicians, and public employees act to further their own economic interests in establishing and enforcing public policy. (Chapter 5)

Public Goods -- Goods that are non-rival in consumption and subject to the non-exclusion principle. Cf. private goods and quasi-public or quasi-private goods. (Chapter 5)

Pure Competition -- A market structure that has all of the characteristics of perfect competition except consumers and producers having perfect information about product prices, qualities, and availability. (Chapter 9)

Quasi-Public (or Quasi-Private) Goods -- Products which have some characteristics of public goods and some characteristics of private goods. Some of these goods are produced privately, some by government, and some in both the public and private sectors. Cf. non-exclusion principle and non-rival consumption. (Chapter 5)

Quantity Demanded -- The amount of a product that consumers are willing and able to buy at one particular price. (Chapter 1)

Quantity Supplied -- The amount of a product that producers are willing and able to sell at one particular price. (Chapter 1)

Quotas -- Legal or contractual limits on the quantities of a product that may be imported, purchased, or produced. (Chapter 3 & 4)

Rate of Return -- Gains (or losses) expressed as a percentage of the costs of an investment.

Reaction Functions -- Schedules indicating how an imperfectly competitive firm will adjust its behavior -- including its price and output decisions -- in response to actions taken by its competitor(s). (Chapter 13)

Rent -- The payment to those productive resources which economists classify as land (natural resources); also any payment to a resource greater than the minimum payment required to keep it in use in a certain production process. (Chapters 1 and 14)

Rent-seeking Behavior -- All attempts to earn economic rents -- payments greater than competitive wages or profits -- in some cases through government protection against competition or price and income subsidies. (Chapter 15)

Repeated Games -- Settings in which interdependent individuals or organizations make decisions on a particular set of variables, such as price and output levels, in two or more time periods. (Chapter 14)

Reservation Price -- The price at which the expected marginal benefit of additional search is equal to its expected marginal cost. Consumers will purchase a given product at a price that is equal to or less than their reservation price, but continue to search for a better price if a seller's price is higher than their reservation price. (Chapter 14)

Residual Demand -- The portion of a market demand curve showing lower price and higher output levels than the current price and output levels in an industry. This portion of the demand curve is available to firms which are potential entrants into an industry. (Chapter 13)

Resources -- Goods or services that can be used to satisfy wants directly, or indirectly by making other goods and services. (Chapter 1)

Return on Sales -- A profit measure that reflects a firm's mark-up, or "margin," over its costs. Found by dividing a firm's after-tax profits by its dollar volume of sales. (Chapter 7)

Return on Stockholders' Equity -- A measure of corporate profits which expresses after-tax profits as a rate of return on stockholders' net claims against the firm's assets. This measure properly views profits as a return for risk-taking; however, as reported by accountants, it does not adjust for normal profits, which economists view as an implicit cost of doing business. Cf. economic profits. (Chapter 7)

Risk -- The chance of an action leading to different outcomes that affect the well-being of an individual or group, often including both favorable and unfavorable effects; economists typically measure risk by the degree of variance around the expected value of the action. (Chapter 1)

Rival Consumption -- The property of most products in which one person's consumption of a good or service physically uses it up, making those resources unavailable for other people to use.

Scarcity -- The economic condition that exists when human wants exceed the capacity of available resources to satisfy those wants. The problem of scarcity faces individuals and organizations, including governments. (Chapter 1)

Screening -- Identifying product or input quality for prospective buyers and employers by sorting through a large number of products or inputs, and ranking or grading them based on a set of performance requirements and tests. (Chapter 14)

Search -- Collecting product or employment information related to price, quality, personal or firm reputations, product features, and related seller services. (Chapter 14)

Second-degree Price Discrimination -- The form of price discrimination in which a firm charges different prices for an identical product depending on the quantity a consumer purchases, even though the firm's unit costs are not affected by the quantity sold in each transaction. (Chapter 11)

Services -- Activities which satisfy human wants. (Chapter 1)

Sequential Game -- Models of strategic behavior involving two or more "players" (individuals and/or organizations), where each player adopts or modifies a strategy in a particular order which is specified in setting up the game-theory model of the players' behavior. (Chapter 14)

Short Run -- A production period of sufficiently brief duration that at least one productive resource (input) is fixed in quantity. How short this length of time will be varies for different products and industries. Cf. long run. (Chapter 1)

Shortage -- The condition in which, at any price below the equilibrium price, the quantity of a product demanded exceeds the quantity supplied. Shortages are typically ended by price increases, except in cases where legal price ceilings are imposed and rigidly enforced. (Chapter 3)

Shutdown Point -- The price and output level where, in the short run, a firm loses just as much by shutting down as it does by continuing to produce. At any higher price it will minimize losses by continuing to operate; at any lower price it will lose less by shutting down. (Chapter 9)

Signaling -- The role of price or other product characteristics in assuring potential buyers that a product or input comes from a selected group of similar items which have a known average level of quality. (Chapter 14)

510

Simultaneous Relationships -- Relationships such that A is a function of B and, at the same time, B is a function of A. (Chapter 2)

Social Benefits -- All private and, when present, external benefits associated with the production and consumption of a good or service. (Chapter 5)

Social Costs -- All private and, when present, external costs associated with the production and consumption of a good or service. (Chapter 5)

Social Indifference Curve -- A hypothetical curve showing all combinations of two products, or two groups of products, which leave a society equally satisfied. Accordingly, it does not matter to a society on which particular point along a given social indifference curve it happens to be. Each curve in a set of such curves represents a different level of satisfaction; and higher curves represent greater levels of satisfaction. (Chapter 17)

Sole Proprietorships -- Firms owned by an individual or family that are not incorporated or operated as a formal partnership. Owners are personally liable for all actions and debts of the firm, and receive any profits it may earn. (Chapter 7)

Spatial Competition -- A form of nonprice competition, narrowly defined as relating to the physical location of sellers in a market area; used more generally as an analogy to refer to "spacing" among a group of substitute products with different nonprice characteristics. (Chapter 12)

Special-interest Issues -- In the public policy arena, programs with tightly focused benefits and widely diffused costs, or *vice versa*. This results in a small group with strong incentives to work for or against some policies, while the large majority of people will each, individually, gain or loose very little from the policy. (Chapter 5)

Specialization -- Producing a narrow range of goods and services, or even a part of a good or service, rather than being self-sufficient by producing all (or even most) of the things you consume. (Chapter 1)

Stabilization Policies -- Government policies, usually at the national level, designed to promote economic stability by reducing unemployment and inflation while promoting reasonable rates of economic growth. (Chapter 5)

Static Equilibrium -- Points in an economic model which firms or individuals will choose to move to and remain at, as long as the conditions specified in constructing the model do not change. Changes over time can be studied by comparing two or more different static equilibrium positions, which is like comparing snapshots of a subject at different times or from different angles. Truly dynamic analysis is done by tracing the continuous path of adjustments in these variables over time. (Chapter 9)

Statistical Discrimination -- Paying different wages (or charging different prices) to individuals who provide (or receive) identical services, because they are members of groups which, on average, exhibit different characteristics from other groups, and those characteristics have significant economic consequences to the firms buying (or selling) these services. (Chapter 16)

Strategic Behavior -- Actions taken in light of expected actions and reactions by competitors, and which may even be designed to influence their behavior. A key feature of market situations characterized by a high degree of interdependence between firm-- especially oligopoly. (Chapter 13)

Strike -- A work stoppage by workers of a particular industry, firm, or worksite, typically called when a collective bargaining contract has expired and a union wants to put extreme pressure on the firm to reach a new agreement, or at least to resume bargaining. (Chapter 16)

Substitutes -- Two or more goods or services which satisfy the same general set of human wants, and are therefore in direct competition in the marketplace. Examples include different brands of the same product. (Chapter 3)

Substitution Effect -- The change in the quantity of a good or service demanded associated with changes in the relative price of the product, compared to other products which can be used to satisfy the same general set of human wants, and which are not due to a change in consumers' effective buying power or producers' changes in output levels. Price increases always lead to negative substitution effects, price decreases to positive substitution effects. Cf. income effects and output effects. (Chapters 1, 6, and 8)

Sunk Costs -- Costs already incurred that cannot be recovered or avoided; they are therefore not relevant in deciding how to best use economic resources in the present or future. (Chapter 7)

Supply -- A schedule or graph of all possible prices for a product and the quantity of the product that producers are willing and able to sell at each price during a given period of time. (Chapter 1)

Surplus -- The condition in which, at any price above the equilibrium price, the quantity of a product supplied exceeds the quantity demanded. Surpluses are usually ended by price decreases, except in cases where legal price floors are effectively enforced. (Chapter 3)

Tariffs -- Excise taxes on imported goods, often imposed by the government to protect similar goods produced by domestic firms from foreign competition. (Chapter 4)

Target Price -- A support price set by the government (usually for an agricultural product) above the market price. Producers receive the difference between the target price and the market price for each unit sold, paid by the government as a kind of subsidy. (Chapter 4)

Tastes -- Consumers' evaluations of the ability of a good or service to satisfy their wants, relative to other available products. (Chapter 3)

Tax Incidence -- See *economic incidence* and *legal incidence*. (Chapter 4)

Technical Efficiencies -- Production methods or levels that reduce the use of one input without requiring additional units of other inputs, observed for some capital inputs as the scale of production is increased. (Chapter 10)

Technology -- The state of scientific and engineering knowledge concerning production processes for goods and services. (Chapter 1)

Third-degree Price Discrimination -- The form of price discrimination in which a firm charges a discrete number of different prices for its product, based on differences in consumers' demand (especially price elasticity) for the good or service, and *not* on differences in the producers' cost of making and selling those products. (Chapter 11)

Time Value of Money -- The widespread preference of individuals, firms, and governments to value present monetary payments more than future payments of the same dollar amount. (Chapter 15)

Time-series Studies -- Empirical studies which gather data from a relatively small number of units over an extended period of time. Cf. cross-section studies. (Chapter 10)

Tit-for-tat Strategies -- Policies established in an interdependent setting in which individuals and/or organizations respond to others in the same way others act toward them. Cooperation is met with cooperation, competition with competition, treachery with treachery.

Total Cost (TC) -- The sum of fixed and variable costs associated with the production of any given quantity of output. (Chapter 7)

Total Product (TP) -- A schedule or graph showing the maximum quantity of output a firm can produce using one or more fixed inputs and different quantities of a variable input. (Chapter 7)

Total Revenue (TR) -- Total receipts from the sales of a product, calculated by multiplying the number of units sold by the price received for each unit. (Chapter 4)

Total Utility (TU) -- The level of satisfaction a consumer derives from all units of a good or service consumed in a given period of time. (Chapter 6)

Trade Cycles -- Fluctuations in the national level of income, exports, and imports around the average rate of long-term growth for each of these variables. Historically a precursor of the idea of business cycles, but reflecting a greater dependence on commerce, trade, and agriculture, and relatively lower levels of industrialization. (Chapter 2)

Trade-offs -- Giving up some desirable goods, services, or goals in order to attain more of other goods, services, or goals. Cf. opportunity cost. (Chapter 2)

Traditional Economy -- An economic system which relies primarily on custom or historical precedent to determine what goods and services will be produced, how they will be produced, and who will consume them. (Chapter 1)

Transactions Costs -- Costs of making exchanges other than the direct prices of the goods or services that, are traded, but still paid by the producers and/or consumers of these products. Examples include consumers costs of negotiating contracts and acquiring information about product quality, price, or availability. (Chapter 1)

Transfer Payments -- Payments that exactly match the full opportunity cost of using a factor of production in a production process, without providing any economic rents. (Chapter 15)

Turnover Tax -- A kind of sales tax levied by central planners in nations such as the former Soviet Union in order to reduce the quantity demanded of certain goods and services, sometimes to reduce or eliminate the excess demand for these products. (Chapter 1)

Underallocation of Resources -- Stopping the production of a product at a level where the social benefits of the last unit produced are greater than the social costs of producing that unit of output. Cf. external benefits. (Chapter 5)

Union Bargaining Preferences -- A formal representation of a union's objectives in a bargaining situation, typically in a graphical or functional format. (Chapter 16)

Unitary Elastic -- A situation where, in percentage terms, the quantity of a product demanded or supplied responds by exactly the same amount as a change in a product's price. (Chapter 4)

User Fees -- Charges for the use of goods and services provided by government agencies, paid by those who use these products. (Chapter 10)

Usury Laws -- Laws which establish a maximum allowable interest rate on loans, or on a specific type of loan. Usury is a somewhat archaic term which refers to the act of charging an exorbitant rate of interest or, in some cultures, charging any interest at all on a loan. (Chapter 15)

Util -- An idealized measure representing an individual "unit" of consumer satisfaction, so named by the utilitarian philosophers and economists of the early 19th century. (Chapter 6)

Utility -- An abstract measure of consumer satisfaction. (Chapter 6)

Value in Exchange -- The market price for each unit of a good or service produced. Cf. value in use. (Chapter 4)

Value in Use -- A monetary measure of the satisfaction a person receives from the consumption of units of a good or service. Cf. value in exchange. (Chapter 4)

Value of Marginal Product (VMP) -- The dollar value of the additional product a firm produces by hiring an additional unit of a variable input, calculated by multiplying the price for the output times the unit of input's marginal product. The downward-sloping segment of the VMP curve is a perfectly competitive firm's demand curve for the input. (Chapter 14)

Variable Costs (VC) -- Production costs that are directly related to the quantity of output, and which change as the level of output produced changes. (Chapter 7)

Variable Input -- A productive resource which firms may employ in different quantities during the current production period. In the short run, labor is typically a variable input; in the long run all inputs are variable. (Chapter 1)

Vertical Mergers -- Combinations or takeovers involving two firms, in which one firm produces a product used as an input by the other firm. (Chapter 13)

Voucher Programs -- Government assistance programs which provide consumers with additional income that can only be used to purchase a particular product or group of products, such as food, utilities, or education. (Chapter 6)

Wants -- Human desires. Economic wants are for goods and services people would like to have or use. (Chapter 1)

Wage Differentials -- Differences in wage payments established by supply and demand forces in different labor markets, and influenced by a variety of the non-wage aspects of an occupation or worksite. (Chapter 15)

Wage Discrimination -- Paying different wages to workers who perform identical jobs. (Chapter 16)

Wages and Salaries -- The payment to those productive resources which economists classify as labor; in other words, the price of labor. (Chapter 1)

Wealth -- An individual or family's current net worth, calculated by subtracting the market value of all debts from the market value of all assets at a given point in time. (Chapter 3)

Windfall Profits -- Higher returns resulting from an increase in demand or a decrease in supply that are received by owners of units of the affected products which were purchased before the product's price increased. Cf. economic profits and normal profits. (Chapter 6)

Winner's Curse -- A frequently observed outcome in situations involving bidding strategies, in which those who overestimate the value of the auctioned "good" bid most to "win" it, and subsequently incur loses when the true value of the product becomes known.

Zero-sum Game -- A transaction in which one party can gain only if another party experiences an exactly offsetting loss. This contrasts with positive-sum games, such as most voluntary exchanges, in which both sides can gain. (Chapter 1)